Real Estate
Investment
A capital market approach

PEARSON EDUCATION

We work with leading authors to develop the strongest educational materials in business and finance, bringing cutting-edge thinking and best learning practice to a global market.

Under a range of well-known imprints, including Financial Times Prentice Hall, we craft high quality print and electronic publications which help readers to understand and apply their content, whether studying or at work.

To find out about the complete range of our publishing please visit us on the World Wide Web at: www.pearsoned-ema.com

Real Estate Investment

A capital market approach

GERALD R. BROWN
NATIONAL UNIVERSITY OF SINGAPORE
AND
GEORGE A. MATYSIAK
CB HILLIER PARKER LIMITED
CITY UNIVERSITY BUSINESS SCHOOL, LONDON

FINANCIAL TIMES
PRENTICE HALL

An imprint of PEARSON EDUCATION

Harlow, England · London · New York · Reading, Massachusetts · San Francisco · Toronto · Don Mills, Ontario · Sydney
Tokyo · Singapore · Hong Kong · Seoul · Taipei · Cape Town · Madrid · Mexico City · Amsterdam · Munich · Paris · Milan

Financial Times Prentice Hall
An imprint of Pearson Education Limited
Edinburgh Gate
Harlow
Essex CM20 2JE
England

and Associated Companies throughout the world

Visit us on the World Wide Web at:
http://www.pearsoned-ema.com

───────────────────────

First published 2000

ISBN 0 13 020063 8

British Library Cataloguing-in-Publication Data
A catalogue record for this book is available from the British Library

Library of Congress Cataloging-in-Publication Data
A catalog record for this book is available from the Library of Congress

10 9 8 7 6 5 4 3 2 1
04 03 02 01 00 99

Typeset by Meridian Colour Repro Ltd, Pangbourne-on-Thames, Berkshire

Produced by Pearson Education Asia Pte Ltd
Printed in Singapore

Contents

PART *1*

The time value of money and the valuation of cash flows

PART *2*

Risk and return in real estate

PART *3*

Portfolio management

Commonly used symbols

V_j	Capital value of property J
a_t	Income stream in period t
R_t	Rental value in period t
PV	Present value
NPV	Net present value
g	Growth in rental value
p	Rent review period
n	Number of years to the next rent review
$\hat{y}$	Initial yield
y	Equivalent yield
m	Number of discounting or compounding periods per year
r_m	Return on the market portfolio
r_j	Return on asset J
r_f	Risk-free rate of return
r_e	Return on equity
r_d	Return on debt
E	Expectation operator
APR	Annual percentage return
APV	Adjusted present value
$MWRR$	Money-weighted rate of return
$TWRR$	Time-weighted rate of return
β	Beta, or systematic risk
α	Alpha, or abnormal return
$\rho_{i,j}$	Rho, or the coefficient of correlation between assets I and J
$\sigma_{i,j}$	Sigma, or the covariance between assets I and J
$Cov(i,j)$	Covariance between assets I and J

σ_j	Sigma, or the standard deviation of returns on asset J
σ^2_j	Sigma squared, or the variance of returns on asset J
$Var(j)$	Variance of returns on asset J
LPM_n	Lower partial moment of order n
MAD	Mean absolute deviation
Σ	Sigma, or 'the sum of'
Π	Pi, or 'the product of'

Introduction

The changing property market

This book is about creating and adding value through the effective management of property assets. It is not about property valuation, although the estimation of value underpins much of what is covered. Our concern with valuation as a discipline is that it is largely taught from a practical perspective with little reference to the underlying theory of economics and finance. We feel that this has many disadvantages and has held back the development of valuation models in the UK and elsewhere. We have, therefore, broken away from traditional approaches used in valuation textbooks to show that the use of financial concepts and a common financial language can offer many advantages and insights. By adopting this approach we show that the analysis of property can be easily integrated into a capital market framework.

Our aim in writing this book is fairly ambitious. We want to raise the level of understanding of financial and economic principles within the property profession so that the next generation of property investment managers and researchers is equipped to compete with highly skilled managers in other areas of finance. We also want to show that property is an important part of capital markets and can be treated like any other financial asset.

It is clear that many aspects of investment have become increasingly more quantitative and are driven by the economics of supply and demand. By focusing on routine aspects of practice, traditional property valuation courses aim to produce graduates who are able to satisfy the current needs of the profession. Divorcing technique from economics exposes the property profession to the possibility that other professional groups will be better placed to offer high-level investment advice. Failure to acknowledge the integration of property into the financial markets could mean that property managers and advisers do not have the necessary skills to develop techniques and products that will be required in the future. The property profession cannot afford to accept graduates whose role is to maintain the status quo.

Over the last decade the nature of property advice has changed significantly. Many of the larger firms of property advisers have formed links with overseas firms in order to provide a global range of property skills. In addition, many firms have abandoned traditional partnerships in favour of a business structure that enables them to offer worthwhile careers to staff with non-property backgrounds. The fact that the more forward-looking firms now routinely employ economists, mathematicians and econometricians is proof that the nature of the business is changing. Research is now taken more seriously and reflects the view that property is really an information business. These changes have mirrored similar developments in the equities market and point to the growing sophistication of the property sector.

There is, therefore, a greater awareness that property advice cannot be taken in isolation, but must be considered within a mixed asset context. To do this, however, requires skills that many property professionals do not possess. Given that institutional investors are the major players in property investment it is clear that understanding property in a capital market framework is likely to be an important feature of investment advice in the foreseeable future.

There is currently no established theory of property investment that adequately brings together the topics we discuss here. We hope that this book will fill a major gap in the market.

However, property investment is still largely deal-driven and the lack of useful investment advice is reflected in the range of property textbooks that are available. With one or two notable exceptions, they tend to focus on two topics. There are those that tell you how to get-rich-quick by buying and selling at the right time and developing the techniques for closing deals. The others are concerned with the mechanics of how to value property. There is, of course, a similar range of books in the equities market, but there is also a wide range of excellent books that deal with the economics of investment.

The get-rich-quick approach tends to focus on making money in a rising market. The possibility of making a loss is rarely mentioned. However, the market is littered with property developers and investors who have lost considerable sums of money, which shows that there is no guaranteed way to make money in property, unless of course you write a book about how to make money!

As far as valuation textbooks are concerned many authors approach the subject from the point of view that property is a unique asset class which requires special valuation methods. In many cases the economic basis for valuation is either briefly covered or completely ignored, and there is heavy emphasis on the use of yields as a means of selecting property.

There is, of course, nothing wrong with either of these approaches as long as they work. Many ideas that you will come across in finance and economics are based on simple truths. For example, the background to diversification is based on the simple intuition that you shouldn't put all your eggs in one basket. Similarly, investors expect to be compensated for taking on extra risk. The theory of finance has tried to quantify these ideas and in doing so has offered a number of valuable insights into the way different markets operate and are priced.

Why is this book different?

An earlier book by one of the authors, *Property Investment and the Capital Markets,*[1] was written as a monograph describing the results of considering property as a financial asset. In writing this edition we have made a conscious effort to change the style so that it can now be considered as a teaching text.

We have updated many of the analyses and have introduced a number of key features that we believe will help to bridge the gap between financial theory and property investment. As you read through this book you will notice the following.

An approachable style

As this book covers a number of fairly advanced topics we felt that it was important to write it in an approachable style. We have avoided the technical paper approach and have tried to engage the reader in what is going on. We hope that we have been successful. Only time will tell.

Use of notation that is common in finance

We have found that many property research papers have tended to use a form of notation that is different from that which is generally accepted in finance. We believe that greater integration with the financial markets can only be achieved if a common form of notation is used. We have therefore provided a summary (see p. xv) of the finance notation that we have adopted and would encourage readers and researchers to use this as a standard.

Our reason for using finance notation is that it provides a level of clarity which the use of the traditional years purchase (YP) notation cannot offer. Given that most portfolio valuation calculations are undertaken by computer, it is clear that the long-term development of the profession will rely upon making use of a form of notation that is able to offer significant insights into the investment performance of property assets. Traditional notation was never developed with this in mind.

Where appropriate we have, however, shown the link between traditional YP notation and the equivalent expression that would be used in finance.

Use of empirical data

All the main ideas we describe in this book are based on empirical evidence. We believe that this is an important feature of the book and one that differentiates it from other property texts. We have, therefore, avoided using hypothetical examples unless absolutely necessary. As a result, we feel confident that our findings give a clear indication of the limits and strategies that are possible for financial institutions investing in property.

Use of examples and highlighted points

We have made extensive use of examples in order to illustrate important points. In many cases we have also adopted a step-by-step approach where we felt it was necessary to identify the use of specific techniques. We have also highlighted points that we felt were important in reinforcing important ideas.

---

[1] Brown, G.R. (1991) *Property Investment and the Capital Markets*, London, E. & F.N. Spon.

Summaries and summary tables

At the end of each chapter we have provided a summary and summary table of the main points covered. The combination of these two teaching aids should aid revision and help reinforce important ideas.

All proofs are shown in full

We have tried to provide proofs of all the main equations. The reason for doing this is not only to avoid a black box approach to investment and valuation, but also to raise awareness of how important financial relationships can be developed. Our hope is that some students will take these ideas further and develop some new ideas.

Property valuation models and financial theory

We have made a conscious point of showing how the main valuation models are derived. We have found that many students are confused by the use of yields in valuation models because they sometimes fail to see the relationship between yields and rates of return. We have tried to clarify some of these issues and show that valuation is not a separate discipline but relies on financial theory. Although we take a different approach to discussing the basis of valuation models, we don't suggest that students should abandon their valuation textbooks. What we do suggest, however, is that they should try to understand what is being taught in valuation and use the investment framework we identify to appreciate that investment and valuation are two sides of the same coin. To those who teach valuation and investment it is essential to encourage students to appreciate that these areas are closely linked. Although the Royal Institution of Chartered Surveyors (RICS) may have certain professional requirements that need to be met, we believe that it is wrong to teach valuation without some knowledge of the material covered in this book. Similarly, we believe that it is wrong to teach investment without understanding valuation practice.

Advanced topics covered in appendices

We have tried to write a book that will appeal to different groups of readers. You will see that there are a number of appendices attached to most chapters. We have chosen to do this, as opposed to writing separate chapters, so that common material is kept together. We have also written each chapter so that it covers the main material. Depending on the level at which you are reading this book you will always know that the more advanced topics will be covered in the appendices.

Quantitative techniques

One of the most important features in the development of modern property investment is that it has become more quantitative. We have often found that many students entering a course in property investment do not possess the required quantitative skills. We have therefore devoted Chapter 17 to providing an introduction to some of the basic material needed to get the most out of this book. This is not a comprehensive chapter but should provide a good introduction and show the relevance of using quantitative skills in finance.

Instructor's workbook with worked examples and illustrations

This book is also accompanied by an instructor's manual which provides worked examples and tests as well as copies of the main illustrations. This is provided as a teaching aid.

General structure of the book

We have divided the book into three parts. We anticipate that the material could be completed over a period of three years with each part building on the previous one.

Part 1: The time value of money and the valuation of cash flows

This part aims to provide material that is not well covered in the property literature. It starts from a basic introduction to discounted cash flow and leads on to the development of the common valuation models. We then cover some other important issues such as the relationship between valuations and prices. We also show how development projects should be appraised within a cash flow framework and how the choice of discount rate should be made. This material is often misleadingly presented in other property textbooks.

Part 2: Risk and return in real estate

This part of the book provides a formal introduction to risk and return. This is the cornerstone of modern financial theory and represents an important part of the way property assets should be valued. By drawing on samples of commercial property data we provide a comprehensive analysis of the risk–return characteristics of commercial property. We extend these ideas to the construction of property portfolios and discuss how effective diversification actually is in property. We also devote a chapter to the important area of valuation smoothing. This has an impact on the way individual properties are valued, but its effect is more pronounced when considering the performance of high frequency indexes.

Part 3: Portfolio management

The material covered in Part 2 provides the basis for discussing portfolio management. We examine the efficiency of the property market as well as its inflation hedging characteristics. However, the main thrust of this part is on developing portfolio strategies and discussing performance measurement. Part 3 also includes a chapter on quantitative techniques. Although we cover a lot of material, a number of questions remain unanswered. The final chapter covers eleven areas that we believe are not well covered or where current results are not conclusive. There is clearly scope for further research!

Bear in mind, however, that the majority of models that are used in finance and property are based on assumptions that easily break down when applied to practical situations. Even the simplest valuation formulas used by valuers also rely on a number of heroic assumptions. However, without these devices it would not be possible to derive useful, workable models. The majority of models you will encounter in this book are static representations of dynamic situations. The question to ask is not how good the assumptions are but how useful the models are in explaining market behaviour. You should absorb what is being taught, but you should also develop a healthy scepticism and think about ways in which the models can be improved.

Proposed reading schedule

We have written the book so that it can be read at different levels. Our primary focus is the undergraduate and postgraduate market, although much of the material will be of use to property researchers, fund managers and valuers. We don't expect the book to be read from cover to cover like a novel, but we have tried to identify a number of key topics that are important for anyone who is serious about property investment. At the end of this introduction we have indicated those sections that we feel would be of interest to different groups of reader. In putting together the suggested schedule we have assumed that postgraduates will be familiar with most of the undergraduate material. What we have proposed is merely a suggestion, and you are, of course, free to approach the material in any order you find interesting. Our intention is that what is covered will have relevance to those involved in teaching and practising property investment in Europe, Australasia, the Far East and the USA.

You will also see that we frequently interchange the terms real estate and property. Although they have the same meaning, their use in different parts of the world varies. We have chosen not to adopt any fixed style but have used whichever expression seemed to us to be most appropriate.

Proposed reading schedule	Undergraduates	Postgraduates	Fund Managers	Property Researchers	Valuers
PART 1: The time value of money and the valuation of cash flows					
1 Valuation and financial theory: bridging the gap	●	●			●
2 Valuing cash flows	●	●			●
3 Simple freehold valuation models	●	●			●
3A Yields and rent review periods		●	●		●
3B Estimating the growth rate from yields	●		●		●
3C Estimating effective rents		●	●		●
4 Simple leasehold models	●				●
4A Multiple growth models		●			●
5 Mortgages and amortisation	●	●			●
5A Analysing alternative payment methods		●	●		●
6 The term structure of interest rates	●		●	●	●
7 Valuations and prices	●		●	●	●
7A Valuations as a proxy for prices allowing for changing market environments		●	●	●	●
7B Valuation versus valuations		●		●	●
7C The distributional characteristics of valuations		●		●	
7D Commercial property valuation and the margin of error		●	●	●	●
8 Investment decision techniques	●	●			
8A Inflation, financing and taxation	●				
8B Estimating relevant cash flows	●	●			
8C Estimating relevant discount rates	●	●			
8D Allowing for risk in the cash flows		●	●	●	
8E The adjusted present value and residual equity income approach		●	●		
8F Development finance: sources and techniques					
8G Options to invest		●	●	●	
PART 2: Risk and return in real estate					
9 Distributional characteristics of real estate returns	●			●	
9A Inter-asset comparisons		●		●	
9B Statistical measures used to describe distributions		●		●	
9C Arithmetic mean, geometric mean and continuous rates of return	●		●	●	
10 Risk, return and diversification	●		●	●	●
10A Portfolio analysis	●		●	●	
10B Portfolio analysis and index models		●	●	●	
10C Portfolio analysis using alternative risk measures		●		●	
10D The capital asset pricing model (CAPM)		●	●	●	
10E The CAPM with non-marketable assets		●		●	
10F Duration and risk		●	●	●	

Acknowledgements

We would like to thank a number of people who have taken the time to read and comment on parts of this book as it was being written. In particular we would like to acknowledge the help of Dr Liow Kim Hiang of the National University of Singapore, Professor Chau Kwong Wing of Hong Kong University, Professor Neil Crosby of Reading University and Professor Graeme Newell of the University of Western Sydney. We also had a number of anonymous reviews, which helped us to refine our ideas and clarify some areas of confusion. We have also benefited from the comments and suggestions made by many students over several years during which a number of the ideas in this book have evolved. We owe a special debt of gratitude to Catherine Newman and Alison Stanford of Prentice Hall together with Jill Birch, our editorial project manager, who jointly transformed the typescript into a published book.

However, this book could not have been written without the help of the Investment Property Databank (IPD). Virtually all the analyses were undertaken using data collected by IPD. They were generous in both time and information and we would like to acknowledge the contribution that they have made over the last decade in helping to raise the standard of property research. We should point out that the results that we have presented are based on aggregate figures and do not reflect the performance of any single portfolio. Our thanks go to Vida Godson, Ian Cullen, Tony Key and Simon Fairchild.

This book has been developed from *Property Investment and the Capital Markets*, written by Gerald Brown in 1991. In the current work George Matysiak has collaborated as co-author in recognition of the valuable contribution he has made to a number of chapters.

Finally a special mention goes to our wives, Janet and Elizabeth, who were more than tolerant of the long hours it took to put this book together. We dedicate the completed work to them and hope that it will bring them many hours of entertaining reading!

Gerald R. Brown (email: brown@clara.net)
George A. Matysiak (email: matysiak@clara.net)

March 1999

Permissions acknowledgements

Grateful acknowledgement is made for permission to reproduce material in this book previously published elsewhere. Every effort has been made to trace the correct copyright holder, but if any have been inadvertently overlooked the publisher will be pleased to make the necessary arrangement at the first opportunity.

'Get the facts first. You can always distort them later'

Mark Twain

PART 1

The time value of money and the valuation of cash flows

Valuation and financial theory: bridging the gap

Learning objectives

After reading this chapter you will understand the following:

- The importance of present value

- What makes a good investment decision

- Why you need to consider the expected outcome when faced with risk

- How positive net present value can increase the value of a business

Introduction

A financial institution is contemplating the purchase of a property to include in its portfolio. The allocation to property has been declining over the last few years and the fund manager responsible for making the decision is keen to ensure that the performance of the property fund will encourage further investment in this sector. In making the decision the property manager is concerned with not only the value of the property in isolation, but also how that value will be viewed within the context of other assets managed by the institution.

This approach shows that property must be considered as part of a much larger range of investments. This chapter introduces some of the concepts that are important in assessing the value of an asset and paves the way for developing a systematic approach to making property investment decisions. You will learn about the importance of information and present value and how decisions should be made using tools that are economically valid.

The importance of present value

Property investment is concerned with acquiring real assets that are worth more than their cost. Although this is a simple decision rule that is widely followed, in practice it is essential to understand how assets should be valued and the need for well-functioning markets. These are important parts of the investment process and have implications for the way decisions are made.

Unlike stock market investments, property is not frequently traded in an open market and access to information is often limited. Professional valuers have, therefore, to acquire information about comparable transactions and use this as the basis of comparison when making an assessment of value. The need for high quality information has, in recent years, led to the emergence of independent property information services whose role it is to provide information about the market which can be used in making investment decisions.

Given this framework an important question to ask is: Do we need a formal theory of valuation? Surprisingly, the answer is no. If a valuer is using all relevant comparable information concerning a property, then the value arrived at should be within a few percentage points of the true value. In a well-functioning market we can, therefore, take market value as representing true value. Market value is also the present value of the property.

> In a well-functioning market we do not need a formal theory of value.
>
> Market Value = True Value = Present Value

This is an important point that is often misunderstood by some valuers. We will explore this issue in more detail as we introduce more advanced topics. However, it is worth pointing out that the use of sophisticated valuation models does not mean that the resulting valuations will be any better. Some professional valuers have argued strongly for the use of explicit growth models in favour of the more common yield models in the belief that they produce 'more accurate' valuations. There are, however, no economic reasons to believe that the use of such a model should improve the accuracy of valuations.

So why bother with a formal theory of value? The answer to this is also surprising. We need a formal theory of value to tell us what a property is worth. Only with an assessment of the true economic value is it possible to determine whether a property is under- or overpriced. This is a matter for economics and an understanding of the way capital markets work. A property may, for example, be worth more to one person than to another merely because of the way each individual assesses the importance of relevant information.

Making investment decisions

To put this into perspective it is important to develop an intuitive grasp of how investment decisions should be made and the criteria that should be used to aid that process. This can best be illustrated with a simple example.

Let us assume that the property fund manager introduced at the beginning of this chapter is interested in buying an office building. To keep things really simple let us assume that the time horizon for the investment is only one year, the investment carries no risk and that there are no transactions costs. In other words, the fund will incur no expenses when it sells the property after one year. After much searching a suitable proposal is found. The problem facing the fund manager is: how much should be offered in order to induce the owner to part with the property?

In order to answer this the fund manager needs to assess the current market value of the property. A valuer is appointed who, after making a comparison with similar properties, estimates the current open market value at £5,000,000. This figure can also be related to its market value in 12 months' time. Assume, for example, that the return on government securities with a one-year maturity is 5%. This implies that the value of the property in one year should be £5,250,000. Another way of looking at this is to recognise that the demand for property will mean that its value will have increased by 5%. Remember that for this example there is no risk involved, so this outcome is certain.

These two figures are, of course, related. The £5,000,000 is merely the present value of £5,250,000 in one year. The present value rule says that a pound today is worth more than a pound tomorrow. This is because it is possible to invest today's pound so that it will start earning interest immediately.

> Because you have the opportunity to invest, the *present value* rule tells us that a pound (£) today is worth more than a pound (£) tomorrow.

If there is a delayed pay-off it must be compared with what could have been earned by investing today. The present value of the office building can therefore be expressed as follows:

$$PV = \frac{\text{pay-off}}{(1 + r_f)} = \frac{£5,250,000}{(1 + 0.05)} = £5,000,000$$

The present value of £5,000,000 represents the price at which the office building could be sold in the market in order to earn £5,250,000 in twelve months' time. As this is a riskless investment it is also what it would cost to make £5,250,000 in one year's time by investing in government securities.

Because this is the only reasonable price in an open market that would satisfy both the buyer and seller the present value is, therefore, its market price. The return of 5% used in the example is also known as the *opportunity cost of capital* because it represents the return forgone by investing in the project rather than in government securities. The open market value of £5,000,000 therefore represents a fair price.

In arriving at the open market value a comparison was made with comparable properties. The values of the comparables were also adjusted so that they reflected more of the characteristics of the property that had to be valued. This is a bit like an auction where the comparable values represent the bids. Given this information, and coupled with experience, the valuer then arrives at a figure that is intended to represent a fair value for the property in a competitive market.

This, however, is not the end of the story. The fund manager now knows the fair market price, but whether he or she will be better off or not will depend on the final price paid. The amount by which he or she will be better off can be determined by calculating the net present value.

Net present value (NPV) is simply the difference between the present value of the pay-off and the current investment. Remember that this investment only has a life of one year. If we assume that our fund manager has no reason to offer other than the market price, then the net present value can be calculated as follows:

$$NPV = \frac{£5,250,000}{(1 + 0.05)} - £5,000,000 = 0$$

The net present value of zero merely means that the property is correctly priced and that the investor is earning 5% on his or her money.

Let us now assume that the fund manager knows that the owner of the property is desperate to sell the property because of financial difficulties and is prepared to negotiate a keen price in order to raise cash quickly. This represents additional information that is outside the open market situation described above. It gives the fund manager a competitive advantage that is quickly exploited with an offer of £4,500,000. Assuming this is accepted, the amount by which the fund is better off can still be estimated using the net present value rule. Remember, however, that all that has changed is the price that has been offered. This is still a riskless investment so the pay-off in one year's time remains unchanged. The net present value under this deal is:

$$NPV = \frac{£5,250,000}{(1 + 0.05)} - £4,500,000 = £500,000$$

There is a net contribution in value to the fund of £500,000 and the value of the shares of the investment fund will increase in the marketplace by this amount. Although the fund manager is happy with this decision it must also be recognised that the property owner has also made a compensating loss of the same amount.

The assumption of a guaranteed pay-off is clearly unrealistic. The future value of a property cannot be known with certainty. It can only be based on the best forecast given the information known today. We must therefore talk in terms of expected returns and pay-offs over the holding period. To this extent expected return only has meaning at the beginning of the holding period. At the end of the holding period the outcome may be completely different and it is this difference that creates uncertainty in the returns.

> Expected returns only have meaning at the beginning of the holding period.
> At the end of the holding period the outcome may be completely different.

Because of the uncertainty concerning the outcome the fund manager is no longer able to offer as much to secure the office building. As most investors try to avoid risk without losing return, the concept of opportunity cost of capital and net present value is still valid for risky investments. It therefore remains sensible to discount our investment at a rate that is comparable to investments of equivalent risk. How this rate is chosen has yet to be discussed but it is a common belief that the risk premium to be offered for investing in property is close to 2% over the riskless rate of return (this is discussed in Chapter 15, Appendix 15A). The 2% is estimated by making a comparison with other investments in the market that carry equivalent risk. For illustration purposes, it is assumed that a premium of 2% is valid so that the opportunity cost of capital is now 7% p.a. The pay-off in one year of £5,250,000 is assumed to remain the same but is now drafted in terms of expectations. Our property now has the following expected present value:

$$E(PV) = \frac{\text{expected pay-off}}{(1 + r)} = \frac{£5,250,000}{(1 + 0.07)} = £4,906,542$$

To achieve an expected pay-off of £5,250,000 in one year the fund manager can only afford to offer approximately £4,900,000 today. This lower value reflects the need for additional return to compensate for taking on the extra risk.

If £5,250,000 represents a fair estimate of the expected value in one year then, given the rate of return of 7%, it should be possible to observe comparable properties trading at prices close to £4,900,000.

The net present value still makes sense in an uncertain world and can still be used as a decision-making rule. It will, however, be drafted in terms of expectations. In our example, if the fund agreed to buy the property for £4,500,000, the expected net present value would be just over £400,000.

Financial distress

This looks very straightforward. All you have to do is find a property, work out its present value and then make a lower offer that will give a positive net present value. However, many investors rarely have sufficient funds to buy a property outright so they usually end up financing the purchase with borrowed funds. This sometimes leads to financial distress. In our example we looked at a single year and estimated the present value by discounting over a one-year period. We can, however, extend this idea over many periods.

Let us take another look at the expected pay-off example and extend it in perpetuity. At an expected return of 7% p.a. the present value of £4,906,542 would generate a perpetual income stream of £343,458 p.a. The more usual way of interpreting this is to say that a project producing an expected income of £343,458 p.a. in perpetuity would cost £4,906,542 if the required return were 7%. If you don't have this sort of money then the only way you could buy this project would be to borrow part of the asking price. Let's assume that you borrow 80% of the asking price and you take out an interest-only loan costing 5% p.a. This reduces the amount of money you have to find, but you have to make sure that you can pay the interest from the rent received. To find out, you can draw up the following analysis:

Project finance

80% Debt	£3,925,234
20% Equity	£981,308
Total	£4,906,542

Interest on debt at 5%	−£196,261
Income from rent	£343,458
Net income	£147,197

After having paid the interest in each year you would be left with a net income of £147,197 p.a. However, as your equity involvement in the project is only £981,308 you can estimate the return that you are earning as follows:

$$\text{Return on equity} = \frac{£147,197}{£981,308} = 0.15 = 15\% \text{ p.a.}$$

It is important to realise that although your return is much higher than the 7% that was used to value the income stream you haven't created any additional wealth. All you have done is rearrange it! You can see how this works by weighting the return on the debt and equity components as follows:

$$w_d r_d + w_e r_e = r_p$$

where w_d and w_e are the proportion of funds in debt and equity, and r_d and r_e represent the return on debt and equity.

Substituting the appropriate figures gives:

$$(0.8 \times 5\%) + (0.2 \times 15\%) = 7\%$$

This is the same return that would have been earned had you been able to fund the project entirely out of your own equity. Whatever combination of debt and equity that you use you will always get the same answer.

Let us now assume that the market crashes and that interest rates rise to 12% p.a. You are still left with a debt of £3,925,234 but, as you can see, your annual interest payments are now much higher and cannot be supported by the rental income.

Project finance

80% Debt	£3,925,234
20% Equity	£981,308
Total	£4,906,542

Interest on debt at 12%	−£471,028
Income from rent	£343,458
Net income	−£127,570

The return on your equity in this case is −13%.

Because you can't afford to support the loan you are technically insolvent. If your bank is not prepared to let you carry the debt until interest rates drop you will be forced to sell the property. Unfortunately, you may have to do this when the market is depressed and you find that property prices have fallen. Your bank insists that you repay the loan so you end up agreeing a sale at £3,500,000. As this doesn't cover the loan of £3,925,234 you still end up with a debt of £425,234 which the bank will try to recover by forcing you to sell some other assets. A further implication of this sequence of events is that you find it difficult to secure additional funds so your ability to invest is severely reduced.

We have looked at only one property transaction. If you own a property company and this happens to a number of the properties you own, you will see that this sequence of events can have serious implications for future growth. Gearing up the return on equity works well when the market is buoyant and many property developers became extremely wealthy by doing just this. However, as interest rates rise you will see that it is also very easy to become bankrupt. The financial crisis in Asia in the mid-1990s owed a lot to the quality of loans that were secured on poorly performing property and reinforces the view that investment in property can be very risky.

These simple examples illustrate a number of key points that are central to the theme of this book.

- In a well-functioning market, present value is equal to market value.
- Positive net present values represent a net contribution to value.
- The opportunity cost of capital is determined by reference to the return on assets carrying equivalent risk.
- Under risky conditions property valuations are drafted in terms of expectations.
- The expected value of a property depends on the quality of information which is available.
- Gearing up the returns on a property will increase the riskiness of the equity returns.

These are important ideas and have a profound influence on the way property investment decisions should be made. They also raise a number of questions that will be explored in the following chapters. For example:

- How do you estimate the correct discount rate?
- How should properties be valued?
- What happens when you add properties into a portfolio?
- Is it possible to develop a property strategy?
- How should you choose between different asset classes?
- How do you measure the performance of a property portfolio?

Many of the ideas discussed will draw heavily on research that has been undertaken in the area of financial economics. The reason for this is simple. The principles of finance and investment have a broad application and property is not so different that it requires a whole new theory. If a new theory were required, then it would be difficult for investment funds to make a choice between asset classes. The valuation of property and good investment decisions should, therefore, be based on an understanding of the principles of finance.

Before we embark on some of these issues it will be useful to consider the importance of property in relation to other asset classes. A study undertaken by Ibbotson, Siegal and Love (1985) examined a number of aspects of world wealth. One of the reasons for doing this is the idea that a market wealth portfolio is consistent with the concept of diversification and portfolio theory. It is therefore useful to see the relative importance of different asset classes. The results are given in Figure 1.1.

When this was undertaken the total value of world wealth was estimated at US$27,681.5 billion. What is interesting from this illustration is that the proportion of funds committed to property is over 55% of this figure. Property in this case includes both commercial and residential as well as farmland and other interests. By contrast,

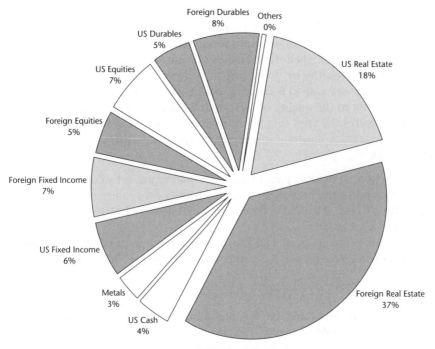

Figure 1.1: Distribution of world wealth, 1984

the equities markets represent only 12% of total world wealth. However, in terms of our understanding of these markets we know far more about the equities market than we do about property. Part of the reason for this is that property only became a seri- ous investment asset class after the Second World War, but the main reason is that databases of property returns were not established until the late 1970s. With this back- ground and the confidentiality that has surrounded many property transactions it is not surprising that our knowledge of this market is not as well developed. However, the scene is changing and there is now a lot of research activity in many parts of the world. This book summarises some of that work.

Summary

In order to make good investment decisions in a well-functioning market you only need a formal theory of valuation in order to tell you what an asset is worth. The difference between its worth and price will tell you whether you have made a profit. This idea works whether you are dealing with riskless or risky assets. The only difference is that when the future is uncertain you have to deal in expected values.

If you are successful in choosing assets that result in a profit, the value of your company will rise. Whenever you are dealing with an uncertain outcome the quality of information you use to make your decisions is very important.

Gearing can enhance your return on equity, but as interest rates rise you run the risk of becoming bankrupt if your level of borrowing is too high.

Problems

1. Why is a positive net present value so important?
2. Why do you need a theory of valuation?
3. What is the importance of a well-functioning market?
4. What is the opportunity cost of capital?
5. What is the relationship between market value and true value?
6. Do sophisticated models give more accurate valuations?
7. What effect does gearing have on your equity returns?
8. What are the implications of gearing up the returns on a property?

Selected reference

Ibbotson, R.G., Siegal, L.B. and Love, K.S. (1985) *The Journal of Portfolio Management,* Vol. 12, No. 1, 4–23.

Valuing cash flows

Learning objectives

After reading this chapter you will understand the following:

- How to value cash flows

- Single- and multiple-period investments

- Annuities

- Sinking funds

- Valuing over periods of less than one year

- Effective interest rates and APRs

- Nominal and real interest rates

This material provides the foundation for valuing all assets and understanding how to evaluate development projects.

Introduction

The purchase of a property conveys certain rights to the investor, one of which is the right to receive an income stream under the terms of a lease. If a property is over-rented how should it be valued?

A financial institution is looking at the possibility of developing a city centre site. There is, however, more than one way to develop the site, each of which would be acceptable in planning terms. How should the choice be made?

Property fund managers frequently face problems such as these and have to make decisions about those options that represent the best value for money. Analysing problems that generate a future stream of cash flows requires a clear understanding of how assets should be valued.

This chapter will introduce you to compounding and discounting, and provide you with the essential tools for valuing and analysing property investment and development problems. These are essential for a clear understanding of the way assets should be valued. We will draw on these ideas in later chapters and show that all valuation models embody these key concepts in some form or other.

Single- and multiple-period investments

The example given in Chapter 1 introduced the time value of money by showing that a pound today is worth more than a pound tomorrow. We related the expected pay-off in one year to the value today by finding the present value. This is a very simple form of valuation model that extends over one period. The concept is exactly the same as investing money in a deposit account at your local bank.

Estimating future values

Assume that you invested £100 in a deposit account offering a return of 5% p.a. At the end of the year your investment would have grown to £105. We can relate the present value (PV) and future value (FV) as follows:

$$PV(1 + r) = FV$$
$$£100(1 + 0.05) = £105$$

Instead of withdrawing the £105 let us now assume that you leave it invested for a further year. What will it be worth at the end of the second year? Using the idea we have just developed we can write down the value at the end of the second year in terms of its value at the beginning of the year:[1]

$$£105(1 + 0.05) = £110.25$$

The value of our fund at the beginning of the second year (i.e., £105) has increased by another 5%. You could, however, have got to the same value in one step. If you assumed that interest rates remained constant in both years you could write its future value as follows:

$$[PV(1 + r)](1 + r) = FV_2$$
$$PV(1 + r)^2 = FV_2$$
$$£100(1 + 0.05)^2 = £110.25$$

If you make no intermediate investments you can generalise the above principle to find the value at any point in the future. The general formula can be written as:

$$PV(1 + r)^n = FV_n \tag{2.1}$$

where $(1 + r)^n$ is the compounding factor.

---

[1] Interest rates are always expressed in decimal form and cash flows are always assumed to arise at the end of a period.

Valuers refer to this as the *amount of one pound.*

Let us now use this formula to find the value of a single deposit of £1,000 invested in a bank at a constant annual rate of interest of 5% for 25 years:

$$£1,000(1 + 0.05)^{25} = FV_{25} = £3,386.35$$

In terms of valuation concepts the £1,000 represents the price that you would have to pay today to receive a single payment of £3,386.35 in 25 years' time assuming that you could earn a constant rate of interest of 5% per annum.

Estimating present values

As we are concerned with valuation concepts we can turn this example round to find the present value. For a single cash flow occurring at any point in the future, its present value can be found by rearranging equation 2.1 as follows:

$$PV = \frac{FV_n}{(1 + r)^n} \tag{2.2}$$

where $\dfrac{1}{(1 + r)^n}$ = the discount factor.

Valuers refer to this as the *present value of one pound.*

Assume you want to build up a lump sum of £50,000 in twenty years' time and interest rates remain constant at 5% p.a. You can use this formula to find out how much it would cost *today* to buy this investment:

$$PV = \frac{£50,000}{(1 + 0.05)^{20}} = £18,844.47$$

Multiple-period cash flows

So far we have considered only single-period cash flows. We can, however, use the same principles to find the present value of a cash flow at any point in time, and because they are all expressed in current terms we can add them together. This is a very useful result for it means that we can use the concept of present value to value a number of cash flows that occur in different periods. We can write the present value of a series of cash flows, $a_1, a_2, a_3, \ldots$ as follows:

$$PV = \frac{a_1}{(1 + r)} + \frac{a_2}{(1 + r)^2} + \frac{a_3}{(1 + r)^3} + \ldots \tag{2.3}$$

A shorthand way of writing this is to use a summation sign.[2]

---

[2] We have provided an introduction to some important mathematical concepts in Chapter 17. None of them requires more than basic algebra.

$$PV = \sum_{x=1}^{x=n} \frac{a_x}{(1 + r)^x}$$

(2.4)

This simple formula can be used to value any investment that produces a series of cash flows at different points in time.

A practical example in which you can use this formula would be the valuation of a short-term lease that generates a guaranteed fixed income stream of, say, £20,000 p.a. for five years. If the appropriate return is 6% p.a. you can work out how much you would have to pay to buy this cash flow.

As it can take some time to become proficient at manipulating cash flows it is worth spending time setting them up on a time line. That way it is easy to see where the cash flows occur and will reduce any errors in discounting. Our leasehold example can be set up as follows:

Each cash flow arises at the end of a year and is discounted back to its present value. Adding them together gives the total present value of £84,247.27. This is what the lease is worth in the marketplace.

Now that you know where each of the cash flows arises you can set them up in a table and discount them in more conventional form (Table 2.1).

If you compare this with the time line shown above, you will see that each of the cash flows is discounted back to its present value at the end of year 0. Because the present values are all expressed at the same point in time, they can be added together.

Table 2.1 ● Cash flow table

End year	Cash flow	Discount factor at 6% p.a.	Present value at end year 0
1	£20,000	0.9434	£18,867.92
2	£20,000	0.8899	£17,799.93
3	£20,000	0.8396	£16,792.39
4	£20,000	0.7921	£15,841.87
5	£20,000	0.7473	£14,945.16
			£84,247.27

This is known as the *value additivity principle*.

> Because present values all occur at the same point in time the *value additivity principle* allows you to add them together.

Rent received in arrears and in advance

Although cash flows are generally assumed to occur at the end of each year it is more common with property leases for rent to be paid in advance. A tenant usually has to pay for the space he or she wishes to rent *before* it can be used. This is the difference between rent being paid *in arrears* and *in advance* and it can make a significant difference in terms of the value of the lease. The reason for this should be clear from the above. Because the table is set up so that rent is received in arrears the first payment of rent occurs at the end of the first year. Its present value is not £20,000, as the delayed receipt reduces its value. In this case the value of the first rental payment is £18,867.92.

If rent is received in advance this no longer happens. The first payment is received at the end of year 0, i.e. at the *beginning* of year 1, and has a present value of £20,000. This effect ripples through each year and increases the overall value of the lease, as follows:

Table 2.2 ● Cash flow table with income received in advance

End year	Cash flow	Discount factor at 6% p.a.	Present value
0	£20,000	1.0000	£20,000.00
1	£20,000	0.9434	£18,867.92
2	£20,000	0.8899	£17,799.93
3	£20,000	0.8396	£16,792.39
4	£20,000	0.7921	£15,841.87
5			
			£89,302.11

Note that you have no cash flow at the end of year 5 although you still have five rental payments. By switching the rental payments from arrears to advance the value of the lease has increased by just over £5,000.

There is a simple relationship between cash flows that are received in arrears and in advance. One is merely the present value of the other:

$$PV_{Arrears} = \frac{PV_{Advance}}{(1 + r)} \qquad (2.5)$$

In our example the values are related as follows:

$$£84,247.27 = \frac{£89,302.11}{(1.06)}$$

By rearranging equation 2.5 you will see that as long as you have a constant interest rate it is a simple matter to convert lease payments received *in arrears* to *in advance* by multiplying by $(1 + r)$. In general terms this can be written as:

$$PV_{Advance} = (1 + r) \sum_{x=1}^{x=n} \frac{a_x}{(1 + r)^x} \qquad (2.6)$$

A Cautionary Tale
Calculations like this are frequently undertaken with spreadsheets using built-in present value functions. These functions adopt a black-box approach to estimating present value and *always* assume that cash flows occur in arrears.

If your lease payments are in advance and you use the spreadsheet function you could easily find that you have valued the lease one period before it starts! Multiplying by $(1 + r)$ will easily correct this problem.

Annuities

An attractive feature of property leases is that they produce a series of constant cash flows. In our example we calculated the present value of each cash flow separately. This is not a problem if only a few periods are involved, but when there are lots of cash flows it is useful to look for some shortcuts. One approach is to recognise that the series of regular cash flows is known as an annuity.

An *annuity* is a regular series of cash flows.

If we can work out a simple expression for the present value of an annuity then we have a valuation formula. It's time to use some algebra!

We will let P equal the present value of a regular series of cash flows of £a p.a. that arise at the end of each year for n years. From what you already know you can write the present value of this cash flow as follows:

$$P = \frac{a}{(1 + r)} + \frac{a}{(1 + r)^2} + \frac{a}{(1 + r)^3} + \ldots + \frac{a}{(1 + r)^n} \qquad (2.7)$$

What you want to do, however, is write this as a single equation so that you don't have lots of intermediate calculations. You therefore need some way of eliminating a lot of the expressions on the right-hand side. The way to do this is to multiply both sides of the equation by $\frac{1}{(1 + r)}$. All this does is change the scale of the equation but it has some useful advantages.

Let's see what happens:

$$\frac{P}{(1 + r)} = \frac{a}{(1 + r)^2} + \frac{a}{(1 + r)^3} + \ldots + \frac{a}{(1 + r)^{n+1}} \qquad (2.8)$$

If you compare this with equation 2.7 you will see that a lot of the expressions are the same. This suggests that if you subtract equation 2.8 from equation 2.7 you could get rid of a lot of the intermediate expressions. This is what happens:

$$P - \frac{P}{(1 + r)} = \frac{a}{(1 + r)} - \frac{a}{(1 + r)^{n+1}} \tag{2.9}$$

This has reduced the number of intermediate expressions, but with a bit of rearrangement it can be simplified further. This requires a bit of extra algebra:

$$P\left[1 - \frac{1}{(1 + r)}\right] = \frac{a}{(1 + r)}\left[1 - \frac{1}{(1 + r)^n}\right]$$

$$P(1 + r)\left[1 - \frac{1}{(1 + r)}\right] = a\left[1 - (1 + r)^{-n}\right]$$

$$P[1 + r - 1] = a[1 - (1 + r)^{-n}]$$

The present value of an annuity can, therefore, be written as follows:

$$P = \frac{a[1 - (1 + r)^{-n}]}{r} \tag{2.10}$$

where $\dfrac{1 - (1 + r)^{-n}}{r}$ = the discount factor.

Valuers refer to this as the *Year's Purchase* (single rate) or the *present value of £1 p.a.*

From this you will see that all you need to value the cash flow is the constant income stream, the discount rate and the number of years. Let's use this on the lease we valued earlier.

The rental payments were £20,000 for five years. We decided that the opportunity cost of capital was 6%. Substituting these figures into equation 2.10 gives the present value as follows:

$$£20,000\left[\frac{1 - (1.06)^{-5}}{0.06}\right] = £84,247.27$$

This is exactly the same value we got in Table 2.1, when we discounted each of the cash flows in arrears. If you want to know the value if the cash flows were received in advance, then you would multiply the expression by $(1 + r)$.

For cash flows received in advance

$$P_{Advance} = (1 + r)\left\{\frac{a[1 - (1 + r)^{-n}]}{r}\right\} \tag{2.11}$$

Using the same figures as before the value of the lease with income received in advance is:

$$P_{Advance} = (1.06)\left\{£20,000\left[\frac{1 - (1.06)^{-5}}{0.06}\right]\right\} = £89,302.11$$

There are many cases where you can use the annuity formula. In Chapter 5, for example, we will use the annuity formula to analyse mortgages. We will also use annuities in Chapter 3 when we start to look at valuation formulas that embody growth. The main advantage in using an algebraic solution is that it enables complex cash flow situations to be analysed in an economically defensible manner.

Sinking funds

Earlier we saw that if you made a single deposit of £1,000 in a bank offering 5% p.a. and left it invested for 25 years it would grow to £3,386.35. But what would happen if you invested £1,000 each year? How much would this investment be worth in 25 years? With a constant cash flow this is very similar to the annuity we have just discussed, except that it is in reverse. In fact, we will soon show you how these two are related.

This type of cash flow is known as a sinking fund and is a way of building up a capital sum at some point in the future. Usually this is required to make a payment for some capital equipment, or for future repairs or the replacement of the capital lost in a lease. Because you are earning interest on the money you invest, the cost of building up the fund will be less than if you had to find the total amount as a single sum at some point in the future.

> A *sinking fund* is a series of regular deposits that earn interest. The final value is often used to fund a major acquisition, or replace some capital equipment at some point in the future.

Let's look at a simple example of how a sinking fund works. Assume that you make five annual deposits of £1,000 and are able to earn interest at 8% p.a. on the sums invested. You make the first investment at the beginning of year 0 and receive the accumulated sum at the end of year 4. Note that this is also the beginning of year 5 so your sinking fund is available for use during the fifth year. The question is, how much is your sinking fund worth at the end of year 4? This is really a compound interest problem which you can set up using a time line.

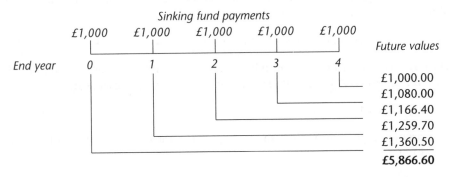

Your fund grows to £5,866.60 by the end of year 4. You should note carefully where the cash flows arise and how they have been compounded. This is important when considering any type of cash flow analysis. Once you are familiar with what is happening on the time line you can write the cash flows in the form of a table as follows:

Table 2.3 ● **Cash flows for a sinking fund**

End year	Cash flow	Years invested	Interest factor at 8%		Final value at End Year 4
0	£1,000	4	$(1.08)^4 =$	1.3605	£1,360.50
1	£1,000	3	$(1.08)^3 =$	1.2597	£1,259.70
2	£1,000	2	$(1.08)^2 =$	1.1664	£1,166.40
3	£1,000	1	$(1.08)^0 =$	1.0800	£1,080.00
4	£1,000	0	$(1.08)^0 =$	1.0000	£1,000.00
					£5,866.60

Now that you can see how this works in practice it is time to use some algebra again to derive a simple model that will estimate the final value of the sinking fund assuming that the deposits are the same in each period. The way to solve this is similar to the method we used for the annuity. The future value, F, can be expressed as follows:

$$F = a(1 + r)^{n-1} + a(1 + r)^{n-2} + \ldots + a(1 + r)^3 + a(1 + r)^2 + a(1 + r) + a \qquad (2.12)$$

It is easier to read this expression from the far right. The last term is just a single payment with no compounding. In our example this is equal to £1,000 at the end of year 4. The next term is just the annual payment compounded for one year, and so on.

When you get to the first term you will see that it equals the annual payment compounded for $(n - 1)$ years. Why have we used $n - 1$ years? The answer to this can be seen from the time line and the table where the first cash flow is only compounded forward for four years. Given that you have made five annual investments the four-year period can be expressed as $n - 1$.

To find a simple expression for the future value you have to eliminate a lot of intermediate terms. To do this you can adopt the same idea we used with the annuity formula, with a slight modification. Because all our cash flows are compounded, we multiply both sides by $(1 + r)$ as follows:

$$F(1 + r) = a(1 + r)^n + a(1 + r)^{n-1} + \ldots + a(1 + r)^3 + a(1 + r)^2 + a(1 + r) \qquad (2.13)$$

Once again there are expressions in both equations that are the same. If you subtract equation 2.12 from 2.13 you will see that a lot of these terms disappear:

$$F(1 + r) - F = a(1 + r)^n - a \qquad (2.14)$$

By rearranging you can write a simple expression for the future value of the cash flows as follows:

$$F[(1 + r) - 1] = a[(1 + r)^n - 1] \tag{2.15}$$

$$F = \frac{a[(1 + r)^n - 1]}{r} \tag{2.16}$$

where $\dfrac{(1 + r)^n - 1}{r}$ = the compounding factor.

Valuers refer to this as the *amount of £1 p.a.*

You can check that it is correct by substituting the values from our example:

$$F = £1,000 \left[\frac{(1.08)^5 - 1}{0.08} \right] = £5,866.60 \tag{2.17}$$

The value of the sinking fund tells you how much the fund will be worth at some point in the future. Often, however, you may want to know how much to invest each year in order to build up a fund. You can use the same formula, but in this case you would find the annual amount, a, by rearranging equation 2.16 to give:

$$a = \frac{Fr}{[(1 + r)^n - 1]} \tag{2.18}$$

Sinking fund example

Assume that the air conditioning plant in your new office building cost £125,000. It has a useable life of 20 years and you anticipate that the replacement cost will rise at the rate of 3% p.a. If you can deposit funds in an account offering 7% p.a. how much should you invest at the end of each year to replace the system in 20 years' time?

First of all you need to know how much the air conditioning system will cost to replace in 20 years' time. This is the future value of £125,000 at 3% p.a. for 20 years.

£125,000 $(1.03)^{20}$ = £225,764

This is the final value that your fund needs to build up to over 20 years. Using equation 2.18 you can work out the annual instalments:

$$\frac{£225,764 \times (1.07)}{(1.07)^{20} - 1} = £5,507$$

By investing £5,507 every year for 20 years in an account paying 7% p.a. in interest, you will build up a fund worth £225,764 and have enough money to replace your air conditioning system. You can see that the reinvestment of the interest is a valuable component in the calculation and reduces the amount you have to save each year. Without the opportunity to earn interest you would need to put aside £11,288 every year for 20 years.

Another way of looking at sinking funds

We mentioned earlier that sinking funds and annuities are related. What they share is a constant cash flow. The only difference is that annuities calculate the present value, whereas sinking funds calculate the future value. We also know that present values and future values are related, which suggests that the final value of a sinking fund can be regarded as the future value of an annuity. A simple way of getting our expression for the value of a sinking fund is to compound the annuity formula to the end of the investment period. This entails multiplying the annuity formula by $(1 + r)^n$. The future value of equation 2.10 can, therefore, be written as:

$$FV = a \left[\frac{1 - (1 + r)^{-n}}{r} \right] (1 + r)^n \tag{2.19}$$

which simplifies to:

$$FV = a \left[\frac{(1 + r)^n - 1}{r} \right] \tag{2.20}$$

This is exactly the same formula derived earlier and shows the value of using financial mathematics to solve valuation problems.

Valuing over periods of less than one year

So far we have considered cash flows and interest rates which have been expressed in annual terms. In many cases, however, cash flows occur at different periods throughout the year. Rents received under a lease can, for example, occur quarterly or monthly as well as being in advance. The methods of valuation discussed above need to take this into consideration.

The first question we need to ask is: what effect would cash flows received throughout the year have on value? Earlier in this chapter we showed that a pound today is worth more than a pound tomorrow. When we discounted cash flows that were received in advance we showed that they were more valuable than cash flows received in arrears. This is because you receive the money earlier. It follows, therefore, that rental payments received throughout the year must be worth more than a single rental payment at the end of the year.

Although cash flows may be spread throughout the year you can still value them using the same techniques we have already described. The important point to bear in mind, however, is that you must be consistent in the way you handle cash flows and discount rates. For example, if your cash flows occur in every quarter then you must value them using quarterly discount rates.

Let's use this idea to modify our annuity formula to value quarterly cash flows. If we assume that the interest rate is quoted as one quarter of the annual rate we can write the value of the annuity over n years as:

$$V = \frac{a}{4} \left[\frac{1 - \left(1 + \frac{r}{4}\right)^{-4n}}{\frac{r}{4}} \right] \tag{2.21}$$

You will see that what we have done is to express the income as one quarter of the annual amount. However, to be consistent we have increased the number of periods over which they are valued by a factor of 4. Let's try a simple example to show how this works.

You are asked to value a lease that has five years to run. The annual rent is £12,000 and the annual return for this type of investment is believed to 12% p.a. The rent is received quarterly in arrears. Substituting these figures into equation 2.21 gives the following:

$$V = \frac{£12,000}{4} \left[\frac{1 - \left(1 + \frac{0.12}{4}\right)^{-(4)(5)}}{\frac{0.12}{4}} \right] = £44,632.42$$

Had the income been received in five equal instalments at the end of each year the lease would have been worth £43,257.31. Receiving the income earlier has increased the value of the lease by just over £1,375.

You could, of course, generalise the above expression to cope with any period. If we let m equal the number of discounting periods per year the present value of an annuity for n years can be written as:

$$V = \frac{a}{m} \left[\frac{1 - \left(1 + \frac{r}{m}\right)^{-mn}}{\frac{r}{m}} \right] \qquad (2.22)$$

which simplifies to:

$$V = \frac{a}{m} \left[\frac{1 - (1 + r_m)^{-mn}}{r_m} \right] \qquad (2.23)$$

where r_m is the rate of interest for the m discounting periods in a year.

Annual percentage return (APR)

Although this appears reasonable it will, in fact, produce incorrect results if the periodic interest rate is quoted as a fraction of the annual rate! The reason for this is to do with the way that interest is calculated in each period. To illustrate the point we will take our example a little further.

The annual interest rate was quoted as 12% so we assumed that the interest in each quarter was 3%. If, however, you compound this interest rate over four quarters you will see that it does not equal 12% p.a. but 12.55% p.a. The way to do this is as follows:

$$(1 + r_{Quarter})^4 = (1 + r_{Annual}) \qquad (2.24)$$

$$r_{Annual} = (1 + r_{Quarter})^4 - 1 \qquad (2.25)$$

$$r_{Annual} = (1 + 0.03)^4 - 1 = 0.1255 \text{ or } 12.55\% \text{ p.a.}$$

The 12.55% is referred to as the *Annual Percentage Rate* (APR). This has such an important effect on loan agreements that you will see the APR quoted on many financing arrangements for mortgages, car loans and credit cards. In Chapter 5 we will look at the effect that APRs have on the calculation of mortgages.

Credit card companies frequently quote the interest rate they charge on a monthly basis. This is because bills are sent out monthly and it makes sense to charge on this basis. However, the difference in cost between different companies can be quite large even though the difference in monthly rates appears to be small.

For example, the difference between a monthly rate of 1.50% and 1.75% is only 0.25%. However, in terms of Annual Percentage Return (APR) the difference is between 19.56% and 23.14%, or 3.58% p.a. Credit card companies generally show the APR they are charging on their monthly statements.

The effective rate of interest

Using the correct rate of interest for cash flows that occur at periods of less than one year is important, so you need to understand what effect it will have on the value of your lease. Let's try to reason this through. In our example you were charged 3% every quarter so you were in effect paying more interest than you should. Remember the annual rate quoted was 12%, but the APR is 12.55%. Because of the extra interest this means that the value of your lease is lower than it should be given that the agreed annual interest rate is 12%. You can, however, work out the correct quarterly rate assuming that the APR is 12%, as follows:

$$r_{Quarter} = (1 + r_{Annual})^{\frac{1}{4}} - 1 \tag{2.26}$$

Substituting the 12% annual rate of return gives:

$$r_{Quarter} = (1 + 0.12)^{\frac{1}{4}} - 1$$

$$r_{Quarter} = 0.02874, \text{ or } 2.874\%$$

This is known as the *effective rate of interest*. Substituting into our annuity formula gives the following valuation:

$$V = \frac{£12,000}{4} \left[\frac{1 - (1 + 0.02874)^{-(4)(5)}}{0.02874} \right] = £45,156.83 \tag{2.27}$$

As expected, the value has increased. In this case the difference is just over £524. Although this is a relatively small figure you will see that with longer leases and higher valued rental streams the effect could be very large.

The *effective rate of interest* is the rate per period which, when compounded, equates to the *annual percentage rate (APR)*.

Real and nominal interest rates

If you were to invest £100 in a bank account offering a return of 6% p.a. you would find that after one year your investment would be worth £106. Although you may be pleased with this result the question you need to ask is: would £106 buy the same quantity of goods as £100 a year earlier? The answer to this question depends on how the general level of prices has changed over the year.

This illustrates the difference between nominal and real rates of interest. In our example the bank offered a guaranteed nominal rate of return of 6% p.a. The £106 you receive is an absolute or *nominal* amount that you could take out of the bank and count. When you make the investment you know in advance what it will be worth at the end of the year. In terms of pounds the amount is certain. This, however, is not the case in terms of purchasing power. This depends on the rate of inflation. If prices have risen over the year your investment will buy less. You won't know what you can really buy until the end of the year. Your *real* return is, therefore, uncertain until you know the rate of inflation over the year.

If we let Δ equal the rate of inflation we can relate real returns, r_r, and nominal returns, r_n, in the following way:

$$(1 + r_n) = (1 + r_r)(1 + \Delta) \tag{2.28}$$

This tells us that the nominal return is equal to the product of the real return and the inflation rate. If you expand this expression you get:

$$r_n = r_r + \Delta + r_r \Delta \tag{2.29}$$

The nominal return is, therefore, the *sum* of the real return and the inflation rate plus the product of the real return and the inflation rate. Unless the inflation rate is high the last term usually has a very small impact on the figures so that the nominal return is often approximated as the sum of the real return and the inflation rate. However, when estimating real rates of return the correct method to use is as follows:

$$(1 + r_r) = \frac{(1 + r_n)}{(1 + \Delta)} \tag{2.30}$$

In our example the nominal return offered by the bank is 6%. If inflation over the year is 2% you can estimate the real return as follows:

$$(1 + r_r) = \frac{(1 + 0.06)}{(1 + 0.02)}$$

$$r_r = 0.0392, \text{ or } 3.92\%$$

Had you just taken the difference between the nominal return of 6% and the 2% rate of inflation you would have arrived at an approximate real rate of return of 4%.

Although the difference is small it can become significant when making a decision to evaluate projects in nominal or real terms. We will show in Appendix 8A that the net present value of a cash flow is the same in both nominal and real returns. If there is a difference, it is probably because of errors in the way the discount rate has been estimated.

Inflation is an important part of the investment process as maintaining purchasing power is an important issue for pension funds. We will examine how effective property has been as a hedge against inflation in Chapter 14.

Summary

The purpose of this chapter has been to introduce you to some of the common ways in which cash flows are valued. We have provided some building blocks on which more complex valuations can be explored. We showed the relationship between future and present values and derived some of the common valuation formulas used by valuers. Although we haven't used the notation frequently adopted by valuers you should find that there is an overlap between what we have provided and what you will find in most valuation textbooks. In order to avoid a black box approach to valuation we have, however, shown how the valuation formulas have been derived.

An important part of valuation is being able to value both irregular and regular cash flows. We showed how to do this and also introduced the concept of the annuity, illustrating how to convert present values in arrears to in advance. Using the same idea we extended the annuity model to value a sinking fund, where regular constant payments are used to arrive at a known future value.

Given that many property leases require rental payments to be made quarterly in advance, we showed how to take account of payments that are made at periods other than once per year. We also discussed annual percentage returns (APRs) and effective rates of interest. The chapter concluded with a brief discussion of real and nominal rates of return.

Chapter 2: Summary table

1. Interest rates are expressed in decimal form.

2. Cash flows use the end period convention.

3. The amount of one pound over n years $\qquad PV(1 + r)^n = FV_n$

4. The present value of one pound over n years $\qquad PV = \dfrac{FV_n}{(1 + r)^n}$

5. The present value of a series of irregular cash flows $\qquad PV = \sum_{x=1}^{x=n} \dfrac{a_x}{(1 + r)^x}$

6. The value additivity principle implies that present values can be added together.

7. The present value of a series of irregular cash flows in arrears can be converted to the present value in advance by multiplying by $(1 + r)$. $\qquad PV_{Advance} = (1 + r)\sum_{x=1}^{x=n} \dfrac{a_x}{(1 + r)^x}$

8. An annuity is a regular series of cash flows. Valuers call this the years purchase (YP) or the present value of £1 p.a.

$$P = \frac{a[1 - (1 + r)^{-n}]}{r}$$

9. If income is received in advance you should use the following formula.

$$P_{Advance} = (1 + r)\left\{ \frac{a[1 - (1 + r)^{-n}]}{r} \right\}$$

10. A sinking fund is a series of regular deposits that earn interest. The final value, F, is often used to fund a major acquisition, or replace some capital equipment at some point in the future. Valuers refer to this as the amount of £1 p.a.

$$F = \frac{a[(1 + r)^n - 1]}{r}$$

11. If the periodic rate of interest is expressed as a fraction of the annual rate, the present value of an annuity can be found from the following formula, assuming that cash flows arise at the end of each period.

$$V = \frac{a}{m}\left[\frac{1 - \left(1 + \frac{r}{m}\right)^{-mn}}{\frac{r}{m}} \right]$$

12. The effective rate of interest is the rate per period which, when compounded, equates to the annual percentage rate (APR).

13. The nominal rate of return is the product of one plus the real rate of return and one plus the rate of inflation.

$$(1 + r_n) = (1 + r_r)(1 + \Delta)$$

Problems

1. You are given a present of £1,000 and decide to invest it in a bank offering 7.5% interest p.a. How much would it be worth in 5 years, 10 years, 15 years, 20 years?

2. Use your results from question 1 to plot the increase in value of your investment.

3. How long would it take for your investment to double in value?

4. Assume that you want to retire in 30 years' time with a lump sum of £500,000. If you were able to invest at 6.5% p.a., how much would you have to deposit today in order to achieve this ambition?

5. From question 4 you will have found that a single lump sum investment is quite substantial. As an alternative you decide to invest a fixed amount each year for 30 years. What would your annual investment need to be in order to build up a fund of £500,000?

6. You invest £200 each year for 10 years at 10% p.a. Draw up a table to show the opening balance for each year, together with the interest earned and the closing balance. How much is your investment worth in ten years' time?

7. You want to make a bid for a lease that produces £12,000 p.a. The tenant has a good business so there is hardly any risk attached to the income. If you use a discount rate of 7.5% p.a., what would the lease be worth if the rent were received quarterly in arrears and quarterly in advance?

8. An investment of £5,000 grows to £14,500 over 15 years. What annual return has been earned?

9. How many years would it take for a single investment of £10,000 to grow to £1,000,000 assuming that you could earn interest at 6.5%?

10. You buy a property and sell it after ten years. The rate of return you have earned on the investment is 14.5% p.a. If the average rate of inflation over the period was 3.75% p.a. what is your real rate of return?

Selected references

Brealey, R.A. and Myers, S.C. (1996) *Principles of Corporate Finance*, 5th edn. New York: McGraw-Hill.

Francis, J.C. and Taylor, R.W. (1992) *Investments*, Schaum's Outline Series. New York: McGraw-Hill.

Jaffe, A.C. and Sirmans, C.F. (1995) *Fundamentals of Real Estate Investment*, 3rd edn. Englewood Cliffs, NJ: Prentice Hall.

Stafford, L.W.T. (1972) *Business Mathematics*, London: MacDonald and Evans.

Simple freehold valuation models

Learning objectives

After reading this chapter you will understand the following:

- How to value perpetual income streams that have no growth

- How to use what you learnt in Chapter 2 to derive the equivalent yield model

- How to value an asset where income is growing at a constant annual rate

- How to value a property where the rent received is subject to periodic growth

- How to relate traditional valuation notation to discounted cash flow models

Introduction

Professional valuers are often required to make an assessment of the price they believe a property will sell for in a competitive market. This is the basis of the RICS definition of open market value. To complete this role efficiently valuers need shorthand ways for estimating present value.

In Chapter 2 we introduced you to some of the basic techniques of financial mathematics. The ideas we have discussed form the basis of many of the valuation models found in practice. Often they are expressed as simple yield models where the income is capitalised in perpetuity.

There is a view held by professional valuers (and some academic valuers!) that simple yield capitalisation models have nothing to do with discounted cash flow. This view also extends to suggesting that using discounted cash flow models to value property will produce more accurate valuations. We show that this is a misconception.

Sophistication has nothing to do with accuracy and simple capitalisation models are based on concepts of discounted cash flow.

In this chapter you will learn about some of the common models used to value income streams in perpetuity. We will start with models that have no growth in income and then extend them to incorporate annual growth. The effect of reviewing the rent at periodic intervals is also analysed. Each of these models becomes more complex and more explicit in the way cash flows are defined. The reason for developing these models is not so they can be used as standard methods of valuation. Property will always be valued with reference to comparable sales and by using simple capitalisation models. The reason for developing sophisticated models is to analyse transactions in a way that provides useful insights concerning market behaviour.

Some advanced topics on yield analysis and over-rented properties are covered in the appendices.

Non-growth models

In Chapter 2 we introduced you to the annuity. If you are not familiar with how we arrived at the annuity formula you should review that section again. We will now show you how this important result can be extended to derive some common valuation models.

To recap, the current price, P, of an annuity is as follows:

$$P = \frac{a[1 - (1 + r)^{-n}]}{r}$$

(3.1)

where a is the initial income stream received at the end of each period, r is the discount rate and n, the number of periods. This is also the present value of £1 p.a.

Annuities in perpetuity

Equation 3.1 provides a valuation over a fixed number of periods. We will now examine what happens when the period over which you have to value the cash flow is infinitely long. This is referred to as a perpetuity. To make the logic easier to follow we will rewrite the annuity formula in a slightly different way. We will also change P to V to denote that it is a valuation model:

$$V = \frac{a\left[1 - \dfrac{1}{(1 + r)^n}\right]}{r}$$

(3.2)

This is exactly the same as equation 3.1. All we have done is to write the negative power as a reciprocal.[1] In this form you will see that as the number of periods, n, gets longer the fraction in the square brackets gets smaller. As the number of periods becomes infinitely long, i.e. a perpetuity, the fraction disappears and the annuity formula reduces to the following:

[1] It is useful to know alternative ways of writing expressions, particularly those that are raised to negative powers. We review this material in Chapter 17.

$$V = \frac{a}{r} \qquad\qquad (3.3)$$

where $\dfrac{1}{r}$ is the discounting factor.

This is our formula for valuing an infinitely long constant income stream. It is a capitalisation model that is based on the concepts of discounted cash flow.

Valuers refer to this as the *Years Purchase (YP) in perpetuity.*

Example

An investment generates a constant income stream of £1,000 p.a. If interest rates are 12% p.a., how much is this income stream worth?
Substituting into the valuation formula gives the following:

$$V = \frac{£1,000}{0.12} = £8,333.33$$

The discount factor in this example is 8.33333 (i.e. 1/0.12). You could, therefore, buy a perpetual income stream of £1,000 p.a. for just over eight times the initial income stream. The number of years times the initial income stream that equals the capital value is often referred to as the *years purchase* or YP for short. You will see that the figure is just the reciprocal of the interest rate. Clearly, the higher the interest rate the smaller the YP.

Table 3.1 shows how the values of an annuity approach a limit as the number of years increases. It also shows that the limit is reached more rapidly as the interest rate is increased.

Table 3.1 ● Annuity values

Number of years	5%	Value of annuity of £1,000 p.a. 10%	20%
5 years	£4,329	£3,791	£2,991
10 years	£7,722	£6,145	£4,194
20 years	£12,462	£8,514	£4,870
50 years	£18,256	£9,915	£4,999
100 years	£19,848	£9,999	£5,000
Perpetuity	£20,000	£10,000	£5,000
Years purchase	20	10	5

The concept of years purchase (YP) has a lot to do with the pay-back period we discuss in Chapter 8. Valuers also use other forms of YP when the cash flows terminate after a number of years. Because these are useful shortcuts for valuing income streams valuers frequently embody these concepts in building up valuations from a series of YP components. We will give an example of this towards the end of this chapter. The valuers' shorthand approach has the virtue of familiarity but it was developed at a time when it was common practice to use valuation tables. The widespread use of computers avoids the need to do this although many valuation programs still make use of YPs. Although this speeds up the calculation process it obscures a detailed understanding of the underlying cash flows. There is also a view that using YPs makes life easier for students because they can avoid a lot of algebra and it gives them familiarity with methods of valuation that are widely used in practice. This is undoubtedly true, but it also places them at a considerable disadvantage when compared with graduates who are trained in finance. Our view is that valuers should understand where YPs come from so that they are able to analyse them in an economically defensible manner.

Income received in advance

The valuation model we have derived assumes that income is received in arrears. If, however, income were received in advance there would be one extra year to account for. You will probably remember that we said that you could convert valuations estimated in arrears to in advance by multiplying by $(1 + r)$. The value of a perpetuity with income received in advance can be expressed as follows:

$$V = \frac{a}{r}(1 + r) \qquad (3.4)$$

$$V = \frac{a}{r} + a \qquad (3.5)$$

You will see from this that all you have to do is add one extra year of income. In our example the value in advance would be £8,333.33 + £1,000 = £9,333.33.

The equivalent yield model

Now that you know how to value an annuity for both a fixed term and in perpetuity you can use these ideas to develop some practical valuation formulas. We will leave the more complex issues of growth for the moment and concentrate on the simple non-growth, equivalent yield model.

The equivalent yield model is probably the most common method used for valuing commercial property and for analysing current transactions. The model is in two parts. The first consists of the current income up to the next rent review. The second part occurs at the review when the income is replaced by the current estimate of rental value, which is then assumed to remain constant in perpetuity. If you let y equal the equivalent yield, R and a the current rental value and passing income and n, the number of years to the next review, you can write the property value as follows:

$$V = \frac{a}{y} + \frac{R - a}{y(1 + y)^n} \tag{3.6}$$

For example, if a property has a current income of £10,000 p.a. and a rental value of £12,500 with 2.5 years to run before the rent is reviewed, you would value the property as follows. The first step would be to make an estimate of the equivalent yield from comparable properties that have recently been sold. Assume you choose a yield of 6.5%, substituting these figures into equation 3.6 gives:

$$V = \frac{£10,000}{0.065} + \frac{(£12,500 - £10,000)}{0.065(1 + 0.065)^{2.5}}$$

$V = £186,705$

Valuers would normally set out this calculation as follows:

Net income	£10,000	
YP in perpetuity @ 6.50%	15.3846	£153,846.15
Marginal income*	£2,500	
YP in perpetuity		
deferred 2.5 years @ 6.50%	13.1435	£32,858.75
Property value		£186,704.90

* The marginal income is the difference between the rental value of £12,500 and the passing income of £10,000.

You will see that the same yield is applied to both the passing income and the rent that is received at the date of the review. This is the equivalent yield.

Most valuation textbooks present valuations using the equivalent yield in this form. Those that also give the formula will tend to express it as a statement of fact without any indication as to how it has been derived. However, if you look at equation 3.6 you will see that it is made up of the present value components that we have already discussed. You can, therefore, derive the equivalent yield model in two ways: the first uses the term and reversion, and the second the layer approach.

Method 1: term and reversion

The first approach is to consider the cash flow in two parts. The first is the annual income, £a for n years up until the next rent review. The second part of the valuation is the reversion to the current rental value, £R, which is assumed to remain at the same level in perpetuity. We have illustrated these cash flows in Figure 3.1.

Assume that you value each cash flow using the equivalent yield, y. You will end up with two present values which you add together. The total value is just the present value of an annuity for n years plus the present value of a perpetuity, discounted back to its present value over n years. You can write this as:

$$V = a \left[\frac{1 - (1 + y)^{-n}}{y} \right] + \frac{R}{y(1 + y)^n} \tag{3.7}$$

Figure 3.1 Term and reversion

Simplifying gives:

$$V = a \left[\frac{(1 + y)^n - 1}{y(1 + y)^n} \right] + \frac{R}{y(1 + y)^n} \tag{3.8}$$

$$V = \frac{a}{y} + \frac{R - a}{y(1 + y)^n} \tag{3.9}$$

This is the equivalent yield model we showed in equation 3.6.

Method 2: the layer approach

The alternative approach to valuing the cash flows is to assume that they consist of two overlapping perpetuities. One part consists of a layer of current rent, £a, which is assumed to continue in perpetuity. The second part is the difference between the current rental value and the current income, £$(R - a)$, which is also assumed to continue in perpetuity. Using the equivalent yield to value both income streams gives a total present value that is the sum of the present value of the two perpetuities. You can represent these cash flows as shown in Figure 3.2.

Expressed in this form the valuation can be written in one step:

$$V = \frac{a}{y} + \frac{R - a}{y(1 + y)^n} \tag{3.10}$$

As long as you make a constant assumption about the yield that is used to discount each cash flow, the term and reversion and layer approaches will give the same valuation.

One of the reasons for using the layer approach is that there is uncertainty about rental values, which suggests that this tranche of income should be valued at a higher rate than the passing rent. However, if the rental value is lower than the passing rent, (i.e. $R < a$), then the equivalent yield model could lead to an overvaluation of the current income unless the equivalent yield is adjusted to take this into account.

You should also be aware that the equivalent yield model includes a rental value

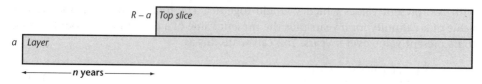

Figure 3.2 The layer approach

that is expressed in current day or real terms, whereas the date of the review takes place at some point in the future. The rental value at the review date, therefore, has the same purchasing power as the current rental value. By contrast, the passing rent is expressed in nominal terms, but is declining in real terms. Because of these differences the economic meaning of the equivalent yield is not clear, other than being the internal rate of return of the cash flows. In addition, the model assumes that the rent is received annually in arrears. An adjustment would have to be made for rent that is received in advance and at other frequencies.

Although these may appear to be serious shortcomings, adjustments for growth and for taking account of income being received in advance and over different periods are usually accommodated in the equivalent yield. There is, therefore, a lot of judgement involved in the choice of yield, as it has to take account of many complex factors. This is where the experience of the valuer plays an important role.

There are clearly a number of problems with the equivalent yield model and it is tempting to abandon it as not being economically defensible. The real question to ask, however, is: will the equivalent yield model produce correct valuations? Despite all its problems the surprising answer is, probably yes! The equivalent yield model is widely used and valuers are familiar with subtle changes in the market that will influence the choice of yield. The principal advantage of the equivalent yield model is that it requires estimates of only two unknown inputs: the rental value and the yield. Evidence of these can be found in the marketplace and the valuer will use his or her experience to arrive at figures that are considered appropriate for the property being valued.

> Although the equivalent yield model suffers from a number of economic short-comings this does not imply that a more sophisticated model will produce more accurate valuations.

Although the equivalent yield is just the internal rate of return of the two cash flows it is also a shorthand way of compensating for the differences in real and nominal cash flows and for allowing for the growth expectations. Making these factors explicit doesn't necessarily mean that valuations will be more accurate. If equivalent yields are part of the common language used by valuers, then they must have economic value. How they are analysed is, however, a separate issue.

Constant growth models

We now turn our attention to valuation models that are more explicit and incorporate growth in income. These are especially important in an inflationary society, as one of the reasons for investing is to maintain the purchasing power of investments in real terms. It has been argued that property is a good investment for hedging against inflation and should, therefore, represent an important component of a mixed asset portfolio. This is an important issue that we will examine more fully in Chapter 14.

We develop two forms of growth model. The first allows the income stream to be reviewed once every year. This is typical of the dividend growth models found in the equity market. The valuation formula we shall develop is frequently referred to as the

Gordon growth model, after the economist who first developed it. The second approach allows the income to be reviewed periodically. This is more representative of the lease arrangement for most commercial properties. Working out the valuation formulas does require some algebra. You can skip this section if you want to move on, but it is worth understanding how the models are derived as they have a direct bearing on how to interpret yields.

The Gordon growth model

Assume you have an investment that generates an initial income of £a at the end of the first year. Instead of remaining at this level the income grows at a constant rate of g% p.a. so that at the end of the second year it takes on a value of $a(1 + g)$. This process is continued so that at the end of the third year the income is $a(1 + g)^2$, and so on. You can write the value of this cash flow in perpetuity as follows:

$$V = \frac{a}{(1 + r)} + \frac{a(1 + g)}{(1 + r)^2} + \frac{a(1 + g)^2}{(1 + r)^3} + \frac{a(1 + g)^3}{(1 + r)^4} + \ldots \to \infty \qquad (3.11)$$

Simplifying this gives:

$$V = \frac{a}{(1 + r)} \left[1 + \frac{(1 + g)}{(1 + r)} + \frac{(1 + g)^2}{(1 + r)^2} + \frac{(1 + g)^3}{(1 + r)^3} + \ldots \to \infty \right] \qquad (3.12)$$

The expression in the square brackets is now in the form of a geometric progression as each term is growing at a constant rate. If you refer to Chapter 17 you will see that there is a very simple expression for the sum of an infinite geometric progression which can be used to find the sum of the series in perpetuity. The expression is:

$$S_\infty = \frac{A}{(1 - R_c)} \qquad (3.13)$$

where A is the first term in the series and R_c is the common ratio between each term. You can apply this to the geometric expression in the square brackets by letting:

$$A = 1 \text{ and } R_c = \frac{1 + g}{1 + r}$$

Substituting this information in equation 3.13 you can write the present value of the constant growth model as:

$$V = \frac{a}{(1 + r)} \left[\frac{1}{1 - \dfrac{(1 + g)}{(1 + r)}} \right] \qquad (3.14)$$

The expression outside the square brackets comes from equation 3.12. Multiplying these together gives:

$$V = \frac{a}{r - g} \text{ subject to } r > g \qquad (3.15)$$

This is our valuation model for an income stream growing at a constant annual rate. It is, however, subject to the return, r, being greater than the growth rate, g. This constraint is important because if r is less than g, you would end up with negative capital values! In addition, if r is equal to g, the capital value would be infinitely large! Although these constraints may seem to restrict the use of the model you need to recognise that the figures for r and g are intended to represent long-term averages, rather than single-period values.

We can also transpose this equation as follows:

$$r - g = \frac{a}{V} \tag{3.16}$$

The initial income divided by the capital value is also known as the income yield, $\hat{y}$. This gives us another way of writing the capital value.

$$V = \frac{a}{\hat{y}} \tag{3.17}$$

You will see that this has exactly the same form as equation 3.3 where we derived the present value of an annuity in perpetuity. The only difference is that the income stream is divided by the rate of return rather than the income yield. The use of the yield implies that there is growth in the income, whereas the use of the rate of return assumes that the income remains constant. The yield is, therefore, the difference between the expected rate of return and the growth rate:

$$\hat{y} = r - g \tag{3.18}$$

> The use of *yields* in a valuation model implies that there is growth in the income stream.

You will see that the valuation model allowing for growth is just a yield capitalisation model. Although the value is found by dividing the current income by a yield, the model is still based on the principles of discounted cash flow.

The important message from this analysis is that a valuation model can incorporate growth even though it is not an explicit part of the model. It just depends on whether you are using yields or returns.

Example

An investment offers an initial income of £1,000 that grows at the rate of 5% p.a. What is this investment worth if interest rates are 6%, 8% and 10% per annum?
Substituting these figures in equation 3.15 gives the values as follows:

Return = 6%

$$V = \frac{£1,000}{0.06 - 0.05} = £100,000$$

Return = 8%

$$V = \frac{\pounds1,000}{0.08 - 0.05} = \pounds33,333$$

Return = 10%

$$V = \frac{\pounds1,000}{0.10 - 0.05} = \pounds20,000$$

You will see that as long as the expected growth remains constant the capital value declines as the interest rate increases.

You can, of course, use this model for analysing investments. Assume, for example, that you analyse an investment with an initial income stream of £2,500 that recently sold for £45,000. If the expected return is estimated as 8.5% you can rearrange equation 3.15 to estimate the expected growth as follows:

$$g = r - \frac{a}{V} \qquad (3.19)$$

$$g = 0.085 - \frac{\pounds2,500}{\pounds45,000}$$

$$g = 0.0294, \text{ i.e. } 2.94\%$$

The periodic growth model

Property investments rarely have rent that is reviewed as frequently as once a year. The common period in the UK is for rent to be reviewed every five years although it used to be as long as seven and fourteen years. The high levels of inflation of the 1970s brought about the trend towards shorter reviews.

The effect of periodic rent reviews causes the profile of the rental income to move up in steps. If, however, you assume that the growth rate is constant, then you can express the rent at the date of the next review in terms of the original rent. For example, assume that a property is let at an initial rent of £1,000 which grows at the rate of 10% p.a. The rent remains constant for five years at which time it is reviewed to its new open market value. Assuming a constant growth rate the new rent can be estimated as $\pounds1,000(1.10)^5 = \pounds1,610.51$. If you continue this process the rent at the next review can be written as $\pounds1,000(1.10)^{10} = \pounds2,593.74$, and so on. This process can be continued indefinitely.

Using what we know about present values the value of the property is just the present value of the stepped income stream in perpetuity. To make the result more general we will assume that the initial rent is £a, the growth rate is g% and the period between rent reviews is p years. We can illustrate the periodic growth in the rental stream as in Figure 3.3.

You will see that each of the rental flows can be regarded as an annuity, fixed for the period between each review. The rent at each review is just the initial rent, £a, inflated

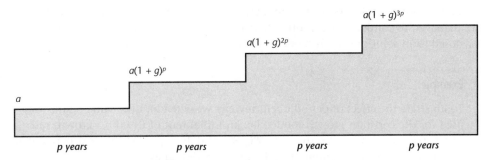

Figure 3.3 Income stream subject to periodic reviews

by the growth rate, $g\%$, over the intervening period. If you remember the formula for an annuity you can write the present value of the income stream as follows:

$$V = \frac{a[1 - (1 + r)^{-p}]}{r} + \frac{a(1 + g)^p}{(1 + r)^p} \frac{[1 - (1 + r)^{-p}]}{r} + \frac{a(1 + g)^{2p}}{(1 + r)^{2p}} \frac{[1 - (1 + r)^{-p}]}{r} + \ldots \to \infty$$

This looks very messy! However, you can simplify it by factoring out the expression for an annuity, which is common to each review:

$$V = \frac{a[1 - (1 + r)^{-p}]}{r} \left[1 + \frac{(1 + g)^p}{(1 + r)^p} + \frac{(1 + g)^{2p}}{(1 + r)^{2p}} + \frac{(1 + g)^{3p}}{(1 + r)^{3p}} \ldots \to \infty \right] \quad (3.21)$$

This looks a bit better, but it is still not very useable. However, the advantage of factoring out the annuity is that the expression in the brackets on the right-hand side is once again in the form of a geometric progression. Having spotted this you use the formula for summing this type of progression. Remember that you will need the first term, A, and the common ratio, R_c. From the above you will see that these can be represented by:

$$A = 1 \text{ and } R_c = \frac{(1 + g)^p}{(1 + r)^p}, \text{ so that } S_\infty = \frac{A}{1 - R_c}$$

If you substitute S_∞ in the valuation formula and simplify the expression you will end up with the following:

$$V = \frac{a[1 - (1 + r)^{-p}]}{r} \left[\frac{(1 + r)^p}{(1 + r)^p - (1 + g)^p} \right] \quad (3.22)$$

Simplifying this gives:

$$V = \frac{a}{r} \left[\frac{(1 + r)^p - 1}{(1 + r)^p - (1 + g)^p} \right] \quad (3.23)$$

This is also subject to the constraint that $r > g$.

Valuers refer to this as the *equated yield* model where the required rate of return is also known as the equated yield.

You will notice that both growth models started with infinitely long cash flows but we managed to condense them into fairly simple compact formulas. These are known as closed form solutions. Each model is expressed in terms of a set of finite variables.

Example

To illustrate the effect of periodic rent reviews we will adopt the same figures we used for the constant growth model, i.e. an initial rent of £1,000, a growth rate of 5% p.a. and expected returns of 6%, 8% and 10% p.a. As this is a periodic growth model we will assume that the rent is reviewed every five years.

Return = 6%

$$V = \frac{£1,000}{0.06} \left[\frac{(1.06)^5 - 1}{(1.06)^5 - (1.05)^5} \right] = £91,003$$

Return = 8%

$$V = \frac{£1,000}{0.08} \left[\frac{(1.08)^5 - 1}{(1.08)^5 - (1.05)^5} \right] = £30,390$$

Return = 10%

$$V = \frac{£1,000}{0.10} \left[\frac{(1.10)^5 - 1}{(1.10)^5 - (1.05)^5} \right] = £18,266$$

For each rate of return the capital value is less than the constant growth model. This, of course, makes sense. With the constant growth model the increase in income is received each year and is, therefore, worth more than if it were deferred for a number of years.

How valuers deal with periodic growth

The model we derived above gives a full representation of how to value cash flows that have periodic growth in income. Valuers do not, however, approach the problem in this way. For a fully rack-rented property, where the passing rent equals the rental value, they value the income stream until the review date as an annuity, and then capitalise the increase in rent in perpetuity at the equivalent yield. The resulting value is then discounted back to its present value and added to the present value of the annuity. The reason for doing this is to make use of notation frequently used by the valuer.

If you start with an initial income of £a, by the date of the next review it will grow to $(1 + g)^p$ where p is the rent review period. We have shown this arrangement in Figure 3.4.

If you were to use the equivalent yield model to value a fully rack-rented property you would just capitalise the initial income stream at the equivalent yield, i.e. $\frac{a}{y}$. You

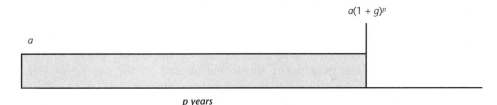

p years

Figure 3.4 How valuers approach the growth problem

might want to refer back to our discussion on the equivalent yield model to see what happens to equation 3.6 when the rental value, R, equals the passing income, a. The yield is assumed to contain information about the periodic review pattern and the growth in rental values. Assuming that there are no changes in these factors you can use the same yield to value the rent at the first rent review. As the resulting value should be the same as capitalising the initial income at the equivalent yield you can write down the following equality:

$$V = \frac{a}{y} = a\left[\frac{1 - (1 + r)^{-p}}{r}\right] + \frac{a(1 + g)^p}{y(1 + r)^p} \text{ subject to } r > g \tag{3.24}$$

The constraint that $r > g$ is still important but you are unlikely to see a reference to this in valuation textbooks.

Equation 3.24 is a simplified form of equation 3.23. In economic terms they will give identical answers. The principal advantage of equation 3.24 is that it makes use of market information concerning yields. With a bit of rearrangement it can be used to estimate the growth rate implied by the yield as follows:

$$(1 + g)^p = y(1 + r)^p \left\{\frac{1}{y} - \left[\frac{1 - (1 + r)^{-p}}{r}\right]\right\} \tag{3.25}$$

This contains both compounding and present value expressions. In order to make use of notation that is familiar to valuers the compounding expressions have to be rewritten as the reciprocal of their present values:

$$(1 + g)^p = \frac{\left\{\frac{1}{y} - \left[\frac{1 - (1 + r)^{-p}}{r}\right]\right\}}{\left[\frac{1}{y} \times \frac{1}{(1 + r)^p}\right]} \tag{3.26}$$

We have already covered each of these expressions in Chapter 2, and expressed them in terms that are familiar to valuers. If you review the material in Chapter 2 you will see that equation 3.26 can also be written as:

$$(1 + g)^p = \frac{YP \text{ in perp at } y\% - YP \text{ for } p \text{ years at } r\%}{YP \text{ in perp at } y\% \times PV \text{ for } p \text{ years at } r\%} \tag{3.27}$$

The implied growth rate can be estimated by substituting the appropriate values.

You will see that in arriving at this expression some contortion of the components in equation 3.25 was required. Despite the fact that the result embraces what is referred to as contemporary valuation methodology, it nevertheless obscures a lot of what is happening in the underlying cash flows. Its main advantage is that it enables valuers to use traditional valuation tables. However, with the widespread use of computers the need to use valuation tables must become less important. All that equation 3.27 does is estimate the growth rate in income implied by the equivalent yield. The inputs are exactly the same as those required in equation 3.23. If a computer program is used to analyse the yield, then it makes more sense to use the correct financial notation.

Expressions such as equation 3.27 have the virtue of familiarity and can be developed for simple cash flows. However, when more complex situations arise it becomes difficult to make use of this notation in a way that provides useful insights, particularly when valuations need to be viewed within a capital market framework. Valuation yields are a logical part of the property market and will always be with us. The analysis of those yields should, however, be made with models that are comparable with other asset classes. Those readers who are interested in property as an investment asset should try to understand and apply the methods of cash flow analysis that are common in finance.

We examine how to analyse yields to estimate implied growth rates in Appendix 3B.

The relationship between valuation models

At first glance it would appear that we have derived a number of valuation models that are unrelated. This, however, is not the case. We could, for example, have written this chapter by starting with the periodic growth model and then changed our assumptions about the frequency of rent reviews and the rate of growth in rental values.

For example, we have shown that the value of a property where the rent grows at the rate of g% p.a., and is reviewed every p years, will take the following form:

$$V = \frac{a}{r}\left[\frac{(1 + r)^p - 1}{(1 + r)^p - (1 + g)^p}\right] \text{ subject to } r > g \tag{3.28}$$

If the rent were reviewed every year the value of p would equal 1 and equation 3.28 would become:

$$V = \frac{a}{r}\left[\frac{(1 + r) - 1}{(1 + r) - (1 + g)}\right] \tag{3.29}$$

which simplifies to:

$$V = \frac{a}{r - g} \text{ subject to } r > g \tag{3.30}$$

This is the same as the constant growth model we derived as equation 3.15.

If, of course, the income showed no growth, then $g = 0$ and equation 3.30 simplifies further to:

$$V = \frac{a}{r} \tag{3.31}$$

There is, therefore, a relationship between these models. This is useful because it gives greater clarity to the interpretation of rates of return and yield and shows how property relates to other assets classes where the income profiles are not subject to periodic review.

Important uses of growth explicit models

In this chapter we have developed a number of valuation models that incorporate growth. It is possible to use these to analyse known transactions so that valuers can develop a picture of expected growth rates. We look at this issue in more detail in Appendix 3B.

One other important use of these models is to estimate a property value formally. If the valuer is able to estimate the expected rate of return and growth rate it is possible to derive a property value. If the property is offered for sale, this figure can then be compared with the offer price. A difference between the two will indicate whether the property is under- or overpriced. A decision as to whether to proceed can then be made using this information.

> One of the most important roles of the valuation model is to determine whether property is under- or overpriced.

The quality of this decision will depend on the estimate of expected return and growth rate. These are complex factors that need to be estimated independently of each other.

Summary

In this chapter we developed some of the common approaches to value and analyse income streams that extend over a number of periods. In particular we analysed perpetual income streams that had no growth as well as those that were subject to both constant and periodic growth. We showed how to adjust these models to take account of rent that is received in advance as well as arrears.

We also derived the equivalent yield model and showed the importance of understanding the yield. When we introduced growth models we also related the more explicit model to traditional valuation notation, but pointed out that it obscured a lot of information about the underlying cash flows and did not fit in well with concepts of modern finance.

The interrelationship between the main valuation models and how they can be derived from each other was also discussed and the chapter closed by highlighting some of the important roles of growth explicit valuation models.

This chapter has three appendices which cover more advanced topics that draw on the information developed so far. The following material is covered.

Appendix 3A: Yields and rent review periods

This appendix shows how to convert yields to account of differences in rent review patterns.

Appendix 3B: Estimating the growth rate from yields

This builds on a topic introduced in Chapter 3 and shows how to estimate the growth rate from property transactions based on the equivalent yield. We show how to do this for fully rented property as well as situations where a property is valued part-way through the rent review period. As this is the more general case we also include a Visual Basic program which can be used with Excel.

Appendix 3C: Estimating effective rents

This appendix shows how to use the discounted cash flow techniques to estimate effective rents when the rental market is distorted by rent free periods and other forms of incentive.

Chapter 3: Summary table

1. A constant annuity in perpetuity is known by valuers as the year purchase (YP) in perpetuity.	$V = \dfrac{a}{r}$
2. If income is received in advance you should use the following formula.	$V = \dfrac{a}{r} + a$
3. The equivalent yield model is the most common valuation model used to value income producing property.	$V = \dfrac{a}{y} + \dfrac{R-a}{y(1+y)^n}$
4. The use of sophisticated models does not imply that valuations will be more accurate.	
5. The present value of an income stream that grows at a constant annual rate is known as the Gordon growth model.	$V = \dfrac{a}{r-g}$
6. The difference between the required return and growth rate is known as the income yield.	$\hat{y} = r - g$
7. Capitalisation models are based on the principles of discounted cash flow.	
8. Valuation models that use yields imply growth in income.	
9. If income is reviewed at periodic intervals you should use the equated yield model.	$V = \dfrac{a}{r}\left[\dfrac{(1+r)^p - 1}{(1+r)^p - (1+g)^p}\right]$
10. Sophisticated valuation models should be used to analyse transactions where the yields and lease structure are known.	
11. One of the most important roles of growth explicit valuation models is to decide whether a property is under- or overpriced.	

Problems

1. Your firm signs a lease for a 10,000 sq. ft office building at £60 per sq. ft. If you assume that the review period is five years and you expect rents to grow at a constant annual rate of 6% p.a., how much would you be prepared to pay for the freehold if the expected return is 12% p.a.?

2. What difference would it make if the rent is paid quarterly in advance?

3. You want to bid for an investment that generates a constant annual income of £2,500 in perpetuity. Assuming that your opportunity cost of capital is 8% p.a., how much would you be prepared to offer?

4. A project generates a constant cash flow of £1,000 at the end of each year for five years. It then increases by 10% and remains constant for the next ten years, after which it drops to £500 and remains at this level in perpetuity. Assuming that the opportunity cost of capital is 9%, how much is this project worth?

Selected references

Baum, A. and Crosby, N. (1995) *Property Investment Appraisal*, 2nd edn. London: Routledge.

Brown, G.R. (1984) Assessing an all-risks yield. *Estates Gazette*, No. 269, 700–6.

Darlow, C. (1983) *Valuation and Investment Appraisal*, London: Estates Gazette.

Enever, N. (1977) *The Valuation of Property Investments*, London: Estates Gazette.

Jaffe, A.C. and Sirmans, C.F. (1995) *Fundamentals of Real Estate Investment*, 3rd edn. Englewood Cliffs, NJ: Prentice Hall.

Lusht, K.M. (1997) *Real Estate Valuation*, Chicago: Irwin.

Whipple, R.T.M. (1995) *Property Valuation and Analysis*, Sydney: Law Book Co.

Appendix 3A
Yields and rent review periods

As part of the process of analysing comparables and yields it is sometimes necessary to compare properties with different rent review patterns. Two identical properties may report different yields if their rent review pattern differs. When comparing yields it is important to ensure that they reflect the same structure. In this appendix we show that the principles developed in Chapters 2 and 3 can be used to estimate the adjustment required to compensate for differences in the frequency of rent reviews.

The principle we follow is that the value of two identical properties should not change merely because the frequency of their rent reviews is different. If this were the case it would be possible to buy a property, change the terms of the lease and resell it at a higher level. By similar reasoning expected rates of return and growth rates will be determined in the marketplace and will not be influenced by changes in the lease structure. The only factors that can change are the rent, which in turn will influence the yield.

Given this background you can express the present value, V, of two fully rented properties that have an initial income of £a and £$â$, a return of $r\%$ p.a., and a growth rate of $g\%$ p.a. The rent review periods are p and $\hat{p}$ as follows:

Rent review period = p

$$V = \frac{a}{r}\left[\frac{(1+r)^p - 1}{(1+r)^p - (1+g)^p}\right] \tag{3A.1}$$

Rent review period = $\hat{p}$

$$V = \frac{â}{r}\left[\frac{(1+r)^{\hat{p}} - 1}{(1+r)^{\hat{p}} - (1+g)^{\hat{p}}}\right] \tag{3A.2}$$

As the values are the same, these two expressions must be equal. Dividing through by V enables them to be expressed in terms of yields. Rearranging to find the ratio of the yields gives the following:

$$\frac{y_p}{y_{\hat{p}}} = \left[\frac{(1+r)^{\hat{p}} - 1}{(1+r)^p - 1}\right]\left[\frac{(1+r)^p - (1+g)^p}{(1+r)^{\hat{p}} - (1+g)^{\hat{p}}}\right] \tag{3A.3}$$

Alternatively, this relationship can be expressed as a factor that can be used to convert yields from one review structure to another.

$$y_p = y_{\hat{p}}\left[\frac{(1+r)^{\hat{p}} - 1}{(1+r)^p - 1}\right]\left[\frac{(1+r)^p - (1+g)^p}{(1+r)^{\hat{p}} - (1+g)^{\hat{p}}}\right] \tag{3A.4}$$

Example

Assume that you have to analyse a fully rented property that has been sold at a yield of 8.1% but has a rent review pattern of fourteen years. You want to use this as a comparable for a property that has a rent review pattern of five years.

From additional research you estimate the expected return and growth rate to be 12% p.a. and 6% p.a. Substituting these figures into equation 3A.4 gives the following:

$$y_5 = y_{14} \left[\frac{(1 + 0.12)^{14} - 1}{(1 + 0.12)^5 - 1} \right] \left[\frac{(1 + 0.12)^5 - (1 + 0.06)^5}{(1 + 0.12)^{14} - (1 + 0.06)^{14}} \right]$$

$$y_5 = y_{14} \left(\frac{3.8871}{0.7623} \right) \left(\frac{0.4241}{2.6262} \right)$$

$$y_5 = y_{14} \, (0.8234)$$

Given that the yield for fourteen-year reviews is 8.1%, you will see that by changing to five-year reviews the yield should be 6.7%.

Once you know the expected rate of return you can use this information to derive a family of yield curves that correspond to different rates of growth. We have done this for a series of common rent review patterns. In Figure 3A.1 we have shown how to find the 6.7% yield based on a five-year rent review pattern, a 12% rate of return and a 6% rate of growth. Figure 3A.3 shows that the yield is 8.1% when the review pattern is fourteen years.

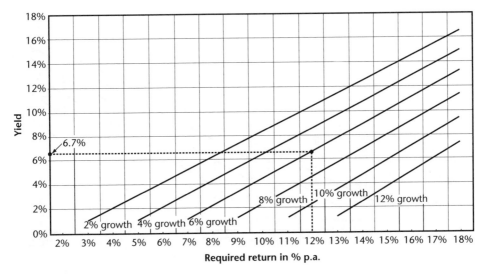

Figure 3A.1 Required yields for five-year reviews

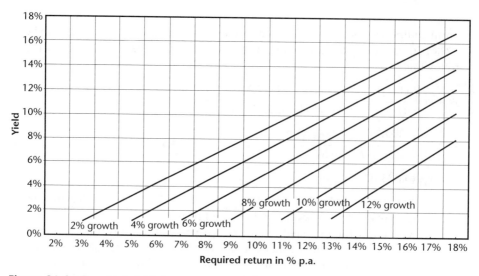

Figure 3A.2 Required yields for seven-year reviews

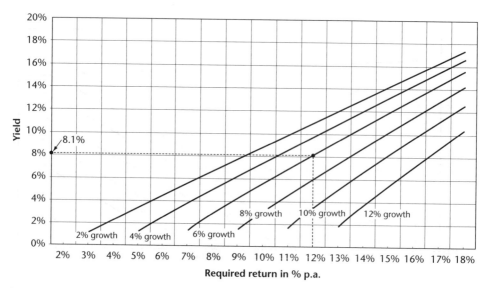

Figure 3A.3 Required yields for fourteen-year reviews

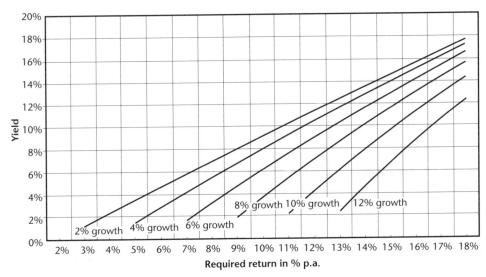

Figure 3A.4 Required yields for 21-year reviews

Appendix 3B
Estimating the growth rate from yields

It is often necessary to estimate the growth rate implied by a yield. Remember that yields are a combination of growth rates and rates of return. If you are not sure why this is the case then you should review Chapter 3. Assuming that you are happy with this concept, it follows that if you make an assumption about the expected return it is possible to derive the expected growth rate. This appendix shows how this can be done.

There is, however, an important economic point that needs to be made. This type of analysis merely produces a growth rate that justifies the capital value of a property. All that the algebra is doing is solving for the unknown factor in the equation. The expected growth calculated in this way may not bear any relationship to market conditions. The approach is really more concerned with checking to see whether the growth rates implied in a particular transaction are in line with market expectations.

A further area in which the calculation of growth rates is relevant is in estimating effective rents. This occurs when a property is over-rented so that the current rent is greater than the rental value. The problem of estimating effective rents is considered in Appendix 3C.

In estimating expected growth rates we shall examine two cases. The first involves a fully rented property and the second a property that is valued part-way through the review period.

1. A fully rented property

In Chapter 3 we showed that the value of a property could, using the equivalent yield model, be expressed as:

$$V = \frac{a}{y} + \frac{R - a}{y(1 + y)^n} \tag{3B.1}$$

where

a = the passing rent
R = the rental value
y = equivalent yield
n = number of years to the next rent review

If the property is fully rented, then the rental value R will equal the passing rent a. In this case the equivalent yield model simplifies to:

$$V = \frac{a}{y} \tag{3B.2}$$

In this form the valuation does not include any reference to the growth rate. However, we showed that the value of a fully rented property could also be written as:

$$V = \frac{a}{r} \left[\frac{(1 + r)^p - 1}{(1 + r)^p - (1 + g)^p} \right] \quad \text{subject to } r > g \tag{3B.3}$$

Combining these equations gives the following:

$$\frac{1}{y} = \frac{1}{r} \left[\frac{(1 + r)^p - 1}{(1 + r)^p - (1 + g)^p} \right] \quad \text{subject to } r > g \tag{3B.4}$$

Note that when the property is fully rented, the income yield is equal to the equivalent yield. Equation 3B.4 can be rearranged to give a closed form solution for the growth rate as follows:

$$g = \left\{ (1 + r)^p - \frac{y}{r} \left[(1 + r)^p - 1 \right] \right\}^{\frac{1}{p}} - 1 \tag{3B.5}$$

Rearranging gives:

$$g = \left[(1 + r)^p \left(1 - \frac{y}{r} \right) + \frac{y}{r} \right]^{\frac{1}{p}} - 1 \tag{3B.6}$$

In this form you will see that you only need to make two intermediate calculations before taking the root. These are $(1 + r)^p$, the amount of £1 over p years, and $\frac{y}{r}$, which is the equivalent yield divided by the expected return.

In Chapter 3 we showed that valuers take a different approach and write this in terms of the years purchase (YP) as follows:

$$g = \left(\frac{YP \text{ in perp at } y\% - YP \text{ for } p \text{ years at } r\%}{YP \text{ in perp at } y\% \times PV \text{ for } p \text{ years at } r\%} \right)^{\frac{1}{p}} - 1 \tag{3B.7}$$

This requires three intermediate calculations before the growth rate can be estimated.

Example

Given a fully rented property with an equivalent yield of 6.7%, a required return of 12% and five-year rent reviews you can estimate what this implies in terms of rental value growth. These are the figures from the example we gave in Appendix 3A.

The implied growth can be estimated by substituting into equation 3B.6 to give:

$$g = [1.7623(1 - 0.5583) + 0.5583]^{\frac{1}{5}} - 1$$

$$g = 5.98\%, \text{ i.e. } 6.00\%$$

To use equation 3B.7 you need to find the corresponding YP values in tables or work them out separately:

$$g = \left(\frac{14.9254 - 3.6048}{14.9254 \times 0.5674} \right)^{\frac{1}{5}} - 1$$

$$g = 5.98\%, \text{ i.e. } 6.00\%$$

You will see that both approaches give the same answer.

2. A property valued part-way through the rent review period

This is a more complex case as it is not possible to derive a closed form solution for the growth rate. It is also the more general case and as it can only be solved by iteration we will not use the YP notation.

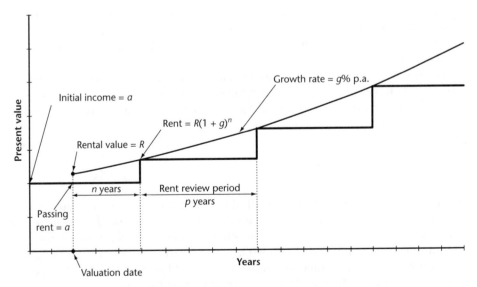

Figure 3B.1 Growth in rental values

Figure 3B.1 illustrates the cash flows at the time of the valuation. You will see that a number of components are involved. There are n years to the next rent review and the rental value at the time of the valuation is R. The passing rent is a. Assuming that the growth rate is g%, this means that the rent at the next review date will be $R(1 + g)^n$.

You can express the value of the property in terms of both an equivalent yield model and as the present value of a perpetually growing cash flow that is valued part-way through a rent review:

$$\frac{a}{y} + \frac{R - a}{y(1 + y)^n} = \frac{a(1 - (1 + r)^{-n})}{r} + \frac{R(1 + g)^n}{r(1 + r)^n}\left[\frac{(1 + r)^p - 1}{(1 + r)^p - (1 + g)^p}\right] \qquad (3B.8)$$

This equation can be solved graphically or by using iteration.

Example

To show how we can solve this we will assume that a property has been valued on an 8.5% yield with 2.5 years to run to the next rent review. The ratio between the passing rent and the current rental value is 0.8. The property has five-year rent reviews and the expected return is 12%.

To solve this graphically these figures are substituted into equation 3B.8. The equation on the left of the equal sign is just the equivalent yield model. As this does not include the growth rate it will remain constant. The right-hand side of the equation is the periodic growth model. The value of this model will be influenced by changes in the growth rate. As this gradually increases, the value will increase. Remember, however, that the growth rate must always be less than the required return. By plotting the constant value and the increasing value for different growth rates you will see that the two lines cross at the point which identifies the growth rate implied by the equivalent yield. Figure 3B.2 shows that this occurs at 4%.

The alternative way is to solve this by iteration. There are two ways to do this. The first is to calculate the difference between the two values and solve for g until the difference is zero. If you use Excel you can set this up using Solver and you should find that the solution is 4% p.a.

If you have a lot of calculations you will find that it is easier to set this up using an Excel function. We have written a program to do this. You will need to create a new module within Excel and type in the following commands. When you run this you will find a new function called RVGrowth listed under the user-defined functions that you can use like any other function in Excel. You could also set this up as an add-in so that the function is then available to every worksheet that you use.

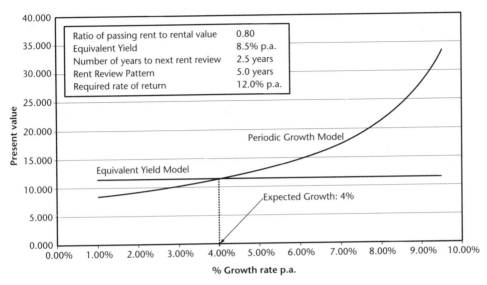

Figure 3B.2 Estimating expected growth

```
'Function RVGrowth() to estimate the rental value growth
'of a property that is valued part way through
'a rent review period
'
'Gerald Brown 1998

Function RVGrowth(Yield, Income, Rental_Value, Exp_Return,
Yrs_to_rev, Rev_period)

    y = Yield
    a = Income
    RV = Rental_Value
    R = Exp_Return
    n = Yrs_to_rev
    p = Rev_period

'Estimate capital value using equivalent yield model

    V = (a / y) + ((RV - a) / (y * (1 + y) ^ n))

'Initialize parameters for iteration routine to find
'the growth rate G.
'L is the lowest value, H is the highest value

    L = -1
    H = R
    R1 = 0
```

```
Start:
  G = (L + H) / 2
  If G = R1 Then GoTo Finish
  R1 = G
  T = 0
  T = ((a / R) * (1 - ((1 + R) ^ -n))) + ((RV * (1 + G) ^ n) /
(R * (1 + R) ^ n)) * ((((1 + R) ^ p) - 1) / (((1 + R) ^ p) - ((1
+ G) ^ p)))

  If T = V Then GoTo Finish
  If T > V Then GoTo Revise
  L = G

  GoTo Start

Revise:
  H = G
  GoTo Start

Finish:
  RVGrowth = G

End Function
```

Appendix 3C
Estimating effective rents

In this appendix we show how it is possible to use the principles we introduced earlier to estimate effective rents. This topic became very important following the collapse of the occupational market in the early 1990s. In order to encourage prospective tenants to lease vacant space it became common for landlords to offer incentive packages. The general form of these packages was to keep the contract rent high but at the same time offer rent-free periods and/or capital incentives so that the effective rent paid by the tenant was much lower.

Introducing these incentives had the effect of distorting the rental market and made it difficult to establish evidence of open market rental values that could be used for rent review purposes. It became necessary, therefore, to analyse rental packages in order to strip out the effect of incentives so that unbiased estimates of the effective open market rental values could be established. We will show that the estimation of effective rent can be solved by assuming that the present value of the rental stream without incentives should be the same as the present value with incentives. If this were not the case, then opportunities would exist for arbitrage, as investors identified those properties that were mispriced as a result of a wrongly valued incentive package.

The starting point for this analysis is to revisit the periodic growth model we derived earlier. The reason for doing this is to consider the riskiness of each of the cash flows in the valuation. With upward-only rent reviews contract rents could be fixed at such high levels that they were likely to stay at a constant level until two or three review periods had elapsed. Under the terms of a lease agreement the obligation to pay rent ranks very highly, so the riskiness of the fixed rent differs from the riskiness of the property market. This raises a general issue concerning risk which we will cover in Part 2. At this stage, however, it is appropriate to point out that cash flows should be discounted at the risk-adjusted discount rate appropriate to those cash flows.

This is particularly important for property, as we have pointed out that a lease agreement really defines two types of risk. Once the rent has been fixed, it remains constant until the next review. The rent payable is, therefore, only subject to the default risk of the tenant. All the uncertainty in the property market occurs at the point when the rent is renegotiated. Once the review has taken place all the property market risk is resolved and the cash flow once again reflects the default risk of the tenant. You will see, therefore, that if the contract rent is fixed at a very high level for long periods it will be exposed to more of the risk of the tenant, and to less of the risk of the property market. In certain cases the whole of the rental cash flow may exhibit the risk characteristics of the bonds issued by the tenant company. These different components of risk need to be incorporated into a valuation model as they could influence the calculation of effective rent.

In Chapter 3 we derived a valuation model with periodic rent reviews assuming that the same discount rate could be applied to all the cash flows. If we recognise that the riskiness of the cash flows differs we can derive a slightly different model. This is relatively straightforward using a financial framework. Relying on traditional property notation would make this more difficult to manipulate and the equations would lose a lot of clarity.

In working out the overall present value we will assume that the annuity component carries the same risk as the bonds of the tenant company, r_b. Each of these present values is then discounted at the review date at the required return for the property, r_j, which reflects the risk of the property market:

$$V = a\left[\frac{1 - (1 + r_b)^{-p}}{r_b}\right] + \frac{a(1 + g)^p}{(1 + r_j)^p}\left[\frac{1 - (1 + r_b)^{-p}}{r_b}\right] + \ldots \infty \qquad (3C.1)$$

where

  a = initial income
  r_b = return on bonds issued by tenant company including a default premium
  r_j = required return p.a. at each rent review
  g = growth rate per annum of effective rent
  p = rent review period

Rearranging gives:

$$V = \left[\frac{1 - (1 + r_b)^{-p}}{r_b}\right]\left[1 + \frac{(1 + g)^p}{(1 + r_j)^p} + \frac{(1 + g)^{2p}}{(1 + r_j)^{2p}} + \ldots \infty\right] \qquad (3C.2)$$

The second part of this expression is in the form of a geometric progression that has a compact solution for the sum to infinity. The valuation formula can, therefore, be expressed as:

$$V = a\left[\frac{1 - (1 + r_b)^{-p}}{r_b}\right]\left[\frac{(1 + r_j)^p}{(1 + r_j)^p - (1 + g)^p}\right] \qquad (3C.3)$$

Rearranging gives:

$$V = \frac{a}{r_b} \frac{(1 + r_j)^p}{(1 + r_b)^p} \left[\frac{(1 + r_b)^p - 1}{(1 + r_j)^p - (1 + g)^p} \right] \tag{3C.4}$$

subject to $r_j > g$ and the information set available at $t = 0$.

It is a simple matter to extend this model to take account of rent received in advance over any period, as well as using periodic discount rates and growth rates. It can also be modified to value an income stream part-way through a rent review.

Estimating the expected return at each rent review

You will see that this model incorporates two rates of return. One reflects the risk of the tenant, r_b, and the other, r_j, the risk of the property market at each review. We can make an assumption about the tenant risk, but we need to estimate the property market risk. Instead of assuming that the discount rates are split into a riskless and risky component, valuers would probably be more familiar with the concept of a single discount rate that is a weighted average of these two components. By substituting an average return, r_k, for r_b and r_j we can obtain the following alternative expression. You will recognise this as the same valuation model we derived in Chapter 3.

$$V = \frac{a}{r_k} \left[\frac{(1 + r_k)^p - 1}{(1 + r_k)^p - (1 + g)^p} \right] \tag{3C.5}$$

This is also subject to $r_j > g$ and the information set that is available at the time the property is valued.

Equations 3C.4 and 3C.5 are equal and with some manipulation it can be shown that:

$$\frac{r_f}{r_k} \frac{[(1 + r_k)^p - 1]}{[(1 + r_b)^p - 1]} \frac{(1 + r_b)^p}{[(1 + r_k)^p - (1 + g)^p]} = \frac{(1 + r_j)^p}{(1 + r_j)^p - (1 + g)^p} \tag{3C.6}$$

As long as you know both the expected return and the expected growth rate it is possible to estimate the expected return at each review. This would, however, have to be solved iteratively.

An alternative approach is possible if the property is fully rack-rented. Using the equivalent yield, y, you can estimate r_j directly as follows:

$$\frac{a}{y} = \frac{a}{r_b} \frac{(1 + r_j)^p}{(1 + r_b)^p} \left[\frac{(1 + r_b)^p - 1}{(1 + r_j)^p - (1 + g)^p} \right] \tag{3C.7}$$

This can be rearranged to give:

$$r_j = \left\{ \frac{r_f (1 + r_b)^p (1 + g)^p}{r_b (1 + r_b)^p - y[(1 + r_b)^p - 1]} \right\}^{\frac{1}{p}} - 1 \tag{3C.8}$$

Determining effective rents in the presence of incentives

The present value of a property let with open market rent reviews or subject to incentives should be the same. If this were not the case mispricing would create profitable opportunities that would create disequilibrium in the market. This, however, could not be sustained for long periods without a structural change in the way valuations were carried out.

Tenant incentives, therefore, merely represent the repackaging of an open market rental stream without altering the capital value. The reason for offering incentives is to provide an inducement to potential tenants to lease a building at a high contract rent.

Crosby (1995) has identified the range of incentives that have dominated the market. These are as follows:

(a) rent-free periods and rent subsidies in addition to normal fitting-out periods
(b) stepped rents and rent capping
(c) cash payments
(d) fitting out costs paid by the landlord
(e) take-back of existing premises
(f) break clauses
(g) lease concessions (for example, capping service charges)

Incentives usually fall into the category of a capital payment made by the landlord to the tenant or a rent-free period. In order to determine the effective rent implied by the incentive package we assume that the open market value of the property, with and without incentives, is equal. Thus:

$$V_{OMV} = V_{CON} - PV_C \tag{3C.9}$$

where

V_{OMV} = Present value of effective open market value rent without incentives

V_{CON} = Present value of the contract rent subject to incentives

PV_C = Present value of capital incentives

This identifies the equilibrium position. It is possible to estimate the effective open market rental value that takes into account the inducement package by imposing the following condition:

$$V_{OMV} - V_{CON} + PV_C = 0 \tag{3C.10}$$

A process of iteration can be used to solve for the effective open market rental value. To illustrate the principles involved Figure 3C.1 shows the cash flows of a property with and without incentives.

From this it will be seen that:

m = multiple of rent review periods
k = contract rent
a = effective rent
g = growth rate p.a. in effective rent
f = rent-free period
q = number of years for contract rent to equal effective market rent
p = rent review period

We already have an expression for the present value of the open market rental value. We now need a similar expression for the contract rent, V_{CON}. This can be written as follows:

$$V_{CON} = \frac{k}{(1 + r_b)^f} \left[\frac{1 - (1 + r_b)^{f-mp}}{r_b} \right] + \frac{a(1 + g)^{mp}}{(1 + r_j)^{mp}} \left[\frac{1 - (1 + r_b)^{-p}}{r_b} \right] \left[\frac{(1 + r_j)^p}{(1 + r_j)^p - (1 + g)^p} \right]$$

(3C.11)

subject to $r_j > g$ and $k > a$.

If capital incentives are involved, this expression would have to be reduced by the present value of any capital payments made by the owner of the property.

In order to estimate the effective open market rent a restriction is imposed which ensures that, after allowing for any capital incentives, the difference between the present values based on open market rents and contract rents is zero. The combined expression is as follows:

$$a \left[\frac{1 - (1 + r_b)^{-p}}{r_b} \right] \frac{[(1 + r_j)^p][1 - (1 + g)^{mp}]}{\{(1 + r_j)^p - (1 + g)^p\}(1 + r_j)^{mp}} - \frac{k}{(1 + r_b)^f} \left[\frac{1 - (1 + r_b)^{f-mp}}{r_b} \right] + PV_c = 0$$

(3C.12)

subject to $r_j > g$ and $k > a$.

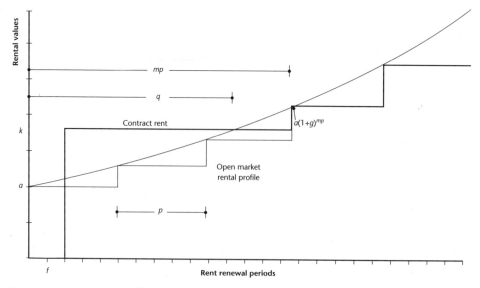

Figure 3C.1 Rental profile of over-rented property and effective rent

Given an assumption concerning the expected growth rate, g, and assuming that the required return at each rent review, r_j, has been estimated, it will be evident that the only remaining unknown in this expression is the *effective open market rental*, a. This can easily be solved by iteration.

It is also a simple matter to amend the equation to allow for rent that is received either in advance or arrears. A further refinement to the model is to allow for rent to be received at intervals other than once a year. It should be noted, however, that both these refinements would make no difference to the estimation of effective open market rental values as the same adjustments are made to both expressions of value. The only time these adjustments become important is when the incentive package includes a capital payment by the owner to the prospective tenant. As these aspects represent minor variations they have been omitted from the analysis.

Identifying when the contract rent increases

Before presenting an example there are two further pieces of information that can be solved from the cash flow information:

1. The number of years for the contract rent to reach the effective open market rent.
2. The number of complete rent review periods before the contract rent is reviewed to the effective open market rent.

These factors are interrelated. The first can be found from the following:

$$k = a(1 + g)^q \tag{3C.13}$$

q = number of years for the contract rent to equal the effective market rent.
By rearranging it can be shown that q can be derived as follows:

$$q = \frac{\ln(k) - \ln(a)}{\ln(1 + g)} \tag{3C.14}$$

Similarly the number of whole rent reviews can be found from:

$$m = \frac{1}{p} \left[\frac{\ln(k) - \ln(a)}{\ln(1 + g)} \right] \tag{3C.15}$$

where m is rounded up to the nearest whole integer.

Example

Assume that a property is let on five-yearly upward-only reviews at a rent of £300,000 p.a. The lease was granted with a rent-free period of 2.5 years and the landlord agreed to make a contribution to the tenant of £100,000 to cover fitting-out costs. Assume that the risk-free rate of return is 8.5% p.a., the default risk of the tenant is 0.5% and the expected open market growth in income is 5% p.a. The expected growth rate could be estimated using the techniques discussed in Appendix 3B. However, it is probably better to estimate this from microeconomic data relating specifically to the property and its location.[1] Assume also that the rent is to be received quarterly in advance.

By substituting these figures into the valuation equation it is possible to solve for the effective rent assuming a range of risk premium figures for the property market. The results are presented in Table 3C.1.

Introducing the incentive package has enabled the contract rent of £300,000 to set at about 60% above the effective market rental value. This simple example also shows that over a relatively narrow range of risk premium figures the effective rental value can change substantially. Estimating the expected return of a fully let rack-rented property is a critical issue and probably the most difficult part of this analysis. From a practical point of view, the easiest way to proceed is to bracket the risk premium figures and give a range within which the effective rent will lie.

Other issues

You will see from these calculations that estimating effective rents is not an easy task and involves many complex issues. Practitioners have, therefore, tried to find simple solutions to the problem. One approach concerns writing off the incentives over a given period. The discussion usually centres on the relative bargaining positions of the lessee and lessor. There are, however, dangers in these approaches, as the calculation of the effective rent becomes an ad hoc process that could lead to the property being wrongly valued.

Table 3C.1 ● Estimation of effective rent

Contract rent	£300,000				
Fitting-out contribution	£100,000				
Rent-free period	2.5 years				
Rent review cycle	5.0 years				
Expected growth	5.00%				
Risk-free rate of return	8.50%				
Tenant default risk	0.50%				
Property risk premium	0.00%	1.00%	2.00%	3.00%	4.00%
Required return	9.00%	10.00%	11.00%	12.00%	13.00%
Return at each review	9.00%	10.20%	11.40%	12.70%	14.10%
Effective rental value (ERV)	£178,705	£183,306	£185,234	£189,835	£194,663
Ratio of ERV to contract rent	59.57%	61.102%	61.74%	63.28%	64.89%
Number of years before growth	10.62	10.12	9.88	9.38	8.86
Number of reviews before growth	3	3	2	2	2

[1] Remember that estimating the growth rate from yields only results in a figure that justifies the capital value. A large sample of yields would be needed to obtain a consensus view of expected growth.

If lease incentives are viewed as a way of repackaging the rental stream then in most cases the writing-off period is not a critical issue. The advantage of setting up the model as described above is that it is possible to determine exactly when the open market rental value will exceed the contract rent. If this period exceeds the term of the lease, then the package is too generous and would have to be renegotiated. In the example given above, if we assume that a lease has been granted for a period of ten years then as long as the risk premium is in excess of 2% p.a. the benefits to the tenant will be written off before a new lease is negotiated. As the present value of the incentive package and the open market rental stream will be the same, then both parties should be satisfied with the deal.

It has also been suggested that the incentives should be written off by the first rent review. Whether this is possible depends on the level at which the contract rent is fixed and the effective rental value in the marketplace derived from comparable evidence. If this was considered to be an essential requirement then a more pragmatic approach could be followed. For example, it would be possible to estimate an effective rent from other leases that do not have this imposition and then constrain the model to establish a contract rent that would be written off by the first review.

If the market is efficient in the way it processes information then lease incentives should not have any effect on the open market valuations. They will, however, distort the rental value market. Disequilibrium in capital values could, however, arise if contract rents are substituted for effective rents, particularly if there is insufficient evidence to derive effective rents or ad hoc methods are used for analysis.

Selected references

Crosby, N. (1995) Lease incentives and inducements: A question of capital or rental incentives? University of Reading. Proceedings of the Pacific Asia Property Research Conference, Singapore.

Jefferies, R. (1994) Lease incentives and effective rents: A decapitalisation model. *Journal of Property Valuation and Investment* **12**, 21–42.

Simple leasehold models

Learning objectives

After reading this chapter you will understand the following:

- How to find the value of a leasehold interest from a perpetuity

- How to value a fixed term cash flow that has annual growth

- How to value a fixed term cash flow that has periodic growth

This chapter illustrates a useful technique for quickly valuing terminating cash flows from cash flows that are valued in perpetuity. It also shows the link between what has been called contemporary methods of valuation and the underlying DCF calculations.

Introduction

In Chapter 3 we discussed how to value different types of perpetual income stream and showed how the common valuation models used in practice could be derived. Often, however, it is necessary to know how to value growth cash flows that terminate after a fixed number of years. A leasehold interest, for example, is the most common form of terminating cash flow model. In this chapter we show how to derive leasehold valuation models from the perpetual valuation models we have already developed. This approach enables complex cash flows to be valued which embody both constant and growing income streams.

The difference between two perpetuities

In Chapters 1 and 2 we showed that whenever you have a cash flow that follows a regular pattern it is possible to value it by using the properties of a geometric progression. In Chapter 17 we describe a number of essential mathematical principles and derive two formulas for a geometric progression. The first is the sum of a fixed number of terms and the second the sum to infinity. We used the formula for the sum to infinity to derive some of the freehold valuation models we introduced in Chapter 3.

In this chapter we switch our attention to valuing terminating leasehold interests. Once again we will not follow the traditional valuation notation, as we want to show the link between freehold and leasehold models. You will see that some of the solutions are quite complex and really should be solved by computer. However, they are still discounted cash flow models and build on the ideas that we have already developed. One advantage of using this approach is that attention focuses on estimating those factors that drive the valuation. A further advantage is that once the general approach is understood, it is possible to apply it to more complex cases than can be handled using traditional notation. Having read this chapter the reader should review some traditional valuation textbooks in order to see the link between the two approaches.

The valuation of leases is a complex issue and there are many academic papers in finance journals that have been written on analysing lease or buy decisions. The valuation profession has, however, absorbed hardly any of this literature, although there are similarities in the issues covered. There are also a number of complex computer programs available designed to help the lease–buy decision. It is also noticeable that none of the finance literature, nor any of these programs, makes use of notation that is common in the property sector. We believe the reason for this is that valuation insights only come from an explicit approach to the definition of cash flows. Modern valuers should take this into consideration if their intention is to compete with other professional groups.

In Chapter 3 we used the properties of geometric progressions to value freehold cash flows that continued in perpetuity. It is also possible to value a fixed-term lease using the sum of a geometric progression for a fixed number of terms. This, however, is not the only way to approach the problem. In this chapter we will show that the valuation of a terminating cash flow can be viewed as the difference between two perpetuities. This approach offers valuable insights into the similarities between the freehold and leasehold interests.

The basis of the approach is the value additivity principle, which implies that you can add and subtract present values. For example, if you know the present value of a perpetuity starting today and a perpetuity starting in ten years' time, for the same cash flow, you can find the value of the ten-year cash flow by subtracting one from the other. This idea is probably better illustrated with a simple example.

Let us assume that you want to find the present value of £100 p.a. for ten years at 10% p.a. You already know how to do this using the annuity formula, but let us look at it in a slightly different way. The present value of £100 p.a. in perpetuity is £1,000, i.e. £100/0.1. Similarly, the present value of £100 p.a. in perpetuity starting in ten years' time is also £1,000, but this must be discounted over the ten-year period to give a present value today of £385.54, i.e. $£1,000/(1.1)^{10}$. The difference between these two present values gives the present value of £100 p.a. for ten years. The answer in this case is £614.46. If you use the annuity formula with the above figures you will get the same answer.[1] You may recognise that this approach is just like finding the distance between a number of locations lying on a straight line. For example, if you know that the distance between points A and C is 400 miles and the distance between points B and C is 250 miles, then the distance between points A and B must be 400 miles − 250 miles, which equals 150 miles.

Now that you know the principles involved you can develop them algebraically to derive some formulas for valuing terminating cash flows. For completeness we will start with zero growth and then cover both constant and periodic growth models. The reason for doing this is to show similarities in the general form of the models that are developed. In all cases you will need to find the present value of a perpetual cash flow starting at the end of year zero and at the end of year n and then find the difference. We will refer to these as $V_{0,0}$ and $V_{0,n}$.

Zero growth models

This is the simplest form of model in which you have a constant cash flow for a fixed number of years. The present values of the two perpetuities, n years apart, are as follows:

Present value at end year zero of perpetual cash flow, a

$$V_{0,0} = \frac{a}{r} \tag{4.1}$$

Present value at end year n of perpetual cash flow, a

$$V_{0,n} = \frac{a}{r(1 + r)^n} \tag{4.2}$$

The difference between these perpetuities, V_n, gives the present value of the constant cash flow a for n years:

$$V_n = V_{0,0} - V_{0,n} = \frac{a}{r} - \frac{a}{r(1 + r)^n} \tag{4.3}$$

This simplifies to:

$$V_n = a \left[\frac{1 - (1 + r)^{-n}}{r} \right] \tag{4.4}$$

This is the annuity formula we derived in Chapter 2, which can also be written as follows:

$$V_n = \frac{a}{r} \left[1 - \frac{1}{(1 + r)^n} \right] \tag{4.5}$$

[1] The present value of the £1,000 annuity for ten years can be written as:

$$V = £1,000 \left[\frac{1 - (1.1)^{-10}}{0.1} \right] = £614.46$$

This shows that the valuation is made up of two parts. The expression outside the square brackets is just the capital value of the fixed income stream in perpetuity. The expression inside the square brackets is a factor that reduces this value by recognising that the cash flow is only received for a fixed term of n years. The product of these two components is a general form that will also appear in the models that take account of growth.

Example

Find the value of a lease that pays a fixed amount of £1,500 p.a. for 15 years. The expected return is assumed to be 10% p.a. Substituting these figures into equation 4.5 gives:

$$V_{15} = \frac{£1,500}{0.1}\left[1 - \frac{1}{(1.1)^{15}}\right]$$

$$V_{15} = £15,000[0.7606]$$

$$V_{15} = £11,409.12$$

Constant growth model

You will recall from Chapter 3 that the present value of a perpetual cash flow, which is growing at a constant annual rate, has a simple closed form solution. We derived this as the Gordon growth model. You can use this result to derive the present value of a constantly growing cash flow that terminates after n years.

Present value at end year zero of perpetual cash flow, a, growing at g% p.a.

$$V_{0,0} = \frac{a}{r - g} \qquad (4.6)$$

Present value at end year n of perpetual cash flow, a, growing at g% p.a.

$$V_{0,n} = \frac{a(1 + g)^n}{(r - g)(1 + r)^n} \qquad (4.7)$$

Equation 4.6 is just the Gordon growth model we derived in Chapter 3. In equation 4.7 the cash flow after n years has grown to $a(1 + g)^n$. This continues to grow at the constant annual rate of g% p.a. It is capitalised in perpetuity and then discounted back to its present value over the period of n years. The present value of the growing cash flow for the fixed period of n years is just the difference between equations 4.6 and 4.7:

$$V_n = V_{0,0} - V_{0,n} = \frac{a}{(r - g)} - \frac{a(1 + g)^n}{(r - g)(1 + r)^n} \qquad (4.8)$$

Simplifying gives:

$$V_n = \frac{a}{(r-g)} \left[1 - \frac{(1+g)^n}{(1+r)^n} \right] \text{ subject to } r > g \tag{4.9}$$

The constraint that $r > g$ is still important. You should also note that it has the same general form as equation 4.5. The expression on the left of the square brackets is the present value in perpetuity of a constantly growing cash flow. The expression in the square brackets is a factor that reduces the present value to reflect the fact that the cash flow is only received for a fixed number of years.

Example

We will use the same figures as above but assume that the income stream is growing at the rate of 4% p.a. Substituting these figures into equation 4.9 gives:

$$V_{15} = \frac{£1,500}{(0.10 - 0.04)} \left[1 - \frac{(1.04)^{15}}{(1.10)^{15}} \right]$$

$$V_{15} = £25,000(0.5689)$$

$$V_{15} = £14,221.71$$

Periodic growth model

This situation covers a terminating lease where the growing income stream is reviewed at periodic intervals. To make the mathematics more tractable we will assume that the period over which the lease is being valued, i.e. n, is a multiple of the review periods. If we let $n = mp$ where m is an integer representing the number of review periods, p, it will be evident that the initial income, a, which is growing at the rate g% p.a., will after n years be equal to $a(1 + g)^{mp}$. You can use this to value the two perpetuities as follows:

Present value at end year zero of perpetual cash flow, a, growing at g% p.a., which is subject to periodic reviews every p years

$$V_{0,0} = \frac{a}{r} \left[\frac{(1+r)^p - 1}{(1+r)^p - (1+g)^p} \right] \tag{4.10}$$

Present value at end year n of perpetual cash flow, a, growing at g% p.a., which is subject to periodic reviews every p years

$$V_{0,mp} = \frac{a(1+g)^{mp}}{r(1+r)^{mp}} \left[\frac{(1+r)^p - 1}{(1+r)^p - (1+g)^p} \right] \tag{4.11}$$

The difference in present values is, therefore:

$$V_n = V_{0,0} - V_{0,mp} = \frac{a}{r} \left[\frac{(1+r)^p - 1}{(1+r)^p - (1+g)^p} \right] \left[1 - \frac{(1+g)^{mp}}{(1+r)^{mp}} \right] \tag{4.12}$$

subject to $r > g$.

Once again this is in the same general form of the value of a perpetuity that is adjusted by a factor reflecting the number of periods over which the cash flow is received.

Example

We will use the same figures as before, but will also assume that the period between reviews is five years. Note that the period of the lease is 15 years, which is an exact multiple of the rent review period so that $m = 3$. Substituting these figures into equation 4.12 gives:

$$V_{15} = \frac{£1,500}{0.10} \left[\frac{(1.10)^5 - 1}{(1.10)^5 - (1.04)^5} \right] \left[1 - \frac{(1.04)^{15}}{(1.10)^{15}} \right]$$

$$V_{15} = £23,251.2(0.5689)$$

$$V_{15} = £13,226.87$$

The present value in this case is lower than the constant growth model. This reflects the fact that the income remains constant between rent reviews.

In this final example we have assumed that there are no fixed ground rents being paid. Where this does occur it is possible to amend the formulas we have derived to take this into consideration. The ground rent is just another cash flow that can be easily valued. The DCF approaches we have illustrated are capable of handling a wide variety of cases. Although the mathematics is more complex than valuers would normally use, the advantage is that the valuation of the cash flows can be written in a more explicit manner. This has significant advantages when it comes to analysing leasehold interests.

Summary

This chapter has shown how to use some simple ideas involving discounted cash flow to value terminating leasehold interests. We showed that leasehold values could be estimated as the difference between the value of two perpetuities that are a fixed number of years apart. Using this idea we showed an alternative way of estimating the present value of fixed income for a given number of years. This resulted in the annuity formula that we had derived earlier.

By extending this idea to incorporate growth we derived two further models that took account of both constant and periodic growth. We also showed that all these models had the same general form.

Appendix 4A: Multiple growth models

This chapter has one appendix covering the more advanced topic of multiple growth models. This recognises the fact that the constant growth model is an approximation and that a more realistic approach may incorporate valuation periods in which the growth rate changes.

Chapter 4: Summary table

1. Terminating leasehold interests can be valued as the difference between two perpetuities that are separated by the number of years corresponding to the term of the lease.

2. The present value of a fixed cash flow for n years can be written as:

$$V_n = \frac{a}{r}\left[1 - \frac{1}{(1+r)^n}\right]$$

3. The present value of a cash flow for n years that is growing at a constant annual rate of $g\%$ p.a. can be written as:

$$V_n = \frac{a}{(r-g)}\left[1 - \frac{(1+g)^n}{(1+r)^n}\right]$$

4. The present value of a cash flow that is subject to periodic growth every p years, where the number of years n is a multiple of the review period, such that $n = mp$, can be written as:

$$V_n = \frac{a}{r}\left[\frac{(1+r)^p - 1}{(1+r)^p - (1+g)^p}\right]\left[1 - \frac{(1+g)^{mp}}{(1+r)^{mp}}\right]$$

5. Each of these present values has the same general form. They represent a perpetuity multiplied by a factor that reduces their value to account for the fact that the cash flow is received for a fixed period.

Problems

1. Use the sum of a geometric progression, given in Chapter 17, for a fixed number of terms and derive the formulas given in this chapter. You should find that they are the same.

2. A property generates a profit rent of £280,000 for the unexpired term of six years of a lease. Assuming that the required return is 18% p.a., what is the value of lease?

3. You have to value a 15-year lease that is subject to review every five years. The growth in rental values is 4.5% p.a. and the expected return is 12% p.a. If the property is fully rented at a rental value of £25,000, what is it worth?

4. What would the value be if you valued it as a freehold?

5. What would the value of the 15-year lease be if the rent was reviewed annually?

Selected references

Baum, A. and Crosby, N. (1995) *Property Investment Appraisal*, 2nd edn. London: Routledge.

Brealey, R.A. and Myers, S.C. (1996) *Principles of Corporate Finance*, 5th edn. New York: McGraw-Hill.

Darlow, C. (1983) *Valuation and Investment Appraisal*, London: Estates Gazette.

Fraser, W.D. (1984) *Principles of Property Investment and Pricing*, 1st edn. London: Macmillan.

Jaffe, A.C. and Sirmans, C.F. (1995) *Fundamentals of Real Estate Investment*, 3rd edn. Englewood Cliffs, NJ: Prentice Hall.

Lusht, K.M. (1997) *Real Estate Valuation*, Chicago: Irwin.

Whipple, R.T.M. (1995) *Property Valuation and Analysis*, Sydney: Law Book Co.

Appendix 4A
Multiple growth models

Up to this point we have assumed that rental value growth remains constant at a fixed rate in perpetuity. This, however, is only an approximation and recent experience shows that rental value growth is likely to show considerable variation. A more realistic approach to defining cash flows in a DCF framework would take account of periods of high and low growth.

In this appendix we present a general model that builds on the concepts we have already developed. It shows that by combining the ideas discussed in this chapter it is possible to develop a model that can cope with any combination of growth rates. Once again the principal advantage of this type of model is to use it for analysing transactions.

For simplicity we will consider a three-period model and assume that growth takes place over a fixed number of reviews. Each period of growth can therefore be valued as if it were a terminating cash flow. We will use the following notation:

a = initial rental value
n_j = number of rent reviews in period j
p = rent review period in years
g_j = growth in rental value in period j
r = expected rate of return

For the first period of growth, $j = 1$, and the present value can be expressed as:

$$\frac{a}{r}\left[\frac{(1 + r)^p - 1}{(1 + r)^p - (1 + g_1)^p}\right]\left[1 - \frac{(1 + g_1)^{n_1 p}}{(1 + r)^{n_1 p}}\right] \quad \text{subject to } r > g_1 \qquad (4A.1)$$

For the second period of growth, $j = 2$, and the present value can be expressed as:

$$\frac{a}{r(1 + r)^{n_1 p}}\left[\frac{(1 + r)^p - 1}{(1 + r)^p - (1 + g_2)^p}\right]\left[1 - \frac{(1 + g_2)^{n_2 p}}{(1 + r)^{n_2 p}}\right] \quad \text{subject to } r > g_2 \qquad (4A.2)$$

For the third period of growth, $j = 3$, and the present value can be expressed as:

$$\frac{a}{r(1 + r)^{p(n_1 + n_2)}}\left[\frac{(1 + r)^p - 1}{(1 + r)^p - (1 + g_3)^p}\right]\left[1 - \frac{(1 + g_3)^{n_3 p}}{(1 + r)^{n_3 p}}\right] \quad \text{subject to } r > g_3 \quad (4A.3)$$

This process can, of course, be continued indefinitely. The total present value is just the sum of the equations. A simple example will show more clearly what is happening. Assume that you wish to value a property that is let at its full rental value of £1,000 p.a. After having researched the market you forecast that the growth in rental value will be 8% p.a. for the first two reviews, 2% p.a. for the next three reviews, after which it will revert to its normal growth rate of 4% p.a. in perpetuity. If the expected return is 10% p.a. and the rent review periods are every five years the present value can be estimated using equations 4A.1–4A.3. The results are summarised in Table 4A.1.

Table 4A.1 • Present value of multiple growth model

Initial rental value: £100 p.a.
Rent review period: 5 years
Expected return: 10% p.a.

Period	Growth rate: g	Number of reviews: n	Present value
1	8% p.a.	2	£724.90
2	2% p.a.	3	£315.03
3	4% p.a.	∞	£143.07
			£1,183.00

Notice that in the final period the growth rate is assumed to continue in perpetuity. In this case the number of review periods included in the valuation is infinitely long so that the final expression in the last equation simplifies to 1.0.

Although the principles are relatively straightforward, you will see that the valuation equation soon becomes complex and needs to be solved using a computer. We have also assumed a constant rate of return for each period. This too is a simplification as it is based on the assumption that the yield curve is flat. Further realism could be introduced by allowing the discount rate to change in each period.

Mortgages and amortisation

Introduction

The first four chapters have developed some useful financial tools that are widely used in practice. As you develop your skill in applying these models you can use them for analysing and valuing a wide range of investments. We will build on these ideas in later chapters.

This chapter is, however, devoted to one major area that affects most of us during our lives – the mortgage. The purchase of a house is usually supported by a mortgage with repayments being made over long periods. For most people the commitment to a series of long-term payments is the only way that a high-value purchase can be arranged. Because the mortgage periods tend to be lengthy there are opportunities for substantial overpayment if the calculation of the repayments is incorrect. In many cases, however, mortgages are linked to other investment products, such as life insurance, so that it becomes difficult to disentangle the various components from the regular monthly payments.

The principles involved in setting up a mortgage are also used in hire purchase transactions. You will see that you have already learnt the basic techniques in the previous chapters. However, as long as you know how to set up a mortgage repayment table you can use this information to analyse a wide range of financial transactions. We will focus on the different forms of mortgage and how the calculation of interest can result in differences in payment.

The mortgage repayment table

A mortgage is a way of paying off, or amortising, a loan over a fixed period with a series of regular payments. This is just another example of the use of an annuity in which the repayments include a proportion of both capital and interest. The *mortgage repayment table* is just a way of showing how the payments are decomposed into capital and interest. You should remember the annuity formula from Chapter 2. We will use this in the following example.

Example

You decide to buy a small office building costing £150,000 and take out a fixed-term loan over five years at 10% p.a. The loan is to be repaid in five equal instalments starting at the end of the first year. Using the annuity formula you can estimate the annual repayments as follows:

$$V = a \left[\frac{1 - (1 + r)^{-n}}{r} \right] \qquad (5.1)$$

With the exception of the annual payment, a, everything else in this formula is known as follows:

$V = £150,000$

$r = 10\%$, i.e. 0.1

$n = 5$ years

We can find the annual repayment by substituting these figures into equation 5.1 to give:

$$£150,000 = a \left[\frac{1 - (1 + 0.1)^{-5}}{0.1} \right]$$

$£150,000 = 3.79a$

$a = £39,569.62$

> The annual repayment of £39,569.62 not only includes a proportion of capital but also of interest. However, the relative proportion of capital and interest changes over time. Table 5.1 shows how this figure can be split into its component parts.

Let's take a look at the first line. This shows your position during the first year. At the beginning of the year you start with an opening balance of £150,000. At the end of the year you make your first payment of £39,569.62. Part of this payment is interest on the opening balance of £150,000. At 10% p.a. the interest charged during the year is £15,000. If you subtract this from your annual payment of £39,569.62 you are left with an amount of capital which can be used to reduce the initial debt. In the first year the figure is £24,569.62 (i.e. £39,569.62 – £15,000.00). By the end of the year you have paid off part of the loan and are left with a closing balance of £125,430.38 (i.e. £150,000 – £24,569.62). This figure now becomes your opening balance at the beginning of the second year.

If you repeat this process in each year you will see that the loan is gradually being reduced. By the end of the fifth year the initial loan has been paid off, or *fully amortised*. This type of repayment scheme is sometimes referred to as a table mortgage.

If you follow the table through each year you will see that although the annual payments remain constant, the interest payments gradually get smaller as the reduction in capital increases. This can be clearly seen in Figure 5.1, which shows how the annual repayment of £39,569 is split into capital and interest and the relative proportion of these components change over time.

You will see that the interest payments represent a relatively high proportion of the annual repayment in the early years, although this reduces towards the end of the loan. This is a significant point if borrowers are able to obtain tax relief on interest payments. The argument is that the greatest tax relief is available in the early years of the loan because most of the annual repayment is made up of interest. This observation has led to insurance companies and building societies selling *endowment mortgages*, which are intended to offer the benefits of tax efficiency. The principle involved is to delay the repayment of the loan until the end of the term by building up an investment fund which should accumulate to at least the amount borrowed. If the fund does

Table 5.1 ● Mortgage repayment table assuming interest rate of 10% p.a.

Years	Opening balance	Annual repayment	Interest payment	Reduction in capital	Closing balance
0–1	£150,000.00	£39,569.62	£15,000.00	£24,569.62	£125,430.38
1–2	£125,430.38	£39,569.62	£12,543.04	£27,026.58	£98,403.80
2–3	£98,403.80	£39,569.62	£9,840.38	£29,729.24	£68,674.56
3–4	£68,674.56	£39,569.62	£6,867.46	£32,702.16	£35,972.40
4–5	£35,972.40	£39,569.62	£3,597.24	£35,972.38	£0.00
		£197,848.10	£47,848.12	£150,000.00	

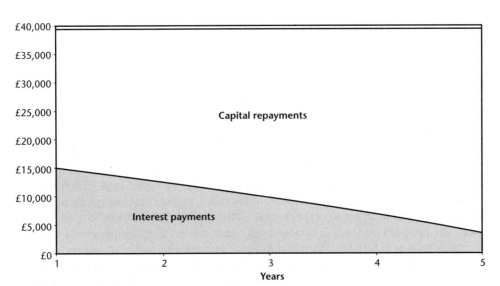

Figure 5.1 Total annual repayments split into capital and interest

well it is possible for the borrower to end up with a surplus after having paid off the loan. We shall look at the structure of the endowment fund in the next section. Before we do this, however, it is useful to look at some of the total figures given in Table 5.1.

Over the five-year period the total amount repaid is £197,848.10, of which £47,848.12 is interest. For some loan agreements, particularly for car purchase, it is not unusual to find the total amount repaid to be expressed as an annual percentage of the amount borrowed. This gives an optimistic view of the interest charged and appears to give the impression that the loan may be relatively cheap. For example, you can calculate the annual rate as follows:

$$r = \left[\frac{Total\ payments}{Amount\ borrowed} \right]^{\frac{1}{Term}} - 1 \qquad (5.2)$$

$$r = \left[\frac{£197,848}{£150,000} \right]^{\frac{1}{5}} - 1 = 5.69\%\ \text{p.a.}$$

This is about half the interest rate being charged and clearly appears attractive. At first sight there doesn't appear to be anything wrong with this calculation. You have borrowed £150,000 and over the five years you pay back £197,848. However, this rate would only be true if you made one single repayment of £197,848 at the end of five years. The reason the interest rate appears lower than the 10% rate being charged is because the capital is gradually being paid off throughout the term of the loan. If, however, you were able to enter into a contract which required only a single payment at the end of five years it is unlikely that the lender would be happy with an interest rate that was less than the original figure of 10% p.a. You can easily calculate the amount that you would need to repay the full amount of £150,000 after five years by applying what you have learnt about compound interest:

Repayment = £150,000(1 + 0.1)^5 = £241,576.50

As this is £43,728 greater than required by paying in instalments you will see that the lower rate of interest is really a financial sleight of hand designed to give the impression that you are getting a cheap loan.

Endowment mortgages

It has been common practice in the UK for borrowers to obtain tax relief on loans for house purchase. The benefits of this practice have gradually been reduced over a number of years and it is likely that in the future it will be eliminated. Currently, it is possible for borrowers in the UK to obtain tax relief on their interest payments at the rate of 10% on the first £30,000 borrowed. This reduces the effective rate of interest paid. The tax relief on interest is taken into consideration in salary payments through a system known as MIRAS, which stands for *mortgage interest relief at source*.

To illustrate the principle behind the endowment mortgage we will use the same example as given in Table 5.1. In this case, however, we have to make allowance for the tax relief and calculate the payments on a net of tax basis. The gross interest being charged is 10%. On a net of tax basis at the rate of 10%, i.e. $t = 0.10$, you can estimate the interest rate as follows:

$$r_{net} = r_{gross} (1 - t) \tag{5.3}$$

$$r_{net} = 10.00(1 - 0.10)$$

$$r_{net} = 9.0\%$$

This rate, however, applies only to the first £30,000 borrowed. The remainder of the loan would be charged at 10% p.a. Given this information you can calculate the weighted average rate of interest being charged on the total loan of £150,000.

$$r_{average} = 9.0\% \frac{£30,000}{£150,000} + 10.00\% \frac{£120,000}{£150,000}$$

$$r_{average} = 9.80\% \text{ p.a.}$$

You can see that the tax relief has slightly reduced the annual interest rate. This will also reduce the annual repayment. You can see this as follows by substituting the average rate into annuity formula:

$$£150,000 = a \left[\frac{1 - (1 + 0.098)^{-5}}{0.098} \right]$$

$$£150,000 = 3.81a$$

$$a = £39,367.65$$

Without the tax relief your annual payment was £39,569.62, so this represents a saving of £202 p.a.

Table 5.2 ● Repayment table for an endowment mortgage at 9.80% p.a.

Years	Opening balance	Annual repayment	Interest at 9.8%	Investment fund	Closing balance
0–1	£150,000.00	£39,367.65	£14,700	£24,667.65	£150,000
1–2	£150,000.00	£39,367.65	£14,700	£24,667.65	£150,000
2–3	£150,000.00	£39,367.65	£14,700	£24,667.65	£150,000
3–4	£150,000.00	£39,367.65	£14,700	£24,667.65	£150,000
4–5	£150,000.00	£39,367.65	£14,700	£24,667.65	£150,000
		£196,838.25	£73,500	£123,338.25	

However, one of the features of the endowment mortgage is to get the greatest advantage from the tax relief. In order to do this none of the capital is paid off until the end of the term so that the mortgage repayment table needs to be amended. The main change is that there is no reduction in the interest payments per year so that the borrower gets the maximum benefit from the tax relief. Table 5.2 shows how to set this up.

If you compare Table 5.2 with Table 5.1 you will see that, in this example, the total payments made are £1,009 less than the repayment mortgage. However, the total interest payments are much greater. For the repayment mortgage the proportion is 24% (i.e. £47,848/£197,848) and for the endowment mortgage it is 37% (i.e. £73,500/£196,838). As no capital is repaid, the endowment mortgage creates a fund of £24,667.65 p.a. which, if invested, should grow to cover the amount of the outstanding fund.

> The endowment mortgage embodies the principles of both an annuity and a sinking fund. Its main advantage is to make use of the tax relief on interest. This benefit has in recent years been reducing.

You should recognise this as a *sinking fund*, which has fixed regular payments each year that grow to the terminal value. In this case you know both the terminal value (£150,000) and the regular payment (£24,668) so you can solve for the breakeven rate required for the investment. To simplify matters you can assume that there is no commission or other cost(s) involved in managing the fund. Using the sinking fund formula from Chapter 2 you get the following:

$$£150,000 = £24,668 \left[\frac{(1 + r)^5 - 1}{r} \right]$$

$r = 0.098$, i.e. 9.80% p.a.

This, of course, is just the net of tax rate used to calculate the mortgage.

The endowment mortgage just repackages the loan in a slightly different way from a repayment loan and, as no additional costs have been introduced, this is the return that we should expect. The benefit of this approach comes if the fund is able to earn a return in excess of this figure. If this is possible when the loan is paid off there should be a reasonable surplus.

In principle this sounds fine. However, the value of the fund depends on the performance of the stock market and the costs associated with managing the fund. In fact, the risk of the fund is different from the risk of the loan. The fund risk is affected by conditions in the stock market whereas the risk of the loan is a function of the default risk of the borrower. Borrowers should be aware of these differences in risk. We will, however, delay the discussion concerning risk until Part 2. What is clear from the above, however, is that, excluding all costs, an endowment mortgage will break even if the fund is able to earn the same rate of interest as the loan. To put this another way, this arrangement will break even if the difference between the mortgage rate and the investment rate is completely absorbed by management costs. Given that the difference could easily be in the order of 5–8% p.a., this would represent a substantial amount in management costs.

Fund performance, management costs and endowment mortgages received a lot of publicity following the collapse of the UK stock market in 1987. First, the performance of the underlying funds, in many cases, proved to be insufficient to cover the value of the outstanding loans. Many borrowers were forced into a position where they had to make additional top-up payments in order to pay off the loan at the end of the term. Second, the position was exacerbated by the high costs of managing the funds particularly as most were *front-loaded*. In other words, most of the commissions paid to agents were made in the first few years of the loan so that the fund value showed little increase until the later years. In fact, it is not unusual to find the cash-in value of the fund in the first few years to be less than the amount paid to cover the mortgage. This severely disadvantaged those borrowers who wanted to sell after a few years and move to another property as they had not paid off any of the capital borrowed and could end up with a negative fund value. In these cases the borrower is relying solely on inflationary increases in the value of the property to build up equity. During the UK recession of the early 1990s the value of many residential properties reduced dramatically. In some cases the value of a property became less than the outstanding loan. This led to what became known as *negative equity*.

Often, repayment and endowment mortgages are set up with a supporting life insurance policy to cover the loan in the event that the borrower dies before it is fully repaid. In addition, the loans usually require some form of building insurance. These are costs on top of the mortgage repayment.

Changes in interest rates

The loan agreements we have illustrated so far have been based on fixed interest payments. This arrangement is known as a *fixed rate mortgage* (FRM). In practice, however, it is not unusual to have variable rate loans in which the interest rates change over time. These are referred to as *adjustable rate mortgages* (ARMs). In this situation the repayment is recalculated every time there is a change in interest rates and is based on

Table 5.3 • Mortgage repayment table with a change in interest rate

Years	Interest	Opening balance	Annual repayment	Interest payment	Reduction in capital	Closing balance
0–1	10%	£150,000.00	£39,569.62	£15,000.00	£24,569.62	£125,430.38
1–2	10%	£125,430.38	£39,569.62	£12,543.04	£27,026.58	£98,403.80
2–3	5%	£98,403.80	£36,134.72	£4,920.19	£31,214.53	£67,189.27
3–4	5%	£67,189.27	£36,134.72	£3,359.46	£32,775.26	£34,414.01
4–5	5%	£34,414.01	£36,134.72	£1,720.70	£34,414.01	£0.00
			£187,543.40	£37,543.39	£150,000.00	

the amount needed to pay off the loan over the remainder of the term. You can see how this works in Table 5.3 where we have re-estimated Table 5.1 with a change in the interest rates half-way through the period of the loan from 10% to 5%.

You will see that up until the end of year 2 the figures are exactly the same as in Table 5.1. However, at the beginning of year 3 the interest rate drops to 5% and as a result the annual repayments change. The way you calculate the revised payment is as follows. The opening balance at the beginning of year 3 is £98,403.80. This has been brought forward from the end of the previous year. The loan now has three more years to run before it is fully discharged. You can regard this as taking out a new loan of £98,403.80 which has to be paid off over three years at 5% p.a. Using the annuity formula again gives the revised payment:

$$£98,403.80 = a \left[\frac{1 - (1 + 0.05)^{-3}}{0.05} \right]$$

$$£98,403.80 = 2.72a$$

$$a = £36,134.72$$

Substituting this new figure gives the repayment schedule as shown in Table 5.3.

Changing the repayment period

During those periods when mortgage interest rates were very high it became common practice for building societies to offer the alternative of increasing the payment or extending the loan period. This, however, also works in reverse whenever there is a reduction in interest rates. In the example above the annual repayment at 10% was estimated to be £39,569.62. When the interest rate dropped to 5% we estimated the repayment to be £36,134.72 but kept the overall term of the loan unchanged at five years. However, we could have decided to keep the same payments but accept a shorter repayment period. You can estimate the revised repayment period by once again using the annuity formula:

$$£98,403.80 = £39,569.62 \left[\frac{1 - (1 + 0.05)^{-n}}{0.05} \right]$$

Rearranging gives:

$$2.487 = \frac{1 - (1 + 0.05)^{-n}}{0.05}$$

$$1.142 = (1.05)^n$$

The value of n can be found by taking logs:

$$\ln(1.142) = n\ln(1.05)$$

$$n = 2.722 \text{ years}$$

In this example, by keeping the payments constant, it is possible to pay off the loan about three and a half months early.

Payments over less than one year

The examples we have considered so far have made the assumption that there is only one payment per year. However, most mortgages generally require borrowers to make payments every month. The principles we have discussed above still apply, but it is important to make sure that the monthly interest rate is calculated correctly.

Building societies often estimate the monthly payment by taking one twelfth of the annual payment. The main problem with this approach is that the lender is able to invest these funds on a monthly basis, but the benefit to the borrower of payment by instalment is not taken fully into consideration. An alternative approach followed by building societies is to take one twelfth of the interest rate and use this as the basis for calculating the monthly payment.

You should, however, recall our discussion on annual percentage returns (APRs). The rate of interest charged per month should compound forward to the APR. If, however, the interest charged is only one twelfth of the annual rate it will be evident that this is not the case. Let's look at a simple example.

A building society offers an APR of 7% p.a. and requires its borrowers to make monthly payments. To be consistent with the APR the interest charged per month should, when compounded, be equal to the APR. In our case the building society takes one twelfth of this rate as the monthly rate, i.e. 0.583%. Let's compound this over one year to see what annual rate this implies.

$$r_{ann} = (1 + r_{mon})^{12} - 1$$

$$r_{ann} = (1.00583)^{12} - 1$$

$$r_{ann} = 0.0723, \text{ or } 7.23\% \text{ p.a.}$$

In this case the building society is charging more interest than it should. Clearly this has an impact on the total amount paid over the term of the loan.

Let us look at the effect of the different methods of payment on the total amount paid over the term of a typical loan. For example, assume you want to buy a house and have to borrow £80,000 over a term of 25 years. The annual percentage rate (APR) is quoted at 7.00% p.a. As described above you can calculate the monthly payments in three ways.

1. Annual payment method

With this approach you just estimate the annual payment and divide it by 12.

$$£80,000 = a \left[\frac{1 - (1 + 0.07)^{-25}}{0.07} \right]$$

$$£80,000 = 11.654a$$

$$a = £6,864.84 \text{ p.a.}$$

The monthly payment is, therefore, £572.07 and the total amount paid over 25 years is £171,621 assuming no changes in the rate of interest.

Now that you know the monthly payment it is possible to work out what this implies in terms of monthly and annual interest rates. This can be found by substituting the monthly interest payments into the annuity formula. The monthly rate in this case is 0.594% or 7.36% p.a.

2. Annual interest method

As an alternative to the above you could also have taken one twelfth of the interest rate and estimated the monthly payments over the total number of periods. In this case the interest would be 0.07/12 or 0.0058, i.e. 0.58% per month. This monthly rate is equivalent to an annual figure of 7.23%. This rate can be substituted into the annuity formula to estimate the monthly payment. Note that you have to use 300 months not 25 years.

$$£80,000 = a \left[\frac{1 - (1 + 0.00583)^{-300}}{0.00583} \right]$$

$$£80,000 = 141.487a$$

$$a = £565.42 \text{ per month}$$

The total payment over the term of the loan is this case is £169,627.

3. Effective interest method

The alternative approach for estimating the monthly interest correctly allows for the fact that the annual rate is expressed as an APR. Using the method discussed in Chapter 2 you can calculate the monthly payments as follows:

$$r_{mon} = (1 + r_{ann})^{\frac{1}{12}} - 1$$

$$r_{mon} = (1.07)^{\frac{1}{12}} - 1$$

$$r_{mon} = 0.00565, \text{ i.e. } 0.565\% \text{ per month}$$

Table 5.4 ● **Alternative methods of estimating monthly payments based on loan of £80,000 over 25 years**

Method of interest calculation	Monthly interest	APR	Monthly payment	Total payment over term of loan	Overpayment over term
1. Annual payment	0.594%	7.36%	£572.07	£171,621	£5,348
2. Annual interest	0.583%	7.23%	£565.42	£169,627	£3,354
3. Effective interest	0.565%	7.00%	£554.25	£166,273	£0

This figure can now be substituted into the annuity formula to estimate the monthly payments over 300 months:

$$£80,000 = a \left[\frac{1 - (1 + 0.00565)^{-300}}{0.00565} \right]$$

$$£80,000 = 144.34a$$

$$a = £554.25 \text{ per month}$$

Over the term of the loan the total amount paid will be £166,273.70. Table 5.4 summarises the results and shows the amount of overpayment that can occur when the monthly payment is calculated in different ways.

You will see that there are significant differences that can lead to a substantial overpayment over the 25-year term of the loan. In each case the APR is different, even though the quoted interest rate is 7.0% p.a.

The correct method of calculating periodic payments is to use the effective interest rates so that they are related to the APR. Other methods will overstate the payments.

Appendix 5A presents the above in a mathematical framework so that differences in payment structure can easily be evaluated.

Reducing the payment period

One further option offered by lenders is for borrowers to make more frequent payments. This is usually every two weeks and is offered as a way of reducing the period of the loan. Let us look at how this would work in practice. For this example assume you take out a loan of £80,000 over 25 years at an annual rate of interest (APR) of 6.5%.

Instead of paying monthly the lender offers the opportunity to pay half the monthly instalment at fortnightly intervals. In practice this means that you will make 26 fortnightly payments instead of 24 half-monthly payments. You will therefore pay more per year under this arrangement than under a normal monthly repayment scheme. The first step is to work out the monthly payment.

Given an APR of 6.5% the monthly interest is as follows:

$$(1 + r_{mon})^{12} = (1 + r_{ann})$$

$$r_{mon} = (1 + r_{ann})^{\frac{1}{12}} - 1$$

$$r_{mon} = (1.065)^{\frac{1}{12}} - 1$$

$$r_{mon} = 0.00526 \text{ or } 0.526\% \text{ per month}$$

Substituting this into the annuity formula gives the monthly payment required over the period of 300 months (i.e. 25 years × 12 months).

$$\pounds 80,000 = a \left[\frac{1 - (1 + 0.00526)^{-300}}{0.00526} \right]$$

$$\pounds 80,000 = 150.71a$$

$$a = \pounds 530.81$$

However, instead of paying £530.81 per month you agree to pay half this amount, i.e. £265.40 every two weeks. Because there are 26 fortnights in one year, the total annual amount paid is £6,900.47 instead of £6,369.72 if the instalments were paid monthly.

Because you are making fortnightly payments you need to know the correct rate of interest per period in order to calculate what effect the accelerated payments will have on the repayment period. This is calculated in the same way you estimated the monthly interest:

$$r_{fortnightly} = (1 + r_{ann})^{\frac{1}{26}} - 1$$

$$r_{fortnightly} = (1.065)^{\frac{1}{26}} - 1$$

$$r_{fortnightly} = 0.00243, \text{ i.e. } 0.243\% \text{ per month}$$

Now that you know both the fortnightly payment and the interest rate you can solve for the repayment period. This is found by substituting these figures into the annuity formula and solving for the number of years.

$$\pounds 80,000 = \pounds 265.40 \left[\frac{1 - (1 + 0.00243)^{-26n}}{0.00243} \right]$$

You will notice that we have used $26n$ to express the total number of years, n, in terms of the number of fortnights. This equation is, however, a little tricky to solve but there are two ways it can be tackled. One way is to solve it iteratively by changing the values of n until the difference between the left- and right-hand side of the equality is equal to zero. Alternatively it can be solved by rearranging and taking logs, as follows:

$$301.432 \times 0.00243 = [1 - (1 + 0.00243)^{-26n}]$$

Rearranging to eliminate the negative power gives the following:

$$\frac{1}{0.2675} = (1.00243)^{26n}$$

$$3.7380 = (1.00243)^{26n}$$

Taking logs of both sides:

$$\ln(3.7380) = 26n\ln(1.00243)$$

$$n = \frac{\ln(3.7380)}{26[\ln(1.00243)]}$$

$$n = 20.895 \text{ years}$$

This is approximately 20 years and 11 months. Thus, by paying more rapidly it is possible, in this case, to reduce the term of the loan by just over four years. The total amount paid over this revised term is £144,184, i.e. 20.895 × 26 × £265.40. Had the payments been monthly the total amount paid for the full term would have been £159,243, i.e. 25 × 12 × £530.81. The amount you have saved is £15,059.

The saving in this case is quite substantial, but it is really an illusion. The lender will not present you with a cheque for £15,059. All that is happening is that you are paying back capital at a much faster rate and are, therefore, reducing the amount of gearing in the financing package. Further 'savings' could be made by paying back more. Paying half the monthly payment every fortnight is an arbitrary figure. Any amount could be used over any interval. The limit to this arrangement is to take out a loan for £80,000 and immediately pay it back. This would give the impression that you are making a saving of £79,243, i.e. (£159,243 – £80,000), over someone who is paying monthly. Paying off the loan immediately has removed all the gearing and clearly shows that this arrangement is a financial illusion. If interest rates are lower than the growth in the capital value of the property, then it will generally pay to borrow.

Summary

This chapter has shown how financing arrangements can often be considered as the repackaging of simple annuities and sinking funds. Once you know this then it is possible to analyse alternative financing deals.

We showed how to set up a mortgage repayment schedule and then extended this to take account of mortgages that were repaid with an endowment. We gave an example of a fixed rate mortgage and showed how to estimate the repayments with an adjustable rate mortgage. We also showed how to re-estimate the loan repayment period whenever the interest rate changes, assuming the repayments remained constant.

The calculation of the interest rate is an important component of a mortgage, particularly when repayments are made monthly. We showed how mortgage lenders have different ways of calculating monthly interest and payments, and how this can significantly affect the total amount paid over the term of a loan. The chapter closed with a discussion of how to reduce the term of the loan by making accelerated payments.

Appendix 5A: Analysing alternative payment methods

This chapter has one appendix in which we develop a mathematical model for estimating the overpayment that will occur with different funding arrangements.

Chapter 5: Summary table

1. The mortgage is just another example of how to use the annuity formula.	$V = a \left[\dfrac{1 - (1 + r)^{-n}}{r} \right]$
2. Over the life of a mortgage the annual rate is just the rate of return that equates the total payments with the initial loan. This assumes, however, that only two cash flows are involved.	$r = \left(\dfrac{Total\ payments}{Amount\ borrowed} \right)^{\frac{1}{Term}} - 1$
3. Endowment mortgages do not repay any capital but build up an investment fund to cover the loan at the end of the term. The basis of this is the sinking fund. Endowment mortgages were designed to make use of the tax relief available on interest payments.	$FV = a \left[\dfrac{(1 + r)^n - 1}{r} \right]$
4. Repayments using an adjustable rate mortgage can be simply estimated using the annuity formula.	
5. It is also possible to alter the repayment period when interest rates change by keeping the repayments constant.	
6. When payments are made monthly, building societies use a wide range of calculation. The correct method is to use the effective rate of interest based on the known APR.	$r_{mon} = (1 + r_{ann})^{\frac{1}{12}} - 1$
7. Accelerated payments can reduce the effective period of a loan. This is really an illusion as accelerated payments just remove the gearing in the loan.	

Problems

1. You borrow £20,000 from a bank and agree to repay it over ten years. The bank offers a rate of interest of 9.5% p.a. Assuming that you make payments at the end of each year, what are your annual repayments?

2. Draw up a repayment schedule to show how the loan would be paid off.

3. What would the repayments be if the instalments were paid in advance?

4. The bank offers the opportunity to repay on a monthly basis. Assuming that you repay monthly in arrears, what would your repayments be?

5. The ABC Mortgage Company offers you £200,000 to buy a house over 20 years and tells you that your total repayments will only represent a cost to you of 5.9% p.a. You're impressed, as every other company you approached was charging 14% p.a. You think that you have got a good deal, but how much is it really costing?

6. You decide not to use the ABC Mortgage Company but instead borrow the £200,000 from your friendly bank. They are able to offer you a deal at a fixed rate of 12% p.a. They tell you that the monthly repayments are £2,231.31 but you can repay the loan in fortnightly instalments. What difference would this make to the term of your mortgage?

Selected references

Brealey, R.A. and Myers, S.C. (1996) *Principles of Corporate Finance*, 5th edn. New York: McGraw-Hill.

Darlow, C. (1983) *Valuation and Investment Appraisal*, London: Estates Gazette.

Francis, J.C. and Taylor, R.W. (1992) *Investments*, Schaum's Outline Series, New York: McGraw-Hill.

Lusht, K.M. (1997) *Real Estate Valuation*, Chicago: Irwin.

Whipple, R.T.M. (1995) *Property Valuation and Analysis*, Sydney: Law Book Co.

Appendix 5A
Analysing alternative payment methods

In this appendix we build some simple models that compare the different methods of calculation discussed in Chapter 5. The models can be used to estimate the periodic overpayment based on the outstanding loan. We shall use the following notation:

V = amount of loan outstanding
n = number of years of loan outstanding
m = number of payment periods p.a.
a = annual mortgage repayment
a_m = periodic payment
$\hat{a}_m$ = periodic payment based on effective interest rate
r_m = return per period
r = annual percentage return APR

Given the APR the effective interest rate per period can be estimated as:

$$r_m = (1 + r)^{\frac{1}{m}} - 1 \tag{5A.1}$$

The payment per period can be found by substituting into the annuity formula:

$$V = \hat{a}_m \left[\frac{1 - (1 + r_m)^{-mn}}{r_m} \right] \tag{5A.2}$$

Rearranging gives the payment as:

$$\hat{a}_m = \frac{V.r_m}{[1 - (1 + r_m)^{-mn}]} \tag{5A.3}$$

This is the correct payment per period based on the effective rate of interest. This is the base case payment to be used for estimating the amount of overpayment per period.

Apart from this base case two other methods of calculating the periodic payments were discussed in the text. These were based on the annual payment and the annual interest. We can write these as follows.

Case A. Annual payment method

In this situation the periodic payment is just the annual payment divided by the number of compounding periods per year:

$$V = a \left[\frac{1 - (1 + r)^{-n}}{r} \right] \tag{5A.4}$$

Rearranging to find the annual payment gives:

$$a = \frac{V.r}{[1 - (1 + r)^{-n}]} \tag{5A.5}$$

The payment in each period is, therefore:

$$\frac{a}{m} = \frac{V.r}{m[1 - (1 + r)^{-n}]} \tag{5A.6}$$

The overpayment per period, based on the outstanding loan, is just the difference between equation 5A.6 and 5A.3:

$$\left[\frac{a}{m} - \hat{a}_m\right] = V\left\{\frac{r}{m[1 - (1 + r)^{-n}]} - \frac{r_m}{[1 - (1 + r_m)^{-mn}]}\right\} \tag{5A.7}$$

Example

Assuming an outstanding loan of £100,000 and an APR of 8.5% you can estimate the overpayment per month, based on a term of 25 years.

The first step is to estimate the effective rate of interest from equation 5A.1 as follows:

$$r_m = (1 + 0.085)^{\frac{1}{12}} - 1$$

$$r_m = 0.00682$$

Substituting into equation 5A.7 gives:

$$£100,000\left\{\frac{0.085}{12[1 - (1 + 0.085)^{-25}]} - \frac{0.00682}{[1 - (1 + 0.00682)^{-300}]}\right\}$$

$$£100,000(0.00814 - 0.00784)$$

£30 per month

Assuming no change in interest rates, this represents a total overpayment of £9,000 over 25 years.

Case B. Annual interest method

In this case the interest per period is calculated by dividing the annual interest by the number of compounding periods per year. The periodic payment can, therefore, be written as:

$$V = a_m\left[\frac{1 - \left(1 + \dfrac{r}{m}\right)^{-mn}}{\dfrac{r}{m}}\right] \tag{5A.8}$$

This can be rearranged to give the following periodic payment:

$$a_m = \frac{V.r}{m\left[1 - \left(1 + \dfrac{r}{m}\right)^{-mn}\right]} \tag{5A.9}$$

The overpayment per period, based on the outstanding loan, is just the difference between equation 5A.9 and 5A.3:

$$(a_m - \hat{a}_m) = V \left\{ \frac{r}{m\left[1 - \left(1 + \dfrac{r}{m}\right)^{-mn}\right]} - \frac{r_m}{[1 - (1 + r_m)^{-mn}]} \right\} \qquad (5A.10)$$

Using the same example as above the overpayment per period can be written as:

$$£100,000 \left\{ \frac{0.085}{12\left[1 - \left(1 + \dfrac{0.085}{12}\right)^{-300}\right]} - \frac{0.00682}{[1 - (1 + 0.00682)^{-300}]} \right\}$$

£100,000(0.00805 – 0.00784)

£21 per month

Assuming no change in the interest rate, this represents a total overpayment of £6,300 over 25 years.

Conclusion

The expressions we have derived are based on simple annuity formulas and can be used on a period-by-period basis to estimate the overpayment that occurs when there are differences in the calculation of the periodic payments. The formulas can also be adjusted to allow for tax relief on interest payments.

The term structure of interest rates

Learning objectives

After reading this chapter you will understand the following:

- The relationship between spot rates, redemption yields and the yield curve

- The importance of forward rates

- How to estimate the term structure of interest rates

- The theories that have been proposed to explain the term structure

Introduction

The principles of valuation we have discussed so far have assumed that interest rates remain constant over time. However, an examination of the financial pages of many newspapers will show that gilt interest rates vary and depend on the number of years to maturity. The relationship between interest rates and the term to maturity can be described by means of a yield curve. If this is not flat, then the use of a constant discount rate in a valuation model could lead to errors.

Spot rates, redemption yields and the yield curve

In Chapter 2 we showed you how to value cash flows. Let us now go back to first principles and establish some new ideas.

Assume that you only have one cash flow, £a, which arises at the end of the first year. This cash flow is assumed to be default free and has the following present value,

$$V = \frac{a}{(1 + r_1)} \qquad (6.1)$$

Assume now that you have another cash flow of £a, which arises at the end of the second year. The present value can now be written as:

$$V = \frac{a}{(1 + r_1)} + \frac{a}{(1 + r_2)^2} \qquad (6.2)$$

In the first example, r_1 is today's *one-period spot rate*. In the second example, r_2 is today's *two-period spot rate*. A sequence of *spot rates* is known as the *term structure of interest rates*.

Instead of having a sequence of spot rates for each period it is possible to have one single rate, which would give the same present value. We could, therefore, write the second example as:

$$V = \frac{a}{(1 + r)} + \frac{a}{(1 + r)^2} \qquad (6.3)$$

The rate used in this case is just the internal rate of return or the *redemption yield*. As long as we know the price, the term to maturity and the sequence of cash flows it is

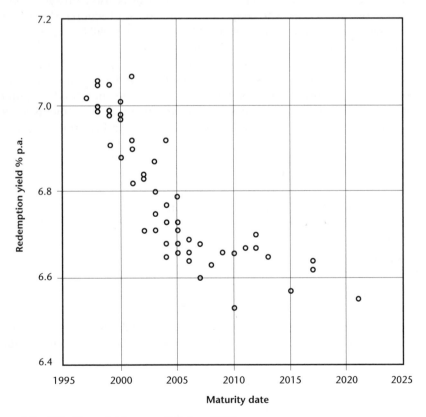

Figure 6.1 UK gilts – yield curve, October 1997

possible to calculate the redemption yield. A graph of redemption yields for different maturities identifies what is known as the *yield curve*. Figure 6.1 shows the yield curve in October 1997 based on redemption yields and maturity dates for the UK gilt market.

The general slope in this case is downward, i.e. long-term returns are generally lower than short-term returns. This, however, is not always the case. The shape of the yield curve can sometimes be flat, upward-sloping or it may even be humped.

Forward interest rates

An alternative way of looking at the term structure of interest rates is to estimate the *forward interest rate*. This is just a single period rate of interest occurring at some point in the future, which can be estimated from the sequence of spot rates. Given that a market exists for both long- and short-term loans this implies a forward market for loans similar to a commodities futures market. You can use this principle to estimate forward interest rates.

Assume that you have some spare money that you want to invest for two years. You have two options. You could invest in a bond for one year at a known rate of interest. This would be today's one-year spot rate. At the end of the year you take what you have earned and invest it in another one-year bond. This is also a one-year spot rate but it starts in one year's time. The problem with this course of action is that you don't know what next year's one-year spot rate is going to be so you will be exposed to some uncertainty concerning the final value of your investment.

The alternative strategy would be to invest in a two-year spot rate. Given that you know the one-year spot rate, this second option effectively locks in a *forward rate* for the second year. With this information you can calculate the one period forward rate.

Let us assume that today's spot rates for one- and two-year investments are 9.5% and 10.00%. You can write an equation that relates these investment options as follows:

$$(1 + 0.095)(1 + f_2) = (1 + 0.10)^2$$

Rearranging to find the forward rate in the second period gives:

$$f_2 = \frac{(1.10)^2}{(1.095)} - 1$$

$$f_2 = 0.11 \text{ or } 11.0\%$$

As long as you have a sequence of spot rates it is possible to estimate the forward rate over any period in the future. You can generalise the above example as follows:

$$f_{n-m,t+m} = \left[\frac{(1 + r_{n,t})^n}{(1 + r_{n-m,t})^{n-m}} \right]^{\frac{1}{n-m}} - 1 \tag{6.4}$$

This can be interpreted as the $(n-m)$ period forward rate commencing in period $(t-m)$. The period t represents the date on which the rates are established. This looks very complex but assume that you want to estimate a five-year forward rate today, which will commence in five years' time. Assume that the yield curve is rising and the spot rates for five- and ten-year bonds are 6.0% and 6.5%. From this you can summarise all the information you need to work out the five-year forward rate:

$t = 0$

$n = 10$ years

$m = 5$ years

$r_n = 6.5\%$, i.e. 0.065

$r_m = 6.0\%$, i.e. 0.060

Substituting these figures into equation 6.4 gives the following:

$$_0f_{10-5,0+5} = \left[\frac{(1 + 0.065_{10,0})^{10}}{(1 + 0.060_{10-5,0})^{10-5}} \right]^{\frac{1}{10-5}} - 1$$

$$_0f_{5,0} = \left(\frac{1.8771}{1.3382} \right)^{\frac{1}{5}} - 1$$

$_0f_{5,0} = 0.07$, i.e. 7.0% p.a.

Although the ten-year spot rate is 6.5%, the five-year forward rate in five years' time is 7.0%.

Valuation and the term structure

An important part of the analysis of a property is the valuation of its cash flows so that a comparison can be made with its market price. This will help you decide whether a property is under- or overpriced. One way to do this is to use the equivalent yield model and base your decisions on a careful choice of yield. The alternative is to be more explicit in the way you define your cash flows. We developed some of these models in Chapter 3, but made an assumption that the same discount rate should be used in each period. Doing this meant that we could arrive at closed form solutions for the valuation formulas. In terms of the term structure of interest rates we used the redemption yield.

This has important implications for valuation. Assume, for example, that you wanted to value a ten-year lease that had a rent review after five years. The initial rental income is £1,000 but is reviewed to £1,500 in year 5. Assume that there is no default risk so that you can use the bond market rates to estimate the required return.

If you ignored the slope of the yield curve we would probably use the 6.50% p.a. spot rate on a ten-year bond as the appropriate rate. Using the annuity formula you would value the cash flows as follows:

$$V = £1,000 \left[\frac{1 - (1 + 0.065)^{-5}}{0.065} \right] + \frac{£1,500}{(1 + 0.065)^5} \left[\frac{1 - (1 + 0.065)^{-5}}{0.065} \right]$$

$V = £8,705.40$

However, from our discussion on term structure you know that the forward rate for the first five years is 6.00% and this rises to 7.00% for the second five years. Taking this into consideration gives the following value:

$$V = £1,000 \left[\frac{1 - (1 + 0.060)^{-5}}{0.060} \right] + \frac{£1,500}{(1 + 0.060)^5} \left[\frac{1 - (1 + 0.070)^{-5}}{0.070} \right]$$

$V = £8,808.22$

Taking the slope of the yield curve into consideration you will see that the value of the lease has increased. In the first example a constant discount rate was used. This caused the early cash flows to be undervalued. Similarly, if the yield curve were falling this would also give rise to a different value.

Understanding the slope of the yield curve is important in valuing long-lived investments such as property. This, however, is very rarely done in practice and could lead to properties being mispriced. We say *could*, because the market generally values property by making use of initial and equivalent yields. As these are combinations of many factors we cannot be sure that they have not adjusted for changes in the slope of the yield curve.

> As a general principle cash flows should be discounted using returns that are derived from the underlying spot rates in each period.

Estimating the term structure

The yield curve shown in Figure 6.1 is based on redemption yields. This is just the internal rate of return of the cash flows from the bonds with different maturities. Redemption yields are not, however, very useful for estimating the term structure because they are sensitive to differences in cash flow. What is needed is a sequence of pure discount bonds. These are government securities that have only a single payment on maturity. The yields on these securities represent the spot rates for given maturities. A smooth line drawn through the spot rates will give the term structure of interest rates. Depending on how the discount bonds are traded the sequence of spot rates may not, however, be smooth. Some of the bonds may not have been traded so there may be jumps in the series. In addition to this there may be gaps if there are maturities with no observations. In order to overcome these difficulties it is common to estimate the term structure using some form of smoothing technique.

One such method is based on a technique known as spline smoothing, which relates discount factors to a cubic function of the time to maturity. Given a series of observed spot rates the discount factor relating to the spot rate can be expressed as a cubic function of the term to maturity. Algebraically we can summarise this as follows:

$d_n = \beta_0 + \beta_1 n + \beta_2 n^2 + \beta_3 n^3$

where

d_n = discount rate for maturity n

β = regression coefficient

We can illustrate this with the following simplified example. Assume that you have a series of annual observed spot rates which has some gaps in the sequence. For each spot rate you estimate the discount rate and use this as the dependent variable in the above equation. The fitted values from the regression equation will give the smoothed discount factors from which the spot rates for each maturity, r_n, can be estimated using the following.

The discount factor for each spot rate can be written as:

$$d_n = \frac{1}{(1 + r)^n} \tag{6.5}$$

The discount rates come from the regression equation so it is possible to rearrange equation 6.5 to give the spot rates for a sequence of maturity dates:

$$r_n = \left(\frac{1}{d_n}\right)^{\frac{1}{n}} - 1 \tag{6.6}$$

Table 6.1 summarises the results. Using the observed spot rates in the second column the regression equation has the following parameters:

$d_n = 1.01116 - 0.04779n - 0.00238n^2 + 0.00015n^3$

Table 6.1 ● Estimating the term structure

Years to maturity n	Observed spot rate	Discount factor d_n	Estimated discount factor	Estimated spot rate r_n
1	4.56	0.96	0.96	4.04
2	4.66	0.91	0.91	4.99
3	5.60	0.85	0.85	5.55
4	6.20	0.79	0.79	6.02
5			0.73	6.45
6	7.00	0.67	0.67	6.87
7	7.30	0.61	0.61	7.27
8	7.50	0.56	0.55	7.67
9	8.10	0.50	0.50	8.05
10	8.50	0.44	0.45	8.40
11	8.60	0.40	0.40	8.72
12			0.36	8.99
13	9.10	0.32	0.32	9.18
14	9.20	0.29	0.29	9.25
15	9.30	0.26	0.27	9.16

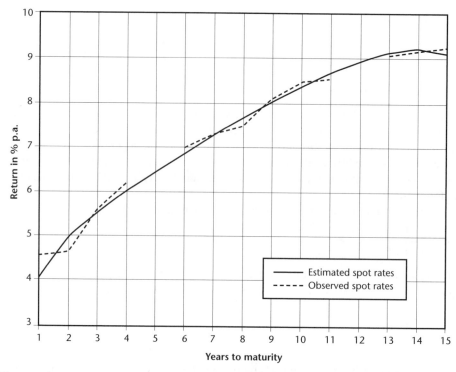

Figure 6.2 Using spline regression to estimate spot rates

The smoothed spot rate curve identifies the term structure. This provides the correct base line for use in discounted cash flow models of valuation. The fitted spot rates and observed spot rates are plotted in Figure 6.2.

Explaining the term structure

You will see from Table 6.1 that there is a difference between short- and long-term rates. Often the spot rate curve is upward-sloping. Sometimes, however, it is downward-sloping. A number of theories have been proposed to explain the difference between long- and short-term rates. These can be generalised into *the expectations hypothesis* and the *market segmentation hypothesis*.

The expectations hypothesis

The expectations hypothesis has a number of forms. These include pure expectations, liquidity preference and the preferred habitat hypotheses.

The *pure expectations hypothesis* suggests that forward rates represent expected future rates. An upward-sloping yield curve would, therefore, imply that short-term rates would rise in the future. Similarly a downward-sloping yield curve would suggest that short-term rates in the future would fall. Under this hypothesis long-term rates can be regarded as the average of a sequence of short-term forward rates. You can represent this algebraically as follows:

Table 6.2 ● Present value calculation with a rising term structure

End year	Forward rate	Spot rate	Discount factor	Cash flow	Present value
1	4.00%	4.00%	0.9615	£100.00	£96.154
2	5.00%	4.50%	0.9158	£100.00	£91.575
3	6.00%	5.00%	0.8639	£100.00	£86.392
4	7.00%	5.49%	0.8074	£100.00	£80.740
5	8.00%	5.99%	0.7476	£100.00	£74.759
					£429.620

$$r_n = [(1 + r_1)(1 + r_2)(1 + r_3)(1 + r_4)(1 + r_5) \ldots (1 + r_n)]^{\frac{1}{n}} - 1 \tag{6.7}$$

For example, if you have the following sequence of one-year forward rates, i.e. 4%, 5%, 6%, 7% and 8% you would estimate the five-year spot rate as follows:

$$r_5 = [(1.04)(1.05)(1.06)(1.07)(1.08)]^{\frac{1}{5}} - 1$$

$r_5 = 0.599$, i.e. 5.99% p.a.

With the rising yield curve the long-term rate is higher than the current short-term rate. Reversing the sequence of returns would give the same average return, but in this case the long-term rate would be lower than the short-term rate. We previously examined what would happen to a lease with fixed cash flows if you failed to take account of the term structure. We also pointed out that you should use the spot rate for each period in which the cash flow arises. In the example above we showed how to estimate the five-year spot rate from the series of five, one-year forward rates. You could also estimate the spot rate for the periods from one to five in the same way. This would then give the appropriate discount factors for each cash flow.

If you assume that you are valuing a project that has a cash flow of £100 in each year you would estimate the present value for a term structure that is rising as shown in Table 6.2.

Table 6.3 ● Present value calculation with a falling term structure

End year	Forward rate	Spot rate	Discount factor	Cash flow	Present value
1	8.00%	8.00%	0.9259	£100.00	£92.593
2	7.00%	7.50%	0.8654	£100.00	£86.535
3	6.00%	7.00%	0.8164	£100.00	£81.637
4	5.00%	6.49%	0.7775	£100.00	£77.749
5	4.00%	5.99%	0.7476	£100.00	£74.759
					£413.273

The spot rate in each year is calculated by substituting the one-year forward rates into equation 6.7.

You can estimate the present value for a falling term structure by reversing the sequence of rates. This is shown in Table 6.3.

The present value in this case is lower because the higher spot rates at the start of the cash flow have a greater discounting effect. Note also that the five-year spot rate of 5.99% is the same in both cases. Had you used this rate to discount the cash flows the present value would be £421.345. The shape of the yield curve and the underlying spot rates could therefore have a significant effect on valuations. However, we don't know whether the yield models incorporate the effects of changes in the term structure.

> Although the term structure of interest rates can have an effect on valuations we are not sure whether traditional yield models fully reflect the changes.

The liquidity preference hypothesis

The pure expectations hypothesis, however, ignores the fact that there is greater risk associated with holding long-term bonds so that investors normally expect to be compensated for the increase in uncertainty. This view has led to a modified version of pure expectations known as the liquidity preference hypothesis.

This approach suggests that in order to induce investors to take on the extra risk of holding longer-term bonds, they should be compensated with a return that is greater than the average of the forward rates suggested by the pure expectations hypothesis. Long-term rates should, therefore, embody a risk premium that increases uniformly with the term to maturity.

The preferred habitat hypothesis

An alternative argument accepts the risk premium proposal suggested above, but rejects the view that it must rise uniformly with an increase in maturity. The preferred habitat hypothesis suggests that the yield curve is made up of independent maturity segments and the yield in each segment is determined by supply and demand.

As the supply and demand in a given segment may not match, investors will be encouraged to shift to other maturity segments. As a result of moving from their preferred habitat investors, therefore, expect to be compensated with a risk premium that is related to their attitude to risk.

The market segmentation hypothesis

The market segmentation theory also suggests that the yield curve is made up of independent maturity segments. In addition, the theory argues that investors are unwilling to shift from their preferred habitat in order to take advantage of supply and demand differences within different segments. The shape of the yield curve is, therefore, determined by supply and demand within each segment.

The evidence does not generally support this view. Investors do tend to move into other market segments when there are differences in supply and demand. Support, therefore, shifts back to the preferred habitat hypothesis.

Summary

This chapter has shown the importance of understanding the term structure of interest rates and how it is likely to affect valuations. It is clearly more relevant when dealing with models that are explicit in analysing cash flows as the discount rate in each period becomes more important. We are not sure whether the subtle adjustments to yields made by valuers are sufficient to compensate for changes in the yield curve. We do know, however, that valuers are aware of these issues. Changes in yields also reflect other economic issues that may influence expected growth.

We showed the difference between spot rates, redemption yields and forward rates and illustrated the importance of the yield curve. We also showed how to estimate the term structure from a series of spot rates with different maturities.

The chapter closed with a discussion on the alternative arguments that have been put forward to explain the term structure.

Chapter 6: Summary table

1. The term structure of interest rates relates the return on government securities to the term to maturity.

2. The yield curve represents the theoretical zero coupon spot rates to the term to maturity.

3. A forward rate is a single period rate of interest occurring at some point in the future.

$$f_{n-m,t+m} = \left[\frac{(1 + r_{n,t})^n}{(1 + r_{n-m,t})^{n-m}} \right]^{\frac{1}{n-m}} - 1$$

4. Valuation models that assume a flat yield curve could result in property assets being mispriced.

5. Cash flows should be discounted at rates that are based on the underlying structure of spot rates.

6. There are a number of sophisticated models available for identifying the theoretical spot rates. This chapter illustrated a method using spline regression. The fitted discount rates can be converted to the spot rates using the following:

$$r_n = \left(\frac{1}{d_n} \right)^{\frac{1}{n}} - 1$$

7. A number of theories have been proposed for explaining the term structure of interest rates. These include:

- the pure expectations hypothesis
- the liquidity preference theory
- the preferred habitat hypothesis
- the market segmentation hypothesis

Problems

1. What is meant by the term structure of interest rates?

2. What is the difference between a spot rate and a forward rate of interest?

3. What do you understand by the term redemption yield?

4. Why should the shape of the yield curve be important in determining the value of a property?

5. Do you think that property yields adequately adjust for changes in the slope of the yield curve?

6. What shapes can the yield curve take?

7. What theories have been suggested to explain the term structure of interest rates?

Selected references

Brealey, R.A. and Myers, S.C. (1996) *Principles of Corporate Finance*, 5th edn. New York: McGraw-Hill.

Hicks, J.R. (1946) *Value and Capital*, 2nd edn. London: Oxford University Press.

Meiselman, D. (1962) *The Term Structure of Interest Rates*, Englewood Cliffs, NJ: Prentice Hall.

Michaelsen, J.B. (1973) *The Term Structure of Interest Rates*, Monetary Economics, New York: Intext Educational Publishers.

Nelson, C.R. (1972) *The Term Structure of Interest Rates*, New York: Basic Books.

Valuations and prices

Learning objectives

After reading this chapter you will understand the following:

- Why it is important that in the long term, valuations should act as a good proxy for prices

- The effect of behavioural issues and how they influence the way valuations are formed

- The issues involved in testing whether valuations are a good proxy for prices

Introduction

The techniques we have discussed so far have been concerned with the ways in which property can be valued. In the absence of an active sales market in property, valuations assume great importance. Most property portfolio decisions are, for example, based of valuations, not prices. Given their importance and widespread use one aspect that needs to be considered is whether valuations are indeed a good proxy for prices.

This is an important issue as it has important implications concerning the way the market operates. As you will see, if, on average, valuers are unable to arrive at reliable estimates of market prices the property industry would be thrown into disarray.

The importance of valuations

If valuations are an accurate reflection of information they should indicate the best way in which to allocate resources. Thus, in considering the value of information we are also looking at issues relating to the efficiency of the property market. We will delay our discussion on efficiency until Chapter 13. For the moment we will focus on the way buyers and sellers interpret information and how that influences the distribution of valuations and prices.

Because valuations are a reflection of the way information is interpreted it has been suggested that providing a single value for a property may give a misleading impression, and that a range of values would be more meaningful. Although this sounds plausible, clients really need to have a single point estimate of value. This is particularly true if they are paying a fee for the valuation. It would be difficult to justify paying a fee to a valuer if he or she presented a valuation report saying that a city office building is worth somewhere in the region of £3–5 million! What this does indicate is that there is uncertainty surrounding estimates of value and that different valuers have different views, depending on how they interpret information relevant to the property in question.

In a well-functioning market this is what you would expect. It is differences in opinion concerning the value of an asset that causes trades to take place. If everybody had the same view concerning values there would be no incentive to earn abnormal returns. We are also going to delay a discussion of abnormal returns, as it is related to risk and return, which we will develop in Part 2. We will therefore assume that the value of a property will have some distribution, which is related to the way information is interpreted.

Valuations can cover a number of different requirements, some of which are given in the following list:

- open market value
- current use value
- redevelopment value
- insurance value
- mortgage value
- stock exchange value
- going concern value

Some of these are specialist valuations reflecting a specific subset of information. However, each can be drafted in very general terms that take the following form:

$$E(V) = f(a,b,c,d,e,f, \ldots) \tag{7.1}$$

where $a, b, c, d, \ldots$, represent a range of factors that influence the valuation. Depending on the type of valuation being undertaken the weight applied to each of the factors will vary. Note also that we have expressed the valuation in terms of expectations, $E(V)$, because you cannot be certain about the value of each factor.

Each of the valuations mentioned above will vary, not only between each other but also from period to period depending on the type of information that is relevant and how the valuer assesses that information. Current use values, for example, will reflect the existing use of a property on the assumption that planning permission would not be granted for any material development. Similarly, redevelopment value will reflect more of the future potential of the property assuming that planning permission would be granted. In this case the option to redevelop has value. The probability of the redevelopment going ahead needs to be estimated as this will influence the final value.

Embedded real options of this nature are an important aspect of property valuation and are only just beginning to enter the literature on valuation theory.

Of the values referred to above *open market value* is the most important from the investment point of view. This is intended to represent the following:

> An opinion of the best price at which the sale of an interest in property would have been completed unconditionally for cash consideration on the date of valuation, assuming:
>
> a) a willing seller;
> b) that, prior to the date of valuation, there had been a reasonable period (having regard to the nature of the property and the state of the market) for the proper marketing of the interest, for the agreement of the price and terms and for the completion of the sale;
> c) that the state of the market, level of values and other circumstances were, on any earlier assumed date of exchange of contracts, the same as on the date of the valuation;
> d) that no account is taken of any additional bid by a prospective purchaser with a special interest; and
> e) that both parties to the transaction had acted knowledgeably, prudently and without compulsion.

> *RICS Appraisal and Valuation Manual*
> *Practice Statement*, 4 .2, 1995

These are the assumptions recommended by the RICS under which open market values should be estimated. It is important to note that under the current definition, open market value is drafted in terms of the best value that can be achieved and that the subset of information is very clearly specified. The use of the expression *best value* does imply something about the shape of the distribution from which the final value is decided.

Assume it is possible to sample a large number of valuers so that a probability distribution of open market values could be constructed for a single property. The shape of the distribution would tell you whether the RICS definition of open market value implies that valuers should be trying to estimate the mean, median or mode of the distribution. As it is generally not possible to get large numbers of valuers to provide full independent valuations of a single property we have, as an alternative, simulated the distribution of valuations based upon an established time series of rental value growth and total returns. You can find the results of this exercise in Appendix 7A.

Our analysis shows that the shape of the distribution is positively skewed. This is what you should expect, as the lowest property value is bounded by zero, but there is no upper limit. The choice of *best value* for a positively skewed distribution is, therefore, the mean or expected value. This also ties in with the common use of expected return, which is also based on the use of expected values.

This, however, is not the end of the story as far as open market values are concerned, as we are also interested to know whether a distribution of values is likely to be the same as a distribution of prices for the same property. In other words, are all players in the market using the same subset of information when assessing open market values?

Given a distribution of values, the price at which a property trades in the market ought to be chosen randomly from the distribution of values. Valuations and prices do not have to coincide, but you need to be sure that, on average, buyers and sellers are using the same subset of information so that no significant bias exists between values and prices. This is an important point as it affects the whole working of the professional market. To make this point more precise we need to introduce the concept of an equilibrium market. If the supply and demand for property are in balance then, on average, you would expect open market values to be equal to open market prices. If this is not the case, then it would give rise to two important implications that would affect professional property advice:

● property advice based on valuations would have little value,
● performance measurement based on valuations would have no meaning.

These points must be understood in relation the subset of information under consideration. The hypothesis that valuations are a good proxy for prices is valid only for the same subset of information. If, for example, open market values are being compared with special purchase prices, then the relationship breaks down. The information subset has changed and because it differs from the open market approach it could signal an opportunity to earn abnormal profits. The difficulty with this approach is that it can only be operationalised if we have a formal model of equilibrium values. This is something we shall introduce in Part 2.

> When supply and demand are in equilibrium, valuations should be a good proxy for prices. This is what you would expect over long periods. If it were not the case then professional advice would be worthless and performance measurement would have no meaning.

Prices are formed within a framework where buyers and sellers bid against each other until an agreed price is reached. If you assume that buyers and sellers both have access to the same set of information both parties will arrive at their own view of value from the same probability distribution. The price at which a property sells will depend on the relative strength of buyers and sellers in different market environments and the interpretation they place on the information. In an equilibrium market, for example, the number of sellers will be matched by an equal number of buyers and valuations and prices should be close to each other. In other market environments, however, the relative strength of buyers and sellers will be different and this will give rise to prices being systematically higher or lower than values. It will also mean that buyers and sellers face different probability distributions. The reason for this is that if valuers strictly adhere to the RICS definition of open market value then they should also try to establish a value that implies an equilibrium market. This is consistent with the concepts of equilibrium asset pricing models that you will find in the economics literature. At any point in time, however, the distribution of prices may reflect issues that are specific to the parties involved.

> The RICS definition of open market value implies that markets are in equilibrium. This is a benchmark against which buy–sell decisions should be made. This is also consistent with the economic concept of equilibrium asset pricing models.

In bull markets, for example, there are likely to be more buyers than sellers so that prices may exceed values. There may be cases where overinflated prices are paid for some properties that cannot be justified in terms of the evidence. By contrast, in a bear market the number of sellers will exceed the number of buyers and prices will tend to be lower than their corresponding values. At some times there may also be a number of distressed sales that would improve the bargaining strength of potential buyers.

In addition to the relative strength of buyers and sellers we also want to introduce the concept of 'sticky' valuations. This is particularly important because it affects the probability distribution of values. We have pointed out that the RICS definition of open market value is based on the principle of equilibrium markets. Although this is not specifically referred to in the definition of open market value it is nevertheless implied by assuming a willing seller and excluding special purchasers. Other parts of the definition reinforce the concept of an equilibrium market. One implication of this view is that valuers will respond to new information as it arises and will continually reflect this in a change in value.

In practice this does not happen. Values can remain unchanged for long periods or may be adjusted by a constant amount over a number of periods. Given that valuers have to assess information in an intuitive way these effects may arise for a number of reasons. For example:

- the threshold of information may be too small to cause the valuer to make a change until the cumulative effect becomes significant;
- abnormal changes in the market may not be fully reflected in a change in value, as client pressure may encourage valuers to move gradually towards a new equilibrium level;
- valuations may be undertaken by sample so that the average change in a group of values is applied to all other properties in a portfolio;
- many properties may only be valued annually so that intermediate valuation dates record no change.

The combination of these effects will reduce the volatility of changes in property values. This is more important at the portfolio level. However, in terms of the relationship between individual valuations and prices the effect of sticky values could give a misleading impression of a mismatch in the market and may imply that, at certain times, there has been a structural shift or a bias between valuations and prices.

We will return to the idea of sticky values when we discuss smoothing in property indexes, as this is an important issue. We now have enough information to examine how we should test the correspondence between valuations and prices.

Valuations versus prices

Analysing a sample of properties that have both a transaction price and a contemporaneous independent valuation we can test the hypothesis that valuations act as a good proxy for prices. It should be clear from the above that this is a test of an equilibrium market relationship. In other words, if you were able to strip out the effect of different market environments you should be able to observe a strong correspondence between valuations and prices. In this general form, this is not a testable statement.

What is needed is a model that relates valuations and prices so that a testable hypothesis can be proposed.

Let us assume that observed values and prices are equal to their expected values together with a random error term. You can state this algebraically as:

$$V_t = \bar{V}_t + e_t \tag{7.2}$$

$$P_t = \bar{P}_t + u_t \tag{7.3}$$

In this expression V_t and P_t are the observed value and price in period t, and $\bar{V}_t$ and $\bar{P}_t$ are their expected values. The difference between what is observed and what is expected is captured in the error terms e_t and u_t. In an equilibrium market, where the number of buyers is matched by an equal number of sellers, the expected value should be equal to the expected price. By making this assumption we can rearrange and simplify these equations as follows:

$$V - e_t = P_t - u_t \tag{7.4}$$

Combining the error terms gives:

$$V_t = P_t + \omega_t \tag{7.5}$$

To test whether valuations are a good proxy for prices you can write this in the form of a regression equation as follows:

$$V_t = \alpha_1 + \beta_1 P_t + \eta_t \tag{7.6}$$

If you have a sample of valuations and prices in period t, you can test whether valuations are a good proxy for prices by examining the regression coefficients. If our hypothesis is correct in an equilibrium market, you should expect to see a one-to-one correspondence between valuations and prices. In terms of the regression model you will be testing to see whether the slope of the coefficient β_t is statistically indistinguishable from 1.0. In addition, you will also be testing to see whether the intercept term a_t is statistically indistinguishable from zero.

The model drafted above relates valuations to prices. The reason for this is that information on prices is intended to explain valuations. However, tests of valuations as a proxy for prices are not really trying to establish any causal relationship. It would be just as valid to have a regression equation that has prices as the dependent variable and valuations as the independent variable. We will discuss the results using both forms of the equation in this chapter and also in the appendices. Before we do that, however, let us look a little more closely at the regression coefficients.

The slope coefficient

Remember that our valuation model is intended to describe an equilibrium market so that the number of buyers should be matched by an equal number of sellers. When you examine the results of a regression of valuations on prices (or prices on valuations) you should only expect to see a slope coefficient that is statistically indistinguishable from 1.0 if the market is in equilibrium. In other market environments you may see slope coefficients that are statistically different from 1.0. All this is telling us is that the market is not in equilibrium. The slope coefficient will tell you the average percentage difference between valuations and prices in different market environments. If you run this analysis over a number of different periods, you should expect to see the slope coefficient varying round 1.0.

As most of the analyses have tended to use prices as the dependent variable the slope coefficient will be greater than 1.0 in a bull market and less than 1.0 in a bear market. Over long periods you would, however, expect the average slope coefficient to be close to 1.0. However, we don't really know what constitutes a long period.

> The slope coefficient can differ from 1.0 depending on market conditions. In the long term the coefficient should on average be close to 1.0. However, we don't really know what constitutes a long period.

The intercept term

In an equilibrium market you would expect the intercept term to be statistically indistinguishable from zero. However, in many cases interpretation of the intercept term is difficult. The reason for this is that the intercept is likely to represent a combination of a number of factors. For example, there will often be a lag between the date of the valuation and the date of the sale. Depending on market conditions this could give the impression that there has been a structural shift between valuations and prices. However, valuations could also be 'sticky' and pick up information from previous periods. This too could affect the coefficient. In the simple bivariate model we described, you can't be sure what the combined effect of these factors is likely to be. The intercept term is picking up a number of factors that are difficult to separate, so you can't place too much credence on what it is really telling you.

One implication of this, however, is that tests of valuations versus prices which just look at the average percentage difference between the two figures is likely to give a misleading impression of valuation accuracy. If, for example, your sample contains a lot of sticky valuations the percentage difference between these figures and the sales prices will not tell you a great deal about how valuers interpret information. The reason for this is that some of the valuations may reflect behavioural factors that have nothing to do with the estimation of equilibrium values. The regression model, therefore, provides a much richer framework for examining how good valuers are at interpreting information. Let's now turn to some results.

Analysis of results

An important point, which arises from the above discussion, is the need to ensure that the valuations and prices used in the analysis reflect open market, or equilibrium market conditions. There are two ways to do this. One is to use a sample of properties that have all abnormal sales and valuations filtered out. The other way is to specifically build different market conditions into the model. We will present the results of the first approach in this chapter and cover the second in Appendix 7A.

Table 7.1 ● **Valuations versus prices, 1975–80**

	a_1	β_1	$\bar{R}^2$
Coefficient	–0.20	1.02	0.99
Standard errors	0.05	0.02	

The first test of valuations as a proxy for prices was undertaken by Brown (1985) using a sample of 29 properties collected over the period 1975–80. The sample covered a broad spectrum of types and quality, and consisted of transaction prices together with the most recent prior independent valuation. The 29 properties were taken from a much larger sample by excluding all transactions that covered special purchasers or forced sales. In addition, each of the valuations had to be undertaken on an open market basis. Any valuation that was for a specific purpose was excluded. This simple process ensured that, as far as possible, both prices and valuations were consistent with the RICS definition of open market value. Before the analysis was run the data were converted into units per square foot to compensate for differences in the absolute size of the properties. They were also normalised by taking logs. By letting V and P

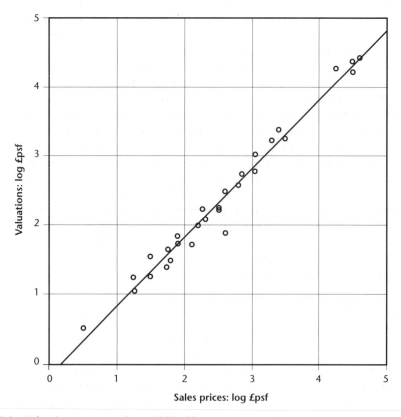

Figure 7.1   Valuations versus prices, 1975–80

represent the open market valuations and prices the regression model used in this analysis took the following form:

$$\ln(V_t) = \alpha_t + \beta_1 \ln(P_1) + e_t \tag{7.7}$$

The result of regressing valuations onto prices is given in Table 7.1.

These are also summarised in Figure 7.1.

The one-to-one relationship appears to be confirmed as the slope coefficient is statistically indistinguishable from 1.0. In addition the high $\bar{R}^2$ value indicates that prices explain about 99% of the variation in valuations. Both these results are encouraging and lend weight to the belief that valuers are doing a good job of impounding information into values. The intercept term is, however, significantly different from zero. Given our earlier comments we should not place too much emphasis on the significance of this coefficient. We know that the valuations and prices were not undertaken at exactly the same time and this may contribute to the shift away from zero. Over the period of the analysis the market was rising, so a negative intercept is consistent with the view that the general level of prices had increased relative to their earlier valuations. Other factors, however, may also have contributed to the non-zero intercept. Because there are difficulties in interpreting this coefficient the intercept does not tell us a great deal about the accuracy of valuations, even though it is statistically significant.

Following this early work the Investment Property Databank (IPD) and Drivers Jonas undertook a more extensive analysis (Drivers Jonas 1988) using a sample of 1,442 properties taken from the IPD database. Each of the properties was sold between January 1982 and March 1988 and had at least two open market valuations in the two consecutive years prior to the sale. All the valuations occurred between January 1980 and December 1987.

Various tests were undertaken but the principal one concerned an examination of prices versus valuations. The regression model differed from the analysis given above as prices were used as the dependent variable:

$$P_t = \alpha_1 + \beta_1 V_t + \eta_t \tag{7.8}$$

As we are not really concerned with establishing a causal relationship between prices and values, it doesn't matter which way round the regression is formulated.

The data were adjusted for heteroskedasticity by converting prices and values to units per square foot. The transformed data results were sufficiently normal so that no further adjustment was required. Although no information was given to indicate whether the prices represented open market transactions it is assumed that with such

Table 7.2 ● **Prices versus valuations, January 1982–March 1988**

	a_1	β_1 (Valuations)	R^2
Coefficient	3.56	1.061	0.934

Source: IPD/Drivers Jonas.

a large sample the effect of special situations could be diversified away. No tests for significance were supplied but the results of the basic model are shown in Table 7.2.

These results show a slope coefficient, β_1, which is again close to 1.0 and confirms the previous findings. The high $\bar{R}^2$ value in this case suggests that valuations explain a high proportion of the variability in prices. Because the model has used valuations as the independent variable the positive intercept could be consistent with the fact that the market was rising during the period of the analysis.

Further analyses were undertaken which included the lag between the valuation and the transaction date. These showed that the intercept term was unstable and was probably statistically indistinguishable from zero and that the lag term was significant. The basic hypothesis that there is a one-to-one relationship between valuations and prices remained unchanged.

Both of these analyses are reassuring from the point of view of the valuation profession since they add credence to the proposition that valuers are correctly interpreting information. If this were not the case, then the validity of professional advice would be thrown into disarray.

Since these early studies IPD have provided an analysis of prices versus valuations on an annual basis. Table 7.3 summarises the results from 1982 to 1996.

You will see from these results that the intercept term varies over a wide range of figures. With the exception of 1983 they are all significantly different from zero. However, we are more concerned with the magnitude of the slope coefficients and how these can be interpreted in terms of market conditions.

1992 and 1996 have coefficients that are statistically indistinguishable from 1.0, indicating that the market was in equilibrium.

Table 7.3 ● Prices versus valuations, 1982–96

	a_1	Standard error	β_1 (Valuations)	Standard error	R^2	n	Market
1982	3.24	0.36	1.09	0.02	0.94	164	Bull
1983	0.24	0.39	1.18	0.02	0.91	321	Bull
1984	6.07	0.38	1.05	0.00	0.97	276	Bull
1985	5.10	0.27	1.05	0.01	0.97	370	Bull
1986	2.43	0.32	1.06	0.00	0.95	560	Bull
1987	2.57	0.41	1.18	0.01	0.90	801	Bull
1988	−0.85	0.35	1.27	0.01	0.91	998	Bull
1989	7.28	0.35	1.18	0.01	0.91	738	Bull
1990	8.45	0.26	0.96	0.01	0.95	453	Bear
1991	8.91	0.27	0.95	0.01	0.94	605	Bear
1992	1.23	0.19	0.99	0.01	0.97	498	Equilibrium
1993	2.51	0.21	1.02	0.01	0.96	889	Bull
1994	6.15	0.30	1.06	0.01	0.92	828	Bull
1995	−2.08	0.26	1.02	0.01	0.96	957	Bull
1996	2.20	0.22	1.01	0.01	0.95	1007	Equilibrium
82–96	3.20	0.30	1.07	0.01	0.94	9465	Bull

Source: Investment Property Databank.

1990 and 1991 have slope coefficients significantly less than 1.0. These years indicate a bear market.

1982–89 and 1993–95 have slope coefficients which are significantly greater than 1.0. These would indicate bull market conditions.

The results of a regression analysis undertaken over the whole period show a slope coefficient that is statistically greater than 1.0. This would indicate that over the period 1982–96 the market was generally bullish. From these figures it will be seen that prices, on average, were about 7% higher than open market valuations. The property market during this period was generally buoyant, even up to the period following the stock market crash in 1987. The high prices indicated by this analysis are probably the result of abnormal transactions, which were outside the definition of open market value.

US research

The use of regression analysis as a means of investigating the relationship between valuations and prices for commercial property has been largely confined to UK studies. In the US similar tests have generally focused on the percentage difference between valuations and prices. For example, a study undertaken by Miles, Guilkey, Webb and Hunter in 1982, using a total sample of 469 commercial property transactions over the period 1979–90, showed a relatively small percentage difference between valuations and prices. Their results are summarised in Table 7.4.

This analysis does not, however, control for open market valuations and prices. Over the eleven-year period covered by the analysis the effect of different market environments generally cancel each other out and show that, on average, prices exceeded valuations by about 1.6%. The authors of this study argue that these results are appropriate for determining whether valuations are an unbiased estimate of prices over time. However, in order to examine the reliability of valuations they also examined the average *absolute* differences. These results are summarised in Table 7.5.

In this case the average absolute percentage difference between prices and values increased to 10.7%. It is not clear what reliability can be placed on these figures, as the information set used to estimate the values could be different from those used to estimate prices. In an additional analysis, the authors investigated whether properties

Table 7.4 ● Average percentage difference between prices and values. US data

	Pre-1986	1986–1 to 1987–3	1987–4 to 1990–4	All
All property	0.078	0.023	−0.033	0.016
Office	0.060	0.001	−0.067	−0.022
Retail	0.030	0.005	−0.027	0.005
Industrial	0.105	0.049	−0.013	0.040

Source: Miles, Guilkey, Webb and Hunter, 1982.

Table 7.5 ● Average absolute percentage difference between prices and values. US data

	Pre-1986	1986–1 to 1987–3	1987–4 to 1990–4	All
All property	0.127	0.088	0.103	0.107
Office	0.096	0.090	0.119	–0.108
Retail	0.097	0.051	0.072	0.075
Industrial	0.152	0.108	0.099	0.119

Source: Miles, Guilkey, Webb and Hunter, 1982.

that are more likely to be sold at a price that differs substantially from the valuation have common characteristics. Their results show that buyers and sellers place more weight on current market conditions, in addition to the future of local markets, than valuers.

Australian research

A more recent study by Newell and Kishore (1998) has examined the relationship between prices and valuations based on a sample of 218 commercial properties in Sydney, Australia. The total value of the sales was AUS$15.5 billion and we summarise the results of regressing prices on valuations in Table 7.6.

In each case the slope coefficient is statistically indistinguishable from 1.0; the intercept terms are also indistinguishable from zero and the $\bar{R}^2$ values are very high. These results are consistent with the UK regressions and show that, internationally, valuers are generally doing a good job of impounding information into values.

This is an important finding that needs to be developed in other parts of the world. In order to make a valid comparison of international property investment it is essential to know that local valuations are, on average, a good proxy for prices. In some countries where valuation practice is not well developed this relationship may not hold.

Table 7.6 ● Regression of prices versus values: Commercial property 1987–96, Sydney, Australia

	α	ß	R^2	n
All property	0.828 (1.351)	0.979 (0.012)	0.969	218
Office	2.968 (2.709)	0.982 (0.019)	0.964	101
Retail	1.167 (1.220)	0.976 (0.015)	0.973	117

Note: Standard errors in brackets.

Summary

This chapter has discussed the importance of valuations in terms of the way the market operates. Given the importance of the RICS definition of open market value it was shown that valuations should be a good proxy for open market prices. If this were not the case then it would have important implications for the way that the property market operates. In particular:

- professional advice would have little value;
- performance measurement would be invalid.

We also showed that valuations could be sticky and that prices could respond to abnormal situations. The joint effect of these influences could give a misleading impression of valuation accuracy unless they are specifically allowed for in an analysis. Tests of valuations, as a proxy for prices, is therefore concerned with how groups of valuers, as well as buyers and sellers, interpret the same information under open market conditions. The results showed that in a simple model, which does not specifically allow for changing market environments, differences could be observed between valuations and prices on a year-by-year basis. If, however, the effect of changing market conditions are filtered out, so that open market valuations are compared with open market prices, then valuations appear to be a good proxy for prices.

Appendix 7A: Valuation as a proxy for prices allowing for changing market conditions

This appendix develops the analysis described in Chapter 7 to incorporate the effect of changing conditions that would cause the market to be in disequilibrium. We show that when this is accounted for, the intercept term and slope coefficients have a much stronger interpretation.

Appendix 7B: Valuations versus valuations

This appendix updates an earlier analysis that examines whether valuations prepared by one firm are a good proxy for valuations of the same properties prepared by another firm.

Appendix 7C: The distributional characteristics of valuations

We referred to this appendix in Chapter 7 and here undertake a simulation of the full range of valuations that are possible for a valuation. We show that the distribution of valuations is positively skewed.

Appendix 7D: Commercial property valuation and the margin of error

This appendix addresses an important issue relating to the margin of error that is likely to exist between two valuers who try to assess the value of the same property. There have been a number of cases of negligence that revolve around this issue. This appendix sheds light on the magnitude of the margin of error that should be expected.

Chapter 7: Summary table

1. The RICS definition of open market value implies an equilibrium market-pricing model.

2. Expected values can be expressed as a function of a number of different factors. $E(V) = f(a, b, c, d, e, f, \ldots)$

3. Valuation and prices do not have to be the same all the time. In an equilibrium market buyers and sellers should be using the same set of information.

4. On average you should expect valuations to be a reasonably good proxy for prices. If this did not occur the following would happen:
   ● property advice based on valuations would be invalid;
   ● performance measurement based on valuations would have no meaning.

5. The RICS definition of open market value is consistent with the economic concept of equilibrium asset pricing models.

6. Valuations are often influenced by behavioural issues that can distort their relationship with prices.

7. In the UK tests of valuations versus prices are usually based on regression models of the following form. $V_t = \alpha_1 + \beta_1 P_t + \eta_t$

8. The Investment Property Databank in the UK undertake an analysis of valuations versus prices on an annual basis using the following model. $P_t = \alpha_1 + \beta_1 V_t + \eta_t$

9. Research in the US has generally focused on an analysis of the percentage difference between valuations and prices.

10. Research in Australia has followed the UK precedent and has found similar results.

Problems

1. Why is it important to ensure that in the long term there is a one to one relationship between valuations and prices?

2. What factors are likely to cause this relationship to break down?

3. In a regression of valuations versus prices how would you interpret a slope coefficient of 0.98 that was significantly different from 1.0?

4. What credence can you place on the interpretation of the intercept term?

5. Critically discuss the RICS definition of open market value in relation to the concept of equilibrium market asset pricing models.

6. If valuations were never a good proxy for prices, what would this imply for the property profession?

7. If valuations are 'sticky', what effect would this have of the relationship between valuations and prices?

Selected references

Brown, G.R. (1985) Property investment and performance measurement: a reply. *Journal of Valuation* **4** (1), 33–44.

Brown, G.R. (1991) *Property Investment and the Capital Markets*, London: Chapman & Hall.

Brown, G.R. (1992) Valuation accuracy: developing the economic issues. *Journal of Property Research* **9**, 199–207.

Cullen, I. (1990) Property valuation: fact or fiction? Paper presented at IBC conference *Property in the Portfolio - A Strategic Asset?* London: IBC Ltd.

Drivers Jonas (1988) *Technical Appendix to the Variance in Valuations*. London: Investment Property Databank.

IPD/Drivers Jonas (1988) *The Variance in Valuations*. London: Investment Property Databank.

Lizieri, C. and Venmore-Rowland, P. (1991) Valuation accuracy: a contribution to the debate. *Journal of Property Research* **8** (2), 115–22.

Lizieri, C. and Venmore-Rowland, P. (1993) Valuations, prices and the market: a rejoinder. *Journal of Property Research* **10** (2), 77–84.

Miles, M., Guilkey, D., Webb, B. and Hunter, K. (1992) An empirical evaluation of the reliability of commercial appraisals 1978–1990. *Prudential Real Estate Investors*, Working paper.

Newell, G. and Kishore, R. (1998) Are valuations an effective proxy for property sales? *The Valuer and Land Economist* **35** (2), 150–4.

Appendix 7A
Valuation as a proxy for prices allowing for changing market environments

In Chapter 7 we argued that a one-to-one relationship between valuations and prices would exist only if the property market were in equilibrium. The logic for this follows from recognising that the RICS definition of open market value implies an equilibrium market. As a result, the one-to-one relationships will not hold if supply does not equal demand.

The simple models we described in Chapter 7 included properties that were collected over several years and made no allowance for changes in market environment. The only exception to this has been the ongoing IPD study which has examined the relationship on a year-by-year basis. The results showed that the market moved in and out of equilibrium, although there was a general trend towards a bull market. Measured over long periods we should not expect the slope coefficient to differ from 1.0 as this would imply consistent bias between valuations and prices. So far, however, the IPD analysis covers the period 1982–96 only and this may not be long enough to cover fully all market environments. We can, however, incorporate the effect of different market environments by using dummy variables. This is what we do in this appendix.

Defining the model

In Chapter 7 we suggested that observed values and prices could be expressed in terms of their equilibrium value plus a random error term. There may, however, be times when observed values and prices reflect some bias. The size of the bias will depend on market conditions and the amount of comparable sales information that is available. For example, in a bull market you would expect to see many transactions taking place so that comparable evidence is plentiful. When estimating current value, valuers will use their previous estimate together with as much comparable sales evidence as possible. They will, however, place greater weight on the sales information. This is, in effect, a simple updating rule, which expresses current values as a weighted average of current observed market prices and previous valuations. You can write this as follows:

$$V_t = k\bar{P}_t + (1 - k)V_{t-1} \tag{7A.1}$$

$$0 \le k \le 1$$

In this expression k represents the weight applied to the observed market prices, $\bar{P}_t$. You will see from this expression that as k approaches 1.0 more weight will be given to the observed market price. When k is exactly equal to 1.0 current values will equal current prices and the market is in equilibrium. As k approaches zero more weight will be given to the previous valuation. This is more likely to happen during bear markets when there is less comparable sales information available.

The process we have just described is known as *smoothing* and is something we will discuss in more detail in Chapter 12. For the purpose of relating this to valuations and prices all you need to know is that in different market environments current estimates of open market value can be greater or less than market prices. How they differ depends on the volume and quality of comparable sales evidence. You can incorporate this effect by revising the expressions for valuations and prices as follows:

$$\bar{V}_t = V_t + \hat{V}_t + e_t \tag{7A.2}$$

$$\bar{P}_t = P_t + \hat{P}_t + u_t \tag{7A.3}$$

where $\hat{V}_t$ and $\hat{P}_t$ represent abnormal errors caused by different market environments which are not captured in the error term.

If you assume as before that in equilibrium values and prices are equal you can rewrite these equations as follows:

$$\bar{P}_t = \bar{V}_t + (\hat{P}_t - \hat{V}_t) + \eta_t \tag{7A.4}$$

In regression form this can be written as:

$$\bar{P}_t = \beta_0 + \beta_1 \bar{V}_t + \varepsilon_t \tag{7A.5}$$

where $\beta_0 = (\hat{P}_t - \hat{V}_t)$ \tag{7A.6}

You will see from this expression that the intercept term captures structural differences inherent in the simple bivariate model. However, we also know that the property market moves through periods of bull and bear markets. Given our comment on smoothing, valuers may under- or over-react in different market environments so that the simple regression model may be misspecified.

One implication of excluding relevant variables is that estimates of included coefficients in the misspecified equation will be biased. This is known as the *omitted variables* problem. If changes in market environments are considered important in explaining values and prices, then it is important that they are allowed for in the regression equation.

This is the basis of the approach followed by Matysiak and Wang (1995). In examining the relationship between prices and valuations they used a sample of 317 properties with valuations and sales prices from 1973 to 1991 covering the following market environments:

Although this covers a longer period than the IPD analysis reported in Chapter 7 you will see that the simple annual regressions for 1987–91 match the market environments identified by the IPD results.

Table 7A.1 ● Changing market environments, 1973–91

Period	Market environment
1974–75	Bear
1977–79	Bull
1987–89	Bull
1990–91	Bear

Table 7A.2 ● Expected coefficients for different market environments

Market environments	Coefficients
Stable	$\beta_0 = 0$
Stable	$\beta_1 = 1$
Bear (1974 to 75)	$\beta_2 < 0$
Bull (1977 to 79)	$\beta_3 > 0$
Bull (1987 to 89)	$\beta_4 > 0$
Bear (1990 to 91)	$\beta_5 < 0$

The model Matysiak and Wang developed included dummy variables for each of the market environments as follows:

$$\ln P_t = \beta_0 + \beta_1 \ln V_t + \beta_2 \delta_1 + \beta_3 \delta_2 + \beta_4 \delta_3 + \beta_5 \delta_4 + \mu_t \tag{7A.7}$$

where $\ln P_t$ and $\ln V_t$ are the logs of prices and values and δ_t is a dummy variable representing the date of each paired valuation and price.

The dummy variables have the following values:

$\delta_1 = 1$ in 1974–75, 0 otherwise
$\delta_2 = 1$ in 1977–79, 0 otherwise
$\delta_3 = 1$ in 1987–89, 0 otherwise
$\delta_4 = 1$ in 1990–91, 0 otherwise

This is a much richer approach than the simple bivariate model and provides greater insights into the valuation process. By taking the market environments into account the coefficients in the regression model should take on the values in Table 7A.2.

The first stage of the analysis involved running a simple bivariate regression. The results are as follows:

Table 7A.3 ● Bivariate regression results, 1973–91

Regressor	Coefficient	Standard error	t-ratio
Intercept	–0.1298	0.08984	–1.44 (0.15)
lnV	1.0136	0.00703	144.15 (0.00)

$\bar{R}^2 = 0.985$, standard error of equation = 0.214, p-values for zero coefficients are reported in parentheses

The intercept term is statistically indistinguishable from zero. This differs from the analyses covered in Chapter 7 and is probably a result of the 18 years of data covering different market environments.

The t-statistic for the slope coefficient being equal to 1 is 1.93 (i.e. 0.0136/0.00703). As this is less than 1.96 the one-to-one relationship between values and prices cannot be rejected at the 5% level. At the 10% level, however, the t-statistic exceeds 1.645 so that the one-to-one relationship is firmly rejected. This result implies that, on average, valuers understated the eventual selling price.

Table 7A.4 ● Regression coefficients with all market environments included, 1973–91

Regressor	Coefficient	Standard error	t-ratio
Intercept	0.03428	0.10089	0.34
lnV	0.99926	0.00802	124.53
Bear 1974–75	– 0.01126	0.00381	– 2.96*
Bull 1977–79	0.00288	0.00297	0.97
Bull 1987–89	0.00908	0.00245	3.71*
Bear 1990–91	0.00029	0.00335	0.09

$\bar{R}^2$= 0.986, standard error of equation = 0.207. For market the environment variables, the absolute critical value for a one-tailed t-test = 1.65 at the 5% level and 2.33 at the 1% level; * indicates coefficient is significant at the 1% level.

Given our earlier observations it would appear, however, that this simple regression model is misspecified. Table 7A.4, therefore, summarises the analysis by including dummy variables for each of the market environments.

The intercept term remains indistinguishable from zero. What is more important, however, is that the *t*-test on the coefficient for valuations undertaken during stable market conditions shows that it is indistinguishable from 1 at the 1% level of significance. This is a much stronger statistical result than that obtained in the simple bivariate case.

The one tailed *t*-tests for the different market environments showed significant impacts during the bear market of 1974–75 and the bull market of 1987–89. The negative coefficient implies that values exceeded prices during a falling market, but were lower than prices in a rising market. The coefficients in both these markets were significant at the 1% level.

The coefficient for the bull market of 1977–79 was insignificant, although it had the correct sign. The coefficient for the bear market of 1990–91 is highly insignificant. This could be attributed to the low level of transactions in this period. The analysis

Table 7A.5 ● Regression coefficients for significant market environments, 1973–91

Regressor	Coefficient	Standard error	t-ratio
Intercept	0.02831	0.09514	0.30
lnV	0.99979	0.00750	133.25
Bear 1974–75	– 0.01126	0.00373	– 3.02*
Bull 1978	0.00780	0.00455	1.72**
Bull 1987–89	0.00898	0.00232	3.87*

$\bar{R}^2$= 0.986, standard error of equation = 0.206. For market the environment variables, the absolute critical value for a one-tailed t-test = 1.65 at the 5% level and 2.33 at the 1% level; * indicates coefficient is significant at the 5% level, and ** indicates significance at the 1% level.

was also extended to include specific year impacts within the non-significant bull and bear markets. Only 1978 proved to be statistically significant. This year was, therefore, included in the subsequent analysis. The re-estimated results are shown in Table 7A.5.

The broad conclusion is that valuations tend to exceed prices in falling markets and to be below prices in rising markets. These results are also consistent with those reported by Webb (1994), based on the analysis of properties that were sold from the Russell NCREIF Property Index in the US. Webb's figures show that appraisals lag market changes, being lower than prices in bull markets and higher than prices in bear markets.

The important finding from this analysis is that, taking the influence of different market environments into consideration, the one-to-one relationship between valuations and prices, in an equilibrium market, becomes much stronger. This adds weight to our belief that the RICS definition of open market value is consistent with the economic concept of equilibrium asset pricing models. It would, therefore, appear that in equilibrium markets valuers are doing a good job of impounding information into valuations.

Selected references

Matysiak, G.A. and Wang, P. (1995) Commercial property market prices and valuations: analysing the correspondence. *Journal of Property Research* 12 (3), 181–202.

Webb, R.B. (1994) On the reliability of commercial appraisals:an analysis of the properties sold from the Russell-NCREIF Index (1978–1992). *Real Estate Finance* 11 (1), 62–5.

Appendix 7B
Valuation versus valuations

If valuations are a good proxy for prices it is also reasonable to assume that valuations prepared by one firm should be a good proxy for valuations prepared by another firm. If both firms have access to the same set of information, then although they may interpret that information differently, at the portfolio level they should be statistically indistinguishable from each other.

You can test this hypothesis by taking a group of properties that have regular valuations prepared by two different firms. This can occur when one firm is employed to provide check valuations in order to reveal any bias that may be present. In both cases the firms involved are formally appointed to undertake the valuations.

Regressing the valuations onto each other would produce a model of the following form, where X and Y represent the firms involved:

$$X = \beta_0 + \beta_1 Y + e \qquad (7B.1)$$

If inter-firm valuations are a good proxy for each other then β_0 should be statistically indistinguishable from zero, and β_1 should be indistinguishable from 1.0.

This proposition represents a more stringent test than valuations versus prices. Our discussion in Chapter 7 and Appendix 7A concerning the regression of valuations on prices allowed the intercept term to differ from zero and the slope coefficient to differ from 1.0 in response to different market environments. The coefficients only equalled zero and 1.0 under conditions of market equilibrium. However, in a test of valuations versus valuations different market environments should not have any effect on the intercept and slope coefficients. Irrespective of market conditions the intercept term should always be indistinguishable from zero and the slope coefficient should always be indistinguishable from 1.0. If this were not the case then it would indicate that different firms were processing the same information in completely different ways in response to changing conditions in the market. If this practice were widespread, then it would throw the valuation profession into disarray. We will now look at the results of a study covering the period 1981–84 and a more recent analysis that extends this initial work over the period from 1983 to 1985.

Valuations versus valuations, 1981–84

To date there has only been one published study to test the proposition that valuations prepared by one firm are a good proxy for valuations prepared by another firm (Brown 1985, 1991). The relationship between the valuations prepared by different firms was analysed using a group of 26 properties, all from the same fund, with valuations over the four-year period 1981–84. One firm was employed to undertake the valuations and another firm was appointed to prepare independent check valuations. Neither was aware of the valuations prepared by the other firm. However, both firms did have access to the same set of information.

The data were converted to values per square foot and normalised by taking logs. The results are summarised in Table 7B.1.

In all cases the β_0 coefficients are close to zero and statistically insignificant. The β_1 coefficients are also statistically indistinguishable from 1.0 implying that, throughout the valuation range, both firms are valuing in the same way. The one-to-one relationship between valuations should not be misconstrued as implying that the valuations for individual properties are identical. It is still possible to see reasonable differences. At the portfolio level the differences should be diversified away. The amount of scatter shown in Figure 7B.1 illustrates the differences that can occur when valuations are prepared by different firms. The R^2 values are all high, indicating that the valuations prepared by firm X explain about 98% of the variation in the valuations prepared by firm Y.

Table 7B.1 ● Regression results of inter-firm valuations

	β_0	Standard error	β_1	Standard error	$\bar{R}^2$
1981	0.108	0.138	0.985	0.035	0.98
1982	0.071	0.122	0.993	0.030	0.98
1983	−0.002	0.100	1.003	0.029	0.98
1984	0.000	0.123	1.006	0.025	0.99

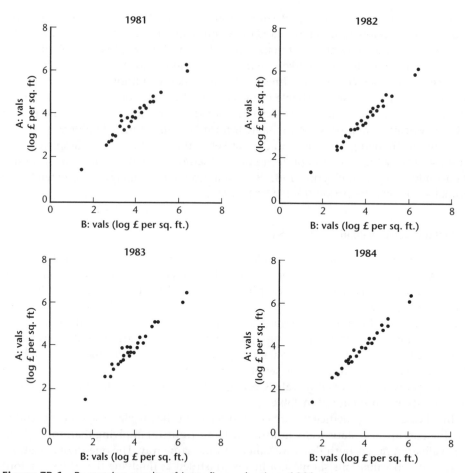

Figure 7B.1 Regression results of inter-firm valuations 1981–4

Valuations versus valuations, 1983–85

Table 7B.2 reports the results of a more recent analysis in which firm A prepared check valuations for firms B, C, D and E. In this case the data were transformed by taking logs. In the following regressions the valuations prepared by firm A were the dependent variable.

Although the sample sizes varied, only two of the portfolios analysed showed coefficients that differed from their test values. Aggregating the whole sample the intercept term is statistically indistinguishable from zero and the slope coefficient is indistinguishable from 1. The results for the full sample are also shown in Figure 7B.2.

Given that these analyses have been based on a sample of average properties and assuming that the results are representative of the whole market, then valuations prepared by different firms appear to be good substitutes for each other. Underlying this is the principle that both firms have access to the same or similar databases of comparable information. Bias would occur if the information subset being used by each firm differed.

Table 7B.2 ● Regression results of inter-firm valuations

	Firms	β_0	Standard error	β_1	Standard error	$\bar{R}^2$	n
1983	D	−0.506	0.761	1.042	0.058	0.979	9
1984	E	0.506	2.194	0.963	0.156	0.927	5
1985	B	−0.221	0.167	1.017	0.012	0.996	29
1985	B	−0.095	0.444	1.007	0.032	0.986	16
1985	C	−0.154	1.091	1.012	0.082	0.933	12
1985	B	0.884**	0.469	0.938**	0.033	0.991	9
1985	B	1.055*	0.445	0.931*	0.031	0.972	28
1985	B	−0.003	0.909	1.003	0.065	0.960	12
83–85	ALL	0.118	0.171	0.994	0.012	0.982	120

* indicates significant at the 5% level; ** indicates significance at the 10% level.

The above results suggest, however, that on average there is no evidence of bias between valuations prepared by different firms. They also show that if valuers make use of the same information, it should not be possible for professional firms to compete with each other purely on the quality of their valuations. Competitive advantage can only be achieved by offering a range of additional services.

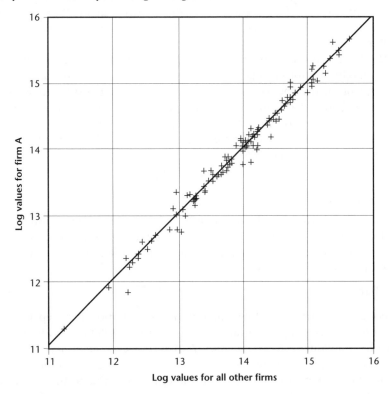

Figure 7B.2 Values versus values, 1983–5

Selected references

Brown, G.R. (1985) Property investment and performance measurement: a reply. *Journal of Valuation* **4** (1), 33–44.

Brown, G.R. (1991) *Property Investment and the Capital Markets*, London: Chapman & Hall.

Appendix 7C
The distributional characteristics of valuations

In Chapter 3 we introduced a number of models which are frequently used to value or analyse property. We also pointed out that valuations are drafted in terms of expectations, but didn't say much about the shape of the distribution from which those valuations are derived. This is, nevertheless, an important issue as it has a direct bearing on the distribution of returns.

The value of a property is a professional estimate of what it is expected to sell for at the date of the valuation. This principle is embodied into the RICS definition of open market value. Expected values will, however, be subject to variation depending on how valuers interpret those factors that contribute to value. The RICS Mallinson Report (1994) recognised this fact, but also suggested that the uncertainty may vary in different market conditions and that valuers need to quantify this in some way.

One of the important issues that arise from understanding the uncertainty in valuations is the ability of different valuers to produce valuations within a given percentage of the mean value. It has been argued that if a valuation lies outside a given margin of error, then the valuer has been negligent in some way. The key to understanding this issue is knowing something about the distribution of valuations. We will discuss the margin of error in Appendix 7D. In this appendix we are concerned only with the shape of the distribution of capital values. As it is not possible to obtain large samples of independent valuations for a single property we will simulate the distribution based on the valuation model we developed in Chapter 3. By using historic information over different periods we can also examine how the distribution changes in different market environments.

Methodology

In algebraic terms we can describe our approach as follows. Given an initial income the expected value $E(V_t)$ of a property can be expressed as a function of its expected return $E(r_t)$ and expected growth rate $E(g_t)$, both of which are conditional on the set of information (ϕ_t), available at time t.

$$E(V_t) = f[E(r_t), E(g_t)] | \phi_t \tag{7C.1}$$

The expected value will, therefore, come from a distribution that depends on the distribution of returns and growth rates. These in turn will depend on how they are interpreted by individual valuers. Equation 7C.1 is, however, an *ex-ante* model based on what valuers expect is going to happen. As expectations cannot be directly observed in the marketplace we can, as an alternative, estimate the shape of the distribution by using historic information.

Given a time-series of historic returns and growth rates, over a given period, and assuming they are drafted in nominal terms, it is possible to express the average value over that period as follows:

$$\bar{V}_t = f[\bar{r}_t, \bar{g}_t]$$

(7C.2)

where

$\bar{V}_t$ = average capital value

$\bar{r}_t$ = average total return

$\bar{g}_t$ = average rental value growth rate

Assume, for example, that you collected annual returns and rental value growth rates on a yearly basis for ten years. The average of each set of figures would give you an indication of what investors expected the returns and growth rates over that ten-year period to be. If you substituted the average values into a valuation model based on equation 7C.2 you would get one estimate of the capital value based on the conditions that applied over that ten-year period.

As each annual return and growth rate is equally likely to happen, a distribution of average capital values can be obtained for the sub-period by continually resampling random paired data values. Each resampling of the data produces a new mean return and growth rate, which can be substituted into a valuation model to produce one realisation of a possible market value. Continually repeating this process produces a distribution of the population of the capital values for the market conditions that prevailed over the period. This process is known as bootstrapping.

The principle behind bootstrapping is explained in detail in Efron and Tibshirani (1993). The technique is valuable for estimating the distributional characteristics of a population derived from small sample sizes. It is based on the assumption that the samples used are unbiased and representative of the population. In this case by continually replicating the sample with replacement it is possible to simulate the complete distribution of mean valuations. Although it is assumed that the returns and growth rates in each sub-period are independent, it is important to ensure that each return is paired with its contemporaneous growth rate. Changes in market conditions affecting the covariance between returns and growth rates are, therefore, preserved in the simulation.

We used the IPD annual index to estimate the mean total return and growth rate over a series of overlapping ten-year periods. A ten-year period was chosen so that the data covered two rent review periods. This provides sufficient information for the bootstrapping and also enables the effect of changes in market conditions on valuation uncertainty to be monitored over a reasonably long period. It would, of course, be possible to use other periods. Given the length of the data sample the use of ten-year periods provides a reasonable compromise. Because we are isolating ten-year periods the bootstrapping process we have adopted assumes that the market conditions will prevail in perpetuity. This enables the impact of a specific set of market conditions on the uncertainty in valuations to be examined. By advancing the sample period on a year-by-year basis the effect of different market conditions can be examined over time.

We simulated the distribution of capital values by using the constant growth model derived in Chapter 3. Assuming an initial income of £1 p.a. and a rent review period of five years the expected value can be estimated using the following expression:

$$\bar{V} = \frac{1}{\bar{r}} \left[\frac{(1 + \bar{r})^5 - 1}{(1 + \bar{r})^5 - (1 + \bar{g})^5} \right] \quad \text{Subject to } \bar{r} > \bar{g} \tag{7C.3}$$

The constraint that $\bar{r} > \bar{g}$ is important. If the total return were less than the growth rate, then equation 7C.3 would give negative capital values. Remember, however, that valuations are drafted in terms of expectations. In expectations format this condition should always apply. However, this may not always be the case in an *ex-post* framework. There may, for example, be situations when the sampling process gives mean growth rates that exceed mean returns, resulting in negative values. Similarly, it may be possible for the mean return and mean growth rates to be equal. This would result in an infinitely large capital value. For the resampling process to be consistent with the constraint imposed by equation 7C.3 only values of $\bar{r}$ that are greater than $\bar{g}$ are included in the simulation. Casual inspection of equation 7C.3 suggests, however, that the distribution of capital values should be positively skewed. We would expect to see some very high values but there will be a lower limit of zero.

The period for our analysis was 1980–95. The bootstrapping procedure starts by taking the first ten-year period and randomly sampling ten paired returns and rental value growth rates. The average value for the sampled total returns and growth rates were calculated and substituted into equation 7C.3 to give the first estimate of the expected capital value. We repeated this procedure 2,000 times, screening out those cases where the average return was less than the average growth rate, and obtained a distribution of capital values for the first ten-year period. After 2,000 replications we advanced the sample period by one year and repeated the whole process. We analysed a moving window of ten-year periods until we reached 1995.

The data used in this study were taken from the Investment Property Databank (IPD) Annual Index covering the period 1980–95. The property included in the index represents the performance of typical commercial property held by UK institutional funds. Table 7C.1 summarises the composition of the index as at December 1995.

Annual total returns and rental value growth rates are estimated from these data as inputs into a mean capital value model. Although the sample size has increased over time it is assumed that the statistics used in each period are representative of general market conditions.

Table 7C.1 ● IPD Annual Index composition as at December 1995

	All property*	Retail	Office	Industrial
Total capital value £m	47,867	21,158	18,819	6,767
ERV £m	3,822	1,768	1,402	604
Number of properties	12,302	5,918	3,849	1,949
Number of funds	207			

Source: Investment Property Databank (IPD). * Figures include 'other' property types.

Table 7C.2 • Retail sector: Distributional characteristics of sample statistics and bootstrapped capital values

Retail	Sample statistics				Bootstrapped results			
	Mean total return	Std error	Mean RV growth	Std error	Mean capital value	Std error	Skew	Coeff of var
1981–90	0.12	0.03	0.10	0.01	39.16	27.09	1.90	0.69
1982–91	0.11	0.03	0.09	0.02	41.31	27.03	1.82	0.65
1983–92	0.10	0.03	0.08	0.02	40.30	27.02	1.90	0.67
1984–93	0.11	0.03	0.07	0.02	28.83	22.12	2.58	0.77
1985–94	0.11	0.03	0.06	0.02	25.64	20.26	2.85	0.79
1986–95	0.10	0.03	0.06	0.02	26.07	20.50	2.77	0.79
1981–95	0.11	0.02	0.06	0.02	21.97	11.60	2.40	0.53

Results

Tables 7C.2–7C.5 show, for each sector, the distributional characteristics of rental value growth and total returns for ten-year sub-periods taken from the annual data. The distributional characteristics of the derived capital values are also shown after bootstrapping the data 2,000 times.

The strong positive skewness of capital values is confirmed by these results. Property, therefore, has the potential for high capital values. Table 7C.2 also shows that the skewness progressively increased during the boom period during the 1980s, peaking in the 1985–94 period, but has since declined. Thus market conditions can influence the shape of the distribution of capital values. Figure 7C.1 shows the bootstrapped simulation for the retail sector over the whole sample period 1981–95.

The general shape of the distribution is common to all sectors. Because it is positively skewed the mean value will be greater than both the mode, i.e. the *most frequently occurring value*, and the median, i.e. *the mid-point* of the distribution.

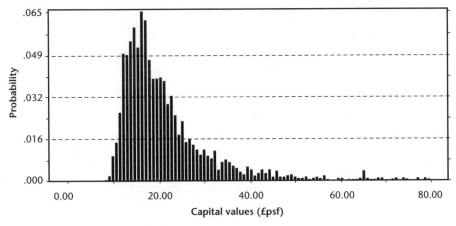

Figure 7C.1 Distribution of retail valuations 1981–95

Table 7C.3 ● Office sector: Distributional characteristics of sample statistics and bootstrapped capital values

Office	Sample statistics				Bootstrapped results			
Bootstrapped Period	Mean total return	Std error	Mean RV growth	Std error	Mean capital value	Std error	Skew	Coeff of var
1981–90	0.12	0.04	0.10	0.03	44.83	26.13	1.69	0.58
1982–91	0.09	0.04	0.08	0.04	47.99	25.60	1.56	0.53
1983–92	0.08	0.04	0.05	0.05	38.12	24.20	2.05	0.64
1984–93	0.09	0.04	0.04	0.05	23.13	19.08	2.91	0.83
1985–94	0.10	0.04	0.03	0.05	18.74	14.66	3.67	0.78
1986–95	0.09	0.05	0.02	0.05	18.61	14.68	3.91	0.79
1981–95	0.09	0.03	0.03	0.03	18.49	9.43	2.48	0.51

Assuming that the distribution of capital values always remains positively skewed in an *ex-ante* framework, the use of the *mean* will be consistent with the notion of *best price* within the definition of open market value adopted by the RICS.

Similar results were obtained for the other sectors and are summarised in Tables 7C.3–7C.5.

The general decline in property values is clear from these tables and reflects the changing market conditions over the 15-year period. As the mean values declined it will also be seen that their standard errors also declined. Although this would seem to indicate that valuations have become less variable, the coefficient of variation shows that the volatility of the office and retail sectors has in fact increased. The coefficient of variation adjusts for the differences in the size of the capital value and provides a relative measure of volatility.[1] The industrial sector shows only a slight decline in volatility with less variation over each of the sub periods.

Table 7C.4 ● Industrial sector: Distributional characteristics of sample statistics and bootstrapped capital values

Industrial	Sample statistics				Bootstrapped results			
Bootstrapped Period	Mean total return	Std error	Mean RV growth	Std error	Mean capital value	Std error	Skew	Coeff of var
1981–90	0.12	0.03	0.10	0.01	39.16	27.09	1.90	0.51
1982–91	0.11	0.03	0.09	0.02	41.31	27.03	1.82	0.51
1983–92	0.10	0.03	0.08	0.02	40.30	27.02	1.90	0.50
1984–93	0.11	0.03	0.07	0.02	28.83	22.12	2.58	0.55
1985–94	0.11	0.03	0.06	0.02	25.64	20.26	2.85	0.50
1986–95	0.10	0.03	0.06	0.02	26.07	20.50	2.77	0.46
1981–95	0.11	0.03	0.04	0.02	13.38	4.55	2.27	0.34

[1] You might want to review some of these concepts in Chapter 17.

Table 7C.5 ● All property: Distributional characteristics of sample statistics and bootstrapped capital values

Industrial	Sample statistics					Bootstrapped results			
Bootstrapped Period	Mean total return	Std error	Mean RV growth	Std error		Mean capital value	Std error	Skew	Coeff of var
1981–90	0.12	0.03	0.10	0.02		41.20	24.81	1.77	0.60
1982–91	0.10	0.03	0.08	0.03		43.67	25.91	1.85	0.59
1983–92	0.09	0.04	0.06	0.03		37.20	23.47	2.12	0.63
1984–93	0.10	0.04	0.05	0.04		24.41	19.88	2.95	0.81
1985–94	0.10	0.04	0.05	0.04		20.86	17.54	3.65	0.84
1986–95	0.10	0.04	0.04	0.04		19.94	15.74	3.57	0.79
1981–95	0.10	0.03	0.04	0.02		20.59	12.33	4.05	0.60

The simulated distributions indicate that property values are likely to be positively skewed. A large portfolio of randomly selected property values is also likely to exhibit positive skewness. We can illustrate this by plotting a distribution of the 120 property valuations we analysed in Appendix 7B. This is shown in Figure 7C.2. Skewness in property weights can have important implications in terms of performance measurement. We shall return to this issue in Part 3.

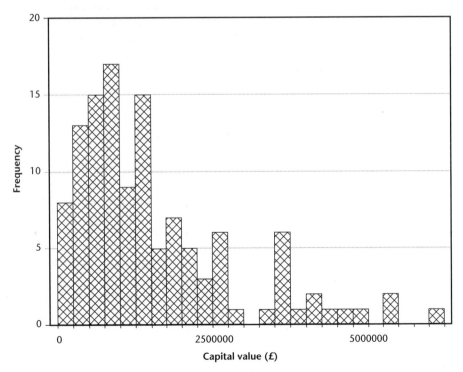

Figure 7C.2 Distribution of property values

Ranking the sector valuations over the 15-year period, in terms of the coefficient of variation, shows that the retail sector was the most volatile, followed by the office and industrial sectors.

The definition of open market value

The starting point for our discussion of the distribution of values was the RICS definition of open market value, which relies heavily on the concept of *best price*.

Unfortunately, the RICS do not provide a statistical definition of best price although it is widely assumed that it relates to some measure of central tendency.[2] The question that arises is, should best price relate to the mean, median or mode of a distribution? The choice only becomes important if the distribution of values is not symmetrical. The analysis we have undertaken shows that valuations are positively skewed so that the choice of which measure to use does become important.

For a distribution of values that is positively skewed the value of the mean will exceed both the median and the mode. This implies that the mean is also consistent with the concept of best price that could be achieved, even though the mode represents the most likely valuation. Thus in terms of the RICS definition of open market value the mean would appear to be the correct measure to use.

An alternative way of looking at this is to recognise that the economic value of a property should be determined within a capital market framework. This implies that valuations should be present values. The expected value of a property is, therefore, the present value of its expected future cashflows discounted at the expected rate of return. If the present value rule is to be applied consistently across all asset classes, it follows that valuers should estimate the mean of the distribution of capital values. Rates of return estimated from changes in the median or mode of a distribution will not be consistent with calculation of the expected rate of return.

Selected references

Brown, G.R. (1985) Property investment and performance measurement: a reply. *Journal of Valuation* **4** (1), 33–44.

Brown, G.R. (1992) Valuation accuracy: developing the economic issues. *Journal of Property Research* **9** 199–207.

Brown, G.R. (1996) Analysing ground rents. *The New Zealand Property Journal* **67** 19–24.

Efron, B. and Tibshirani, R. (1993) *An Introduction to the Bootstrap*, London: Chapman and Hall.

Hager, D. and Lord, D. (1985) *The Property Market, Property Valuations and Property Performance Measurement*. London: Institute of Actuaries.

Hutchison, N., MacGregor, B.D., Nanthakumaran, N., Adair, A. and McGreal, S. (1996) *Variations in the Capital Valuations of UK Commercial Property*, London: RICS.

Mallinson, M. (1994) *Report of the President's Working Party on Commercial Property Valuations*, The Mallinson Report, London: RICS.

Whipple, R.T.M. (1995) *Property Valuation and Analysis*, Sydney: Law Book Co.

---

[2] See Whipple (1995) for a discussion of the issues concerning the definitions of value and how these relate to alternative statistical measures of central tendency.

Appendix 7D
Commercial property valuation and the margin of error

How accurate is a commercial property valuation?

It seems reasonable to assume that two equally informed valuers should be able to arrive at estimates of value for the same property that are close to each other. But are we expecting too much of our valuers? After all, a valuation is just a professional *estimate* of what a commercial property is expected to sell for. If the difference between two values is large, does this mean that one of the valuers runs the risk of facing a case of negligence?

The main issue in negligence cases is whether a group of independent valuers can arrive at valuations for a property that are either the same or likely to lie within a 'small' margin of error of each other. Why this has become an issue is that since the Singer and Friedlander court case in 1977, the valuation profession has become saddled with an arbitrary estimate of the margin of error. A figure of 5–10 per cent between independent valuations is widely believed to be applicable under all conditions.

This may, however, be stretching credibility a little too far. In this appendix we will argue that the degree of confidence that can be attached to *any* margin of error is likely to vary under different circumstances. We will show that the probability of two valuations falling within a specified range of each other can vary considerably. The margin of error will depend on both the uncertainties in each valuation and the level of 'implied' agreement between valuers on expected outcomes. By using some basic statistics we will show you how to quantify the odds of a valuation lying within a given margin of error.

Valuations, information and uncertainty

The starting point is to recognise that all valuations are a reflection of the quality of available information. This is a point we have stressed on a number of occasions. A simple freehold property let on five-year rent reviews with an initial income of £1 can, for example, take on a wide range of values depending on the assumptions used to estimate the *expected* return and rental value growth. Table 7D.1 summarises the value of a hypothetical property based on the views of four different valuers.

The first point to note is that the expected rental value growth rates and returns in each case are uncertain and therefore imply that they come from a probability distribution. Consequently, the expected capital value will also have a probability

Table 7D.1 ● Possible range of valuations for a single property

	Valuer A	Valuer B	Valuer C	Valuer D
Expected growth p.a.	4.00%	4.00%	8.00%	8.00%
Expected return p.a.	12.00%	10.00%	12.00%	10.00%
Expected value	£11.64m	£15.50m	£21.68m	£43.24m

distribution, indicating that there will be a range of possible outcomes. The figures in Table 7D.1 show that the range can be quite large; but which is wrong or negligent?

It is not possible to answer this question without knowing how each valuer has estimated the inputs to the valuation. At one end valuer A believes that the property is fairly risky and considers that the growth prospects are poor. At the other end valuer D takes a more optimistic view and believes that growth prospects are much better. In both cases the valuers involved are able to justify the inputs and do not appear to have produced negligent figures, even though they all lie way outside a range of ±10% of each other and the two other valuations.

In this simple case the highest valuation is almost four times greater than the lowest valuation. All this shows, however, is that well informed valuers can have different views concerning the prospects for a property that give rise to differences of opinion as to the true value. You should also bear in mind that this is also the way competitive markets operate. It is the difference in opinion concerning values that causes assets to be actively traded. This is important in understanding the margin of error. The legal implication is that two valuers who independently examine the available information concerning a property should come to exactly the same view. If there is a difference it should be very small. The real question is, how similar do the opinions of the two valuers have to be to ensure that the difference in values is very small? This is what we shall try to answer in this appendix.

Margin of error

This brief discussion suggests that the margin of error is made up of the following components:

● the uncertainty in individual valuations
● the correlation between different valuers' assumptions used in their calculations

By making use of this information it is possible to arrive at a simple expression that you can use to quantify the uncertainty surrounding the margin of error. To develop this further, it is necessary to estimate the probability of the difference between two valuations, for the same property, lying within a given margin of error.

Suppose valuers A and B have been fully briefed and are assumed to share the same set of information concerning a property. Depending on market conditions, the valuations they each arrive at can take on a range of figures that can be described in terms of an expected value and a measure of dispersion round that value. In statistical terms the dispersion is referred to as the standard deviation. Because both valuers share the same information it is assumed that the uncertainty surrounding their best estimates is the same, implying they have identical distributions.

Our real interest, however, is in the *difference* between the valuations prepared by A and B which, ideally, should have an expected value of zero. However, because there is uncertainty in the valuations prepared by each valuer the difference will also be uncertain. It is this uncertainty that defines the margin of error. What we want to do is quantify the probability of two valuations falling within a specified given range. Working this out requires a little statistics, but the calculation is straightforward.

The valuations prepared by A and B, which we refer to as V_A and V_B, come from identical distributions. The measure of uncertainty surrounding each valuation is represented by the standard deviation. The only other piece of information that is needed is the correlation between all the possible valuations that can be prepared by valuers A and B. The correlation can be interpreted as the extent to which the two valuers process information in the same way. If the correlation is high, then both valuers have similar views concerning their estimates of expected return and expected rental value growth. Using these definitions you can write some simple expressions for the difference between the expected values prepared by A and B together with the dispersion of this difference.

Given the assumption that each valuer possesses the same information, the expected value of the difference between the valuations will be zero:

$$E(V_A - V_B) = 0 \qquad (7D.1)$$

This, of course, is what you are hoping for, as both valuers should arrive at the same figure. Unfortunately, this rarely happens. There will be some uncertainty surrounding this difference that you can quantify by writing an expression for the variance of the difference between the values:

$$Var(V_A - V_B) = VarV_A + VarV_B - 2\rho_{V_A V_B}\sigma_{V_A}\sigma_{V_B} \qquad (7D.2)$$

If both valuers share the same information you can assume that the variance of their valuations will be the same. Making this simplification and taking the square root to express equation 7D.2 in standard deviation terms gives:

$$\sigma_{(V_A-V_B)} = \sigma_V \sqrt{(1 - \rho_{V_A V_B})} \qquad (7D.3)$$

This equation offers some insights into the distribution of the difference between valuations. For example, if the variability in the valuations, $\sigma_{V_A} = \sigma_{V_B} = 0$, is equal to zero, there would be no uncertainty in the valuations and, clearly, no uncertainty in the difference between valuations. You could, however, have a different situation in which there is a lot of uncertainty surrounding each valuation. Furthermore, the uncertainty in the *difference* between valuations also depends on the level of agreement between the valuers concerning their valuation calculations. As noted above, this is measured by the correlation between the estimates prepared by each valuer, $\rho_{V_A V_B}$.

If there were perfect agreement, high- or low-value estimates of expected return and rental value growth would be *exactly* mirrored by each valuer. In this case $\rho_{V_A V_B} = +1$ and the dispersion of the difference between the valuations would once again be equal to zero. As the correlation declines the uncertainty in the difference between valuations begins to increase.

With this background let's look at a simple example. Two valuers are asked to value a property which they estimate as having an expected capital value of £40 million and an associated dispersion of £60 million around this figure. Let us also assume that the degree of agreement between the valuers is given as 0.98. We can use this information to work out the dispersion of the difference between the two estimates. Substituting these figures into equation 7D.3 gives:

$$\sigma_{(V_A-V_B)} = £60\text{m} \sqrt{(1-0.98)} = £12\text{m}$$

Even though there is a high degree of agreement between the valuers there is, nevertheless, a lot of uncertainty surrounding the difference between their valuations.

The importance of the figure just calculated is that it can be used to estimate the probability that the difference in valuations will lie within some margin of error. Although this requires some additional calculation, for the most part this only involves looking up a figure in a statistical table. By assuming that the uncertainty surrounding a valuation follows a *normal distribution*, you can calculate what is known as the z statistic. This is just the distance that the target difference in values lies from the expected difference of zero:

$$z = \frac{Target(diff) - E(diff)}{\sigma_{(V_A-V_B)}} \qquad (7D.4)$$

In this calculation the target difference is the margin of error and can be expressed as a percentage of the average value. For example, assume that our interest is in a margin of error of ±10%. In our example this is 10% of £40 million, or £4 million. In other words, you would expect the two valuations to be within £4 million of each other if they are to lie within a margin of error of 10%.

The expected difference in valuations should of course be zero. Knowing that the dispersion of the difference is £12 million as calculated above, you can substitute these figures into equation 7D.4 to give the following z value:

$$z = \frac{£4-£0}{£12} = 0.33$$

You can interpret this by saying that the target difference of £4 million is 0.33 standard deviations away from zero. By referring to a statistical table of areas under a normal curve, you can translate this into the proportion of a normal distribution that this figure represents. In our example the area is 0.1293, or 12.93%. As the 10% error may be either positive or negative you need to double this to 25.86%.

This is the figure that you are interested in as it quantifies the margin of error. Given our assumptions you can say that there is a 25.86% probability, or the odds are roughly 1 in 4, that the two valuations will lie within ±10% of each other.

Estimating the inputs

You can see that as the probability of lying within the margin of error depends on both the uncertainty in valuations and the correlation between the opinion of valuers, it is unlikely to remain constant. Both components need to be estimated separately which, in practice, may be difficult.

Uncertainty in valuations

In our example we measured the uncertainty using the standard deviation of the valuations. This is not an easy figure to estimate but it is important to realise that it is supposed to capture the complete distribution of valuations that embraces all possible outcomes. It is difficult to offer guidance on a typical figure as it depends on many factors influencing expectations. In Appendix 7C we simulated the distribution of values and also estimated the coefficient of variation *(COV)*. This is a way of standardising the uncertainty in the valuations and is just the ratio of standard deviation to expected value. We showed that the *COV* generally lay within the range 0.50–0.85. By contrast IPD, as part of their regular study on valuations versus prices, have also reported the average value and standard deviation per sq. ft of the valuations of properties that were sold from their database. On the basis of this evidence the average coefficient of variation is in the order of 1.20. This may represent an upper limit as it is based on a large sample of different properties whereas our concern is with the coefficient of variation for an individual property. A simulation exercise may, however, offer one way of estimating this figure.

The value of using the coefficient of variation is that it can be directly interpreted as the uncertainty in the valuation and is independent of the capital value of the property.

Correlation of opinion between valuers

If information is poor or incomplete this will have an effect on the implied agreement between valuers on how certain factors influence value. You can relate this to the availability of comparable information and the current state of the market. If there is a lot of uncertainty in the market and comparable evidence is poor or non-existent, then you would expect to see a lower correlation between valuers' estimates. Our research suggests, however, that the correlation figure would probably be in excess of 0.9. Although this appears high, small movements away from this figure can make a large difference in the probabilities regarding the margin of error.

Uncertainty and the margin of error

To give an idea of the range of figures involved in estimating the margin of error, Table 7D.2 provides estimates of the odds of any valuation lying within a specified margin of error. The calculations assume that the percentage difference between valuations follows a normal distribution although in practice a skewed distribution may be more appropriate.

For each margin of error, four levels of uncertainty regarding the valuation are provided. These are expressed as the coefficient of variation so that the higher the figure the greater the uncertainty. We have also expressed each probability figure in terms of the odds that any two valuations will lie within the specified margin of error.

You will see that, for each level of correlation, as the coefficient of variation in the valuations increases the odds that two valuations will lie within the margin of error begins to lengthen. For example, there is 1 chance in 3 that two valuations will lie within 5% of each other when the coefficient of variation is 0.6 and the correlation between the opinions of two valuers is 0.98. Under different market conditions the coefficient of variation could increase to 1.00 and the odds of lying within the 5% margin of error increases to 1 chance in 5. Other positions within the table can be interpreted in a similar way. As you increase the margin of error the odds will of course shorten, and this is what Table 7D.2 shows.

Table 7D.2: Valuation odds and the margin of error

Margin of error	Coefficient of variation of valuations	Correlation between valuers' estimates of valuation inputs					
		1.00	0.98	0.96	0.94	0.92	0.90
		Odds that valuation will lie within the specified margin of error					
5%	0.60	1	3	4	5	6	7
	0.80	1	4	6	7	8	9
	1.00	1	5	7	9	10	11
	1.20	1	6	9	10	12	13
10%	0.60	1	2	2	3	3	3
	0.80	1	2	3	4	4	5
	1.00	1	3	4	4	5	6
	1.20	1	3	4	5	6	7
15%	0.60	1	1	2	2	2	2
	0.80	1	2	2	2	3	3
	1.00	1	2	2	3	3	4
	1.20	1	2	3	4	4	5

The correlation between valuers' estimates is restricted to a 'likely' range.

There are three important points that come out of this analysis of margin of error:

1. None of the figures gives any indication of negligence. The fact that the odds are 1 in 10 that two valuations may lie within 5% of each other does not imply negligence. To make this judgement would require an investigation as to how the components used in the valuation have been arrived at. Only by careful examination of the assumptions used to estimate the value is it possible to make a statement about negligence. What is more likely to be a problem is bias, where one valuer clearly misinterprets or omits valuable information when forming a valuation.
2. The odds that two valuations will lie within a given margin of error will vary in relation to changes in market conditions.
3. Small changes in the agreement between valuers, or in the uncertainty surrounding valuations, can have a substantial impact on how the margin of error is interpreted.

Unless the uncertainty in valuations and the agreement between valuers can be quantified, it is not possible to make strong statements about the probability of any two valuations lying within a given margin of error. Legal cases of negligence that focus solely on the margin of error, without reference to the way market conditions affect the difference between valuations, are failing to address some important issues in valuation.

CHAPTER *8*

Investment decision techniques

Learning objectives

After reading this chapter you will understand the following:

- How financial theory relates to project appraisal

- How to analyse development projects

- How to use a residual analysis

- Common methods of investment appraisal using cash flow analysis

- Which methods of analysis maximise shareholder wealth

This chapter includes a number of appendices that deal with specific topics relating to project appraisal.

Introduction

A development company is about to embark on a new project and is anxious to know whether it will be profitable. The intention is to sell the completed project to a financial institution so that it can be included in its investment portfolio. Both the developer and the financial institution need to know what methods of analysis are most appropriate for evaluating project viability.

Although this raises a number of important questions it is not unusual for major financial decisions to be made using *ad hoc* methods of analysis that rely more on rules-of-thumb than financial theory. Although we can't be sure about the quality of decisions made using *ad hoc* methods of analysis, we feel that it is important to consider how to appraise projects using the ideas that we have discussed in the previous chapters. There should, therefore, be a link between project appraisal and financial theory.

The rationale for investment

In this chapter we will concentrate on the techniques needed to analyse the viability of projects. Our intention is to identify methods of analysis that can be regarded as being economically defensible. Although we will illustrate the points by using simple examples the principles involved can easily be applied to more complicated projects.

Companies involved in the commitment of scarce resources try to allocate them in a way that offers benefits to shareholders. Plans for capital expenditure are, therefore, usually summarised in a capital budget, which identifies suitable projects and their estimated cost. The whole process is referred to as *capital budgeting*. There are two important strands to this process: one is *strategic* and the other *economic*. The strategic aspect is concerned with the overall philosophy of the company and whether the commitment of resources is in line with the aims and objectives of the firm. The economic aspect is just as important and is concerned with the financial viability of the proposed projects. Clearly, the two are interlinked, as there is little point in proposing a profitable project that does not fit in with the overall vision of the company.

A number of activities contribute to a capital budgeting analysis. In all cases, however, it is essential to separate the investment decision from the funding decision. In other words, projects should be evaluated without reference to the way in which they are financed. This is an important point as the effects of financing are only important if the company pays taxes. We discuss this issue in more detail in Appendix 8A. Many property textbooks that cover development appraisal fail to make a distinction between the investment and financing decisions and are unwittingly perpetuating bad practice. In this case it is not enough to say that the methods of analysis are widely used in practice. Bad practice can result in poor decisions, which is not in the best interests of the investors.

> The decision to invest in a project is separate from the decision to finance the project. Projects should be evaluated without reference to the way they are financed.

This raises two important points that need to be emphasised at this stage:

- interest payments incurred on debt should not be included in the project cash flows;
- the cost of debt will enter the analysis indirectly through the required rate of return used to discount the cash flows.

It is not uncommon to see debt payments being included as part of the cash flows of a project. This is not necessary to evaluate the profitability of a project. If, however, debt payments are included, it is important to ensure that the correct discount rate is being used to evaluate the cash flows. We will return to these points later.

The capital budgeting process

The whole process of capital budgeting follows four distinct activities:

- *Screening*: where a range of suitable projects that fit into the overall objectives of the firm is identified.
- *Evaluation*: where the viability of each project is analysed. This will involve discussion with architects and other members of the professional team concerning the best way to develop a site.
- *Implementation*: where the project is taken from the design to contract and construction stages.
- *Auditing*: where the viability of the project is re-examined after all the costs are known.

Each of these is important in its own right. However, in this chapter we are going to focus solely on the area of evaluation and will examine a number of cash flow approaches that are considered to be economically valid. We will, however, begin by reviewing some of the *ad hoc* techniques used in practice and will show that the net present value (NPV) approach is the only method of analysis that is consistent with the objective of maximising shareholder wealth.

We have included a number of appendices that address more advanced topics. Although we will be anticipating some of the material to be covered in Part 2 it is nevertheless appropriate that the issues be discussed at this stage. The remainder of this chapter will focus on development appraisal as the evaluation of investments and the construction of property portfolios is something that we will cover in more depth in the remainder of this book.

The residual analysis

This is the simplest form of analysis widely used in the property industry. As its name implies, the method of analysis evaluates the difference between the project costs and sales values and arrives at a residual figure. Depending on how the analysis is set up the residual figure can either represent the profit or land value. Let's take a look at this in more detail.

The main components consist of:

- net development value or sales value (*S*)
- land value (*L*)
- development costs (*C*)
- interest charges (*I*)
- profit (*P*)

Although each of these can be split into many sub-components, they nevertheless represent the main cost groups. The residual valuation therefore takes either of the following forms.

Estimating the profit (P)

This is just the difference between the sale proceeds and the sum of all the cost elements. You can write this as follows:

$$P = S - (L + C + I) \tag{8.1}$$

Estimating the land value (L)

By making an assumption about the profit (P) equation 8.1 can be rearranged to give the land value:

$$L = S - (C + I + P) \tag{8.2}$$

In order to arrive at single figures for use in the analysis a number of simplifying assumptions have to be made. We can illustrate this by showing the whole development process on a time line (Table 8.1).

You will see that this involves three distinct phases:

1. *The land acquisition phase.* This can be a number of months before the construction starts and therefore includes design and pre-contract work needed before construction can start.
2. *The construction phase.* This covers the period it takes to construct the project.
3. *The letting and sales phase.* This covers the time required after completion for the project to be let and then sold.

Although this provides a general overview of the basic phases in a development, it is nevertheless a simplified view of reality. Developers try to minimise their exposure to risk wherever possible. For example, it is unlikely that they will buy a site unless they are sure that the development will go ahead. It would not be unusual, therefore, for a developer to take out an option before committing to buying a site. This gives the developer freedom to investigate alternative ways of developing the site and maybe to submit an outline planning application. If these investigations are successful, the developer will exercise the option, otherwise it is allowed to lapse.

In this preliminary stage developers sometimes minimise their exposure by transferring risk on to professional consultants. In this case the consultant in effect holds an option to receive fees, which can only be exercised if the project goes ahead. The consultant can therefore complete a lot of valuable preliminary work at no cost to the

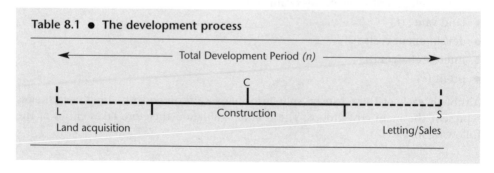

Table 8.1 ● The development process

developer. This procedure is very common where a developer is bidding for a site.

Some developers also build up land banks, and develop them progressively over a number of years. This is another form of option in which the decision to delay development has value. We will discuss some of these issues in Appendix 8F. The general point we wish to make is that property projects often have embedded options that can have an important influence on the decision to invest.

Example

The residual approach can best be illustrated by a simple example. Assume that you are interested in buying and developing a city office site that has an asking price of £4m. The rental value is estimated to be £14 per sq. ft and you are able to borrow funds at 8% p.a. Armed with this information you set up the following residual appraisal and estimate your gross profit as in Table 8.2:

Table 8.2 • A residual appraisal

Project details			
Land cost		£4,000,000	£4,000,000 L
Rental value	£14 per sq. ft		
Building area	100,000 sq. ft		
Interest rate	8.00%		
Site acquisition period	6 months		
Construction period	12 months		
Letting and sales	6 months		
Residual appraisal			
Net development value			
Net to gross ratio	80%		
Net lettable area	80,000 sq. ft		
Rental income p.a.		£1,120,000	
Capital value at	5.50%	£20,363,636	
Less costs	2.50%	£509,091	
		£19,854,545	£19,854,545 S
Development costs			
Construction cost			
100,000 sq. ft at	£100 per sq. ft	£10,000,000	£10,000,000

Professional fees *(expressed as a percentage of construction costs)*

Architect	5.00%	£500,000
Quantity surveyor	2.00%	£200,000
Structural engineer	2.00%	£200,000
Mechanical engineer	1.50%	£150,000
Site investigation		£10,000
		£1,060,000 £1,060,000

Table 8.2 continued

Development fees			
Planning fees	£3,000		
Building Regulation fees	£10,000		
	£13,000	£13,000	

Finance arrangement fees			
Bank arrangement fee	£20,000		
Legal fees for developer and bank	£50,000		
	£70,000	£70,000	
		£11,143,000	£11,143,000 C

Interest charges

Half development cost over the construction period

Cost	£5,571,500		
Interest	8.00%		
Period	12 months	£445,720	

Total development cost over letting/sales period

Cost	£11,143,000		
Interest	8.00%		
Period	6 months	£437,145	

Land cost over total development period

Cost	£4,000,000		
Interest	8.00%		
Period	24 months	£665,600	
		£1,548,465	£1,548,465 I

Profitability measures	
Gross Profit i.e. S – (L + C + I)	£3,163,080 P
Profit as a percentage of total cost P/(L + C + I)	18.95%
Rent as a percentage of total cost Rent/(L + C + I)	6.71%

You will see that although this residual appraisal is made up of a number of components, it follows the format we described above. To make this clearer we have also included the notation that relates to our equations for calculating gross profit and land value.

Using these figures you stand to make a profit of just over £3 million, which represents 18.95% of your total costs. If your profitability cut-off rate is, say, 15%, then this indicates that the project is worth undertaking. Another way of looking at profitability is to express the annual rent as a percentage of total costs. In this case it is 6.71%. Given that the rental income was capitalised at 5.5% this figure appears to represent a reasonably comfortable margin.

This example works out the profitability of the project. Another use of the residual analysis is to estimate the land value. This is particularly useful when a bid has to be put in for a site. Equation 8.2 showed how this could be worked out in principle. However, you have to go a little further than this to make it work in practice as the residual calculation includes elements of interest on both the land and construction cost. Let's see how you can do this.

Equation 8.2 gave the land value as:

$$L = S - (C + I + P)$$

In this expression I represents the total interest. It is however made up of two components: the interest on construction, I_C, and the interest on land, I_L. You will see from the example above how these have been calculated. As the land is held over the whole of the development period, n, the total interest paid can be written as:

$$I_L = L(1 + r)^n - L \qquad (8.3)$$

Substituting this back into the land value equation gives:

$$L = S - \{C + I_C + L[(1 + r)^n - 1] + P\} \qquad (8.4)$$

$$L = \frac{S - C - I_C - P}{(1 + r)^n} \qquad (8.5)$$

You will see from this that the land value is now expressed as a present value. This is, of course, what you would expect. It represents the residual value at the end of the development period discounted back to the beginning of the development period.

You can calculate the land value from this equation if you know the profitability (P) in absolute terms. This, however, is not very useful as the absolute profit depends on the total expenditure, including the unknown land value. The way round this is to express profitability in percentage terms, as we did in the appraisal. If you call the percentage profitability p you can express the absolute profitability, P, as a proportion of total costs as follows:

$$p = \frac{P}{L + C + I_C + I_L} \qquad (8.6)$$

As you already have an expression for I_L, you can substitute this into equation 8.6 to give:[1]

$$p = \frac{P}{\{L + C + I_C + L[(1 + r)^n - 1]\}} \qquad (8.7)$$

Rearranging gives the absolute profitability as follows:

$$P = p[C + I_C + L(1 + r)^n] \qquad (8.8)$$

You now have an expression for the gross profit, P, expressed as a percentage of the construction cost, C, the interest on construction, I_C, the land value, L, the interest rate, r, and the development period, n. By substituting this into the land value expression you will get the following:

$$L = \frac{S - (1 + p)(C + I_C)}{(1 + r)^n(1 + p)} \qquad (8.9)$$

[1] If you feel that the construction time and the sales period are likely to vary, you could also express I_C as a function of these components.

This can be simplified to:

$$L = \frac{1}{(1 + r)^n} \left[\frac{S}{(1 + p)} - C - I_c \right] \tag{8.10}$$

You can now try some figures from our residual value example:

S = £19,854,545
C = £11,143,000
I_c = £882,865
r = 0.08
n = 24 months, i.e. 2 years

By using the profitability figure of 18.95% calculated from the residual you get a land value very close to £4 million as follows:

$$L = \frac{1}{(1.08)^2} \left[\frac{£19,854,545}{(1 + 0.1895)} - £11,143,000 - £882,865 \right]$$

L = £4,000,034

This just confirms the figures used in the residual calculations. If, however, you were only prepared to accept the project if your profitability figure was 20%, you could use this formula to show that you could only afford to offer £3,874,819 for the land:

$$L = \frac{1}{(1.08)^2} \left[\frac{£19,854,545}{(1 + 0.20)} - £11,143,000 - £882,865 \right]$$

L = £3,874,819

The residual value approach, therefore, has a number of uses and has the virtue of being fairly easy to set up on a spreadsheet. It also has a number of problems that will become obvious in the remainder of this chapter. Despite its shortcomings we cannot say that the use of the residual value approach will lead to wrong investment decisions. In fact, if the market is generally using the residual value approach to estimate land values, then it clearly has value. The residual in this case gives a good indication of the order of magnitude that would be acceptable to bid for a plot of land. The value at which the site trades is, however, determined in an auction framework by a process of bidding which does not depend on any form of valuation model.

The residual approach should only be regarded as a means of estimating the order of magnitude of either the land value or profitability. Although it does include some rudimentary cash flow analysis it breaks a number of rules. In particular it includes the interest charges as part of the analysis, so it is not clear how you should regard the importance of the profitability measures.

Some important questions

If the decision to proceed with a development is made on the basis of using a residual valuation, there are a number of important questions that need to be asked:

- Will taking on the project increase the value of the firm?
- Does the gross profit adequately compensate for risk?
- How sensitive is the project to changes in each of the cost elements?
- Are the profitability measures a good indication of the value of the project?
- Is the basis of the analysis economically valid?

An issue underlying these questions is: *who benefits from good investment decisions?* The answer to this is that it is the shareholders of the company undertaking the development. This is an economic matter. If shareholder wealth is increased by good investment decisions, they will tend to invest more in the company. Over time the value of the company will increase and shareholders will be happy.

> Investment decisions should be made on behalf of the shareholders of a company. Good investment decisions should aim to maximise shareholder wealth.

If investment decisions are consistently poor, then shareholders will withdraw their funds and seek more profitable investment opportunities elsewhere. As the shareholders are the ultimate owners of a company, methods of analysis used to evaluate projects should be concerned with the effect that investment decisions have on maximising shareholder wealth.

The real problem with the residual method of analysis is that you can't be sure that shareholder wealth is being considered because the return that shareholders seek does not form part of the calculation. To take our understanding of investment appraisal further we need to consider the position of the shareholder and review some other methods of analysis that are widely used in practice.

Common methods of investment appraisal

In this section we will briefly cover some other methods of analysis that are used to evaluate investment projects. This will provide a framework for developing an approach that can be regarded as being economically defensible. We will cover the following methods:

- Pay-back
- Discounted pay-back
- Return on investment
- Internal rate of return
- Net present value

Pay-back

The pay-back period for a project is just the time it takes to recover the initial investment. We can illustrate this idea by calculating the pay-back period for the projects shown in Table 8.3.

For project A the positive cash flows exactly equal the £4,000 cash outlay in year 3 so the pay-back period is 3 years. Project B pays back its initial outlay sometime

Table 8.3 ● The pay-back period

Year	Project A	Project B	Project C
0	−£4,000	−£11,000	−£10,000
1	£1,000	£4,500	£3,000
2	£1,000	£7,500*	£4,000
3	£2,000*	£1,000	£1,000
4	£3,000	£1,000	£1,000
5	£2,000	£1,000	£1,000*
6		£1,000	
Pay-back period	3 years	1.87 years	5 years

*Pay-back period

during year 2. We calculate the exact pay-back period by finding how much of the initial outlay is outstanding at the end of year 1. Following our initial outlay of £11,000 we receive £4,500 in year 1 so that we still have £6,500 to be recovered. If the cash flows occur evenly over the course of each year we can express the £6,500 as a proportion of the £7,500 in year 3. In this case it is 0.87, so that the pay-back period is 1.87 years.

The pay-back period for project C calculated in the same way is found to be exactly five years.

The choice of project is made on the basis of some agreed cut-off period. Projects with a pay-back less than the cut-off period are accepted. Those with a pay-back greater than the cut-off period are rejected. If the cut-off period in our example is assumed to be two years, then only project B would be accepted.

Decision Rule: PAY-BACK
Accept a project if the pay-back period is less than an agreed cut-off period.

Shortcomings of the pay-back rule

This simple example shows that the pay-back period is found by just adding up the cash flows. The fact that they occur in different time periods and, therefore, have a time value means that the discounting effect is completely ignored. In addition, we have no way of deciding what is an appropriate pay-back period. We have used a figure of two years, but there is no economic reason to support this. It is in effect an arbitrary figure.

Another problem with the pay-back rule is that it treats all projects in the same way, irrespective of their risk. Thus a risky project might be accepted over a safe project merely because it has a shorter pay-back period. The pay-back rule also ignores cash flows that occur after the pay-back period so those potentially profitable projects are rejected.

Table 8.4 ● Comparison of projects using pay-back

Year	Project X	Project Y
0	–£1,000	–£1,000
1	£1,100	£0
2		£4,000
Pay-back period	1 year	2.25 years
NPV at 20%	–£83	+£1,315

The use of a short pay-back period does not always guarantee that the choice will be profitable. Take for example the two projects shown in Table 8.4.

Assuming a cut-off period of two years we would accept project X and reject project Y. If, however, both projects were equally risky and we required a return of 20%, the net present value of project A would be –£83 and for project B it would be £1,315. The pay-back rule has, therefore, led to the wrong decision being made because the time value of money has been ignored and there is a bias towards shorter-term projects. We will discuss net present value shortly.

Many property development projects are short-term. Even relatively complex projects can be built within periods of less than, say, two years so there is a temptation to use a rule-of-thumb that is based on very simple cash flows. However, one of the features of property development projects is that they are usually costly. Given the high capital commitment to property it makes sense to use methods that are economically defensible.

Benefits of the pay-back rule

Despite the shortcomings of the pay-back rule it does have some attractive features. Apart from being easy to use, the fact that it biases decisions towards short-term projects means that liquidity becomes an important issue. Development companies that are having cash flow difficulties may prefer to take on projects with very short pay-back periods, as they will free up cash to help with liquidity problems.

Discounted pay-back

This approach overcomes one of the difficulties of the basic pay-back approach by taking account of the time value of money. The discounted pay-back period is the time it takes for the discounted cash flows to equal the initial investment. Table 8.5 shows how it is calculated, assuming a discount rate of 20% p.a.

The normal pay-back period is shown in the second column and is calculated to be just over three years. The present value of the cash flows is shown in the third column and the pay-back in this case is calculated at 5.25 years. As before the decision to proceed is based on comparing the discounted pay-back period with a predetermined cut-off period. Once again, however, we have no economically defensible way of deciding what the cut-off period should be.

Table 8.5 ● The discounted pay-back

Year	Project A	PV at 20%
0	–£20,000	–£20,000
1	£6,500	£5,416
2	£6,500	£4,514
3	£6,500*	£3,762
4	£6,500	£3,135
5	£6,500	£2,612*
6	£6,500	£2,177
7	£6,500	£1,814
8	£6,500	£1,512
Pay-back period	3.08 years	5.25 years

*Pay-back period

Decision Rule: DISCOUNTED PAY-BACK
Accept a project if the discounted pay-back period is less than an agreed cut-off period.

The only difference between the normal pay-back and discounted pay-back is the fact that the discounted pay-back does take account of the time value of money. Apart from this it has the same advantages and disadvantages. Although the discounted pay-back takes account of the time value of money, it is not widely used. The main reason for this is that it requires a lot of work to set up the cash flows, and calculation of the discounted pay-back is no simpler than calculating net present values.

Return on investment

This is another approach that has the virtue of simplicity. The return on investment (ROI) has a number of definitions. We shall use the two shown in the residual appraisal.

Return on investment based on the gross profit

$$ROI(P) = \frac{\text{Gross profit}}{\text{Total cost}} \tag{8.11}$$

Often the return on investment is expressed as the average annual profit as a percentage of the average annual investment. However, in our case taking an average of the gross profit and total costs will not make any difference.

Using the figures from the residual analysis the return on investment is calculated as follows:

$$ROI(P) = \frac{£3,163,080}{£16,691,465}$$

$ROI(P) = 0.1895$, or 18.95%

As long as this is above some target return then the project is considered acceptable.

Return on investment based on the total rent received

$$ROI(R) = \frac{\text{Rental income}}{\text{Total cost}} \qquad\qquad (8.12)$$

Using the figures from the residual appraisal gives the following:

$$ROI(R) = \frac{£1,120,000}{£16,691,465}$$

$ROI(R) = 0.0671$, i.e. 6.71% p.a.

This figure is usually compared with the yield used to capitalise the income. In the example the yield was 5.50%. As the $ROI(R)$ exceeds this figure it suggests that the project is worth accepting.

> Decision Rule: RETURN ON INVESTMENT
> Accept a project if the return on investment is greater than an agreed target return.

Neither of these returns is comparable with any market-determined rates of return. They are just calculated from accounting figures so there is no economically defensible way to estimate what an appropriate cut-off rate should be. This is particularly true of the first return. In the second case the fact that the return on investment exceeds the yield does not really tell us anything about profitability. The investment yield is just a figure chosen to capitalise the income stream. It represents a combination of expected return and expected growth. Comparing one yield with another does not offer any insights concerning profitability.

Making decisions using cut-off rates

In many cases where return is used as a measure of profitability, the investment decision is often made relative to some fixed cut-off rate. This is often applied irrespective of the riskiness of the project. The danger in this approach is that low-risk/low-return projects will be rejected even though they may be profitable. In addition, some high-risk/high-return projects may also be accepted even though they are in fact unprofitable. The net effect of using a constant cut-off rate is that there is a tendency towards accepting high-risk projects. Over time the risk class of the company will become more risky and investors will require higher rates of return. The use of a constant cut-off rate implies something about the average riskiness of the company. As a decision-making technique it can be improved by using different cut-off rates for different risk groups.

The internal rate of return

We now move on to discuss methods of analysis that use all the cash flows in a project and correctly take account of the time value of money.

The first of these is the *internal rate of return* and is defined as the rate of return which equates the present value of the cash outflows to the present value of the cash inflows. We can write this in the following form:

$$\sum_{t=0}^{n} \frac{c_t}{(1+r)^t} = \sum_{t=0}^{n} \frac{a_t}{(1+r)^t} \tag{8.13}$$

where c_t represents a cash outflow and a_t a cash inflow in period t. The internal rate of return is represented by r. A project is considered profitable if the internal rate of return exceeds the opportunity cost of capital, r.

> Decision Rule: IRR
> Accept a project if the internal rate of return exceeds the opportunity cost of capital.

You will see from this expression that the return cannot be calculated directly but can only be worked out by finding a solution that satisfies this equality. To make the maths a little easier to work out, the internal rate of return is usually solved by making the difference between the present values equal to zero:

$$0 = \sum_{t=0}^{n} \frac{a_t}{(1+r)^t} - \sum_{t=0}^{n} \frac{c_t}{(1+r)^t} \tag{8.14}$$

If you just have one cash flow, then calculating the internal rate of return presents no problem. For example, assume you make a single investment of £100 at the end of year zero and get back £120 at the end of year 1. The internal rate of return is simply 20%. Using equation 8.14 you can write the cash flows as follows:

$$0 = \frac{£120}{(1+r)} - £100$$

$r = 0.2$, or 20%

If, however, you have three cash flows the calculation immediately gets more difficult. For example, assume you have the following:

Table 8.6 ● Estimating the internal rate of return

End year	Cash flow
0	−£100
1	+£60
2	+£70

Writing this as an equation gives:

$$0 = \frac{£60}{(1+r)} + \frac{£70}{(1+r)^2} - £100$$

This is in the form of a quadratic equation, which as you will no doubt remember from school, has two solutions. You will recall that a quadratic equation has the following form:

$$ax^2 + bx + c = 0 \tag{8.15}$$

The solution to this is:

$$x = \frac{-b \pm \sqrt{b^2 - 4ac}}{2a} \tag{8.16}$$

In our example, if we let $x = \dfrac{1}{(1+r)}$ we can write the present value of the cash flows as:

$$0 = £60x + £70x^2 - £100$$

As this is now in the same form as a quadratic equation you can find the solutions using equation 8.16:

$$x = \frac{-£60 \pm \sqrt{£60^2 - 4(£70)(-£100)}}{2(£70)}$$

$$x = 0.841, \text{ or } -1.698$$

You can find what these values imply in terms of the rate of return by substituting into the following:

$$x = \frac{1}{(1+r)}$$

$$0.841 = \frac{1}{(1+r)}$$

$$r = 0.189 \text{ or } 18.90\%$$

For $x = -1.698$ the internal rate of return is -158.9%.

As the number of cash flows increases you will end up with more complex polynomial expressions that have multiple roots. Many of the solutions will not, however, have any economic meaning. In this example the return of -158.9% is difficult to interpret, given the size of the cash flows involved.

Whenever we have a series of complex cash flows, the internal rate of return is usually calculated by computer, using a spreadsheet or a program that specifically handles cash flow analysis. It is, however, possible to solve most problems graphically. Using projects A, B and C from our pay-back example you can calculate the present value of each project over a wide range of discount rates. These are shown in Table 8.7.

Table 8.7 ● Estimating the internal rate of return

Discount rate	Project A	Project B	Project C
0%	£5,000	£4,000	£1,000
2%	£4,409	£3,392	£446
4%	£3,872	£2,827	-£61
6%	£3,383	£2,299	-£526
8%	£2,937	£1,806	-£953
10%	£2,529	£1,345	-£1,347
12%	£2,155	£912	-£1,711
14%	£1,812	£505	-£2,049
16%	£1,496	£122	-£2,362
18%	£1,204	-£239	-£2,653
20%	£936	-£579	-£2,924
22%	£687	-£900	-£3,178
24%	£457	-£1,205	-£3,416
26%	£243	-£1,493	-£3,638
28%	£45	-£1,766	-£3,847
30%	-£140	-£2,026	-£4,044
32%	-£312	-£2,273	-£4,229
34%	-£472	-£2,508	-£4,404
36%	-£622	-£2,731	-£4,569
38%	-£762	-£2,945	-£4,725
40%	-£894	-£3,149	-£4,873

A word of caution If you use a spreadsheet to work out present values the first cash flow is usually assumed to occur at the end of period 1, not the end of period zero. The figures will need to be compounded for one period. It is always wise to check.

You will see that the present values change from being positive to negative as the discount rate increases. Plotting the results in the form of a graph shows this more clearly (Figure 8.1).

The internal rates of return are shown where the graphs cut the present value line at zero. You can estimate the internal rate of return by either reading the figures off the graph or you can interpolate between the positive and negative present values. To show how this works let us look more closely at project B.

From Table 8.7 you will see that the internal rate of return must lie somewhere between 16% and 18% as this is where the present value of zero will be found. If you plot this you can see more clearly where the internal rate of return will lie.

You will see from Figure 8.2 that the present values lie on a downward-sloping curve. If, however, you assume as an approximation that the line is straight you can use the principle of proportional triangles to work out the internal rate of return:

$$\frac{£122}{r - 16\%} = \frac{£239}{18\% - r}$$

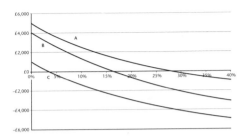

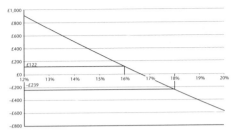

Figure 8.1 Present value of projects at different discount rates

Figure 8.2 Calculating the IRR for project B linear interpolation

Note that you are not interested in the signs of the present values as you are just comparing the proportion of two triangles. Solving this expression gives an internal rate of return of 16.68%.

Using a spreadsheet we found the internal rates of return for projects A, B and C to be 28.47%, 16.66% and 3.75%. If the projects are independent and have the same risk, you would accept those that exceed the opportunity cost of capital. If this was set at 15%, then projects A and B would be accepted and project C rejected. If, however, the projects were mutually exclusive so you could only accept one, the internal rate of return approach would lead you to accept project A. Mutual exclusivity is something that occurs quite frequently with property development proposals. Although it is possible to develop a site in a number of ways, it is only possible to proceed with one proposal.

An important point to note when using the internal rate of return to select projects is that the opportunity cost of capital is not the same as the borrowing rate. It is a market-determined rate and depends on the riskiness of the asset.

> The opportunity cost of capital is not the same as the borrowing rate. It is market-determined and depends on the riskiness of the asset.

We have seen that the decision rule for the internal rate of return is to accept those projects that exceed the opportunity cost of capital. This, however, is only valid when the present value curve is downward-sloping as shown in the illustration. There are, however, times when this does not happen so that a project can have multiple internal rates of return. The problem usually occurs when there is more than one sign change in the cash flow. In a phased property development project this is something which can happen quite frequently. Take, for example, the cash flows in Table 8.8.

A computer spreadsheet will show that the internal rate of return is 21.23%. However, if you were to plot the present value of this cash flow over a wide range of discount rates you would end up with the result shown in Figure 8.3. This shows a present value profile that is both downward- and upward-sloping with two more internal rates of return at approximately 90% and 200%. The total number of returns

Table 8.8 ● Cash flows in £000s for a phased project

Year	Project A
0	−£200
1	£1,200
2	−£2,200
3	£1,200
4	−£10
5	£100

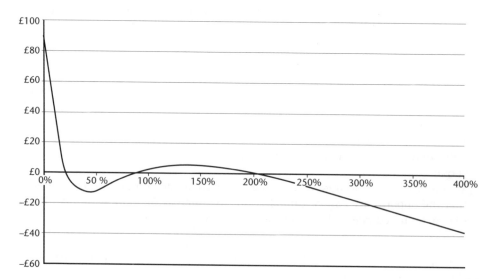

Figure 8.3 Multiple rates of return

depends on the number of sign changes. In our example we have five sign changes so the total number of returns could be five, three or one.

The real question is, how do you make a decision to invest when faced with multiple returns? The answer to this relies on using the net present value rule.

Net present value (NPV)

We have already come across net present value. We used it to estimate the internal rate of return by ensuring that the NPV was equal to zero. We also used it to develop some valuation models. If you discount a series of positive and negative cash flows the surplus value will represent the net present value. This can be positive or negative. Algebraically, the NPV for a project can be written as:

$$NPV = \sum_{t=0}^{n} \frac{a_t}{(1 + r_p)^t} - \sum_{t=0}^{n} \frac{c_t}{(1 + r_p)^t} \qquad (8.17)$$

where r_p represents the opportunity cost of capital. The decision rule is to accept those projects that have a positive NPV. Take for example the simple cash flow in Table 8.9.

Table 8.9 ● Estimating the net present value

End year	Cash flow	PV factor at 8% p.a.	Present value
0	−£500	1.0000	−£500.00
1	£200	0.9259	£185.18
2	£200	0.8573	£171.46
3	£200	0.7938	£158.76
		Net Present Value	£15.40

The discount rate of 8% represents the opportunity cost of capital and is a reflection of the riskiness of the project. The NPV in this case is positive so the project is worth accepting. In fact, the decision rule is to accept those projects where the NPV is greater than zero.

Decision Rule: NET PRESENT VALUE
Accept a project if the net present value is greater than zero when discounted at the opportunity cost of capital.

Net present value has another attractive feature. You will recall from our discussion on valuation that present values can be added together. This is the *value additivity principle*, and implies that once you know the NPV for one project you can add it to the NPV for other projects. A portfolio of positive NPVs will increase the overall value of a company.

Another important aspect of NPV is that it represents an increase in value in absolute terms and will do so irrespective of the nature of the cash flows. It is, therefore, a superior method of analysis when compared with the internal rate of return, which measures increases in value in relative terms.

In many cases decisions made using NPV will be the same as those using the internal rate of return. However, there may be times when they conflict. This will happen when the downward-sloping present value curves cross. Table 8.10 illustrates this point.

Assume you have two mutually exclusive projects, A and B. Because they are mutually exclusive you can choose only one project and must reject the other. If you plot the NPVs over a wide range of discount rates you will get two downward-sloping lines which cross each other. This is illustrated in Figure 8.4.

Table 8.10 ● Mutually exclusive projects

End year	A	B
0	–£10,000	–£10,000
1	£500	£6,000
2	£3,000	£3,000
3	£6,000	£2,000
4	£3,500	£1,000

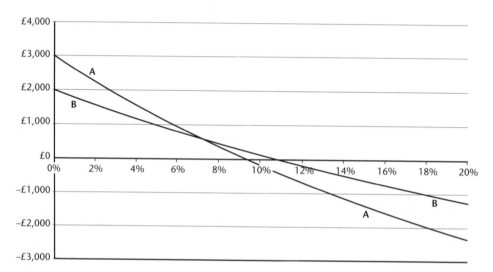

Figure 8.4 Mutually exclusive investment decisions

The choice of investment depends on the opportunity cost of capital and how this relates to the crossover point. If the opportunity cost of capital is less than the crossover rate, then project A is superior to project B. At higher rates, project B is superior.

In order to find the crossover rate all you have to do is subtract the cash flows for each project and find the internal rate of return of the difference. Table 8.11 shows the internal rate of return for project A and B as well as the difference. It also shows the NPVs for A and B at 6% and 8%.

The internal rate of return of the difference between the two cash flows is 7.28% and is shown in Figure 8.4. You will see that the ordering of the projects differs on either side of this rate.

If you had to make a choice between A and B it is clear that the IRRs imply that B is superior to A. On the basis of NPV the answer depends on the opportunity cost of capital. Although both techniques include all the cash flows in each project it is clear that only one technique can be correct.

Table 8.11 • Analysing mutually exclusive projects

End year	A	B	A – B
0	–£10,000	–£10,000	£0
1	£500	£6,000	–£5,500
2	£3,000	£3,000	£0
3	£6,000	£2,000	£4,000
4	£3,500	£1,000	£2,500
IRR	9.36%	10.75%	7.28%
NPV @ 6%	£951.7	£801.7	
NPV @ 8%	£370.6	£450.3	

The reinvestment rate

The NPV uses a single discount rate when comparing each project. The discount rate is a market-determined figure that represents the opportunity cost of capital. This is the only rate to use if the intention is to maximise shareholder wealth. If you decide that the correct opportunity cost of capital is 6%, then the appropriate project to choose is A. The internal rate of return does not, however, discount cash flows at the opportunity cost of capital, it uses the internal rate of return. This is also known as the *reinvestment rate*.

> The NPV and IRR make different assumptions concerning the reinvestment rate.

The NPV and IRR make different assumptions concerning the reinvestment rate. The NPV assumes that investors can reinvest at the opportunity cost of capital. This is the correct assumption concerning the reinvestment rate. The IRR, by contrast, assumes that investors can reinvest at the internal rate of return. For holders of project A this means that investors are assumed to be able to reinvest at 9.36% p.a. and for project B the rate is 10.75% p.a. Given that both projects have the same risk, why should it be possible to reinvest at different rates, particularly when the opportunity cost of capital for both projects is known to be 6%?

This, of course, doesn't make sense. The only valid investment decision is to use the net present value. This handles all conflicts of mutual exclusivity and provides an unambiguous measure of profitability in absolute terms.

Requirements of decision-making techniques

In the light of the above discussion we can now identify the essential requirements for a method of analysis that can be regarded as economically valid. We can list these as follows.

- All cash flows should be included in the analysis.
- Cash flows should be discounted at the opportunity cost of capital.
- The method of analysis should aim to maximise shareholder wealth.
- The choice between mutually exclusive projects should be on the basis of maximising shareholder wealth.
- Projects should be capable of being analysed separately.

Given this list of requirements it will be evident that NPV is the only valid method of analysis to use.

We introduced the residual method of analysis at the beginning of this chapter. It should be clear by now that, although widely used, it is not a very good indicator of profitability. Let's look at each of the points in turn:

1. It does not include all the cash flows in the project. It uses an approximation of the cash flow profile. On short-term projects this may be acceptable, but it could introduce errors.
2. The cash flows are not discounted at the opportunity cost of capital. In most cases interest is calculated on the basis of the rate at which funds are borrowed.
3. Because of inconsistencies concerning cash flow and the opportunity cost of capital, it is not clear whether the analysis is consistent with the concept of maximising shareholders' wealth.
4. The measure of absolute profitability is not a present value. It is a figure that arises at the end of the development period. If several projects are being analysed it would be wrong to add their profit figures together if their development periods differ.

In addition to these points you should be aware that the residual appraisal is sometimes not very clear about how to handle inflation. The capital value is based on current rental values and capitalisation rates, but the total costs are projected into the future. There is inconsistency here. Furthermore the residual profit completely ignores any reference to taxation when estimating profitability. Given that net of tax funds are used to pay for the project this represents another shortcoming.

So, the residual method of analysis doesn't stand up too well in terms of the requirements we have set. Nevertheless it still has value, just as pay-back and return on investment have value. These approaches should be regarded as being appropriate for initial screening purposes. If a project looks good using the simple approaches we have described, then it would probably justify taking the analysis further.

The agency principle

Before concluding this chapter it is important to reinforce the idea that shareholders' wealth is the present value of a project's cash flows discounted at the market-determined opportunity cost of capital. This is also the decision rule that should be followed by the managers of companies, irrespective of the business area. All shareholders have to do is ensure that the managers are following this decision rule.

There is clearly a difference between the ownership and management of a company. There is no reason to believe, however, that the managers of a company will always be pursuing the shareholders' best interests. The managers could, for example, recommend that a project be accepted as it could influence their position within the company or affect their annual bonus. This is what is known as the *agency principle*. The owners of a company, i.e. the shareholders, may have to incur costs to ensure that the managers are acting in the interests of the owners. They will, therefore, trade off the cost of monitoring the managers against the rewards they offer. This is a complex issue that may have an optimal solution.

An important implication of managers not increasing shareholders' wealth is that the source of funds available to a company may dry up. It is not unreasonable to assume, therefore, that managers should pursue a policy of maximising shareholder wealth. To this end NPV is the only sensible decision-making technique to use.

> Sensible investment decisions should try to maximise shareholder wealth. The use of net present value is consistent with this objective.

Summary

Our main objective in this chapter has been to show that the aim of good investment is to maximise shareholders' wealth. Shareholders are the owners of a company so financial decisions should be made from their point of view. If this idea is applied consistently, it follows that methods of analysis based on *ad hoc* techniques may only increase shareholders' wealth merely by chance. We also pointed out that the decision to invest in a project is separate from how you would finance a project. This distinction is important in terms of understanding methods of appraisal. Most traditional property textbooks that deal with development appraisal fail to make this distinction.

With these points in mind we examined a number of common appraisal techniques. We started with the residual method, as it is probably one of the most common approaches used in the property industry. We showed how it could be used to estimate profitability or land value. We also showed that it does suffer from a number of shortcomings that can only be rectified by using a more formal cash flow approach.

We also discussed other methods of analysis such as payback, discounted payback and return on investment. Each of these relies on *ad hoc* decision rules that have no close link with modern financial theory. We showed, for example, that the use of a constant cut-off rate of return could encourage companies to reject profitable projects and lead them into areas of high risk. The chapter closed by introducing formal methods of analysis that make use of the time value of money and incorporate the concept of discounted cash flow. The net present value rule was shown to be the only method of analysis that provides a measure of absolute profitability that is consistent with maximising shareholders' wealth. The drawback to using net present value is that it requires an estimate of the opportunity cost of capital. This relies on an understanding of the riskiness of the asset and is not easy to estimate for individual projects. Understanding risk is an issue we discuss in depth in Part 2. We do, however, introduce some of the issues in Appendix 8C as it is an important part of project appraisal.

This chapter has a number of appendices that cover advanced topics that are relevant in the context of evaluating projects.

Appendix 8A: Inflation, financing and taxation

This appendix covers some of the issues we raised in Chapter 8 and highlights the need to be consistent in the way cash flows are drafted.

Appendix 8B: Estimating relevant cash flows

Our assumption in this appendix is that net present value should be used to estimate the viability of a project. As most appraisals are set up using a spreadsheet it is, therefore, important to understand the main elements of a cash flow analysis. This appendix covers the main topics.

Appendix 8C: Estimating relevant discount rates

The net present value rule requires an estimate of the opportunity cost of capital. This is not the rate at which the project is financed. This appendix describes a number of ways of estimating an appropriate figure.

Appendix 8D: Allowing for risk in the cash flows

So far we have assumed that all the cash flows are known. In reality this is not the case so it is relevant to consider how you would simulate the uncertainty in the project. This appendix introduces you to some of the issues involved.

Appendix 8E: The adjusted present value and residual equity income approach

This appendix covers two advanced topics related to net present value. The adjusted present value rule is a method of analysis that specifically values the side-effects of taxation caused by borrowing. The residual equity income approach is a method of analysis that does include funding as part of the cash flows but makes an allowance for this when discounting the residual cash flows.

Appendix 8F: Development finance: sources and techniques

This appendix briefly reviews the main sources and techniques of finance used in property. The emphasis is on showing how the risks are shared between the developer and the lender.

Appendix 8G: Options to invest

Although we have stressed the importance of the net present value rule it is clear that a number of projects have embedded options or there may be some value attached to delaying the decision to invest. This appendix raises these issues. A detailed understanding of these topics is likely to be important in the future.

Chapter 8: Summary table

1. Capital budgeting is the term used to describe plans for capital expenditure. It involves four phases: screening, evaluation, implementation and auditing.

2. Project appraisal should make a distinction between the investment decision and the funding decision.

3. The residual analysis is widely used in the property industry to estimate profitability or land value. It does, however, suffer from a number of shortcomings.

4. Valid methods of analysis should answer the following questions:

   ● Will taking on the project increase the value of the firm?
   ● Does the gross profit adequately compensate for risk?
   ● How sensitive is the project to changes in each of the cost elements?
   ● Are the profitability measures a good indication of the value of the project?
   ● Is the basis of the analysis economically valid?

5. Investment decisions should be made on behalf of the shareholders of a company. The intention should be to maximise shareholders' wealth.

6. Pay-back and discounted pay-back relate to the time it takes to recover the initial investment.

   In both cases accept the project if the pay-back period is less than the agreed cut-off period.

7. Return on investment is an accounting measure of profitability and can be based on gross profit or rental income.

   Accept a project if the return on investment is greater than some agreed target return.

8. Using arbitrary cut-off rates can cause some profitable projects to be rejected and over time will gradually increase the riskiness of the firm.

9. The internal rate of return (IRR) uses all the cash flows and correctly takes account of the time value of money. The IRR is, however, a relative measure of profitability and is sensitive to the sign changes in the cash flows. It is possible, therefore, to have multiple rates of return.

Accept a project if the IRR exceeds the opportunity cost of capital.

10. The net present value (NPV) is found by discounting the project cash flows at the opportunity cost of capital.

Accept a project if the NPV is greater than zero.

11. Net present values are an absolute measure of profitability and can be added together. This is known as the value additivity principle.

12. In mutually exclusive cases the ranking of projects can sometimes differ depending on whether the IRR or NPV is used. Using the NPV will, however, always give the correct ranking.

13. The NPV and IRR make different assumptions concerning the reinvestment rate.

14. Decision-making techniques should incorporate the following requirements:

● All cash flows should be included in the analysis
● Cash flows should be discounted at the opportunity cost of capital
● The method of analysis should aim to maximise shareholders' wealth
● The choice between mutually exclusive projects should be on the basis of maximising shareholder wealth
● Projects should be capable of being analysed separately

15. The agency principle is concerned with ensuring that managers make decisions that are in the best interests of the owners of a company. This can be violated if managers take decisions that could improve their own position within the company.

16. Managers should pursue a policy of wealth maximisation. This requires the use of net present value as the economically valid decision-making technique.

Problems

1. A development project having a cost of £3,000,000 generates a constant annual rental stream at the end of each of the following ten years of £420,000. What is the pay-back period? Assuming that the opportunity cost of capital is 8.00% p.a., is this project profitable?

2. You have been asked to evaluate a project which has the following setting up cash outflows over a period of three years:

   End Year 0 £250,000
   End Year 1 £350,000
   End Year 2 £450,000

   After completion the project lies dormant for two years before it generates an income stream. The first year of income is £200,000. The second year it rises to £300,000. By the third year it has reached £500,000. It stays at this level for three years and then the project is scrapped with a zero value.

   Assuming that the appropriate rate of return is 10% p.a., is this project profitable?

3. You have been appointed as consultant to a developer and you have to advise on the viability of a project that is being planned. You are given the following information. The land cost is £2,500,000 and the project is planned to consist of 150,000 sq. ft of offices. It will take about one year to build and six months after completion before it is fully let. The cost of construction is £125 per sq. ft and the developer is able to borrow at 9% pa. Your research suggests that the rental value is currently £30 per sq. ft and you expect that the project could be capitalised at 6.5%.

   Given this information prepare an initial residual valuation to estimate the profitability of this project. If the opportunity cost of capital is 11% prepare an outline cash flow and compare the net present value with the residual appraisal.

4. You represent a company that has to decide on whether to proceed with one of three investment opportunities it has under consideration. The cash flows for each of the projects are as follows:

Project	Investment	1	2	3	4	5
				Years		
A	£5,000	£800	£1,000	£350	£1,250	£3,000
B	£7,500	£1,250	£3,000	£2,500	£5,000	£5,000
C	£4,000	£600	£1,200	£1,200	£2,400	£3,000

   Assuming that the appropriate return is 12% per annum which project would you recommend?

5. Using a wide range of discount rates draw a graph of NPV against rate of return for each project.

Selected references

Brealey, R.A. and Myers, S.C. (1996) *Principles of Corporate Finance*, 5th edn. New York: McGraw-Hill.

Darlow, C. (1984) *Valuation and Development Appraisal*, London: Estates Gazette.

Isaac, D. (1996) *Property Development Appraisal and Finance*, London: Macmillan.

Jaffe, A.C. and Sirmans, C.F. (1995) *Fundamentals of Real Estate Investment*, 3rd edn. Englewood Cliffs, NJ: Prentice Hall.

Lusht, K.M. (1997) *Real Estate Valuation*, Chicago: Irwin.

Appendix 8A
Inflation, financing and taxation

In Chapter 8 we examined a number of different techniques for analysing projects. We showed that net present value (NPV) was the only rule that adequately allowed for all the cash flows, offered a measure of profitability in absolute terms, and was consistent with maximising shareholder wealth.

In order to use NPV in practice you have to ensure that the cash flows and discount rates are used in a consistent manner. We showed that the residual method of analysis has a number of problems that can only be addressed using a cash flow approach. In this appendix we will address three important topics which affect cash flows: inflation, financing and taxation.

Inflation

The opportunity cost of capital is determined by reference to other assets with equivalent risk. It is a market-determined return and embodies investors' expectations concerning inflation. Interest rates quoted in the marketplace are therefore in *nominal* terms, because they incorporate the effects of expected inflation. The return on Government securities, building society rates, bank borrowing and lending rates are all in nominal terms.

The nominal opportunity cost of capital, r_n, is made up of two components: the risk free rate of return, r_f, plus a premium, p, which offers compensation for taking on risk. You can write the nominal return as follows:

$$r_n = r_f + p \tag{8A.1}$$

The risk-free rate is also made up of two components: the real riskless rate of return, r_{fr}, and the expected change in the general price level per period, Δ. This is the expected rate of inflation or deflation. Incorporating these elements gives a more detailed expression for the components that make up the nominal return:

$$r_n = r_{fr} + \Delta + p \tag{8A.2}$$

As nominal returns incorporate the effects of inflation, cash flows must also be expressed in the same form when undertaking a discounted cash flow analysis. In fact, to be more general all we need to say is that you have to be consistent in the way you draft both cash flows and discount rates.

NOMINAL CASH FLOWS should be discounted using NOMINAL DISCOUNT RATES
REAL CASH FLOWS should be discounted using REAL DISCOUNT RATES

It doesn't really make any difference which approach you adopt as the net present value will be the same in both cases. We can illustrate this as follows.

Assume that you want to invest in a project costing £100,000. Based on current costs you estimate the cash flow profile over the five-year life of the project. You also look at similar projects and decide that the opportunity cost of capital should be 12% p.a. With this information you can work out the net present value as follows.

Table 8A.1 ● Estimating the net present value

End year	Cash flow	Discount factor at 12% p.a.	Present value
0	–£100,000	1.0000	–£100,000
1	£20,000	0.8929	£17,857
2	£25,000	0.7972	£19,930
3	£30,000	0.7118	£21,353
4	£30,000	0.6355	£19,066
5	£20,000	0.5674	£11,349
		Net present value	–£10,455

As the net present value is negative this would indicate that the project is not worth accepting. However, closer examination of the cash flows indicates that they have been drafted using today's values and are, therefore, expressed in real terms. For example, the cash flow of £20,000 at the end of year 5 represents what £20,000 would buy today. Because they are drafted in real terms the cash flows are not consistent with the nominal return used in the discounting.

To make economic sense of the analysis you can do either of the following:

● Convert the cash flows in nominal terms.
● Convert the discount rate into a real rate of return.

We will do both!

Let us assume that the expected rate of inflation is 5% p.a. You can convert each of the cash flows into nominal terms so that they have a purchasing power appropriate for the period in which they occur. This is shown in Table 8A.2.

Discounting at the nominal rate of 12% p.a. now gives a net present value of £3,100, indicating that the project is in fact profitable.

The alternative way of dealing with this problem is to leave the cash flows as they are, but to convert the nominal discount rate into a real rate. We showed in Chapter 2 that the relationship between nominal and real returns can be expressed as:

$$(1 + r_n) = (1 + r_r)(1 + \Delta) \tag{8A.3}$$

Table 8A.2 ● NPV using nominal cash flows

End year	Cash flow	Revised cash flow	Discount factor at 12% p.a.	Present value
0	–£100,000(1.05)^0	–£100,000	1.0000	–£100,000
1	£20,000(1.05)^1	£21,000	0.9829	£18,750
2	£25,000(1.05)^2	£27,563	0.7972	£21,973
3	£30,000(1.05)^3	£34,729	0.7118	£24,719
4	£30,000(1.05)^4	£36,465	0.6355	£23,174
5	£20,000(1.05)^5	£25,526	0.5674	£14,484
			Net present value	£3,100

Table 8A.3 ● NPV using a real discount rate

End year	Cash flow	Discount factor at 6.67% p.a.	Present value
0	−£100,000	1.0000	−£100,000
1	£20,000	0.9375	£18,750
2	£25,000	0.8789	£21,973
3	£30,000	0.8240	£24,719
4	£30,000	0.7725	£23,174
5	£20,000	0.7242	£14,484
		Net present value	£3,100

You can rearrange this to give the following real rate of return:

$$r_r = \left(\frac{1 + r_n}{1 + \Delta}\right) - 1 \qquad (8A.4)$$

Using the figures from the above example:

$$r_r = \frac{1 + 0.12}{1 + 0.05} - 1$$

$r_r = 0.0667$, i.e. 6.67%

You will see that this is not quite the same as subtracting 5% from 12%. Although the difference is small, it would nevertheless give rise to errors in the NPV calculation.

Having calculated the real rate of return you can now use it to discount the original cash flows (Table 8A.3).

Once again the NPV is £3,100, confirming that there is no difference between discounting in real or nominal terms, as long as consistency is maintained throughout. If you compare this with the figures given in Table 8A.2 you will also see that the present value of the cash flow in each period is the same.

In this example we have used only one rate of inflation. The choice of inflation rate really depends on the cash flows. In complex development projects it would not be unusual to have sales values inflating at a different rate to construction costs.

Financing

In Chapter 8 we made the point that it was unnecessary to take account of funding when evaluating a project. Although this may seem to be an unfamiliar idea it is based on the principle that the value of a project will not alter merely by the way it is financed. This is *proposition 1* developed by Modigliani and Miller (1958) as part of what is known as the MM hypothesis. Consequently, if a project is profitable on its own, then the addition of funding will only improve the return to the shareholders.

This is an important idea which implies that it is easier to increase shareholders' wealth through good investment decisions rather than through skilful financing decisions. This, of course, raises the critical question, does financing matter? As we shall see, the answer depends on the tax status of the investor.

It is easier to increase shareholders' wealth through good investment decisions rather than through skilful financing decisions.

Let us examine the effect of introducing debt into a project or a company.

A company is just a collection of projects, which are financed in different ways. Each project has, therefore, a value (V), which is made up of the sum of two sources of funding namely debt (D) and equity (E). This can be compared with a balance sheet. On one side you have the total assets (V), which are matched by the liabilities of debt (D) and equity (E). The returns on each of these sources of funds will differ in relation to their risk. The weighted average of the two returns will equal the asset or project return. You can write this as follows:

$$r_p = wr_d + (1 - w)r_e \tag{8A.5}$$

where

r_p = return on asset or project
r_d = return on debt
r_e = return on equity.

The proportion of funds represented by debt and equity can be written as:

$$\text{Debt proportion:} \quad w = \frac{D}{D + E} \tag{8A.6}$$

$$\text{Equity proportion:} \quad (1 - w) = \frac{E}{D + E} \tag{8A.7}$$

You will see from this that you can't suddenly change the value of the project merely by changing the way it is funded. This doesn't make sense, otherwise identical projects would sell at different prices. In an active market the demand for lower-valued projects would force their prices up and the lack of demand for higher-valued projects would force their prices down. It wouldn't take long before the market adjusts for the mispricing. The return on the project can, therefore, be assumed to be fixed. If you also assume that the return on debt is fixed, then the only factor in equation 8A.7 that can change is the return on equity. As the proportion of debt used to fund a project changes the return on equity also changes to maintain the same project return.

Assume, for example, that a project has an expected return of 12% p.a. and is financed with 60% of debt costing 8% p.a. From this information you can find out what the expected return on equity should be in order to maintain the same project value. Substituting these figures into equation 8A.5 gives:

$$0.12 = 0.6(0.08) + (1 - 0.6)r_e$$

$$r_e = 0.18, \text{ i.e. } 18\% \text{ p.a.}$$

This shows that by borrowing funds to finance the project it is possible to increase the return on equity. As the shareholders have provided the 40% of equity the high return is clearly welcome. You will also see that by using a higher proportion of debt you can increase the return on equity. It is tempting therefore to go on increasing the proportion of debt. Table 8A.4 shows what happens to the return on equity, r_e, if you do this.

You will see that in order to maintain the project return at 12% the return on equity increases as the proportion of debt increases.

There is, however, a cost associated with gearing up the returns in this way. High returns are also accompanied by increases in risk that could lead to bankruptcy. Although we have shown a constant return of 8% on the debt, in reality this will increase as the proportion of debt increases. In fact, as you get closer to 100% debt you would expect the return to be the same as the return on the project. The reason for this is that at 100% debt funding the lender now owns all the equity in the project and would expect the same return as the project, i.e. 12%. You will see that this is the case by substituting $w = 1$ in the formula we used to calculate the return on equity.

If this were a development project the relationship between developer and lender would change. At 100% debt financing the developer is really taking on the role of project manager. The developer may be prepared to do this for either a fixed fee or a percentage of the profits.

The above discussion shows that if the value of the project doesn't change as we introduce debt, then it is not necessary to include debt as part of the cash flows when undertaking a viability appraisal. We can show that this is the case using a simple example.

Assume that a project costing £100 has a value in one year of £115. The project is correctly priced and has an opportunity cost of capital of 15%. Let us also assume that you finance the purchase of the project with 70% debt costing 10% p.a. The first step is to calculate the return on equity. Rearranging equation 8A.5 in terms of the return on equity gives:

$$r_e = \frac{r_p - wr_d}{1 - w} \tag{8A.8}$$

Substituting the information on the project gives:

$$r_e = \frac{0.15 - 0.7(0.1)}{1 - 0.7}$$

$r_e = 0.2667$, i.e. 26.7%

Table 8A.4 ● Increasing the proportion of debt in a project

Proportion of funds		Return on debt	Return on project	Return on equity
Debt	Equity	r_d	r_p	r_e
0.5	0.5	0.08	0.12	0.16
0.6	0.4	0.08	0.12	0.18
0.7	0.3	0.08	0.12	0.21
0.8	0.2	0.08	0.12	0.28
0.9	0.1	0.08	0.12	0.48

This is the return that you expect on the equity invested in the project. You can set this up in cash flow terms as follows:

Table 8A.5 ● Project cash flows with 70% debt

| | | End year cash flows | |
	End year	0	1
Project cost		−£100.00	
Borrowings		+£70.00	
Interest on debt			−£7.00
Repayment of debt			−£70.00
Sales value			+£115.00
Residual equity		−£30.00	+£38.00

The final line in this table represents the residual equity after allowing for all the debt payments. It is, therefore, the geared cash flow and should be discounted at the geared return on equity in order to find the NPV. The rate to use in this case is the return on equity of 26.70% p.a.

$$NPV = -£30.00 + \frac{£38.00}{(1 + 0.267)}$$

$$NPV = 0$$

The fact that we have a zero NPV shows that the project is correctly priced.

If, however, you had no funding but assumed that the project was wholly equity financed you would end up with the cash flow shown in Table 8A.6.

As you have no funding the return of the residual equity must equal the return on the project. Substituting the figures into equation 8A.8 gives:

$$r_e = \frac{0.15 - 0.0(0.1)}{1 - 0.0}$$

$r_e = 0.15$, i.e. 15.0%

Table 8A.6 ● Project cash flows with 0% debt

| | | End year cash flows | |
	End year	0	1
Project cost		−£100.00	
Borrowings		£0	
Interest on debt			£0
Repayment of debt			£0
Sales value			+£115.00
Residual equity		−£100.00	+£115.00

Discounting the residual equity at 15% p.a. also gives an NPV of zero.

As long as you are consistent about risk and the discount rates you use it will not make any difference to the NPV. You can, therefore, assume that the project is wholly equity financed and concentrate on making good investment decisions. It follows, therefore, that the funding decision is separate from the investment decision.

This, however, is only true in a world without taxes. We, therefore, have to consider the effect that taxes have on the investment decision.

Taxation

Every investment has a tax side-effect. If the government offers tax relief on borrowed funds, then the value of the project will increase by the present value of the tax shield.

Borrowing money to finance the purchase of a house is a good example of using a tax shield. Because the government allows tax relief on a proportion of the interest payments they are in effect reducing the cost of borrowing. Someone who is able to take advantage of the tax relief will be better-off in comparison to someone else who cannot do this, even though they both borrow the same amount.

We saw above that the value of a project does not depend on how it is financed. But this is true only in a world without taxes. In a world with taxes the value of a project can be considered in two parts.

Project value	=	Value if wholly equity financed	+	Value of tax side-effects

You can incorporate this idea into the simple example we have already used. Let us assume that the project is financed with 70% debt costing 10% p.a. and that the tax rate is 25%.

Table 8A.7 ● Equity financing

		End year cash flows	
	End year	0	1
Project cost		−£100.00	
Sales value			+£115.00
Residual equity		−£100.00	+£115.00
Present value at 15% p.a.		−£100.00	+£100.00
	NPV assuming 100% equity	**£0.00**	
Debt financing			
Borrowings		£70.00	
Interest on debt at 10%			−£7.00
Tax shield at 25%			£1.75
Present value of tax shield at 15%			£1.52
	NPV of tax shield	**£1.52**	

We have discounted the tax shield at 15% because its risk is determined by the project cash flows. The value of the project is, therefore, the sum of the two NPVs which, in this case, amounts to £1.52. Thus, by borrowing and assuming you pay tax, you are able to increase the value of the project. Note that in this case the total project value comes entirely from the tax side-effect. In some cases the NPV of the project, assuming 100% equity finance, could be negative. However, the project could still be profitable if the present value of the tax shield is large. If the tax benefits of borrowing are suddenly withdrawn, then the investor will be exposed to the profitability of the underlying project. This highlights the need to separate the investment decision from the financing decision.

> Every investment has a tax side-effect. If the government offers tax relief on interest payments the present value of the tax shields can add value to a project.
> In terms of assessing the viability of a project, funding is only important if there are tax side-effects.

There are three methods that are used to allow for the effects of tax when appraising a project. They are:

● Adjusted Present Value (APV)
● Weighted Average Cost of Capital (WACC)
● Residual Equity Income (REI)

We have briefly described the adjusted present value approach. Appendix 8E covers the methods in more detail.

Selected references

Brealey, R.A. and Myers, S.C. (1996) *Principles of Corporate Finance*, 5th edn. New York: McGraw-Hill.

Modigliani, F. and Miller, M.H. (1958) The cost of capital, corporation finance and the theory of investment. *American Economic Review* **48**, 261–97.

Appendix 8B
Estimating relevant cash flows

We have shown that the viability of a project depends on taking into consideration all the cash flows generated by a project. In this appendix we will consider which cash flows are relevant. This is especially important when setting up an analysis using a spreadsheet.

The only cash flows that are relevant for capital budgeting purposes are the *incremental net of tax cash flows*. Let us look at this in a little more detail.

Incremental cash flows

This represents the difference between the cash flows for a company with and without the project. Only those elements that affect the total cash flows of the firm if the project is accepted should, therefore, be considered. If you look at this in development terms, then construction costs are clearly relevant because the cash flow of the company will change by taking on the project. What would not be relevant, however, would be to apportion part of the firm's overheads to the project. These are costs that the firm would incur irrespective of whether the project goes ahead.

Taxation (t)

All cash flows must be expressed on a net of tax basis. The reason for this is that the initial cash outflows are paid from the net of tax income of the company. Taking on a project will also affect the tax position of the firm, so it is important to measure cash flows after taking account of tax.

A new development, for example, will generate both income, in the form of sales, and expenditure, in the form of construction costs. Once these have been estimated the incremental effect on the company is estimated and the tax can then be deducted to give the after tax cash flow.

Often, there is a delay between incurring a tax liability and actually paying it. By setting up the cash flows on a spreadsheet it is possible to incorporate the tax payments at the correct point in time when they occur.

Operating cash flows

Operating cash flows cover both the expenditure, (E), and the sales, (S), which contribute to the incremental cash flows.

Depreciation (D)

Depreciation is not, strictly speaking, a cash flow item. It is included here because it affects the amount of tax that is paid. Where depreciation is included in a cash flow it is usual to include a balancing amount that neutralises its effect after tax has been calculated.

Depreciation may be more relevant for a company that is building, say, a new warehouse for its own use. In some cases it may be possible to depreciate a proportion of the cost of construction over a fixed number of years. This would effectively reduce the tax burden to the investor. A developer constructing a building for sale may not have access to many depreciable items. Nevertheless, it is an important aspect when estimating taxation and therefore needs to be considered.

The net of tax operating cash flows: NOTCF

We can identify the above components in the cash flow analysis as follows:

   C: Costs and other expenditure

S: Sales and other revenue
D: Depreciation
t: Tax rate

In any period you can estimate the net of tax operating cash flows from the following expression,

$$NOTCF = (S - C - D)(1 - t) + D \qquad (8B.1)$$

The first part of this expression is just the difference between the sales (S) and the costs (C) reduced by the depreciation (D). Multiplying this by $(1 - t)$ gives the after tax cash flow. The second part of the equation just adds back the depreciation so that it is taken out of the net of tax cash flow calculation. This procedure should be followed in each period of analysis.

Having established the cash flows in a project the next step is to find their present value using a relevant discount rate. This is covered in Appendix 8C.

Selected references

Brealey, R.A. and Myers, S.C. (1996) *Principles of Corporate Finance*, 5th edn. New York: McGraw-Hill.

Rao, R.K.S. (1987) *Financial Management*, New York: Macmillan.

Shapiro, A.C. (1991) *Modern Corporate Finance*, New York: Macmillan.

Appendix 8C
Estimating relevant discount rates

So far we have referred to discounting cash flows at the opportunity cost of capital, or the expected rate of return. This is a market-determined rate of return that reflects the riskiness of the asset. We have been careful to point out that this is not the rate at which a project is financed. Estimating the expected rate of return is a complex issue that involves an understanding of risk and return which we will cover in detail in Part 2. However, it is such an important topic in the context of appraising investments that it is appropriate to raise some of the issues at this stage.

Taking account of risk in a project

The expected rate of return can be split into two components: the risk-free rate of return and a premium for bearing risk. Whatever method of analysis is used to estimate the expected rate of return they all share the aim of trying to identify, as accurately as possible, the risk premium.

This is not, however, the only way to take account of risk. As an alternative to adjusting the discount rate, risk can be incorporated directly into the cash flows. The interpretation of the output in this case requires some care and is considered separately in Appendix 8D. In this appendix we will discuss five ways in which the discount rate can be estimated.

1. Risk grouping
2. Risk ratios
3. The capital asset pricing model
4. The arbitrage pricing theory
5. The weighted average cost of capital

1. Risk grouping

Although this is the simplest approach it nevertheless has some appeal because it recognises that project cash flows should be discounted at a rate that reflects their risk. The way it works is to identify a range of risk premium groupings that reflect low, medium and high-risk projects. These are after tax premium figures used to discount after tax cash flows. You might, for example, use the following groupings:

Table 8C.1 ● Risk groupings

Risk group	Risk premium
Low risk	0%–3%
Medium risk	3%–6%
High risk	6%–10%

When undertaking an appraisal you decide which group is most appropriate for the project. The opportunity cost of capital can, therefore, be estimated by adding one of the risk premium figures to the risk-free rate of return.

Although this approach is intuitively appealing, it nevertheless suffers from a number of shortcomings:

- It is not clear how the risk groupings are determined. If they are based on some notion of total risk, then this is the incorrect measure of risk to use because it ignores the importance of diversification. This is a major area of investment theory and we discuss it fully in Part 2.
- The risk premium figures are also difficult to determine. Why should the risk premium figures be as shown in this table? Higher or lower figures would be just as appropriate.
- The risk premium figures may be related to a company and not to the project. This is not a reliable approach to estimating the opportunity cost of capital for individual projects.

Risk grouping is, however, an improvement on using a constant cut-off rate. It is quite common for firms to select a target cut-off rate which they use to screen every project. This is applied irrespective of risk. We mentioned this in Chapter 8 and pointed out that it would cause firms to reject profitable, low-risk projects and accept unprofitable, high-risk ones.

2. Risk ratios

An alternative to the risk grouping approach is to use risk ratios. In this method the risk of a project is related to the average risk of the firm. We can express this as follows:

$$E(r_p) = r_f + \frac{\sigma_p}{\sigma_k} \; (\bar{r}_k - r_f)$$

(8C.1)

where

$E(r_p)$ = expected rate of return for project
r_f = risk-free rate of return
$\bar{r}_k$ = average return for firm
σ_p = total risk of project
σ_k = total risk of firm

The risk ratio is calculated by comparing the standard deviation of the project with the standard deviation of the firm. Alternatively, the ratio of the two risks could be assessed subjectively. Managers may have a view that a particular project is, say, 10% or 15% more risky than the average undertaken by the firm. In this case the risk ratio would be estimated directly as 1.1 or 1.15.

This approach is a slightly more formal way of dealing with differences in risk than the risk grouping approach. It is still, however, an approximation of what is happening in reality because it ignores the effect of diversification.

As a first attempt though it does at least bias decision-making in the right direction.

3. The capital asset pricing model (CAPM)

This is probably the most rigorous method used for estimating the opportunity cost of capital. As it is such an important model we will describe in more detail how it developed in Part 2. We just present the main result here and show how it can be adapted to estimate the opportunity cost of capital for projects. The important point to note is that the CAPM holds for all assets. This includes financial securities as well as real assets. It is, therefore, valid to use the model for estimating expected returns for projects.

> The capital asset pricing model holds for all assets. This includes both financial securities as well as real assets. It can therefore be used to estimate the expected return for individual projects.

The main form of the CAPM is as follows:

$$E(r_p) = r_f + \beta_p [E(r_m) - r_f]$$

(8C.2)

This expresses the expected return on a project in terms of the risk-free rate of return and a risk premium, which is related to its market risk, β_p. The advantage of this approach is that it recognises that each project has a different level of market risk which will influence its expected return. Market risk is a special type of risk that is related to the contribution that the asset makes to a well-diversified portfolio.

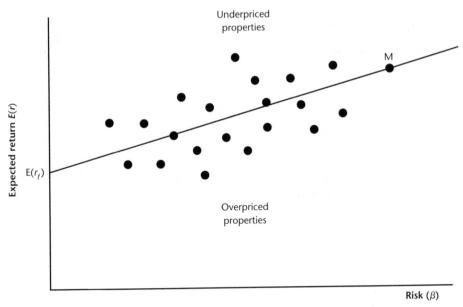

Figure 8C.1 Choosing projects using the capital asset pricing model

The CAPM can be used to identify those projects that are under- or overvalued. This is illustrated in Figure 8C.1, which relates a group of projects to their expected returns.

This shows a number of projects that lie above and below an upward-sloping line known as the *security market line (SML)*. This line represents the trade-off between risk and return for all assets. In expectations form the line is upward-sloping. In other words, you would expect to be compensated with higher returns by taking on higher levels of risk. There is, of course, a difference between what you expect and what actually happens. If, however, you know the expected return you can use this to price the asset. Whether your expectations are realised is another matter.

The CAPM is intuitively appealing. In Figure 8C.1 those projects that lie above and below the line are under- and overpriced. Those that lie on the line are correctly priced. The fact that some assets are under- and overpriced implies that there is relationship between expected return and net present value. We can show this by assuming that you invest in a project costing £100 that has an expected sales value of £115 in one year. The expected return for the project is 15%. At the time you make the investment your expectation is that over the year the return should be 15%. At the end of year 1 you will know the outcome and can compare the realised return with your expectations. The difference will tell you whether the asset was under- or overpriced when you bought it. We will consider the following three possible outcomes at the end of year 1:

A: The sales value is equal to £115
B: The sales value is equal to £120
C: The sales value is equal to £90

The results of calculating the realised return, the NPV and the abnormal return are shown in Table 8C.2.

Table 8C.2 ● Net present value and expected returns

	End Year 0	End Year 1	Expected return	Realised return	PV (S)	NPV	Abnormal return
	Cost C	Sales S	E(r)	r	at E(r)	PV(S)–C	r–E(r)
A	£100.00	£115.00	0.15	0.15	£100.00	£0.00	0.00
B	£100.00	£120.00	0.15	0.20	£104.30	£4.30	0.05
C	£100.00	£90.00	0.15	–0.10	£78.26	–£21.74	–0.05

You should note that the risk class of the asset hasn't changed, so the expected return of 15% is the correct figure to use to discount the sales value. The realised return is just the internal rate of return of the cash flows over the year. The abnormal return is the difference between what you realised and what you expected.

For case A the sales value is in line with expectations so the NPV and abnormal return are both zero. This indicates that you paid the correct price for the asset. If, however, the outcome is like case B the realised return at 20% is now in excess of what you expected. The NPV and the abnormal return are both positive, indicating that the asset was underpriced when you bought it. By contrast, case C has a negative NPV and abnormal return and indicates that the asset is overpriced. This simple example also includes the elements of performance measurement, which we cover in Part 3.

In order to make use of the CAPM for project appraisal you need to estimate the market risk, β_p, for each asset. When estimating this for financial securities it is common to have a time-series of returns so that it can be determined by regression analysis. However, for most assets a time-series of returns is unlikely. This is particularly so for a new development. This does not invalidate the use of the CAPM because you are really interested in knowing the expected risk of the asset, not what it has been in the recent past. Using regression analysis to measure market risk is usually taken as a starting point for estimating expected risk. Where there is no history of returns an alternative approach is needed.

There are two ways that this can be done. One is to use a *scenario approach* and the other is to use the *pure play approach*.

Estimating market risk using the scenario approach

The scenario approach requires an estimate of the expected outcome for both the market and a property over a defined time horizon under different economic conditions. It is probably easier to use when appraising single properties rather than complex cash flows arising from a development. It is also easier to implement over short periods as it is difficult to make reliable estimates of future outcomes when the time horizon is very long. Let's look at an example.

Example

Assume that you have a five-year investment time horizon and would consider disposing of a property if the performance within that period is not satisfactory. To simplify your analysis you identify three economic conditions that are likely to exist. These are above-average growth, average growth and below-average growth. Knowing the current purchase price for a property you forecast the value in five years' time for each of these scenarios.

The property you are thinking of buying costs £1,000,000 and generates an income stream of £50,000 p.a. The next rent review is in five years' time so that intermediate changes in income can be ignored. Using the best forecasting methods available you construct the following table:

Table 8C.3 ● Forecasting the outcome for a project over a five-year time horizon

Current value	Income p.a.	Economic conditions	Expected value in five years	IRR
£1,000,000	£50,000	Above-average growth	£3,000,000	27.99%
£1,000,000	£50,000	Average growth	£2,000,000	18.77%
£1,000,000	£50,000	Below-average growth	£1,100,000	6.75%

A probability is assigned to each outcome and a similar estimate is made for the returns on the property market over the next five years. This is shown in Table 8C.4.

Table 8C.4 ● Forecasting the outcome for the market over a five-year time horizon

Economic conditions	Prob.	Property market return r_m	Property return r_p
Above-average growth	0.30	20.00%	27.99%
Average growth	0.60	11.00%	18.77%
Below-average growth	0.10	4.00%	6.76%

Given this information you can now estimate the expected return for the property. You can also estimate the market risk by calculating the variance and covariance.

Expected returns

The expected return for the market and the property is just the weighted average of the respective outcomes.

The property market

$E(r_m)$ = (0.30 × 20.00%) + (0.60 × 11.00%) + (0.10 × 4.00%)
= 13.00%

The property

$E(r_p)$ = (0.30 × 27.99%) + (0.60 × 18.77%) + (0.10 × 6.75%)
= 20.33%

The market risk of the property

In order to estimate the market risk of the property you will need to estimate the variance of the market and the covariance between the returns on the property and the market. The background to these calculations is explained in detail in Part 3.

Variance of returns for the property market

$$Var(r_m) = E[r_m - E(r_m)]^2$$

$$= 0.30(20.00 - 13.00)^2 + 0.60(11.00 - 13.00)^2 + 0.10(4 - 13.00)^2$$

$$= 25.20\%$$

(8C.3)

Covariance of returns

$$Cov(r_p, r_m) = E\{[r_p - E(r_p)][r_m - E(r_m)]\}$$

$$= 0.30[(27.99 - 20.33)(20.00 - 13.00)]$$

$$+ 0.60[(18.77 - 20.33)(11.00 - 13.00)]$$

$$+ 0.10[(6.75 - 20.33)(4.00 - 13.00)]$$

$$= 30.19\%$$

(8C.4)

Market risk of project

Given the covariance and variance you can estimate the market risk as follows:

$$\beta_p = \frac{Cov(r_p, r_m)}{Var(r_m)}$$

(8C.5)

$$\beta_p = \frac{30.19}{25.20} = 1.198$$

The property is, therefore, assessed as being about 20% more risky than the market. The expected return over the next five years can be estimated from the security market line assuming that the five-year risk-free rate of return is 6.00% p.a.

The expected return

$$E(r_p) = r_f + \beta_p[E(r_m) - r_f]$$

(8C.6)

$$E(r_p) = 6.00 + 1.198(13.00 - 6.00)$$

$$E(r_p) = 14.39\%$$

Given the economic conditions specified, you have estimated the *ex-post* return for the property to be 20.33%. The forecast abnormal return for the property can be found by subtracting the expected return. In this case the figure is 5.94% (i.e. 20.33% − 14.39%). As this is positive it indicates that if you bought the property, it would add value to your firm by generating a positive net present value. The effect of transactions costs should also be taken into consideration to determine whether the abnormal return remains positive in the event of a sale. Note that even if the abnormal return drops to zero, the property would still earn a gross return of 14.39% p.a.

Estimating market risk using the pure play approach

This technique is more appropriate when estimating the market risk of development projects that have complex cash flows. If a quoted development company specialises in one type of property only you can make use of its published beta for estimating the market risk of similar projects.

If, however, your company decides to undertake a completely different type of development, or if it does not have a published beta, you would have to derive a project beta by using information from other companies that are experienced in the area you are moving into. These are called *pure play* companies.

The principle behind the pure play technique is to recognise that the return on the assets of a company is the weighted average of the return on debt and equity. As the beta of the company assets, β_p, are unobservable they have to be estimated from the following:

$$\beta_p = \beta_d \frac{D}{D + E} + \beta_e \frac{E}{D + E} \tag{8C.7}$$

where D and E represent the market values of debt and equity and β_d and β_e are their market risk. This equation can also be expressed in terms of weights:

$$\beta_p = \beta_d w_d + \beta_e w_e \tag{8C.8}$$

If the pure play firm pays taxes, then the proportion of debt and equity will be different from those implied in this relationship. We can take this into consideration as follows.

The tax shield available as a result of obtaining tax relief on interest payments can be written as:

$$\text{Tax shield} = D.r_d t \tag{8C.9}$$

where D is the market value of debt. If the company has perpetual debt the tax shield can be capitalised in perpetuity:

$$\text{Tax shield} = \frac{D.r_d t}{r_d} \tag{8C.10}$$

which simplifies to:

$$\text{Tax shield} = D.t \tag{8C.11}$$

You know that the value of the firm with debt $(D + E)$ must equal the value (A) of the firm without debt, plus the value of the tax shield $(D.t)$, thus:

$$D + E = A + D.t \tag{8C.12}$$

$$A = D(1 - t) + E \tag{8C.13}$$

The proportion of equity, w_e, in a firm is given by the market value of the equity divided by the value of the firm without debt. We can write this as:

$$w_e = \frac{E}{A} = \frac{E}{D(1 - t) + E} \tag{8C.14}$$

Similarly, the proportion of debt is given by:

$$w_d = \frac{D}{A} = \frac{D}{D(1-t)+E} \tag{8C.15}$$

Substituting these weights to find the project beta gives:

$$\beta_p = \beta_d \frac{D}{D(1-t)+E} + \beta_e \frac{E}{D(1-t)+E} \tag{8C.16}$$

If you also make the simplifying assumption that the beta of debt is zero, you end up with the following expression for the project beta:

$$\beta_p = \frac{\beta_e}{1+\dfrac{D}{E}(1-t)} \tag{8C.17}$$

To use this in practice you will need to find as many companies as possible that undertake the type of project that your company is interested in. This will give an average estimate for the equity beta, β_e. If you also know the average proportion of debt and equity and the tax rate you can estimate the project beta from equation 8C.17.

Example

Assume that you have found a number of suitable pure play companies and have found that the average equity beta is 1.25. Assume also that the average amount of debt and equity is £50 million and £20 million. Property companies tend to have very high levels of debt. If the average tax rate is 20% you can substitute these figures into equation 8C.17 to find the project beta:

$$\beta_p = \frac{1.25}{1+\dfrac{50}{20}(1-0.20)}$$

$$= 0.42$$

This can now be used to estimate the expected rate of return. Strictly speaking this is a single period rate of return. In a discounted cash flow framework it can be extended for use over several periods, but doing so relies on the assumption that both the term structure of interest rates and the market risk do not change. Both of these assumptions are acts of faith, but in the absence of any other economically defensible method for estimating the expected rate of return this approach is worth considering.

4. The arbitrage pricing theory (APT)

The CAPM is not the only equilibrium-pricing model that can be used to estimate the expected rate of return. One alternative is to use arbitrage pricing theory (APT). This is a more general theory than the CAPM and is based on the principle that two port-folios that have the same sensitivity to a group of factors must offer the same returns to avoid arbitrage profits. In equilibrium the expected return can be expressed as:

$$E(r_p) = r_f + \beta_{p_1}[E(r_1) - r_f] + \beta_{p_2}[E(r_2) - r_f] + \beta_{p_3}[E(r_3) - r_f] \qquad (8C.18)$$

where, in this example, the expected return is related to the sensitivity of three factors.

Although this model overcomes many of the objections to the CAPM it is likely to be difficult to use for analysing property because of the problems of estimating both the relevant factors and the sensitivity to those factors. Assuming these problems could be overcome the model would be used in the same way as the CAPM.

5. The weighted average cost of capital (WACC)

This is a traditional method for estimating the required rate of return. It takes the cost of equity and debt and combines them into a weighted average related to the market values of debt and equity. The formula for the WACC is:

$$WACC = w_d r_d (1 - t) + w_e r_e \qquad (8C.19)$$

where

w_d and w_e represent the market value weights of debt and equity
r_d = cost of debt
r_e = geared or levered cost of equity
t = corporate tax rate

The return on equity is the geared cost of equity because it reflects the fact that the firm is using debt. You can find the geared cost of equity from the capital asset pricing model.

Example

Assume that the gross interest on debt is 9.00% and that the corporate tax rate is 46%. Assume also that the β of the company is 1.35 and the risk-free rate of return is 6%.

If the expected market risk premium is 8.5% you can estimate the geared return on equity as:

$$E(r_e) = r_f + \beta_e[E(r_m) - r_f]$$

$$E(r_e) = 0.06 + 1.35(0.085)$$

$$= 0.1748 \text{ or } 17.48\%$$

In this calculation the risk-free rate of return is expressed gross of tax. The reason for this is that the firm must earn 6% after corporate taxes so that its shareholders can earn a risk-free return of 6%. Having estimated the geared return on equity, the WACC can be calculated using the market value weights. Assuming that w_e and w_d are 0.3 and 0.7, you can calculate the WACC as follows:

$$WACC = 0.3[9.00(1 - 0.46)] + 0.7(17.48)$$

$$= 13.69\%$$

Although the WACC is a commonly used approach it is based on figures derived from the firm which are not directly applicable to the analysis of an individual project.

> The weighted average cost of capital should only be used on projects that have the same financial structure as the firm.

The WACC, therefore, becomes a cut-off rate which is applied to all projects irrespective of risk. It will work, however, if the majority of projects that the firm takes on have a similar financial structure to the firm. If, however, the firm moves into a new area of development then the WACC is likely to produce misleading results.

Selected references

Brealey, R.A. and Myers, S.C. (1996) *Principles of Corporate Finance*, 5th edn. New York: McGraw-Hill.

Francis, J.C. (1986) *Investments*, 4th edn. New York: McGraw-Hill.

Francis, J.C. and Taylor, R.W. (1992) *Investments*, Schaum's Outline Series, New York: McGraw-Hill.

Jaffe, A.C. and Sirmans, C.F. (1995) *Fundamentals of Real Estate Investment*, 3rd edn. Englewood Cliffs, NJ: Prentice Hall.

Lusht, K.M. (1997) *Real Estate Valuation*, Chicago: Irwin.

Rao, R.K.S. (1987) *Financial Management*, New York: Macmillan.

Shapiro, A.C. (1991) *Modern Corporate Finance*, New York: Macmillan.

Sharpe, W.F. (1985) *Investments*, 3rd edn. Englewood Cliffs, NJ: Prentice Hall.

Appendix 8D
Allowing for risk in the cash flows

There are two ways to allow for risk when analysing the viability of a project. One is to discount the expected cash flows using a risk-adjusted expected rate of return and the other is to model risk directly in the cash flows. In this appendix we will describe how to allow for risk in the cash flows using a simulation model and also through sensitivity analysis.

Modelling risk using simulation

In each period the cash flows from a project are made up of a number of elements that have uncertain values. If you are able to model the uncertainty of each element you can use this information to provide some insight into the uncertainty surrounding the value of the project. In principle this is what is involved in a simulation. It is a computer solution in which the final outcome is generated by randomly selecting from a range of possible outcomes. This is an appealing way to handle a development or investment proposal but it is not without its problems. We can illustrate these by considering two ways in which simulation is normally undertaken.

Simulating NPVs and IRRs

Assuming that you are able to model the uncertainty in the cash flows it is possible to obtain a distribution of the NPVs. The question that arises is, what discount rate should be used? As you have taken risk into consideration in the cash flows it would be double counting to use a risk-adjusted discount rate. For this reason it is usually suggested that the distribution of NPVs should be estimated using the risk-free rate of return.

However, you still have a problem. By using the risk-free rate of return you are in effect obtaining a distribution of NPVs assuming that all the uncertainty about the cash flows is resolved between each period. As the uncertainty is not resolved in this way it is difficult to know what the distribution of NPVs actually means.

An alternative way of tackling this problem is to obtain a distribution of internal rates of return. Once this is known you can make statements about the probability that a given outcome is likely to occur. This also has the advantage that a distribution of internal rates of return is also a measure of the total risk of the project.

Simulating the expected value of the cash flows

Another way in which simulation can be used is to estimate the expected value of the periodic cash flows. The reason for doing this is because some of the component cash flows may not be estimated in terms of their expected value. Some may come from different shaped distributions. When they are combined they may well produce an expected value that differs from the sum of the estimated values. If, however, you are able to simulate the expected values you can estimate the NPV by discounting at the expected rate of return. Remember that the NPV is calculated by using a risk-adjusted discount rate. You are, therefore, discounting expected cash flows with an expected rate of return. Any further risk adjustment would be double counting. The advantage of this approach is that it leads to a single NPV figure. The decision to accept or reject the project is therefore made in an unambiguous way.

Probability statements can still be made, but in this case they are confined to the likelihood that a single cash flow will lie within a certain range. This information may be helpful for management, as it would identify those periods when the project is at its most risky.

Example

We can illustrate these two approaches by examining a simple development cash flow. Assume that you represent a company that has a quoted beta of 0.78 and a capital structure of 40% debt and 60% equity. The company is paying tax at the rate of 46% and the risk-free rate of return is taken as 6% p.a. The plan is to undertake a development that is likely to take three years to complete and has the following cash flows.

Table 8D.1 ● Project cash flows

End year	0	1	2	3
Land cost	-£4,000,000			
Sales			£5,000,000	£15,000,000
Building costs		-£3,000,000	-£7,000,000	-£1,000,000
NOTCF	-£2,200,000	-£1,650,000	-£1,100,000	£7,700,000

Note that the net of tax cash flows (NOTCF) come from the equation we used in Appendix 8B.

Before considering the simulation you can also estimate the expected rate of return on the assets of the company. (This comes from Appendix 8C.)

$$\beta_p = \frac{\beta_e}{1 + \dfrac{D}{E}(1 - t)} \tag{8D.1}$$

$$\beta_p = \frac{0.78}{1 + \dfrac{0.4}{0.6}(1 - 0.46)}$$

$$\beta_p = 0.57$$

Assuming that the market premium is 8.5% the expected return on the assets of the company is:

$$r_p = 6.00\% + 0.57(8.5\%)$$

$$r_p = 10.85\% \text{ p.a.}$$

You can now consider running a simulation on the development cash flows. In order to do this you need to describe a suitable distribution for each cash flow in the project. This is not an easy task and involves considerable skill in estimating the range within which each of the cost items lie. There is a wide range of possible distributions that can be used to help with this decision. A detailed discussion is outside the scope of this book and readers are referred to the texts that deal with this topic. For a full description of the issues involved, see Byrne (1996). We have summarised the assumptions that we used in the simulation in Table 8D.2.

The shape of the net cash flows is found by randomly selecting from the distributions in each period to arrive at a combined distribution. If you do this many times you can plot out the results on a period-by-period basis. The results of sampling from the distributions 2,000 times are shown in Figure 8D.1.

Table 8D.2 ● Distributional assumptions for cost elements

Cost item	End year	Estimated cost	Distribution	Min.	Max.	St. Dev.
Land	0	£4.0m	Triangular	£3.6m	£4.4m	
Costs	1	£3.0m	Triangular	£2.7m	£4.0m	
Sales	2	£5.0m	Normal	—	—	£0.5m
Costs	2	£7.0m	Triangular	£6.3m	£10.m	
Sales	3	£15.0m	Normal	—	–	£1.50m
Costs	3	£1.0m	Triangular	£0.9m	£1.1m	

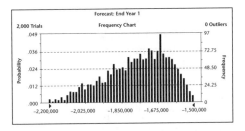

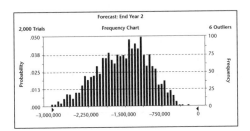

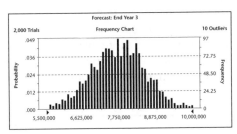

Figure 8D.1   Distribution of end year cash flows – end year 0–3

The simulations in this case were performed using an add-in to Microsoft Excel[1] called Crystal Ball. You will see that there is considerable uncertainty concerning the cash flows on a period-by-period basis. We have also assumed that the cash flows in each period are independent. This does not always happen. A change in one cost component may affect another component in a predictable way. An increase in rental values may, for example, cause an increase in capital values. These two components are, therefore, positively correlated. Other components may exhibit different degrees of correlation. With modern simulation packages this type of interrelationship is quite easy to handle.

From this simple simulation you can summarise the distribution of each end year cash flow as shown in Table 8D.3.

[1]Crystal Ball version 4.0c, Decisioneering Inc., Denver, Colorado.

Table 8D.3 ● Distribution of simulated end year cash flows

End year	Expected cash flow	Standard deviation	Coefficient of variation
0	−£2,198,445	£89,808	0.041
1	−£1,772,500	£150,058	0.085
2	−£1,538,797	£534,813	0.348
3	£7,706,516	£810,623	0.105
NPV at 10.85%	£608,668		

By adjusting for the absolute size of the cash flows the coefficient of variation shows that the greatest variability occurs at the end of the second year. This implies that the risk could be reduced if the cash flow components in this year could be assessed with greater accuracy.

Because this analysis enables you to estimate the expected value of the cash flows they can then be discounted at the expected rate of return of 10.85% to give an NPV of £608,668. As this is positive it indicates that the project is worth pursuing. You will see that the expected cash flows differ slightly from the estimated cash flows shown in Table 8D.1. Discounting these at the same rate gives an NPV of £1,069,977. However, as these are not the expected cash flows this would imply that your project is £461,309 more profitable than it actually is.

Once you have a distribution of cash flows in each year you can use this information to simulate a distribution of internal rates of return. This is shown in Figure 8D.2.

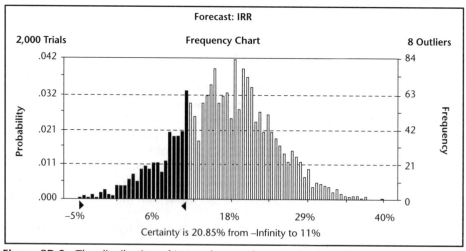

Figure 8D.2 The distribution of internal rates of return

We have once again assumed that the total cash flows in each period are independent of each other. You could make an assumption concerning the relationship
between cash flows in each period and arrive at a slightly different distribution of
returns.

The mean of this distribution is 17% with a standard deviation of 7%. With this
information it is possible to make probability statements concerning certain outcomes. For example, you have already estimated the expected rate of return to be
10.85%. Given the distribution of returns, it is possible to estimate the probability that
the actual outcome will be less than this figure. You can find the probability by using
a bit of statistical theory to calculate the distance that the expected return of 10.85%
is from the mean of the distribution. This is known as the z-value.[2]

$$P\left(z < \frac{x - \bar{x}}{\sigma}\right) \tag{8D.2}$$

$$P\left(z < \frac{10.85\% - 17\%}{7\%}\right)$$

$$P(z < -0.879)$$

By referring to tables of the areas under a normal curve you can convert the z-value
into a probability of 0.3106 or 31.06%. This represents the area under the curve from
the mean to the point of interest. As the z-value is negative this is the area to the left
of the mean. What you are interested in, however, is the area below 10.85%. You can
find this by subtracting 31.06% from 50%. This gives a probability of 18.94% that the
actual return will be less than the expected return of 10.85%. This figure has been
calculated on the assumption that the underlying distribution is normal. Using
the simulation obtained from Crystal Ball the probability can be calculated directly
from a frequency count. In this case it is slightly higher at 20.85%. This is shown in
Figure 8D.2.

As 10.85% is the expected rate of return, another way of looking at this is to
recognise that 20.85% is the probability that the NPV will be less than zero. In general
terms you can say that there is approximately 1 chance in 5 that the project will break
even with an NPV of zero. We can also use these figures to calculate the abnormal
return. This is just the difference between the mean internal rate of return and the
expected rate of return, i.e. 6.15% (17% − 10.85%).

It is not unusual to find that investors would want to exceed the expected rate of
return by a margin to compensate for additional risks. This provides a hurdle rate for
accepting a project that can also be incorporated into a probability statement. If you
assume a margin of 3% over the expected return we can estimate the probability that
the actual return will be less than the expected return plus 3%. In this case the figure
is 34.50%, or approximately 1 chance in 3.

[2] Chapter 17 contains a review of some basic statistical ideas.

Modelling risk using sensitivity analysis

Because the cash flows in each period are built up from other cash flows it is often useful to know how sensitive the NPV is likely to be if each of the components changes. The reason for doing this is to isolate those factors that are likely to have the greatest impact on NPV. This can cut down the amount of time involved in a simulation analysis by identifying those factors that are likely to contribute most to risk.

We can illustrate the most common method of sensitivity analysis by using the figures from the above example. All the cash flows in the example have been estimated on the basis of being their most likely value. Our example has only three cash flow elements, i.e. the land cost, sales values and construction costs. A full analysis would, of course, have many more cost elements. You can examine the effect on the NPV by changing, in turn, each of the elements by ±10% while leaving the others at their most likely value. A summary of the results is given in Table 8D.4, after discounting at the expected rate of return of 10.85%.

Table 8D.4 ● Sensitivity of project to 10% change in cost elements

Cost element	NPV with 10% increase	NPV with 10% decrease
Land cost	£849,360	£1,289,360
Sales	£1,898,849	£2,398,874
Building costs	£566,810	£1,571,910

The NPV calculated by discounting the most likely values is £1,069,360. It should be noted, however, that the net present value rule requires the *expected values* not the *most likely* values to be discounted. You will see from the simulation given above that there is a considerable difference in NPV.

The sensitivity analysis assumes that all the values will increase or decrease by 10%. Although this makes the calculations easy, it is however likely to be unrealistic in the majority of cases. A 10% increase in sales values may not be comparable with a 10% increase in construction costs. An alternative way of handling this is to express each of the cost components in terms of their most optimistic and pessimistic values. Once this has been done, the effect on the NPV can be estimated by taking, in turn, the most optimistic and pessimistic value for each component while keeping all other components fixed at their most likely value. The difference in NPVs will indicate the cost components that are likely to have the greatest impact on risk. The results of this approach are summarised in Table 8D.5.

This analysis shows the factor that contributes most to the risk of the project is the sales value. In fact, it has a significantly greater effect than changes in the building cost and shows that this element needs the most refinement. Changing

Table 8D.5 ● **Analysing the sensitivity of each cost component**

Cost element	Most optimistic NPV	Most pessimistic NPV	Difference in NPVs
Land cost	£1,289,360	£849,360	£440,000
Sales	£3,557,817	−£1,419,097	£4,976,914
Building costs	£1,571,910	£809,989	£2,381,899

We have calculated the most optimistic and pessimistic values from the data used in the simulations. For those variables that have assumed a normal distribution we have used three standard deviations as representing the optimistic and pessimistic bounds.

each of the elements by fixed amounts does not have the same impact on the final outcome.

Although this approach requires more information it provides more useful results. In addition, most of the information required for estimating the most optimistic and pessimistic values is also needed to run the simulation analysis.

Selected references

Byrne, P. (1996) *Risk, Uncertainty and Decision-making in Property Development*, London: E. & F.N. Spon.

Hertz, D.B. (1964) Risk analysis in capital investment. *Harvard Business Review* **42** (1), 95–106.

Hertz, D.B. and Thomas, H. (1983) *Risk Analysis and its Applications*, Chichester: John Wiley & Sons.

Hertz, D.B. and Thomas, H. (1984) *Practical Risk Analysis: An Approach through Case Histories*, Chichester: John Wiley & Sons.

Hillier, F.S. (1963) The derivation of probabilistic information for the evaluation of risky investments. *Management Science* **9** (3), 443–57.

Hillier, F.S. (1965) Supplement to the derivation of probabilistic information for the evaluation of risky investments. *Management Science* **11** (3), 485–7.

Phyrr, S.A. (1973) A computer simulation model to measure the risk in real estate investment. *AREUEA Journal* **1** (1), 48–78.

Wagle, B. (1967) A statistical analysis of risk in capital investment projects. *Operational Research Quarterly* **18** (1), 13–33.

Appendix 8E
The adjusted present value and residual equity income approach

Although it is usual for companies to borrow in order to finance a series of ongoing projects, it is not unusual for funding arrangements to be tied to specific projects. This could happen if a small developer carries out one project at a time. Funding

Table 8E.1 ● Project and company details

Project details	
Gross building area	75,000 sq. ft
Net to gross ratio	0.85
Net lettable area	63,750 sq. ft
Vacancy rate	0.05 p.a.
Building cost (including all fees)	£125 per sq. ft
Total building cost	£9,375,000
Land cost	£6,000,000
Valuation details	
Rental value	£20 per sq. ft
Annual rent	£1,275,000 p.a.
Growth rate in income	0.04 p.a.
Initial cap rate	0.065
Cap rate on sale	0.075
Financial details	
Company tax rate	0.450
Riskless return	0.060
Borrowing rate	0.090
Equity market risk premium	0.085

arrangements in this case will generally be more expensive than through corporate borrowing where the risk of a portfolio of projects will be less than the risk of a single project.

In Appendix 8C we showed how to allow for the effect of borrowing and taxation in estimating a weighted average cost of capital. In this appendix we will examine how taxation and borrowing can be taken into consideration in the cash flows. We will examine the results of two methods of analysis: the *Adjusted Present Value (APV)* and the *Residual Equity Income (REI)* approaches. We will illustrate these approaches using a simple project.

You are contemplating the construction of a 75,000 sq. ft office building. The intention is to hold it for ten years and then sell it on. We have summarised the main items of the project and your company in Table 8E.1.

Your company uses the capital value of the project as collateral for a loan. At a yield of 6.5% the initial rental of £1,275,000 has a value of £19,615,385. You approach a lending institution with a view to borrowing enough money to fund both the land and construction costs of £15,375,000. The institution considers that this is a risky venture but because of your track record they are prepared to offer you a maximum loan of 50% of the capital value, i.e. £9,807,692. This is to be repaid by a mortgage over a ten-year period. The remainder has to be provided from your own resources. The financial structure of your project is, therefore, as follows:

Table 8E.2 ● The financial structure of the project

Collateral project value		£19,615,385
Land value	£6,000,000	
Construction value	£9,375,000	
Total		£15,375,000

Funding arrangement		Weight
Amount borrowed (50% collateral value)	£9,807,692	64%
Equity to be provided by developer	£5,567,308	36%
Total	£15,375,000	100%

Given that this is the type of package you will be offered, you have to decide whether the project is profitable. You can analyse this in two ways.

The adjusted present value (APV)

The adjusted present value approach assumes that a project has two sources of value, i.e. the project and the tax side-effects. By valuing these elements separately it is possible to arrive at an adjusted present value. This is just the sum of two present values.

Adjusted present value = Present value of project when wholly equity financed + Present value of tax side-effects

The method of calculation is in four steps.

Step 1. Estimate the project rate of return

This is the rate of return assuming that your project is financed with 100% equity. In order to estimate this you need to work out the beta for the project. We described how to do this in Appendix 8C. If your company is well established and is listed on the stock market, then it will probably have a published beta. If not, then you will have to use the pure play approach. Let us assume that the traded equity of your company has a beta of 1.35. This, however, is not the project beta. You know the split of debt and equity and the tax rate so you can estimate the project beta as follows:

$$\beta_p = \frac{\beta_e}{1 + \dfrac{D}{E}(1-t)} \tag{8E.1}$$

$$\beta_p = \frac{1.35}{1 + \dfrac{0.64}{0.36}(1-0.45)}$$

$$\beta_p = 0.69$$

This is the average beta for the projects undertaken by your firm. At this stage you could make an adjustment to the beta if you think that your project is significantly different to those generally undertaken by your firm. We will leave it at 0.69. Using the CAPM and assuming that the average equity risk premium for the market is 8.5% you can estimate the expected return for the project as:

$$E(r_p) = 0.06 + 0.69(0.085)$$

$$E(r_p) = 0.1187, \text{ i.e. } 11.87\%$$

This provides a measure of the expected return for the project. You can now use this to estimate the NPV assuming that it is financed solely with equity. This is step 2.

Step 2. Estimate the base case NPV assuming project is wholly equity financed

The cash flows for the project are summarised in Table 8E.3.

Table 8E.3 ● Project equity cash flows

End year	0	1	2	3	4	5	6	7	8	9	10
Income			£1,275,000	£1,275,000	£1,275,000	£1,275,000	£1,275,000	£1,551,232	£1,551,232	£1,551,232	£1,551,232
Vacancies			-£63,750	-£63,750	-£63,750	-£63,750	-£63,750	-£77,562	-£77,562	-£77,562	-£77,562
Land costs	-£6,000,000										
Building costs		-£9,375,000									
Running costs				-£250,000			-£250,000			-£250,000	
Sales value											£20,683,099
Net of tax cash flow	-£3,300,000	-£5,156,250	£666,188	£528,688	£666,188	£666,188	£528,688	£810,519	£810,519	£673,019	£12,186,224

Discounting the net cash flows at 11.87% gives a base case NPV of -£990,417. On this basis the project is not profitable. However, this is not the end of the story. You need to consider the tax relief that you would get on the interest you are paying on the loan. This is covered in step 3.

Step 3. Estimate the present value of the tax shield

We have assumed in this example that you repay the loan using a ten-year mortgage at 9% p.a. By setting up a mortgage repayment table you can discount the tax shield in each period at 9%. You should not use the expected return of 11.87% because the repayments do not carry the same risk as the project. The general principle is that the discount rate you use should reflect the risk of the cash flows. Table 8E.4 summarises the present value of the tax shield.

Table 8E.4 ● Estimating the present value of the tax shield

Year	Opening balance	Repayment	Interest at 9% p.a.	Capital repayment	Closing balance	Tax shield at 45%	PV tax shield
1	£9,807,692	£1,528,235	£882,692	£645,543	£9,162,149	£397,212	£364,414
2	£9,162,149	£1,528,235	£824,593	£703,642	£8,458,507	£371,067	£312,320
3	£8,458,507	£1,528,235	£761,266	£766,970	£7,691,537	£342,570	£264,527
4	£7,691,537	£1,528,235	£692,238	£835,997	£6,855,540	£311,507	£220,680
5	£6,855,540	£1,528,235	£616,999	£911,237	£5,944,303	£277,649	£180,453
6	£5,944,303	£1,528,235	£534,987	£993,248	£4,951,055	£240,744	£143,548
7	£4,951,055	£1,528,235	£445,595	£1,082,641	£3,868,414	£200,518	£109,690
8	£3,868,414	£1,528,235	£348,157	£1,180,078	£2,688,336	£156,671	£78,628
9	£2,688,336	£1,528,235	£241,950	£1,286,285	£1,402,051	£108,878	£50,130
10	£1,402,051	£1,528,235	£126,185	£1,402,051	£0	£56,783	£23,986

PV £1,748,375

The present value of the tax shield in this case is £1,748,375. You will see that this is larger than the base case NPV. The effect that this has on the overall profitability of your project is covered in step 4.

Step 4. Estimate the APV

You can calculate the APV by adding the base case NPV to the present value of the tax shields:

APV = –£990,417 + £1,748,375

APV = £757,958

Your project is now profitable, but only because you have been able to take advantage of the tax shields. If this project was being undertaken by a non-tax paying organisation the APV would be –£322,005 assuming everything else remained unchanged. This clearly shows that the tax status of the developer can have an important influence on profitability. For example, a project may be unprofitable from the point of view of a non-tax paying institution, but the same project may be profitable for a tax-paying developer.

The adjusted present value separates project viability from the present value of the tax shields. If the level of borrowing is high the tax shields could contribute a lot to project profitability. However, tax shields are only available if a firm is in a tax-paying situation.

As the tax position could easily change it may not be wise to make investment decisions on projects where most, if not all, of the profitability comes from the tax shields. We have also assumed that the loan is repaid using a mortgage. The APV can, however, handle a wide range of repayment options. It can also handle periods when the firm is in a non-tax paying situation so that it is a very flexible way of analysing projects.

The APV, therefore, shows where the profitability is coming from. Other methods of analysis are generally not able to do this.

The residual equity income (REI)

The main feature of the APV is that it analyses the debt and equity parts of a project separately. However, developers often incorporate the debt payments as part of the cash flow and then analyse the residual equity cash flow. There are fewer steps involved in this process but the choice of discount rate is not so obvious.

The cash flows are the same as the APV but the loan repayment schedule is also included. There are three steps involved in calculating the REI.

Step 1. Estimate the residual equity cash flow

This is shown in Table 8E.5 after including the loan repayment schedule taken from the mortgage calculations given in Table 8E.4.

Table 8E.5 ● Cash flow for residual equity income

End year	0	1	2	3	4	5	6	7	8	9	10
Income			£1,275,000	£1,275,000	£1,275,000	£1,275,000	£1,275,000	£1,551,232	£1,551,232	£1,551,232	£1,551,232
Vacancies			-£63,750	-£63,750	-£63,750	-£63,750	-£63,750	-£77,562	-£77,562	-£77,562	-£77,562
Land costs	-£6,000,000										
Building costs		-£9,375,000									
Running costs				-£250,000			-£250,000			-£250,000	
Sales value											£20,683,099
Net of tax cash flow	-£3,300,000	-£5,156,250	£666,188	£528,688	£666,188	£666,188	£528,688	£810,519	£810,519	£673,019	£12,186,224
Loan repayment	£9,807,692	-£645,543	-£703,642	-£766,970	-£835,997	-£911,237	-£993,248	-£1,082,641	-£1,180,078	-£1,286,285	-£1,402,051
Interest at 9%		-£882,692	-£824,593	-£761,266	-£692,238	-£616,999	-£534,987	-£445,595	-£348,157	-£241,950	-£126,185
Tax benefits at 45%		£397,212	£371,067	£342,570	£311,507	£277,649	£240,744	£200,518	£156,671	£108,878	£56,783
Residual equity	£6,507,692	-£6,287,274	-£490,981	-£656,978	-£550,541	-£584,399	-£758,804	-£517,199	-£561,046	-£746,339	£10,714,771

The bottom line is the cash flow after taking account of the debt repayments and the tax relief on the debt. This raises an important question as to how to discount the residual equity. This is covered in step 2.

Step 2. Estimate the present value of the residual equity income

You have estimated the residual equity income stream and need to find its present value. The question that remains, however, is: what rate should be used?

As you have included the debt repayment as part of the cash flow the residual equity income stream is now a geared cash flow and should be discounted at the geared rate of return. This is easily found because you know that the quoted beta of your geared company is 1.35 so you can use this to find the required return:

$$E(r_e) = 0.06 + 1.35(0.085)$$

$$E(r_e) = 0.1748, \text{ i.e. } 17.48\%$$

Discounting the residual equity income stream at 17.48% p.a. gives an NPV of £1,198,900.

Conclusions

You will see from a comparison of the APV and REI approaches that it is possible to arrive at different answers using different methods of analysis. It is also possible to arrive at the same answers, but this only occurs under fairly restrictive conditions concerning the way the debt capacity of the firm is estimated. The choice of method depends on what data are available. The residual equity income approach is, however, open to misuse because the correct discount rate is frequently not used. For example, the borrowing rate is often used to discount the cash flows.

The adjusted present value approach does require more work to set up, but you will see that it does more than just separate the present value of the project from the tax side-effects. Where it has particular value is in its ability to deal with complex tax payments. A development company may move in and out of a tax-paying position and may have tax credits from previous periods. The weighted average cost of capital approach uses a single discount rate that cannot take account of changes in the tax-paying status of the developer. Similarly, the residual equity income approach is unable to deal with this type of problem.

Selected references

Brealey, R.A. and Myers, S.C. (1996) *Principles of Corporate Finance*, 5th edn. New York: McGraw-Hill.

Franks, J., Broyles, J.E. and Carleton, W.T. (1985) *Corporate Finance: Concepts and Applications*, California: Kent Publishing Company.

Locke, S.M. (1990) Property investment analysis using adjusted present values. *Appraisal Journal* (July), 373–8.

Tirtiroglu, D. (1997) Valuation of real estate assets using the adjusted present value method. *Journal of Property Finance* **8** (1), 7–23.

Appendix 8F
Development finance: sources and techniques

In Chapter 8 we pointed out that the way a project is financed is not important to the investment decision unless there are valuable tax side-effects. Good investment decisions are, therefore, better than good financing decisions. You should avoid gearing up the returns on a project unless you believe that the forecast return will exceed the expected return. If you introduce borrowing into this equation, the rate of interest you pay, as a developer, will depend on the proportion of risk that you take on. At one extreme a funding institution might provide all the finance for the project, but in return would expect to receive the full development return. At the other extreme the developer might provide the majority of the equity finance and the institution would then provide a small proportion of debt. In this case the institution would charge normal lending rates.

You will see from this brief discussion that the relationship between developer and lender is all to do with risk-sharing. As many funding arrangements can be quite complex it is useful to bear this idea in mind.

> As the funding arrangement for many projects can be very complex it is useful to bear in mind that the relationship between developer and lender is all to do with risk-sharing. This defines the role that each takes on and the rewards that they can earn.

Access to finance is, of course, essential, as it is an important part of bringing a project to fruition. This appendix briefly reviews the sources of finance that are available and the types of financing techniques that are used. We will also show you how the risks are shared.

Sources of finance

There are two sources of finance generally available: debt or equity. Debt finance can come from a number of different sources and will include the following:

● the main clearing banks
● overseas banks
● merchant banks
● insurance companies
● pension funds
● finance houses
● building societies

The motivation for becoming involved in development will differ for each of these organisations. They will also have different attitudes to risk and this will influence both the degree of involvement and the type of project they would be prepared to finance.

Insurance companies and pension funds

For example, insurance companies and pension funds occasionally allocate a proportion of their resources to property development as well as investment. However, they are usually risk-averse as they have a long-term liability to provide pensions and will almost certainly minimise their exposure by funding only prime opportunities in which a high proportion of space has been pre-let.

Bank funding

When property is performing well banks are often keen to provide development finance. In the past they have done this even though some of the investment decisions were probably poor. We have pointed out that gearing up the returns on an investment only makes sense if the forecast returns exceed the expected returns. Failure to separate the investment decision from the financing decision and the prospect of earning commission on new loans may well have been a contributory factor. Many banks, therefore, suffered badly when property markets around the world collapsed. As a result of these experiences banks have become more risk-averse. High street banks, for example, favour projects that are pre-let and will lend up to 60% of the development costs only.

Other banks are prepared to take on a greater proportion of risk and will fund speculative developments, but only if they have their own in-house expertise in property. They will nevertheless still aim to minimise their exposure by lending over short periods and imposing severe penalties.

Equity investors

Equity investment is usually provided in terms of cash by the developer or an individual. Some banks or financial institutions may be prepared to invest their own equity but would clearly wish to minimise their risk exposure. Landowners may also use the value of their land as equity. This form of finance carries the greatest risk. It can also offer high returns unless the development becomes unprofitable. In this case the equity investors will run the risk of losing most of their funds.

Other lending institutions adopt a similar approach.

Financing techniques

There are many different financing arrangements available for development projects. In fact, it is probably fair to say that the ready supply of capital during the 1980s contributed to the severity of the subsequent property crash. We will outline a few of the techniques that are used and show how the development risk can shift. The methods we shall include are:

● forward funding
● forward commitment
● project finance

Forward funding

In this arrangement the financial institution provides all the funding for the project and takes on both the development and leasing risk. To compensate for this risk the final value is discounted by capitalising the income stream at a yield that is 1% above comparable investment properties. The developer in this case is paid only a management fee but has the possibility of sharing in the profits of the development above its discounted value, if it is successful.

The value to the institution is that it provides an opportunity to offer shareholders high returns. The risk, however, has clearly shifted to the funding institution. Although the institution may not have any in-house development expertise it is able to acquire this by paying the developer a project management fee. The developer does bear some of the risk, but only in the development profit.

Forward commitment

Some institutions do not want to be involved in development but are happy to enter into a forward commitment to buy the completed project, which it then has to let. The developer becomes responsible for financing the project and will probably do this by borrowing from a commercial bank. The advantage of this arrangement to the developer is that the bank will lend against the forward commitment.

You will see from this arrangement that the institution takes none of the development risk, but all of the leasing risk. Some of this may, however, be offset during the construction period. The development risk is now split between the developer and the commercial bank.

Project finance

Although many larger developers will draw on a pool of funds to finance a series of ongoing projects it is not unusual for funding to be tied to a specific project. This is known as project financing. It is often organised for large projects and many involve a group of banks. They will generally lend between 60% and 80% of the project cost, which is then secured by taking out a first charge against the project. The developer provides the remaining equity. In this arrangement the whole of the developer's equity is exposed to the risk of the property market. If the project is successful the developer is able to take all the profit. The bank, by contrast, will not share in the development profit but will be exposed to the risk of default of the developer.

Project finance is often used to fund large developments and sometimes involves a consortium of banks. The development of the Channel Tunnel is an example of where this type of finance has been used.

Although this list is not exhaustive it should give you an idea of some of the main issues involved, particularly the way risk is shared between different parties.

Selected references

Calatchi, R.F. and Rosenberg, S.B. (1992) *Property Finance: An International Perspective*, London: Euromoney Books.

Finnerty, J.D. (1996) *Project Financing: Asset-based Financial Engineering*, Wiley Frontiers in Finance, New York: John Wiley & Sons.

Isaac, D. (1996) *Property Development Appraisal and Finance*, London: Macmillan.

Appendix 8G
Options to invest

In our discussion on appraising investments we arrived at the conclusion that net present value is the sensible decision rule to follow if your intention is to maximise shareholder wealth. This model is, however, widely used on the assumption that it is an all-or-nothing approach to investment. You either accept a project because it is profitable or you reject it if it is unprofitable. If you are not able to proceed with a project it is assumed to disappear.

At first sight this seems quite sensible. However, there is a qualification that needs to be added. Accepting a project should only be made as long as it doesn't prevent you from taking on some other competing project. When you add this caveat the whole role of decision-making suddenly changes. Let's look at what this means in practice.

Assume you are a developer faced with the prospect of redeveloping a site. You undertake an analysis based on the best estimates you have today and arrive at a net present value that is just positive. As an alternative you may have used these estimates to decide how much to bid for a site. If you are successful your company will, however, hardly show any increase in value. This may seem disappointing but buying the site conveys more than just the opportunity to undertake a one-off investment. As a developer you are buying the rights to the investment. One such right would be the opportunity to delay construction. Depending on how long you are prepared to wait then a number of opportunities present themselves:

- Rental values might increase more than you had anticipated so the capital value of the project increases.
- Alternative uses for the site may be possible at some point in the future that would significantly increase the value.
- Interest rates may change so that the project looks more favourable.

Each of these can be considered as a call option. If you look at the net present value rule again you will see that if you were to undertake a development today this would imply that you were not exercising your option to take on competing opportunities in the future. Every project, therefore, competes with itself, delayed in time.

From this simple example you will see that every project consists of two types of option. One is concerned with changes to the nature of the project brought about by future events. This would include such aspects as changes in planning legislation, which would give life to previously infeasible projects. The additional investment required to take on the new project may be regarded as the exercise price of a real option. These are embedded options that confer additional net present value to your firm. The second type of option concerns all projects and arises through changes in interest rates. Not every project contains real options but every project will, however, contain an option on the change in interest rates.

What is important about considering projects in an options framework is that the greater the uncertainty concerning future events the greater the value of the option. You can also look at these issues within a valuation framework. The value of a building is just the present value of its expected future cash flows. The valuation models we have described have all assumed that the interest rate used is constant over time. If, however, there is a lot of uncertainty in interest rates, then this will confer additional present value. The building may also have embedded options that are related to future development opportunities. A more general expression of value should take these additional aspects into consideration. The presence of options therefore enhances the value of a project as follows:

$$\text{Valuation} = \frac{\text{Present}}{\text{value}} + \frac{\text{Value of}}{\text{real option}} + \frac{\text{Value of}}{\text{interest rate}} \atop \text{option}$$

Valuing real options

Valuing real options is not something that can easily be done using the Black-Scholes option-pricing model. This was developed for pricing financial securities and assumes a finite life for the option. The valuation of real options relies more on the use of decision trees. We can illustrate some of the principles involved using a very simple example.

Let us assume that you are involved in a project that could be let to a number of tenants producing a total annual rental income of £50,000. The construction costs amount to £750,000 so the viability of the project could be assessed as shown in Table 8G.1.

As the net present value is positive it is worth commencing development now as acceptance of the project would represent an increase in the current value of the company.

However, as an alternative, let us assume that there is a possibility that if you delayed construction for a year you could let the project to a major client at £60,000 p.a. This outcome is not guaranteed, so you place a probability of 50% on its happening. Letting it at the lower rental of £50,000 would still be feasible but under this scenario it too has a probability of 50%.

Table 8G.1 ● Value of project if commenced today

End year 0	
Project income	£50,000
Capital value at 5%	£1,000,000
Project cost	£750,000
NPV end year 1	**£250,000**

You are now faced with an option. Either build today and secure a known rental stream, or delay for one year and face an uncertain income stream. The choice will depend on whether the present value of the option to wait exceeds the current present value. You can analyse this as follows. In one year you will have the following:

Table 8G.2 ● Valuing the option to delay development

End year 1	
Project income	£55,000
(£60,000 × 0.5) + (£50,000 × 0.5)	
Capital value at 5%	£1,100,000
Project cost	£750,000
NPV end year 1	**£350,000**

As this is a risky option you can discount the outcome at 20% to give a present value of £292,000. This now exceeds the present value of building today so it would appear to be worthwhile waiting as the value of the option increases the current value of your firm.

This is just one example in which the option to delay development can create value. The renewal of a lease can also be considered as an option and this is an area that has already attracted a lot of interest. There are many others and this area of research is likely to grow in the future.

Selected references

Black, F. and Scholes, M. (1972) The pricing of options and corporate liabilities. *Journal of Political Economy* **81** (637), 659.

Cox, S., Ross, S.A. and Rubinstein, M. (1979) Option pricing: a simplified approach. *Journal of Financial Economics* **9** (September), 229–63.

Grenadier, S.R. (1995) The valuation of leasing contracts: a real options approach. *Journal of Financial Economics* **38**, 297–331.

Margrabe, W. (1978) The value of an option to exchange one asset for another. *Journal of Finance* **33** (March), 177–86.

Quigg, L. (1993) Empirical testing of real option-pricing models. *Journal of Finance* **XLVIII** (2), 621–40.

Rendleman, R. and Bartter, B. (1979) Two state option pricing. *Journal of Finance* **34** (December), 1093–110.

Van Horne, J. (1995) *Financial management and policy*, 10th edn. Englewood Cliffs, NJ: Prentice Hall International.

PART 2

Risk and return in real estate

CHAPTER *9*

Distributional characteristics of real estate returns

Learning objectives

After reading this chapter you will understand the following:

- The principal measures used to describe distributions

- The distributional characteristics of individual properties and portfolios

- How correlated property returns are with each other

- How correlated property returns are across sectors

- How correlated property returns are with other assets

- The effect of different measurement periods on the return statistics

The material in this chapter provides the key components to understanding diversification in property.

Introduction

Despite the institutional interest in commercial property, surprisingly little is known about the distributional characteristics of individual property returns. Studies in this area have been considerably hampered by the lack of reliable data. Nevertheless, an understanding of the distributional characteristics of property returns is important because it plays a key role in making investment decisions.

In this chapter we will look at the distributional characteristics of returns observed on a group of properties. Using real property information gives a clearer idea of the investment characteristics of property and enables us to relate property to other asset classes. We can, therefore, establish a framework which we will later use to develop portfolio models and examine issues such as investment strategy and performance measurement. Our concern is with rates of return measured at both the individual property and index levels as well as with different reporting periods. You will see that the distributional characteristics differ with different reporting periods so that it is important to understand how these will influence investment decisions.

In comparison with the equities market our knowledge of the distributional characteristics of property is still relatively limited. This has been the result of confidentiality and insufficient data. This position is gradually changing. Good quality data are now more readily available and our understanding of this sector is improving. There is still, however, a long way to go.

Rates of return

The *rate of return* is one of the key investment performance measures used in both financial economics and investment decision-making. There are a number of reasons why the rate of return is used:

1. It is a scale-free measure which does not depend on the size of the investment. Assume, for example, that you invested £100 and £1,000 in two separate bank accounts and at the end of the year they increased to £106 and £1,060. Both investments would have earned an identical rate of return of 6%. The size of the return is not influenced by the size of the investment.
2. Many financial models are framed in terms of the rate of return. In Chapter 10 we introduce the capital asset pricing model (CAPM) and arbitrage pricing theory (APT). Both of these are economic models that have been developed for explaining expected returns. The net present value (NPV) and discounted cash flow (DCF) framework we discussed in Part 1 both rely on understanding and using rates of return.
3. The investment characteristics of an asset can be described in terms of the statistical distribution of its returns.

At its simplest level the total return over a given holding period can be estimated from a present value calculation, as follows:

$$P_0 = \frac{P_1 + a_1}{(1 + r)} \qquad (9.1)$$

where P_0 is the price at the end of period 0, and P_1 is the price at the end of period 1. The income received during the holding period is given by a_1 and the return is represented by r. By rearranging, the holding period return can be expressed as:

$$r = \frac{P_1 - P_0 + a_1}{P_0} \qquad (9.2)$$

This works over any holding period.

Assume, for example, you bought a property costing £125,000, which you then sold for £130,000 three months later. Over the three-month period you also received £1,800 in rent. You would calculate the return you earned as follows:

$$r = \frac{£130,000 - £125,000 + £1,800}{£125,000}$$

$r = 0.0544$ or 5.44% per quarter

Note that this is a quarterly return because all the figures relate to the three-month holding period. You could, of course, convert this to its annual equivalent as follows:

$r_{ann} = (1 + 0.0544)^4 - 1$

$r_{ann} = 0.236$ or 23.6% p.a.

In this example we have used prices. In most real estate cases, however, you would have to use valuations because property does not trade frequently enough to generate a regular time series of prices. This is the approach you should use when estimating the returns for individual properties. At the index level, however, the calculation becomes more complex. We discuss this more fully in Chapter 16, where we cover performance measurement.

To get a clearer idea of the characteristics of property returns observed in the market we have based our analysis on a sample of properties, taken from institutional property portfolios.

Sample data

Our main interest in this chapter is in looking at the distributional characteristics of returns for both individual properties and portfolios. Our results are based on a sample of properties drawn at random from the Investment Property Databank (IPD) monthly database and cover two non-overlapping periods:

December 1987 to November 1992, and
December 1992 to November 1997.

Monthly rates of return and capital growth rates for individual properties were provided by IPD. Given the strict data confidentiality constraints that bind IPD, the only other disclosed information about the properties was their broad use classification of retail, office and industrial. The dataset consists of 40 retail, 30 office and 30 industrial properties. We will use this sample in various ways throughout the remainder of the book. For example, in Chapter 11 we will examine the effectiveness of constructing property portfolios. In Chapter 12 we will look at smoothing issues. As this is such an important dataset we first examine how the sample compares with the full IPD monthly index.

The data are split into two sub-periods, 1987–92 and 1992–97. As these cover different phases of the market we have analysed them separately.

Comparison of sample with the IPD Index, 1987–92

The first stage of our analysis combines the sample returns for each sector into separate indexes and then compares the returns with the IPD Index sector profiles.

Figures 9.1a–d show the profiles of total rates of return for each of the sample sectors compared with their IPD counterpart over the period December 1987 to November 1992. Also shown is an equally weighted index consisting of all the properties in the sample compared with the IPD All Property Index.

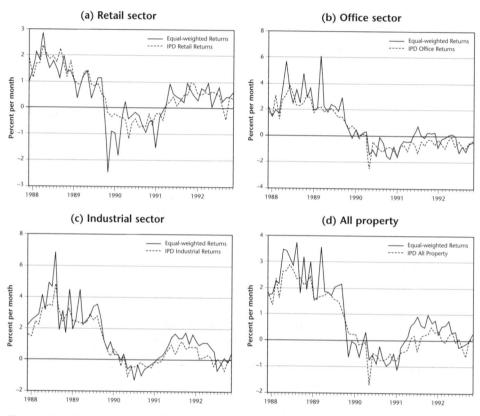

Figure 9.1a–d Comparison of sample and IPD returns, 1987–92

Each of the sample sectors appears to track its IPD counterpart well. The strength of the association between the dataset and the corresponding IPD sector can be quantified by looking at the coefficient of correlation. These are shown in Table 9.1.

Table 9.1 ● Correlation between sample and IPD sector returns, 1987–92

Sample sector	Number of properties	Correlation with corresponding IPD sector
Retail	40	0.83
Office	30	0.88
Industrial	30	0.92
All Property	100	0.92

The high correlations imply a strong association between the sample and the much larger IPD Index.

Comparison of sample with the IPD Index, 1992–97

The equivalent details for the period December 1992 to November 1997 are shown in Figures 9.2a–d. The corresponding correlation coefficients are shown in Table 9.2.

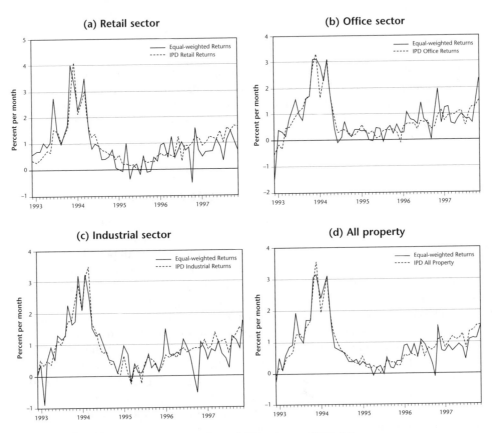

Figure 9.2a–d Comparison of sample and IPD returns, 1992–97

Once again, the correlation measures confirm the high degree of association between the constructed sample portfolios and the IPD sectors. The figures in the second period are marginally higher than the first period.

At the aggregate level, therefore, the sample of data appears to reflect the broad behaviour of the IPD sector indices. This gives us some confidence that our results are likely to be fairly representative of the behaviour of the wider UK real estate investment market.

Table 9.2 ● Correlation profiles, 1992–97

Sample sector	Number of properties	Correlation with corresponding IPD sector
Retail	40	0.84
Office	30	0.87
Industrial	30	0.85
All Property	100	0.93

In both sub-periods the sample rates of return are highly correlated with their equivalent IPD sector. The sample data, therefore, track the broad pattern of market movements reported by the IPD Monthly Index over the ten-year period. The data can, therefore, be regarded as being representative of the types of properties found in the IPD Monthly Index.

The distributional characteristics of real estate returns

A common assumption underlying much financial theory is that rates of return are independent, follow a normal distribution and have constant variance. This last assumption implies that the variation in returns is the same in all periods. In Chapter 10 we introduce the Markowitz approach to portfolio construction. This, however, is based on a constant mean-variance assumption. These two parameters are also known as the first and second moments of a distribution. Despite the assumption that they should be constant the returns in other investment markets, such as equities, suggest that non-normality is more likely to exist in the short term rather than the long term.

Many studies of equity performance have found that a normal distribution does not adequately describe individual stock returns. The distributions of returns often have what is known as 'fat tails' and are more peaked than would be expected with a normal distribution. It is useful, therefore, to investigate how property returns compare with a normal distribution. In Appendix 9B we describe some of the measures commonly used in analysing distributions. The two frequently used measures are skewness and kurtosis.

Skewness

This can be described as the degree of asymmetry of a distribution around its mean. Positive skewness indicates a distribution with an asymmetric tail extending towards more positive values. Conversely, negative skewness indicates a distribution with an asymmetric tail extending towards more negative values. A symmetrical distribution will have a skewness value of zero. Figures 9.3a and b illustrate positively and negatively skewed distributions.

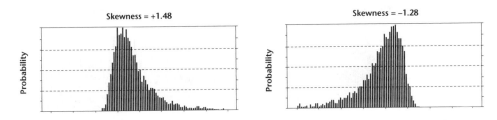

Figure 9.3a and b Positively and negatively skewed distributions

The shape of a distribution of returns can vary as market conditions change. A dramatic example of this occurred when the equity markets suffered a major adjustment after the stock market crash in October 1987. This caused returns to be negatively skewed. One explanation for this is that equity prices fall in value at a greater speed than they increase. It should be noted that if skewness is a feature of the data, an interesting question is whether or not it is priced.

Kurtosis

A second distributional characteristic is referred to as kurtosis. This characterises how peaked or flat is a distribution. When measured relative to a normal distribution a kurtosis value in excess of 3 imply that the distribution is more peaked than normal with fat tails. Kurtosis values less than 3 indicate a relatively flat distribution with narrow tails. The returns on many financial assets exhibit positive kurtosis. An intuitive explanation for its existence is that prices or returns stay relatively close to their average value, with a higher frequency than would be expected under a normal distribution. Positive kurtosis implies that the probabilities of obtaining extreme values are higher than predicted by a normal distribution. This would seem to reflect the reality of the marketplace when large market surprises may tend to induce large movements in markets and in property values. On the other hand, when there is relatively little news there may be little market activity with the result that there is little change in price. In other words, the experience is likely to be one of significant market movement or little or no movement. High kurtosis, therefore, implies a greater probability of market extremes, both for jumps in value and for crashes. Figures 9.4a and b illustrate different forms of kurtosis. A strongly peaked distribution has what is known as *leptokurtosis*. A flatter distribution has *platykurtosis*. A normal distribution has *mesokurtosis*.

Kurtosis also reflects what is known as the 'fat tails' phenomenon. These occur when there are long periods when changes in price or value are relatively small but are interrupted by occasional large changes. One interpretation of kurtosis is that it reflects the tendency for new information to arrive infrequently and in large 'lumps'.

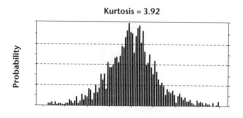 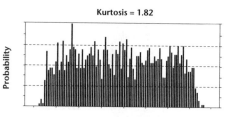

Figure 9.4a and b Leptokurtosis and platykurtosis

Furthermore, the bunching of new information may also lead to high variation of changes in price or valuation. This is likely to be a feature of the commercial property market where a common basis of valuation is the use of comparable evidence. There may be times when there is a lot of comparable evidence and, on other occasions, little evidence. The arrival of information will not, therefore, be uniform. We discuss the effect of information on prices in more depth in Chapter 13.

> The combination of skewness and kurtosis will contribute to different volatilities for different risk classes of investment.

Combining skewness and kurtosis

In addition to providing information about the distributional features of the rates of return, the skewness and kurtosis measures can also be used in combination to assess whether or not the data come from a normal distribution. A test that makes use of these measures is one proposed by Jarque and Bera (1980). The intuition underlying this makes use of the fact that for normally distributed data the skewness and excess kurtosis will be equal to zero. The Jarque–Bera (JB) statistic tests whether or not these values are *jointly* equal to zero. The JB statistic follows a chi-squared distribution with two degrees of freedom so that the critical value when testing for normality is 5.99. We show how this is estimated in Appendix 9B.

Return characteristics of individual properties

Given this background on returns and how to measure their distributional charac-teristics we can now look at the results produced by our data.

For each sector within our sample we have estimated a number of characteristics for each property. These include the average return, standard deviation, skewness, kurtosis and the JB statistic. Tables 9.3 and 9.4 show the average of these statistics, together with the minimum and maximum values for the sample of properties within each sector. These give a good indication of the range of values that you would expect from individual properties.

Table 9.3 ● Distribution of individual property returns, monthly from December 1987 to November 1992

Sector		Average return in % per month	Standard deviation in % per month	Skewness	Kurtosis	JB statistic
Retail	Mean	0.47	2.76	0.12	12.45	382.44
(40 properties)	Min	−0.63	1.30	−3.03	4.84	4.92
	Max	1.45	4.92	4.52	32.92	2388.00
Office	Mean	0.84	3.92	1.64	11.62	429.86
(30 properties)	Min	−0.70	1.69	−1.93	2.99	0.21
	Max	2.69	7.75	5.54	37.30	3417.13
Industrial	Mean	1.47	3.41	1.10	9.92	227.61
(30 properties)	Min	0.88	1.73	−4.36	3.37	0.89
	Max	2.44	5.25	3.32	29.37	2012.95

Table 9.4 ● Distribution of individual property returns, monthly from December 1992 to November 1997

Sector		Average return in % per month	Standard deviation in % per month	Skewness	Kurtosis	JB statistic
Retail	Mean	0.91	2.44	1.48	14.73	707.77
(40 properties)	Min	0.21	0.57	−4.59	5.01	14.55
	Max	1.67	5.13	7.54	57.96	8119.96
Office	Mean	0.86	2.39	0.36	14.05	617.74
(30 properties)	Min	−0.29	0.96	−6.28	3.54	0.82
	Max	1.41	5.09	4.97	45.28	4863.61
Industrial	Mean	0.85	2.32	−0.01	14.91	576.13
(30 properties)	Min	−7.03	0.76	−5.73	4.96	13.79
	Max	8.49	4.88	4.12	39.71	3679.28

The general impression these figures portray, at the monthly level, is that the distribution of returns for individual properties is highly peaked and positively skewed. Whilst providing an overview, the average figures conceal the underlying variability of the individual property returns within each sector. Taking this into consideration we find that over the ten-year period, and using a 5% level of confidence, only five properties out of a sample of 200 could be regarded as being drawn from a normal distribution. This result would seem to rule out the proposition that the monthly returns are drawn from a normal distribution.

As these results are based upon monthly *valued* properties true changes in the market may only be partially incorporated into the return series. We discuss this in more detail in our chapter on smoothing. It would appear that with high frequency data sub-optimal approaches to valuation are likely to account for the high kurtosis observed in the results. This effect is known as stickiness and we discuss it in more detail in Appendix 12A. Over longer holding periods we would expect this effect to be less pronounced. Converting the data to quarterly returns gives the results summarised in Tables 9.5 and 9.6.

Compared with the monthly data, the quarterly figures for both periods show that the average kurtosis is smaller for all sectors. This is also reflected in the JB statistics where the number of normally distributed quarterly returns increases dramatically, when compared with the monthly figures.

To give a clearer indication of how the return interval influences the shape of the distributions we have summarised, in Table 9.7, the number and percentage of properties that could be considered to have normally distributed returns.

For the quarterly returns, a higher proportion of properties is normally distributed in the first sub-period. This reflects the lower average level of kurtosis in that period. As the measurement period increases from monthly to quarterly the returns tend towards normality.

This is an important finding which we can develop further by using annual returns. To examine this issue IPD provided annual returns on 250 properties from each sector of the market over a ten-year period 1987–96. The results of this analysis are summarised in Table 9.8.

Table 9.5 ● **Distribution of individual property returns, quarterly from December 1987 to November 1992**

Sector		Average return in % per quarter	Standard deviation in % per quarter	Skewness	Kurtosis	JB statistic
Retail	Mean	1.46	5.45	0.19	5.09	12.59
	Min	−1.54	2.77	−1.72	2.66	0.01
	Max	4.35	10.96	2.66	11.17	79.13
Office	Mean	2.64	8.08	0.73	4.44	10.86
	Min	−1.98	3.42	−1.37	1.86	0.10
	Max	8.50	16.14	2.91	11.55	89.09
Industrial	Mean	4.54	7.21	0.65	4.42	7.42
	Min	2.71	3.53	−2.00	2.26	0.63
	Max	7.55	11.28	2.28	9.18	49.21

Table 9.6 ● Distribution of individual property returns, quarterly from December 1992 to November 1997

Sector		Average return in % per quarter	Standard deviation in % per quarter	Skewness	Kurtosis	JB statistic
Retail	Mean	2.79	5.08	1.29	6.50	29.73
	Min	0.64	1.25	−1.55	2.51	0.55
	Max	5.13	9.58	3.90	17.01	214.28
Office	Mean	2.66	5.37	1.02	8.45	46.80
	Min	−0.77	2.03	−3.39	4.62	2.27
	Max	4.38	9.80	3.33	14.20	142.80
Industrial	Mean	2.62	4.91	0.57	6.83	31.10
	Min	0.14	1.47	−3.17	2.72	0.08
	Max	4.04	10.08	3.31	14.15	140.15

Table 9.7 ● Number of properties with normally distributed returns

Sector	Number of properties	Monthly data		Quarterly data	
		1987–92	1992–97	1987–92	1992–97
Retail	40	0 (0%)	0 (0%)	21 (53%)	13 (33%)
Office	30	3 (10%)	1 (3%)	19 (63%)	2 (11%)
Industrial	30	1 (3%)	0 (0%)	22 (73%)	7 (23%)
Total	100	4 (4%)	5 (5%)	62 (62%)	22 (22%)

The average skewness figures are now much closer to zero and the kurtosis figures much closer to 3. The average JB figures are also lower implying that the distributions of annual valued returns are much closer to being normal. The number and proportion of annual valued properties with normal returns is summarised in Table 9.9.

Comparing these figures with those given in Table 9.7 it is clear that as the reporting interval between valuation dates increases the probability that individual property returns will be drawn from a normal distribution also increases. One possible reason for this is that new information arrives randomly and continuously so its cumulative effect is likely to have greater impact as the period between valuations increases.

A strong conclusion that emerges from these results is that as the holding period increases individual property returns tend to be more normally distributed.

Table 9.8 ● Distribution of individual property returns, annual, 1987–96

Sector		Average return in % p.a.	Standard deviation in % p.a.	Skewness	Kurtosis	JB statistic
Retail	Mean	11.93	18.54	0.42	3.14	2.076
(250 properties)	Min	2.70	5.66	−1.73	1.36	0.022
	Max	25.98	51.98	2.56	7.77	20.398
Office	Mean	11.25	22.58	0.39	2.85	1.62
(250 properties)	Min	−7.46	4.69	−1.52	1.42	0.01
	Max	28.50	73.73	2.34	7.15	16.29
Industrial	Mean	16.73	20.03	0.66	3.08	2.21
(250 properties)	Min	10.06	7.31	−1.30	1.42	0.01
	Max	24.40	50.51	2.54	7.73	20.09

Table 9.9 ● Number of annually valued properties with normally distributed returns

Sector	Number of properties	Annual data 1987–96
Retail	250	227 (91%)
Office	250	235 (94%)
Industrial	250	232 (93%)
Total	750	694 (93%)

Return characteristics of portfolios

Interesting though these results are, institutional investors do not generally hold individual properties, but combine them into portfolios. It is, therefore, important to look at the distributional characteristics of portfolios.

The figures shown in Tables 9.10–9.13 are based on equally weighted portfolios where the returns were estimated for each sector by taking the average of the individual property returns in each period.

Table 9.10 ● Distribution statistics for equal-weighted sector monthly total returns, December 1987 to November 1992

Sector	Average return (%)	Standard deviation in % per month	Skewness	Kurtosis	JB statistic
Retail	0.47	1.00	−0.44	3.53	2.64
Office	0.84	1.84	0.88	3.25	7.92
Industrial	1.47	1.68	0.81	3.55	7.35

For the period December 1987 to November 1992 (Table 9.10), we cannot reject at the 5% level the possibility that the distribution of returns for the retail portfolio comes from a normal distribution. We can, however, reject this for the other sectors. Note that the JB statistics are much smaller than the statistics we estimated for individual properties. Even at the monthly level they tend towards the critical chi-squared value of 5.99 in the test for normality. Combining properties into portfolios can, therefore, have a powerful impact on the distributional characteristics. The other noticeable feature is that the standard deviations for each sector during 1987–92 are quite high. This is not unexpected as the sample returns covered both the stock market and property crash. This was a period of considerable uncertainty. A summary of the more recent sub-period December 1992 to November 1997 is given in Table 9.11.

Table 9.11 ● Distribution statistics for equal-weighted sector monthly total returns, December 1992 to November 1997

Sector	Average return (%)	Standard deviation in % per month	Skewness	Kurtosis	JB statistic
Retail	0.91	0.89	1.47	5.60	38.66
Office	0.86	0.85	0.88	4.49	13.37
Industrial	0.85	0.77	0.89	4.72	15.34

This period was less volatile and this is reflected in the lower standard deviations. However, the lower activity in the market has caused an increase in the kurtosis, from which it will be seen that normality is clearly rejected for all three sectors.

A similar picture emerges when we compare the quarterly returns over each sub-period. These are summarised in Tables 9.12 and 9.13.

Table 9.12 ● Distribution statistics for equal-weighted sector quarterly total returns, December 1987 to November 1992

Sector	Average) return (%)	Standard deviation in % per quarter	Skewness	Kurtosis	JB statistic
Retail	1.46	2.71	−0.04	2.41	0.30
Office	2.64	5.19	0.50	1.72	2.22
Industrial	4.54	5.03	0.74	3.12	1.82

Table 9.13 ● Distribution statistics for equal-weighted sector quarterly total returns, December 1992 to November 1997

Sector	Average return (%)	Standard deviation in % per quarter	Skewness	Kurtosis	JB statistic
Retail	2.79	3.14	2.83	11.25	83.44
Office	2.66	3.00	2.75	11.16	80.65
Industrial	2.62	2.71	2.50	10.12	63.17

For the earlier period, normality of quarterly returns cannot be rejected for any of the sectors. The low levels of skewness and kurtosis over the period have contributed towards the normal distributions. The more recent period, however, confirms the results we obtained with the monthly data.

Table 9.14 ● Distribution statistics for equal weighted sector annual total returns, 1987–96

Sector	Average return (%)	Standard deviation in % p.a.	Skewness	Kurtosis	JB statistic
Retail	10.75	10.87	0.18	2.13	0.37
Office	10.61	14.00	0.47	2.05	0.74
Industrial	17.02	13.26	0.72	2.55	0.94

Normality is overwhelmingly rejected for all three sectors over the period December 1992 to November 1997.

Using our annual sample covering the period 1987–96 the evidence of normality is much stronger. This is shown in Table 9.14.

Table 9.15 ● Normality of portfolio returns

	Portfolio size	1987–92 Monthly	Quarterly
Retail	40	✓	✓
Office	30	×	✓
Industrial	30	×	✓
		1992–97 Monthly	Quarterly
Retail	40	×	×
Office	30	×	×
Industrial	30	×	×
		1987–96 Annual	
Retail	250	✓	
Office	250	✓	
Industrial	250	✓	

We have covered a lot of material on the distributional characteristics of property returns at both the individual and portfolio levels. Our real interest is in understanding portfolio returns, as this is an important part of portfolio management. We have, therefore, summarised our results by identifying those sectors and periods in which the portfolio returns could be considered to be drawn from a normal distribution. This is shown in Table 9.15.

It is evident that market conditions play an important role in determining the distributional characteristics of portfolio returns. So does the reporting interval. The annual portfolio returns are consistently normal, whereas the results for the other frequencies are mixed. Our results at the annual level are also influenced by the large sample size. We will look at the effect of adding more properties into a portfolio in Chapter 11.

Comparison with the IPD Index

So far our analysis has been confined to relatively small samples of data. It is useful, however, to compare the statistics of a total portfolio consisting of all 100 properties with similar figures estimated for the IPD Monthly Index. Tables 9.16 and 9.17 summarise the distributional characteristics for each sub-period.

The effect of different market conditions has quite an effect on the distribution of returns. In the first period the returns appear to be fairly well behaved for both the 100-property portfolio and the IPD Index. The returns for both portfolios appear to come from a normal distribution. During the second period there is evidence of skewed returns and leptokurtosis. The JB statistic clearly shows that the portfolio returns for both the portfolio and the index were not normally distributed.

Table 9.16 ● Distribution statistics for equal-weighted all properties index, monthly returns, December 1987 to November 1992

Index	Average % per month	Standard deviation in % per month	Skewness	Kurtosis	JB statistic
100 properties	0.88	1.33	0.52	2.27	4.08
IPD monthly	0.63	1.15	0.38	2.01	3.86

Table 9.17 ● Distribution statistics for equal-weighted all properties index, monthly returns, December 1992 to November 1997

Index	Average (%)	Standard deviation in % per month	Skewness	Kurtosis	JB statistic
100 properties	0.88	0.77	1.47	4.95	30.92
IPD monthly	0.91	0.75	1.61	5.93	47.43

The corresponding figures for quarterly returns are shown in Tables 9.18 and 9.19.

Table 9.18 ● Distribution statistics for equal-weighted all properties index, quarterly returns, December 1987 to November 1992

Index	Average (%)	Standard deviation in % per quarter	Skewness	Kurtosis	JB statistic
100 properties	2.73	3.89	0.46	1.96	1.61
IPD monthly	1.93	3.45	0.46	1.71	2.11

Table 9.19 ● Distribution statistics for equal-weighted all properties index, quarterly returns, December 1992 to November 1997

Index	Average (%)	Standard deviation in % per quarter	Skewness	Kurtosis	JB statistic
100 properties	2.70	2.91	2.94	11.78	93.05
IPD monthly	2.78	2.13	1.10	3.59	4.35

The pattern of non-normal returns persists for the 100-property portfolio over the later five-year period, but not for the IPD Index. Again, the quarterly figures show that the volatility of real property returns in the first five-year period was higher than in the second five-year period.

By using the annual sample it is also possible to compare a portfolio of 750 properties with the IPD Annual Index consisting of approximately 13,500 properties. A summary of these results is shown in Table 9.20.

Table 9.20 ● **Distribution statistics for equal value-weighted all properties index, annual returns, 1987–96**

Index	Average (%)	Standard deviation in % p.a.	Skewness	Kurtosis	JB statistic
750 properties	12.79	12.41	0.50	2.24	0.65
IPD annual	10.04	13.14	−0.03	1.81	0.60

The sample portfolio performed better than the IPD Annual Index over the ten-year period and had lower volatility. In neither case could we reject the hypothesis that the returns were drawn from a normal distribution.

The results we have presented in this section have provided a fairly comprehensive overview of the distributional characteristics of property at both individual and portfolio levels. Clear messages emerge that have an important bearing on portfolio construction and strategy.

● The distribution of individual property returns tends towards normality as the reporting period increases. This is almost certainly influenced by the arrival of information and the way valuers are able to respond to that information.
● Combining properties into portfolios also increases the probability that the distribution of returns will approach normality.
● Portfolio size and market conditions play an important role in determining whether the distribution of portfolio returns will be normal.
● Relying on average results over a given period is unlikely to provide a reliable guide to future performance.

The correlation structure of returns

In Chapter 10 we will discuss the effect of diversification in property portfolios and will introduce the single index model. This is an important model in portfolio theory and is based on the assumption that all investment returns are, to a greater or lesser extent, affected by some common factor. In other words, the returns on individual properties are not independent but exhibit some degree of correlation. Chapter 11 takes this further and addresses the issue of portfolio construction, where it is necessary to take account of inter-asset correlations. As this is one of the principal factors influencing portfolio diversification it is important to understand the range of correlation coefficients that you are likely to encounter between the returns on individual properties within each sector of the market.

A summary of the correlation coefficients between individual properties at monthly and quarterly intervals is given in Tables 9.21 and 9.22.

Table 9.21 ● Average correlation coefficients between properties, December 1987 to November 1992

Sector		Monthly returns	Quarterly returns
Retail	Mean	0.134	0.281
(40 properties)	Min	−0.449	−0.502
	Max	0.799	0.845
Office	Mean	0.213	0.442
(30 properties)	Min	−0.126	−0.172
	Max	0.814	0.870
Industrial	Mean	0.228	0.443
(30 properties)	Min	−0.179	−0.139
	Max	0.697	0.876

Table 9.22 ● Average correlation coefficients between properties, December 1992 to November 1997

Sector		Monthly returns	Quarterly returns
Retail	Mean	0.144	0.307
(40 properties)	Min	−0.438	−0.478
	Max	0.731	0.914
Office	Mean	0.128	0.218
(30 properties)	Min	−0.398	−0.771
	Max	0.720	0.903
Industrial	Mean	0.098	0.198
(30 properties)	Min	−0.399	−0.667
	Max	0.774	0.942

Compared with other major asset classes, these coefficients are generally low. Although market factors have an influence on the movement of property returns it is evident that other non-systematic factors are of considerable importance. Property is a heterogeneous form of investment so that returns tend to be influenced by factors specific to individual properties. For example, individual property returns will be influenced by location, the type of tenant, covenant, the age of the property, its general condition, lease structure, and so on. This fits in well with conventional wisdom. It is frequently reported that the three most important factors affecting property performance are location, location and location. This is just another way of saying that property returns are influenced by factors specific to each property. For these reasons it is not unusual to find low correlation figures. This is an important point because it is the correlation between individual asset returns that determines how effective diversification is likely to be. We investigate this in Chapter 11.

Tables 9.21 and 9.22 show that there is an increase in the correlation going from monthly to quarterly data. This could be caused by the way information is incorporated into valuations. Such intertemporal valuer behaviour is known to cause this effect. However, even at the annual level the correlation coefficients still remain relatively low. These figures are shown in Table 9.23.

Table 9.23 ● Average correlation coefficients between properties, 1987–96

Sector		Annual returns
Retail	Mean	0.395
(250 properties)	Min	−0.798
	Max	0.991
Office	Mean	0.425
(250 properties)	Min	−0.830
	Max	0.989
Industrial	Mean	0.464
(250 properties)	Min	−0.871
	Max	0.991

Factors influencing the performance of property tend to be very specific so that individual property returns are not highly correlated. This has important implications in terms of diversification.

In addition to the above we are also interested in knowing how the returns for individual properties are correlated between sectors. Tables 9.24 and 9.25 summarise these figures for both monthly and quarterly returns.

Table 9.24 ● Average correlation coefficients between sectors, December 1987 to November 1992

Sector		Monthly returns	Quarterly returns
Retail–Office	Mean	0.129	0.279
	Min	–0.529	–0.679
	Max	0.698	0.881
Retail–Industrial	Mean	0.132	0.294
	Min	–0.336	–0.464
	Max	0.611	0.839
Office–Industrial	Mean	0.213	0.423
	Min	–0.112	–0.164
	Max	0.695	0.885

Table 9.25 ● Average correlation coefficients between sectors, December 1992 to November 1997

Sector		Monthly returns	Quarterly returns
Retail–Office	Mean	0.130	0.226
	Min	–0.475	–0.679
	Max	0.765	0.882
Retail–Industrial	Mean	0.113	0.241
	Min	–0.557	–0.775
	Max	0.803	0.871
Office–Industrial	Mean	0.115	0.211
	Min	–0.560	–0.806
	Max	0.776	0.872

For both sub-periods the average quarterly correlation figures are approximately double the monthly returns. Using annual returns we get the correlation coefficients in Table 9.26.

Table 9.26 ● Average correlation coefficients between sectors, 1987–96

Sector		Annual returns
Retail–Office	Mean	0.395
	Min	–0.798
	Max	0.991

Table 9.26 continued

Retail–Industrial	Mean	0.425
	Min	–0.830
	Max	0.989
Office–Industrial	Mean	0.464
	Min	–0.871
	Max	0.991

The figures shown in these tables are similar to the range of correlation coefficients between properties within sectors which we showed in Tables 9.21–9.23. This is an important finding because it tells us that we are unlikely to get a significant improvement in risk-reduction by diversifying across different sectors of the market. The conventional view that diversifying across property sectors helps to reduce risk does not appear to be valid.

The correlation of real estate returns with other assets

So far we have looked at real estate returns in isolation. We are, however, also interested in the way the returns on property co-vary with other assets. This is important because it will influence the contribution that property has in a mixed-asset portfolio. We can examine this at the portfolio level by estimating the cross-correlation coefficients between both our property sample and the IPD Index, together with two other growth investments, namely the FT All Share and the FT Property Share indexes.

Tables 9.27 and 9.28 show the correlation coefficients between the rates of return for each of the two five-year sub-periods for both monthly and quarterly data. The equally weighted portfolios consist of 100 properties made up of 40 retail, 30 industrial and 30 office.

Table 9.27 ● Inter-asset correlation coefficients, 1988–92

	Monthly data		Quarterly data	
Index	IPD Index	Equal-weighted	IPD Index	Equal-weighted
FT All Share	0.086	0.104	0.216	0.250
FT Property	0.288	0.260	0.420	0.418

The figures in Table 9.27 show that the IPD Index and the 100-properties portfolio are more highly correlated with property shares than with the FT All Share index. Also, the strength of association increases as we move from monthly to quarterly data. This implies that there is some association between real property and the property share market. Note, however, that this is not strong. At the quarterly level the correlation coefficient is approximately 0.4. Another way of considering this is to say that the real property market only accounts for about 16% (i.e. 0.4×0.4) of the variation of returns in the property share market. In Table 9.28 we examine the second five-year sub-period and show that the correlation is even less.

Table 9.28 ● Inter-asset correlation coefficients, 1993–97

Index	Monthly data		Quarterly data	
	IPD Index	Equal-weighted	IPD Index	Equal-weighted
FT All Share	−0.078	−0.115	−0.014	0.199
FT Property	−0.022	0.016	0.046	0.100

The strength of the association between the FT property index and the two property portfolios is much weaker, with the correlation coefficients having fallen significantly in value. The monthly frequency data also show a reversal in the previously positive relationship between the two property portfolios and the FT All Share index. At the quarterly level the real property market now explains less than 1% of the variation in returns in the property share market. An important implication of this finding is that holding property company shares cannot be regarded as a substitute for investing in real property.

Investing in property shares is not a substitute for investing in real property.

These results provide a cautionary warning. Although the data used have been arbitrary, in the sense that they are divided into two five-year periods, it will be evident that there are significant differences between the variances and correlation coefficients between each of the sub-periods. From these figures one immediate implication is clear. The choice of data period used in calculating the various measures needs to be carefully considered. Although it may appear sensible to use all available data in arriving at the variance and correlation measures, this is not advisable, as the derived measures will be some average figure reflecting all previous market environments. Using historic averages in areas such as portfolio construction is likely to result in misleading results. As you will see in Chapter 10, portfolio theory is drafted in terms of expectations. Ideally, what is required are forward-looking measures of expected performance.

Summary

The results reported in this chapter suggest that the returns for individual properties are likely to have originated from non-normal distributions. This clearly has implications in areas such as portfolio theory, where this assumption is generally required. However, the key issue is not whether property returns are normally distributed but whether the departure from normality is likely to make a significant difference in terms of applying the theory. Portfolio theory has, for example, resulted in the development of a number of important insights into asset pricing and the way investors behave. Apart from considering the practical aspects of constructing efficient portfolios, one of our main interests lies in the insights that modern financial theory can have in areas such as property valuation, asset allocation and portfolio strategy.

This chapter also examined the correlation structure of property returns. These appear to be consistently low for all frequencies of data and are almost certainly caused by factors that are specific to individual properties. These include location, tenant and lease structure, and so on. One of the advantages of this is that the low correlation between assets improves diversification. The figures are on average lower than you would get with equities which implies that it should be possible to achieve greater levels of risk reduction in a property portfolio than in an equity portfolio. This is something we shall return to in Chapter 11.

In addition we showed that the correlation between property returns and other assets is generally low, implying that property is potentially useful in terms of constructing mixed-asset portfolios. Having established some results that describe the characteristics of property returns, we can build on this information to provide a better understanding of property as an investment asset.

This chapter has three appendices:

Appendix 9A: Inter-asset comparisons

This provides a more detailed analysis of how property correlates with other asset classes. This is a key component in understanding property in a portfolio context.

Appendix 9B: Statistical measures used to describe distributions

In this appendix we cover the main statistical measures used to describe distributions.

Appendix 9C: Arithmetic mean, geometric mean and continuous rates of return

It is important to understand that returns can be measured in more than one way. This becomes important when you have to consider the performance of portfolios. This appendix provides this information.

Chapter 9: Summary table

1. For individual properties monthly returns do not appear to come from a normal distribution. There is some evidence of normality for quarterly returns and annual returns tend to be normally distributed.

2. At the portfolio level a similar picture emerges. The returns of monthly valued portfolios are not normally distributed. There is some evidence of normality for quarterly valued portfolios and the returns on annual valued portfolios tend to be normally distributed.

3. As the holding periods increase individual property returns tend to be more normally distributed.

4. Combining properties into portfolios increases the probability that the distribution of returns will approach normality.

5. Portfolio size and market conditions play an important role in determining whether the distribution of portfolio returns will be normal.

6. The average correlation between individual properties within sectors tends to be low for all reporting periods. The low correlation is influenced by factors that are specific to individual properties.

7. The average correlation between sectors is in the same order as the average correlation between individual properties. This implies that diversifying across sectors may offer no significant advantages over diversifying within sectors.

8. The correlation figures increase as the reporting interval increases.

9. The correlation of property returns with other asset classes is generally low. This implies that property will offer diversification benefits in a mixed-asset context.

10. The correlation between property returns and the FT Property Share index is low. This implies that property shares should not be regarded as being a good substitute for investment in real property.

Problems

1. What are the advantages of using rates of return to describe the characteristics of property?

2. What are the most common measures used to describe a distribution?

3. Skewness and kurtosis can be combined into a single measure that can be used to test for normality. What is that measure?

4. What effect does the reporting interval for property have on the normality of returns?

5. The correlation between individual properties tends to be low. What property factors contribute to this low correlation?

6. The correlation between real property and property shares is also low. Does this imply that property shares are a good substitute for investing in property?

Selected references

Fama, E.F. (1965) The behavior of stock market prices. *Journal of Business* **38** (1), 34–105.

Fama, E.F. (1976) *Foundations of Finance*, Oxford: Blackwell.

Hawawini, G. (1983) Why beta shifts as the return interval changes. *Financial Analysts Journal* (May–June), 73–7.

Jarque, C.M. and Bera, A.K. (1987) A test for normality of observations and regression residuals. *International Statistical Review* **55**, 163–72.

Markowitz, H.M. (1952) Portfolio selection. *Journal of Finance* **12** (March), 77–91.

Markowitz, H.M. (1959) *Portfolio Selection: Efficient Diversification of Investments*, A Cowles Foundation Monograph, New Haven: Yale University Press.

Officer, R.R. (1972) The distribution of stock returns. *Journal of the American Statistical Association* **67**, 807–12.

Young, M.S. and Graff, R.A. (1995) Real estate is not normal: a fresh look at real estate returns distributions. *Journal of Real Estate Finance and Economics* **10**, 225–59.

Appendix 9A
Inter-asset comparisons

In this appendix we provide additional information concerning the performance of property in relation to other asset classes. This is an important issue because investment decisions are often made within a mixed-asset framework. Competition for funds is, therefore, decided by comparing the relative performance of different asset classes.

We will focus on monthly and quarterly total returns over the sub-periods we used in Chapter 9. These are December 1987–November 1992 and December 1992–November 1997. The reason for this is that asset allocation decisions are often made at frequencies of less than one year. However, we will also provide results based upon annual data from 1970 to 1997 so that a more comprehensive view of inter-asset comparisons can be made.

Monthly and quarterly data

A comparison of correlations and variances for monthly and quarterly returns over the periods 1987–92 and 1992–97 is made using the following data.

Asset class	Name	Abbreviation
Equities		
	FT All Share index	FT-All
	FT Property Share index	FT-Prop
Real Estate		
All Property	IPD All Property Monthly Index	IPD-All
	Equal-weighted sample (100 properties)	EW-All
Retail	IPD Retail Sector	IPD-Ret
	Equal-weighted sample (40 properties)	EW-Ret
Office	IPD Office Sector	IPD-Off
	Equal-weighted sample (30 properties)	EW-Off
Industrial	IPD Industrial Sector	IPD-Ind
	Equal-weighted sample (30 properties)	EW-Ind

Inter-asset correlations

Table 9A.1 summarises the correlation between the return on equities and the property market. For the period 1987–92 you will see that property is more highly correlated with the FT Property Share index than with the FT All Share index. Although the figures are less than 0.5 these results do show that property shares reflect some of the movement in the property market.

Table 9A.1 ● Inter-asset correlation coefficients, 1987–92

Index	Monthly data		Quarterly data	
	FT All Share Index	FT Property Share Index	FT All Share Index	FT Property Share Index
IPD-All	0.086	0.288	0.216	0.420
EW-All	0.104	0.260	0.250	0.418
IPD-Ret	0.038	0.223	0.214	0.400
EW-Ret	0.093	0.222	0.234	0.419
IPD-Off	0.116	0.327	0.199	0.428
EW-Off	0.057	0.244	0.181	0.396
IPD-Ind	0.056	0.228	0.227	0.382
EW-Ind	0.139	0.243	0.290	0.370

Table 9A.2 ● Inter-asset correlation coefficients, 1992–97

Index	Monthly data		Quarterly data	
	FT All Share Index	FT Property Share Index	FT All Share Index	FT Property Share Index
IPD-All	−0.078	−0.022	−0.014	0.046
EW-All	−0.115	0.016	0.199	0.099
IPD-Ret	−0.067	−0.017	0.015	0.062
EW-Ret	−0.077	0.100	0.237	0.167
IPD-Off	−0.083	−0.029	−0.048	0.029
EW-Off	−0.100	0.000	0.193	0.066
IPD-Ind	−0.084	−0.018	−0.025	0.041
EW-Ind	−0.151	−0.100	0.131	0.021

This relationship breaks down for the period 1992–97, shown in Table 9A.2, which covers the time after the UK property market collapsed. The co-movement between property shares and real property therefore appears to be stronger when the property market is performing well.

In Table 9A.3 we summarise the monthly cross-correlations and returns statistics for the property market, as represented by the IPD monthly index, and other asset classes. This analysis covers a much longer period from January 1987 to June 1998.

This shows strong correlation between each sector of the property market but low correlation with the other asset classes. The low inter-asset correlation would imply that property is good for diversification purposes. It should be borne in mind, however, that the property returns are highly smoothed so that their risk is understated. We will look at this issue in Chapter 12.

Table 9A.3 ● Inter-asset cross-correlations and return statistics, monthly from January 1987 to June 1998

	IPD				RPI	T-Bills	FT		Gilts	
	All	Ind	Off	Ret	RPI	T-Bills	All Share	Props	10-Year	15-Year
IPD-All	1.000									
IPD-Ind	0.925	1.000								
IPD-Off	0.964	0.888	1.000							
IPD-Ret	0.934	0.808	0.819	1.000						
RPI	-0.003	0.085	0.032	-0.084	1.000					
T-Bills	-0.252	-0.013	-0.176	-0.417	0.344	1.000				
FT All Share	-0.015	0.001	0.006	-0.044	-0.099	-0.065	1.000			
FT Prop	0.097	0.081	0.124	0.067	-0.112	-0.211	0.784	1.000		
10-Year Gilts	-0.116	-0.147	-0.133	-0.053	-0.118	-0.056	0.298	0.335	1.000	
15-Year Gilts	-0.087	-0.123	-0.106	-0.023	-0.117	-0.074	0.298	0.343	0.996	1.000
	All	Ind	Off	Ret	RPI	T-Bills	All Share	Props	10-Year	15-Year
Mean Return	0.834	1.083	0.742	0.814	0.360	0.691	1.335	1.142	1.034	1.057
St. Dev.	0.937	1.067	1.166	0.821	0.486	0.236	4.088	5.326	2.072	2.262

Table 9A.4 ● Standard deviations for 1987–92

Index	Monthly data (% per month)			Quarterly data (% per quarter)		
	1987–92	1987–90	1990–92	1987–92	1987–90	1990–92
FT-All	3.97	3.53	4.35	7.17	5.53	8.47
FT-Prop	5.48	4.31	6.23	10.88	8.96	11.49
IPD-All	1.15	1.07	0.40	3.45	3.04	1.05
EW-All	1.33	1.33	0.61	3.89	3.62	1.67
IPD-Ret	0.88	0.94	0.51	2.59	2.71	1.38
EW-Ret	1.00	1.20	0.59	2.71	3.14	1.53
IPD-Off	1.53	1.27	0.36	4.49	3.42	0.66
EW-Off	1.84	1.67	0.64	5.19	4.09	1.51
IPD-Ind	1.39	1.30	0.52	4.22	3.80	1.42
EW-Ind	1.68	1.65	0.85	5.03	4.69	2.41

Table 9A.5 ● Standard deviations for 1992–97

Index	Monthly data (% per month)			Quarterly data (% per quarter)		
	1992-97	1992-95	1995-97	1992-97	1992-95	1995-97
FT-All	2.42	2.80	1.95	4.56	5.84	2.63
FT-Prop	3.81	4.44	3.05	8.38	11.00	4.40
IPD-All	0.75	0.95	1.08	2.13	2.65	1.16
EW-All	0.77	0.97	0.40	2.91	3.84	0.85
IPD-Ret	0.79	0.97	0.48	2.21	2.66	1.35
EW-Ret	0.89	1.09	0.48	3.14	4.07	0.85
IPD-Off	0.75	0.97	0.37	2.10	2.70	0.99
EW-Off	0.85	1.08	0.51	3.00	4.01	1.00
IPD-Ind	0.74	0.96	0.37	2.14	2.71	1.04
EW-Ind	0.77	0.95	0.46	2.71	3.53	0.93

Asset risk

Tables 9A.4 and 9A.5 show the relative volatility of each asset class in standard deviation terms measured over five-year, three-year and two-year periods.

All the property returns are much less volatile than equities. This can be partly attributed to aggregation effects. Table 9A.5 shows that all sectors exhibited some reduction in risk during 1992–97.

Long-term annual data

One of the problems with using short-term property returns is that cross-correlations between property valuations can cause the volatility of property returns to be

Table 9A.6 ● Inter-asset cross-correlation and returns statistics, 1970–97

	IPD All Property	Equities	Bonds	RPI	T-Bills
IPD All Property	1.000	0.173	0.060	−0.052	−0.265
Equities		1.000	0.695	0.239	−0.021
Bonds			1.000	−0.017	0.047
RPI				1.000	0.529
T-Bills					1.000

	IPD All Property	Equities	Bonds	RPI	T-Bills
Mean Return	12.356	20.285	13.156	8.315	9.907
St. Dev.	10.875	33.696	16.938	5.828	3.131

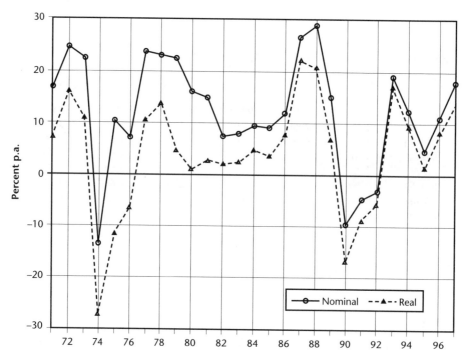

Figure 9A.1 Property returns in nominal and real terms

understated. This can be overcome, to some degree, by using annual return data. The smoothing in this index is much lower and, as a result, the correlations with other assets are probably more reliable.

Table 9A.6 summarises the inter-asset correlation and return statistics covering the period 1970–97.

This provides some interesting information on the performance of property over long periods. For example, property shows low positive correlation with equities and

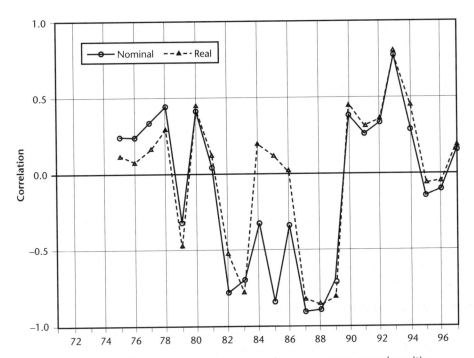

Figure 9A.2 5-year rolling correlation coefficients between property and equities

bonds but is negatively correlated with both inflation (RPI) and Treasury Bills (T-Bills). Property is good as a diversifying asset, but even over a 27-year period did not provide a hedge against inflation. The risk characteristics show that property has about one third of the volatility of equities.

These figures just present a static view of performance and it is more than likely that there is a lot of variation in each of the figures. For example, in Figure 9A.1 we show the returns on property over the period 1971–97 in both nominal and real terms. You will see that there were significant negative real returns during the two major property crashes in 1974 and 1990.

If investors in property have holding periods in the order of five years, then the correlation between property and equities over this time horizon could assume some importance. In Figure 9A.2 we show five-year rolling correlation coefficients between the returns on property and equities from 1971 to 1997. These are shown in both nominal and real terms.

You will see that there was a long period during the whole of the 1980s when the correlation was negative. Although this was partly eliminated in real terms there appear to be strong reasons for holding property in a portfolio that included equities.

Selected references

Ball, M., Lizieri, C. and MacGregor, B.D. (1998) *The Economics of Commercial Property Markets*, London: Routledge.

Ibbotson, R.G., Siegal, L.B. and Love, K.S. (1985) World wealth: Market values and returns. *Journal of Portfolio Management* (Fall), 4–23.

Lee, S. (1989) Property returns in a portfolio context. *Journal of Valuation* **7**, 248–58.

MacGregor, B.D. and Nanthakumaran, N. (1992) The allocation to property in the multi-asset portfolio: the evidence and theory reconsidered. *Journal of Property Research* **9**, 5–32.

Miles, M., Hartzell, D. and Guilkey, D. (1990) A different look at commercial real estate returns. *AREUEA Journal* **18**, 403–30.

Newell, G. and Matysiak, G.A. (1997) An empirical investigation into the presence of chaotic behaviour in UK property markets. *Royal Institution of Chartered Surveyors.*

Ross, S.A. and Zisler, R. (1991) Risk and return in real estate. *Journal of Real Estate Finance and Economics* **4** (2), 175–90.

Appendix 9B
Statistical measures used to describe distributions

In this appendix we describe the statistical measures we used in Chapter 9 to describe the distribution of returns.

Moments of a probability distribution

The returns from any asset are usually described in terms of four moments. These are the mean (M1), variance (M2), skewness (M3) and kurtosis (M4). Each of these can be related to both historic and future returns.

First moment: mean or expected value (M1)

The first moment is generally measured relative to the origin of a distribution and indicates its location, or central tendency. Depending on whether historic or future returns are used it is known as the mean or expected value.

Using future returns data the expected return is given as:

$$E(r) = \sum_{i=1}^{n} p_i r_i \tag{9B.1}$$

where p_i represents the probability associated with each return r_i, the sum of all the probabilities adds up to 1.

Alternatively, using historic data the mean return would be calculated from:

$$\bar{r} = \frac{1}{n} \sum_{i=1}^{n} r_i \tag{9B.2}$$

This is just the average of all the historic returns assuming that they each had an equal probability of occurring.

When analysing returns data it is sometimes useful to estimate the first moment about the mean rather than the origin. In this case the first moment will be zero for both future and historic data. Using future returns:

$$M1 = \sum_{i=1}^{n} p_i \left[r_i - E(r_i) \right] = 0 \qquad (9B.3)$$

and using historic returns:

$$M1 = \frac{1}{n} \sum_{i=1}^{n} [r_i - \bar{r}] = 0 \qquad (9B.4)$$

Higher order moments, which we discuss below, are generally estimated relative to the mean.

Second moment: variance (M2)

The variance is a measure of dispersion about the mean or expected value. Using future returns it can be estimated as follows:

$$M2 = \sigma^2 = \sum_{i=1}^{n} p_i \left[r_i - E(r_i) \right]^2 \qquad (9B.5)$$

Using historic returns we have:

$$M2 = \sigma^2 = \frac{1}{n} \sum_{i=1}^{n} (r_i - \bar{r})^2 \qquad (9B.6)$$

Taking the square root of M2 results in the standard deviation.

For reasons we shall discuss in Chapter 12, the second moment of real estate returns is sometimes understated. This means that the observed variance for valuation returns is much lower than the true variance, had transaction prices been available. This is known as *smoothing* and results in a trade-off between risk and return that appears much better than other assets that are frequently traded.

Third moment: skewness (M3)

Skewness measures how lopsided the distributions are. As discussed in Chapter 9, it would occur if a return series had a tendency to have a large number of high or low returns. It is calculated by taking the cube of the deviations from the mean as this magnifies the effect of the sign. For future returns skewness is estimated from the following:

$$M3 = \sum_{i=1}^{n} p_i [r_i - E(r_i)]^3 \qquad (9B.7)$$

Using historic returns we have:

$$M3 = \frac{1}{n} \sum_{i=1}^{n} (r_i - \bar{r})^3 \qquad (9B.8)$$

In both cases the skewness can be normalised by dividing by the cube of the standard deviation. This enables distributions with different degrees of skewness to be compared:

$$S = \frac{M3}{\sigma^3} \tag{9B.9}$$

The normalised skewness of a symmetric distribution, such as a normal distribution, is equal to zero. As explained in Chapter 9, a positive value of S means that the distribution has a long tail to the right, and a negative value implies that the distribution has a long tail to the left. Examples of skewed distributions were shown in Chapter 9 in Figures 9.3(a) and 9.3(b).

Skewness
A normal distribution has a skewness value equal to zero.
A positively skewed distribution has a long tail to the right.
A negatively skewed distribution has a long tail to the left.

Fourth moment: kurtosis (M4)

Kurtosis measures the peakedness or flatness of a distribution. In order to calculate its value, it is necessary to compute the fourth powers of the deviations. Using future returns kurtosis is computed as follows:

$$M4 = \sum_{i=1}^{n} p_i[r_i - E(r_i)]^4 \tag{9B.10}$$

Using historic returns:

$$M4 = \frac{1}{n} \sum_{i=1}^{n} (r_i - \bar{r})^4 \tag{9B.11}$$

Kurtosis can also be normalised by dividing by the standard deviation raised to the fourth power. This enables the characteristics of different distributions to be compared.

$$K = \frac{M4}{\sigma^4} \tag{9B.12}$$

A normal distribution has a kurtosis value equal to 3. A distribution with a value in excess of 3 is said to be fat-tailed, which means that the probability of observing extreme values is greater than that for a normal distribution. Such a distribution is peaked and is described as being *leptokurtic*. If kurtosis is less than 3 the distribution is flat relative to the normal, and is described as being *platykurtic*. A normal distribution is said to be *mesokurtic*. Sometimes a measure of excess kurtosis is reported. These represent values in excess of three and provide an indication of kurtosis relative to a normal distribution. Examples of kurtosis were shown in Chapter 9 in Figures 9.4(a) and 9.4(b).

Kurtosis
A normal distribution has a kurtosis value equal to 3. This is known as mesokurtosis.
A peaked distribution has a kurtosis value in excess of 3. This is known as leptokurtosis.
A flat distribution has a kurtosis value less than 3. This is known as platykurtosis.

Testing for normality

Each of the four moments describes a certain characteristic of a distribution. If you were able to take all these into consideration you would be interested to know whether a given distribution represents a significant departure from normality. The standard way of evaluating whether a distribution departs from normality is to use the Jarque–Bera (JB) test. This compares the sample skewness and excess kurtosis with the values they would take on under normality. In statistical terms, based on 'large' samples, the JB statistic has a chi-squared distribution with two degrees of freedom. At the 5% level the critical value for the chi-squared distribution with two degrees of freedom is 5.99. If the calculated JB statistic exceeds this figure the hypothesis that the returns are normally distributed is rejected. The JB statistic is estimated using the following expression:

$$JB = \frac{n}{6}\left[S^2 + \frac{(K-3)^2}{4} \right] \qquad (9B.13)$$

Measures of association

The above statistics help to describe the characteristics of individual returns. However, we also need to know something about the association of returns with other assets. The common measures used are the covariance and coefficient of correlation, which we next describe.

Covariance

An important statistic that is central to the development of portfolio theory is the covariance. This describes how pairs of asset returns move relative to each other. It can be estimated from the following:

$$Cov(r_i, r_j) = \frac{1}{n-1}\sum (r_i - \bar{r}_i)(r_j - \bar{r}_j) \qquad (9B.14)$$

Coefficient of correlation

As the covariance is measured in the same units as the variables it is sometimes difficult to interpret. This can be overcome by dividing by the product of standard deviation of each variable to give what is known as the coefficient of correlation:

$$\rho_{r_i r_j} = \frac{1}{n-1} \frac{\sum (r_i - \bar{r}_i)(r_j - \bar{r}_j)}{\sigma_{r_i} \sigma_{r_j}} \tag{9B.15}$$

In this form it is scale-free and lies within the range –1 to +1 depending on whether the variables being analysed are negatively or positively correlated. This is an important part of portfolio construction and we discuss it further in Chapter 10.

Selected references

Bera, A.K. and Jarque, C.M. (1981) An efficient large-sample test for normality of observations and regression residuals. *Australian National University* (WP 040).

Gujarati, D.N. (1995) *Basic Econometrics*, 3rd edn, New York: McGraw-Hill.

Hill, C., Griffiths, W. and Judge, G. (1997) *Undergraduate Econometrics*, New York: John Wiley & Sons.

Jarque, C.M. and Bera, A.K. (1987) A test for normality of observations and regression residuals. *International Statistical Review* 55, 163–72.

Appendix 9C
Arithmetic mean, geometric mean and continuous rates of return

Arithmetic and geometric mean returns

In Chapter 9, we estimated the average rates of return for our sample of properties by using the arithmetic mean as the measure of central tendency. This is fairly standard practice when describing a distribution as the arithmetic mean is also used in the calculation of standard deviation and other higher moments. We discussed the higher moments in Appendix 9B. If, however, you are concerned with measuring investment performance over several periods, the arithmetic mean does not provide a good measure of return on investment.

To illustrate why this is the case assume that you invest £1,000 in projects A and B that have the following annual returns over three years.

Table 9C.1 ● Investment returns for projects A and B

Project	Year 0	Year 1	Year 2	Year 3	Average
A		50.00%	10.00%	–39.39%	6.87%
	£1,000	£1,500	£1,650	£1,000	
B		–50.00%	25.00%	60.00%	11.67%
	£1,000	£500	£625	£1,000	

The average return for project B appears to have outperformed investment A. However, had you invested £1,000 in each project you will see that by the end of year 3 your investment has not changed in value. On this basis the average return is zero. The problem with taking the arithmetic average is that each of the returns could be earned on different portfolio values. What you are really concerned with is the *value relative* for the portfolio over the investment holding period. We therefore need a constant rate of return per period which, when compounded, would have resulted in an equivalent investment. This can be measured by using the *geometric mean return*.

If you have an investment with returns in each of n periods the geometric mean return r_g is given by the following:

$$r_g = [(1 + r_1)(1 + r_2)(1 + r_3) \ldots (1 + r_n)]^{\frac{1}{n}} - 1 \tag{9C.1}$$

Using the returns for project A you can estimate the geometric mean return, allowing for some small rounding errors, as follows:

$$r_g = [(1.50)(1.10)(0.61)]^{\frac{1}{3}} - 1 = 0.22\%$$

The calculation involved taking the third root of the product of each of the annual returns. When there are a lot of returns involved this can be tedious. An alternative approach is to rearrange equation 9C.1 as follows:

$$(1 + r_g)^n = (1 + r_1)(1 + r_2)(1 + r_3) \ldots (1 + r_n) \tag{9C.2}$$

Taking logs gives:

$$\ln(1 + r_g) = \frac{1}{n} \sum_{i=1}^{n} \ln (1 + r_i) = a \tag{9C.3}$$

In this expression a is the average of all the logged returns. You can solve for r_g as follows:

$$r_g = e^a - 1 \tag{9C.4}$$

You can calculate the value of a for Project A by taking the average of the logs of $(1 + r)$ from Table 9C.1:

$$a = \tfrac{1}{3} [\ln(1.50) + \ln(1.10) + \ln(0.61)]$$

$$a = \tfrac{1}{3} (0.405 + 0.095 - 0.494) \doteq 0$$

Substituting into equation 9C.4 gives the geometric mean return:

$$r_g = e^0 - 1 = 0\%$$

The geometric mean return will always be less than the arithmetic mean return except when the returns in each period are the same. In this case the arithmetic and geometric mean returns will be equal.

Table 9C.2 ● The IPD annual return, 1980–97

	Total return	Index
1980		100.0
1981	15.0	115.0
1982	7.5	123.7
1983	7.6	133.1
1984	8.6	144.6
1985	8.3	156.5
1986	11.1	173.8
1987	25.8	218.6
1988	29.7	283.5
1989	15.4	327.1
1990	−8.4	299.6
1991	−3.2	290.1
1992	−1.7	285.2
1993	20.0	342.1
1994	12.0	383.2
1995	3.5	396.8
1996	10.0	436.3
1997	16.8	509.6

Continuous rates of return

Assume that you want to estimate the geometric mean return using the IPD All Property Annual Index. The returns are summarised in Table 9C.2.

You can estimate the geometric mean return over the 17-year period using the index numbers. (As an exercise, you can also confirm the result by using logs as described above.)

$$r_g = \left(\frac{509.6}{100.0}\right)^{\frac{1}{17}} - 1 = 10.05\% \text{ p.a.}$$

This is an equivalent annual rate of return. If you continuously compounded at this rate for 17 years your investment would have shown an increase of 509.6%. Note that the arithmetic average return is 10.47% p.a.

The relationship between discrete returns and continuous returns can, therefore, be expressed as follows:

$$1 + r = \left(1 + \frac{k}{n}\right)^n \tag{9C.5}$$

Where k is the continuous rate of return and n is the number of compounding periods.

As n gets large it can be shown that, in the limit, the right-hand side of equation 9C.5 simplifies to e^k. If you substitute this value and take logs you get:

$$1 + r = e^k \tag{9C.6}$$

$$\ln(1 + r) = k \tag{9C.7}$$

This shows that the continuous rate of return is equal to the log of the discrete rate of return. It is often more convenient to work in continuous returns. For relatively small returns there is little difference in the figures, but for high values taking logs has the effect of shrinking them towards the mean. The reason for this is that the distribution of log returns tends towards a normal distribution. Given that much of portfolio theory is based on the assumption of normally distributed returns this suggests that there are advantages to working in continuous returns. For most work in finance the differences are not significant. In the area of performance measurement, however, the differences are important.

Risk and return

You will see in Chapter 10 that portfolio theory is drafted in terms of expectations. The question that needs to be asked is, what measure of return should be used to estimate future expected returns? The answer to this depends on whether your intention is to estimate the return for a single year or for a multi-year horizon.

If you are concerned with only a single period return then the best estimate to use, based on historic evidence, is the arithmetic mean return. If, however, you are more concerned with the value of your investment over a number of periods then, based on past experience, you should use the geometric mean return. (See Appendix 10A for an example of using the geometric mean return in an asset allocation framework.)

Risk, return and diversification

Introduction

Imagine that you have been retained to advise a client who has to make a choice between two properties. Both properties are from the same sector but are located in different parts of the country. They have the same asking price and you have to advise on which is the more attractive as an investment. To offer your client sound advice you will have to go much further than just looking at prices. You need to consider the uncertainty surrounding the prices and the effect that this will have on the investment decision.

So far we have made passing reference to the importance of risk. In this chapter we will begin to explore this issue in a more formal way and show how risk and return are used to make investment decisions. We will introduce you to the basic concepts of diversification and portfolio theory and show how these lead to a general theory of asset pricing. This chapter provides a brief overview of a number of important topics which we will draw on throughout the rest of this book.

Diversification and portfolio theory

Portfolio theory is based on the assumption that diversification reduces risk. Most of the research in this area and the subsequent development of the *capital asset pricing model* (CAPM) has related to investment in equities. The theory, however, is not solely confined to stock market investments, but can be applied to all risky assets.

This is often a source of confusion. Difficulties really only arise because of limited information concerning the risk–return characteristics of real assets. When you begin to look at property it is evident that it consumes a major proportion of investment funds at both the personal and institutional levels. For many people, the commitment of funds to house purchase far outweighs that which would be allocated to equities. The risk–return profile of their total assets will, therefore, be heavily dependent on their property holdings. The same is also true of financial institutions. In fact, property represents a major proportion of investment wealth throughout the world. In Chapter 1 we showed that property accounted for over 50% of the world's wealth. Given this background it is appropriate to consider property in a portfolio context.

Enter Harry Markowitz

The pioneering work of Markowitz (1959) resulted in a radical reappraisal of the way investors behave and laid the way for the development of what became known as *capital market theory*.

By defining a portfolio of assets in terms of their risk, return and covariance, Markowitz developed a model that could identify the optimal proportion of funds to hold in each asset. For a given level of risk the resulting portfolio was considered efficient because it offered the maximum expected return. The alternative approach was to minimise risk for a given rate of return. In Appendix 10A we illustrate the principles involved in a simple portfolio analysis. Before Markowitz showed how to handle this problem quantitatively the selection of assets was largely undertaken in a subjective manner.

> Although portfolio theory and its subsequent development into the capital asset pricing model have focused on equity shares the theory has a general application and can be applied to all risky assets.

The key to understanding diversification is to recognise that portfolio risk can only be reduced by investing in a minimum of two assets where the pattern of their returns do not move in perfect lockstep. We can illustrate this idea by combining, in equal proportions, two assets with negatively correlated returns. Table 10.1 and Figure 10.1 summarise the returns for assets A and B over a period of 14 years.

Table 10.1 ● Asset and portfolio returns: negative correlation

Years	A	B	Portfolio
1	0.00%	8.00%	4.00%
2	4.00%	5.00%	4.50%
3	8.00%	4.00%	6.00%
4	2.00%	10.00%	6.00%
5	−1.00%	8.00%	3.50%
6	−10.00%	6.00%	−2.00%
7	−9.00%	9.00%	0.00%
8	−6.00%	8.00%	1.00%
9	0.00%	3.00%	1.50%
10	2.00%	−8.00%	−3.00%
11	−2.00%	2.00%	0.00%
12	10.00%	−2.00%	4.00%
13	4.00%	−2.00%	1.00%
14	8.00%	−8.00%	0.00%
Average	0.71%	3.07%	1.89%
St. Dev.	6.09%	5.99%	2.82%
Correlation A, B	−0.56		

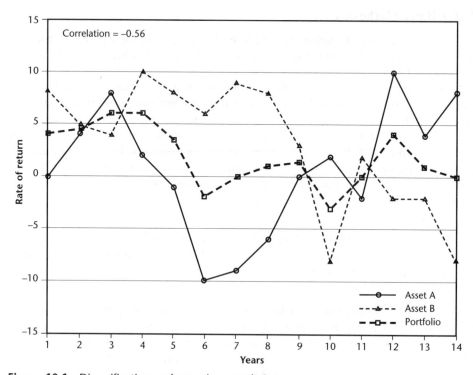

Figure 10.1 Diversification and negative correlation

We have also calculated the average return and standard deviation of returns for both assets and the portfolio. You will see that by combining A and B in equal proportions the portfolio return is just the average of the individual returns but the risk of the portfolio, in this case, is less than half the risk of holding each asset in isolation. Plotting the returns over time shows that the variability of the portfolio is considerably reduced.

The diversification benefits arise in this case from the fact that the returns on A and B tend to move in opposite directions. The coefficient of correlation between the two returns is −0.56. If A and B represented two properties in different locations this movement would indicate that their returns were influenced by different economic factors. You may, for example, have no prior expectation that their returns should move together. Property A may be a retail development and property B may be an office building. If interest rates suddenly increase this will mean less disposable income for individuals to spend, which could depress the returns from the retail property. By contrast, the office building may be less affected by this announcement so you would not be surprised to find that the office returns are not correlated with the retail property.

It would, of course, be unusual to find large groups of properties that have negatively correlated returns. There are usually some common factors that cause all returns to be positively correlated to some degree. We can illustrate the effect that this would have on the portfolio risk by changing the signs of the returns on property B. This is shown in Table 10.2.

Changing the signs causes the correlation coefficient to change from negative to positive. The portfolio return of −1.18% is still the average of returns for properties A

Table 10.2 ● Asset and portfolio returns: positive correlation

Years	A	B	Portfolio
1	0.00%	−8.00%	−4.00%
2	4.00%	−5.00%	−0.50%
3	8.00%	−4.00%	2.00%
4	2.00%	−10.00%	−4.00%
5	−1.00%	−8.00%	−4.50%
6	−10.00%	−6.00%	−8.00%
7	−9.00%	−9.00%	−9.00%
8	−6.00%	−8.00%	−7.00%
9	0.00%	−3.00%	−1.50%
10	2.00%	8.00%	5.00%
11	−2.00%	−2.00%	−2.00%
12	10.00%	2.00%	6.00%
13	4.00%	2.00%	3.00%
14	8.00%	8.00%	8.00%
Average	0.71%	−3.07%	−1.18%
St. Dev.	6.09%	5.99%	5.34%
Correlation A, B	0.56		

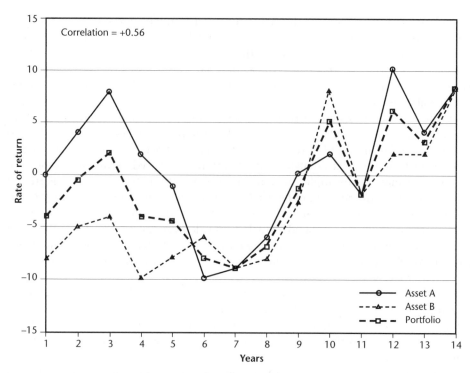

Figure 10.2 Diversification and positive correlation

and B, but the portfolio risk now shows only a small amount of reduction. You can see this in Figure 10.2.

The correlation coefficient, therefore, has an important effect on diversification. In fact, if the returns on two assets were perfectly negatively correlated it would be possible to create a portfolio that would eliminate risk altogether. Appendix 10A develops this idea further and shows how risk changes as the correlation structure changes. Perfect negative correlation is, however, difficult to find in practice. Although most portfolios do show the benefits of diversification it is unlikely to find risk being eliminated. There is therefore a limit to diversification.

This simple example offers some important messages.

● The most important factor influencing the risk of the portfolio is the correlation coefficient. If you can locate assets that are negatively correlated you can reduce the risk of your portfolio. However, the combination of less than perfectly correlated assets will also reduce risk.
● Those assets that are negatively correlated will be highly prized. You would, therefore, be prepared to pay more to secure those assets because of their diversification benefits.

You should begin to see that diversification is likely to be an important factor in determining the price of an asset. You should also see that the components that determine portfolio performance are the expected return, a measure of risk and the coefficient of correlation between the asset returns.

Those assets that have negatively correlated returns with other assets will be valuable for reducing portfolio risk. There will, therefore, be high demand for those assets and their prices will be bid up.

The contribution that an asset makes to diversification is an important factor determining the price of that asset.

Combining property returns

So far we have looked at portfolio risk in a hypothetical framework. To put this into context we can illustrate the effect of diversification by using real property data. Figure 10.3 shows these ideas applied to a portfolio consisting of two randomly selected properties with monthly returns over the period from 1986 to 1995. We have assumed that the portfolio consists of 40% of funds in property 1 and 60% in property 2.

We summarise the results of this analysis in Table 10.3.

Although the return on the portfolio is negative this represents an improvement on holding property 2 in isolation. What is more important, however, is the reduction in risk that has been achieved. This is less than separately holding each property and clearly shows that diversification has a powerful effect in a property portfolio. The reduction in risk has come about as a result of the low correlation between the returns on each property. In this case the correlation is 0.072, and by combining the properties into a portfolio the risk has been reduced by approximately 23% over the average. This is quite substantial and shows the benefits of diversification in property.

In Chapter 11 we investigate what the limits of diversification for property are likely to be. You will recall from Chapter 9 that the coefficient of correlation between

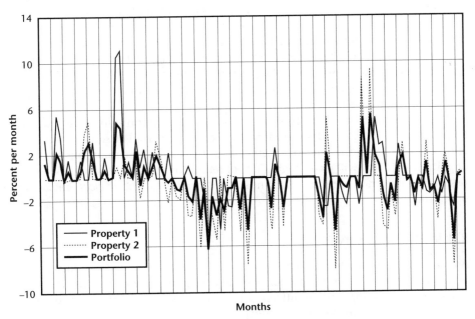

Figure 10.3 Combining property returns 1986–95

Table 10.3 ● A simple two-asset portfolio

	Average return % per month	Standard deviation in % per month
Property 1 (40%)	0.28	2.24
Property 2 (60%)	−0.48	2.66
Portfolio (1 + 2)	−0.18	1.89

Coefficient of correlation between properties 1 and 2 is 0.072.

individual properties is generally low. We argued that this was because of differences in location, lease structure, the type of tenant, and so on. Our simple portfolio example illustrates how powerful these differences can be when you start to combine properties into portfolios.

> The correlation of returns between individual properties will be influenced by factors specific to those properties. These will include the location, type of tenant, the lease structure and so on.
> Differences in these factors will give rise to low correlation which will contribute to improved diversification benefits for property portfolios.

This analysis represents the simple two-asset case in which we have made assumptions concerning the proportion of funds that can be invested in each asset. Generally speaking, however, you would be considering a large number of opportunities. If you were investing in equities you would also have a lot of control over the proportion of funds that could be invested in each asset. For any combination of assets it is possible to plot the position of the portfolio on a graph of risk against return. As the proportion of funds in each asset alters, the position of the resulting portfolio will change. Plotting all the combinations onto a graph will give rise to an area of all possible portfolios. These are shown in Figure 10.4.

The enclosed area in Figure 10.4 is referred to as the opportunity set of portfolios. Points such as A, B, C and D represent total investment in a single security. Only those portfolios that lie on the line XY are efficient as there is no other portfolio within the opportunity set that will give a higher rate of return for the same level of risk, or lower risk for the same rate of return. The line XY is referred to as the *efficient frontier* of the opportunity set.

Risk indifference curves

An optimal portfolio for each investor will lie somewhere on the line XY. The investor's attitude and preference for risk will determine the exact point. This can be found by constructing a risk indifference curve that represents the preferred trade-off between risk and return for an individual.

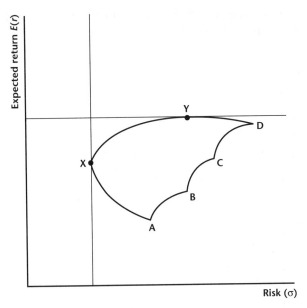

Figure 10.4 Opportunity set of portfolios

In Figure 10.5 investor A has a different attitude to risk to investor B. Although they both accept the same riskless rate of return investor A is prepared to take on more risk for each increase in return. Investor B by contrast is only prepared to accept a small amount of additional risk.

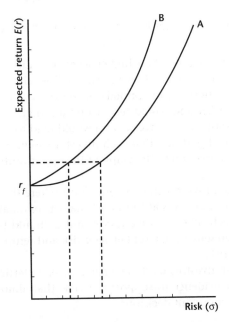

Figure 10.5 Risk indifference curves for investors A and B

As the riskless return changes each investor will have a family of risk indifference curves that are roughly parallel to each other. These are shown in Figure 10.6.

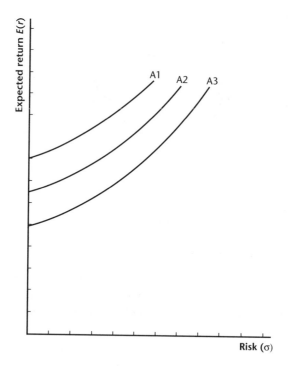

Figure 10.6   Risk indifference curves for investors with changes in the rate of interest

Each curve in Figure 10.6 represents a higher level of utility for investor A. It is possible to have an infinite number of curves that follow similar profiles for each investor. When it comes to choosing an optimal portfolio you will see from Figure 10.5 that investor A is a risk-seeker and would tend to hold a higher proportion of risky assets. Investor B, by contrast, is a risk-averter and would tend to hold less risky assets. You can identify the optimal portfolio that each investor should hold by plotting the family of risk indifference curves on to the graph of the opportunity set. This is shown in Figure 10.7.

You will see that for each investor there is one point where the indifference curve just touches the efficient frontier. It is at this point that the optimal efficient portfolio has been identified for each investor. Investors A and B should be happy with this outcome because they represent a trade-off between risk and return that satisfies their individual preferences to risk.

Generally speaking most investors tend to be risk-averse, preferring less risk to more risk. There is considerable evidence to support the view that almost all investors are risk-averse when making important decisions.

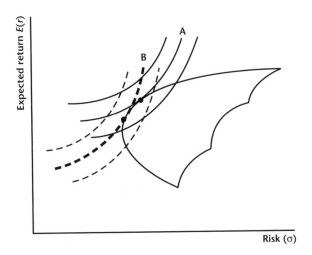

Figure 10.7 Risk indifference curves and the opportunity set

Assumptions used in portfolio models

One point we need to emphasise is that the portfolio model we have discussed is, technically speaking, a single period model. This is the way the theory has been developed although there is nothing to say what would be regarded as a single period. Other assumptions on which this analysis is based are as follows:

● Investors aim to maximise the single-period expected utility of their terminal wealth and choose among alternative portfolios on the basis of the mean and variance of return.
● Investors' risk estimates are proportional to the variability of the returns they visualise.
● All assets are perfectly divisible and marketable and there are no transaction costs.
● There are no taxes.
● For any given risk class, investors prefer a higher to a lower return.

Given the above it can be shown that the expected return and variance of returns for a portfolio can be expressed as follows.

Expected returns

$$E(r_p) = \sum_{i=1}^{n} x_i E(r_i) \tag{10.1}$$

Variance of returns

$$Var(r_p) = \sum_{i=1}^{n} \sum_{j=1}^{n} x_i x_j \sigma_{ij} \tag{10.2}$$

where

$E(r_p)$ = expected return on portfolio P

$Var(r_p)$ = variance of returns on portfolio P

x_i = proportion of funds invested in the ith asset

σ_{ij} = covariance of returns between the ith and jth asset

Another way of looking at the variance of the portfolio is to recognise that it is the sum of all the asset variances together with the covariances. We can therefore write the portfolio variance as:

$$Var(r_p) = \sum_{i=1}^{n} x_i^2 \sigma_i^2 + \sum_{i=1}^{n} \sum_{\substack{j=1; \\ j \neq i}}^{n} x_i x_j \sigma_{ij} \tag{10.3}$$

We will use this expression when we show how the inputs can be simplified.

The standard portfolio problem

The standard portfolio problem is, therefore, to select all values of x which minimise the portfolio variance subject to two constraints. The first is that the expected return on the portfolio is achieved and the second is that the total proportion of funds invested should not exceed 100%.

By selecting an expected return the optimal weight for each investment is calculated in order to minimise the portfolio variance. Successive repetitions of this procedure produce the efficient frontier. Markowitz developed a quadratic programming algorithm that enabled the efficient frontier to be identified. Although this process plots out the efficient frontier it does not identify which portfolio would be most suitable for an individual investor. As described above, the final choice depends on the particular preferences of the individual to risk and return.

In practice the mean-variance approach requires a significant amount of input data. Not only does each asset need to be described in terms of its mean and variance, it is also essential to estimate the covariance between each pair of assets. It is this aspect of portfolio analysis that causes the most problems. If you applied this approach to a portfolio consisting of 100 properties we would need to estimate 100 expected returns and variances together with 4,950 covariance terms. In fact the number of covariance terms increases exponentially as the number of assets in the analysis increases.

Ex-post versus ex-ante analysis

Strictly speaking, portfolio analysis requires estimates of expected returns, variances and covariances values. Although you may have historic data these are only a guide to what is required for the analysis. This point is important when considering the construction of property portfolios. Institutions often buy new properties to add to a portfolio. By definition, a time-series of returns for a new property would not be available. This, however, does not invalidate this type of analysis. The property analyst has to make a judgement concerning the expected value of each of the parameters. In fact, even if historic data were available it would still be necessary to adjust the figures to arrive at expected values. This approach also applies to the construction of stock portfolios. Investment is an *ex-ante* decision.

> Portfolio analysis is drafted in terms of expectations. Historic data can only provide evidence of past performance and should be adjusted to take account of market expectations before they can be used in a portfolio analysis.

The problem with solving the portfolio problem in an *ex-ante* framework really comes in trying to arrive at what the expected values should be. It may be possible to make a reasonable estimate of expected returns, but it is more difficult to arrive at some estimate of dispersion. Estimating the covariance is even more difficult. Apart from the fact that it is difficult to visualise how expected returns are likely to move relative to each other, the number of estimates required soon becomes very large. Markowitz recognised this problem and suggested that the data requirements could be significantly reduced if the returns on individual assets were related to some common factor.

Enter William Sharpe

It wasn't until 1963, however, that a model was developed by William Sharpe that built on these ideas. This became known as the *single index* or, more generally, the *market model*. It is the intuition behind the single index model that has led on to the development of a general theory of asset pricing.

Building on the work of Markowitz, Sharpe developed a model for stock portfolios that related security returns to the performance of some index of business activity. He suggested that the return on any security could be determined solely by random factors and the relationship with some common index. Given this assumption the equation for the return on security j in period t relative to an index of market movements, m, could be written as follows:

$$r_{jt} = \alpha_j + \beta_j r_{mt} + e_{jt} \tag{10.4}$$

α_j and β_j are constants for security j, and r_m is the return on the underlying common index. The observed returns for security j in period t (i.e., r_{jt}) are determined by the common relationship with the market index and the random error term, e_{jt}. We will look more closely at the statistical basis of the model in Appendix 10B. For the moment notice that the relationship we have described is linear, as can be seen in Figure 10.8.

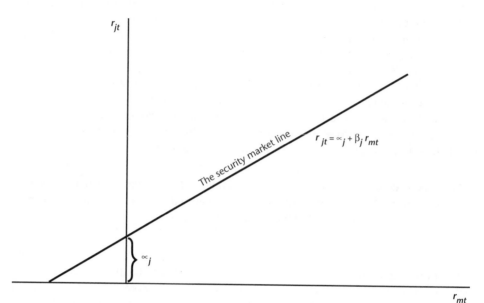

Figure 10.8 Single Index Model

The error term in this model embodies a number of very important assumptions:

- the average of the error terms is zero, i.e. $E(e) = 0$
- the variance of the error term is constant
- the error term is uncorrelated with the index, i.e. $Cov(e_{jt}, r_{mt}) = 0$
- the error terms have no serial correlation, i.e. $Cov(e_{jt}, e_{jt+n}) = 0$
- the error terms for one asset are uncorrelated with the error terms for another asset

Given the above and the equation relating returns to an index you can derive the following simple formulas for any asset.

Expected return for asset j

$$E(r_j) = \alpha_j + \beta_j r_m \tag{10.5}$$

Variance of returns for asset j

$$\sigma_j^2 = \beta_j^2 \sigma_m^2 + \sigma_{ej}^2 \tag{10.6}$$

Covariance of returns between assets i and j

$$\sigma_{ij} = \beta_i \beta_j \sigma_m^2 \tag{10.7}$$

You will see that by relating the returns on an asset to the returns on some common index it is possible to obtain, indirectly, all the inputs for a portfolio analysis. All that is required for a portfolio of n assets are estimates of α, β, and σ^2_e for each asset in addition to r_m and σ^2_m. The total number of calculations in this case is now $3n + 2$. Once these have been determined all the other inputs can be estimated from the above equations. A full portfolio analysis would require $\dfrac{(n^2 + 3n)}{2}$ inputs to be estimated, so this is clearly a substantial reduction. We have provided an example of how the single index model works in practice in Appendix 10B.

If the assumptions of the single index model hold we have another way of writing the expected return and variance of a portfolio.

Portfolio expected return

We have already shown that the portfolio return can be written as:

$$E(r_p) = \sum_{i=1}^{n} x_i E(r_i)$$

Using the single index model you can write this as:

$$E(r_p) = \sum_{i=1}^{n} x_i \alpha_i + \sum_{i=1}^{n} x_i \beta_i r_m \qquad (10.8)$$

Portfolio variance

We showed earlier that the portfolio variance could be split into its variance and covariance components as follows:

$$Var(r_p) = \sum_{i=1}^{n} x_i^2 \sigma^2_i + \sum_{i=1}^{n} \sum_{\substack{j=1; \\ j \neq i}}^{n} x_i x_j \sigma_{ij}$$

The single index model provides expressions for the variance and covariance that you can substitute to give:

$$Var(r_p) = \sum_{i=1}^{n} x_i^2 \beta_i^2 \sigma^2_m + \sum_{i=1}^{n} \sum_{\substack{j=1; \\ j \neq i}}^{n} x_i x_j \beta_i \beta_j \sigma^2_m + \sum_{i=1}^{n} x_i^2 \sigma^2_{ei} \qquad (10.9)$$

Alternatively, this can be written as:

$$Var(r_p) = \sum_{i=1}^{n} \sum_{j=1}^{n} x_i x_j \beta_i \beta_j \sigma^2_m + \sum_{i=1}^{n} x_i^2 \sigma^2_{ei} \qquad (10.10)$$

Although this appears complicated its value lies in the smaller number of estimates required to compute the portfolio variance.

The model we have derived has described returns in relation to a single index of market movements. In doing this we imposed a number of conditions on the properties of the error term in the single index model that enabled us to derive fairly simple models for use in a portfolio analysis. In comparison with a full portfolio analysis the results are, however, approximations that depend on whether the assumptions we have imposed have been violated. It turns out that in some cases there is some correlation between the error terms between individual assets whereas we had assumed that this would be zero. What this implies is that there are other factors besides a general market effect that help to explain returns. Including other indexes in the model could pick up these extra factors. This approach led to the development of *multi-index* models. We briefly discuss this in Appendix 10B.

Capital market theory

Following the development of portfolio theory, a number of researchers began to examine the implications of all investors adopting the rationale of Markowitz portfolio diversification. The results of this research have given rise to what has become known as *capital market theory*. This represented a major leap forward in our understanding of investment and has had a significant impact on the theory and practice of investment appraisal and valuation. The way in which capital market theory evolved from portfolio theory can be described as follows.

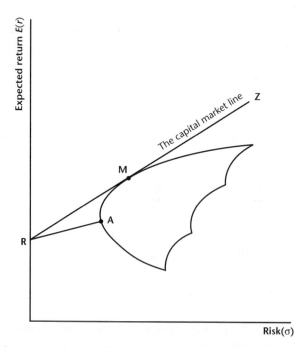

Figure 10.9 Investment in a risk-free asset

It has been shown that those portfolios that lie on the efficient frontier dominate all other portfolios in the opportunity set. It has also been shown that the optimal portfolio for any investor can be constructed for any investor once the investor's risk indifference curve has been established. This implies that it is not possible to achieve a portfolio that is more efficient than one that lies on the efficient frontier. This was assumed to be the case until it was realised that an investor could construct a portfolio that would lie outside the opportunity set by investing in a risk-free asset such as government securities in addition to a risky portfolio lying on the efficient frontier. We illustrate this in Figure 10.9.

Given the opportunity to invest in a risk-free asset you are in effect creating a simple two-asset portfolio. Let's look at the variance of a portfolio that consists of two assets.

The riskless asset is R and the risky portfolio, A, lies on the efficient frontier. Assume that you invest $x\%$ of your funds in the riskless asset. You can write the variance of this two-asset portfolio by rewriting the portfolio variance as follows:

$$Var(r_p) = x^2\sigma^2_R + (1 - x)\sigma^2_A + 2x(1 - x)\rho_{R,A}\sigma_R\sigma_A \qquad (10.11)$$

In this two-asset portfolio one of the assets is riskless and the other is a risky portfolio lying on the efficient frontier. By definition the riskless asset must have a variance of zero and will be uncorrelated with the risky portfolio. By assuming that $\sigma_R = 0$ and $\rho_{R,A} = 0$ you can simplify this expression to give:

$$Var(r_p) = (1 - x)^2\sigma^2_A \qquad (10.12)$$

Taking the square root gives:

$$\sigma_p = (1 - x)\sigma_A \qquad (10.13)$$

In standard deviation terms you will see that the risk of the portfolio is linear.

By altering the proportion of funds invested in the riskless asset and the risky portfolio it is possible to create any portfolio lying on a straight line between these two assets. You could, however, move on to a higher risk indifference curve if the line joining the risky and riskless portfolios was tangential to the opportunity set. In Figure 10.9 this is represented by the line RMZ. By altering the proportion of funds invested in R and M it is possible to create any portfolio between these two points. These are known as lending portfolios. Similarly, by borrowing at the riskless rate and investing in M it is possible to create any portfolio lying along the portion MZ. These are known as borrowing portfolios. Let's consider a numerical example to show how this happens.

Example

We will use Figure 10.9 to illustrate this example. Assume that you can borrow or lend any amount of money at the riskless rate R and that the only investments available to you are property. The point M on Figure 10.9 represents an index of property market movements in which you are able to buy shares. Each share in the index costs £10,000. After some research you estimate that over the next year there is a 60% chance that the market will rise by 10% and a 40% chance that it will rise by 50%. Given this information you estimate the expected return and standard deviation of the market returns as follows:

Expected market return

$$E(r) = \sum_{i=1}^{2} p_i r_i \tag{10.14}$$

$$E(r) = 0.6(10\%) + 0.4(50\%) = 26\%$$

Standard deviation of market returns

$$\sigma = \sqrt{\sum p_i (r_i - E(r_i))^2} \tag{10.15}$$

$$\sigma = \sqrt{0.6(10\% - 26\%)^2 + 0.4(50\% - 26\%)^2}$$

$$\sigma = \sqrt{384\%} = 19.59\%$$

You are able to borrow at 7.5% so the expected return on property looks good. You buy £50,000 worth of shares in the index with your own money but decide to gear up your returns by borrowing an extra £10,000 at the riskless rate which you also use to invest in the index. The expected return and standard deviation on your portfolio is shown in Table 10.4.

Table 10.4 ● Performance of a borrowing portfolio

	Market forecasts	
Borrowing portfolio	10% increase	50% increase
Total equity available	£50,000	£50,000
Amount borrowed	£10,000	£10,000
Total invested in risky portfolio	£60,000	£60,000
Increase in value at end of year	£66,000	£90,000
Repayment of loan	–£10,000	–£10,000
Interest on loan	–£750	–£750
Net value of portfolio	£55,250	£79,250
Return on equity over one year	10.50%	58.50%
Probability of outcome	0.60	0.40
Expected return (equation 10.14)	29.70%	
Standard deviation (equation 10.15)	23.50%	

The calculations of the expected return and standard deviation are exactly the same as we have shown above. You will see that by borrowing funds to gear up your investment you have managed to increase your expected overall return from 26% to 29.70%, but your risk has also increased from 19.59% to 23.50%.

Let us suppose that you didn't want to take on so much risk. Instead of borrowing funds to invest in the risky portfolio you decide to invest some funds in the riskless investment. Assume that in this case you invest £25,000 in government securities that offer the same riskless return of 7.5%. Your portfolio would now look like this:

Table 10.5 ● Performance of a lending portfolio

	Market forecasts	
Lending portfolio	**10% increase**	**50% increase**
Total equity available	£50,000	£50,000
Amount invested in riskless asset	–£25,000	–£25,000
Total invested in risky portfolio	**£25,000**	**£25,000**
Increase in value at end of year	£27,500	£37,500
Repayment of loan portfolio	£25,000	£25,000
Interest received on loan portfolio at 7.5%	£1,875	£1,875
Net value of portfolio	£54,375	£64,375
Return on equity over one year	8.75%	28.75%
Probability of outcome	0.60	0.40
Expected return (equation 10.14)	**16.80%**	
Standard deviation (equation 10.15)	**9.80%**	

The expected return has reduced, but so has the risk. Each of these options lies on a straight line connecting the riskless return to the return on the property index. This example is summarised in Figure 10.10.

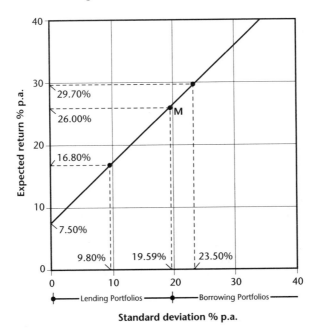

Figure 10.10 Borrowing and lending portfolios

The market portfolio

Although we have used a property index in this example you could, however, extend this idea so that the index consists of all risky assets. In this case it takes on a special meaning and is referred to as the *market portfolio* (M). You can still create portfolios that lie along a line from the riskless return to the market portfolio, and beyond, but the line is now known as the *capital market line* (CML). The importance of this is that the CML dominates all other portfolios within the opportunity set. Rational investors will, therefore, seek to lie at some point along the CML by buying some combination of M, because these portfolios represent the optimal efficient set of portfolios. The expected return on all *efficient portfolios* is just a linear function of the standard deviation of the market portfolio.

The separation theorem

What we have described embodies an important idea known as the *separation theorem*. Given the assumptions identified earlier, all rational investors will hold combinations of only two portfolios, i.e. the market portfolio (M) and the riskless asset (R). Each investor will make a choice concerning their risk–return preferences and then decide how to finance the purchase of the market portfolio. The risk-aggressive investor, A, will, for example, borrow funds at R and invest in M whereas the risk-averse investor will divide funds between M and R.

The separation theorem implies that, irrespective of whether investors seek risk or are averse to risk, they should all hold the same combination of risky assets. They differ in their attitude to risk merely by the way they finance their portfolios.

How diversification affects value

So far we have shown how diversification can reduce risk. We will now show you how diversification can also affect value. Let us assume that you have two assets, X and Y. They both generate an income stream of £1,000 p.a. but have different expected returns and risks. If the income is received in perpetuity you can estimate the value of the cash flows by capitalising at the expected rate of return.[1] Table 10.6 summarises the data.

Table 10.6 ● The value of assets X and Y

Portfolio	Cash flow	E(r)	St. Dev.	Capital value
X	£1,000 p.a.	10%	20%	£10,000
Y	£1,000 p.a.	20%	50%	£5,000

[1]We showed how to value a perpetuity in Chapter 3.

If you assume that the asset returns are perfectly negatively correlated you can find the proportion of funds to invest in X and Y that will completely eliminate risk.[2] This occurs when 71.4% of funds are invested in Y and 28.6% of funds are invested in X. As this completely eliminates risk you know that the expected return on your portfolio must also equal the riskless return. If this is taken as 7.5% the capital value of the new portfolio is as follows:

$$V_{X+Y} = \frac{£286 + £714}{0.075} = \frac{£1,000}{0.075} = £13,333$$

Even though you have created a new portfolio by making lower value investments you have increased the value of the portfolio because of the benefits of diversification. The negative correlation between X and Y has reduced the risk so that the portfolio cash flow is discounted at a lower rate. You will see from this that assets that reduce risk will command a high price because they can increase value.

Systematic and specific risk

The capital market line identifies the relationship between total risk and the expected return of portfolios after diversification. However, when you begin to look at individual assets you will find that part of their total risk can be attributed to common factors. This is known as *systematic risk*. It is the minimum level of risk that remains after diversification across a large number of randomly selected assets. The variability that cannot be attributed to the common factors can therefore be diversified away. This is known as *unsystematic* or *specific risk*.

Total risk can be split into two parts: systematic and unsystematic risk.
Systematic risk is also known as *market risk*. It is the risk that remains after diversification and affects all assets to some degree.
Unsystematic risk is also known as *specific risk*. It is the risk that is attributable to individual assets and can be diversified away in large portfolios.

If a portfolio is large enough it is possible for the specific risk to be diversified away completely so that all that is left is the systematic risk. If you apply this idea to property you will see that there are a number of factors that influence returns which you can classify as either systematic or specific risk. Some of these are listed in Table 10.7.

You will see that there are more specific risk factors than systematic factors. By building portfolios of property it is therefore possible to eliminate a lot of the risk of holding single properties. Diversification is an important issue in property portfolios

[2]With perfect negative correlation the proportion of funds to invest in portfolio X in order to minimise the portfolio risk can be estimated from $\dfrac{\sigma_Y}{\sigma_X + \sigma_Y}$ i.e. $w_x = \dfrac{50}{20 + 50} = 0.714$.

Table 10.7 ● Decomposition of property risk into systematic and specific risk

Systematic risk	Specific risk
General economic condition	Tenant
Changes in finance rates	Location
Taxation	Constructional aspects
	Building quality
	Legal constraints
	Depreciation

that is not well understood by practitioners. We will look at how effective diversification in property is likely to be in Chapter 11. The effectiveness of diversification does, however, have an important impact on the performance of property portfolios. We will consider this aspect in more detail in Chapter 16.

Partitioning the variance

You can get a better idea of the sources of risk if you revisit the single index model. You will recall that this relates the returns on any asset to some index of market activity:

$$r_{jt} = \alpha_j + \beta_j r_{mt} + e_{jt} \tag{10.16}$$

If you take the variance of this expression you can show that the total variation in returns comes from two sources. This is known as *partitioning the variance*:

$$Var(r_{jt}) = Var(\alpha_j + \beta_j r_{mt} + e_{jt}) \tag{10.17}$$

Expanding the expression on the right-hand side gives:

$$Var(r_{jt}) = \beta_j^2 Var(r_{mt}) + Var(e_{jt}) \tag{10.18}$$

This can also be written as:

Total risk = Systematic risk + Specific risk

where

Systematic risk = $\beta_j^2 Var(r_{mt})$

Specific risk   = $Var(e_{jt})$

By partitioning the variance in this way it is easy to see that the variability of returns comes from two sources. As assets are combined into portfolios the specific risk portion diversifies away until it eventually disappears.

The security market line and the capital asset pricing model

We showed earlier that the capital market line (CML) consists only of efficiently diversified portfolios. Efficiently diversified portfolios, therefore, consist only of systematic risk. This determines their expected return. When you begin to look at the risk of individual assets you know that they will carry both systematic risk and specific risk. Individual assets are, therefore, more risky than portfolios lying on the CML. They will lie within the opportunity set and can only be a part of the market portfolio through the process of successful diversification.

Let's look again at the equation of the single index model:

$$r_{jt} = \alpha_j + \beta_j r_{mt} + e_{jt} \tag{10.19}$$

By taking expectations and given that the expected value of the error term is zero you will arrive at the following:

$$E(r_{jt}) = \alpha_j + \beta_j r_{mt} \tag{10.20}$$

The single index model in equation 10.19 is just the equation of a regression model relating the returns on the asset to the market. The expected returns in equation 10.20 are just the fitted values from the equation. The slope of the line, β_j, relating returns on the asset to the market is a measure of systematic risk. An upward-sloping line indicates that the returns are positively correlated with the market, whereas a downward-sloping line indicates negative correlation.

Positive values of beta imply that the asset returns are positively correlated with the market.
Negative values of beta imply that asset returns are negatively correlated with the market.

Example

To illustrate the importance of beta in understanding performance we have shown in Table 10.8 the results of an analysis in which the monthly returns from a property are regressed against the Richard Ellis monthly index.

Table 10.8 ● Regression of the returns for a single property against the Richard Ellis monthly index

	Intercept	Beta	$\bar{R}^2$	Observations
Property returns	−0.004	0.754	0.103	80
Standard errors	0.005	0.237		

These are also summarised in Figure 10.11.

This property has a volatility, or beta coefficient, of 0.75. This is statistically indistinguishable from 1.0 and indicates that as the market moves up we would expect the returns on the property to move in the same general direction. The $\bar{R}^2$ value is, however, only 0.103, indicating that the property market explains only about 10% of the variation in returns of this property. The remaining 90% are explained by other factors specific to the property. With such a low $\bar{R}^2$ value you should not be surprised to find the performance of this property to be completely different from the market on a period-by-period basis.

The $\bar{R}^2$ value can also be interpreted as a measure of diversification. The figure we have shown in this example is typical of most properties. It is only by combining properties into portfolios that the level of diversification will increase.

From our discussion on diversification you will recall that the single most important factor that influences the success of diversification is the covariance of returns. Successful diversification involves combining assets that have low or negative covariance with each other. It follows, therefore, that the demand for these assets will be high. As a result their prices will be bid up. Assets that have high covariance will experience less demand and have lower values. Systematic risk, or beta, is another

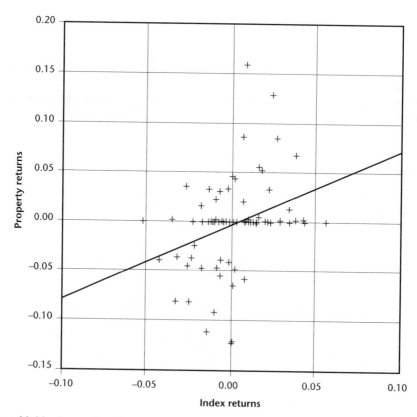

Figure 10.11 Regression of property returns on the Richard Ellis index

measure for covariance. Low beta assets will tend to have low expected returns and high values, whereas high beta assets will have high expected returns and low values.

Systematic risk, or beta, is a measure of covariance.
Low beta assets will have low expected returns and high values.
High beta assets will have high expected returns and low values.
As systematic risk is a measure of covariance it is the appropriate measure of risk to use for pricing individual assets.

Thus, in equilibrium the expected return on an asset is a positive linear function of its covariance of returns with the market. As systematic risk is a measure of covariance it is the appropriate measure of risk to use for pricing individual assets. The relationship between systematic risk and expected return is identified by the *security market line* (*SML*). In equilibrium every asset will lie on the SML and off the CML. Efficient portfolios will lie on both the CML and the SML because they consist only of systematic risk. The relationship between expected return and systematic risk is shown in Figure 10.12.

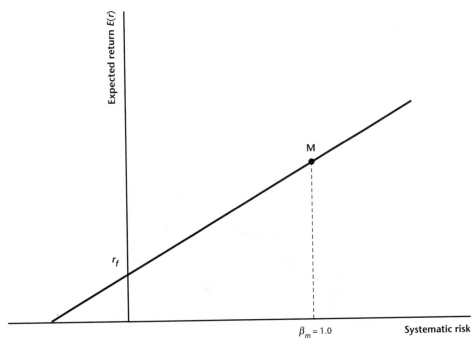

Figure 10.12 The security market line

You will see from this that the security market line (SML) looks similar to the capital market line (CML). There is a positive relationship between expected return and risk and the line cuts the vertical axis at the risk-free rate of return. However, the SML also extends beyond the risk-free return to cut the horizontal axis. This occurs because systematic risk is a measure of covariance and can be both positive and negative. The CML plots expected return against total risk, which is always positive.

The expected return on any asset, j, can be related to the security market line using the following equation:

$$E(r_j) = r_f + \beta_j[E(r_m) - r_f]$$

(10.21)

This is known as the *capital asset pricing model (CAPM)*. It relates the expected return of an asset to the risk-free rate of return plus a premium for bearing risk. This latter component is the risk premium for the market scaled by a factor related to the systematic risk of the asset. The CAPM is probably one of the most important models developed over the last thirty years and formally relates the expected return of an asset to its risk class.

The application of risk indifference curves shown earlier can also be applied to the security market line. You can still maximise your utility by moving onto the highest risk indifference curve. If an asset or portfolio is correctly priced in relation to the market, then it will lie on the security market line. The expected return derived from this line will give a net present value of zero when used to discount the asset's cash flows. If, however, an asset or portfolio is underpriced it will lie above the security market line. If you hold such an asset or portfolio you will be able to move on to a higher risk indifference curve and thus maximise your utility. What is equally important is that the portfolio or asset will generate a positive net present value. Figure 10.13 summarises the security market line and the risk indifference curves.

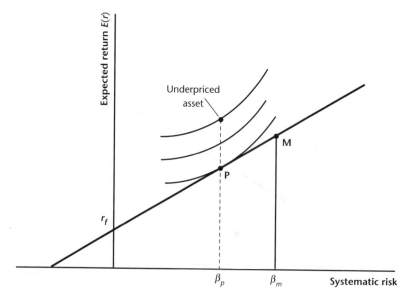

Figure 10.13 Risk indifference curves and the SML

It should be evident from the above that selecting portfolios or assets with positive net present values is entirely consistent with maximising utility. Our earlier proposition that investors should aim to follow a strategy that maximises net present value, therefore, remains valid within the risk–return framework outlined above. Estimating systematic risk is, therefore, an important factor in understanding the valuation process.

> Assets that are correctly priced will lie on the security market line.
> Underpriced assets lie above the line. They will maximise utility and contribute to positive net present values.
> Overpriced assets lie below the line and will contribute to negative net present values.

The security market line embodies an important idea concerning the way assets are priced. It identifies a positive relationship between expected return and risk. In a pricing framework, however, it is not total risk that is important. The relevant risk is systematic or non-diversifiable risk. The fundamental insight is that the price of an asset is determined by its contribution to a diversified portfolio. Investors are not willing, therefore, to pay a premium for bearing risk that can be diversified away.

> The price of an asset is determined by its contribution to a diversified portfolio. Investors are not willing to pay a premium for bearing risk that can be diversified away.

Systematic risk is, therefore, the appropriate measure of risk to use for diversified portfolios. However, even if investors are unable to hold diversified portfolios, systematic risk is still important for the simple reason that investors are not compensated for all the risk they take on. Systematic risk, therefore, determines the correct opportunity cost of capital to use when assessing an investment project. This will apply irrespective of the diversification policy being pursued. Although a property may be extremely risky in total risk terms its contribution to the risk of a mixed-asset portfolio may well mean that it has low systematic risk. It is for this reason that the risk premium for property is often quoted as approximately 2%.

The two beta trap

The capital asset pricing model we have just described is an important economic model that relates the expected returns on an asset to the market portfolio. A key part of the model is the estimation of beta relative to the market portfolio. The mathematics of this model looks exactly the same as the single index model. In fact we also used beta to measure the sensitivity of the returns on an asset relative to an index. It is because of these similarities that confusion often arises.

The *single index model* is just a simplified way of estimating the inputs for a portfolio analysis. It doesn't make any assumptions about the use of a market portfolio and is statistically sound.

In contrast to this the *capital asset pricing model* relies on identifying a market portfolio and measuring risk relative to that portfolio. The market portfolio is, however, unobservable and is difficult to proxy as it is supposed to contain every risky asset in the market. For the capital asset pricing model to work completely you would have to find the market portfolio. As yet, nobody has succeeded in doing this.

You will see that there are important differences between these approaches. As a result the capital asset pricing model is difficult to prove. In the property world some practitioners reject the capital asset pricing model as being invalid. However, they also confuse this with the single index model and reject that as well. This is wrong. You may not be able to prove the capital asset pricing model, but the implications of the single index model and estimation of beta relative to some index is still valid.

> Although you may reject the capital asset pricing model as being difficult to prove, the single index model and the estimation of beta relative to an index still remains valid.
> You do not require the capital asset pricing model to use the single index model.

This is an important point. Later on we will discuss a risk-adjusted approach to examine performance measurement. In order to do this we don't need to assume that the capital asset pricing model works. All we require is some way of ranking the risk of individual properties relative to an index of property market movements. This is a straightforward application of the single index model.

Summary

We have covered a lot of material in this chapter.

We showed that investors make decisions by considering both risk and return, and how portfolios could be constructed that would maximise the trade-off between risk and return. By developing this idea we were able to show that if all investors adopted the same investment rationale, portfolio theory was central to understanding how expected returns should be estimated.

In developing this idea we showed how it led to a general theory of asset pricing. The important insight in this was that risk could be split into two parts, systematic and specific risk, and that investors would only be compensated for the risk they could not diversify away. This component of risk, therefore, identifies the expected return and is the most important component affecting the price of an asset.

Although property is commonly valued using yields, this does not imply that these ideas have no value in the property industry. Given that yields are just a combination of expected returns and growth rates it is important to know how the expected returns are determined. Our understanding of yields and how property is priced will improve with a better understanding of these issues.

This chapter has six appendices which cover some of the issues raised in more detail.

Appendix 10A: Portfolio analysis

This includes an analysis of a two-asset portfolio. We then show how the techniques can be extended to analyse the asset allocation problem of a portfolio consisting of property, equities and bonds.

Appendix 10B: Portfolio analysis and index models

In this appendix we show how the single index model can be used to estimate the inputs for a portfolio analysis. We also introduce multi-index models.

Appendix 10C: Portfolio analysis using alternative risk measures

In Chapter 10 we made use of variance as the main measure of risk. This, however, is not the only risk measure that has been used in applying portfolio theory. In this appendix we discuss the coefficient of variation, semi-variance, mean absolute deviation and lower partial moments.

Appendix 10D: The capital asset pricing model (CAPM)

This appendix includes a formal derivation of the capital asset pricing model.

Appendix 10E: The CAPM with non-marketable assets

One of the features of property is that it is indivisible and can, therefore, be difficult to market. There are other assets that suffer from this problem and this appendix shows how the CAPM can be amended to take this aspect into consideration. The result is a more general form of CAPM.

Appendix 10F: Duration and risk

We pointed out in Chapter 10 that portfolio theory is drafted in terms of expectations so that a measure of expected risk is required. In this appendix we develop a model based on duration that can be used as a basis for estimating expected risk.

Chapter 10: Summary table

1. Portfolio theory is about minimising risk for a given level of return or maximising return for a given level of risk.

2. Portfolio theory has a general application and can be applied to all risky assets.

3. The most important factor influencing portfolio risk is the correlation between asset returns.

4. Assets that have low or negative correlation with other assets will be in high demand and their prices will be bid up.

5. The correlation between the returns on individual properties will be influenced by factors specific to those properties. These include location, type of tenant, the lease structure, and so on.

   The correlation of returns between individual properties tends to be low.

6. Given an opportunity set of portfolios the choice will depend on the investor's attitude to risk.

   Attitude to risk can be identified by risk indifference curves.

7. Portfolio theory is based on the following assumptions:
   ● Investors aim to maximise the single-period expected utility of their terminal wealth and choose among alternative portfolios on the basis of the mean and variance of return.
   ● Investors' risk estimates are proportional to the variability of the returns they visualise.
   ● All assets are perfectly divisible and marketable and there are no transaction costs.
   ● There are no taxes.

   For any given risk class, investors prefer a higher to a lower return.

8. A portfolio can be described in terms of its expected return and variance assuming that the weight of each of its assets does not exceed 100%.

   The expected return is:

   $$E(r_p) = \sum_{i=1}^{n} x_i E(r_i)$$

   The variance is:

   $$Var(r_p) = \sum_{i=1}^{n} \sum_{j=1}^{n} x_i x_j \sigma_{ij}$$

9. Portfolio theory is drafted in terms of expectations. Historic returns are only used as a guide to estimate the parameters. What are needed are forecasts.

10. The single index model was introduced as a means of simplifying the number of terms required in the analysis. It relates the returns on an asset to an index of market movements.

11. Using the single index model the expected return, variance and covariance can be estimated as follows:

Expected return:
$$E(r_j) = \alpha_j + \beta_j r_m$$

Variance:
$$\sigma_j^2 = \beta_j^2 \sigma_m^2 + \sigma_{ej}^2$$

Covariance:
$$\sigma_{ij} = \beta_i \beta_j \sigma_m^2$$

12. Given the opportunity to invest in the risk-free rate of return it is possible to create portfolios that lie outside the Markowitz efficient frontier.

The capital market line joins the risk-free return to the market portfolio.

13. The separation theorem tells us that there are only two portfolios in the market: the riskless portfolio and the market portfolio.

The choice of risk and returns for an individual will depend on how he or she finances his or her portfolios.

14. All assets and portfolios can be split into systematic risk and specific risk.

Systematic or market risk cannot be diversified away. Specific risk can be diversified away.

15. Investors will only pay for that portion of risk that cannot be diversified away. The capital asset pricing model relates expected return to systematic risk.

$$E(r_j) = r_f + \beta_j[E(r_m) - r_f]$$

16. Assets that lie on the security market line are correctly priced. Under- and overpriced assets lie above or below the line.

Problems

1. Why is the correlation between asset returns important for diversification?
2. Why is correlation so important in determining the price of an asset?
3. What do you understand by the term 'efficient frontier'?
4. Should a portfolio analysis always be based on historic data?
5. What is the purpose of the single index model?
6. Why would borrowing and lending make a difference to the risk of a portfolio?

7. What is the market portfolio, and why is it so important in terms of asset pricing?

8. What is the separation theorem?

9. What is the difference between systematic and specific risk?

10. What is the capital asset pricing model?

11. What is the difference between beta measured relative to an index and beta measured relative to the market portfolio?

Selected references

Elton, E.J. and Gruber, M.J. (1981) *Modern Portfolio Theory and Investment Analysis*, 5th edn. New York: John Wiley & Sons, Inc.

Fama, E.F. (1976) *Foundations of Finance*, Oxford: Blackwell.

Fama, E.F. and Miller, M.H. (1972) *The Theory of Finance*, Hinsdale, Illinois: Dryden Press.

Francis, J.C. (1986) *Investments*, 4th edn. New York: McGraw-Hill.

Francis, J.C. and Archer, S.H. (1979) *Portfolio Analysis*, Prentice-Hall Foundations of Finance Series, 2nd edn. Englewood Cliffs, NJ: Prentice-Hall Inc.

Haugen, R.A. (1993) *Modern Investment Theory*, 3rd edn. Englewood Cliffs, NJ: Prentice-Hall International.

Markowitz, H.M. (1984) The 'two beta' trap. *Journal of Portfolio Management* **11** (1), 12–20.

Rudd, A. and Clasing, H.K. (1982) *Modern Portfolio Theory: The Principles of Investment Management*, Homewood, Illinois: Dow Jones-Irwin.

Sharpe, W.F. (1970) *Portfolio Theory and Capital Markets*, McGraw-Hill Series in Finance, New York: McGraw-Hill.

Sharpe, W.F. (1985) *Investments*, 3rd edn. Englewood Cliffs, NJ: Prentice Hall.

Appendix 10A
Portfolio analysis

In Chapter 10 we discussed the background to constructing efficient portfolios. In this appendix we will illustrate how this works in practice using a simple two-asset portfolio. We will then show how the principles can be used in a mixed-asset portfolio consisting of property, equities and bonds in order to investigate the asset allocation problem.

A two-asset portfolio

First, we will show the effect that changes in the correlation between property returns can have on the risk of a portfolio. Assume that you own two properties, A and B, that have expected returns and standard deviations as shown in Table 10A.1.

The proportion of funds invested in A can vary between 0% and 100% and the coefficient of correlation between A and B is either -1, 0 or $+1$. From this information it is possible to estimate the expected return and standard deviation of the portfolio for different proportions of A and B by using the equations we gave in Chapter 10. You will recall that the portfolio expected return and standard deviation could be written as:

$$E(r_p) = \sum_{i=1}^{n} x_i E(r_i)$$

(10A.1)

For a two-asset portfolio $n = 2$. You can, therefore, write the returns for A and B as $r_1 = r_a$ and $r_2 = r_b$. In addition the proportion of funds invested in A and B can also be written so that $x_1 = x_a$ and $x_2 = x_b$. By also expressing x_b in terms of x_a you can rewrite equation 10A.1 as follows:

$$E(r_p) = x_a E(r_a) + (1 - x_a)E(r_b)$$

(10A.2)

You will see that the expected return is just the weighted average of the two returns.

As far as the portfolio variance is concerned this is a more complex calculation as it depends on the coefficient of correlation between A and B. The variance can be written as:

$$\sigma_p^2 = \sum_{i=1}^{n} \sum_{j=1}^{n} x_i x_j \sigma_{ij}$$

(10A.3)

Table 10A.1 ● Risk and return of two assets

Asset	Expected return	Standard deviation
Property A	6%	3%
Property B	8%	4%

Table 10A.2 ● Two-asset portfolio risk and return

Amount invested in A (%)	Portfolio expected rate of return (%)	Portfolio standard deviation (%)		
		Case 1 $P_{ab} = -1$	Case 2 $P_{ab} = 0$	Case 3 $P_{ab} = +1$
100	6.00	3.00	3.00	3.00
75	6.50	1.25	2.46	3.25
50	7.00	0.50	2.50	3.50
25	7.50	2.25	3.09	3.75
0	8.00	4.00	4.00	4.00

By expressing the covariance in terms of the coefficient of correlation between A and B this can be expanded to:

$$\sigma_p^2 = x_a^2 \, \sigma_a^2 + (1 - x_a)^2 \, \sigma_b^2 + 2x_a \, (1 - x_a)P_{ab}\sigma_a\sigma_b \qquad (10A.4)$$

The portfolio standard deviation is just the square root of equation 10A.4.

By varying the proportion of funds invested in property A and making an assumption about the coefficient of correlation it is possible to estimate the expected return and standard deviation for a range of portfolios. The results are given in Table 10A.2.

Case 1. Perfect negative correlation

When the returns are perfectly negatively correlated, as in case 1, you will see that the portfolio standard deviation both reduces and then increases rapidly. In fact, there is a point when the risk can be eliminated completely.

Case 2. Zero correlation

In this case the risk gradually reduces and then increases. Risk cannot be completely eliminated.

Case 3. Perfect positive correlation

When the asset returns are perfectly positively correlated there is no reduction in risk.

This simple two-asset case provides a clear example of how important the correlation structure is likely to be when considering diversification. Figure 10A.1 summarises the range of portfolios in risk–return space for the correlation structures shown above. Point X also shows that with perfect negative correlation it is possible to choose a proportion of funds to invest in A and B that will eliminate risk completely.

This is clearly an important idea and Figure 10A.1 shows the boundary for all feasible portfolios when the coefficient of correlation lies within the range of −1 to +1. This is represented by the triangle AXB. Depending on the coefficient of correlation all

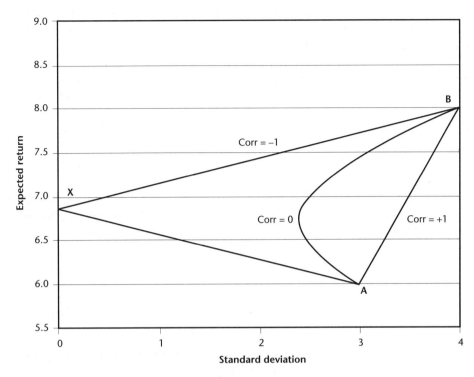

Figure 10A.1 Two-asset portfolios in risk-return space

other portfolios will lie within this triangle. We have also shown the profile of port-folios when the coefficient of correlation is zero.

This simple example incorporates two important ideas that are common to all port-folios: *minimum risk* and *efficient portfolios*.

Minimum risk portfolios

Depending on the correlation structure there will be some proportion of funds that will minimise portfolio risk. With a two-asset portfolio it is possible to derive a simple model to do this.

First, consider what would happen if the assets were perfectly correlated, so that $\rho_{ab} = 1$. Substituting into equation 10A.4 gives:

$$\sigma_p^2 = x_a^2 \sigma_a^2 + (1 - x_a)^2 \sigma_b^2 + 2x_a (1 - x_a)\sigma_a \sigma_b \tag{10A.5}$$

You can factorise this to give:

$$\sigma_p^2 = [x_a \sigma_a + (1 - x_a)\sigma_B]^2 \tag{10A.6}$$

In terms of standard deviation:

$$\sigma_p = x_a \sigma_a + (1 - x_a)\sigma_B \tag{10A.7}$$

You will see from this that when the asset returns are perfectly positively correlated the portfolio risk is just a linear combination of the risk of each asset. All combinations of A and B lie on a straight line, as shown in Figure 10A.1.

This linear relationship only exists when $\rho_{ab} = 1$. Substituting other values for ρ_{ab} into equation 10A.4 will result in a quadratic equation, so there will be some value of x_a that will cause the portfolio risk to be minimised. You can find this by differentiating equation 10A.4 with respect to x_a and setting the result equal to zero. If your school algebra is up to it you can differentiate equation 10A.5 to give:

$$\frac{d\sigma^2_p}{dx_a} = 2x_a\sigma^2_a - 2(1 - x_a)\sigma^2_b + 2(1 - x_a)\rho_{ab}\sigma_a\sigma_b - 2x_a\rho_{ab}\sigma_a\sigma_b \qquad (10A.8)$$

This measures the slope at each point along the curve given by equation 10A.5. To find the minimum value you set this equal to zero and solve for the proportion of funds to invest in property A:

When $\dfrac{d\sigma^2_p}{dx_a} = 0$

$$x_a = \frac{\sigma_b(\sigma_b - \rho_{ab}\sigma_a)}{\sigma^2_a + \sigma^2_b - 2\rho_{ab}\sigma_a\sigma_b} \qquad (10A.9)$$

This is a general equation for a two-asset portfolio. From this you can examine cases 2 and 1 when the coefficient of correlation is either 0 or –1.

Zero correlation

The proportion of funds to invest in asset A can be found by substituting $\rho_{ab} = 0$ into equation 10A.9. This gives:

$$x_a = \frac{\sigma^2_b}{\sigma^2_a + \sigma^2_b} \qquad (10A.10)$$

Using the figures from Table 10A.1 the portfolio risk is minimised when:

$$x_a = \frac{4^2}{3^2 + 4^2} = 0.64$$

Substituting $x_a = 0.64$ and $\rho_{ab} = 0$ in equation 10A.4 provides an estimate for the minimum risk:

$$\sigma^2_p = 0.64^2(3^2) + (1 - 0.64)^2 (4)^2 = 5.76\%$$

$$\sigma_p = 2.40\%$$

This is known as the *minimum variance portfolio* or MVP. You can confirm this value from Figure 10A.1.

Perfect negative correlation

For perfect negative correlation you can find the proportion of funds to invest in property A by substituting $\rho_{ab} = -1$ in equation 10A.9.

When $\rho_{ab} = -1$,

$$x_a = \frac{\sigma_b(\sigma_b + \sigma_a)}{\sigma_a^2 + \sigma_b^2 + 2\sigma_a\sigma_b} \qquad (10A.11)$$

Factorising the bottom line and simplifying gives:

$$x_a = \frac{\sigma_b}{\sigma_b + \sigma_a} \qquad (10A.12)$$

Using the example in Table 10A.1 the proportion of funds to invest in A to minimise risk is given by:

$$x_a = \frac{4}{4 + 3} = 0.571$$

With perfect negative correlation this is the proportion of funds to invest in property A that should completely eliminate risk. Substituting $x_a = 0.571$ and $\rho_{ab} = -1$ in equation 10A.4 gives:

$$\sigma_p^2 = (0.571)^2(3)^2 + (1 - 0.571)^2(4)^2 - 2(0.571)(1 - 0.571)(3)(4)$$
$$\sigma_p^2 = \sigma_p = 0$$

This can also be confirmed in Figure 10A.1.

Efficient portfolios

We introduced the idea of efficient portfolios in Chapter 10. A portfolio is said to be efficient if it offers the highest rate of return for a given level of risk or lowest risk for a given rate of return. Figure 10A.1, for example, shows that if the correlation is $\rho_{ab} = -1$ all portfolios that lie along the line XB have higher rates of return for each level of risk than portfolios lying along the line XA. Investors would, therefore, prefer to choose a combination of A and B that will ensure that they lie along XB because this will maximise their trade-off between risk and return.

All portfolios lying along XB are said to be efficient. In fact, all portfolios that lie on the curve between the minimum risk portfolio and the highest risk–return portfolio will be considered efficient for a given correlation structure. In our example, if the correlation coefficient between A and B is zero, the minimum risk portfolio would be constructed by investing 64% in asset A and 36% in asset B. We showed the calculations for this above. Efficient portfolios will lie between this point and point B and would be formed by increasing the proportion of funds invested in B.

A three-asset portfolio

The example given above illustrates some important points and as we only used two assets the calculations were fairly straightforward. Moving to a three-asset portfolio introduces more complexity. Although it is still possible to complete the calculations by hand it is nevertheless better to use an optimiser. This also gives us the opportunity to consider a real problem that deals with how much to invest in property, equities and bonds. This is a common asset allocation problem faced by financial institutions and represents a good application of portfolio theory. Before we start, however, it is important to realise that our analysis is based on an historic dataset. Our allocations will, therefore, be *ex-post* but will be correct given the data series we used. Investors are, however, more interested in *ex-ante* allocations. Unless you believe that historic performance is a good guide to future performance you would need to amend the parameters before using them in a portfolio model.

Table 10A.3 ● Annual returns for property, equities and bonds

	Property	Equities	Bonds
1971	16.90	45.20	35.30
1972	24.80	16.30	−10.00
1973	22.80	−28.30	−12.30
1974	−13.70	−51.70	−22.20
1975	10.50	150.90	39.00
1976	7.30	−0.80	15.00
1977	23.90	49.00	45.00
1978	23.30	6.90	−1.50
1979	22.60	8.00	4.90
1980	16.20	33.30	20.70
1981	15.00	14.30	2.40
1982	7.50	30.70	52.60
1983	7.80	28.40	16.20
1984	9.50	29.80	10.40
1985	9.20	19.80	12.60
1986	11.80	25.90	12.50
1987	26.80	7.10	16.40
1988	29.10	10.40	8.20
1989	15.20	36.00	7.40
1990	−9.30	−9.80	7.90
1991	−4.70	20.00	18.20
1992	−3.30	20.80	19.10
1993	19.00	27.90	25.10
1994	12.40	−5.60	−8.40
1995	4.50	23.80	17.60
1996	10.80	16.80	7.60
1997	17.80	22.60	15.50

Source: IPD Annual Index, 1998.

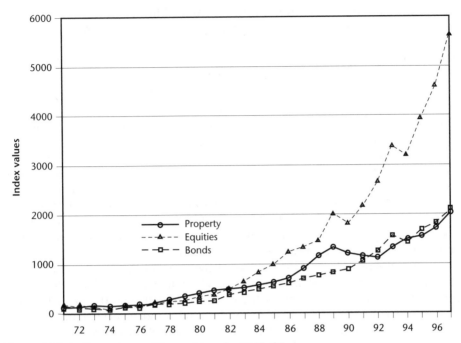

Figure 10A.2 Property, equities and bonds, 1971–97

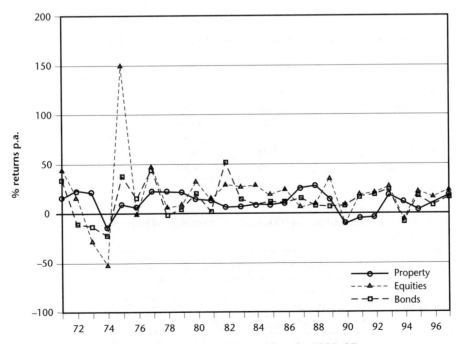

Figure 10A.3 Total returns: property, equities and bonds, 1991–97

The data we will use are taken from the IPD Annual Index and cover a long-term total return series from 1970 to 1997 for property, equities and bonds. These are summarised in Table 10A.3.

Figure 10A.2 plots these figures in index form and shows that over the period 1971–97 the equity market offered the best performance.

The performance of the property and bond markets was similar, but as will be seen from Figure 10A.3, the volatility of each of the markets differed.

You can get a better indication of the performance of each asset class by summarising their distributional characteristics. These are given in Table 10A.4.

The high return associated with equities was also accompanied by higher risk. Note also that the returns for property were negatively skewed whereas equities and bonds were positively skewed. As far as normality is concerned we can't reject the proposition that the property and bond returns were normal, but we can reject this proposition for the equity market. This will affect our allocations as our model is based on the assumption of normally distributed returns. We will relax this assumption when we look at other measures of risk in Appendix 10C.

These statistics provide a general picture of the shape of the distribution for each asset class. As you are interested to know what allocations you should use in a multi-period context you can use the geometric mean return (although the standard deviation is calculated with reference to the mean) and standard deviation. The other information you require is the correlation between each of the assets. These are summarised in Table 10A.5.

You will notice that property is not highly correlated with either equities or bonds. This implies that it is good for diversifying the risk in a mixed-asset portfolio. However, using a different period will result in different figures.

Table 10A.4 ● Distributional characteristics of asset classes, 1971–97

	Property	Equities	Bonds
Arithmetic mean	12.36	20.29	13.16
Geometric mean	11.82	16.11	11.93
Standard deviation	10.88	33.70	16.94
Skewness	−0.68	1.77	0.29
Kurtosis	2.96	10.11	3.26
Jarque–Bera	2.06	70.89	0.44

Table 10A.5 ● Correlation coefficients between asset classes, 1971–97

	Property	Equities	Bonds
Property			
Equities	0.173		
Bonds	0.059	0.695	

The general portfolio model

To solve the asset allocation problem the portfolio model is usually set up in the following form:

$$\text{Minimise } \sigma^2_p = \sum_{i=1}^{n} \sum_{j=1}^{n} x_i x_j \sigma_{ij} \tag{10A.13}$$

subject to

$$1. \sum_{i=1}^{n} x_i = 1 \tag{10A.14}$$

$$2. \sum_{i=1}^{n} x_i \bar{r}_i = \bar{r}_p \tag{10A.15}$$

$$3. x_i \geq 0 \quad i = 1, \ldots, n$$

All this means is that the portfolio variance is to be minimised subject to three constraints. The first tells you that the sum of all the weights should add up to 1. In other words, all the funds you have available for investment are fully used. The second constraint tells you that the weighted average of the returns is equal to the target return on the portfolio. The third constraint ensures that the weight associated with each investment is greater than or equal to zero.

By setting up the problem in this way you can trace out the efficient frontier by choosing a target return and then solving for the proportion of funds that would minimise the portfolio variance. By increasing the target return from the return on the minimum variance portfolio up to the maximum return portfolio you end up with a series of portfolios that trace out the efficient frontier.

This is a quadratic programming problem because it involves squared terms in the variance expression. If you are not sure why this is the case take a look at equation 10A.5 where we expanded the variance to include two assets. The weights attached to each of the variance terms were squared. There are a number of software packages available to solve this type of problem. We have used an optimiser and have summarised the results in Table 10A.6. It is also possible, however, to set up this problem using a spreadsheet that is able to solve equations. Excel, for example, has an add-in called Solver which could be used to estimate the optimal proportion of funds to invest in each asset. We will leave this as an exercise.

You will see that as the expected return on the portfolio increases so does the risk. This, of course, is what you would expect although the relationship is not linear. Each of the portfolios lies on a curve as shown in Figure 10A.4.

By combining different proportions of the three assets it is possible to achieve a portfolio that gives a better trade-off between risk and return than by holding each asset in isolation. You will also see from Table 10A.6 that as the expected return on the portfolio increases the allocations shift towards equities. We have plotted the allocations to each asset class for each portfolio in Figure 10A.5.

Table 10A.6 ● Optimal allocations for three-asset portfolio, 1971–97

Portfolio	MVP	1	2	3	4	5	6	7	8	9
Exp.Ret.%	11.84	12.32	12.79	13.26	13.73	14.21	14.68	15.15	15.63	16.10
Port.S.D.	9.39	10.57	12.28	14.47	17.17	20.20	23.42	26.77	30.21	33.70
Allocations										
Property	71.98	72.97	74.30	66.32	55.26	44.21	33.16	22.11	11.05	0.00
Equities	0.00	11.28	22.57	33.68	44.74	55.79	66.84	77.89	88.95	100.00
Bonds	28.02	15.75	3.12	0.00	0.00	0.00	0.00	0.00	0.00	0.00

Note: MVP = minimum variance portfolio.

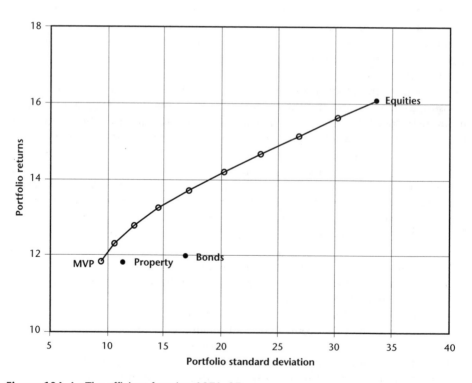

Figure 10A.4 The efficient frontier, 1971–97

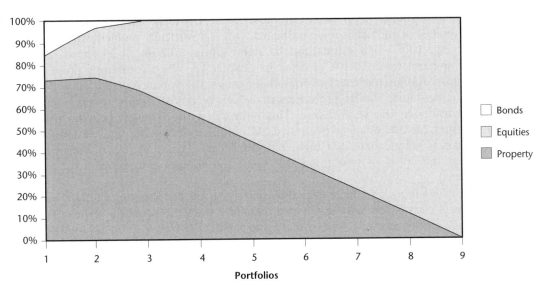

Figure 10A.5 Asset allocation, 1971–97

This shows that the allocation to bonds drops out very quickly. As the return on the portfolio increases the allocation to property steadily declines. This illustration shows the full range of possible allocations. Your choice of portfolio will depend on your attitude to risk and return. For example, let us assume that you have undertaken these calculations on behalf of a financial institution. Let us also assume that it has a target return of 15% p.a. In order to achieve this return and minimise its risk the institution should hold 25.89% in property and 74.11% in equities. This answer assumes, however, that the distribution of returns and the correlation structure you observed over the period 1971–97 remains unchanged. If you don't believe this, then you will have to make your own assumptions and re-estimate the model.

Error maximisation and other issues

Before we complete this section we need to sound a warning note concerning the use of optimisation models. The allocations that we have shown above are mathematically correct but they sometimes don't tie in with the allocations observed in practice. For example, Table 10A.6 shows that at the lower levels of expected return the allocation to property exceeds 70% and dominates all other assets. In fact, over the range of returns covered in Table 10A.6 the allocation to property is much higher than observed in practice. There are a number of possible explanations for this.

● Optimisation models tend to favour those assets where the expected return is overestimated or the risk is underestimated. This is a particular problem with real estate, especially when estimating the returns from indexes. It is known as smoothing and we discuss it in detail in Chapter 12. When combining properties into portfolios the effect of smoothing causes the variance of the portfolio to be understated. Similar problems can be observed with equity indexes, but not generally to the same degree. This means that the trade-off between risk and return for real estate is overstated. As optimisation models tend to favour those assets where there is a high trade-off between risk and return, you will see that the effect of smoothing will cause the allocation to property to be overstated.

● The portfolio models we have used also assume that the distribution of returns for each asset class is normally distributed. In many cases the distributions may be positively or negatively skewed so that using standard deviation as an appropriate measure of risk may be inappropriate. There are, however, other models of risk that are less restrictive. See Appendix 10C.

● Asset allocation is really an *ex-ante* exercise. Historic data may not be a good guide to what investors *expect* to happen. The allocations we have shown are, therefore, conditional on the information we have used.

Asset allocation is not, therefore, a mechanical exercise involving the use of historic data. To be undertaken properly it requires careful forecasts of the inputs if it is to provide meaningful results. Portfolio theory does, however, provide a good framework for providing usable solutions.

Selected references

Blundell, G. and Ward, C.W.R. (1987) Property portfolio allocation: a multi-factor model. *Land Development Studies* **4**, 145–56.

Byrne, P. and Lee, S. (1994) Computing Markowitz efficient frontiers using a spreadsheet optimiser. *Journal of Property Finance* **5** (1), 58–66.

Byrne, P. and Lee, S. (1995) Is there a place for property in the multi-asset portfolio? *Journal of Property Finance* **6** (3), 60–83.

Firtenberg, P., Ross, S.A. and Zisler, R. (1988) Real estate: the whole story. *Journal of Portfolio Management* (Spring), 23–32.

Fogler, H.R. (1984) 20% in real estate: Can theory justify it? *Journal of Portfolio Management* **10** (2), 6–13.

MacGregor, B.D. and Nanthakumaran, N. (1992) The allocation to property in the multi-asset portfolio: the evidence and theory reconsidered. *Journal of Property Research* **9**, 5–32.

Matysiak, G.A. (1993) Optimizing property portfolio holdings: a scenario based approach. *Journal of Property Finance* **4** (3/4), 68–75.

Michaud, R.O. (1989) The Markowitz optimisation enigma: is 'optimised' optimal? *Financial Analysts Journal* (Jan./Feb.), 31–42.

Rydin, Y.J., Rodney, W. and Orr, C. (1990) Why do institutions invest in property? *Journal of Property Finance* **1** (2), 250–8.

Webb, J. and Rubens, J. (1988) How much in real estate?: A surprising answer. *Journal of Portfolio Management* (Spring), 10–13.

Appendix 10B
Portfolio analysis and index models

The portfolio models we illustrated in Appendix 10A used a small number of assets and were relatively easy to solve. However, as soon as you are faced with much larger portfolios the problem of estimation becomes more difficult. This is not because of computational power but because the number of parameters needed to set up the model increases significantly as more assets are added.

In order to optimise the proportion of funds to invest in each asset in your portfolio you need to estimate the expected rate of return, the variance of returns and the covariance for each asset. If you want to do this in an *ex-ante* framework, then each of these elements has to be estimated using forecasts.

The number of expected returns will come from the following expression:

$$E(r_p) = \sum_{i}^{n} x_i E(r_i) \tag{10B.1}$$

If you have a portfolio with 100 assets you will need to estimate 100 expected returns.

The number of variance and covariance terms comes from the expression for the variance of a portfolio:

$$\sigma^2_p = \sum_{i=1}^{n} \sum_{j=1}^{n} x_i x_j \sigma_{ij} \tag{10B.2}$$

We showed in Chapter 10 that you could also write this as the sum of the variances and covariances.

$$\sigma^2_p = \sum_{i=1}^{n} x_i^2 \sigma_i^2 + \sum_{i=1}^{n} \sum_{\substack{j=1; \\ j \neq i}}^{n} x_i x_j \sigma_{ij} \tag{10B.3}$$

This also shows that the number of variance terms equals the number of assets. The double summation sign, however, captures the number of covariance terms. The double summation is just another way of writing a matrix. In fact, the whole expression for the portfolio variance comes from what is known as a variance–covariance matrix. You can get a better idea of the number of elements involved if we illustrate the components in this matrix. This is shown in Table 10B.1, and is just another way of writing equation 10B.2.

Table 10B.1 ● The variance–covariance matrix

	1	2	3	4	- - - - - - -	n
1	Cov(1,1)	Cov(1,2)	Cov(1,3)	Cov(1,4)	- - - - - - -	Cov(1,n)
2		Cov(2,2)	Cov(2,3)	Cov(2,4)	- - - - - - -	Cov(2,n)
3			Cov(3,3)	Cov(3,4)	- - - - - - -	Cov(3,n)
4				Cov(4,4)	- - - - - - -	Cov(4,n)
n					- - - - - - -	Cov(n,n)

In this matrix we have shown n assets. Each cell shows how the assets covary with every other asset. The top row, for example, shows how asset 1 covaries with all other assets from 1 to n. The first term, $Cov(1,1)$, represents the covariance of asset 1 with itself. You will recall that this is just another way of writing the variance of asset 1. In fact, all the covariance terms lying on the diagonal can be replaced by their respective variances. The upper triangle contains all the covariance terms. As the lower triangle is just a mirror image of the upper triangle, it is only necessary to estimate the covariance terms in the upper triangle.

Knowing the structure of this matrix it is possible to estimate the total number of covariance terms. You can find this by adding up the total number of terms in the upper triangle:

$$\text{Number of covariance terms} = \frac{n^2 - n}{2} \qquad (10B.4)$$

For small portfolios this is not a problem. If, however, you have a portfolio consisting of 100 assets, you will need to estimate 4,950 covariance terms in addition to 100 expected returns and variances. Apart from the volume of figures required, the estimation of covariance is not an intuitive exercise. These problems severely restricted the use of the standard portfolio model until the process was simplified. This came about with the introduction of the single index model in 1963.

The single index model

The single index model was developed by Sharpe (1963) and was based on a suggestion by Harry Markowitz. The starting point was to recognise that the returns on an asset are to some degree related to the performance of the market. This enables the return on an asset to be captured by a simple linear relationship:

$$r_{it} = \alpha_i + \beta_i r_{mt} + \varepsilon_{it} \qquad (10B.5)$$

where

r_{mt} = return on a general market index in period t

ε_{it} = random return for asset i in period t

α_i and β_i are constants

This is just an ordinary least squares regression model that requires the following assumptions concerning the error term:

● The mean value for the error term is zero, i.e. $E(\varepsilon_{it}) = 0$
● The variance of the error term is constant
● The errors are uncorrelated with r_{it}, i.e. $Cov(\varepsilon_{it}, r_{it}) = 0$
● The errors are serially uncorrelated, i.e. $Cov(\varepsilon_{it}, \varepsilon_{it+n}) = 0$
● The error terms between assets are uncorrelated.

If these assumptions hold true, then the regression parameters α_i and β_i will be unbiased, minimum variance estimates of the true regression parameters. The β coefficient provides an indication of how responsive the returns on an asset will be in relation to the returns on the market index. Values greater than 1.0 imply an aggressive asset, whereas a value less than 1.0 implies a defensive asset.

From these assumptions it is possible to simplify the inputs required in a portfolio analysis.

The expected return

The expected return can be estimated from equation 10B.5 by noting that $E(\varepsilon_{it}) = 0$:

$$E(r_{it}) = \alpha_i + \beta_i E(r_{mt}) \tag{10B.6}$$

The variance of returns

The deviation of the observed return from its expected value is just the difference between equations 10B.5 and 10B.6:

$$r_{it} - E(r_{it}) = (\alpha_i + \beta_i r_{mt} + \varepsilon_{it}) - [\alpha_i + \beta_i E(r_{mt})] \tag{10B.7}$$

$$r_{it} - E(r_{it}) = \beta_i [r_{mt} - E(r_{mt})] + \varepsilon_{it} \tag{10B.8}$$

The variance of r_{it} can however be expressed as:

$$Var(r_{it}) = E[r_{it} - E(r_{it})]^2 \tag{10B.9}$$

Substituting equation 10B.8 for the deviation in the square brackets you can see that equation 10B.9 can be written as:

$$Var(r_{it}) = \beta_i^2 Var(r_{mt}) + Var(\varepsilon_{it}) \tag{10B.10}$$

This provides an alternative way of expressing the variance of an asset in terms of the market variance.

The covariance term

You can write the covariance between assets i and j as:

$$Cov(r_{it}, r_{jt}) = E\{[r_{it} - E(r_{it})][r_{jt} - E(r_{jt})]\} \tag{10B.11}$$

This is just the product of two deviations. Another way of writing these is as follows:

$$r_{it} - E(r_{it}) = \beta_i[r_{mt} - E(r_{mt})] + \varepsilon_{it} \tag{10B.12}$$

$$r_{jt} - E(r_{jt}) = \beta_j[r_{mt} - E(r_{mt})] + \varepsilon_{jt} \tag{10B.13}$$

Recalling that the expected value of the error terms is zero the covariance can be written as:

$$Cov(r_{it},r_{jt}) = \beta_{it}\beta_{jt}Var(r_{mt}) \tag{10B.14}$$

You can see that the single index model enables each component to be related to the returns on a market index. The principal advantage is the reduction in the number of terms required to estimate the inputs for a portfolio analysis. In Table 10B.2 we have compared the number of terms required by the Markowitz and single index models.

The Markowitz model requires the inputs to be estimated directly, whereas most of the inputs for the single index model come from the results of regressing the returns on each asset against the returns on some market index. You can see what a difference

Table 10B.2 ● Number of parameters required for the Markowitz and single index models

Markowitz model		Single index model	
Parameter	Number	Parameter	Number
$E(r_{it})$	n	α_i	n
$Var(r_{it})$	n	β_{it}	n
$Cov(r_i,r_j)$	$\dfrac{n^2 - n}{2}$	$Var(\varepsilon_{it})$	n
		$Var(r_{mt})$	1
		$E(r_{mt})$	1
Total number of terms:	$\dfrac{n^2 + 3n}{2}$	Total number of terms:	$3n + 2$

Table 10B.3 ● Number of assets required to compute the efficient frontier

Number of assets	Markowitz model	Single index model
10	65	32
20	230	62
30	495	92
40	860	122
50	1,325	152
100	5,150	302

this makes in Table 10B.3 where we compare the total number of parameters required to estimate the efficient frontier for portfolios of different size.

The single index model was also developed to reduce the amount of computing time needed to run a full portfolio analysis. With the increasing availability of cheap, fast computers this aspect is no longer a major concern. However, the single index model still plays an important role in portfolio management and performance measurement. We will discuss this in more depth in Part 3.

Example

To show how the single index model works in practice we will estimate the variance and covariance terms for two properties by using the IPD annual index as the reference index. The returns for properties A and B together with the IPD index over the period from 1983 to 1997 are given in Table 10B.4.

Table 10B.4 ● Annual returns, 1983–97

	Property A	Property B	IPD
1983	20.00	2.20	7.79
1984	6.50	5.66	9.52
1985	35.00	8.22	9.17
1986	45.00	14.23	11.75
1987	35.57	45.00	26.75
1988	23.40	36.20	29.08
1989	2.30	14.00	15.15
1990	−26.00	3.00	−9.29
1991	−45.40	−4.30	−4.68
1992	−13.00	−11.56	−3.28
1993	2.25	−15.00	19.00
1994	5.80	0.25	12.44
1995	11.30	8.56	4.49
1996	12.60	21.00	10.81
1997	14.60	11.00	17.85

With such a small sample it is, of course, possible to estimate the parameters directly from the data. We will, therefore, estimate these figures using historic data so that they can be compared with the results estimated using the single index model. The main parameters are summarised in Table 10B.5.

Table 10B.5 ● Summary statistics

	Property A	Property B	IPD
Mean	8.66	9.23	10.44
St. Dev.	22.85	15.45	10.40
Cov(A,B)	203.11		

In order to use the single index model you need to regress the returns of each property on the IPD index in order to estimate α and β. As an alternative to running a full regression analysis we have used two Excel functions, *intercept* and *slope*, to work out these figures and summarise them as follows:

Table 10B.6 ● Regression statistics

	Property A	Property B
Intercept α	−7.04	−0.73
Slope β	1.50	0.95

Both properties have negative intercepts, implying that over the period 1983–97 their average performance was not as good as the market as a whole. The slope coefficient for property A is greater than 1.0, implying that it is more volatile than the market. Property B has a slope coefficient that is much closer to the market.

The only other piece of information you require is the residual standard deviation. This is also part of the standard output from a regression package, although some packages estimate the figures differently from the way they estimate standard deviation. For clarity we have estimated these figures manually. The first step is to calculate the deviation of each return from its predicted value. For property A this would be:

$$r_{at} - E(r_{at}) = r_{at} - (\alpha_a - \beta_a r_{mt}) \tag{10B.15}$$

Using the figures from Tables 10B.4 and 10B.6 the deviation in 1983 equals 15.36% as follows:

$$20.00 - [-7.04 + 1.50(7.79)] = 15.36\%$$

The second step involves squaring this figure to give the residual variance in 1983. Table 10B.7 summarises the calculations for each year.

You now have estimates for the intercept and slope coefficients, together with the residual standard deviations for both properties. You can use the single index model to estimate the expected return, variance and covariance as follows.

Expected returns

The expected returns for Property A and B can be estimated from equation 10B.6 as follows:

$$E(r_{it}) = \alpha_i + \beta_i E(r_{mt})$$

$$E(r_a) = -7.04 + 1.50(10.44) = 8.66\%$$

$$E(r_a) = -0.73 + 0.95(10.44) = 9.23\%$$

If you refer to Table 10B.5 you will see that these are the same as the historic figures.

Table 10B.7 ● Estimating the residual standard deviation

		Property A			Property B	
	r_a	$E(r_a)$	$[r_a - E(r_a)]^2$	r_b	$E(r_b)$	$[r_b - E(r_b)]^2$
1983	20.00	4.68	234.83	2.20	6.70	20.26
1984	6.50	7.28	0.61	5.66	8.35	7.26
1985	35.00	6.76	797.47	8.22	8.02	0.04
1986	45.00	10.64	1180.50	14.23	10.49	14.00
1987	35.57	33.20	5.63	45.00	24.81	407.78
1988	23.40	36.70	176.89	36.20	27.03	84.08
1989	2.30	15.76	181.05	14.00	13.73	0.07
1990	−26.00	−21.00	24.95	3.00	−9.60	158.81
1991	−45.40	−14.07	981.41	−4.30	−5.20	0.81
1992	−13.00	−11.97	1.05	−11.56	−3.87	59.15
1993	2.25	21.54	371.96	−15.00	17.40	1050.02
1994	5.80	11.68	34.55	0.25	11.15	118.72
1995	11.30	−0.29	134.23	8.56	3.55	25.09
1996	12.60	9.23	11.37	21.00	9.59	130.17
1997	14.60	19.80	27.07	11.00	16.30	28.13
			Residual variance 277.57			Residual variance 140.29

	Residual standard deviation	16.66% p.a.		Residual standard deviation	11.84% p.a.

Variance

The variance of returns can be estimated from equation 10B.10 as follows:

$$Var(r_{it}) = \beta_i^2 Var(r_{mt}) + Var(\varepsilon_{it})$$

$$Var(r_a) = (1.50)^2(10.40)^2 + (16.66)^2 = 522.12$$

$$\sigma_a = 22.85\%$$

$$Var(r_b) = (0.95)^2(10.40)^2 + (11.84)^2 = 238.70$$

$$\sigma_a = 15.45\%$$

These are also the same as the historic figures.

Covariance

The covariance between A and B can be estimated from equation 10B.14:

$$Cov(r_{it}, r_{jt}) = \beta_{it}\beta_{jt} Var(r_{mt})$$

$$Cov(r_a, r_b) = (1.50)(0.95)(10.40)^2 = 155.15$$

You will see that this figure is different from the historic covariance of 203.11. The reason for this is that the single index model assumes that the correlation between the residuals of A and B is zero. This was a condition of the single index model. Using historical data takes account of any historic covariance that may exist between A and B.

The single index model, therefore, offers a close approximation to the full portfolio model developed by Markowitz. Although there are errors in this estimation technique the model does provide answers that are close to the full optimisation approach.

Multi-index models

By adopting the single-index model you are making the assumption that the covariance between the returns on individual assets can be explained by just one factor, usually the market. In a multi-index framework you can attribute the covariance to two or more factors. The value of this approach is that there are likely to be a number of factors influencing returns that the single index model is unable to capture. In a property context it would possible to envisage the returns being influenced by regional or economic effects that are not fully reflected in an index of property market movements.

Although a multi-index model is useful in helping to explain the sources of variation in the returns of individual assets its main use has been in trying to obtain better estimates of the variance–covariance structure for use in an optimisation model. We present the results of the multi-index model without proof. The references provide further information.

The return on any asset can be expressed in terms of its movement with a number of indices.

$$r_i = \alpha_0 + \beta_1 r_1 + \beta_2 r_2 + \beta_3 r_3 + \ldots + \beta_n r_n + u_i \tag{10B.16}$$

The expected return can therefore be expressed as:

$$E(r_i) = \alpha_0 + \beta_1 E(r_1) + \beta_2 E(r_2) + \beta_3 E(r_3) + \ldots + \beta_n E(r_n) \tag{10B.17}$$

The variance of returns can be written as:

$$Var(r_i) = \beta_1^2 Var(r_1) + \beta_2^2 Var(r_2) + \ldots + \beta_n^2 Var(r_n) + Var(u_i) \tag{10B.18}$$

Similarly the covariance can be written as:

$$Cov(r_i r_j) = \beta_{i1} \beta_{j1} Var(r_1) + \beta_{i2} \beta_{j2} Var(r_2) + \ldots + \beta_{in} \beta_{jn} Var(r_n) \tag{10B.19}$$

Given a multi-index framework it will be evident that there will be an infinite number of models that can be used to predict the correlation structure. Although it has been shown that multi-index models do not perform any better than single-index models this is, nevertheless, a potentially valuable area for research. The principal advantage probably comes from trying to explain the factors that influence return. This could lead to an improvement in portfolio strategy and asset allocation.

Selected references

Cohen, K.J. and Pogue, J. (1967) An empirical evaluation of alternative portfolio selection models. *Journal of Business* **46** (April), 166–93.

Elton, E.J. and Gruber, M.J. (1981) *Modern Portfolio Theory and Investment Analysis*, 5th edn. New York: John Wiley & Sons.

Fama, E.F. (1976) *Foundations of Finance*, Oxford: Blackwell.

Francis, J.C. (1986) *Investments*, 4th edn. New York: McGraw-Hill.

Francis, J.C. and Archer, S.H. (1979) *Portfolio Analysis*, Prentice-Hall Foundations of Finance Series, 2nd edn. Englewood Cliffs, NJ: Prentice-Hall Inc.

Haugen, R.A. (1993) *Modern Investment Theory*, 3rd edn. Englewood Cliffs, NJ: Prentice-Hall International.

Jacob, N.L. (1974) A limited diversification portfolio selection model for the small investor. *Journal of Finance* (June), 847–56.

Levy, H. and Sarnat, M. (1984) *Portfolio and Investment Selection: Theory and Practice*, Englewood Cliffs, NJ: Prentice-Hall International.

Sharpe, W.F. (1963) A simplified model for portfolio analysis. *Management Science* IX (2), 277–93.

Sharpe, W.F. (1970) *Portfolio Theory and Capital Markets*, McGraw-Hill Series in Finance, New York: McGraw-Hill.

Sharpe, W.F. (1971) Mean-absolute-deviation characteristic lines for securities and portfolios. *Management Science* **18** (2), B1–B13.

Sharpe, W.F. (1985) *Investments*, 3rd edn. Englewood Cliffs, NJ: Prentice Hall.

Appendix 10C
Portfolio analysis using alternative risk measures

The development and use of the Markowitz models we introduced in Chapter 10 have been based on two critical assumptions:

1. The choice of portfolio by an individual is assumed to be made on the basis of maximising utility.
2. Asset returns are assumed to be normally distributed so that they can be completely described in terms of the mean and variance.

Each of these conditions is sufficient but not necessary to operationalise portfolio models.

The utility assumption, for example, implies that investors can derive a risk indifference curve that fully describes their attitude to risk and return. This is not easy, as each investor will have a different view of the trade-off between risk and return so that the shape of the utility function could be very irregular. If the choice of portfolio is being made by an investment institution representing the interests of many investors then it becomes less clear what form the utility function should take. One way round these problems is to assume that the utility function is quadratic. Although this is clearly an assumption, it at least makes the mathematics of choice much easier to handle.

If you don't impose the requirement of quadratic utility then the justification for using the Markowitz approach rests on assuming that asset returns are normally distributed. But this too is only an approximation of what happens in practice. We showed in Chapter 9 that real estate returns are not normally distributed and the shape of the distribution is influenced by the interval between reporting dates and the way information is incorporated into valuations. Asset returns generally tend to be positively skewed and can be transformed so that they are approximately normal by taking the log of $(1 + r)$. By using continuous returns the effect of skewness can, therefore, be reduced. The reason for assuming that returns are normally distributed is that the mathematics required in mean-variance optimisation models is much easier to handle. It also has the added advantage that concepts of risk employing the standard deviation or variance are generally better understood.

Other measures of risk

The above discussion highlights the fact that the optimisation of asset weights in a traditional mean-variance portfolio analysis represents an approximation of observed investor behaviour. The problem centres on defining a suitable measure that adequately represents the way investors perceive risk. Although standard deviation is attractive it assumes that investors will regard returns above the mean in the same light as returns below the mean. This, however, is unlikely. Most investors are generally not too worried about how much they will make but are concerned with how much they will lose.

Given this difficulty a number of other measures of risk have been proposed which are not as restrictive in terms of the shape of the distribution. Some more easily lend themselves to being used in portfolio analysis than others. Those that have been proposed include the following:

● Coefficient of variation
● Semi-variance
● Mean absolute deviation
● Lower partial moments

This list is not exhaustive and interested readers should consult the references for more information. In this appendix we will briefly describe each of these measures and show how they can be used in a portfolio context.

Coefficient of variation (CV)

This is a measure of relative variability and is found by dividing the standard deviation by the expected value. In returns form:

$$CV = \frac{\sigma_r}{E(r)} \tag{10C.1}$$

The coefficient of variation is a way of adjusting for scale differences when measuring risk. It is therefore more applicable to those situations where risk is measured in absolute rather than relative values. The following example illustrates its use. Assume you want to compare two projects that have the expected values and standard deviations shown in Table 10C.1.

Although project A has a smaller standard deviation it is more risky than project B. The coefficient of variation has made an adjustment for differences in scale between the projects.

Table 10C.1 ● Using the coefficient of variation (COV) to compare projects

Project	Expected value	Standard deviation	Coefficient of variation (COV)
A	£100,000	£300,000	3.00
B	£1,000,000	£2,500,000	2.50

Table 10C.2 ● Using the coefficient of variation (COV) with project returns

Project	Expected return	Standard deviation	Coefficient of variation (COV)
X	3.0%	2.0%	0.67
Y	30.0%	20.0%	0.67

Often, however, the COV is used to make a comparison between projects using rates of return, where risk is measured in relative terms. In a portfolio context it would, therefore, be possible to optimise the weights attached to each investment so that the COV is minimised. This approach, however, still relies upon the mean-variance framework. Although the idea of minimising the ratio of risk to expected return may sound attractive it should be noted that standard deviation is a measure of relative risk and so is already in a form that it is directly comparable with the risk of other assets. If used without care the COV can, therefore, produce odd results. Consider for example, the figures given in Table 10C.2.

The coefficients of variation for projects X and Y are identical even though project Y is ten times more risky than project X. In a portfolio context that relied on COV both projects would be considered equally desirable. It is true to say, however, that the risk per unit of return is the same for both projects. A further problem can arise, however, as the expected return approaches zero. This could happen if historic data are being used to estimate the figures. In this case the COV would imply that the project carried infinite risk!

Semi-variance

Markowitz suggested the use of semi-variance as a measure of risk on the assumption that investors were more likely to be concerned with returns below rather than above some target value. The semi-variance can be written as follows:

$$SV = \frac{1}{T} \sum_{t=1}^{T} Max[0,(h - r_t)]^2 \qquad (10C.2)$$

subject to $h < r_t$; where h is a target rate of return.

The most common choices for h are the risk-free rate of return, the expected rate of return and zero. Note also that if the target rate of return, h, is equal to the expected return and the distribution is symmetrical, the semi-variance will give the same results as the variance.

If you assume a target return equal to the expected rate of return you would calculate the semi-variance as follows:

Table 10C.3 ● Calculating the semi-variance

Asset returns r_t	Max[0,$(h - r_t)$]	Max value squared
15.10	0.00	0.00
6.70	0.00	0.00
5.50	0.00	0.00
12.67	0.00	0.00
8.24	0.00	0.00
−5.00	10.03	100.64
−11.50	16.53	273.31
2.50	2.53	6.41
4.56	0.47	0.22
11.55	0.00	0.00
Mean $E(r)$ 5.03		38.06
Target (h) 5.03		

The semi-deviation is 6.17, which is the square root of the semi-variance.

Because the semi-deviation measures only the values below the target return its covariance with the semi-deviation of other assets will not be symmetrical. In a portfolio context it is necessary, therefore, to estimate the cosemi-variance. This aspect is beyond the scope of this book.

Mean absolute deviation (MAD)

The mean absolute deviation does not rely on any assumptions about the shape of a distribution and can therefore be used where the normal distribution is too restrictive. It is calculated by ignoring the signs of the deviations, and can be estimated using the following equation:

$$MAD = \sum_{t=1}^{T} p_t |r_t - E(r_t)| \tag{10C.3}$$

where p_t is the probability attached to each return.

Using historical data the MAD would be calculated from the following:

$$MAD = \frac{1}{T} \sum_{t=1}^{T} |r_t - E(r_t)| \tag{10C.4}$$

Using the figures from Table 10C.3 you would calculate the MAD as follows:

Table 10C.4 ● Calculating the mean absolute deviation

	Asset returns r_t	$r_t - E(r)$	Absolute deviation
	15.10	10.07	10.07
	6.70	1.67	1.67
	5.50	0.47	0.47
	12.67	7.64	7.64
	8.24	3.21	3.21
	-5.00	-10.03	10.03
	-11.50	-16.53	16.53
	2.50	-2.53	2.53
	4.56	-0.47	0.47
	11.55	6.52	6.52
Mean $E(r)$	**5.03**		**MAD: 5.91**

The MAD has a number of attractive features that make it useful in a real estate context. Fama (1965), for example, has pointed out that MAD is more stable over time than the standard deviation as it gives less weight to outliers. *Ex-post* MADs therefore offer a useful guide as an *ex-ante* measure of risk irrespective of the time horizon. An additional important advantage of MAD is its ability to estimate risk measures from small samples. This is especially important in a real estate context where the number of assets in a portfolio could exceed the number of periods over which risk is being measured. The standard portfolio model cannot handle this problem as the covariance matrix becomes singular and cannot be inverted.

The only example of MAD being applied to the optimisation of a real estate port-folio is by Byrne and Lee (1997). They show that the MAD of a portfolio of m assets with returns over T periods can be solved using the following optimisation model:

Minimise

$$MAD_p = \frac{1}{T} \sum_{t=1}^{T} \left| \sum_{i=1}^{m} [r_{it} - E(r_i)]x_i \right| \tag{10C.5}$$

subject to:

1. $\displaystyle\sum_{i=1}^{m} x_i = 1$

2. $\displaystyle\sum_{i=1}^{m} x_i \bar{r}_i = \bar{r}_p$

3. $0 \leq x_i \leq 1$

Table 10C.5 ● Asset allocation using mean absolute deviations, 1981–97

Sector	Maximum return	11% target	Minimum return
Retail	0.00%	82.43%	0.00%
Office	0.00%	17.57%	100.00%
Industrial	100.00%	0.00%	0.00%
Portfolio return	11.58%	11.00%	8.72%
MAD risk	8.31%	5.94%	10.82%

Although this minimisation problem is set up in the same form as the standard portfolio model the important difference is that the MAD for the portfolio does not contain any covariance terms. The reason for this is that the MAD approach seeks to minimise an absolute variation which does not have the same scaling as the variance. As this does not involve any quadratic terms, the optimisation becomes a linear programming problem. It is, therefore, easier to solve than a similar quadratic programming problem in variance terms, although the results have to satisfy the constraints we have identified.

If the distribution of returns is, however, symmetrical then the MAD will produce the same set of portfolios as a model drafted in terms of standard deviations.

To illustrate the use of MADs in an asset allocation framework we summarise in Table 10C.5 the percentage of funds that should have been invested in each sector of the UK property market over the period 1981–97. The data for this analysis are the IPD annual total returns. The table shows allocations for the minimum and maximum returns together with a target of 11%.[1]

We shall return to these data in the following section.

Lower partial moments (LPM)

Lower partial moments represent a more general class of model that are not only distribution-free, but also recognise that skewness is an important consideration when it comes to making investment decisions. For example, if two assets have the same expected return and variance, investors would view these as being equivalent unless they have some knowledge concerning the skewness of returns. With this additional information investors would prefer the asset with the greatest positive skewness. The logic behind this is that investors are much happier with above-target returns but less happy with below-target returns.

Different investors may, however, view above- and below-target returns in different ways. The *n-degree lower partial moment* captures different degrees of risk-aversion in the following equation:

$$LPM_n(h) = \frac{1}{T} \sum_{t=1}^{T} Max[0, (h - r_t)]^n \tag{10C.6}$$

[1]We wish to thank Peter Byrne of Reading University for undertaking these calculations.

where n represents the degree of lower partial moment and h represents the target return.

You will see that equation 10C.6 is exactly the same as our equation for semi-variance. In fact, semi-variance is just a special case of a lower partial moment when $n = 2.0$.

You will also see from equation 10C.6 that the calculation of the lower partial moment ignores returns that are above the target and penalises returns that are below the target. This seems to fit in well with the way many investors behave in practice. The degree of lower partial moment, n, therefore tells you something about the risk-aversion of investors. As n increases, investors become increasingly unhappy with returns that are below the target. This represents increasing risk aversion. In contrast, as n reduces, investors are more willing to accept below-target returns and as a result become less risk-averse.

The calculation of the lower partial moments is shown in Table 10C.6. In this case we have used the expected return as the target value, h. You will see that the calculation of LPM(2) is exactly the same as the semi-variance given above.

In order to trace out the efficient frontier the optimisation is exactly the same as the standard portfolio model except that the variance is replaced with the lower partial moment relating to the degree of risk-aversion.

You can see how risk-aversion affects the proportion of funds invested in different assets by examining a simple asset allocation problem using the IPD annual total returns for each sector of the market over the period 1981–97. In Table 10C.7 we have summarised the geometric mean and standard deviation for each sector and, on the assumption that the risk-free rate of return over the period was 9.0%, have also estimated their reward-to-risk ratios. This is just the difference between the mean and risk-free return divided by the standard deviation. We have also estimated similar reward-to-risk ratios based on lower partial moment degrees of 0.5 and 3.0. Using

Table 10C.6 ● Calculating lower partial moments

Asset returns	$Max[0, (h-r_i)]$	LPM(0.5)	Increasing risk-aversion LPM(1.0)	LPM(2.0)	LPM(3.0)
15.10	0.00	0.00	0.00	0.00	0.00
6.70	0.00	0.00	0.00	0.00	0.00
5.50	0.00	0.00	0.00	0.00	0.00
12.67	0.00	0.00	0.00	0.00	0.00
8.24	0.00	0.00	0.00	0.00	0.00
−5.00	10.03	3.17	10.03	100.64	1,009.63
−11.50	16.53	4.07	16.53	273.31	4,518.31
2.50	2.53	1.59	2.53	6.41	16.23
4.56	0.47	0.69	0.47	0.22	0.11
11.55	0.00	0.00	0.00	0.00	0.00
Mean $E(r)$ 5.03	Average:	0.95	2.96	38.06	554.43
Target (h) 5.03	LPM Root:	0.90	2.96	6.17	8.22

Table 10C.7 ● **Reward-to-risk measures for IPD total returns, 1981–97**

Sector	Mean	St. Dev.	Reward-to-risk measures (ranking shown in brackets)		
			St. Dev.	LPM: 0.5	LPM: 3.0
Retail	11.49	7.75	0.32 (1)	3.48 (1)	0.314 (2)
Office	8.72	11.62	−0.02 (3)	−0.11 (3)	−0.02 (3)
Industrial	11.58	10.63	0.24 (2)	1.44 (2)	0.38 (1)

Table 10C.8 ● **Allocation to each sector using mean variance and LPM analysis, 1981–97**

Sector	Percentage allocation to each sector		
	Mean variance	LPM: 0.5	LPM: 3.0
Retail	100.00%	48.77%	37.71%
Offices	0.00%	18.46%	19.20%
Industrial	0.00%	32.77%	43.09%

lower partial moments enables us to examine the effect of risk-aversion for different groups of investor. As the degree of LPM increases investors become more risk-averse.

The important point to notice about this table is that using standard deviation in the reward-to-risk calculation results in a ranking of assets that is not influenced by the investor's attitude to risk. In this example investors would rank them in the order: retail, industrial and then office. However, by using reward-to-risk measures that incorporate risk-aversion you will see that this ranking is the same as an investor who is happy to take on additional risk. The more risk-averse investor (LPM: 3.0) ranks the assets in the order of industrial, retail and then offices.

In terms of asset allocation, using mean variance analysis shows no allocation to the office sector over the period 1981–97. Using a target return of 11.0% the mean variance model shows that investors should have invested 100% of their funds in the retail sector. This result does not, however, tie in with observed practice as investors did allocate funds to each of the sectors. One reason for this could be due to differences in the risk-aversion of different groups of investor. Alternatively, investors' expectations could have been different from those revealed in the historic data. It could also be a data problem, but that is another story. We summarise the allocation to each sector using mean variance analysis and LPM analysis in Table 10C.8 based on a target return of 11.0% p.a.

You will see that by incorporating risk-aversion into the model there is now some allocation to each sector. As investors become more risk-averse the main allocations switch from retail to industrial while the allocation to the office sector stays fairly close to 20%. It is also interesting to note that the MAD analysis selected an allocation of 17.57% to offices. These brief analyses could imply that investors should aim to keep a core holding of offices in the order of 20% and then adjust the proportion of funds they hold in retail and industrial property in relation to their attitude to risk.

Although this example does show that different levels of risk-aversion can be included in the asset allocation problem the main disadvantage of using lower partial moments is that the analysis is not well understood. However, this will change in time.

Selected references

Ang, J.S. and Chua, J.H. (1979) Composite measures for the evaluation of investment perform-ance. *Journal of Financial and Quantitative Analysis* **14** (2), 361–84.

Byrne, P. and Lee, S. (1997) Real estate portfolio analysis under conditions of non-normality: the case of NCREIF. *Journal of Real Estate Portfolio Management* **3** (1), 37–46.

Fama, E.F. (1965) The behavior of stock market prices. *Journal of Business* **38** (1), 34–105.

Francis, J.C. and Archer, S.H. (1979) *Portfolio Analysis*, Prentice-Hall Foundations of Finance Series, 2nd edn. Englewood Cliffs, NJ: Prentice-Hall Inc.

Konno, H. (1988) Portfolio optimisation using L_1 risk function. IHSS Report 88–9 Tokyo, Institute of Technology: Institute of Human and Social Sciences.

Konno, H. (1989) Piecewise linear risk functions and portfolio optimisation. *Journal of the Operations Research Society of Japan* **33**, 139–56.

Konno, H. and Yamazaki, H. (1991) Mean absolute deviation portfolio optimisation model and its application to the Tokyo Stock Market. *Management Science* **37** (5), 519–31.

Levy, H. and Sarnat, M. (1984) *Portfolio and Investment Selection: Theory and Practice*, Englewood Cliffs, NJ: Prentice-Hall International.

Nawrocki, D.N. (1983) A comparison of risk measures when used in a simple portfolio selection heuristic. *Journal of Business Finance and Accounting* **10** (2), 183–94.

Nawrocki, D.N. (1991) Optimal algorithms and lower partial moments: Ex post results. *Applied Economics* **23** (March), 465–70.

Nawrocki, D.N. and Staples, K. (1989) A customised LPM risk measure for portfolio analysis. *Applied Economics* **21** (February), 205–18.

Saunders, A., Ward, C.W.R. and Woodward, R. (1980) Stochastic dominance and the performance of UK unit trusts. *Journal of Financial and Quantitative Analysis* **15** (2), 323–30.

Young, M.S. and Graff, R.A. (1995) Real estate is not normal: a fresh look at real estate returns distributions. *Journal of Real Estate Finance and Economics* **10**, 225–59.

Appendix 10D
The capital asset pricing model (CAPM)

In this appendix we provide a mathematical derivation of the capital asset pricing model.

The CAPM

In Chapter 10 we showed that only efficient portfolios lie on the capital market line. All other portfolios lie below the line. By investing funds in the inefficient portfolio, J, and the market portfolio, M, it is possible to construct another portfolio represented by Q in Figure 10D.1.

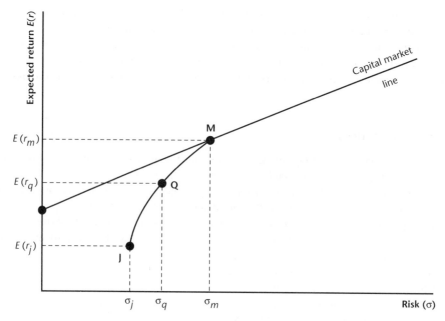

Figure 10D.1 The capital market line and inefficient portfolios

Assuming that some proportion x of available funds is invested in asset J the expected return and standard deviation of portfolio Q can be written as:

$$E(r_q) = xE(r_j) + (1 - x)E(r_m) \tag{10D.1}$$

$$\sigma^2_q = x^2\sigma^2_j + (1 - x)^2\sigma^2_m + 2x(1 - x)Cov(j,m) \tag{10D.2}$$

The shape of the curve JQM will depend on the correlation between portfolios J and M. In addition, as you move along the line JQM its slope will change as the proportion of funds invested in J and M changes. At point M it will be equal to the slope of the capital market line as this is where the two curves touch. The slope at this point is important because it implies that all the specific risk in the portfolio has been diversified away, leaving only the systematic component.

To find the slope of the curve at point M you need to differentiate equation 10D.2 with respect to x. You can do this in two parts by letting $w = \sigma^2_q$ and substituting into equation 10D.2.

$$w = x^2\sigma^2_j + (1 - x)^2\sigma^2_m + 2x(1 - x)Cov(j,m) \tag{10D.3}$$

Differentiating w with respect to x gives:

$$\frac{dw}{dx} = 2x\sigma^2_j + 2(1 - x)\sigma^2_m + 2(1 - 2x)Cov(j,m) \tag{10D.4}$$

You now need to express σ_q in terms of w and differentiate the result with respect to w:

$$\sigma_q = w^{\frac{1}{2}} \tag{10D.5}$$

Differentiating gives:

$$\frac{d\sigma_q}{dw} = \frac{1}{2} w^{\frac{-1}{2}} \qquad (10D.6)$$

Substituting for w gives:

$$\frac{d\sigma_q}{dw} = \frac{1}{2\sigma_q} \qquad (10D.7)$$

By using the chain rule you can find $\dfrac{d\sigma_q}{dx}$ as follows:

$$\frac{d\sigma_q}{dx} = \frac{d\sigma_q}{dw} \cdot \frac{dw}{dx} = \frac{x\sigma_j^2 - (x-1)\sigma_m^2 + (1-2x)Cov(j,m)}{\sigma_q} \qquad (10D.8)$$

This provides an expression for the slope of the curve JQM in terms of the change in portfolio risk relative to the proportion of funds invested in asset J.

What you are interested in is the change in the expected return, $E(r_q)$, of the portfolio Q relative to its risk, σ_q. You can find this in two steps. First differentiate equation 10D.1 with respect to x:

$$\frac{dE(r_q)}{dx} = E(r_j) - E(r_m) \qquad (10D.9)$$

Second, multiply this by the reciprocal of equation 10D.8:

$$\frac{dE(r_q)}{d\sigma_q} = \frac{dE(r_q)}{dx} \cdot \frac{dx}{d\sigma_q} = \frac{\sigma_q[E(r_j) - E(r_m)]}{x\sigma_j^2 - (x-1)\,\sigma_m^2 + (1-2x)\,Cov(j,m)} \qquad (10D.10)$$

At point M there will be no funds invested in asset J so that $x = 0$ and σ_q must, by definition, equal σ_m. Substituting these into equation 10D.10 gives:

$$\frac{dE(r_q)}{d\sigma_q} = \frac{\sigma_m[E(r_j) - E(r_m)]}{Cov(j,m) - \sigma_m^2} \qquad (10D.11)$$

This is the slope of the curve JQM at point M. This must, however, equal the slope of the line $r_f M$. You can, therefore, write equation 10D.11 as:

$$\frac{\sigma_m[E(r_j) - E(r_m)]}{Cov(j,m) - \sigma_m^2} = \frac{E(r_m) - r_f}{\sigma_m} \qquad (10D.12)$$

Simplifying gives:

$$E(r_j) - E(r_m) = [E(r_m) - r_f] \left[\frac{Cov(j,m)}{\sigma_m^2} - 1 \right] \qquad (10D.13)$$

By letting

$$\frac{Cov(j,m)}{\sigma_m^2} = \beta_j \qquad (10D.14)$$

equation 10D.13 simplifies to:

$$E(r_j) = [E(r_m) - r_f][\beta_j - 1] + E(r_m) \tag{10D.15}$$

which gives the standard form of the capital asset pricing model as:

$$E(r_j) = r_f + \beta_j[E(r_m) - r_f] \tag{10D.16}$$

This is Sharpe's derivation of the security market line. Other derivations such as those by Fama and Lintner take a slightly different approach but arrive at the same general result.

Selected references

Elton, E.J. and Gruber, M.J. (1981) *Modern Portfolio Theory and Investment Analysis*, 5th edn. New York: John Wiley & Sons.

Fama, E.F. (1968) Risk, return and equilibrium: Some clarifying comments. *Journal of Finance* **XXIII** (1), 29–39.

Fama, E.F. (1971) Risk, return and equilibrium. *Journal of Political Economy* **79** (1), 30–55.

Fama, E.F. (1976) *Foundations of Finance*, Oxford: Blackwell.

Fama, E.F. and Miller, M.H. (1972) *The Theory of Finance*, Hinsdale, Illinois: Dryden Press.

Francis, J.C. and Archer, S.H. (1979) *Portfolio Analysis*, Prentice-Hall Foundations of Finance Series, 2nd edn. Englewood Cliffs, NJ: Prentice-Hall Inc.

Levy, H. and Sarnat, M. (1984) *Portfolio and Investment Selection: Theory and Practice*, Englewood Cliffs, NJ: Prentice-Hall International.

Lintner, J. (1965) Security prices, risk and maximal gains from diversification. *Journal of Finance*, 587–615.

Sharpe, W.F. (1964) Capital asset prices: A theory of market equilibrium under conditions of risk. *Journal of Finance* (Sept.), 425–42.

Appendix 10E
The CAPM with non-marketable assets

Our discussion on portfolio models and the capital asset pricing model (CAPM) has rested on the assumption that all assets are marketable and infinitely divisible. In practice, however, we know that this is not the case. Individuals often hold assets that are non-marketable. The most obvious of these is human capital. This can be regarded as an asset in which the returns are received by way of future income and cannot be separated from the individual and sold on the open market. Real estate can sometimes be non-marketable. It cannot be traded as freely as company stocks and also involves high transaction costs. Non-marketable assets are, therefore, an important part of the portfolio of individuals and this clearly raises important issues concerning the construction of optimal portfolios.

We showed in Chapter 10 that assets are priced in relation to their contribution to a portfolio containing every asset in the marketplace. Tests of the traditional form of CAPM have only been partially successful, as they have generally used a stock market index to represent the market portfolio. This is clearly a simplification if investors generally hold some proportion of non-marketable assets.

Mayers (1972) has, however, developed an asset-pricing framework that incorporates non-marketable assets. As this is particularly relevant in a real estate context it is worth introducing the topic. We will only present the background and main results and will leave it to the interested reader to pursue the relevant references.

A portfolio with non-marketable assets

Each investor, i, is assumed to hold a portfolio with an end-of-period value E_i, such that:

$$E_i = \sum_{j=1}^{n} (x_{ij}\bar{R}_j) + \bar{R}^N_i - (1 + r_f)D_i \tag{10E.1}$$

where
x_{ij} = proportion of the total market value of the firm j held by investor i
r_f = risk-free rate of return
$\bar{R}_j$ = end-of-period capital value of firm j
$\bar{R}^N_i$ = end-of-period capital value of non-marketable assets held by investor i
D_i = current value of the debt held by investor i.

You will see that equation 10E.1 expresses the value of the portfolio in absolute terms. The variance of equation 10E.1 can also be expressed in value terms as:

$$V_i = \sum_{j=1}^{n} \sum_{k=1}^{n} x_{ij}x_{ik}Cov(R_j,R_k) + Var(R^N_i) + 2 \sum_{j=1}^{n} x_{ij}Cov(R^N_i, R_j) \tag{10E.2}$$

Mayers argues that investors will choose values of x_{ij} and D_i that maximise their utility. By using a Lagrangian multiplier and differentiating with respect to x_{ij} and D_i he derives an expression for the CAPM that takes account of non-marketable assets.

Note that summing all assets from 1 to n is equivalent to setting $R_j = R_m$, i.e. the market value of all assets. These can also be expressed in terms of rates of return by recognising that $\bar{R}_j = P_j(1 + \bar{r}_j)$ and $\bar{R}_m = P_m(1 + \bar{r}_m)$. By also letting $P_{m+N} = P_m + P_N$ and $r_{m+N} = \left(\dfrac{P_m}{P_{m+N}}\right)r_m + \left(\dfrac{P_N}{P_{m+N}}\right)r_N$ Mayers shows that the expected return of an asset can be written as:

$$\bar{r}_j = r_f + \cfrac{Cov(r_j r_{m+N})}{\left[\dfrac{P_m}{P_{m+N}} Var(r_m) + \dfrac{P_N}{P_{m+N}} Cov(r_N r_m)\right]} (\bar{r}_m - r_f) \tag{10E.3}$$

Expanding the covariance term in the numerator and rearranging gives:

$$\bar{r}_j = r_f + \cfrac{\bar{r}_m - r_f}{Var(r_m) + \dfrac{P_N}{P_m} Cov(r_N r_m)} \left[Cov(r_j r_m) + \dfrac{P_N}{P_m} Cov(R_j R_N) \right] \tag{10E.4}$$

where the market price of risk is given by:

$$\frac{\overline{r}_m - r_f}{Var(r_m) + \dfrac{P_N}{P_m} Cov(r_N r_m)} \tag{10E.5}$$

Equation 10E.4 represents a more complex version of the capital asset pricing model we showed in Chapter 10. In fact, the standard CAPM is just a special case of a more general model that takes account of non-marketable assets. For example, if you assumed that an investor held no non-marketable assets, the value of P_N would be zero. Substituting this into equation 10E.4 you will see that the expected return can be expressed as:

$$\overline{r}_j = r_f + \frac{Cov(r_j r_m)}{Var(r_m)}(\overline{r}_m - r_f) \tag{10E.6}$$

In its more familiar form this can be expressed as:

$$\overline{r}_j = r_f + \beta_j(\overline{r}_m - r_f) \tag{10E.7}$$

The market price of risk in this case is given by:

$$\frac{\overline{r}_m - r_f}{Var(r_m)} \tag{10E.8}$$

Comparing equations 10E.5 and 10E.8 you will see that the slope of the trade-off between risk and return is lower when suggested by the standard CAPM. This conclusion rests on the assumption that the return on the total of all non-marketable assets is positively correlated with the return on the market. It also depends on the proportion of non-marketable assets relative to marketable assets.

The Mayers model offers a number of valuable insights. For example, it addresses the situation where transactions costs for a class of assets are so large that trading in them becomes prohibitively expensive. Similarly, some assets could be so large in terms of value that there may only be one or two prospective buyers in the market. This is not unusual in real estate where a single building could have a capital value that exceeds that of a major company and there may only be one or two possible buyers. The Mayers model could, therefore, offer some insight into the pricing of liquidity in real estate.

One important point raised by Mayers CAPM is that in the presence of non-marketable assets investors will face different efficient frontiers so that the separation theorem no longer remains valid. Investors do not, therefore, hold the same risky portfolio. Nevertheless the relationship between the relevant measure of risk and the price of an asset is still linear even when non-marketable assets are introduced.

Tests of the capital asset pricing model have generally used a stock market index as representing the market portfolio. This is clearly a simplification as many non-traded assets are excluded. Mayers' model provides a framework for dealing with the missing asset problem.

Selected references

Elton, E.J. and Gruber, M.J. (1981) *Modern Portfolio Theory and Investment Analysis*, 5th edn. New York: John Wiley & Sons.

Francis, J.C. and Archer, S.H. (1979) *Portfolio Analysis*, Prentice-Hall Foundations of Finance Series, 2nd edn. Englewood Cliffs, NJ: Prentice-Hall Inc.

Mayers, D. (1972) Nonmarketable assets and capital market equilibrium under uncertainty. In: Jensen, M.C. (ed.) *Studies in the Theory of Capital Markets*, New York: Praeger Publishers Inc.

Mayers, D. (1973) Nonmarketable assets and the determination of capital asset prices in the absence of a riskless asset. *Journal of Business* **46** (2), 258–67.

Mayers, D. (1976) Nonmarketable assets, market segmentation and the level of asset prices. *Journal of Financial and Quantitative Analysis* **11** (1), 1–12.

Appendix 10F
Duration and risk

In this appendix we develop a simple model that can be used to estimate both the systematic and total risk of property. The approach we adopt does not rely on historical data but estimates expected risk using the concept of duration estimated from traditional valuation models. The measures of risk are, therefore, *ex-ante* and in the spirit of the models developed in portfolio theory.

Deriving the market risk

We covered the background to freehold valuation models in Chapter 3 and showed how you could derive the equivalent yield model. This is the most common valuation model used in the market. For property *J*, you would write its value as follows:

$$V_j = \frac{a_j}{y_j} + \frac{(R_j - a_j)}{y_j(1 + y_j)^n} \tag{10F.1}$$

Where a_j is the passing rent, R_j is the current rental value, y_j is the equivalent yield and n represents the number of years to the next rent review.

Irrespective of the economic validity of this model it will be clear that changes in value are a function of changes in the equivalent yield. Thus the percentage change in value, using continuous compounding, can be related to its duration, D_j, as follows:

$$\frac{dV_j}{V_j} = -D_j dy_j \tag{10F.2}$$

Over a short period you can express the rate of return on property *J* as:

$$r_j = \frac{V_j + a_j + dV_j}{V_j} \tag{10F.3}$$

Substituting from 10F.2 gives:

$$r_j = 1 + \frac{a_j}{V_j} - D_j dy_j \tag{10F.4}$$

From the capital asset pricing model the systematic risk of property J, relative to the market portfolio, could be expressed as follows:

$$\beta_j = \frac{cov(r_j, r_m)}{\sigma^2(r_m)} \tag{10F.5}$$

$$\beta_j = \frac{\rho(r_j, r_m)\sigma(r_j)}{\sigma(r_m)} \tag{10F.6}$$

Substituting for r_j from equation 10F.4 gives the following:

$$\beta_j = \frac{-D_j\rho(dy_j, R_m)\sigma(dy_j)}{\sigma(R_m)} \tag{10F.7}$$

Given that equation 10F.4 also has a similar representation for the market you will see that equation 10F.7 can also be written as:

$$\beta_j = \frac{D_j}{D_m} \frac{\rho(dy_j, dy_m)\sigma(dy_j)}{\sigma(dy_m)} \tag{10F.8}$$

Thus, the systematic risk of a property investment is related to duration and the covariance of changes in the property yield relative to changes in the market yield.

Another way of looking at this is to recognise that the yield component on the right-hand side of this equation is just the slope coefficient of changes in property yields relative to changes in property market yields:

$$\beta_j = \frac{D_j}{D_m} \beta_{y_j y_m} \tag{10F.9}$$

Estimating the duration

To use this model in practice you need to estimate the duration of property. Duration can be thought of as an approximate change in price for a small change in yield. A duration of 15 would, for example, imply that if yields changed by 1%, prices would change by approximately 15%. This is a good way to think of duration but it is only approximate because the relationship between duration and yields is not quite linear.

From equation 10F.1 the duration of the equivalent yield model can be written as:

$$D_j = -\frac{dV_j}{dy_j} \cdot \frac{(1 + y_j)}{V_j} \tag{10F.10}$$

The partial derivative of V_j with respect to y_j can be expressed as:

$$\frac{dV_j}{dy_j} = -\frac{a_j}{y_j^2} - \frac{(R_j - a_j)}{y_j(1 + y_j)^n} \left[\frac{1}{y_j} + \frac{n}{(1 + y_j)} \right] \tag{10F.11}$$

The duration of a property can, therefore, be expressed in terms of its equivalent yield as follows:

$$D_j = \left\{ \frac{a_j}{y_j^2} + \frac{(R_j - a_j)}{y_j(1 + y_j)^n} \left[\frac{1}{y_j} + \frac{n}{(1 + y_j)} \right] \right\} \cdot \frac{(1 + y_j)y_j(1 + y_j)^n}{a_j(1 + y_j)^n + (R_j - a_j)} \tag{10F.12}$$

A similar expression also exists for the duration of the property market. Note that when the number of years to the next rent review is equal to zero the duration reduces to:

$$D_j = \frac{(1 + y_j)}{y_j} \tag{10F.13}$$

The systematic risk of the UK property market

Using monthly data from the IPD index equation 10F.8 can be used to estimate the systematic risk of each property sector relative to the property market as a whole. Although our derivation of systematic risk has relied on the capital asset pricing model we are really only concerned with the volatility of each sector relative to the property market. To extend this to a full asset pricing framework would require a market index that contained every risky asset. This is not currently available. However, in a performance measurement and strategy framework relative volatility is still an important measure of risk.

For simplicity we have assumed that the number of years to the next rent review remains constant at 2.5 years. IPD publish information concerning the total rental value and income received on a monthly basis. This is used as the basis for deriving the duration each month.

The covariance term in equation 10F.8 is estimated using ordinary least squares regression. The results are given in Table 10F.1.[1]

Using the slope coefficients from this analysis together with equation 10F.9 the time varying measures of systematic risk are summarised in Figure 10F.1.

The statistics for each sector are given in Table 10F.2.

The retail sector has the highest market risk and the industrial sector the lowest. This would imply that the retail sector offers the highest expected return and the industrial sector the lowest. The office sector beta is close to 1. The ranking of systematic risk ties in well with market expectations. The highest growth sector is generally regarded as being retail with the lowest being industrial.

Table 10F.1 ● OLS of sector yields versus market yields

Dep Var		Intercept	Slope	R^2
Retail	Δy	0.0053	0.9607	
		(0.0071)	(0.0735)	0.595
Office	Δy	−0.0001	1.0990	
		(0.0058)	(0.0597)	0.744
Industrial	Δy	−0.0179	0.8578	
		(0.0070)	(0.0731)	0.543

Standard errors in brackets.

[1] See Brown (1999) for an alternative approach using time varying parameters.

Table 10F.2 ● Average *ex-ante* estimates of systematic risk

Beta	Retail	Office	Industrial
Mean value	1.099	1.026	0.715
St. Dev.	0.039	0.063	0.045

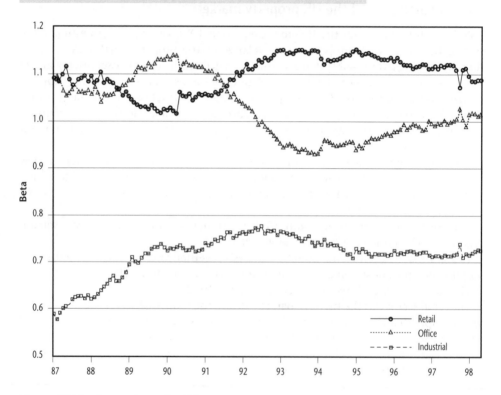

Figure 10F.1 *Ex-ante* betas for UK property sectors

The graph also shows a strong negative correlation between the beta of the office and retail sectors (−0.968). The expected return on these sectors should, therefore, be strongly negatively correlated. This relationship could, however, be a function of the way the model is specified. For example, we have assumed that changes in duration relative to changes in the yield are linear. The true relationship is more likely to be curvilinear. This aspect would be captured by what is known as convexity and the model could be modified to incorporate this effect. If, however, the negative relationship between the office and retail sectors is shown to hold it could have important implications in terms of strategy.

As this model estimates *ex-ante* risk it is difficult to test. Historical data are bound to be influenced by actual events so that the relationship between *ex-post* and *ex-ante* measures of risk may not be strong.

Estimating the total risk of individual properties

Assets with a long duration tend to be more volatile than assets with a short duration. As duration changes over time you should also expect to see the total risk of assets changing. You can investigate this by developing a simple model for total risk.

From equation 10F.2 we have an expression for the change in value divided by the original value. This is just another way of expressing the growth rate. By taking the variance of equation 10F.2 you can arrive at an expression for the standard deviation of the capital growth:

$$Var(g) = D_j^2 Var(dy_j) \qquad\qquad (10F.14)$$

Taking the square root gives:

$$\sigma_g = D\sigma_{dy_j} \qquad\qquad (10F.15)$$

This equation produces risk estimates on a period-by-period basis. The resulting figures, when annualised, are very similar to estimates based on time-series data. For example, using the IPD All Property monthly capital growth data in equation 10F.15 we estimated an average risk figure over the period January 1987 to May 1998 of 3.67% p.a. The risk figure estimated directly from the IPD data is 3.32%. The difference may be due to the fact that convexity has not been incorporated into the model.

These risk estimates merely confirm the IPD data. There are other issues concerning smoothing that would affect these risk estimates. These are dealt with in Chapter 12.

These models represent a starting point for estimating *ex-ante* risk. We will make use of them when we examine performance measurement. Although much remains to be done, our belief is that it is better to make some attempt to quantify the risk in property investment rather than ignore it completely. Some simplifications are necessary to operationalise the models. However, these are no more restrictive than simplifications that are used in other areas of financial economics.

Selected references

Boquist, J.A., Racette, G.A. and Schlarbaum, G.G. (1975) Duration and risk assessment for bonds and common stocks. *Journal of Finance* **XXX** (5), 1360–5.

Brown, G.R. (1999) Duration and risk. Paper presented at the AREUEA/AsRES Internatiuonal Real Estate Conference in Maui, 4–8 May.

Casabona, P.A., Fabozzi, F.J. and Francis, J.C. (1994) How to apply duration to equity analysis. *Journal of Portfolio Management* (Winter), 52–8.

Dym, S.I. (1991) Measuring the risk of foreign bonds. *Journal of Portfolio Management* (Winter), 56–61.

Fabozzi, F.J. (1996) *Bond Markets, Analysis and Strategies*, 3rd edn. Englewood Cliffs, NJ: Prentice-Hall International.

Gould, J.B. and Sorensen, E.H. (1996) Duration: A factor in equity pricing. *Journal of Portfolio Management* (Fall), 38–43.

Hamelink, F., MacGregor, B.D., Nanthakumaran, N. and Orr, A. (1998) The duration of UK commercial property. *University of Aberdeen*. Paper presented at the ERES/AREUEA conference, Maastricht, June 1998.

Hopewell, M.H. and Kaufman, G.G. (1973) Bond price volatility and term to maturity: A generalized respecification. *American Economic Review* **63** (4), 749–53.

Jarrow, R. (1978) The relationship between yield, risk and return of corporate bonds. *Journal of Finance* **XXXIII** (4), 1235–40.

Lanstein, R. and Sharpe, W.F. (1978) Duration and security risk. *Journal of Financial and Quantitative Analysis* (Proceedings Issue – November), 653–68.

Livingston, M. (1978) Duration and risk assessment for bonds and common stocks: A note. *Journal of Finance* **XXXIII** (1), 293–5.

Reilly, F.K. and Sidhu, R.S. (1980) The many uses of bond duration. *Financial Analysts Journal* (July–August), 58–72.

Ward, C.W.R. (1988) Asset pricing models and property as a long term investment: The contribution of duration. In: MacLeary, A.R. and Nanthakumaran, N. (eds) *Property Investment Theory*, pp. 134–45. London: E & F.N. Spon.

Constructing property portfolios

Learning objectives

After reading this chapter you will understand the following:

- The implications of portfolio theory in understanding risk-reduction and portfolio size

- The difference between risk-reduction and diversification

- How effective diversification is likely to be in a property portfolio

- How value weighting affects diversification

Introduction

Indivisibility and lack of liquidity in the property market would seem to rule out any interest by investors in trying to construct efficient portfolios. This, however, is not the case. Professional advice is often concerned with making recommendations about portfolio decisions. Although there is a clear implication by investors that diversification is worth pursuing it is not clear that in this area professional advisers are offering advice that has any sound economic basis.

The principle of diversification is well known to investors in property although there are few empirical studies concerned with the reduction in risk and portfolio size. Assessments of diversification tend to be qualitative in nature with little quantitative content. A central issue in this debate concerns the number of properties that investors should hold. This is important not only in terms of property but also in a mixed-asset context.

In this chapter we will investigate how effective diversification in real estate is likely to be. As you will see this can have important implications in terms of developing a portfolio strategy.

Background

The analysis of risk-reduction and portfolio size related to stock portfolios has been well documented and several studies have been carried out to investigate the effect of adding more assets into a portfolio has on the standard deviation of portfolio returns. See, for example, Evans and Archer (1968) and Elton and Gruber (1977). This work has also been extended to cover the impact of investing internationally (Solnik, 1974).

One of the most quoted studies on risk-reduction and portfolio size is by Evans and Archer (1968). Recognising that the total variation in portfolio returns can be split into two parts, i.e. systematic and unsystematic risk, they argued that the reduction in risk must be a function of unsystematic risk. That is the part of risk that can be diversified away. As your portfolio increases in size and approaches the market, you should expect the variation in portfolio returns to approach the systematic level. The relationship between portfolio size and variance of returns should, therefore, be a declining, asymptotic function. Markowitz (1959) first identified this in relation to stock portfolios. As a reminder the variance of returns of a portfolio consisting of n assets can be expressed as:

$$\sigma_n^2 = \sum_{j=1}^{n} x_j^2 \sigma_j^2 + \sum_{j=1}^{n} \sum_{\substack{k=1; \\ k \neq j}}^{n} x_j\, x_k\, \sigma_{jk} \tag{11.1}$$

If you assume that each asset carries the same value this can be simplified as follows:

$$\sigma_n^2 = \frac{1}{n}\, \bar{\sigma}^2 + \frac{n-1}{n}\, \bar{\sigma}_{jk} \tag{11.2}$$

where

σ_n^2 = variance of portfolio consisting of n equally weighted stocks
$\bar{\sigma}^2$ = average variance of all stocks
$\bar{\sigma}_{jk}$ = average covariance between all stocks
n = number of stocks

You will see that as the number of assets increases, the portfolio variance gradually reduces until it reaches the average covariance between all stocks:

$$\sigma_n^2 = \bar{\sigma}_{jk} \tag{11.3}$$

Evans and Archer showed that by maintaining equal investment in each asset most of the reduction in risk occurs within a portfolio holding between 15 and 20 stocks. The method Evans and Archer used to investigate diversification was randomly to construct portfolios of increasing size and to calculate the average standard deviation of returns. Repeating the process many times enabled the relationship between portfolio risk and the number of stocks to be established. Using this methodology to analyse the same problem in property terms introduces two further complications: the lack of data and the indivisibility of property.

As you build up a property portfolio you can't easily invest in a small portion of a building. This means that the percentage contribution that each property makes to a portfolio is important in terms of risk-reduction. Although similar problems can arise in stock portfolios, choosing the proportion of funds to invest in each asset is generally within the control of the investor. However, in trying to analyse the effectiveness of portfolio construction in relation to risk-reduction, it is useful to construct a model based on the assumption of equal investment and compare this with the results obtained by simulating some value-weighted property portfolios.

The major problem, however, is the lack of data, coupled with the confidentiality that surrounds many of the figures relating to valuations and transactions. Although there is considerable interest in understanding portfolio construction there still remains a great reluctance to release data. Despite these difficulties it has been possible to investigate the reduction in risk and portfolio size by using data collected by one of the authors together with additional data provided by the Investment Property Databank (IPD).

The first UK study in this area (Brown 1985) was based on a sample of 135 properties with total returns collected over the period from January 1979 to December 1982. The properties were typical of commercial properties acquired by institutional investors and were of differing age and quality. There was no attempt to bias the sample to include only prime-quality property. The advantage of this sample was that it incorporated a continuous time-series of valuations that were prepared on a monthly basis. The data not only included changes in capital value but also income received, together with expenditure incurred. From the resulting time-series, continuously compounded monthly rates of return were estimated. Although the period covered was short it did have the advantage of being based on a verifiable sample of data.

A more up-to-date sample was provided from the IPD database and consisted of a random sample of properties drawn from each sector of the market covering two separate periods, i.e. monthly returns from December 1987 to December 1992 and from December 1992 to December 1997. For both sub-periods the total sample size was 130 properties. In no case was it possible to identify any specific property. All that was known was that they were representative of typical institutional investments. In addition to monthly data IPD also provided a random sample of properties with annual returns covering the period 1987–96. The total sample size in this case was 750 properties.

These samples have enabled us to make a full investigation of the effect of risk-reduction and portfolio size using UK property covering different market conditions.

All the valuations were prepared on an open market basis and followed the Royal Institution of Chartered Surveyors (RICS) definition of open market value. It will be recalled that this is defined as:

> An opinion of the best price at which the sale of an interest in property would have been completed unconditionally for cash consideration on the date of valuation, assuming:
>
> (a) a willing seller;

(b) that, prior to the date of valuation, there had been a reasonable period (having regard to the nature of the property and the state of the market) for the proper marketing of the interest, for the agreement of the price and terms and for the completion of the sale;

(c) that the state of the market, level of values and other circumstances were, on any earlier assumed date of exchange of contracts, the same as on the date of the valuation;

(d) that no account is taken of any additional bid by a prospective purchaser with a special interest; and

(e) that both parties to the transaction had acted knowledgeably, prudently and without compulsion.

RICS Appraisal and Valuation Manual
Practice Statement 4.2, 1995

The information subset is clearly defined. Because of the infrequent nature of sales in the property market our analysis is based on valuations. One of the features of using an open market approach to valuation is that comparable data in the form of known transaction prices are frequently used as a reference point in order to establish a current valuation. Chapter 7 explored the relationship between valuations and prices and showed that given contemporaneous open market valuations and sales prices for the same group of properties, valuations can serve as a good proxy for their equivalent sales price. This statement only holds true, of course, if sales prices and valuations both represent open market conditions and the market were in equilibrium. The effect of special factors, such as a forced sale or disposal to a tenant at a concessionary price, could introduce bias into the relationship so that the definition of open market value will no longer be valid.

This relationship between valuations and prices is important for two reasons:

1. If valuations are a good proxy for prices, then investment research undertaken using valuations will be equivalent to similar research using prices. Portfolio advice based on valuations will also be valid. This is important in terms of investigating risk-reduction and portfolio size. Furthermore, if there is a change in the information set which enables a difference to be identified between a valuation and a potential transaction price, this could lead to a position of profitable arbitrage, assuming due allowance is made for both risk and trading costs.

2. Institutions holding property as part of a mixed-asset portfolio will try to make asset allocation decisions on the basis of changes in valuation. These decisions will hold true only if valuations and prices are a good proxy for each other.

Methodology

In Chapter 9 we covered the distributional characteristics of the data. This section will draw on this information to investigate how effective diversification is likely to be in property.

In Chapter 9 we showed that the correlation between the returns on individual properties is low. Although this is advantageous in terms of risk-reduction, this advantage can easily be eroded if there are considerable differences in the value weighting of individual properties. This is an important issue in portfolio construction. If, however, we bypass the additional problems caused by unequal property values we can investigate, as a separate issue, the effect that property correlation has on diversification. We can then compare our results with those obtained by simulating the construction of value-weighted portfolios.

The importance of examining portfolios of equal-valued properties is not as unrealistic as it may sound. Another way of looking at this is to regard the portfolios as representing what a naïve investor should do if he or she had no forecasting skill. Any departure from equal weighting would imply that the investor is placing bets on the performance of individual properties.

> Equal investment in each property is equivalent to assuming that investors have no forecasting ability.

When Evans and Archer analysed diversification they argued that the reduction of risk in a portfolio is inversely proportional to the number of assets held. This can be expressed formally as:

$$\sigma_n = A + B\left(\frac{1}{n}\right) \tag{11.4}$$

where

σ_n = standard deviation of returns on portfolio of n assets
A and B = constants

By assuming equal investment in each asset the values of A and B can be estimated by regressing the average risk of a portfolio of increasing size against the reciprocal of the number of properties held. Trying to apply the same approach to property is not, however, a practical proposition. Even though the constraint of value weighting can be dropped, the small sample of properties available for analysis within each sector makes it impossible to estimate the average risk for portfolios of increasing size without double counting. An alternative approach is therefore required.

You should note from equation 11.4 that Evans and Archer assumed that it is the reduction in the *standard deviation* of returns that is inversely related to the number of assets. The Markowitz model shown in equation 11.2 implies that the reduction in risk for an equally weighted portfolio is related to the *variance* of returns. Equation 11.4 should therefore be written as follows:

$$\sigma_n^2 = A + B\left(\frac{1}{n}\right) \tag{11.5}$$

The difference is not trivial. Using the Evans and Archer model in standard deviation terms assumes that risk reduces at a much faster rate than in variance terms. As portfolio sizes increase the risk reduction curves using equation 11.4 and the square root of equation 11.5 will coincide, but over the critical region of 10–20 properties there can be significant differences. In our analysis we will follow the Markowitz approach and assume that reduction in risk is related to the variance of returns.

As long as you are able to estimate the values for A and B in equation 11.5 you can easily prepare a series of risk-reduction profiles for each sector of the market. As an alternative to using regression analysis you can estimate these parameters by setting the risk-reduction equation equal to the variance of an equally weighted portfolio:

$$A + B \left(\frac{1}{n} \right) = \frac{1}{n} \bar{\sigma}^2 + \frac{n-1}{n} \bar{\sigma}_{jk} \qquad (11.6)$$

For a portfolio consisting of a single asset, $n = 1$ and this simplifies to:

$$A + B = \bar{\sigma}^2 \qquad (11.7)$$

This is just the average variance of all the assets.

Similarly for a very large portfolio, n will approach infinity and the equation simplifies to:

$$A = \bar{\sigma}_{jk} \qquad (11.8)$$

This is the average covariance. It is the systematic risk of a portfolio in variance terms for the asset class under consideration. Using these simplifications it is possible to estimate the parameters needed for the risk-reduction profiles.

Risk-reduction and portfolio size using monthly returns

By setting up the monthly returns data reported in Chapter 9 in a matrix we can estimate the average variance and covariance for each sector and sub-period. Separate data samples were available for three non-overlapping periods from 1979 to 1996. There

Table 11.1 ● Risk-reduction parameters

Monthly returns

	Average variance $\bar{\sigma}^2$	Average correlation coefficient $\bar{\rho}$	Coefficient A	Coefficient B	Sample size
January 1979 to December 1982					
Retail	37.760	0.060	2.859	34.901	46
Office	15.490	0.120	1.750	13.740	50
Industrial	19.300	0.080	1.316	17.984	39
All property	*21.970*	*0.095*	*1.951*	*20.019*	*135*
December 1987 to November 1992					
Retail	7.519	0.134	0.800	6.719	40
Office	15.252	0.213	2.886	12.367	30
Industrial	11.508	0.228	2.454	9.054	30
All property	*11.035*	*0.133*	*1.626*	*9.410*	*100*
December 1992 to November 1997					
Retail	5.975	0.144	0.647	5.328	40
Office	5.697	0.128	0.543	5.154	30
Industrial	5.355	0.098	0.428	4.926	30
All property	*5.706*	*0.126*	*0.530*	*5.176*	*100*

was, however, a gap between December 1982 and December 1987. Table 11.1 summarises the estimated coefficients.

By substituting each of the coefficients for *A* and *B* into equation 11.5 you can track
the effectiveness of risk-reduction for each sector in different market environments.
We have converted the figures to annual standard deviations and plotted them in
Figures 11.1a–11.1c. The same scale has been used for each figure so you can compare
the changes in risk in different market environments.

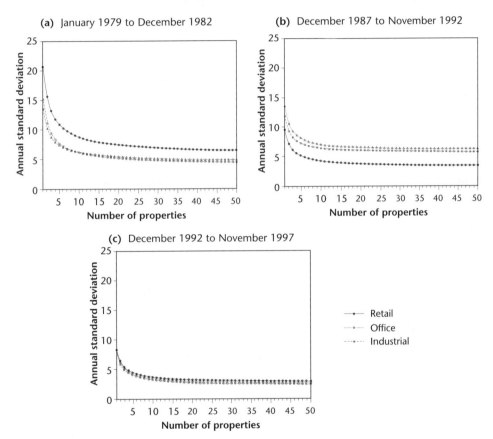

Figure 11.1a–c Risk-reduction and portfolio size

Although the samples in each sub-period are different these illustrations tell an
interesting story about risk-reduction over the period 1979–97.

The retail sector, for example, was most risky during 1979–82. This was a time when
expected returns in this sector were at their highest with a lot of activity in new
development. The periods 1987–92 and 1992–96 covered the stock market crash of
1987 and the subsequent collapse of the property market in 1992. The riskiness of the
retail sector reduced during these periods, indicating that the return expectations were
lower. Notice that in all periods the ranking of the office and industrial sectors remains
the same with offices always being more risky than industrial. The greatest change in
the risk seems to take place in the retail sector.

> The market risk for each sector can vary in different market conditions. The most volatile in terms of the ranking of market risk appears to be the retail sector.

If you estimate the average covariance for each sector you are assuming that all the residual risk has been diversified away. You can, therefore, use this to estimate the beta for each sector relative to the property market. You can do this as follows:

We can write the sector variance, σ_s^2 as:

$$\sigma_s^2 = \beta_s^2 \sigma_m^2 \tag{11.9}$$

Where σ_m^2 represents the variance of the property market, consisting of all sectors, and β_s is the systematic risk of the sector. Taking the square root and rearranging gives the sector beta as:

$$\beta_s = \frac{\sigma_s}{\sigma_m} \tag{11.10}$$

Table 11.2 summarises the sector betas in each of the sample periods compared with the ordinary least squares regression estimates.

Table 11.2 ● Comparison of proxy and OLS betas for each sector

	Proxy β (equation 11.10)	OLS estimates β	Standard error	$\bar{R}^2$
1979–82				
Retail	1.21	1.300	0.120	0.811
Office	0.95	0.999	0.059	0.858
Industrial	0.82	0.700	0.108	0.469
1987–92				
Retail	0.70	0.634	0.054	0.710
Office	1.33	1.297	0.063	0.881
Industrial	1.22	1.190	0.055	0.890
1992–97				
Retail	1.10	1.099	0.051	0.891
Office	1.01	0.981	0.062	0.817
Industrial	0.89	0.886	0.063	0.778

The period 1987–92 covered the collapse of the UK stock market and the start of the recession. The property market went into decline with very little development and investment taking place. The higher income yields associated with industrial property offered a potential for higher returns and this is reflected in the increased beta of this sector. If, however, you ignore this period as being unrepresentative of general market conditions it will be seen that the ranking of the betas in the other periods indicates that the market expects the highest returns in the retail sector and the lowest returns in the industrial sector.

You can gain further insights into the changing market conditions by examining the percentage reduction in risk in each sub-period. These are summarised in Tables 11.3–11.5.

Table 11.3 ● Percentage reduction in risk assuming equal weighting in each property

| | Risk-reduction and portfolio size: January 79 to December 82 | | | |
| | | | Percentage reduction in standard deviation | |
Number of properties	Retail	Office	Industrial	Portfolio
1	0	0	0	0
2	27	25	27	26
3	38	36	38	37
4	45	42	45	44
5	49	46	50	48
10	59	55	60	58
20	65	60	66	63
30	67	62	68	65
40	69	63	70	67
50	69	64	51	67
100	71	65	72	69
1,000	72	66	74	70

Table 11.4 ● Percentage reduction in risk assuming equal weighting in each property

| | Risk-reduction and portfolio size: December 87 to November 92 | | | |
| | | | Percentage reduction in standard deviation | |
Number of properties	Retail	Office	Industrial	Portfolio
1	0	0	0	0
2	26	23	22	24
3	36	32	31	34
4	43	37	36	40
5	47	41	39	44

Table 11.4 continued

Risk-reduction and portfolio size: December 87 to November 92			
		Percentage reduction in standard deviation	
Number of properties	Retail	Office	Industrial	Portfolio
---	---	---	---	---
10	56	48	46	52
20	61	52	50	56
30	63	54	51	58
40	64	54	52	59
50	65	55	52	59
100	66	56	53	61
1,000	67	56	53	62

Table 11.5 ● Percentage reduction in risk assuming equal weighting in each property

Risk-reduction and portfolio size: December 92 to November 97			
		Percentage reduction in standard deviation	
Number of properties	Retail	Office	Industrial	Portfolio
---	---	---	---	---
1	0	0	0	0
2	26	26	27	26
3	36	37	38	37
4	42	43	44	43
5	46	47	49	48
10	56	57	59	57
20	61	63	65	63
30	63	65	67	65
40	64	66	68	66
50	64	66	69	67
100	66	68	70	68
1,000	67	69	72	69

Generally speaking it would appear that you should be able to achieve reductions in risk close to 70% over the risk of the average property. During 1987–92, however, this was closer to 60%, implying that it was more difficult to diversify away the risk of holding property. These tables, together with the graphs, show that most of the reduction in risk occurs within the first 10–20 properties. Beyond this point the rate at which the risk reduces falls dramatically.

Risk-reduction and portfolio size using annual data

Before comparing our results with some real portfolios we will examine risk-reduction and portfolio size using annual data. The reason for doing this is that monthly returns are more susceptible to behavioural issues in the way the individual valuations are undertaken. This tends to introduce characteristics into the returns of portfolios that are not present in the underlying properties. By using annual data this problem is considerably reduced. The drawback, however, is that the number of returns for each property is smaller.

Our analysis in this case was undertaken using annual total returns based on the anonymous random sample of properties selected from the IPD database. The sample consisted of 250 properties from each sector. Setting these up in a variance–covariance matrix enabled the risk-reduction parameters to be estimated as before. A summary of the figures is given in Table 11.6.

Table 11.6 ● Risk-reduction parameters using annual data

Annual returns December 1987 to December 1996	Average variance $\bar{\sigma}^2$	Average correlation coefficient $\bar{\rho}$	Coefficient A	Coefficient B	Sample size
Retail	309.29	0.395	105.43	203.85	250
Office	458.79	0.425	175.53	283.26	250
Industrial	361.05	0.463	157.41	203.64	250
All property	376.39	0.407	138.38	238.00	250

We have substituted these parameters into equation 11.5 and have plotted the risk-reduction profiles for each sector in Figure 11.2 in terms of portfolio standard deviations.

The percentage reduction in risk for each portfolio size is summarised in Table 11.7.

The sample used in this analysis embraces two of the periods covered by the monthly data. You will see that the ranking of the sectors is the same as the 1987–92 period covered by the monthly data. There are, however, differences in the percentage reduction in risk. In comparison with the monthly data the figures are lower. The reason for this is differences in the cross-correlation between property returns. If you

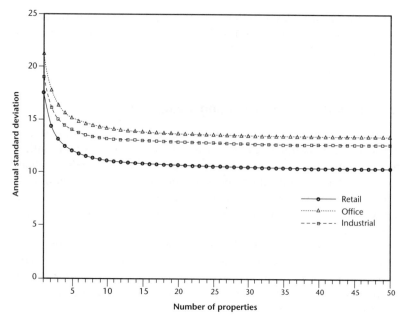

Figure 11.2   Risk-reduction and portfolio size: Annual returns, December 1987 to December 1996

Table 11.7 ● Risk-reduction parameters using annual data

Risk-reduction and portfolio size: annual returns December 1987 to December 1996
Percentage reduction in standard deviation

Number of properties	Retail	Office	Industrial	Portfolio
1	0	0	0	0
2	18	17	15	17
3	25	23	21	24
4	29	27	24	25
5	31	29	26	30
10	36	33	29	34
20	39	36	32	37
30	40	37	33	38
40	40	37	33	38
50	40	37	33	38
100	41	38	34	39
1,000	42	38	34	39

refer to Chapter 9 you will see that as the reporting frequency increases so the cross-correlation also increases. This implies that it is not so easy to reduce risk. Part of these differences may be due to the way information is impounded into valuations over different reporting intervals.

The principal difference between the two sets of results is that the systematic risk at the annual level is much higher than the equivalent annual monthly figures. The systematic risk is just the average covariance, represented by A in the risk-reduction equations. We have summarised these figures in Table 11.8 in terms of annual standard deviations for both the monthly and annual samples. In order to use the same period covered by the annual returns we have estimated an annual equivalent from the monthly data by weighting the variance in the periods from 1987–92 and 1992–97 to cover the same period as the annual returns.[1]

Table 11.8 ● Comparison of annual standard deviations

| | Annual standard deviations, 1987–96 | | |
	Monthly data annual equivalent risk	Annual data observed annual risk	Ratio
Retail	2.96	10.27	3.47
Office	4.71	13.25	2.81
Industrial	4.32	12.55	2.90
All property	3.70	11.76	3.18

In arriving at the annual standard deviation from the monthly data all we have done is convert the monthly systematic risk to its annual equivalent. This merely involves multiplying the monthly variance by 12 and then taking the square root of the result. There is, however, a considerable difference between using this approach and the annual systematic risk that is estimated directly from annual returns. We have already mentioned smoothing in index returns and the difference in figures could be caused by this effect. As the portfolios increase in size, smoothing generally increases and the portfolio standard deviation reduces. We will cover this in Chapter 12. However, you will see from Table 11.8 that the annual returns give a standard

---

[1] Each of the monthly samples covered five years, or 60 months. The systematic variance for the retail sector from 1987 to 1992 was 0.80%. The figure for the period from 1992 to 1997 was 0.647%. We re-weighted these to find an average figure for the period from 1987 to 1996 by taking 60 months in the first period and 48 months in the second period. The calculation was as follows. The average variance per month = [60(0.800)+48(0.647)]/108 or 0.732%. The annual equivalent of 2.96% was estimated from $\sqrt{12(0.732)}$.

deviation that is almost three times as large as the monthly conversion. When we examine ways of removing smoothing we also find that it increases risk by a factor of almost three.

Risk-reduction and value-weighted portfolios

Our discussion so far has assumed equal investment in each property. As this is not possible in practice it is useful to examine how effective reduction in risk is likely to be when value weighting is taken into consideration. We have, therefore, constructed some value-weighted portfolios by randomly selecting properties from each sector of the market. In this analysis we have used the data from 1979–82 because a complete time-series of value changes was available for each property. We will consider some other issues of portfolio construction when we examine the implications for portfolio strategy in Part 3.

In constructing the portfolios the approach we adopted was intended to replicate what a fund manager would do in putting together a property portfolio. The only difference was that the properties were chosen at random, whereas the fund manager will probably follow some selection criteria and could well increase the capital value of successive acquisitions as the portfolio increases in capital value. Whether any particular strategy followed by a fund manager is superior to random selection is open to debate. When we examine performance measurement in Part 3 we will show the evidence for consistent superior performance is not good in the property sector. This implies that random selection might do just as well. This, of course, raises a number of issues that we will defer until Part 3.

We examined the value-weighted reduction of risk for each sector as follows. We started by choosing at random a single property from the sample of available properties within each sector. This provided time-series information over the holding period so that the first mean return and standard deviation could be estimated. Another property was then randomly selected and the cash flows and capital values added to the first property. From the amalgamated cash flow the second mean return and standard deviation was computed. The process was continued by randomly selecting properties and adding them to the portfolio until all properties within each sector were exhausted. Our value-weighted risk-reduction profiles for one simulation within each sector are shown in Figures 11.3a–11.3c. Also shown on the graphs are the sector risk-reduction profiles we estimated earlier, together with the risk-reduction profile applicable to the portfolio. In estimating this profile we wanted to take account of the value weighting so that the risk-reduction parameters were obtained by regressing the variance of returns for the value-weighted portfolios against the reciprocal of the number of the properties. The resulting profile represented the naïve investor constructing an equally weighted portfolio with the same risk-reduction characteristics as the value-weighted portfolio.

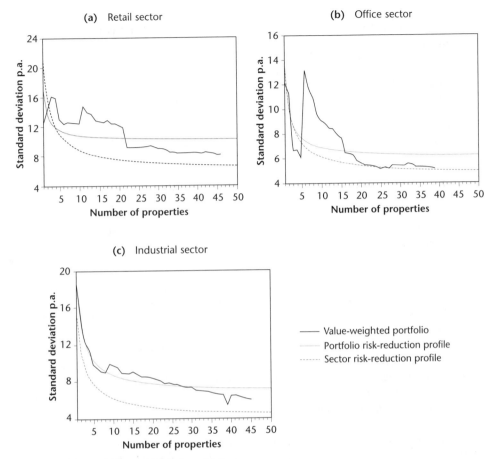

Figure 11.3a–c Value-weighted portfolio

There are two points that need to be stressed in interpreting these results:

1. The effect of differences in capital value of each property will skew the performance of the portfolio towards the risk-return characteristics of the largest valued properties. We examine this issue in Appendix 11E.
2. The systematic risk of each portfolio could change as each new property is added to the portfolio.

The combination of these effects will mean that when value weighting is taken into consideration the portfolios will deviate from the risk-reduction profiles that we identified for equal weighting. Morrell (1993) has also investigated this aspect. Using the parameters from the regression analysis the results show that the risk-reduction only approximately follows the equally weighted theoretical estimates for each sector. We illustrate this point in Table 11.9.

Table 11.9 ● **Comparison of parameters for value-weighted and equal-weighted portfolios**

Monthly returns Sector	$\sigma^2 = A + B\left(\dfrac{1}{n}\right)$ A	Standard error	B	Standard error	$\bar{R}^2$	n
Retail	8.678	0.691	13.124	3.679	0.21	46
(theoretical)	2.859		34.901			
Office	3.181	0.490	11.462	2.406	0.36	39
(theoretical)	1.750		13.740			
Industrial	3.667	0.153	25.887	0.804	0.96	45
(theoretical)	1.316		17.984			

The coefficients for A and B for each value-weighted sector are significant at the 99% level. In addition, you will see that the A coefficients in all cases are higher and significantly different from the equally weighted values. In other words, given the sample sizes used, and bearing in mind the effect of different property values, the portfolios have not diversified down to the systematic risk level of a naïve investor who had no forecasting skill. In terms of strategy what this means is that the selection skill has caused the investor to take on additional risk. As a result more properties would be required to reduce the level of risk down to what could be considered to be theoretically possible.

Taking on additional risk is only acceptable if it is compensated by additional return. As this is a performance measurement issue we will leave it to Part 3. However, by now you will probably not be surprised to know that in many cases we find that taking on additional risk is not compensated by additional return. Superior investment skill is difficult to find.

Table 11.9 also shows considerable variation in the $\bar{R}^2$ values, although they do indicate that increasing the numbers of properties within a value-weighted real estate portfolio does explain a reasonable proportion of the reduction in risk. As a comparison we have summarised the percentage reduction in risk for both value-weighted and equally weighted portfolios within each sector. As the equally weighted figures represent the limit in terms of risk-reduction Table 11.10 shows that the value-weighted portfolios we constructed in each portfolio still have the potential for further reduction in risk.

Investment in all sectors

It is, of course, unusual for property managers to concentrate their funds in one sector, since they generally argue those spreading funds across each sector of the market

Table 11.10 ● Percentage reduction risk for both value-weighted and equal-weighted portfolios

	Portfolio type	*n*	Percentage reduction in standard deviation
Retail	Value-weighted	46	35.87%
	Equal-weighted	46	69.05%
Office	Value-weighted	39	51.29%
	Equal-weighted	39	63.16%
Industrial	Value-weighted	45	62.12%
	Equal-weighted	45	70.20%

will produce better diversified portfolios. As this is a strong assertion it is useful to undertake the same analysis as above, but to construct portfolios randomly selected from each sector. We employed the same methodology as before with the exception that the portfolio sizes were limited to a maximum of 40 properties.

We have constructed three randomly selected portfolios and have plotted the results in Figures 11.4a–11.4c. On each of these figures we have also plotted the equally weighted profile together with our estimated 95% confidence limits.

The risk-reduction profile for each portfolio is different, but they each lie within the 95% confidence limits. The result of regressing the variance of returns for the value-weighted portfolios against the reciprocal of increasing numbers of properties is given in Table 11.11.

Each of the *A* coefficients differs from the equivalent value for the equally weighted portfolio. In the case of simulations 1 and 3 the higher figures imply that there is still potential to reduce the systematic risk of the portfolios further. The variance of simulation 2 is, however, lower than the equal-weighted portfolio. This is probably due to a fortuitous combination of properties that has focused on low-risk, or low-correlation, properties. Unless it is possible to continue doing this it is probable that adding additional properties will increase the risk.

In terms of standard deviations each of the simulations shows different levels of risk-reduction. These are summarised in Table 11.12.

Even though simulation 2 shows that, with 40 properties, it is possible to achieve a risk-reduction of over 78% this is still within the confidence bands that we have placed on the equal-weighted portfolio.

The results of these simulations clearly illustrate that the risk-reduction potential is quite significant although the profile followed by each portfolio is influenced by the capital value and market risk of the largest properties. The exposure of the portfolio to the performance of these properties can only be minimised by adding a large number of small properties or a smaller number of large properties. In each case it will be seen that by the time the portfolio consists of about 20–30 properties it is approaching its systematic risk level.

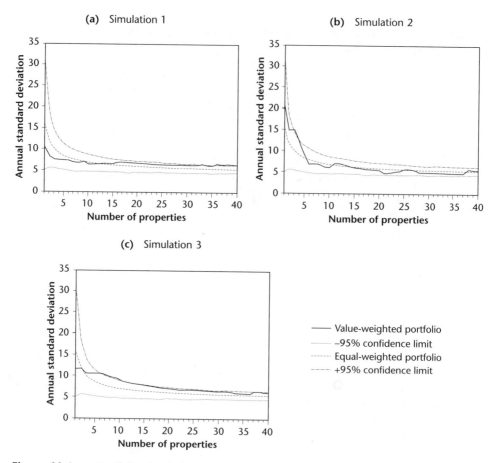

Figure 11.4a–c Portfolio simulations

Table 11.11 ● Comparison of parameters for value-weighted and equal-weighted portfolios

Monthly returns	$\sigma^2 = A + B\left(\dfrac{1}{n}\right)$					
Portfolio	A	Standard error	B	Standard error	$\bar{R}^2$	n
Simulation 1	3.316	0.034	5.553	0.170	0.96	40
Simulation 2	0.805	0.245	37.221	1.219	0.96	40
Simulation 3	3.979	0.286	10.952	1.420	0.60	40
Equal-weighted portfolio	1.951		20.019			

Table 11.12 ● Comparison of risk-reduction of value-weighted and equal-weighted portfolios

	Portfolio type	n	Percentage reduction in standard deviation
Simulation 1	Value-weighted	40	37.57%
Simulation 2	Value-weighted	40	78.64%
Simulation 3	Value-weighted	40	46.64%
	Equal-weighted	40	66.59%

Portfolio diversification

So far our discussion has been concerned with reduction in risk. We have shown that if an investor had no forecasting ability and could invest equal amounts in about 30 properties it would be possible to reduce the level of risk in the portfolio to the systematic level. We also showed that this principle holds with value-weighted portfolios. The risk-reduction in the portfolios was also substantial, varying between 51% and 74% depending on the sector and between 62% and 70% at the portfolio level. Comparable figures in the UK stock market are in the order of 50%. These figures apply to equal-weighted portfolios and assume that the market risk is constant for each portfolio size. The overall reduction in risk does not appear to be influenced by whether the returns are reported monthly or annually.

In Chapter 9 we showed that the correlation between returns for individual properties was low. We argued that this was probably due to factors specific to individual properties such as location, the type of tenant, and so on. We also showed in Chapter 10 that it is the covariance between asset returns that is the most important factor contributing to diversification. The low correlation that we observe between individual property returns, therefore, contributes a lot in terms of risk-reduction. This, however, is not the end of the story. Each property and portfolio carries a high proportion of specific risk. This is risk that has not been diversified away, so for each portfolio size there still remains a lot of uncertainty in the portfolio returns. You can see this from the confidence limits that we have shown in Figures 11.4a–11.4c.

In practical terms what this means is that, depending on the number of properties you hold, the performance of your portfolio in each period is more likely to be influenced by specific rather than market-wide factors. The market will only play a significant role in explaining performance if your portfolio holds a large number of properties.

So far we have looked at risk-reduction and portfolio size. Diversification is, however, concerned with explaining the effect that the market has on the performance of a portfolio. You can define this as:

Diversification is the percentage variation in portfolio returns that can be explained by the market.

If you know a little about regression analysis you may recognise this as explanatory power, which in statistical terms is just the $\bar{R}^2$ value. In fact, if you regressed the returns of a portfolio against an index of property returns then the explanatory power of the regression model would indicate the level of diversification of the portfolio. An alternative way of working this out is to relate it to the figures that we estimated when we looked at risk-reduction and portfolio size.

You can do this by recognising that as the portfolio increases in size it will get progressively more diversified until its returns exactly follow those of the market. You can plot this in the form of a declining asymptotic function as follows:

$$\frac{1}{\bar{R}^2} = X + Y\left(\frac{1}{n}\right) \qquad (11.11)$$

where

$\bar{R}^2$ = coefficient of determination between the portfolio returns and the market
n = number of properties

To solve this equation for each portfolio size you need estimates of X and Y. By using the same logic we adopted earlier it will be evident that as the number of properties increases and approaches infinity the ratio $1/n$ disappears. At this point the portfolio is completely diversified with the market explaining all of its variation in returns so that $\bar{R}^2$ must be equal to 1. Similarly when n is equal to 1 you will get:

$$\frac{1}{\bar{R}^2} = X + Y \qquad (11.12)$$

rearranging and recognising that $X = 1$ gives:

$$\bar{R}^2 = \frac{1}{1 + Y} \qquad (11.13)$$

This gives one expression for $\bar{R}^2$. Another form is to relate it to the total risk of the portfolio:

$$\sigma_p^2 = \beta_p^2\, \sigma_m^2 + \sigma_e^2 \qquad (11.14)$$

Dividing through by the total risk of the portfolio, σ_p^2, you can express $\bar{R}^2$ as:

$$1 = \bar{R}^2 + (1 - \bar{R}^2) \qquad (11.15)$$

where

$$\bar{R}^2 = \frac{\beta_p^2 \sigma_m^2}{\sigma_p^2} \tag{11.16}$$

This is just the market risk of your portfolio divided by its average risk. You already know that the market risk can be written as A and the average risk as $(A + B)$ so you can also write $\bar{R}^2$ as:

$$\bar{R}^2 = \frac{A}{A + B} \tag{11.17}$$

You now have two expressions for $\bar{R}^2$ so you can use them to solve for Y by setting them equal to each other. Combining equations 11.13 and 11.17 gives:

$$\frac{1}{1 + Y} = \frac{A}{A + B} \tag{11.18}$$

which can be rearranged in terms of Y as follows:

$$Y = \frac{A + B}{A} - 1 \tag{11.19}$$

Substituting this back into equation 11.11, and remembering that $X = 1$, gives the following:

$$\frac{1}{\bar{R}^2} = 1 + \left(\frac{A + B}{A} - 1 \right) \frac{1}{n} \tag{11.20}$$

Simplifying gives:

$$\frac{1}{\bar{R}^2} = 1 + \left(\frac{B}{A} \right) \frac{1}{n} \tag{11.21}$$

so that

$$\bar{R}^2 = \frac{nA}{nA + B} \tag{11.22}$$

We already worked out the value of the parameters A and B when we examined risk-reduction. By using the same figures in equation 11.22 you can estimate the percentage diversification of a portfolio in relation to the number of properties held. We have summarised these figures for each sector for the period from December 1979 to January 1982 in Table 11.13.

If you look at these figures you will see that the property market explains a relatively small proportion of the variation in returns for the average property within each sector. The first row of numbers shows that at the portfolio level the market explains only about 9% of the variation in returns of the average property. A similar figure for the stock market is in the order of 30%. It follows from this that it is easier

Table 11.13 ● How portfolio size affects diversification

December 1979 to January 1982	% diversification ($\bar{R}^2$)			
No. of properties	Office	Retail	Industrial	Portfolio
1	0.11	0.08	0.07	0.09
2	0.20	0.14	0.13	0.16
3	0.28	0.20	0.18	0.23
4	0.34	0.25	0.23	0.28
5	0.39	0.29	0.27	0.33
10	0.56	0.45	0.42	0.49
20	0.72	0.62	0.59	0.66
30	0.79	0.71	0.69	0.75
40	0.84	0.77	0.75	0.80
50	0.86	0.80	0.79	0.83
100	0.93	0.89	0.88	0.91
200	0.96	0.94	0.94	0.95
1,000	0.99	0.99	0.99	0.99

to create highly diversified portfolios within the stock market than it is within the property market. Increasing portfolio size does of course increase diversification and this fact is clearly seen in the table.

> The property market explains less than 10% of the variation in returns of the average monthly valued property.
> By contrast the stock market explains about 30% of the variation in returns of the average stock.

Once again you can test the validity of this model by randomly constructing portfolios and estimating the change in the $\bar{R}^2$ value measure relative to the market sample. In this case we have simulated two portfolios and plotted the results in Figure 11.5 relative to the equally weighted portfolio together with the estimated 95% confidence limits.

You will see that simulation 1 stays close to the average line whereas simulation 2 shows greater variation. As these are value-weighted portfolios the greater deviation from the average equal-weighted line indicates the influence of some large-valued properties. You can examine the effect of large-valued properties by regressing the reciprocal of $\bar{R}^2$ against the reciprocal of the number of properties. You will recall that we summarised the relationship between $\bar{R}^2$ and the number of properties in equation 11.21 as follows:

$$\frac{1}{\bar{R}^2} = 1 + \left(\frac{B}{A}\right)\frac{1}{n}$$

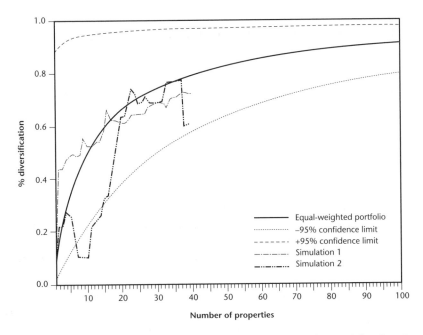

Figure 11.5 Diversification and portfolio size: comparison of value-weighted and equal-weighted portfolios

You can test this model by running the following regression:

$$\frac{1}{\overline{R^2}} = X + Y\,\frac{1}{n} + e \tag{11.23}$$

and then compare the coefficients X and Y with the figures you expected using an equally weighted portfolio. For example, you know that the coefficient X should be equal to 1.0. This should hold for both value-weighted and equal-weighted portfolios. The coefficient for Y should, for an equally weighted portfolio, be the ratio of B divided by A. For our sample of properties covering the period from January 1979 to December 1982 we estimated these as 20.019 and 1.951, giving a Y coefficient of 10.261.

Deviations from these figures in the regression analysis using value-weighted data indicate the effect that large-valued properties have on the performance of the portfolio. The results are given in Table 11.14.

It is difficult to interpret these statistics separately. All you can say is that the small sample size and the effect of value weighting have caused the X coefficients to differ from 1.00 in both simulations. As far as the Y coefficients are concerned you are testing to see whether the coefficients differ from our test value of 10.261. Only simulation 1 differs from this figure. The explanatory power, $\overline{R}^2$, of simulation 1 is much higher than simulation 2. This implies that, overall, simulation 2 was less influenced by large-valued properties.

Table 11.14 ● Analysis of diversification of simulated portfolios

$$\frac{1}{\bar{R}^2} = X + Y.\frac{1}{n} + e$$

Portfolio	X	Standard error	Y	Standard error	$\bar{R}^2$	n
Simulation 1	1.253	0.069	5.432	0.348	0.86	40
Simulation 2	2.192	0.459	11.050	2.278	0.37	40
Equal weighting	1.000		10.261			

The $\bar{R}^2$ values in the table tell us about the explanatory power of our regression model estimated using only 40 observations. However, what you are interested in is an absolute measure of diversification taking account of the portfolio sizes and value weights. You can estimate this from the coefficients given in Table 11.14. There are two statistics that are of interest:

● The effect that the market has in explaining the variation in returns of the average property in each portfolio. This is estimated by setting $n = 1$ in equation 11.23.
● The effect that the market has in explaining the variation in returns of a portfolio holding 40 properties. This is estimated by setting $n = 40$ in equation 11.23.

Example

As an example you know from Table 11.14 that for simulation 1 the X coefficient is 1.253 and the Y coefficient is 5.432.

Explanatory power for the average property (n = 1)

Substituting these coefficients into equation 11.23 gives:

$$\frac{1}{\bar{R}^2} = 1.253 + 5.432$$

$$\bar{R}^2 = 0.149$$

Explanatory power for portfolio holding 40 properties (n = 40)

Substituting these coefficients into equation 11.23 gives:

$$\frac{1}{\bar{R}^2} = 1.253 + 5.432\left(\frac{1}{40}\right)$$

$$\bar{R}^2 = 0.720$$

For simulation 1 the market explains about 15% of the variation in returns of the average property held in the portfolio. By the time the portfolio holds 40 properties the explanatory power has increased to 72%.

We have summarised this analysis in Table 11.15 for both simulations together with the equal-weighted portfolio.

Table 11.15 ● Estimated explanatory power, $\bar{R}^2$, for each portfolio

Portfolio	$n = 1$	$n = 40$
Simulation 1	0.149	0.720
Simulation 2	0.076	0.405
Equal weighting	0.088	0.796

You will see that the portfolio in simulation 2 is only 40% diversified and that the market explains about 8% of the variation in returns of the average property.

You can also compare these figures with the equal-weighted portfolio. In this case the market explains about 9% of the variation in returns of the average property and for a portfolio of 40 properties the diversification increases to approximately 80%. This represents the naïve position of an investor with no forecasting ability. The effect of value weighting has not been able to match the same level of diversification. The reduction in diversification is not a problem as long as it is compensated with better than average performance. That, however, is another story.

Combining risk-reduction and diversification

Our simulations of risk-reduction and diversification have important implications for the development of a portfolio strategy. We will return to this in Part 3, but for the moment it is worth noting that for a portfolio to be considered well diversified the market should explain at least 95% of its variation in returns. Our diversification figures show that in order to achieve this it would be necessary to hold an equal proportion of funds in about 200 properties. With value weighting, the figure is likely to be much larger. The majority of UK property portfolios tend to hold fewer than 30 properties, implying that they are almost certainly poorly diversified. The few that hold close to 200 properties will still find that the effect of value weighting would cause significant differences in diversification unless a number of properties are highly correlated with the market.

Property portfolios can, therefore, show rapid reduction in risk with relatively few properties, but require large numbers of properties in order to be highly diversified. This implies that you could combine these elements in order to provide some insights into the performance of property. We have shown this in Table 11.16 by splitting the total risk of a portfolio into its market and specific risk components and matching this with the reduction in risk and percentage diversification. As the risk figures are expressed in terms of annual standard deviations we also give an example of how the figures have been worked out.

Property portfolios show rapid reduction in risk with relatively few properties but require large numbers of properties to be highly diversified.

From our analysis on risk reduction and portfolio size we showed that, in monthly terms, the reduction in variance of the total portfolio returns over the period January 1979 to December 1982 could be expressed as:

$$\sigma_p^2 = 1.951 + 20.019 \; \frac{1}{n} \tag{11.24}$$

The figures in this equation come from Table 11.1. You can use this equation to estimate the total risk for a portfolio and then split it into its market risk and specific risk components.

For any size portfolio the annual standard deviation can be estimated from the monthly variance by replacing n by the number of properties. We will illustrate two examples, when $n = 1$ and $n = 50$.

Estimating the total risk

When $n = 1$

Monthly variance = 1.951 + 20.019 = 21.970%

Converting this to an annual standard deviation gives:

Annual standard deviation = $\sqrt{21.920 \times 12}$ = 16.24%

When $n = 50$

Monthly variance = $1.951 + \dfrac{20.019}{50}$ = 2.351%

Converting this to an annual standard deviation gives:

Annual standard deviation = $\sqrt{2.351 \times 12}$ = 5.31%

Estimating the market risk

This component can be estimated by assuming that the portfolio holds an infinitely large number of properties. From equation 11.24 the variance simplifies to:

Monthly market variance = 1.951%

Converting this to an annual standard deviation gives:

Annual monthly market risk = $\sqrt{1.951 \times 12}$ = 4.84%

Estimating the specific risk

If you know the total risk and market risk for any portfolio size you can easily estimate the residual risk. Remember, however, that you cannot subtract standard deviations, so you have to work in terms of variances.

When $n = 1$

Annual residual risk = $\sqrt{16.24^2 - 4.84^2} = 15.50\%$

When $n = 50$

Annual residual risk = $\sqrt{5.31^2 - 4.84^2} = 2.19\%$

Estimating the reduction in risk

This is just the percentage reduction in total risk from the average portfolio risk. The reduction in risk for a portfolio holding 50 properties over a portfolio holding one property can be estimated from:

Reduction in risk = $\dfrac{16.24 - 5.31}{16.24}$ = 0.673 or 67.3%

Estimating the portfolio diversification

You can estimate the percentage diversification by expressing the total risk of the portfolio as:

$$\sigma_p^2 = \beta_p^2 \, \sigma_m^2 + \sigma_e^2 \tag{11.25}$$

We showed earlier that the $\bar{R}^2$ value can be expressed as:

$$\bar{R}^2 = \frac{\beta_p^2 \sigma_m^2}{\sigma_p^2} \tag{11.26}$$

As $\beta = 1$ for the whole market you have a simple expression for estimating diversification.

When $n = 1$

$$\bar{R}^2 = \frac{4.84^2}{16.24^2} = 0.088 \text{ or } 8.8\%$$

When $n = 50$

$$\bar{R}^2 = \frac{4.84^2}{5.31^2} = 0.83 \text{ or } 83\%$$

Using each of these calculations Table 11.16 summarises the combined effect of risk-reduction and diversification for a wide range of portfolio sizes based on the period January 1979 to December 1982. The results for our other sample periods are summarised in Appendix 11F.

Table 11.16 ● Risk-reduction and diversification: total portfolio, January 1979 to December 1982

No. of properties	Total risk	Market risk	Specific risk	% risk-reduction	% R̄² diversification
1	16.24	4.84	15.50	0.00	8.88
2	11.98	4.84	10.96	26.22	16.31
3	10.17	4.84	8.95	37.35	22.63
4	9.14	4.84	7.75	43.73	28.05
5	8.45	4.84	6.93	47.94	32.77
10	6.89	4.84	4.90	57.58	49.36
20	5.95	4.84	3.47	63.34	66.10
30	5.61	4.84	2.83	65.48	74.52
40	5.42	4.84	2.45	66.59	79.59
50	5.31	4.84	2.19	67.28	82.98
100	5.08	4.84	1.55	68.71	90.70
200	4.96	4.84	1.10	69.44	95.12
500	4.89	4.84	0.69	69.89	97.99
1,000	4.86	4.84	0.49	70.05	98.98

You can use this table to find a reasonable balance between diversification and risk-reduction. For example, by holding the market average of about 30 properties it should be possible to achieve a level of risk-reduction in the order of 65% and for the market to explain about 75% of the variation in portfolio returns. This, of course, assumes equal weighting. But even with this constraint it will be seen that there is still 2.83% p.a. of specific risk that has not been diversified away. We get a similar figure by using annual data so we can be fairly certain that the majority of commercial property portfolios hold a high proportion of specific risk. As the specific risk figures are so high they will clearly have an important effect on the performance of the portfolio from year to year.

If the above analysis holds true in all periods it indicates that it is extremely difficult to achieve portfolios that are highly diversified. This becomes more acute when the effect of large properties is taken into consideration. As a result, investors will find it virtually impossible to create a portfolio that is capable of tracking an index. Assuming that the average-sized portfolio consists of about 30 properties the amount of specific risk still to be diversified away can be quite substantial and will have a significant effect on periodic performance. Two portfolios following identical policies in terms of buying strategy and sector weighting may find that their returns differ considerably on a period-by-period basis purely because of differences in specific risk.

Because it is very difficult to create highly diversified property portfolios it is virtually impossible to create a portfolio that will track an index.

Applying the same logic to the analysis of property indices reveals that it would be necessary to hold many thousands of properties in order to achieve a portfolio of properties that is a good proxy for market movements. Many of the commercially available indices utilise only a few hundred properties. The foregoing discussion would indicate that there is likely to be a considerable amount of specific risk remaining in these indices. Coupled with this is the problem of smoothing.

Although much work remains to be done in understanding the systematic components of property risk to see if they are constant over time, our research indicates that there is probably little advantage to be gained by diversifying across sectors. Similar levels of risk-reduction can be achieved merely by diversifying within a single sector. If, however, investors can successfully forecast positive abnormal returns for an individual sector, then they would achieve a better trade-off between risk and return by diversifying solely within that sector. Diversification across sectors is probably motivated by the long holding periods associated with property and the difficulty of switching sectors as prospects change.

Whether it is possible for investors to forecast positive abnormal returns successfully is, of course, an empirical matter. If perfect forecasting ability does not exist then our research suggests that investors should pursue some policy of diversification. The findings presented above do show, however, that the common beliefs concerning diversification that are followed by many property investment funds are not as effective as imagined.

Summary

This chapter has taken a quantitative approach to understanding risk-reduction and diversification in property portfolios. The starting point was the portfolio model discussed in Chapter 10. This showed that risk could be split into two parts: systematic and specific. Portfolio risk could only be reduced by eliminating specific risk.

We investigated how effective this was likely to be with property and found that although it is possible to achieve significant reductions in risk it is very difficult to achieve high levels of diversification. A main finding is that high proportions of property portfolios are poorly diversified. For the majority of property portfolios the amount of specific risk per period is high and this will have a major impact on property performance. The chapter closed by pointing out that there appear to be no significant benefits to be gained by diversifying across sectors. The reason for doing this is likely to be motivated by reasons other than diversification.

This chapter has six appendices. The first five present some simple proofs that are based on the assumption that investors have no forecasting skill. Although this may seem restrictive we have no evidence to believe that property investors are able to exploit any mispricing that may exist in the market. In practical terms this means that the optimal solution for the naïve investor is to hold equal amounts in each property. These results, therefore, represent a benchmark against which investors can judge their own performance.

Appendix 11A: Risk-reduction and portfolio size based on equal investment

This provides a proof of the risk-reduction formula used in Chapter 11, together with a measure of diversification and risk-reduction.

Appendix 11B: The relationship between systematic risk, diversification and the inter-asset coefficient of correlation

This shows that for a naïve investor the average diversification, i.e. $\bar{R}^2$, is equal to the average inter-asset coefficient of correlation.

Appendix 11C: Estimating the number of properties required to achieve a given level of diversification

This appendix shows how to estimate the number of properties an investor should hold in order to achieve a given level of diversification.

Appendix 11D: Estimating the portfolio-specific risk

This shows how the specific risk of a portfolio can be estimated from some simple market data.

Appendix 11E: Portfolio diversification and the naïve investor

This appendix introduces the effect that value weighting has on a portfolio. A simple solution takes account of differences in property values and produces an equally weighted equivalent.

Appendix 11F: Risk-reduction and portfolio size: empirical results

This appendix summarises the results of our analysis of risk reduction and portfolio size for different periods based on monthly and annual returns.

Chapter 11: Summary table

1. If you assume equal investment in each asset the total risk of a portfolio can be written as:

$$\sigma_n^2 = \frac{1}{n} \, \bar{\sigma}^2 + \frac{n-1}{n} \, \bar{\sigma}_{jk}$$

2. As the number of assets increases the portfolio risk reduces to the average covariance.

$$\sigma_n^2 = \bar{\sigma}_{jk}$$

3. Starting with the standard portfolio model you can show that the variance of portfolio returns can be written as:

$$\sigma_n^2 = A + B \left(\frac{1}{n} \right)$$

4. Because of small sample sizes estimates for A and B have to be made from the property data. For example, the average variance and the systematic risk can be written in terms of these coefficients as follows:

$$A + B = \bar{\sigma}^2$$
$$A = \bar{\sigma}_{jk}$$

5. The results show that with monthly data there can be significant reductions in risk and the most volatile sector in terms of market risk is retail.

6. Annual data show less reduction in risk. This is due to the higher cross-correlation between property returns.

7. Simulations using value-weighted portfolios show that there can be significant reductions in risk. The effect of value weighting can have an important impact on performance.

8. Risk-reduction is only one part of the portfolio problem.

With equal weighting most of the reduction in risk comes within the first 20–30 properties.

9. Another aspect of portfolio construction concerns diversification. This can be defined as the percentage variation of returns that can be explained by the market.

A portfolio that has about 95% of its variation in returns explained by the market is considered to be well diversified.

10. The relationship between diversification and the number of assets held can be expressed in the following form:

$$\frac{1}{\bar{R}^2} = X + Y \left(\frac{1}{n} \right)$$

11. If the maximum $\bar{R}^2$ value is 1.0 it is possible to write another expression for diversification:

$$\bar{R}^2 = \frac{nA}{nA + B}$$

12. For monthly valued property the market explains less than 10% of the variation in returns. For annual valued property the figure is closer to 35%. These figures are influenced by smoothing issues.

13. Property portfolios show rapid reduction in risk with relatively few properties but require large numbers of properties to be highly diversified.

14. A reasonable balance between risk-reduction and diversification appears to be a holding of approximately 30 properties. This assumes equal weighting.   The amount of specific risk in a portfolio of this size will be close to 3% p.a.

15. Because it is very difficult to construct highly diversified property portfolios it is virtually impossible to create a portfolio that will track an index.

16. Diversifying across sectors does not appear to offer any more benefits than diversifying within a sector.

Problems

1. What factors contribute to risk-reduction in a property portfolio?
2. Why should you make a distinction between risk-reduction and diversification?
3. Are there any advantages to be gained by diversifying across sectors?
4. If you wanted to construct a highly diversified portfolio what proportion of the variation in returns of a property portfolio should be explained by the market?
5. Discuss why you would not always expect commercial property portfolios to track each other closely.
6. Are most commercial property portfolios well diversified?
7. If a property portfolio is poorly diversified what does this imply for performance?
8. Why would you expect a difference between the risk-reduction and diversification characteristics of a portfolio that is valued monthly and one that is valued annually?

References

Brealey, R.A. and Myers, S.C. (1996) *Principles of Corporate Finance*, 5th edn. New York: McGraw-Hill.

Brown, G.R. (1988) Reducing the dispersion of returns in UK real estate. *Journal of Valuation* 6 (2), 127–47.

Brown, G.R. (1991) *Property Investment and the Capital Markets*, London: Chapman & Hall.

Brown, G.R. (1997) Reducing the dispersion of returns in UK real estate portfolios. *Journal of Real Estate Portfolio Management* **3** (2), 1–12. Reprinted from *Journal of Property Valuation* **6** (2) (1988), 127–47.

Elton, E.J. and Gruber, M.J. (1977) Risk reduction and portfolio size: An analytical solution. *Journal of Business* **50** (4), 415–37.

Evans, J.L. and Archer, S.H. (1968) Diversification and the reduction of dispersion. *Journal of Finance* **23** (4), 761–7.

Markowitz, H.M. (1952) Portfolio selection. *Journal of Finance* **12** (March), 77–91.

Markowitz, H.M. (1959) *Portfolio Selection: Efficient Diversification of Investments*, A Cowles Foundation Monograph, New Haven: Yale University Press.

Appendix 11A
Risk-reduction and portfolio size based on equal investment

In this appendix we assume that investors have no forecasting skill so that equal investment in each asset is an optimal investment strategy to follow. We derive an expression for the percentage reduction in risk of an equal-weighted portfolio and show that it is a function of the inter-asset coefficient of correlation.

You will recall from Chapter 10 that the variance of returns of a portfolio consisting of n assets can be expressed as:

$$\sigma_n^2 = \sum_{j=1}^{n} x_j^2 \sigma_j^2 + \sum_{j=1}^{n} \sum_{\substack{k=1; \\ k \neq j}}^{n} x_j x_k \sigma_{jk} \tag{11A.1}$$

where

σ_n^2 = variance of portfolio consisting of n assets
σ_j^2 = variance of asset j
σ_{jk} = covariance between assets j and k
$x_j x_k$ = the proportion of funds invested in assets j and k respectively

By assuming equal investment in each asset equation 11A.1 can be expressed as:

$$\sigma_n^2 = \sum_{j=1}^{n} \left(\frac{1}{n}\right)^2 \sigma_j^2 + \sum_{j=1}^{n} \sum_{\substack{k=1; \\ k \neq j}}^{n} \left(\frac{1}{n}\right)\left(\frac{1}{n}\right) \sigma_{jk} \tag{11A.2}$$

By factoring out $1/n$ from the variances and $(n-1)/n$ from the covariances you can write equation 11A.2 as:

$$\sigma_n^2 = \frac{1}{n} \sum_{j=1}^{n} \left(\frac{\sigma_j^2}{n}\right) + \frac{(n-1)}{n} \sum_{j=1}^{n} \sum_{\substack{k=1; \\ k \neq j}}^{n} \left[\frac{\sigma_{jk}}{n(n-1)}\right] \tag{11A.3}$$

The term in the first bracket is the average variance and the term in the square bracket is the average covariance. In total there are $n(n-1)$ covariances because k cannot equal j. You can therefore write equation 11A.3 as:

$$\sigma_n^2 = \frac{1}{n} \bar{\sigma}_j^2 + \frac{n-1}{n} \bar{\sigma}_{jk} \tag{11A.4}$$

You can simplify this further by assuming that all assets possess the same total risk and equal pairwise correlations. In this case each σ_j equals the average standard deviation, $\bar{\sigma}$, and each ρ_{jk} equals the average correlation coefficient, $\bar{\rho}$, for all j and k. This simplification is appropriate for a naïve investor with no forecasting skill. The average covariance can, therefore, be written as follows:

$$\bar{\sigma}_{jk} = \bar{\rho}\bar{\sigma}^2 \tag{11A.5}$$

By substitution equation 11A.3 can be simplified to:

$$\sigma_n^2 = \bar{\sigma}^2 \left[\bar{\rho} + \left(\frac{1 - \bar{\rho}}{n} \right) \right]$$ (11A.6)

The reduction in risk of a portfolio of size n from the average property risk can be expressed as follows:

$$RR_n = \frac{\bar{\sigma} - \sigma_n}{\bar{\sigma}}$$ (11A.7)

By substitution from equation 11A.6 the reduction in risk will be seen to be a function of the inter-asset correlation coefficient as follows:

$$RR_n = 1 - \left[\bar{\rho} + \left(\frac{1 - \bar{\rho}}{n} \right) \right]^{\frac{1}{2}}$$ (11A.8)

Example

Assume you have no forecasting skill but you have estimated the average property risk to be 18% p.a. You also believe that the property market is likely to explain about 20% of the variation of returns of the average property. If you hold 50 properties and the value of each property is approximately equal, you can use this information to estimate the portfolio risk and the percentage reduction in risk.

Portfolio risk

This comes from equation 11A.6. In this case the average coefficient of correlation is 20%:

$$\sigma_{50}^2 = 0.18^2 \left[0.20 + \left(\frac{1 - 0.20}{50} \right) \right]$$

$$\sigma_{50} = 0.0836 \text{ or } 8.36\%$$

Percentage reduction in risk

This can either come from equation 11A.7:

$$RR_{50} = \frac{0.18 - 0.0836}{0.18} = 0.535$$

Or you can use equation 11A.8:

$$RR_{50} = 1 - \left[0.20 + \left(\frac{1 - 0.20}{50} \right) \right]^{\frac{1}{2}} = 0.535$$

In both cases the reduction in risk is 53.5%.

If you replace $n = 50$ with $n = \infty$ in each of these equations you can find the minimum portfolio risk and maximum percentage reduction in risk. The figures in this case are 8.05% and 55.3%. You will see that with this correlation structure this portfolio is close to the maximum possible. Changes in the value weighting of each property will, of course, affect these figures.

Appendix 11B
The relationship between systematic risk, diversification and the inter-asset coefficient of correlation

In the example we gave in Appendix 11A we made the assumption that the inter-asset coefficient correlation for the average property was also equal to the average R^2 value. In this appendix we show how we arrived at this conclusion.

We will assume that each property in the portfolio has the same beta. This is reasonable if you have no forecasting skill. The total risk of the average property in your portfolio can therefore be written as:

$$\bar{\sigma}^2 = \beta^2 \sigma_m^2 + \sigma_e^2 \tag{11B.1}$$

This is just the average total risk decomposed into its market and specific risk components. Dividing both sides by the average total risk provides an estimate of the portfolio diversification in R^2 terms:

$$1 = R^2 + \frac{\sigma_e^2}{\bar{\sigma}^2} \tag{11B.2}$$

where

$$R^2 = \frac{\beta^2 \sigma_m^2}{\bar{\sigma}^2} \tag{11B.3}$$

This is the average diversification for a single property. It represents the percentage variation in returns, of the average property, that is explained by the market.

If you assume a naïve investor, the market risk component can also be written as the average covariance:

$$\beta^2 \sigma_m^2 = \bar{\rho}\bar{\sigma}^2 \tag{11B.4}$$

Substituting this into equation 11B.3 you will see that for the average property the level of diversification is equal to the average inter-asset coefficient of correlation:

$$R^2 = \bar{\rho} \tag{11B.5}$$

You should note that this only applies in the average property case. As you start to add more properties into a portfolio the R^2 will begin to increase, whereas the average coefficient of correlation will stay the same.

> ### Example
>
> In the example we gave in Appendix 11A we assumed that the market explained about 20% of the variation of returns for the average property held by our naïve investor. From equation 11B.5 you will see that this also implies that the average coefficient of correlation between properties is 0.2.
>
> By adding more properties into the portfolio it becomes more diversified and the R^2 value increases. However, the average coefficient of correlation between properties still remains unchanged.

Appendix 11C
Estimating the number of properties required to achieve a given level of diversification

If you have no forecasting ability you will have no view concerning the prospects for an individual property. However, from an historic time-series of returns you should be able to estimate the average coefficient of correlation between individual properties. If you make an assumption about how diversified you want your portfolio to be, then you can use this information to estimate how many properties you should hold. We show you how to do this in this appendix.

You can write the reduction in risk of a portfolio of size n relative to its average risk as:

$$RR_n = \frac{\bar{\sigma} - \sigma_n}{\bar{\sigma}} \tag{11C.1}$$

A similar expression for an infinitely large portfolio representing the market, m, would be given by:

$$RR_m = \frac{\bar{\sigma} - \sigma_m}{\bar{\sigma}} \tag{11C.2}$$

By writing each of these in terms of their average risk and setting them equal to each other you will arrive at the following:

$$\frac{\sigma_m}{\sigma_n} = \frac{1 - RR_m}{1 - RR_n} \tag{11C.3}$$

Squaring both sides gives an expression for diversification, or R^2.

$$R^2 = \left(\frac{\sigma_m}{\sigma_n}\right)^2 = \left(\frac{1 - RR_m}{1 - RR_n}\right)^2 \tag{11C.4}$$

In Appendix 11A we showed that the reduction in risk for a portfolio of size n could be expressed in terms of the average coefficient of correlation as:

$$RR_n = 1 - \left[\bar{\rho} + \left(\frac{1 - \bar{\rho}}{n}\right)\right]^{\frac{1}{2}} \tag{11C.5}$$

As n approaches infinity this gives the maximum risk reduction for the market:

$$RR_m = 1 - \sqrt{\bar{\rho}}$$ (11C.6)

You now have expressions for the percentage reduction in risk for a portfolio of size n and the market, both of which are in terms of the average coefficient of correlation. Substituting equations 11C.5 and 11C.6 into 11C.4 and simplifying gives:

$$R^2 = \frac{n\bar{\rho}}{n\bar{\rho} + (1 - \bar{\rho})}$$ (11C.7)

This can be rearranged to give the number of properties required to achieve a given level of diversification.

$$n = \frac{R^2 (1 - \bar{\rho})}{\bar{\rho} (1 - R^2)}$$ (11C.8)

$$n = \frac{R^2}{(1 - R^2)} \left(\frac{1}{\bar{\rho}} - 1 \right)$$ (11C.9)

Example

Assume that you have estimated the average coefficient of correlation between properties to be 0.15. Your long-term aim is to construct a portfolio that will be 95% diversified. This means that the property market will explain 95% of the variation in returns of your portfolio. You want to know how many properties you should hold in order to achieve this. You can find this from equation 11C.9.

$$n = \frac{0.95}{(1 - 0.95)} \left(\frac{1}{0.15} - 1 \right)$$

$$n = 108$$

We have rounded up this figure, as you don't normally buy fractions of a property. Assuming you have no forecasting ability and are able to invest equal amounts in each property, this implies that you would need to hold over 100 properties in order to be 95% diversified. In practical terms it will not, of course, be possible to ensure that the value of each property is exactly the same. If you take unequal values into consideration you will need to hold more properties than shown here to compensate for the differences in value.

Appendix 11D
Estimating the portfolio-specific risk

We showed in Chapter 11 that it is very difficult to achieve high levels of diversification in property. As a result the majority of portfolios will carry a lot of specific risk and this will influence performance in each reporting period. In this appendix we show how you can estimate the specific risk for any size portfolio assuming that you have no forecasting ability.

The total risk of a portfolio can be split into its market risk and specific risk components. In general terms this can be expressed as:

$$\sigma_n^2 = \beta^2 \sigma_m^2 + \sigma_e^2 \tag{11D.1}$$

Dividing both sides by the total risk expresses each risk component in terms of its proportion of diversification:

$$1 = R^2 + (1 - R^2) \tag{11D.2}$$

where:

$$R^2 = \frac{\beta^2 \sigma_m^2}{\sigma_n^2} \tag{11D.3}$$

and:

$$1 - R^2 = \frac{\sigma_e^2}{\sigma_n^2} \tag{11D.4}$$

From Appendix 11C we derived the following expression for the number of assets required to achieve a given value for $\bar{R}^2$:

$$n = \frac{R^2}{(1 - R^2)} \left(\frac{1}{\bar{\rho}} - 1 \right) \tag{11D.5}$$

Substituting equations 11D.3 and 11D.4 into 11D.5 gives:

$$n = \frac{\beta^2 \sigma_m^2}{\sigma_e^2} \left(\frac{1}{\bar{\rho}} - 1 \right) \tag{11D.6}$$

The residual risk can be found by rearranging to give:

$$\sigma_e^2 = \frac{\beta^2 \sigma_m^2}{n} \left(\frac{1}{\bar{\rho}} - 1 \right) \tag{11D.7}$$

Example

In order to use equation 11D.7 you need three pieces of information: the portfolio beta, the market variance and the average coefficient of correlation between each property. If you have no forecasting ability your best assumption for the portfolio beta is that it should be equal to the market average of 1.0. You may be able to obtain information about the market variance and the average coefficient of correlation from other data sources. Let us assume that these figures are $\sigma_m = 0.12$ and $\bar{\rho} = 0.2$. If you hold a portfolio of 50 equal-valued properties you can find the specific risk by substituting these into equation 11D.7 to give:

$$\sigma_e^2 = \frac{(1.0)^2 (0.12)^2}{50} \left(\frac{1}{0.20} - 1 \right)$$

$\sigma_e = 0.034$ or 3.4%

This represents the amount of residual risk in the portfolio that has not been diversified away. As your portfolio is assumed to have a beta of 1.0 you can make some probability statements about its expected performance relative to the returns on a market index. For example, if in one year the IPD All Property index reports a total return of 12% you could be 95% certain that your portfolio return will lie within the following range:

$$r_{50} = 12\% \pm 1.96(3.40)$$

i.e. from 5.34% to 18.7%.

This wide range shows how difficult it is to track an index. In some years you will outperform the index, in other years you will underperform. This result is also based on the assumption of equal-valued properties. If you were to relax this you would find that the residual risk would be even higher, as long as you assumed that the average coefficient of correlation remained constant.

Appendix 11E
Portfolio diversification and the naïve investor

Appendices 11A–11D have developed some useful formulas that can be used to gain some insights into the performance of your portfolio. The underlying assumption in developing these ideas has been the notion of the naïve investor. This is someone who has no forecasting ability and who invests the same amount of funds in each asset. This is an optimal strategy which is also based on the assumption that each asset carries the same level of risk and the coefficient of correlation between each asset pair is equal.

In this appendix we investigate the effect of relaxing one of these assumptions, namely differences in asset value. This is clearly important in property investment because it is difficult to decide in advance on the optimal proportion of funds to invest in each property. We derive a simple expression that takes account of the effect of different property values by assuming that investors have no forecasting skill so that their optimal strategy should be to hold equal amounts in each property. The degree to which an investor deviates from this position, by holding properties with different values, provides an indication of the bets he or she is placing on the performance of individual properties.

For investors with no forecasting ability you can consider the equally weighted position to be a benchmark against which the performance of the value-weighted portfolio can be monitored. Two portfolios holding the same number of properties, having the same average property risk and average coefficient of correlation may perform differently because one portfolio has a high proportion of funds concentrated in one or two properties. The model we derive provides a way of estimating an *equally weighted equivalent* number of properties that can be used to make a comparison between portfolios. For the naïve investor this gives a better indication of diversification for each portfolio.

The variance of a value-weighted portfolio P is given by:

$$\sigma_p^2 = \sum_{j=1}^{n} x_j^2 \sigma_j^2 + \sum_{j=1}^{n} \sum_{\substack{k=1; \\ k \neq j}}^{n} x_j x_k \sigma_{jk} \qquad (11E.1)$$

A naïve investor with no forecasting skill will assume that each asset has the same variance and covariance. Given this assumption you can simplify this as follows:

$$\sigma_p^2 = \bar{\sigma}^2 \sum_{j=1}^{n} x_j^2 + \bar{\sigma}_{jk} \sum_{j=1}^{n} \sum_{\substack{k=1; \\ k \neq j}}^{n} x_j x_k \qquad (11E.2)$$

For a naïve investor the average covariance can also be written as:

$$\bar{\sigma}_{jk} = \bar{\rho} \bar{\sigma}^2 \qquad (11E.3)$$

If you substitute this into equation 11E.2 you get:

$$\sigma_p^2 = \bar{\sigma}^2 \left(\sum_{j=1}^{n} x_j^2 + \bar{\rho} \sum_{j=1}^{n} \sum_{\substack{k=1; \\ k \neq j}}^{n} x_j x_k \right) \qquad (11E.4)$$

This gives an expression for the variance of a value-weighted portfolio for a naïve investor. This assumes that the correlation between each property is the same and that the variances for each property are equal.

If you wanted to pursue an optimal investment strategy with these assumptions you should invest equal amounts in each property. The variance of an equal-weighted portfolio with the same risk can, therefore, be written as:

$$\sigma_p^2 = \frac{\bar{\sigma}^2}{n} + \frac{n-1}{n} \bar{\sigma}_{jk} \qquad (11E.5)$$

where n is an equally weighted equivalent number of properties.

This can be simplified to:

$$\sigma_p^2 = \bar{\sigma}^2 \left[\frac{1}{n} + \bar{\rho} \left(\frac{n-1}{n} \right) \right] \qquad (11E.6)$$

In order to find the equal-weighted number of properties, n, that would have the same variance as the value-weighted portfolio you set equations 11E.4 and 11E.6 equal to each other:

$$\bar{\sigma}^2 \left[\frac{1}{n} + \bar{\rho} \left(\frac{n-1}{n} \right) \right] = \bar{\sigma}^2 \left(\sum_{j=1}^{n} x_j^2 + \bar{\rho} \sum_{j=1}^{n} \sum_{\substack{k=1; \\ k \neq j}}^{n} x_j x_k \right) \qquad (11E.7)$$

With a little rearrangement of terms you can derive an expression for an *equally weighted* number of properties that would have the same variance as the value-weighted portfolio:

$$n = \left\{ \frac{1}{1-\bar{\rho}} \left[\sum_{j=1}^{n} x_j^2 + \bar{\rho} \left(\sum_{j=1}^{n} \sum_{\substack{k=1; \\ k \neq j}}^{n} x_j x_k - 1 \right) \right] \right\}^{-1} \tag{11E.8}$$

By recognising that the double summation can also be written as:

$$\sum_{j=1}^{n} \sum_{\substack{k=1; \\ k \neq j}}^{n} x_j x_k = 1 - \sum_{j=1}^{n} x_j^2 \tag{11E.9}$$

and substituting this into equation 11E.8 you will see that the *equal-weighted equivalent* number of properties simplifies to:

$$n = \frac{1}{\sum_{j=1}^{n} x_j^2} \tag{11E.10}$$

You will see from this that both the average variance and the average coefficient of correlation cancel out because they occur in both the value-weighted and equal-weighted expressions of the portfolio variance given in equations 11E.4 and 11E.6. Equation 11E.10, therefore, isolates the effect of differences in the capital value of each property.

Example

You manage two portfolios, A and B, each of which holds ten properties and has a total capital value of £70 million. The properties held in each portfolio are broadly similar, except that the capital values of each of the properties differ. Assuming that you have no forecasting ability you assume that the variance of returns for each property in A and B are the same and the average coefficient of correlation between each property is also the same. Given this information you want to know which portfolio is better diversified.

Table 11E.1 sets out the capital values of each property in portfolios A and B together with their respective weights.

Using equation 11E.10 the reciprocal of the total squared weights gives the equal-weighted equivalent number of properties.

Portfolio A

$$n = \frac{1}{0.184} = 5.43$$

Table 11E.1 ● Property details in portfolios A and B

| Property number | Portfolio A | | | Portfolio B | | |
	Property values £m	Property weights A	Squared weights A	Property values £m	Property weights B	Squared weights B
1	£25m	0.357	0.128	£12m	0.171	0.029
2	£10m	0.143	0.020	£10m	0.143	0.020
3	£7m	0.100	0.010	£9m	0.129	0.017
4	£6m	0.086	0.007	£8m	0.114	0.013
5	£6m	0.086	0.007	£7m	0.100	0.010
6	£5m	0.071	0.005	£6m	0.086	0.007
7	£4m	0.057	0.003	£5m	0.071	0.005
8	£3m	0.043	0.002	£5m	0.071	0.005
9	£2m	0.029	0.001	£4m	0.057	0.003
10	£2m	0.029	0.001	£4m	0.057	0.003
Totals	£70m	1.000	0.184	£70m	1.000	0.113

Portfolio B

$$n = \frac{1}{0.113} = 8.85$$

Given our assumption of no forecasting skill you will see that portfolio A behaves more like an equal-weighted portfolio holding between 5 and 6 properties and portfolio B, by contrast, behaves more like a portfolio holding close to nine properties. On this basis portfolio A is not as well diversified as portfolio B.

If you refer back to equation 11D.7 you will see that we gave an expression for the residual risk in a portfolio in terms of the number of properties, the portfolio beta, the market variance and the average coefficient of correlation. You can use this to compare the residual risks for both portfolios. For our naïve investor the portfolio beta, the market variance and the average coefficient of correlation will all cancel out so that the only factor influencing the residual risk will be the number of properties. Given this background you can write the following:

$$n_A \sigma_A^2 = n_B \sigma_B^2 \qquad (11E.11)$$

where σ_A^2 and σ_B^2 represent the residual risk for portfolios A and B.

In standard deviation terms the ratio of the residual risks can be written as:

$$\frac{\sigma_A}{\sigma_B} = \sqrt{\frac{n_B}{n_A}} \qquad (11E.12)$$

Using the figures in our example:

$$\frac{\sigma_A}{\sigma_B} = \sqrt{\frac{8.85}{5.43}} = 1.28$$

As a result of the different capital values for each property the residual risk of portfolio A will be approximately 28% greater than portfolio B. It is important to be aware that these results only reflect differences in the capital value of each property. All other characteristics of each portfolio remain constant.

Other approaches

The approach we have described is not the only way to tackle the effect of value weighting in a property portfolio. For example, Morrell (1993) has also suggested a coefficient of value skewness (CVS) which is derived from the difference in the specific risk of a value-weighted and equally weighted portfolio. Dividing by the average risk gives a standardised coefficient. (See also Schuck and Brown (1997) for a comment on this approach.)

$$CVS = \frac{\widehat{\sigma}_{vw} - \widehat{\sigma}_{ew}}{\overline{\sigma}} \qquad \text{(11E.13)}$$

where

$\widehat{\sigma}_{vw}$ = specific risk for value-weighted portfolio

$\widehat{\sigma}_{ew}$ = specific risk for equally weighted portfolio

$\overline{\sigma}$ = average property risk

We need to stress that both approaches assume a naïve investor. This implies that each property has the same variance and covariance so that differences in portfolio performance can be explained solely in terms of differences in the capital value of each property. To this extent they are approximations of what is happening in practice. However, in the absence of any forecasting skill both methods do provide a quick and easy way to compare the diversification of a group of portfolios.

Selected references

Morrell, G.D. (1993) Value weighting and the variability of real estate returns: implications for portfolio construction and performance evaluation. *Journal of Property Research* **10**, 167–83.

Schuck, E.J. and Brown, G.R. (1997) Value weighting and real estate portfolio risk. *Journal of Property Research* **14** (3), 169–87.

Appendix 11F
Risk-reduction and portfolio size: empirical results

In this appendix we summarise the results of analysing risk-reduction and portfolio size for each of the sub-periods in our sample. We cover both monthly and annual returns data. This provides a reasonably comprehensive view of the diversification potential of UK property over the 18-year period 1979–97.

Monthly Returns: January 1979 to December 1982

All property

No. of properties	Total risk in % p.a.	Market risk in % p.a.	Specific risk in % p.a.	% risk-reduction	% diversification
1	16.24	4.84	15.50	0.00	8.88
2	11.98	4.84	10.96	26.22	16.31
3	10.17	4.84	8.95	37.35	22.62
4	9.14	4.84	7.75	43.73	28.05
5	8.45	4.84	6.93	47.94	32.76
10	6.89	4.84	4.90	57.58	49.36
20	5.95	4.84	3.47	63.34	66.09
30	5.61	4.84	2.83	65.48	74.51
40	5.42	4.84	2.45	66.60	79.58
50	5.31	4.84	2.19	67.29	82.97
100	5.08	4.84	1.55	68.71	90.69
200	4.96	4.84	1.10	69.45	95.12
500	4.89	4.84	0.69	69.90	97.99
1,000	4.86	4.84	0.49	70.05	98.98
10,000	4.84	4.84	0.15	70.18	99.90

Retail sector

No. of properties	Total risk in % p.a.	Market risk in % p.a.	Specific risk in % p.a.	% risk-reduction	% diversification
1	21.21	5.57	20.46	0.00	6.91
2	15.51	5.57	14.47	26.89	12.92
3	13.06	5.57	11.81	38.41	18.20
4	11.65	5.57	10.23	45.06	22.88
5	10.72	5.57	9.15	49.48	27.06
10	8.54	5.57	6.47	59.73	42.59
20	7.21	5.57	4.58	66.00	59.74
30	6.71	5.57	3.74	68.36	69.00
40	6.44	5.57	3.24	69.61	74.79
50	6.28	5.57	2.89	70.39	78.76
100	5.94	5.57	2.05	72.01	88.12
200	5.76	5.57	1.45	72.85	93.69
500	5.65	5.57	0.91	73.37	97.37
1,000	5.61	5.57	0.65	73.54	98.67
10,000	5.58	5.57	0.20	73.70	99.87

Monthly Returns: January 1979 to December 1982

Office sector

No. of properties	Total risk in % p.a.	Market risk in % p.a.	Specific risk in % p.a.	% risk-reduction	% diversification
1	13.63	4.58	12.84	0.00	11.30
2	10.17	4.58	9.08	25.40	20.30
3	8.72	4.58	7.41	36.07	27.65
4	7.89	4.58	6.42	42.14	33.75
5	7.35	4.58	5.74	46.11	38.91
10	6.12	4.58	4.06	55.09	56.02
20	5.41	4.58	2.87	60.34	71.81
30	5.15	4.58	2.34	62.25	79.26
40	5.01	4.58	2.03	63.24	83.59
50	4.93	4.58	1.82	63.85	86.43
100	4.76	4.58	1.28	65.09	92.72
200	4.67	4.58	0.91	65.73	96.22
500	4.62	4.58	0.57	66.13	98.45
1,000	4.60	4.58	0.40	66.26	99.22
10,000	4.58	4.58	0.12	66.37	99.92

Industrial sector

No. of properties	Total risk in % p.a.	Market risk in % p.a.	Specific risk in % p.a.	% risk-reduction	% diversification
1	15.22	3.97	14.69	0.00	6.82
2	11.12	3.97	10.39	26.92	12.77
3	9.37	3.97	8.48	38.45	18.00
4	8.35	3.97	7.34	45.12	22.64
5	7.68	3.97	6.57	49.55	26.79
10	6.11	3.97	4.65	59.83	42.26
20	5.16	3.97	3.28	66.12	59.41
30	4.79	3.97	2.68	68.50	68.70
40	4.60	3.97	2.32	69.75	74.54
50	4.48	3.97	2.08	70.53	78.54
100	4.24	3.97	1.47	72.16	87.98
200	4.11	3.97	1.04	73.01	93.60
500	4.03	3.97	0.66	73.53	97.34
1,000	4.00	3.97	0.46	73.71	98.65
10,000	3.98	3.97	0.14	73.87	99.86

Monthly Returns: December 1987 to November 1992

All property

No. of properties	Total risk in % p.a.	Market risk in % p.a.	Specific risk in % p.a.	% risk-reduction	% diversification
1	11.51	4.42	10.63	0.00	14.73
2	8.72	4.42	7.51	24.26	25.68
3	7.56	4.42	6.13	34.31	34.14
4	6.91	4.42	5.31	39.96	40.87
5	6.49	4.42	4.75	43.62	46.35
10	5.55	4.42	3.36	51.77	63.34
20	5.02	4.42	2.38	56.41	77.56
30	4.82	4.42	1.94	58.08	83.83
40	4.73	4.42	1.68	58.93	87.36
50	4.67	4.42	1.50	59.46	89.63
100	4.54	4.42	1.06	60.52	94.53
200	4.48	4.42	0.75	61.06	97.19
500	4.44	4.42	0.47	61.39	98.86
1,000	4.43	4.42	0.33	61.50	99.42
10,000	4.42	4.42	0.10	61.60	99.94

Retail sector

No. of properties	Total risk in % p.a.	Market risk in % p.a.	Specific risk in % p.a.	% risk-reduction	% diversification
1	9.50	3.10	8.98	0.00	10.64
2	7.06	3.10	6.35	25.62	19.23
3	6.04	3.10	5.18	36.42	26.32
4	5.45	3.10	4.49	42.57	32.26
5	5.07	3.10	4.02	46.60	37.32
10	4.20	3.10	2.84	55.76	54.35
20	3.69	3.10	2.01	61.13	70.43
30	3.51	3.10	1.64	63.10	78.13
40	3.41	3.10	1.42	64.12	82.65
50	3.35	3.10	1.27	64.75	85.62
100	3.23	3.10	0.90	66.04	92.25
200	3.16	3.10	0.63	66.70	95.97
500	3.12	3.10	0.40	67.11	98.35
1,000	3.11	3.10	0.28	67.24	99.17
10,000	3.10	3.10	0.09	67.37	99.92

Monthly Returns: December 1987 to November 1992

Office sector

No. of properties	Total risk in % p.a.	Market risk in % p.a.	Specific risk in % p.a.	% risk-reduction	% diversification
1	13.53	5.88	12.18	0.00	18.92
2	10.43	5.88	8.61	22.89	31.82
3	9.17	5.88	7.03	32.22	41.18
4	8.47	5.88	6.09	37.40	48.28
5	8.02	5.88	5.45	40.72	53.85
10	7.03	5.88	3.85	48.01	70.00
20	6.48	5.88	2.72	52.07	82.35
30	6.29	5.88	2.22	53.50	87.50
40	6.19	5.88	1.93	54.23	90.32
50	6.13	5.88	1.72	54.68	92.11
100	6.01	5.88	1.22	55.58	95.89
200	5.95	5.88	0.86	56.04	97.90
500	5.91	5.88	0.54	56.32	99.15
1,000	5.90	5.88	0.38	56.41	99.57
10,000	5.89	5.88	0.11	56.49	99.96

Industrial sector

No. of properties	Total risk in % p.a.	Market risk in % p.a.	Specific risk in % p.a.	% risk-reduction	% diversification
1	11.75	5.43	10.42	0.00	21.32
2	9.15	5.43	7.37	22.11	35.15
3	8.10	5.43	6.02	31.04	44.85
4	7.52	5.43	5.21	35.97	52.02
5	7.15	5.43	4.66	39.12	57.54
10	6.35	5.43	3.30	45.97	73.05
20	5.91	5.43	2.33	49.74	84.43
30	5.75	5.43	1.90	51.06	89.05
40	5.67	5.43	1.65	51.74	91.56
50	5.62	5.43	1.47	52.15	93.13
100	5.53	5.43	1.04	52.98	96.44
200	5.48	5.43	0.74	53.40	98.19
500	5.45	5.43	0.46	53.65	99.27
1,000	5.44	5.43	0.33	53.74	99.63
10,000	5.43	5.43	0.10	53.81	99.96

Monthly Returns: December 1992 to November 1997

All property

No. of properties	Total risk in % p.a.	Market risk in % p.a.	Specific risk in % p.a.	% risk-reduction	% diversification
1	8.27	2.52	7.88	0.00	9.29
2	6.12	2.52	5.57	26.08	17.00
3	5.20	2.52	4.55	37.13	23.50
4	4.68	2.52	3.94	43.46	29.06
5	4.33	2.52	3.52	47.63	33.86
10	3.55	2.52	2.49	57.15	50.59
20	3.08	2.52	1.76	62.82	67.19
30	2.90	2.52	1.44	64.91	75.44
40	2.81	2.52	1.25	66.01	80.38
50	2.76	2.52	1.11	66.68	83.66
100	2.64	2.52	0.79	68.07	91.10
200	2.58	2.52	0.56	68.79	95.34
500	2.55	2.52	0.35	69.23	98.08
1,000	2.53	2.52	0.25	69.37	99.03
10,000	2.52	2.52	0.08	69.51	99.90

Retail sector

No. of properties	Total risk in % p.a.	Market risk in % p.a.	Specific risk in % p.a.	% risk-reduction	% diversification
1	8.47	2.79	8.00	0.00	10.83
2	6.30	2.79	5.65	25.56	19.54
3	5.39	2.79	4.62	36.32	26.70
4	4.87	2.79	4.00	42.45	32.69
5	4.53	2.79	3.58	46.46	37.78
10	3.76	2.79	2.53	55.56	54.84
20	3.31	2.79	1.79	60.90	70.83
30	3.15	2.79	1.46	62.85	78.46
40	3.06	2.79	1.26	63.86	82.93
50	3.01	2.79	1.13	64.49	85.86
100	2.90	2.79	0.80	65.77	92.39
200	2.84	2.79	0.56	66.42	96.05
500	2.81	2.79	0.36	66.82	98.38
1,000	2.80	2.79	0.25	66.96	99.18
10,000	2.79	2.79	0.08	67.08	99.92

Monthly Returns: December 1992 to November 1997

Office sector

No. of properties	Total risk in % p.a.	Market risk in % p.a.	Specific risk in % p.a.	% risk-reduction	% diversification
1	8.27	2.55	7.86	0.00	9.53
2	6.12	2.55	5.56	26.00	17.40
3	5.21	2.55	4.54	37.00	24.02
4	4.69	2.55	3.93	43.30	29.65
5	4.35	2.55	3.52	47.44	34.50
10	3.56	2.55	2.49	56.90	51.30
20	3.10	2.55	1.76	62.51	67.82
30	2.93	2.55	1.44	64.58	75.97
40	2.84	2.55	1.24	65.66	80.82
50	2.78	2.55	1.11	66.32	84.05
100	2.67	2.55	0.79	67.70	91.33
200	2.61	2.55	0.56	68.40	95.47
500	2.58	2.55	0.35	68.84	98.14
1,000	2.56	2.55	0.25	68.98	99.06
10,000	2.55	2.55	0.08	69.11	99.91

Industrial sector

No. of properties	Total risk in % p.a.	Market risk in % p.a.	Specific risk in % p.a.	% risk-reduction	% diversification
1	8.02	2.27	7.69	0.00	7.99
2	5.89	2.27	5.44	26.52	14.80
3	4.98	2.79	4.44	37.82	20.68
4	4.46	2.27	3.84	44.33	25.79
5	4.12	2.27	3.44	48.62	30.29
10	3.32	2.27	2.43	58.53	46.49
20	2.84	2.27	1.72	64.51	63.47
30	2.67	2.27	1.40	66.74	72.27
40	2.57	2.27	1.22	67.92	77.66
50	2.51	2.27	1.09	68.64	81.29
100	2.39	2.27	0.77	70.14	89.68
200	2.33	2.27	0.54	70.92	94.56
500	2.29	2.27	0.34	71.40	97.75
1,000	2.28	2.27	0.24	71.56	98.86
10,000	2.27	2.27	0.07	71.71	99.89

Annual Returns: 1987 to 1996

All property

No. of properties	Total risk in % p.a.	Market risk in % p.a.	Specific risk in % p.a.	% risk-reduction	% diversification
1	19.40	11.76	15.43	0.00	36.77
2	16.04	11.76	10.91	17.31	53.76
3	14.76	11.76	8.91	23.94	63.56
4	14.07	11.76	7.71	27.49	69.93
5	13.64	11.76	6.90	29.71	74.41
10	12.73	11.76	4.88	34.36	85.32
20	12.26	11.76	3.45	36.81	92.08
30	12.10	11.76	2.82	37.65	94.58
40	12.01	11.76	2.44	38.08	95.88
50	11.96	11.76	2.18	38.33	96.67
100	11.86	11.76	1.54	38.85	98.31
200	11.81	11.76	1.09	39.10	99.15
500	11.78	11.76	0.69	39.26	99.66
1,000	11.77	11.76	0.49	39.31	99.83
10,000	11.76	11.76	0.15	39.36	99.98

Retail sector

No. of properties	Total risk in % p.a.	Market risk in % p.a.	Specific risk in % p.a.	% risk-reduction	% diversification
1	17.59	10.27	14.28	0.00	34.09
2	14.40	10.27	10.10	18.12	50.85
3	13.17	10.27	8.24	25.13	60.81
4	12.51	10.27	7.14	28.89	67.41
5	12.09	10.27	6.39	31.25	72.11
10	11.22	10.27	4.51	36.22	83.80
20	10.75	10.27	3.19	38.86	91.18
30	10.59	10.27	2.61	39.76	93.95
40	10.51	10.27	2.26	40.22	95.39
50	10.46	10.27	2.02	40.50	96.28
100	10.37	10.27	1.43	41.05	98.10
200	10.32	10.27	1.01	41.33	99.04
500	10.29	10.27	0.64	41.50	99.61
1,000	10.28	10.27	0.45	41.56	99.81
10,000	10.27	10.27	0.14	41.61	99.98

Annual Returns: 1987 to 1996

Office sector

No. of properties	Total risk in % p.a.	Market risk in % p.a.	Specific risk in % p.a.	% risk-reduction	% diversification
1	21.42	13.25	16.83	0.00	38.26
2	17.81	13.25	11.90	16.86	55.34
3	16.43	13.25	9.72	23.29	65.02
4	15.70	13.25	8.42	26.72	71.25
5	15.24	13.25	7.53	28.86	75.60
10	14.28	13.25	5.32	33.34	86.10
20	13.77	13.25	3.76	35.70	92.53
30	13.60	13.25	3.07	36.50	94.90
40	13.51	13.25	2.66	36.91	96.12
50	13.46	13.25	2.38	37.16	96.87
100	13.36	13.25	1.68	37.65	98.41
200	13.30	13.25	1.19	37.90	99.20
500	13.27	13.25	0.75	38.05	99.68
1,000	13.26	13.25	0.53	38.10	99.84
10,000	13.25	13.25	0.17	38.14	99.98

Industrial sector

No. of properties	Total risk in % p.a.	Market risk in % p.a.	Specific risk in % p.a.	% risk-reduction	% diversification
1	19.00	12.55	14.27	0.00	43.60
2	16.10	12.55	10.09	15.27	60.72
3	15.01	12.55	8.24	21.01	69.87
4	14.43	12.55	7.14	24.04	75.56
5	14.08	12.55	6.38	25.92	79.44
10	13.33	12.55	4.51	29.83	88.55
20	12.95	12.55	3.19	31.87	93.92
30	12.81	12.55	2.61	32.56	95.87
40	12.75	12.55	2.26	32.91	96.87
50	12.71	12.55	2.02	33.12	97.48
100	12.63	12.55	1.43	33.55	98.72
200	12.59	12.55	1.01	33.76	99.36
500	12.56	12.55	0.64	33.89	99.74
1,000	12.55	12.55	0.45	33.93	99.87
10,000	12.55	12.55	0.14	33.97	99.99

CHAPTER *12*

Valuation smoothing

Learning objectives

After reading this chapter you will understand the following:

- How market imperfections can influence the way properties are valued

- How valuers use information about current prices and recent valuations in order to estimate current values

- Why using the most recent valuation can be regarded as being optimal and does not imply any inefficiency in the way valuers operate

- How the aggregation of valuations reduces the variation in returns

Introduction

Assets that are freely traded in a competitive market provide a useful reference point for determining the value of other assets. This principle is widely adopted in real estate markets, where comparable sales evidence is frequently used as the basis for establishing the value of non-traded properties. Unfortunately, the competitive market model does not offer an accurate representation of the way real estate markets work in practice. Imperfections in the way the market operates can create valuations that are smoothed versions of their true market prices.

There are, however, two distinct processes at work. One is concerned with the valuation of individual properties, whereas the other is with the effect of aggregating groups of properties into indexes. The distinction is important as much of the literature in this area is concerned with removing the effect of smoothing at the index level.

In Chapter 11 we examined the systematic risk of each sector of the property market and found that, in terms of annual standard deviations, our figures differed considerably from those estimated directly from annual data. The annualised monthly risk understated the annual risk by a ratio of approximately 3 to 1.

In this chapter we introduce you to the concept of smoothing. This phenomenon is widely observed in property indices where the variability of returns is understated relative to the average return. As a result the trade-off between risk and return for property appears more favourable than expected. This has a direct bearing on areas such as asset allocation and diversification. Smoothing is an important issue and reflects the way valuers behave. Understanding the principles involved will, therefore, lead to closer integration between property and other asset classes.

More technical aspects concerning smoothing are covered in the appendices.

Competitive market imperfections

In a competitive market it is often necessary, for investment purposes, to estimate the proportion of funds that should be allocated to real estate. In Chapter 10 we discussed the mean-variance model and showed that it could be used to solve the asset allocation problem. However, in order for this model to provide useful answers it requires unbiased estimates of the risk of each asset. For those markets that are freely traded this presents no problem. Unfortunately, the absence of traded prices in the real estate market means that risk has to be inferred from valuations that are estimated from limited information on market transactions. The critical issue here is whether the valuation returns are a true reflection of the underlying market prices.

Quan and Quigley (1989) have shown that, as far as price formation is concerned, real estate markets have three important features that differentiate them from normally competitive Walrasian auction markets. These are:

1. Incomplete information about the attributes of individual properties so that buy and sell decisions are made with only partial knowledge.
2. Periods of costly search incurred by potential buyers.
3. The lack of a central marketplace so that prices are the result of private negotiation between buyer and seller.

These imperfections lead to market prices that, in the short run, can differ from what would be expected in a competitive market. To put this another way, transaction prices for identical properties are likely to vary. Imperfections in the market can also give rise to dispersion in valuations. We discussed this in Appendix 7D where we focused on quantifying the margin of error between valuations.

Using comparable sales to estimate values

One of the most common methods of valuation relies upon using comparable sales evidence as the basis for estimating the value of similar non-traded property. It has frequently been argued that this approach causes valuation to be *backward-looking* and as a result the smoothed versions of true market value do not fully reflect current market information. This implies that smoothing results from poor valuation practice or possibly even incompetence. Quan and Quigley (1989, 1991), however, take a different view. They approach the valuation problem by specifying a price model for the real estate market and then use this to deduce the relationship between market information and transaction prices. Given this approach they then ask what optimal strategy should a valuer follow?

Their analysis shows that the optimal value for any property can be represented as the weighted average of the previous value and the most recent comparable transaction prices. Smoothing, therefore, arises from the relative variability of general market price uncertainty and that associated with the property being valued. This insight shows that smoothing has nothing to do with problems concerning methodology or incompetence amongst valuers.

> The optimal updating strategy for valuers is to use the weighted average of the previous value and the most recent comparable transaction prices.
> This is a logical procedure and does not imply any problems concerning valuation methodology or incompetence amongst valuers.

Estimating prices

The job of the valuer is to make use of as much information as possible concerning an observed transaction price, P_t^T, in order to estimate the value V_t of a non-traded property. The relative negotiating strength between a buyer and seller determines the price at which a property sells.

The buyer's position

The *buyer* estimates a threshold price for a property, P^b, above which he or she is not prepared to make a bid. The threshold price represents the expected true price, P, subject to the set of information, I^b, that is available to the buyer. The information set reflects a wide range of physical characteristics concerning the property. As the buyer does not possess complete information concerning the property the threshold price will differ from the true price by an error term, e^b. You can write this as follows:

$$P = E(P|I^b) + e^b \equiv P^b + e^b \qquad (12.1)$$

The seller's position

The *seller* also estimates a threshold price for the property, P^s, below which he or she is not prepared to accept offers. This also reflects the true price, but in this case it is subject to the set of information, I^s, available to the seller. Like the buyer, the seller does not possess a complete set of information so that the threshold price for the seller also differs from the true price by an error term, e^s. You can write this as follows:

$$P = E(P|I^s) + e^s \equiv P^s + e^s \qquad (12.2)$$

Equations 12.1 and 12.2 define the range within which a transaction P^T will take place. For example, transactions will not occur above the highest threshold price for the buyer or below the lowest threshold price for the seller. It is helpful to view these positions as follows:

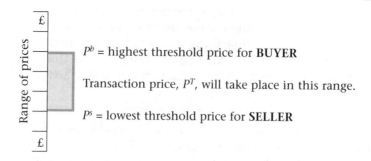

P^b = highest threshold price for **BUYER**

Transaction price, P^T, will take place in this range.

P^s = lowest threshold price for **SELLER**

The price at which the transaction takes place will depend on the negotiating strength of each party. Buyers and sellers, therefore, play a game in which the payoff is the profit that each will make. As they each want to maximise their respective profits they will reach a form of non-cooperative agreement, known as a Nash equilibrium. This is named after the US mathematician John Nash, who developed the concept in the 1950s. The transaction price will, therefore, lie somewhere in between the two thresholds, as follows.

$$P^T = wP^s + (1 - w)P^b \tag{12.3}$$

where w is an arbitrary weight that lies in the range $0 \leq w \leq 1$.

The weighting scheme represents the relative bargaining strength that exists between buyers and sellers. If, for example, $w = 1$ the transaction price will be equal to the seller's threshold price, indicating a buyer's market. Conversely when $w = 0$ this would indicate a seller's market.

Rearranging equations 12.1 and 12.2 in terms of P^b and P^s, and substituting into equation 12.3, gives the following expression for the transaction price:

$$P^T = w(P - e^s) + (1 - w)(P - e^b) \tag{12.4}$$

which simplifies to:

$$P^T = P - we^s - (1 - w)e^b \tag{12.5}$$

You could also write this as:

$$P^T = P + [w(e^b - e^s) - 1] \tag{12.6}$$

This shows that an observed transaction price P^T for a property represents a noisy signal of the true market price, P. The expression in the square brackets is just the error attached to the true market price. However, as this price is unobservable it is the noisy transaction price, P^T, that the valuer has to use to estimate the value of a comparable non-traded property.

Estimating values

In order to see how the valuer uses this information you have to make an assumption about the evolution of the true market price. One reasonable approach is to assume that it evolves as a random walk so that:

$$P_t = P_{t-1} + \eta_t \tag{12.7}$$

where[1]

$$\eta_t \sim NID(0, \sigma_\eta^2)$$

$$E(\eta_t \eta_{t-j}) = 0 \text{ for all } j$$

This assumption may not be too restrictive given that information arrives randomly. In addition, random walk models are frequently used in finance to describe the way in which asset prices evolve.

Assume also that the valuer has access to a set of previously observed transactions. This forms a set of relevant information I_{t-1} such that:

$$I_{t-1} \equiv (P_1^T, P_2^T, P_3^T, ..., P_{t-1}^T) \tag{12.8}$$

From equation 12.5 you know that each transaction price can be represented as the true market price plus some error. Following this approach you can write the transaction price in period t as the sum of the true market price P_t and a random error term v_t:

$$P_t^T = P_t + v_t \tag{12.9}$$

where $v_t \sim NID(0, \sigma_p^2)$

The random error term in this case includes factors such as search costs, as well as the conditions of the sale.

The valuer now has a previous set of transaction information, I_{t-1}, together with the latest transaction price P_t^T. Assuming that true market prices follow a random walk Quan and Quigley (1991) show that valuers will adopt an optimal updating procedure so that current estimates of value are related to their previous value plus a prediction error between the current transaction price and the previous valuation. Writing this in full you have:

$$E(P_t | P_t^T, I_{t-1}) = E(P_t | I_{t-1}) + k[P_t^T - E(P_t | I_{t-1})] \tag{12.10}$$

The left-hand side of equation 12.10 is the expected true market price, P_t, subject to the set of information concerning the current transaction price P_t^T and the previous history of transactions, I_{t-1}. This is just another way of expressing the current value. You can simplify this by replacing this term by the current value, V_t. The right-hand side of equation 12.10 can be interpreted in a similar way. In this case the expected true market price, P_t, based solely on the previous transactions history, can be represented as V_{t-1}.

If you substitute these into equation 12.10 you get:

$$V_t = V_{t-1} + k(P_t^T - V_{t-1}) \tag{12.11}$$

[1]This just tells you that the random term has a mean value of zero and is normally distributed. The second part tells you that each of the changes in price is random over any time period.

Rearranging gives:

$$V_t = kP_t^T + (1 - k)V_{t-1} \text{ where } 0 \leq k \leq 1 \tag{12.12}$$

The current market value is, therefore, the weighted average of the unobserved current transaction price, P_t^T and the previous valuation, V_{t-1} where the weight k is known as the smoothing parameter. In the next section we will consider how this can be estimated.

Equation 12.12 represents a simple updating rule that is derived from a model that explains the way in which transactions prices are formed. This does not represent a backward-looking approach to valuation. It represents an optimal use of information in order to arrive at the current estimate of value.

Estimating the smoothing parameter

By assuming that the current transactions price and the previous valuation, P_t^T and V_{t-1} are independent of each other you can, from equation 12.12, write the variance of the current valuation as:

$$Var(V_t) = k^2 Var(P_t^T) + (1 - k)^2 Var(V_{t-1}) \tag{12.13}$$

As valuers are naturally concerned about the uncertainty in their valuations it makes sense to find a value of k that will minimise this variance. You can find this by differentiating equation 12.13 with respect to k and setting the result equal to zero:

$$\frac{dVar(V_t)}{dk} = 2kVarP_t^T - 2(1 - k)Var(V_{t-1}) \tag{12.14}$$

When this is equal to zero you get:

$$2(1 - k)Var(V_{t-1}) = 2kVarP_t^T \tag{12.15}$$

$$k = \frac{Var(V_{t-1})}{Var(V_{t-1}) + Var(P_t^T)} \tag{12.16}$$

You can simplify this by assuming that the variance of V_{t-1} is equal to the variance of V_t. You also know that V_t is equal to the expected value of the true market price, P_t, subject to all the available information concerning current and previous transactions, I_{t-1}. As the true market price follows a random walk you can, from equation 12.7, write the variance of V_{t-1} as:

$$Var(V_{t-1}) = Var(V_t) = \sigma_{MP}^2 \tag{12.17}$$

From equation 12.9 you can also write the variance of the transaction price P_t^T as:

$$Var(P_t^T) = \sigma_{TP}^2 \tag{12.18}$$

Substituting these into equation 12.16 gives the following value for k:

$$k = \frac{\sigma_{MP}^2}{\sigma_{MP}^2 + \sigma_{TP}^2} \tag{12.19}$$

where $0 \leq k \leq 1$.

This version of k shows that smoothing in valuations arises from the relative uncertainty in general market prices and individual transactions. If these two sources of uncertainty are the same then $k = 0.5$. This implies that valuers give as much weight to the latest transaction price as they would to the previous valuation. Equation 12.19 also implies that the smoothing parameter will not remain constant but will change as the two components of uncertainty change. We model the effect that this is likely to have on the profile of the smoothing parameter in Appendix 12B.

> Smoothing in valuations arises from the relative uncertainty in general market prices and individual transactions.

Backing out the implied transaction prices

One of the advantages of this approach is that it is possible to back out a profile of implied transactions by rearranging equation 12.12 as follows:

$$P_t^T = \frac{V_t - (1-k)V_{t-1}}{k} \tag{12.20}$$

An important assumption in this model is that the smoothing parameter remains constant over time. However, as this is derived from two sources of variability, both of which change over time, it is unlikely that this will hold true. As this is a fairly complex issue we consider it in more depth in Appendix 12B. We show that, over time, there is a lot of variability in the evolution of the smoothing parameter and this can affect the profile of the backed-out implied market prices.

As investors are frequently concerned with the profile of returns it is useful to consider what effect the choice of parameter is likely to have on the profile of backed-out returns. We can investigate this by using equation 12.20 to back out an implied price series using both a time-varying and constant smoothing parameter and then compare the effect on the profile of returns. Before doing this we can examine the relationship between the variance in prices and values by using a bit of algebra.

To make things a little clearer we will rewrite equation 12.20 as follows:

$$P_t^T = \frac{1}{k} V_t - \left(\frac{1-k}{k}\right) V_{t-1} \tag{12.21}$$

The variance of the implied transaction prices can be written as:

$$VarP_t^T = \left(\frac{1}{k}\right)^2 VarV_t + \left(\frac{1-k}{k}\right)^2 VarV_{t-1} - 2\left(\frac{1}{k}\right)\left(\frac{1-k}{k}\right)\rho_{V_tV_{t-1}}\sigma_{V_t}\sigma_{V_{t-1}} \tag{12.22}$$

If you assume that the variance of current and lagged valuations are equal you can write an expression for the ratio of the variance of implied transaction prices and values as follows:[2]

---

[2]Equation 12.23 uses transaction prices and valuations. By taking the log of first differences of prices and valuations you can rewrite this in returns form, i.e.

$$\frac{Var(r_t^T)}{Var(r_t)} = \frac{1}{k^2}\left\{1 + (1-k)[(1-k) - 2\rho_{r_tr_{t-1}}]\right\}$$

$$\frac{VarP_t^T}{VarV_t} = \frac{1}{k^2} \left\{ 1 + (1-k)[(1-k) - 2\rho_{V_t V_{t-1}}] \right\} \qquad (12.23)$$

If you set the value for k at too low a level the ratio of the variances will be large, resulting in an implied volatility of market prices that will be greater than valuation variability. When k is equal to 1 valuers will rely solely on comparable market evidence and the variance of implied transaction prices and values will be equal.

The other factor influencing the ratio of the variances is the correlation between current and lagged valuations. What equation 12.23 shows, therefore, is that the ratio of variances lies on a surface. If you plot this in terms of standard deviations you obtain Figure 12.1.

As the smoothing parameter approaches zero the ratio of the standard deviations increases. If, for example, the valuer places a lot of weight on previous valuations the smoothing parameter will be very low. In this case the ratio of standard deviations becomes large. Similarly, as the correlation between current and lagged values reduces

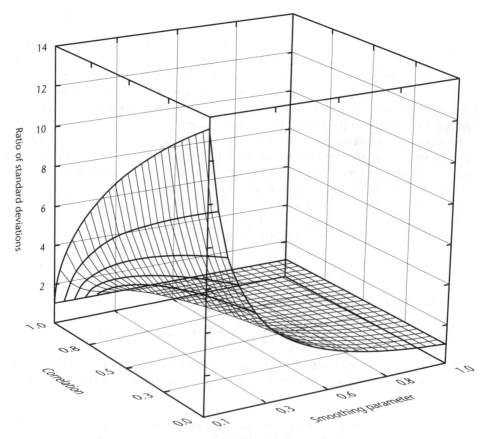

Figure 12.1 Plot of ratio of standard deviations, smoothing parameters and correlation

this also causes an increase in the ratio of standard deviations. Taking both these effects into consideration, changes in the ratio will lie at different points on the surface plot. It should be clear from this that you should expect the variance to change over time, as market conditions will influence the choice of smoothing parameter.

We have investigated this effect by using a time-varying parameter model to estimate the changing profile of the smoothing parameter. We used a sample of 30 properties for which we had monthly capital growth rates over the period 1987–96. We estimated the time-varying smoothing parameter and then used this to back out the growth profile of implied transaction prices. A comparison with the growth in values is given in Figure 12.2.

You will see from this illustration that the growth in values constructed from the index is much less volatile than the implied growth in prices. This is clear evidence of smoothing and reinforces the need to adjust valuation returns to take this effect into consideration.

Further details of the analysis are given in Appendix 12B from which it will be seen that the average time-varying parameter is 0.57. Using this in a constant parameter model to back out the growth in implied transaction prices it is possible to compare the growth profile with the time-varying profile derived above. This is shown in Figure 12.3.

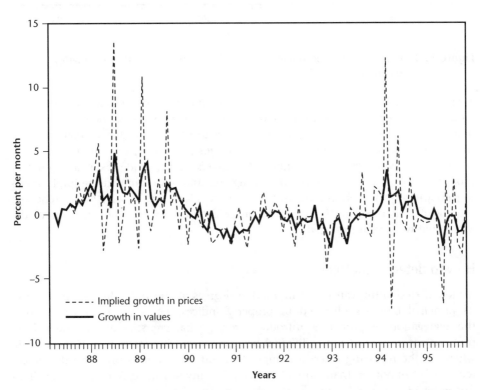

Figure 12.2 Comparison of adjusted and unadjusted monthly capital growth rates

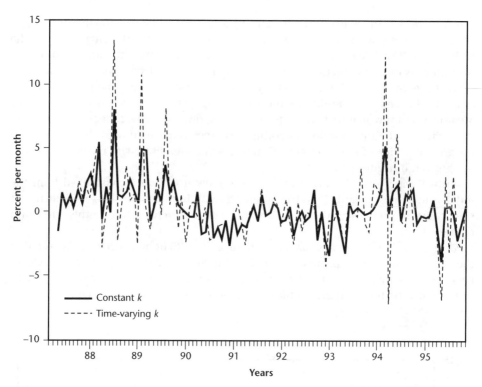

Figure 12.3 Implied growth in prices: comparison of constant and time-varying parameters

There is clearly a difference between the two profiles. This implies that constant parameter models may produce invalid results, particularly during periods when the market is volatile. Models that pick up changes in volatility in the market are more likely to produce better results. At present this area is relatively unexplored.

Professor David Geltner, of Cincinnati University, has undertaken a significant proportion of the research in the smoothing area and has examined the implications of smoothing on valuation returns. We have provided a list of selected references at the end of this chapter which provide more detailed information on some of the topics that we have introduced.

How to detect smoothing

Although smoothing can occur in varying degrees at the individual property level its principal effect is observed in property indices. The reason for this is that the aggregation of properties introduces return characteristics at the index level that are not present at the individual property level. The effect is also more acute whenever the reporting interval is more frequent. The returns on monthly indices tend to be smoother than annual indices. We investigate this in more detail in Appendix 12A.

(a) IPD Monthly Index

(b) IPD Annual Index

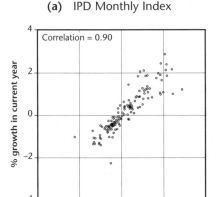

Figure 12.4a–b Cross-correlations

One way to test for the presence of smoothing is to plot the index returns against the returns lagged by one period. If new information arrives randomly, then you would not expect to see a strong association between current and lagged returns. However, if the returns were smoothed, then you would expect to see a positive relationship. We can illustrate this by comparing the smoothing in both monthly and annual returns. These are shown in Figures 12.4a and 12.4b for capital growth in the IPD All Property, monthly and annual indices.

You can see from these illustrations that changes in monthly values are much more strongly associated over time than changes in annual values. The coefficient of correlation figures of 0.90 and 0.44 measures the association between current growth and growth lagged by one period. These figures are also known as the first-order serial correlation coefficients, ρ. The higher the figure the greater the association over time, which in this case means that the monthly index has a much higher level of smoothing than the annual index. In fact, if the first-order serial correlation coefficient is in excess of 0.25 this indicates that smoothing is present. (See Appendix 12D.)

You can use the correlation coefficients as a means of *approximating* the smoothing parameter. From equation 12.12 you can write the following approximation:[3]

$$k \approx 1 - \rho \tag{12.24}$$

Using our results gives:

Monthly smoothing parameter

$$k \approx 1 - 0.90 = 0.10$$

---

[3]Regressing the dependent variable on to its value, lagged by one period, gives a slope coefficient that is equal to the first-order serial correlation coefficient, i.e. ρ_x. From equation 12.12 you will see that $\rho = 1 - k$.

Annual smoothing parameter

$$k \approx 1 - 0.44 = 0.56$$

These are only approximate figures because the relationship used to estimate the correlations is assumed to be linear. We know, however, that the relationship is likely to change over time. In addition, the aggregation of monthly capital growth figures to create an index creates problems that can cause the smoothing parameter to be under-stated. If, however, you take these figures at face value the monthly smoothing parameter implies that current values are estimated using only 10% of the information concerning comparable transactions. At the annual level this increases to 56%. There is clearly inconsistency in these figures, as you would not expect the importance of transaction information to change in this way.

We have already pointed out that smoothing causes the variance of returns to be understated. You can use these smoothing parameters to estimate by how much the risk should be increased. This is just an application of equation 12.23 written in terms of growth:

$$\frac{Var\ g_t^T}{Var\ g_t} = \frac{1}{k^2} \left\{ 1 + (1-k)[(1-k) - 2\rho_{g_t g_{t-1}}] \right\} \tag{12.25}$$

Taking the square root gives the factor by which the risk would be increased after the smoothing has been taken out.

Monthly risk adjustment factor

$$\frac{Var\ g_t^T}{Var\ g_t} = \frac{1}{0.1^2} \left\{ 1 + (1-0.1)[(1-0.1) - 2(0.9)] \right\} = 19$$

Taking the square root gives an adjustment factor of 4.36.

Annual risk adjustment factor

$$\frac{Var\ g_t^T}{Var\ g_t} = \frac{1}{0.56^2} \left\{ 1 + (1-0.56)[(1-0.56) - 2(0.44)] \right\} = 2.57$$

Taking the square root gives an adjustment factor of 1.60.

The monthly figure is almost certainly overstated. You will see from equation 12.25 that the adjustment is very sensitive to the choice of smoothing parameter. As this gets closer to $k = 0$ the adjustment factor approaches infinity. We investigate the estimation of the smoothing parameter in Appendix 12B.

Smoothing is clearly an important issue that needs to be addressed. We know that the smoothing parameter is time-varying but we still don't know the best way to remove smoothing from a valuation index.

Do valuers act in an optimal manner?

One of the assumptions we have made in this chapter is that valuers act in an optimal manner when updating their valuations. We then showed that it was possible to derive an updating rule in which current estimates of value could be formed from the weighted average of observed comparable transaction prices and the most recent valuation. This does, however, raise an important question as to whether valuers do operate in an optimal manner. The answer to this probably has more to do with behaviour than with economics.

For example, valuers are often required to estimate the value of large groups of properties for portfolio purposes. They may have to do this at frequent intervals so that at a purely practical level it may not be possible to evaluate each property within the optimal framework described above. Shortcuts have to be taken. One approach frequently used is to estimate the value of a sample of properties in a portfolio and to use the average change to adjust the value of the remaining properties. In other situations market information may be considered insufficient to influence the valuer to update the previous estimate. This effect may continue for a number of months before the build-up of information is large enough to trigger a change. Each of these effects results in a sub-optimal approach to valuation.

As far as smoothing is concerned these sub-optimal effects tend to introduce characteristics into the distribution of valuation returns that do not exist in the true market price returns. The effects tend to be more severe in frequently valued properties. We discussed the distributional characteristics of property in Chapter 9. You will recall that the distribution of monthly returns tended to be peaked. This is evidence that a high proportion of the changes in value cluster round a constant figure. We estimated this by measuring the leptokurtosis. We also showed that as the interval between valuation dates increased the distributions tended to approach normality.

One of the important effects of sub-optimal valuation practice is that changes in value, for groups of properties in single periods, tend to be correlated across samples. This cross-correlation tends to smooth out a lot of the true variation in returns and therefore introduces much higher serial correlation than would normally be expected in the returns at the index level. Again, this tends to be more acute with high-frequency indices.

Sub-optimal valuation practice is concerned with behavioural issues. This does not imply any flaw in methodology, but recognises that professional valuers are faced with the practical problem of preparing valuations in a market that is not frequently traded. The information used to form a valuation may, therefore, be incomplete. As valuers respond to this in different ways this has led to a growing body of literature dealing with behavioural issues. This is a valuable strand of research that is likely to add to our understanding of smoothing. See, for example, Levy (1998).

Summary

In this chapter we pointed out that imperfections in the market could lead to differences in market prices for identical properties. Following Quan and Quigley

(1991) we showed that if true market prices follow a random walk, valuers would arrive at valuation estimates by weighting current comparable sales evidence with their most recent valuation. Although this would appear to imply that valuers are relying on historic information Quan and Quigley show that this is an optimal updating strategy for valuations.

The choice of weight used to form the current valuation is known as the smoothing parameter. Once this is known it is possible to back out the implied transaction prices. The smoothing parameter is likely to change over time as it is made up of two sources of variability, neither of which is constant.

Many of the issues surrounding valuation are concerned with the way valuers respond to information. These are behavioural issues that can introduce characteristics into a series of property valuation returns that are not present in the true market returns. There is a growing body of literature that is investigating the behavioural aspects of valuation and it is likely that this could provide a valuable link between expected and reported returns.

This chapter has five appendices that investigate more advanced topics related to smoothing and risk adjustment procedures.

Appendix 12A: Sticky valuation processes and aggregation effects

This appendix explains why high-frequency indexes exhibit much higher serial correlation than low-frequency indexes.

Appendix 12B: Valuation smoothing without temporal aggregation

In this appendix we avoid the problems of temporal aggregation by estimating time-varying smoothing parameters at the individual property level.

Appendix 12C: Estimating the volatility of terminal wealth

Scaling up the variance of a monthly series to its quarterly or annual equivalent can result in misleading estimates of the volatility of the terminal wealth if the original series has high levels of serial correlation. This appendix describes two ways in which this can be overcome.

Appendix 12D: Random walk processes and aggregation effects

This appendix describes the key result developed by Working (1960) showing that the aggregation of random elements round the reporting date can result in positive serial correlation.

Appendix 12E: Removing smoothing with autoregressive models

Autoregressive models have been widely used to remove the effect of smoothing from property indices. In this appendix we describe the techniques that have been used.

Chapter 12: Summary table

1. Property markets suffer from the following imperfections:
   - incomplete information about the attributes of individual properties so that buy and sell decisions are made with only partial knowledge,
   - periods of costly search incurred by potential buyers,
   - the lack of a central marketplace so that prices are the result of private negotiation between buyer and seller.

2. Given these imperfections transaction prices for identical properties are likely to vary.

3. If market prices follow a random walk it is possible to show that valuations can be formed as the weighted average of comparable transaction prices and the most recent valuation. The weight, k, is also known as the smoothing parameter.

   $V_t = kP_t^T + (1 - k)V_{t-1}$
   subject to $0 \le k \le 1$

4. This is an optimal updating rule and does not imply any flaws in valuation methodology or negligence on the part of the valuer.

5. The smoothing parameter can be shown to come from the relative uncertainty in market prices and transaction prices.

   $k = \dfrac{\sigma_{MP}^2}{\sigma_{MP}^2 + \sigma_{TP}^2}$

6. As both sources of uncertainty will change, the smoothing parameter is likely to be time-varying.

7. Smoothing is more likely to be a problem at the index level. The aggregation of properties into an index causes the variation in returns to be understated.

8. You can detect smoothing in an index by examining the first-order serial correlation. A figure in excess of 0.25 would indicate that some smoothing is present.

9. Smoothing is more acute in monthly property indices than annual indices.

10. The first-order serial correlation coefficient can be used to obtain an approximate estimate of the smoothing parameter.

$$k \approx 1 - \rho$$

11. You can also use the smoothing parameter to estimate the factor by which the variance should be increased.

$$\frac{Var\ g_t^T}{Var\ g_t} = \frac{1}{k^2}\left\{1 + (1 - k)[(1 - k) - 2\rho_{g_t g_{t-1}}]\right\}$$

12. Note that as the smoothing parameter approaches zero the adjustment factor approaches infinity.

13. Valuers don't always use an optimal approach to update their valuations. Behavioural issues often influence them. They may for example be influenced by client pressure or use shortcuts in response to the flow of information.

14. These additional factors can also introduce smoothing into property returns.

Problems

1. What do you understand by the term smoothing?

2. Why is smoothing likely to be an issue in valuation and portfolio management?

3. Why should the price for identical properties differ?

4. Does smoothing imply that valuers are using a flawed methodology?

5. What is the optimal strategy for valuers to follow?

6. What formula would you use to relate current values to comparable transaction prices and previous values?

7. How would you detect whether smoothing existed in an index of property returns?

8. Is smoothing more likely to be a problem if valuations are undertaken annually or monthly?

9. What are the sources of uncertainty that contribute to the smoothing parameter?

10. What behavioural issues are likely to influence smoothing in valuations?

Selected references

deRoos, J.A. (1994) Smoothing in the appraisal of real estate. Cornell University, Working paper.

Diaz, J. (1990) The process of selecting comparable sales. *The Appraisal Journal* (October), 533–40.

Diaz, J. (1997) An investigation into the impact of previous expert estimates on appraisal judgement. *Journal of Real Estate Research* **13** (1), 57–66.

Diaz, J. and Wolverton, M.L. (1998) A longitudinal examination of the appraisal smoothing hypothesis. *Real Estate Economics* **26** (2), 349–58.

Edelstein, R.H. and Quan, D. (1995) How does appraisal smoothing bias real estate returns measurement? University of California, Working Paper No. 95–240, Haas School of Business.

Geltner, D. (1989a) Bias in appraisal based returns. *AREUEA Journal* **17** (3), 338–52.

Geltner, D. (1989b) Estimating real estate's systematic risk from aggregate level appraisal-based returns. *AREUEA Journal* **17** (4), 463–81.

Geltner, D. (1991) Smoothing in appraisal based returns. *Journal of Real Estate Finance and Economics* **4**, 327–45.

Geltner, D. (1993a) Estimating market values from appraisal values without assuming an efficient market. *Journal of Real Estate Research* **8** (3), 325–45.

Geltner, D. (1993b) Temporal aggregation in real estate return indices. *AREUEA Journal* **21** (2), 141–66.

Giacotto, C. and Clapp, J. (1992) Appraisal based real estate returns under alternative market regimes. *AREUEA Journal* **20** (1), 1–24.

Levy, D.S. (1998) Client influence on reported values. University of Auckland, Paper presented at the RICS Cutting Edge, Property Research Conference, De Montfort University, UK.

Quan, D. and Quigley, J. (1989) Inferring an investment return series for real estate from observations on sales. *AREUEA Journal* **17** (2), 218–30.

Quan, D. and Quigley, J. (1991) Price formation and the appraisal function in real estate markets. *Journal of Real Estate Finance and Economics* **4** (2), 127–46.

Ross, S.A. and Zisler, R. (1987) Managing real estate portfolios, Part 3: A close look at equity real estate risk. In: *Real Estate Research*. Goldman Sachs.

Appendix 12A
Sticky valuation processes and aggregation effects

In Chapter 12 we argued that there might be behavioural issues that could influence the profile of returns for individual properties. At certain times these issues may have an influence across samples of properties within a portfolio. Large numbers of current valuations could, therefore, pick up the influence of other current or lagged valuations. Taken over time this is known as *serial cross-correlation*. The effect causes individual valuations to appear sticky and can introduce smoothing at the index level that is not present at the individual property level.

In this appendix we draw a distinction between cross-sectional and temporal sticky valuation processes that influence smoothing at the index and individual property levels. We develop a simple model that embodies both random and sticky processes and show that it is successful in explaining smoothing in commercial property indices at different frequencies.

Sticky valuations and prices

We showed in Chapter 12 that if valuers follow an optimal updating rule they form estimates of current value by weighting comparable transaction evidence with the most recent valuation. However, if you observe the profile of property values you will see that, depending on the frequency of valuation, there are often long periods when there is no change in value. One rationalisation for the way values are adjusted is that there are costs associated with making changes in value, so that it may be optimal to adjust them by discrete amounts towards some underlying equilibrium level. For commercial property, there are a number of situations where this might arise, for example:

- Large portfolios may be selectively valued by sample. Within a large portfolio it may not be cost-effective formally to appraise every property when frequent valuations are required. In this case a representative sample of properties is valued and the average change is then applied to the remaining properties.
- Many properties may be formally valued annually, with 'intermediate' values being recorded as showing no change. This may be particularly evident with quarterly data.
- The valuer may not consider 'small changes' in information to be important enough to warrant a change in value. Over time, however, the accumulation of information reaches a threshold that causes the valuer to make a change.
- There may be situations where clients are unhappy with large changes in value, particularly in bear market conditions. In these cases the valuer may be encouraged to change values progressively towards the new market level. The effect may alter as market conditions change.

In Figure 12A.1 we have summarised the profile of capital values for four properties that have been selected at random from the IPD monthly database. The stepped profile is very clear, suggesting that changes in value are not a continuous process. You

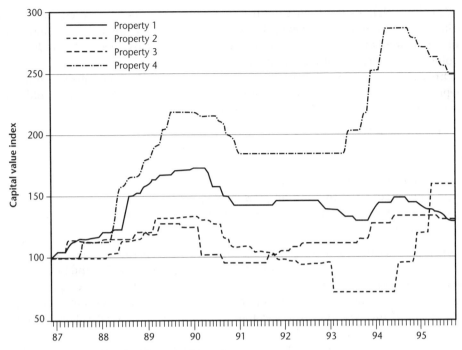

Figure 12A.1 Profile of sticky monthly values

will see that there are long periods of either no change or a constant rate of change towards some new underlying value.

Each of the adjustment processes shown in Figure 12A.1 suggests that individual property values may be *sticky*. There are times when all the valuations move in the same general direction. At other times there is no relationship between values. This effect is likely to be influenced by changes in the market environment, the availability of comparable information and other factors that influence the valuation process. A *sticky valuation model* can therefore be regarded as an imperfect information model.

Sticky value models

The optimal valuation model we discussed in Chapter 12 can also be considered within the framework of sticky values. You will recall that current values can be expressed in the following form:

$$V_t = kP_t^T + (1 - k)V_{t-1} \qquad (12A.1)$$

where

V_t = current open market value appraised at time t

P_t^T = current market price, obtained from comparables

k = smoothing parameter, $0 \leq k \leq 1$

Values of k that are less than 1 imply a sticky appraisal process, with current values being related to previous values. If however k is equal to 1, then current values are equal to market prices. If the evolution of market prices is assumed to be random the evolution of values will also be random.

Other forms of sticky price model allow the evolution of sticky values to follow a stepped adjustment process. For example, following Mussa (1981), we could also represent the change in sticky values as follows:

$$\Delta V_t = \Delta \bar{P}_t + \phi(\bar{P}_{t-1} - V_{t-1}) \tag{12A.2}$$

where

ΔV_t = change in sticky values V_t

$\Delta \bar{P}_t$ = change in the equilibrium price level $\bar{P}_t$

ϕ = speed of convergence $(0 < \phi \leq 1)$ of sticky values to the equilibrium price level

In this model the value at time t is adjusted in relation to the degree of disequilibrium that exists at time $t-1$. The speed of convergence is related to the frequency of changes in appraisals. Thus, the more frequent the change the quicker the convergence towards the equilibrium price level. Note also that, as ϕ approaches 1, $V_t = \bar{P}_t$. Again, if the evolution of prices follows a random walk, then values must also follow a random walk.

Equation 12A.2 also shows that there is a difference between the change in individual values and changes in the general level of equilibrium prices. Individual values will remain constant over a fixed interval and then adjust to their equilibrium value. By contrast, an index comprising a number of values should move continuously and adjust towards the equilibrium market price level. Thus, assuming that individual values are established using a sticky model of the form described above, an index of values should move continuously in and out of equilibrium. This would be consistent with the competitive framework generally found in the capital markets.

Using the concept of sticky values we can revisit the issue of volatility and serial correlation in valuation-based indexes.

Aggregation in property indices

A property index is made up entirely of valuations. As shown above, each valuation will represent a combination of both random and sticky elements. At the index level the random elements will be uncorrelated. By contrast the sticky elements will be highly correlated across the sample.

We can illustrate the joint effect that this would have on an index by assuming that the sequence of returns for an individual property is random. At first sight this may seem unrealistic. However, you will see from Table 12A.1 that the average first-order serial correlation for individual properties is indistinguishable from zero for both monthly and annual valuations. For comparison purposes we have also shown the first-order serial correlation coefficients for the index returns. These are all significantly different from zero for the monthly series. Only the office sector differs from zero at the annual level.

Table 12A.1 ● First-order serial correlation for average and index returns

	Sample averages		Sample indexes		
	Mean	St. Dev.	Mean	St. Dev.	Sample
Monthly returns					
December 87–November 92					
Retail	0.143	0.156	0.769*	0.123	40
Office	0.220	0.152	0.795*	0.123	30
Industrial	0.191	0.137	0.848*	0.123	30
December 92–November 97					
Retail	0.134	0.125	0.632*	0.123	40
Office	0.227	0.228	0.717*	0.123	30
Industrial	0.162	0.186	0.656*	0.123	30
Annual returns					
Retail	0.092	0.292	0.329	0.237	250
Office	0.163	0.298	0.465*	0.237	250
Industrial	0.124	0.254	0.334	0.237	250

*Indicates that the coefficient is significantly different from zero at the 5% level.

The interesting point to notice from this table is that the serial correlation figures are all based on formal commercial valuations that incorporate the effect of smoothing. You will see that at the individual property level smoothing has little impact on serial correlation, irrespective of the interval over which the returns are measured. However, at the index level serial correlation is significantly higher for monthly growth than annual growth. The high serial correlation in the monthly index cannot, therefore, be explained solely in terms of smoothing. Cross-correlation effects are likely to play an important role.

Adopting the assumption that individual property returns are random over time you can simulate the effect of a sticky value process as follows.

Step 1. Construct a series of random returns

Assume that individual property returns have a zero mean and a standard deviation of 0.01. Randomly sampling from a normal distribution gives the series shown in Figure 12A.2. As you are also interested in the serial correlation you can plot current returns against returns lagged by one period. This is shown in Figure 12A.2b.

The scatter of returns is, as expected, random and this is confirmed by the serial correlation coefficient of –0.12. You can use the returns on the random series to plot an index of values. To do this you need to specify that values follow a random walk, and can be written as:

$$V_t = V_{t-1} + e_t \tag{12A.3}$$

This just tells you that the current value is equal to the previous value plus a random error. If you start with an initial value of 100 (i.e. $V_{t-1} = 100$) and add the random change in value you will get the next value. Repeating this process produces an index similar to Figure 12A.3.

You will see that this has all the characteristics of a stock market index.

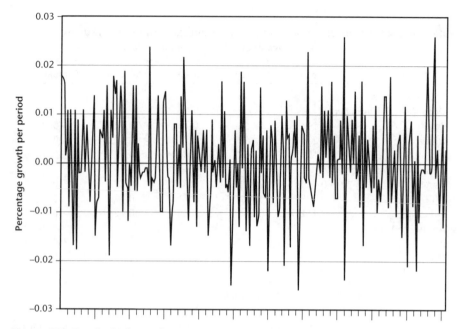

Figure 12A.2a Periodic random returns

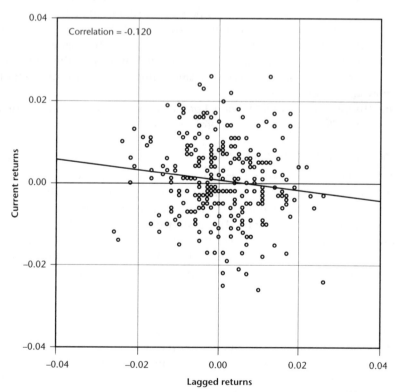

Figure 12A.2b Correlation between current and lagged returns for a random series

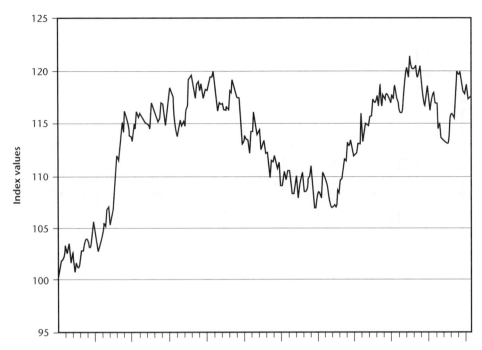

Figure 12A.3   Index of random values

Step 2. Introduce a sticky value process

If all valuations followed a random process, then combining them into an index would produce another random process. If the valuations take place at slightly different times then there will be some averaging round the index dates and this will introduce some serial correlation. We look at this in Appendix 12D.

Assume that a proportion of the valuations in your index are not adjusted in response to the arrival of new information but reflect behavioural factors such as those identified at the beginning of this appendix. A typical case would be where properties are valued by sample. A large number of properties may change in value, in response to the average change in a small number of properties. Some effects may persist over time, particularly if the change in value of a group of properties reflects information over several periods. Other processes may have a similar outcome.

One way you can approximate the effect of sticky value processes is to construct a new series by assuming that changes in value occur at discrete intervals and represent the average of the random returns over the previous period. Figure 12A.4a shows what happens if you do this. We have assumed that a change in value occurs once every six observations and is equal to the average of the previous six random changes. The correlation between current and lagged returns in this case has increased to 0.812, as shown in Figure 12.4b.

This illustrates just one process. In practice there will be many different processes happening at the same time affecting a large number of properties. If you plot the sticky return profile you will end up with a smoother version of the random series as shown in Figure 12A.5.

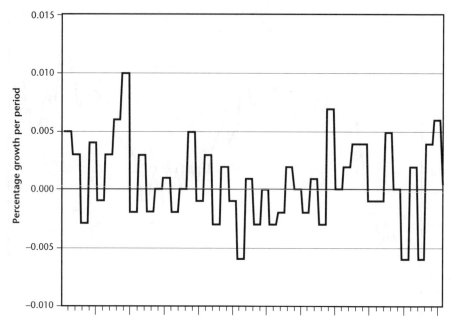

Figure 12A.4a Periodic sticky returns

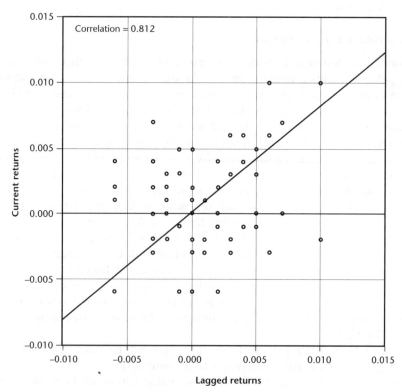

Figure 12A.4b Correlation between current and lagged returns for a sticky series

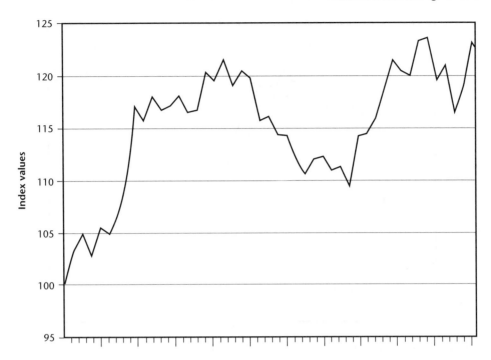

Figure 12A.5 Index of sticky values

Step 3. Combine the random and sticky valuation processes

We have pointed out that a property valuation series can consist of two components – one that is random and the other that follows a sticky process. You have simulated these series separately so it only remains to combine them to create a new series.

For purposes of illustration you can assume that the index contains a high proportion of sticky values. This is more likely to be the case with a high-frequency index. You can construct a new index by assuming that 85% of the index comprise sticky returns and the remaining 15% represent random returns. If you do this you can compare the profile of your sticky index with the random index. This is shown in Figure 12A.6.

The correlation between current and lagged return for the combined index is shown in Figure 12A.7.

You will see from these illustrations that the profile of index numbers tends to overshoot and undershoot the random series. This is the same effect that you get with a high-frequency property index. The correlation structure shown in Figure 12A.7 is 0.660 and is also reminiscent of a high-frequency index.

We have summarised the statistics for each of the indexes so that you can see how the combined index is made up from the combination of two processes. These are shown in Table 12A.2. We have also shown that the serial correlation of the combined series is approximately equal to the weighted average of the individual correlations. You should also note that the standard deviation of the random series is 3.33 times

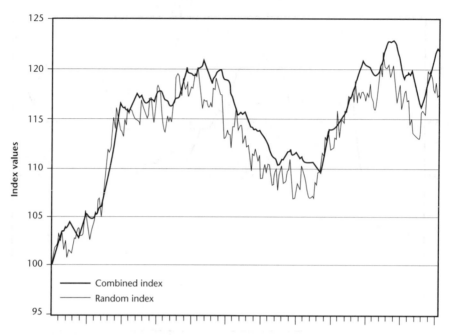

Figure 12A.6 Comparison of combined and random indexes

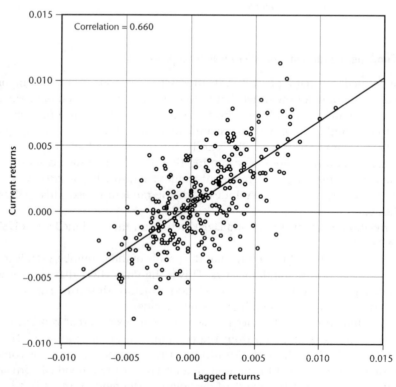

Figure 12A.7 Correlation between current and lagged returns for combined series

Table 12A.2 ● Comparison of random and sticky valuations

	Standard deviations	Serial correlation
Random series	0.010	–0.120
Sticky series	0.003	0.812
Combined series	**0.003**	**0.660**
Weighted serial correlations:	0.15 *(random)* + 0.85 *(sticky)*	0.672

larger than the sticky series. If you refer back to Chapter 9 you will see that this is close to the ratio that you would get if you compare the annualised monthly standard deviation with annual figures.[1]

This illustration shows that the serial correlation in a property index will depend on the proportion of random and sticky valuation components. You would also expect the ratio of these components to change as the frequency of the index changes. You can formalise this process as follows.

Aggregate serial correlation and variance in the presence of sticky prices

The efficient market hypothesis[2] implies that security prices follow a martingale process, a special case of which is the random walk model in which price changes are not predictable. From our discussion it will be evident that in the presence of sticky prices the evolution of valuations will not follow a random walk. Nevertheless, the random nature of asset prices is such an important component of price determination we shall assume that a valuation index consists only of random walk and sticky price processes. The valuation series is, therefore, assumed to be a weighted average of these two components. Although this is a simplification of reality, it should capture a high proportion of the underlying features evident in the market.

Given this simplification you can assume that the returns from a *pure* sticky process are perfectly correlated but are independent of the random walk component. The serial correlation structure of the combined processes can be considered to be a weighted average of these two effects, where the weights are related to the proportion of sticky and random valuations to the total number of valuation elements within an index.

Assume that an index is made up of a series of segments, where each segment can represent a month, quarter or a year. Within each segment there are m valuation elements that are averaged to form the index. The m valuation elements are split into two independent components, where one part consists of a series of k_s sticky

---

[1] As an example the average retail standard deviation from Tables 9.10 and 9.11 is approximately 0.95% per month. If you annualise this you get 3.27%, i.e. $\sqrt{0.95^2 \times 12}$. The annual standard deviation over a similar period, given in Table 9.14, is 10.87%. The ratio of the standard deviations is 1:3.32.

[2] See Chapter 13.

valuations and the remainder, $m-k_s$, follow a random walk. Given that the changes in sticky values are assumed to be perfectly positively correlated, the first-order serial correlation coefficient of the changes in the k_s valuations will be equal to 1 and will have a variance of zero.

Following Working (1960), it can be shown that if a series of $(m-k_s)$ random valuations is averaged between index dates, the first-order serial correlation, ρ, of the first differences can be approximated by:

$$\rho = \frac{(m-k_s)^2 - 1}{2[2(m-k_s)^2 + 1]} \tag{12A.4}$$

The variance of the first differences can also be shown to be:

$$Var(r_p) = \frac{2(m-k_s)^2 + 1}{3(m-k_s)^2} Var(r_{m-k_s}) \tag{12A.5}$$

where

$Var(r_p)$ = variance of the portfolio of the smoothed series
$Var(r_{m-k_s})$ = variance of random series

The relative weight of sticky appraisals and random appraisals, i.e. k_s/m and $(1-k_s/m)$, can be used to adjust the serial correlation as follows:

$$\rho = \left(1 - \frac{k_s}{m}\right)\left\{\frac{(m-k_s)^2 - 1}{2[2(m-k_s)^2 + 1]}\right\} + \frac{k_s}{m} \tag{12A.6}$$

For large values of m this simplifies to:

$$\rho \cong 0.25 + 0.75\frac{k_s}{m} \tag{12A.7}$$

Note that if k_s is zero this converges to 0.25 at the aggregate level. The models that have been proposed in the literature to remove smoothing at the aggregate level have assumed that the first-order serial correlation should be zero. This is inconsistent with the findings of Working (1960). If the serial correlation coefficient for an index of returns is known, equation 12A.7 can be rearranged to give the sticky ratio as follows:

$$\frac{k_s}{m} = \frac{1}{3}[4\rho - 1] \tag{12A.8}$$

The variance of the combined series can also be converted into average variances for each component and then weighted by the proportion that each component represents of the whole segment. Assume also that the index is made up of a combination of sticky valuations having a variance $Var(r_{k_s})$, that are assumed to be independent of the random walk process. The portfolio variance $Var(r_p)$ can, therefore, be expressed as:

$$Var(r_p) = \left(\frac{m-k_s}{m}\right)^2 \left(\frac{2(m-k_s)^2 + 1}{3(m-k_s)^2}\right) Var(r_{m-k_s}) + \left(\frac{k_s}{m}\right)^2 Var(r_{k_s}) \tag{12A.9}$$

where

m = total number of appraisal elements per segment
k_s = number of sticky appraisals per segment
$m-k_s$ = number of random appraisals per segment
$Var(r_{k_s})$ = variance of changes in sticky appraisals

When $k_s = 0$ the series has no sticky appraisals and approximates the underlying random walk. An index that is constructed from a relatively small number of valuations spread over the interval between index dates will, therefore, have a variance of returns that will rapidly approach 2/3 of the true variance. Thus, if true valuations follow a random walk the factor required to adjust the smoothed variance will converge to 1.5. In terms of standard deviation the figure is 1.22.

When $k_s = m$ the index consists entirely of sticky valuations and the variance of the appraised series will be equal to the variance of the changes in the combined sticky value processes. As the proportion of sticky valuations in the index increases the variance of the appraised returns will converge to the variance of the sticky value processes.

With regard to serial correlation, equation 12A.6 implies that given the two appraisal processes, there will be a family of serial correlation curves that will be related to the proportion of sticky appraisals to random appraisals in an index. These are shown in Figure 12A.8.

It will be evident from the above that, depending on the ratio of random to sticky values in an index, it is quite possible to observe high levels of serial correlation. Any

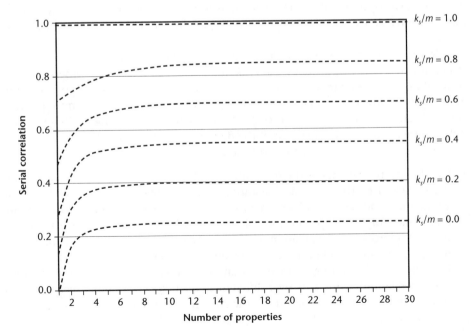

Figure 12A.8 Serial correlation and the sticky ratio k_s/m

changes in serial correlation, as a result of increasing the number of properties, will depend on the relative proportion of values that follow a random walk to sticky prices. In this context market conditions may play an important role. If there is a plentiful supply of comparable evidence, then changes in value are more likely to be random. If a high proportion of values are sticky, then there is likely to be evidence of positive serial cross-correlation at the aggregate level as groups of sticky values move in the same general direction.

This process is not confined to the property market. Evidence from the securities market suggests, however, that it is an important component explaining the serial correlation structure of stock market returns. For example, Cohen et al. (1986) suggest that:

> for a diversified index made up of a large number of positive beta securities, positive serial cross-correlations will dominate the individual securities serial correlations, thereby inducing positive serial correlation in the index regardless of the signs of the individual-security serial correlations.

If the sticky price process is a pervasive factor in the formation of property valuations, this is likely to be the dominant factor in explaining the high levels of serial correlation in valuation indices. This is, of course, an empirical issue.

Forecasting the serial correlation

We have argued that the proportion of sticky valuations in an index is an important component in explaining both the variance and serial correlation structure. Although the ratio of sticky appraisals to total appraisals is unobservable, equation 12A.8 shows that it is possible to obtain this figure as long as the serial correlation coefficient is known.

However, we want to test this model for predicting the serial correlation so it is more important to estimate the sticky ratios (k_s/m) independently of the observed serial correlation. The procedure we used is described in Brown and Matysiak (1998). Using monthly, quarterly and annual returns we estimated the sticky ratios using a different approach and forecasted the serial correlation in commercial property indexes over different frequencies. A comparison of the figures is given in Table 12A.3.

There are two points to note from this table.

1. The sticky ratio declines as the reporting period increases. This is what you should expect. Properties that are valued at annual intervals are more likely to pick up new information and be less influenced by other groups of values than those that are valued monthly. High proportions of properties have formal annual valuations. Shortcut approaches to valuation are less likely in these cases. As a result, at the annual level, only small proportions of valuations are sticky.
2. Secondly, there is a strong positive association between our estimated and observed serial correlation coefficients over different frequencies. The model seems to do a reasonable job in forecasting the coefficients. In fact the correlation between the figures is in excess of 0.99.

Table 12A.3 ● Sticky ratio (k_s/m) and estimated serial correlation coefficients

	Sticky ratio k_s/m	Estimated serial correlation (Eq 12A.7)	Observed serial correlation
IPD Monthly Index: 1987–96			
All property	0.85	0.89	0.89
Retail	0.81	0.85	0.86
Office	0.81	0.86	0.87
Industrial	0.85	0.89	0.90
JLW Quarterly Index: 1977–96			
All property	0.76	0.81	0.77
Retail	0.49	0.62	0.58
Office	0.69	0.77	0.71
Industrial	0.66	0.75	0.75
IPD Annual Index: 1980–95			
All property	0.28	0.46	0.43
Retail	0.19	0.39	0.35
Office	0.38	0.53	0.52
Industrial	0.11	0.33	0.29

IPD: Investment Property Databank.
JLW: Jones Lang Wooton.

Stickiness of individual valuations over time

So far the discussion has focused on the serial correlation introduced into an index caused by the aggregation of sticky valuation processes and serial cross-correlation. However, we are also interested to know whether, for individual properties, stickiness in valuations is pervasive over time. If this were the case then the variance of returns for individual properties would be severely biased.

In order to develop this analysis we express the variance of returns for a single property as the weighted average of its random and sticky components *over time*. Assume that over n valuations for the same property, κ represents the number of valuations that are sticky. There are, therefore, $(n - \kappa)$ random valuations. We will assume, as before, that the sticky values are independent of the random values. The variance of returns for a single property, j, can, therefore, be written as a weighted average of these two components:

$$Var(r_j) = \left(1 - \frac{\kappa}{n}\right)^2 Var(r_{n-\kappa}) + \left(\frac{\kappa}{n}\right)^2 Var(r_\kappa) \tag{12A.10}$$

where $\dfrac{\kappa}{n}$ = temporal sticky ratio.

Given that $Var(r_\kappa)$ is unobservable we shall assume that it is equal to $Var(r_j)$ so that equation 12A.10 can be rewritten as:

$$Var(r_j)\left[1 - \left(\frac{\kappa}{n}\right)^2\right] = \left(1 - \frac{\kappa}{n}\right)^2 Var(r_{n-\kappa}) \tag{12A.11}$$

Table 12A.4 ● Temporal sticky ratios, $\frac{\kappa}{n}$ for individual properties

Minimum	0.00
Mean	0.13
Maximum	0.39

If you assume that the variance of the random component, $Var(r_{n-\kappa})$, can be approximated from an autoregressive model[3] it is possible to solve equation 12A.11 to estimate the temporal sticky ratio for a sample of individual properties.

Our concern in this case is with monthly valued properties as their higher frequency could contribute to persistence in value changes over time. Using a sample of 30 monthly valued properties Table 12A.4 summarises the range of temporal sticky ratios we obtained.

This clearly shows that, *over time*, the proportion of valuations that can be regarded as sticky is relatively small, even though the valuations are at monthly intervals. Although there may be periods when values are sticky, over time the market should correct these discrepancies so that values converge to their equilibrium level.

This result is not unexpected and ties in well with our serial correlation figures in Table 12A.1. You should note that we are not dealing with an index so that the random component of returns should have zero serial correlation. As a result the sticky ratio for individual properties is directly comparable to the serial correlation.

As the serial correlation at the individual property level is low, we can conclude that smoothing at the index level does not necessarily imply smoothing at the individual property level.

Selected references

Barkham, R. and Geltner, D. (1994) Unsmoothing British valuation-based returns without assuming an efficient market. *Journal of Property Research* **11**, 81–95.

Blundell, G. and Ward, C.W.R. (1987) Property portfolio allocation: a multi-factor model. *Land Development Studies* **4**, 145–56.

Brown, G.R. and Matysiak, G.A. (1997) Sticky valuations, aggregation effects and property indices. Paper presented at the AREUEA International Real Estate Conference, 31 May–2 June 1997.

Cohen, K.J., Maier, S.F., Schwartz, R.A. and Whitcomb, D.K. (1986) *The Microstructure of Securities Markets*, Englewood Cliffs, NJ: Prentice Hall.

Edelstein, R.H. and Quan, D. (1995) How does appraisal smoothing bias real estate returns measurement? University of California, Working paper No. 95–240, Haas School of Business.

Fisher, J.D., Geltner, D. and Webb, B. (1994) Value indices of commercial real estate: a comparison of index construction methods. *Journal of Real Estate Finance and Economics* **9**, 137–64.

---

[3] We discuss the use of autoregressive models in smoothing in Appendix 12D.

Geltner, D. (1989) Estimating real estate's systematic risk from aggregate level appraisal-based returns. *AREUEA Journal* **17** (4), 463–81.

Geltner, D. (1991) Smoothing in appraisal based returns. *Journal of Real Estate Finance and Economics* **4**, 327–45.

Geltner, D. (1993) Estimating market values from appraisal values without assuming an efficient market. *Journal of Real Estate Research* **8** (3), 325–45.

Giacotto, C. and Clapp, J. (1992) Appraisal based real estate returns under alternative market regimes. *AREUEA Journal* **20** (1), 1–24.

Kiley, M.T. (1996) The lead of output over inflation in sticky prices. Federal Reserve Board, Washington, Working paper 96–33.

Lai, T.-Y. and Wang, K. (1998) Appraisal smoothing: the other side of the story. *Real Estate Economics* **26** (3), 511–35.

Matysiak, G.A. and Wang, P. (1995) Commercial property market prices and valuations: analysing the correspondence. *Journal of Property Research* **12** (3), 181–202.

Mussa, M. (1981) Sticky prices and disequilibrium in a rational model of the inflationary process. *American Economic Review* **71**, 1020–7.

Quan, D. and Quigley, J. (1989) Inferring an investment return series for real estate from observations on sales. *AREUEA Journal* **17** (2), 218–30.

Quan, D. and Quigley, J. (1991) Price formation and the appraisal function in real estate markets. *Journal of Real Estate Finance and Economics* **4** (2), 127–46.

Ross, S.A. and Zisler, R. (1991) Risk and return in real estate. *Journal of Real Estate Finance and Economics* **4** (2), 175–90.

Working, H. (1960) Note on the correlation of the first differences of averages in a random chain. *Econometrica* **28**, 916–18.

Appendix 12B
Valuation smoothing without temporal aggregation

In Chapter 12 we showed that if valuers follow an optimal updating rule they would estimate current valuations as the weighted average of comparable sales evidence and the most recent valuation. We also argued that the weight applied to these components, also known as the smoothing parameter, is likely to vary over time and will depend on the availability of comparable evidence.

If you try to estimate the smoothing parameter using an index of property values you will find that you can't easily separate valuation smoothing from the effects of aggregation caused by the serial cross-correlation between properties when they are combined into an index. In this appendix we avoid this problem by estimating the smoothing parameter at the individual property level. We also allow it to vary over time, as it will be influenced by changes in market conditions affecting the availability of comparable information.

The optimal updating rule

We showed in Chapter 12 that if true market prices follow a random walk the optimal estimate of current market value at time t, i.e. V_t, can be obtained from:

$$V_t = kP_t^T + (1 - k)V_{t-1} \tag{12B.1}$$

where

V_t = current open market appraised value in period t

P_t^T = current market price, obtained from comparables

$$k = \frac{\sigma_{MP}^2}{\sigma_{MP}^2 + \sigma_{TP}^2} \quad \text{subject to } 0 \le k \le 1$$

σ_{MP}^2 = uncertainty in general market prices

σ_{TP}^2 = uncertainty in transaction prices

Equation 12B.1 shows that the valuer's estimate of current value is the weighted average of recent comparable market prices and the previous estimate of value. The weight, k, is known as the smoothing parameter and is determined by the relative uncertainty in general market prices and individual transactions.

The model shown in equation 12B.1 assumes, however, that the value of k remains constant over time, so that valuers use the same updating rule *under all market conditions*. Quan and Quigley (1991) suggest, however, that the position filter can be made more realistic by employing a Kalman algorithm. This approach recognises that the smoothing parameter, k, can change over time in response to different market conditions and the level of uncertainty attached to particular deals.

Estimating a time-varying smoothing parameter

The appeal of using a time-varying approach can be seen if there are few comparables. In this case there will be greater uncertainty in individual transactions which would cause the value of k to fall. In these situations valuers would be more likely to place greater emphasis on their previous valuation figure. Variations of this nature are to be expected and this leads to changes in the value of k.

In order to avoid the effect of temporal aggregation we discussed in Appendix 12A we have estimated the smoothing parameter at the individual property level from a random sample of 30 properties provided by the Investment Property Databank (IPD). The data were drawn from each sector of the market, but no details were provided about the types of property or their location. The sample provided a monthly time-series of capital growth for each property over the period from December 1986 to October 1995. By constructing an equal-weighted index, the aggregate features of the 30 properties could be compared with the IPD monthly index. Figures 12B.1a and 12B.1b show that the profiles of the equal-weighted index generally track the IPD monthly index. The overall aggregate profile of the 30 properties also suggests that, as a group, their performance over the period was higher than the average as measured by the IPD monthly index. The sample of properties does, however, appear to track overall market movements and can be regarded as being representative of an above-average group within the index.

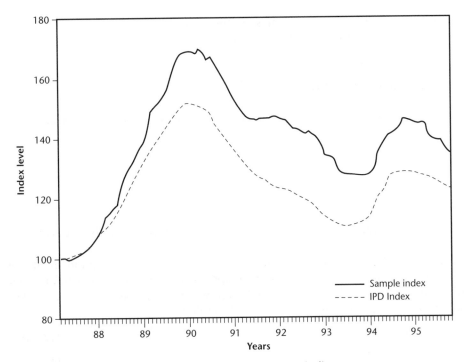

Figure 12B.1a Comparison of IPD and sample property indices

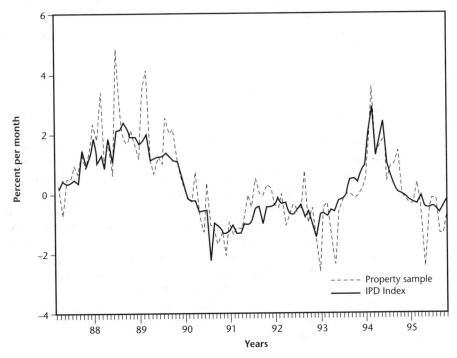

Figure 12B.1b Comparison of monthly capital growth rates

In order to estimate a time-varying smoothing parameter, k, the empirical counterpart of equation 12B.1 needs to be estimated:

$$V_t = \alpha_t + \beta_t V_{t-1} + \omega_t \qquad (12\text{B}.2)$$

where ω_t is a random error term.

The coefficients in equation 12B.2 have a time subscript, reflecting the fact that they are allowed to vary each month. If you compare this with equation 12B.1 you will see that:

$$\alpha_t = k_t P_t^T$$

and

$$\beta_t = (1 - k_t)$$

These are time-varying vectors and given estimates of β_t the monthly values of k_t can be obtained.

In order to solve this regression model you need to make an assumption about how the parameters in the model evolve. One approach is to assume that information arrives in a random fashion, so the evolution of both parameters follows a random walk. You can write the coefficients α_t and β_t as follows:

$$\alpha_t = \alpha_{t-1} + \lambda_t \quad \text{where} \quad \lambda_t \sim NID(0,\ \sigma_\lambda^2) \qquad (12\text{B}.3)$$

$$\beta_t = \beta_{t-1} + \varepsilon_t \quad \text{where} \quad \varepsilon_t \sim NID(0,\sigma_\varepsilon^2) \qquad (12\text{B}.4)$$

where λ_t and ε_t are random error terms that are normal and identically distributed, with $E(\lambda_t) = E(\varepsilon_t) = E(\lambda_t \varepsilon_t) = 0$.

In principle, the variable nature of the parameters in equations 12B.3 and 12B.4 enables them to capture changes in market conditions. By reformulating the system in 'state-space' form, equation 12B.2 can be written as a measurement equation and the parameter profiles given by 12B.3 and 12B.4 as transition equations. Employing maximum likelihood estimation and the Kalman filter it is possible to estimate the parameter values. The estimation of this system of equations is described in Harvey (1993).

Within the framework of the Quan and Quigley (1989) model discussed above, once the value of k is known the implied property market prices, P_t^T, can be backed out from equation 12B.1. A number of studies have attempted to back out an index of market prices on the assumption that there is no serial correlation in the underlying growth series. However, because individual property valuations do not occur at the same point in time, and because of the impact of temporal aggregation, a lower limit on the first-order serial correlation structure should be approximately 0.25, if the underlying changes in prices are random (Working 1960). In a market that is a fair game,[1] this figure may be exceeded. Although significant serial correlation may be present in a backed-out series of market prices, this does not imply that investors are able to secure abnormal returns on a consistent basis, after allowing for transaction costs. Consequently, we do not have any prior expectations as to the extent of serial correlation present in a backed-out price series.

---

[1] We discuss what is meant by a fair game in Chapter 13.

The evolution of the smoothing parameter

Using this model we estimate the time-varying values of k_t for each of the 30 properties. Seven of the properties had constant parameters over the whole period with values ranging from 0.046 to 0.922. The remaining 23 properties exhibited considerable variation in the smoothing parameter. The results are summarised in Table 12B.1 and plotted in Figure 12B.2.

You will see that there was a decline in the average value of the smoothing parameter from 1987 to late 1989. A possible explanation for the decline may be the following. During the boom conditions of 1987–89 there may have been a larger mismatch between valuations and prices, leading to an undervaluation relative to prices, than that expected under relatively stable market conditions (Matysiak and

Table 12B.1 ● Average values of smoothing parameters k_t, March 1987 to October 1995

Grand mean	0.5699
Average monthly maximum	0.6224
Average monthly minimum	0.4958
Standard deviation	0.0364

Note: The shorter time period for the results reflects the fact that a number of observations are lost when the Kalman filter is initialised.

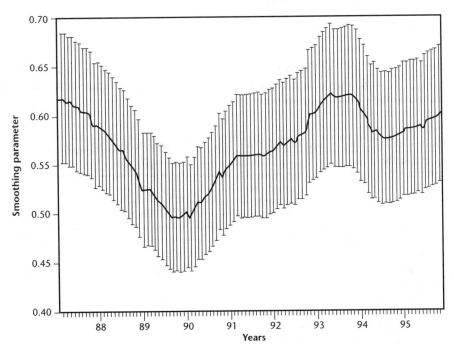

Figure 12B.2 Average monthly time-varying smoothing parameter (±1 standard error)

Wang 1995). Other things being equal, an increase in the uncertainty concerning transaction prices relative to market prices would lead to a reduction in the smoothing parameter k_t. However, there would have been an offsetting effect. First, the growth in market prices would have introduced greater market volatility, and second, the greater number of transactions in an active market should lead to less uncertainty in comparables. However, the combined effect may have been less than that of any undervaluation in these market conditions, with the result that there was an increase in valuation uncertainty. As the UK property market collapsed at the end of 1989, the lower smoothing parameter is indicative of valuers placing less emphasis on comparable transaction evidence. With fewer transactions there is a greater likelihood of more uncertainty between transactions prices and valuations and, consequently, more transactions noise. The smoothing parameter gradually increased up until 1993 after which time it again began to decline, although not to the same degree as in the late 1980s. There has been some recovery since the early 1990s.

The UK evidence for time-varying smoothing parameters corresponds with the results obtained by deRoos (1994) in the USA using data on hotels and motels. In this analysis the smoothing parameter was found to vary when estimated for different sub-periods.

Backing out the implied market prices

In order to gain further insight into the performance of the underlying market prices, the estimated time-varying parameters for each of the properties were used to back out the implied market prices as follows:

$$\frac{V_t - (1 - k_t)V_{t-1}}{k_t} = P_t^T \qquad\qquad\qquad (12\text{B}.5)$$

The implied prices for the 30 properties were also aggregated into an equally weighted portfolio. The resulting average implied price index is shown in Figure 12B.3 together with the average valuation-based series.

Table 12B.2 ● **Comparison of volatility figures of portfolio consisting of 30 properties**

	First-order serial correlation	Standard deviation	Ratio of standard deviations
Monthly index values			
Valuations	0.972	17.042	
Implied prices	0.830	18.093	1:1.06
Monthly changes			
Valuations	0.717	1.359	
Implied market prices	−0.448	7.354	1:5.41

Note: All figures cover the period December 1986 to October 1995.

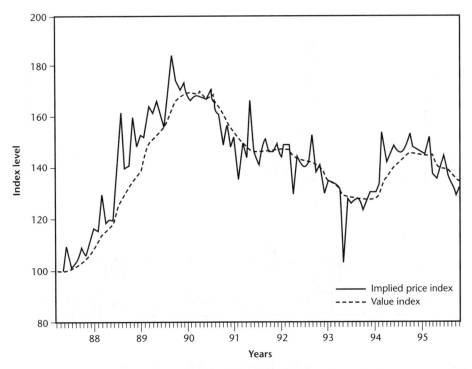

Figure 12B.3 Comparison of value and implied price indices

You will see that there is considerably more volatility in the backed-out implied price series than in the valuation-based series. Table 12B.2 provides some comparison statistics.

You will see that the first-order serial correlation for the changes in the valuations is 0.717. This drops to −0.448 for changes in the monthly implied prices.

The figures in Table 12B.2 also show that the volatility of monthly capital growth in implied market prices exceeds the valuation series volatility by a factor of 5.41. As this is much higher than expected, further insights can be obtained by examining the standard deviation ratio of implied prices and valuations for each of the individual properties. The ratios for all 30 properties are shown in Figure 12B.4, from which you will see that four properties appear to dominate the sample. In the sample of 30 properties this excessive volatility is not diversified away and gives an exaggerated view of the underlying volatility of the aggregate implied price series.

Removing these outliers from the sample and recalculating the implied market price index results in the profile shown in Figure 12B.5.

By removing these outliers the volatility of changes in implied prices drops from 7.354% to 2.920% per month. The ratio in this case is 2.15, which represents a 60% reduction over the original estimate of 5.41.

Although a monthly index is a valuable tool in property investment analysis, if inappropriate unsmoothing adjustments are applied to the index in order to back out a series of implied market prices the resulting figures may be unreliable.

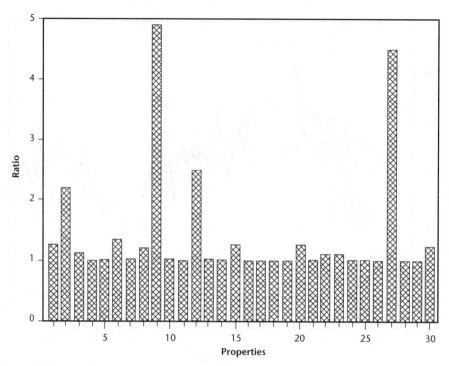

Figure 12B.4   Ratio of standard deviation of implied prices to values

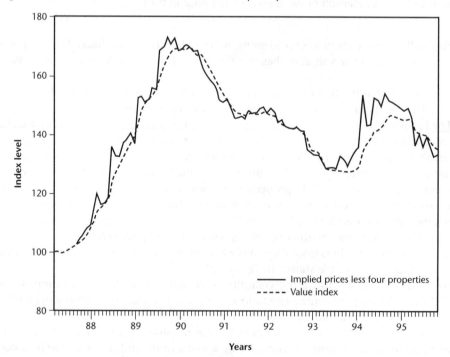

Figure 12B.5   Comparison of value and implied price index less four properties

Selected references

Barkham, R. and Geltner, D. (1994) Unsmoothing British valuation-based returns without assuming an efficient market. *Journal of Property Research* **11**, 81–95.

Blundell, G. and Ward, C.W.R. (1987) Property portfolio allocation: a multi-factor model. *Land Development Studies* **4**, 145–56.

Brown, G.R. and Matysiak, G.A. (1998) Valuation smoothing without temporal aggregation. *Journal of Property Research* **15** (2), 1–15.

Brown, G.R. and Matysiak, G.A. (1995) Using commercial property indices for measuring portfolio performance. *Journal of Property Finance* **6** (3), 27–38. Paper presented at the RICS Cutting Edge Conference, Aberdeen, 1995.

Brown, G.R. and Matysiak, G.A. (1997) Sticky valuations, aggregation effects and property indices. Paper presented at the AREUEA International Real Estate Conference, 31 May–2 June 1997.

deRoos, J.A. (1994) Smoothing in the appraisal of real estate. Cornell University, Working paper.

Fisher, J.D., Geltner, D. and Webb, B. (1994) Value indices of commercial real estate: a comparison of index construction methods. *Journal of Real Estate Finance and Economics* **9**, 137–64.

Geltner, D. (1989) Estimating real estate's systematic risk from aggregate level appraisal-based returns. *AREUEA Journal* **17** (4), 463–81.

Geltner, D. (1991) Smoothing in appraisal based returns. *Journal of Real Estate Finance and Economics* **4**, 327–45.

Geltner, D. (1993) Estimating market values from appraisal values without assuming an efficient market. *Journal of Real Estate Research* **8** (3), 325–45.

Giacotto, C. and Clapp, J. (1992) Appraisal based real estate returns under alternative market regimes. *AREUEA Journal* **20** (1), 1–24.

Harvey, A.C. (1993) *Time Series Models*, New York: Harvester-Wheatsheaf.

Lizieri, C. and Satchell, S. (1996) Property company performance and real interest rates: a regime-switching approach. University of Reading, Working paper in Land Management, No. 45, Department of Land Management & Development.

Maitland-Smith, J. (1996) Value indices of commercial real estate: a Markov switching process? University of Reading, Discussion Papers in Urban & Regional Economics, No. 115, Department of Economics.

Matysiak, G.A. and Wang, P. (1995) Commercial property market prices and valuations: analysing the correspondence. *Journal of Property Research* **12** (3), 181–202.

Quan, D. and Quigley, J. (1989) Inferring an investment return series for real estate from observations on sales. *AREUEA Journal* **17** (2), 218–30.

Quan, D. and Quigley, J. (1991) Price formation and the appraisal function in real estate markets. *Journal of Real Estate Finance and Economics* **4** (2), 127–46.

Ross, S.A. and Zisler, R. (1991) Risk and return in real estate. *Journal of Real Estate Finance and Economics* **4** (2), 175–90.

Working, H. (1960) Note on the correlation of the first differences of averages in a random chain. *Econometrica* **28**, 916–18.

Appendix 12C
Estimating the volatility of terminal wealth

Let us assume that you invest £100 in a project that offers an expected return of 2% per month. This return is not, however, guaranteed so you won't know how much you have earned until one month has elapsed. However, you know something about the risk of the project and are able to estimate that the standard deviation of returns is 10% per month. This additional information now enables you to make some probability statements. For example, you could say with 95% certainty that the actual outcome at the end of the month will lie within the following range.[1]

Expected growth	$= £100 + 2.00\% = £102.00$
95% confidence limits	$= £100 + (2.00\% \pm 1.96 \times 10.00\%)$
+ 95%	$= £100 + 21.60\% = £121.60$
− 95%	$= £100 - 17.60\% = £82.40$

Although you expect the investment to grow to £102.00 it could easily lie in the range of £82.40 to £121.60.

Instead of withdrawing your funds at the end of one month you decide to take a well-earned rest, travel round the world for a few years and leave your investment to grow. The question that arises is, in what range will your investment lie at the end of different investment horizons? For example, you might want to know the range at the end of one year. Alternatively, if you have been having a really good time you might want to know the range after five years. Estimating the expected value of your fund should present few problems as we covered this in Part 1.

Expected growth over twelve months

This is just the 2% monthly growth compounded over twelve periods:

$$E(g_{12}) = (1 + 0.02)^{12} - 1 = 0.2682 \text{ or } 26.82\% \text{ p.a.}$$

Expected growth over five years

This is just the 2% monthly growth compounded over 60 periods:

$$E(g_{60}) = (1 + 0.02)^{60} - 1 = 2.2810 \text{ or } 228.10\%$$

Estimating the standard deviation is a little more complicated as you have to deal in terms of the variance and then convert the answer back to a standard deviation.

Standard deviation over twelve months

The standard deviation of 10% per month is converted to an annual figure as follows:

$$\sigma_{12} = \sqrt{12 \times 0.10^2} = 0.3464 \text{ or } 34.64\% \text{ p.a.}$$

---

[1] We have assumed that the distribution of return is normal.

Standard deviation over five years

The standard deviation of 10% per month is converted to a five-yearly figure as follows:

$$\sigma_{60} = \sqrt{60 \times 0.10^2} = 0.7746 \text{ or } 77.46\%$$

You will see that as the period increases the risk of the investment also increases. In terms of terminal wealth the further into the future you go the greater the uncertainty in your terminal wealth.

Enter serial correlation

The conversion of risk we have shown is only valid if you expect the time-series of returns to be random. In this case the conversion merely requires the standard deviation to be multiplied by $\sqrt{n.m}$, where n equals the number of periods p.a. and m is the number of years. For monthly returns the annual conversion would be equal to $\sqrt{12 \times 1}$, and for quarterly returns the annual conversion would be $\sqrt{4 \times 1}$. However, if the returns are positively serially correlated this procedure may seriously under-estimate the conversion. The magnitude of the underestimation depends on the covariance of returns in each sub-period.

In this appendix we present two methods that take account of the serial correlation that can be used to estimate the volatility of terminal wealth. One is an exact method that uses continuous returns (Brown and Matysiak 1997), and the other is an approximation using discrete returns (Newell and MacFarlane 1995).

Conversion of risk using continuous rates of return

If you have a sequence of returns that are expressed in continuous time[2] the variance of returns measured over any period will be the sum of the variances and covariances for each sub-period.

If you let the periodic returns r_i be continuously compounded over n periods, the sum of these returns will produce an aggregate return of $\sum_{i=1}^{n} r_i$. The variance of this series, in matrix form, is given by $\sigma_n^2 = e^1 \Omega e$, where e is a column vector of 1s and Ω is the $n \times n$ variance–covariance matrix of all the sub-period returns. You can express this in terms of the serial correlation coefficients as follows:

$$\sigma_n^2 = \sum_{i=1}^{n} \sigma_i^2 + \sum_{i=1}^{n-1} \sum_{j=1}^{n-1} \rho_{ij} \sigma_i \sigma_j \text{ subject to } i \neq j \tag{12C.1}$$

where

σ_n^2 = variance over n sub-periods
σ_i^2 = variance for sub-period i

---

[2] You can convert discrete rates of return to continuous form by taking logs. The continuous form of r is $\ln(1 + r)$.

p_{ij} = coefficient of correlation between i and j

n = number of sub-periods

A time-series is considered to be stationary if its mean, variance and auto-covariances are independent of time. By recognising this, the standard deviations for all i and j will be the same and it will be evident that the covariance terms in Ω will satisfy the following condition:

$$\sigma_{ij} = \sigma_{ji} = \sigma_{i-j} \tag{12C.2}$$

This simplification results in what is known as a Toeplitz matrix. This form of matrix has equal elements on the main diagonal together with equal elements on each parallel sub-diagonal. By recognising the general form of this matrix you can simplify equation 12C.1 to give:

$$\sigma_n^2 = \sigma_i^2 \left[n + 2 \sum_{k=1}^{n-1} (n-k)\rho_{1,k+1} \right] \tag{12C.3}$$

where $\rho_{1,k+1}$ = kth-order serial correlation coefficient.

As long as you know the serial correlation structure for a sequence of returns this expression can be used to estimate the variance of returns over any period. You will also see that if there is no serial correlation the variance of the series reduces to:

$$\sigma_n^2 = n\sigma_i^2 \tag{12C.4}$$

This is the conversion method we used in the example at the beginning of this appendix.

Example

We have used equation 12C.3 to estimate the annual risk of the Investment Property Databank (IPD) monthly capital growth series based on data over the period January 1987 to January 1998. The unadjusted monthly standard deviation and serial correlation structure for the series are summarised in Table 12C.1.

Using equation 12C.3 the conversion from monthly to annual risk can be estimated as follows:

$$\sigma^2 = 0.975^2[12 + 2(47.319)] = 106.638\%$$

Allowing for the serial correlation gives an annual standard deviation of 10.07% p.a.

If the IPD returns were *assumed* to be uncorrelated, the annual standard deviation would have been estimated by $\sigma_n = \sqrt{n\sigma_i^2} = 3.46 \times 0.975 = 3.378\%$ p.a. By ignoring the effect of serial correlation the annualised risk of the IPD capital growth series would have been understated by a factor of 2.98.

The conversion approach we have adopted allows the risk to be estimated over any holding period. To illustrate why this is important we have shown in Figure 12C.1 the 95% confidence bands for the IPD Monthly All Property Capital Growth Index from December 1986 to January 1998 using both the adjusted and unadjusted risk

Table 12C.1 ● **IPD capital growth series, January 1987 to January 1998**

Unadjusted monthly standard deviation = 0.975%

Lag	Serial corr.	No. of terms	Product
1	0.897	11	9.867
2	0.861	10	8.610
3	0.829	9	7.461
4	0.754	8	6.032
5	0.688	7	4.816
6	0.620	6	3.720
7	0.551	5	2.755
8	0.477	4	1.908
9	0.405	3	1.215
10	0.335	2	0.670
11	0.265	1	0.265
			47.319

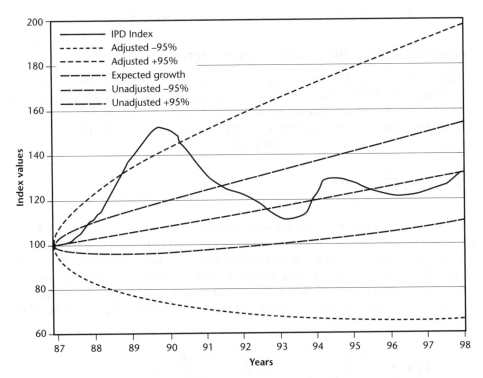

Figure 12C.1   IPD Capital Growth Index December 1986 to January 1998 with
unadjusted and adjusted 95% confidence bands

Table 12C.2 ● IPD Monthly Capital Growth Index, January 1987 to January 1998

Sector	Annualised unadjusted risk in % p.a.	Serial correlation adjusted risk in % p.a. Eqn 12C.3	Ratio of adjusted to annualised risk
All property	3.378	10.070	2.98
Retail	2.921	8.291	2.84
Office	4.184	12.651	3.02
Industrial	3.798	11.097	2.92

measures. The outer bounds in this illustration represent the uncertainty facing an investor who had taken a position in the IPD monthly index in December 1986. The inner bounds represent the uncertainty based on the risk in the IPD index. The outer bounds take into consideration the serial correlation in the index.

You will see that there is a significant difference between the two profiles. An investor in 1986 would expect the profile of capital growth to lie within the outer range. The actual index is also plotted by way of comparison and shows that the risk adjustment provides a more realistic indication of the expected volatility of terminal wealth.

We have also summarised the conversion for each sector in Table 12C.2.

Conversion of risk using discrete rates of return

An alternative approach to converting risk measures has been developed by Newell and MacFarlane (1995). This is based on estimating the variance of the product of a number of discrete returns that are correlated over time.

Let the periodic returns r_i be discretely compounded over n periods. The variance of the product of the n returns can be represented as:

$$\sigma_n^2 = \left\{ Var\left[\prod_{i=1}^{n} (1 + r_i) - 1 \right] \right\} \tag{12C.5}$$

If, for example, the returns are recorded monthly, then $n = 12$ and equation 12C.5 can be used to estimate the annual variance. As with the continuous case this relationship only holds true if the returns are independent over time. If, however, the returns are correlated from period to period, then this procedure will understate the variance. Following Goodman (1960) Newell and MacFarlane show that it is possible to estimate the approximate variance for the product of a number of non-independent variables as follows:

$$\sigma_n^2 \approx \prod_{i=1}^{n} (1 + \mu_i)^2 \left[\sum_{i=1}^{n} \frac{\sigma_i^2}{(1 + \mu_i)^2} + 2 \sum_{i=1}^{n} \sum_{\substack{j=1; \\ i<j}}^{n} \frac{\rho_{ij}\sigma_i\sigma_j}{(1 + \mu_i)(1 + \mu_j)} \right] \tag{12C.6}$$

where

μ_i = mean return in period i

ρ_{ij} = coefficient of correlation between returns in periods i and j

If the returns are assumed to be stationary so that the mean, variance and auto-covariances are independent of time, it is possible to simplify equation 12C.6 as follows:

$$\sigma_n^2 \approx (1 + \mu)^{2n} \left[\frac{n\sigma_i^2}{(1 + \mu)^2} + \frac{2\sigma_i^2}{(1 + \mu)^2} \sum_{i=1}^{n-1} \sum_{j=1}^{n-1} \rho_{ij} \right] \text{ subject to } i \neq j \qquad (12C.7)$$

This can be further simplified to:

$$\sigma_n^2 \approx n\sigma_i^2 (1 + \mu)^{2(n-1)} \left(1 + \frac{2}{n} \sum_{i=1}^{n-1} \sum_{j=1}^{n-1} \rho_{ij} \right) \qquad (12C.8)$$

Given that each parallel sub-diagonal element in the covariance matrix is equal, and the series is stationary, you can write equation 12C.8 as:

$$\sigma_n^2 \approx n\sigma^2 (1 + \mu)^{2(n-1)} \left[1 + \frac{2}{n} \sum_{k=1}^{n-1} (n - k)\rho_{1,k+1} \right] \qquad (12C.9)$$

If you also assume that the mean return, μ, is zero for small intervals of time you can simplify equation 12C.9 to:

$$\sigma_n^2 = \sigma_i^2 \left[n + 2 \sum_{k=1}^{n-1} (n - k)\rho_{1,k+1} \right] \qquad (12C.10)$$

This is the same expression that we derived in equation 12C.3. You will see that by imposing a number of restrictions on the discrete case you end up with a conversion that is equivalent to the continuous case.

Selected references

Brown, G.R. and Matysiak, G.A. (1997) A note on the periodic conversion of measures of risk. *Journal of Property Research* 13, 13–16.

Goodman, L.A. (1960) On the exact variance of products. *American Statistical Association Journal* 55, 708–13.

Newell, G. and MacFarlane, J. (1995) Improved risk estimation using appraisal-smoothed real estate returns. *Journal of Real Estate Portfolio Management* 1 (1), 51–7.

Newell, G. and MacFarlane, J. (1996) Risk estimation and appraisal smoothing in UK property returns. *Journal of Property Research* 13 (1), 1–12.

Appendix 12D
Random walk processes and aggregation effects

In Appendix 12A we mentioned an important result concerning the effect that averaging a series of random returns can have on the serial correlation coefficient of an index (Working 1960). In this appendix we derive this general result.

A random walk can be represented as follows:

$$x_t = x_{t-1} + e_t \qquad (12D.1)$$

where each successive item, x_t, can be represented by the previous item, x_{t-1}, plus a random change, e_t.

The conditional expectation of x_t, given information about x_{t-1}, can be written as:

$$E(x_t | x_{t-1}) = x_{t-1} \qquad (12D.2)$$

This just says that as long as the changes in each of the items are random, your best estimate for x_t, at $t - 1$, is its conditional expectation, x_{t-1}.

Assume now that you want to construct an index made up of the change in value of m items that each follows a random walk. Instead of each item being recorded at the same point in time the index is made up from the average of the items round each index date. In the first period you have m items that can be represented as, x_1, x_2, x_3 ... x_n. In the following period you have another m item that can be represented as:

$$x_{m+1}, x_{m+2}, x_{m+3} \cdots x_{2m}$$

The average of the first set of items can be written as:

$$\bar{x}_1 = \sum_{i=1}^{m} \frac{x_i}{m} \qquad (12D.3)$$

The average of the second set of items can be written as:

$$\bar{x}_2 = \sum_{i-m+1}^{2m} \frac{x_i}{m} \qquad (12D.4)$$

where

$$x_2 = x_1 + e_2$$
$$x_3 = x_1 + e_2 + e_3$$
.
.
.
$$x_m = x_1 + e_2 + e_3 + \ldots + e_m$$
$$x_{m+1} = x_1 + e_2 + e_3 + \ldots + e_{m+1}$$
.
.
.
$$x_{2m} = x_1 + e_2 + e_3 + \ldots + e_{2m}$$

The difference between the averages is, therefore:

$$\Delta_1 = \bar{x}_2 - \bar{x}_1 \qquad (12D.5)$$

$$\Delta_1 = \frac{1}{m} \left(\sum_{i-m+1}^{2m} x_i - \sum_{i=1}^{m} x_i \right) \tag{12D.6}$$

By substituting for each of the x terms given above you can group the error terms as follows:

$$\Delta_1 = \frac{1}{m}[e_2 + 2e_3 + \ldots + (m-1)e_m + me_{m+1} + (m-1)e_{m+2} + \ldots + e_{2m}] \tag{12D.7}$$

This expression has a mean of zero and a variance of:

$$Var(\Delta_1) = \sigma^2 \left(\frac{2m^2 + 1}{3m} \right) \tag{12D.8}$$

By similar logic the covariance term can be written as:

$$cov(\Delta_1, \Delta_2) = \sigma^2 \left(\frac{m^2 - 1}{6m} \right) \tag{12D.9}$$

From equations 12D.8 and 12D.9 the first-order serial correlation coefficient can be written as:

$$\rho = \frac{m^2 - 1}{2(2m^2 + 1)} \tag{12D.10}$$

You will see from this that as the number of terms, m, used to make up the index increases the first-order serial correlation coefficient approaches 0.25. Although the first difference of the component series are uncorrelated the aggregated series is correlated. If an index is made up from data that are averaged between reporting dates, and has a first-order serial correlation coefficient of 0.25, this could imply that the underlying series is, in fact, random. When dealing with property indexes the figure of 0.25 should be regarded as the lower limit in terms of serial correlation.

Selected reference

Working, H. (1960) Note on the correlation of the first differences of averages in a random chain. *Econometrica* 28, 916–18.

Appendix 12E
Removing smoothing with autoregressive models

In Chapter 12 we discussed some of the reasons why valuation-based return series are likely to be smoothed. This is an important issue that affects our interpretation of real estate risk. It is not surprising, therefore, to find that a number of researchers have developed ways of considering how the smoothing can be removed. The reason for doing this is twofold:

1. It may be possible to arrive at measures of risk that more truly reflect the risk class of real estate.

2. It may be possible to back out a series of returns per period that provide a more useful basis for considering real estate in a mixed-asset context.

A number of methods have been proposed for removing the serial correlation in a valuation index. These have included the following:

● subjectively increasing estimates of volatility
● adjusting capitalisation rates
● using equity REIT series
● using a hedged REIT series
● using transaction-based series, and
● using transformed returns series to produce an 'implied' market price series

Those procedures that involve a subjective adjustment of risk measures generally continue to produce low estimates of risk when compared with equities. In addition, the correlation between real estate and equities remains unchanged. In an asset allocation framework this still results in a much higher proportion of real estate than observed in practice.

Using equity REIT returns to determine the volatility of property is based on the premise that equity REITs are more representative of transaction prices than valuations (Chan et al. 1990). Using the Russell-NCREIF property index and the NAREIT equity index over the 1978–91 period, Giliberto (1993) showed that a volatility adjustment factor of 4.8 was required to account for the effect of valuation smoothing. Although the use of listed equity REIT shares to estimate property volatility can be challenged, Giliberto (1993) was able to show that equity REITs do reflect property market factors.

As a compromise between the valuation-based Russell-NCREIF index and the equities-based NAREIT index, Giliberto (1993) developed a hedged REIT index. The extent of smoothing in the Russell-NCREIF index over the period 1978–91 resulted in an adjustment factor of 3.7, with the hedged REIT procedure providing volatility and correlation measures free of appraisal lag and bias.

Transaction-based series have shown some success in local regional analyses (Fisher et al. 1992; Miles et al. 1990; Webb et al. 1992). There is clearly a lot of appeal in developing a transactions-based series. However, as there are considerable problems with data collection it is unlikely that a transaction-based series, at least in commercial real estate, can realistically be achieved (Miles et al. 1991).

In this appendix we focus on those models that adjust for smoothing by using an autoregressive process to generate a derivative version of the underlying price series.

Unsmoothing the returns from real estate

Various models have been proposed for transforming a valuation-based series into an unsmoothed derivative version of the underlying price series. However, in order to develop these models it is necessary to make some assumption about the process generating the unobserved true returns. The common assumption is that the real estate market is efficient so that the returns from period to period are uncorrelated. Many professional valuers certainly take issue with this in the belief that the real estate market is inefficient. Whether the assumption of market efficiency is realistic is, of course, an empirical matter. We consider this further in Chapter 13.

The importance of the efficiency assumption can be seen in the model developed by Blundell and Ward (1987). This was the first published model that used an auto-regressive process to generate a proxy for true market returns. Blundell and Ward suggested that current valuations could be represented as a weighted average of the implied market prices and the valuation in the previous period:[1]

$$V_t = (1 - \alpha)P_t^T + \alpha V_{t-1} \tag{12E.1}$$

where

V_t = valuation at time t
P_t^T = implied market price at time t
α = a constant lying in the range from 0 to 1

You will see that the closer the value of α lies to 1, the more weight is attached to the previous valuation.

A similar expression can be derived for the previous period as follows:

$$V_{t-1} = (1 - \alpha)P_{t-1}^T + \alpha V_{t-2} \tag{12E.2}$$

Subtracting this from equation 12E.1 gives the following:

$$V_t - V_{t-1} = (1 - \alpha)(P_t - P_{t-1}) + \alpha(V_{t-1} - V_{t-2}) \tag{12E.3}$$

If you assume that all the valuations are expressed in log form the difference between the valuations represents continuously compounded rates of return over the period (t–1) to t. You can, therefore, write equation 12E.3 in returns form as:

$$r_t = (1 - \alpha)r_{mt} + \alpha r_{t-1} \tag{12E.4}$$

where

r_t = return derived from the valuation series
r_{mt} = return that would be observed if market prices were correctly captured by valuations

It is at this point that an assumption has to be made about the evolution of r_{mt}. Like other markets it is assumed that the real estate market is weak form efficient and follows a random walk process. This would be the case if valuations were present values. Using this assumption you can write the process generating r_{mt} as:

$$r_{mt} = B + e_t \tag{12E.5}$$

where B is a constant and e_t is a normally distributed random variable with an expected value of zero and is serially uncorrelated for all lags.

Applying the expectations operator to equation 12E.5 gives:

$$E(r_{mt}) = B \tag{12E.6}$$

The expected value of the true market returns is therefore constant with a variance given by:

$$Var(r_{mt}) = Var(e_t) \tag{12E.7}$$

---

[1] You will see that this is similar to the Quan and Quigley model we described in Chapter 12. The only difference is that the smoothing parameter $k = (1 - \alpha)$.

From our expression for $E(r_{mt})$ you can substitute equation 12E.6 into 12E.5 to give:

$$r_t = (1 - \alpha)(B + e_t) + \alpha r_{t-1} \tag{12E.8}$$

$$r_t = B(1 - \alpha) + \alpha r_{t-1} + (1 - \alpha)e_t \tag{12E.9}$$

Applying the expectations operator:

$$E(r_t) = B(1 - \alpha) + \alpha E(r_{t-1}) + (1 - \alpha)E(e_t) \tag{12E.10}$$

If the return series is assumed to be stationary, then $E(r_t)$ will be equal to $E(r_{t-1})$ and the expected value of the error term will be zero. Taking these factors into considera-tion, and dropping the time subscript, equation 12E.10 can be written as:

$$E(r)(1 - \alpha) = B(1 - \alpha) \tag{12E.11}$$

$$E(r) = B = E(r_m) \tag{12E.12}$$

From this you will see that the expected value of the observed series is equal to the expected value of the underlying market series. What will differ, however, is the variance of the market returns. You can see this by taking the variance of equation 12E.9:

$$Var(r_t) = \alpha^2 Var(r_{t-1}) + (1 - \alpha)^2 Var(e_t) \tag{12E.13}$$

Again, assuming that the transformed return series is stationary, the variance of the returns will be constant. Hence $Var(r_t)$ will be equal to $Var(r_{t-1})$ so that equation 12E.13, dropping the time subscripts, can be written as:

$$Var(r) = \frac{(1 - \alpha)^2}{1 - \alpha^2} Var(e) \tag{12E.14}$$

From equation 12E.7 you know that the variance of the error term is also equal to the variance of the true market returns. Substituting into equation 12E.14 gives:

$$Var(r) = \frac{(1 - \alpha)^2}{1 - \alpha^2} Var(r_m) \tag{12E.15}$$

Rearranging in terms of $Var(r_m)$ gives:

$$Var(r_m) = \frac{1 - \alpha^2}{(1 - \alpha^2)} Var(r) \tag{12E.16}$$

Similarly, the implied market returns series can be backed out from equation 12E.4 as follows:

$$r_{mt} = \frac{r_t - \alpha r_{t-1}}{1 - \alpha} \tag{12E.17}$$

This series will have the same mean as the observed, smoothed, return series but will have a greater variance.

Example

By way of illustration we have used this model to unsmooth the IPD capital growth index. Over the period January 1987 to August 1998 the first-order serial correlation coefficient was 0.897, implying a high degree of smoothing. If equation 12E.4 is solved using regression analysis, this figure is also equivalent to the value for α. In terms of the Quan and Quigley model this implies that the smoothing parameter $k = 0.103$ (i.e. $1 - 0.897$).

Using equation 12E.17 the implied market returns can be backed out from the monthly capital growth. Figures 12E.1a and 12E.1b compare the capital growth and index numbers for both the IPD series and adjusted series based on this procedure.

You will see that there are significant differences between the two series, with the capital growth figures showing a lot of variability. The ratio of the standard deviations in this case is 1:4.299. The high volatility arises because we have placed no constraints on the size of the smoothing parameter and have arrived at a figure for k that implies that, over the period 1987–98, valuers used only 10% of the information relating to comparable transactions when forming current valuations. This clearly does not make sense, so that an alternative approach to estimating the smoothing parameter seems more appropriate.

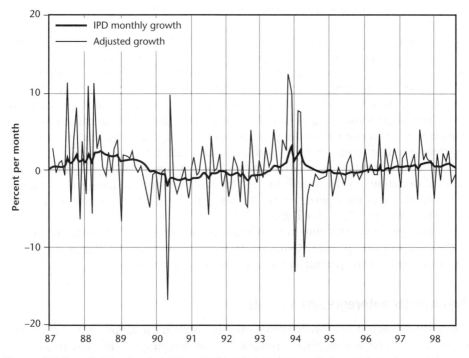

Figure 12E.1a Comparison of IPD monthly all property capital growth and adjusted growth using an autoregressive model

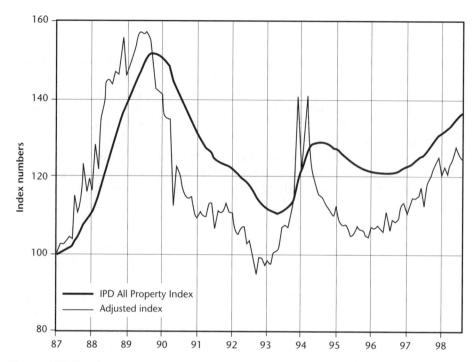

Figure 12E.1b Comparison of IPD monthly All Property Capital Growth Index and adjusted index using an autoregressive model

By assuming that the implied market values of *individual* properties follow a random walk you could argue that the lower limit for the serial correlation in the adjusted growth series should be no less than 0.25. Using equation 12E.17 you can solve for the value of α that would give a backed-out growth series with a first-order serial correlation of 0.25. We estimated this to be 0.654, which gives a smoothing parameter of 0.346. This implies that valuers made use of approximately 35% of the information relating to comparable transactions. A comparison of our constrained growth series and index numbers is shown in Figures 12E.2a and 12E.2b.

There is still substantial volatility, as you would expect, with the ratio of the standard deviations in this case being 1:1.46. The two index profiles are now much closer together and show more of the characteristics of the time-varying adjustment we used in Appendix 12B. (See Figure 12B.5.)

This example shows that the choice of smoothing parameter is critical to the success of the unsmoothing process. Geltner (1993) has also examined the choice of an appropriate smoothing parameter without assuming an efficient market.

Higher-order autoregressive models

The method of adjustment we have described is based on the assumption that returns follow a first-order autoregressive process so that the current observed returns are related to the returns in the previous period. Ross and Zisler (1991), by contrast, expressed current valuation returns as a moving average of the true market returns.

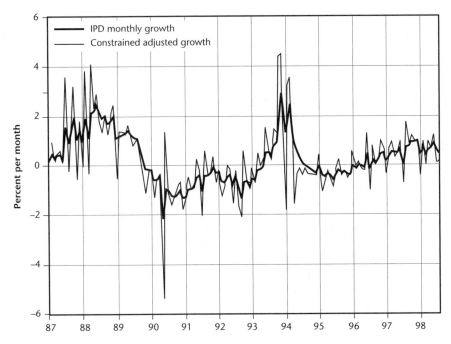

Figure 12E.2a Comparison of IPD monthly all property capital growth and constrained adjusted growth

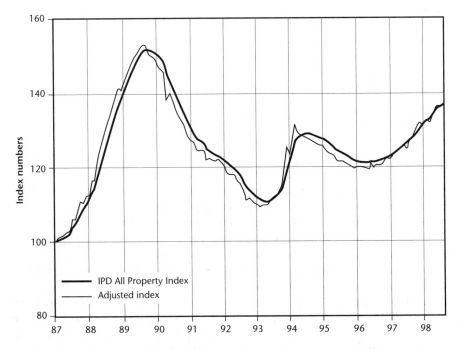

Figure 12E.2b Comparison of IPD monthly All Property Capital Growth Index and constrained adjusted index

Fisher, Geltner and Webb (1992) extended the model proposed by Ross and Zisler in order to generate an unsmooth, informationally efficient liquid market return series. As with the approach adopted by Blundell and Ward this also requires the assumption that returns are uncorrelated over time.

Following their methodology, current valuation-based returns can be expressed as the weighted moving average of market returns as follows:

$$r_t = w_0 r_{m,t} + w_1 r_{m,t-1} + w_2 r_{m,t-2} + \dots + w_i r_{m,t-i} \tag{12E.18}$$

where

r_t = smoothed valuation-based return in period t
$r_{m,t}$ = corresponding true market return
w_i = weight between 0 and 1

This model treats current returns as a noiseless, stationary transfer function. While other models are possible this does at least capture the essence of valuation smoothing present in an aggregate return series such as the IPD index.

Assuming that the true market returns are uncorrelated over time equation 12E.18 can be shown to produce an autoregressive model of the form:

$$r_t = \alpha_1 r_{t-1} + \alpha_2 r_{t-2} + \dots + e_t \tag{12E.19}$$

where $e_t = w_0 r_t$ and $w_0 = 1 - \alpha_1 - \alpha_2 \dots$

Equation 12E.19 indicates that current returns can be related to previous returns by an autoregressive process. Substituting these expressions into equation 12E.18 it is possible, with a bit of rearrangement, to derive the backed-out unobserved market return as follows:

$$r_{mt} = \frac{r_t - \alpha_1 r_{t-1} - \alpha_2 r_{t-2} - \dots}{1 - \alpha_1 - \alpha_2 - \dots} \tag{12E.20}$$

If this is restricted to a lag of one period you will see that it is exactly the same as the Blundell and Ward model given in equation 12E.17.

Estimation issues

Although these models offer similar representations of the underlying market returns they do not provide a way of directly estimating a suitable set of parameter values. The underlying assumption is that property returns are stable over time. However, we have shown in Appendix 12B that this is not the case. Using a constant parameter may provide an unbiased estimate of the true market variance, but the profile of the backed-out market returns may not provide a good indicator of the market returns in each period.

The Fisher, Geltner and Webb approach is more general, and as a result may be more successful in this respect, although there remains the additional problem of deciding how many lags should be included. Although it is possible to use a stepwise regression or Box-Jenkins model to decide this issue, you have no way of knowing whether the resulting specification represents a good reflection of the economics of the returns-generating process. If the parameter value is estimated without reference to the underlying economics, then it is possible that the implied market variance and the backed-out returns profile will both be biased. Equation 12E.16 shows that if the parameter is set too close to 1, the factor needed to adjust the valuation variance becomes much larger than expected and in some cases can approach infinity! This problem is most acute with monthly indices where serial cross-correlation affecting the component properties can induce a strong moving average effect into the returns which then exhibits high serial correlation. We discussed this in Appendix 12A.

It should be evident from the previous appendices that the cross-correlation aspect can introduce a time-varying effect into the estimation process. This suggests that an alternative estimation process may be necessary. It may, for example, be possible to back out the true market returns for a high-frequency index by estimating the market returns from the component properties. With a large number of properties this may not be possible. Other time-varying parameter models, including unobserved component models, may prove to be more successful with high-frequency indexes.

One final point is that each of these models has assumed that the underlying returns-generating process is random. This implies that the first-order serial correlation coefficient for the index returns is zero.[2] Following Working (1960) we argued that an index of averaged returns would have a positive serial correlation that approaches a figure of 0.25. Working also suggests that higher orders of serial correlation should be zero. Our constrained example considered the first-order serial correlation only but it would be possible to extend the model to cover higher-order cases.

Selected references

Blundell, G. and Ward, C.W.R. (1987) Property portfolio allocation: a multi-factor model. *Land Development Studies* **4**, 145–56.

Brown, G.R. (1991) *Property Investment and the Capital Markets*, London: Chapman & Hall.

Brown, G.R. (1993) Valuation and changes in covariance in the UK property market from 1987–92. University of Auckland, Real Estate Research Unit Working Paper No.1, Paper presented at the ARES annual meeting, Key West, Florida, April 1993.

Burns, W. and Epley, D. (1982) The performance of portfolios of REIT's and stocks. *Journal of Portfolio Management* (Spring), 37–42.

Chan, K., Hendershott, P. and Sanders, A. (1990) Risk and return on real estate: evidence from equity REIT's. *AREUEA Journal* **18** (4), 431–52.

Firstenberg, P.B., Ross, S.A. and Zisler, R. (1988) Real estate: the whole story. *Journal of Portfolio Management* (Spring), 23–32.

Fisher, J.D., Geltner, D. and Webb, B. (1992) Historical value indices of commercial real estate. Indiana University, Working paper.

Geltner, D. (1989a) Bias in appraisal based returns. *AREUEA Journal* **17** (3), 338–52.

Geltner, D. (1989b) Estimating real estate's systematic risk from aggregate level appraisal-based returns. *AREUEA Journal* **17** (4), 463–81.

Geltner, D. (1991) Smoothing in appraisal based returns. *Journal of Real Estate Finance and Economics* **4**, 327–45.

---

[2] A random walk also implies that the serial correlation coefficient for all lags is zero.

Geltner, D. (1993a) Estimating market values from appraisal values without assuming an efficient market. *Journal of Real Estate Research* **8** (3), 325–45.

Geltner, D. (1993b) Temporal aggregation in real estate return indices. *AREUEA Journal* **21** (2), 141–66.

Giacotto, C. and Clapp, J. (1992) Appraisal based real estate returns under alternative market regimes. *AREUEA Journal* **20** (1), 1–24.

Giliberto, M. (1990) Equity REIT's and portfolio diversification. *Journal of Real Estate Research* **5**, 259–64.

Giliberto, M. (1993) Measuring real estate returns: the hedged REIT index. *Journal of Portfolio Management* (Spring), 94–9.

Hoag, J. (1980) Towards indices of real estate value and return. *Journal of Finance* **35**, 569–80.

Kuhle, J. (1987) Portfolio diversification and return benefits – common stock versus REIT's. *Journal of Real Estate Research* **2**, 1–9.

Lee, S. (1989) Property returns in a portfolio context. *Journal of Valuation* **7**, 248–58.

Liu, C., Hartzell, D., Grisson, T. and Grieg, W. (1990) The composition of the market portfolio and real estate investment performance. *AREUEA Journal* **18**, 49–75.

MacGregor, B.D. and Nanthakumaran, N. (1992) The allocation to property in the multi-asset portfolio: the evidence and theory reconsidered. *Journal of Property Research* **9**, 5–32.

Miles, M., Guilkey, D. and Shears, D. (1991) A transaction based real estate index: is it possible? *Journal of Property Research* **8**, 203–17.

Miles, M., Hartzell, D. and Guilkey, D. (1990) A different look at commercial real estate returns. *AREUEA Journal* **18**, 403–30.

Ross, S.A. and Zisler, R. (1991) Risk and return in real estate. *Journal of Real Estate Finance and Economics* **4** (2), 175–90.

Webb, B., Miles, M. and Guilkey, D. (1992) Transaction driven commercial real estate returns: the panacea to asset allocation models? *AREUEA Journal* **20**, 325–57.

Webb, J. and Rubens, J. (1988) How much in real estate?: a surprising answer. *Journal of Portfolio Management* (Spring), 10–13.

Wheaton, W. and Torto, R. (1989) Income and appraised values: a re-examination of the FRC returns data. *AREUEA Journal* **17**, 439–49.

PART 3

Portfolio management

CHAPTER *13*

The efficiency of the property market

Learning objectives

After reading this chapter you will understand the following:

- The importance of information in assessing value

- The difference between informational efficiency and operational efficiency

- The role of valuation models

- The different forms of market efficiency

Introduction

One of the most important ideas in modern finance is that prices reflect all knowable information. The value of an asset is, therefore, a reflection of both the quantity and quality of available information.

In a well-ordered society most markets tend to be reasonably efficient. In other words, the prices at which assets sell are on average a fair reflection of their true value. It will be difficult, therefore, to discover assets that are consistently mispriced. An efficient market is also important for developing a framework for asset allocation and performance measurement.

The concept of market efficiency was first proposed in relation to stock and bond markets. It does, however, have general relevance and is particularly important as far as property is concerned since it is frequently suggested that the property market is inefficient.

This chapter looks at the background to market efficiency in relation to the type of information that is relevant to establishing value.

The importance of information in assessing value

If valuations are an accurate reflection of information, then they will indicate the best way in which resources should be allocated. When you are considering factors that may influence the value of a property you are also concerned with the informational efficiency of the property market. Your investigation of the efficiency of the property market should, therefore, say something in answer to the following questions:

● What information is important in assessing value?
● What does this information say about market efficiency?
● Is it possible to earn abnormal returns by obtaining better information about individual properties or locations?

We showed in Part 1 that the most common type of valuation will consist of an expected cash flow, discounted at a rate of return that compensates for the riskiness of the property. You will estimate the expected cash flow by carrying out a detailed survey of the property and its location by reflecting your expectations concerning future potential. The rate of return used to discount the cash flows will reflect the fact that there is a trade-off between risk and return so that high-risk investments will require higher expected returns than low-risk investments. The expected rate of return you choose should also reflect the fact that the property will be valued as part of a large portfolio. This was something you learnt in Part 2.

> The expected rate of return you choose to value a property should reflect the contribution that the property makes to a large, well-diversified portfolio. This principle applies to all risky assets.

Because investors generally combine assets into portfolios they try to diversify away as much of the risk of holding those assets individually. They cannot expect, therefore, to be compensated for the risk they can eliminate, only that risk which remains after diversification. We discussed the importance of this in Chapter 10 and showed that it was the risk that remained after diversification that was important in deciding the rate of return used to discount the cash flows. The notion of considering risk in a portfolio sense is a fundamental concept that applies to all risky assets.

We showed in Chapter 3 that valuations can cover a number of situations that differ in relation to the information that is used, the most common being the *open market valuation*. This is just the present value of the expected cash flows discounted at a rate of interest that reflects the riskiness of the property.

Let's assume that your job is to value a property at regular intervals. Whether or not you realise it, you are concerned with the efficiency of the property market and how it influences your valuation. To put this in a slightly different context, the questions you may want to ask yourself are: what information causes you to change your valuations over time, and how are the changes related to each other? To appreciate the answer to these questions you need to understand what an efficient market means.

The efficiency of the property market

A market is said to be efficient if prices reflect all known information. If valuations are a good proxy for prices, the valuations should reflect all known information. For the property market to operate efficiently all available information must be impounded into valuations.

> A market is considered to be efficient if prices reflect all known information.

We showed in Chapter 7 that as long as the market is in equilibrium valuations appear to be a good proxy for prices. In bull and bear markets there will be a difference because traders and valuers will interpret information in different ways. In the long run, however, you would expect the relationship between valuations and prices to hold.

There is a common belief among professional valuers that the property market is grossly inefficient. They argue that property has a number of characteristics that prevent it from being valued or priced in an efficient manner. For example, property:

● is lumpy
● cannot be sold in small units
● is difficult and slow to sell i.e. illiquid
● incurs high transaction costs

Although these points are important, they only affect the way the market operates. They will not necessarily have an effect on prices or values. What you are really interested in is *allocational efficiency*. In other words, if valuations are a fair reflection of what is happening in the marketplace, then they can provide correct signals for allocating investment funds. Although high trading costs will prevent the market from being *operationally efficient* this is not unique to the property market. Operational efficiency is concerned with ensuring that transactions take place smoothly and without undue delay. You know, however, that there are times when it is difficult to complete a transaction so that delays become inevitable. However, despite these imperfections it is still possible for the property market to be informationally efficient so that values and prices are a fair reflection of the trade-off between risk and return.

Why is efficiency important to the property market?

If a market is efficient, then it will be difficult to earn a return in excess of that which would compensate for the risk of the asset. This is just another way of saying that most assets are fairly priced. In terms of the security market line we introduced in Chapter 10, this means that the asset will lie on the line. Locating an asset that lies above the line will be difficult.

We showed that the security market line can be used to price assets when they are in equilibrium. This is the role of the capital asset pricing model (CAPM). However, the whole pricing structure is worthless unless markets move towards equilibrium. The ideas of efficient markets and of the capital asset pricing model are closely linked so that it is not possible to test each independently.

> Tests of efficient markets assume that markets constantly move towards new equilibrium levels.
>
> Tests of the capital asset pricing model assume that markets are efficient and in equilibrium.

Although from time to time you will see reports that the property market is inefficient this is unlikely to be consistently true. There is little empirical evidence to suggest that the property market is grossly inefficient, particularly if adjustments are made for risk and the information that is used. We will investigate this further in Chapter 16 when we examine performance measurement. On the whole it is probably safe to assume that valuers are probably doing a good job of impounding information into values.

What would happen if property markets were inefficient?

If property markets were inefficient this would imply that valuers would always be able to identify undervalued properties. Positive abnormal returns would be guaranteed.[1] There are, however, two reasons why this is unlikely to happen.

- There are high transaction costs associated with buying and selling property. On average you would expect abnormal returns to disappear after trading costs were taken into consideration.
- If property were consistently mispriced, then other investors would soon move into the market. The increase in competition would cause prices to move towards their equilibrium level, wiping out any abnormal returns.

You will observe these characteristics in many markets. However, they don't imply that you cannot earn abnormal returns, only that it is difficult. Abnormal returns are important to investors as they have a direct bearing on net present value. If you invest in an underpriced property the value of your portfolio will increase by the amount of the net present value earned. Your chances of earning abnormal returns will, however, depend on the level of efficiency and the type of information that is available.

The efficient markets hypothesis

A market is said to be efficient if it responds to all knowable information. This is known as the efficient markets hypothesis.

If the information influencing values is new, then valuations from period to period should be independent of each other. In terms of the question we posed earlier, this means that you would only change the value of a property if you had information that was not incorporated into the current valuation. Because the information is new,

---

[1] Remember that an abnormal return is just the difference between actual and expected returns.

changes in value should be random. This is often a difficult idea for valuers to accept because they frequently believe that their valuations are backward-looking and that current values are related to previous values. We looked at this in Chapter 12 and showed that if individual property values followed a random walk, then the optimal updating rule for a valuer would be to form a weighted average of comparable trans-action evidence and the most recent valuation. The process they follow is entirely logical and does not imply any flaw in methodology.

However, if individual valuations and prices were consistently wrong, it would have important consequences for property investors as they could easily create a money machine! This is a really important issue as far as property is concerned because the profile of returns that you observe from property indices has certain characteristics that obscure the true underlying returns. Let's see what this implies in practice. In Figures 13.1 and 13.2 we have plotted current returns for both the FT Property Share Index and the IPD All Property Index against returns in the previous month. In an efficient market you would not expect to see a strong relationship between current and lagged returns.

The difference is quite marked. The relationship between current and lagged returns for the FT Property Share Index appears fairly random, whereas the association is very

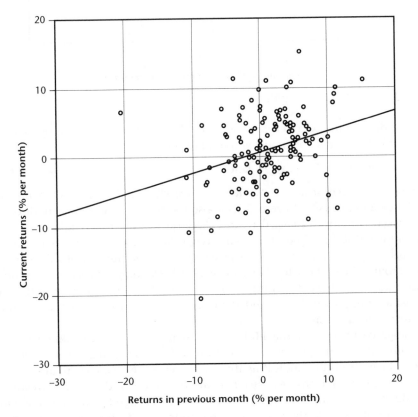

Figure 13.1 FT Property Share Index

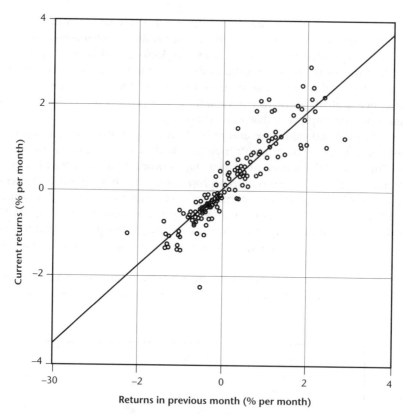

Figure 13.2 IPD All Property Index

strong for the IPD Index. You can get a better idea of what is going on by looking at some regression results. The model you need to run is:

Current Returns = $\alpha + \beta$ (Lagged Returns) + e (13.1)

If there is no relationship between successive changes in value, then the slope coefficient should be close to zero. This is also the same as the coefficient of correlation between current and lagged returns. Because you are using indexes the slope coefficient could still be up to 0.25 even though the component returns are random. This is because each index number is made up of a large number of values that are averaged round the index dates. We discussed the background to this phenomenon in Appendix 12D and showed that it can induce correlation in the returns at the index level that are not present in the underlying assets. Table 13.1 summarises the results of the regression analysis.

The slope coefficient for the FT Property Share Index is 0.30. Although this is statistically different from zero, it is indistinguishable from 0.25. The explanatory power of the model is low, indicating that lagged returns explain less than 10% of the variation in current returns. We have also shown the first-order serial correlation in the residuals and used the Q-test to check whether this is significant. In this case there is a 78% probability that the first-order serial correlation in the residuals is random.

Table 13.1 • Regression of current returns versus lagged returns: monthly data

	α	β	$\bar{R}^2$	Residuals		
				ρ_1	Q-test	Prob
FT Property Share Index	0.78	0.30	0.09	0.02	0.08	0.78
	(0.45)	(0.08)				
IPD All Property Index	0.03	0.89	0.81	−0.26	9.72	0.00
	(0.04)	(0.04)				

Standard errors are in brackets.

Taking all this information together implies that the property share market is, on the whole, efficiently priced.

If you now look at the results for the IPD All Property Index a completely different picture emerges. Here you see that the slope coefficient is 0.89. This is significantly different from both zero and 0.25. The explanatory power of the model shows that lagged returns explain over 80% of current returns. The first-order serial correlation in the residuals is –0.26 and there appears to be no probability that this is zero. Taken together this information seems to imply that the property market is grossly inefficient!

However, we showed in Appendix 12A that if valuations are sticky and there are cross-correlations between individual property returns, then a combination of these processes can induce serial correlation into an index. What you observe in a property valuation index is not what is really happening at the individual property level. With this additional piece of information you can't reject the suggestion that the underlying property market is efficient.

You will recall from Appendix 12A that this phenomenon is most acute at the monthly level. As the interval between index dates increases the stickiness in valuations begins to diminish. For example, using the sample of annual properties we analysed earlier we estimated the regression shown in Table 13.2.

With annual returns the slope coefficient is not significantly different from zero and the lagged returns now explain about 14% of the variation in current returns. The Q-test also shows that there is a 77% probability that the first-order serial correlation in the residuals is zero. Using annual returns implies that changes in valuations are independent of each other. In an efficient market this is what you would expect.

Another important point about the independence of valuations over time is that it implies that valuations are present values so that it will be difficult to consistently earn abnormal returns. These findings imply that the property market is a fair game so that investors will, on average, only be compensated for that part of total risk they cannot eliminate through diversification.

If a market is efficient it is difficult consistently to earn abnormal returns. On average, prices will reflect the risk class in which the asset lies.

Table 13.2 ● Regression of current returns versus lagged returns: annual data

	α	β	$\overline{R}^2$	Residuals ρ_1	Residuals Q-test	Residuals Prob
IPD annual returns	6.84	0.36	0.14	−0.09	0.09	0.77
	(6.08)	(0.34)				

Standard errors are in brackets.

You would expect this principle to apply irrespective of the period over which returns are measured. For example, you would not expect monthly and annual valuations to be both inefficient and efficient at the same time, otherwise it would be possible to create a money machine. We can illustrate this with the following example.

Example

Assume that you want to estimate the expected value of a property one year from today. Over the previous year the return was 15% and, based on your current forecasts, you believe that over the next year the return could be either 5% or 12%. Assume that each of these outcomes is equally likely. In an efficient market the expected increase is just the weighted average of the outcomes. In this case the expected return would be 8.5%.

If, however, the market were inefficient your calculation of return would be influenced by what happened in the previous year. Using the figures for the property market taken from Table 13.1 you could say that the return next year would be 90% of last year's return. In this case it would be 13.5%, i.e. 15.0% × 0.90. However, the regression model also indicated that lagged returns only explained about 80% of current returns. The remaining 20% would come from other factors. We will assume that in this case it would be made up from the expected random change of 1.70%, i.e. 8.50% × 0.2. The total expected return over next year would, therefore, be 12.50%. This is made up from (13.50% × 0.80) + (8.50% × 0.20). We have summarised the outcome of each option in Table 13.3.

Because of inefficiencies in the market you have earned an additional return of 4%. In other market environments the gain may be more or less. The main point is that the expected outcome in this example is closely related to what happened in the previous year.

If the current value of your property were £1,000,000 you would expect the value next year, in an efficient market, to be £1,085,000. In an inefficient market the expected value would be £1,125,000. If the market were inefficient it would imply that you could be 80% certain that the return next year would be 13.50%. With the odds stacked heavily in your favour you could soon create a money machine. Unfortunately, markets don't seem to work this way!

Table 13.3 ● Expected outcome in efficient and inefficient markets

	Return in previous year	Weighting	Return next year	Probability	Weighted return	Expected return
Efficient market	15.00%	0.00	0.00%	0.00	0.00%	
			5.00%	0.50	2.50%	
			12.00%	0.50	6.00%	8.50%
Inefficient market	15.00%	0.90	13.50%	0.80	10.80%	
			8.50%	0.20	1.70%	12.50%
Inefficiency 'gain'						4.00%

Let's look at this example in a slightly different way and assume that investors know that the property market is, in fact, efficient. The correct equilibrium price for your property at the end of the year is, therefore, £1,085,000. If you tried to sell at your inefficient value of £1,125,000 it would be regarded as being overvalued, would attract little interest and stay on the market until equilibrium prices caught up. You can work out how long this is likely to be from a simple present value calculation. Using the expected return of 8.5% the present value of the inefficient value should be equal to the efficient value if normal market conditions prevailed. You can solve for the number of periods before this happens as follows:

$$£1,085,000 = \frac{£1,125,000}{(1.085)^n}$$

Rearranging and taking logs gives:

$$n\log(1.085) = \log(1.037)$$

$$n = 0.44 \text{ years}$$

Assuming that market conditions remain unchanged it would take just over five months for the property to sell.

Let's now look at a slightly different case and assume that you are very keen to sell your property, so that at the end of the year you put it on the market at its original value of £1,000,000. The market would now view your property as being undervalued because it is less than the equilibrium figure of £1,085,000. However, as there is no central marketplace for property it may take a little time before investors realise that the property is underpriced. There is therefore a cost in terms of both time and money associated with trying to locate undervalued properties. Parts of the search costs arise from the fact that professional valuers do not use concepts such as equilibrium value so there is no reference point against which to decide whether a property is under- or overvalued. They tend to offer advice that is largely based on yields. As this is not an explicit equilibrium concept the advice is just as likely to be right as wrong. You will see, therefore, that identifying underpriced properties is likely to be an expensive business, particularly if they are in short supply. For our present value model to work in this case the difference in values would be taken up by search costs. In absolute terms this amounts to £85,000 and would have to cover both research and transaction costs.

An alternative way of looking at this is to find out how long it would take before the value would have to be changed so that it is no longer underpriced. This is also a search cost, but it is now expressed in terms of time and can be solved with the following present value model:

$$£1,085,000 = \frac{£1,000,000}{(1.085)^n}$$

$$n\log(1.085) = \log(0.922)$$

$$n = -0.995 \text{ years, or } -11.9 \text{ months}$$

The negative sign just tells you that in the absence of any other information it could take almost 12 months to locate this property. In practice the period would probably be much less than this if there were a number of buyers actively researching potential opportunities and information is readily available. In an active market potential buyers will bid against each other until the price rises to a point where the search costs disappear.

This is just one example of how the market responds to inefficiencies and adjusts in response to changes in information. There are, of course, other cases that relate to different forms of efficiency. We will discuss these shortly. What is important to appreciate is that markets move in and out of equilibrium so there may be times when some properties appear to be under- or overvalued. If it is possible to identify when this occurs, it may be possible to earn abnormal returns. The difficulty is being able to do this consistently.

> The efficient markets hypothesis does not imply that it is impossible to earn abnormal returns. However, it does imply that abnormal returns cannot be earned consistently from period to period.

If the property market were grossly inefficient all investors would want to buy property because abnormal returns would be guaranteed, and other investment sectors would be abandoned in favour of property. Clearly this doesn't happen, and the reason is probably because the market recognises that, despite what is implied by commercial indices, property is probably fairly valued.

Capitalising on information

If you look at these issues from another point of view and you believe that property markets are completely efficient, then it would be impossible to earn abnormal returns. Without the possibility of being able to do this there would be no incentive to acquire costly information because properties selected at random would generate returns that compensated for their risk.

Markets are not, however, completely efficient. There will always be some mispricing so that abnormal returns can be earned. Finding mispriced properties will not be easy and will also be expensive. However, if investors can capitalise on information, then they may be able to earn abnormal returns. This does, however, require the use of valuation models that are capable of processing information in a useful manner.

Why do you need property valuation models?

It is at this point that the role of valuation models must be questioned. Why, for example, are they needed? In an efficient market the process of buying and selling properties should generate sufficient information which, together with the valuer's experience and knowledge of the properties concerned, should enable current market values to be assessed. Two ideas suggest themselves:

- Valuation models are needed because they formalise the process by which value is assessed and identify the critical factors. They draw on information in the market-place and define the economic relationship between critical variables.
- Valuation models are needed to establish equilibrium market values, which can then be used to determine whether a property is under- or overvalued.

The second suggestion is probably the most important. Clearly, if you can identify a value for a property that reflects current market conditions, and a property is offered for sale below this equilibrium value, then, if bought, the property should generate a rate of return higher than required to compensate for its level of risk. This information would be of immense benefit to property investors. The valuation model is, therefore, trying to identify equilibrium values.

> The main role of valuation models is to estimate equilibrium market values against which the potential sales price of a property can be compared. Any difference between the figures would signal the possibility of earning an abnormal return.

The best estimates of equilibrium value will depend on the quality of information available. Abnormal returns can be earned only by acquiring better information than other investors. By utilising costly information it may be possible to outperform those investors who do not have access to similar information. This outperformance will be more pronounced at the gross level. The critical issue, of course, is whether abnormal returns can be earned net of costs. If by better analysis it is possible to locate properties that are undervalued, then it should be possible to earn abnormal returns. After taking costs into consideration the advantage may be eroded although these principles will still remain valid.

This idea is both simple and compelling and implies that professional property firms are really operating in the information business. However, until the mid-1980s it was common practice for many firms to discard information that had research value. This attitude changed with the widespread use of low-cost computers. In addition, a number of firms established a research function to provide background information and strategic advice. Although the idea is sound, simple economics suggests that the cost of undertaking research has to be less than the potential gains that could be earned by identifying undervalued properties, otherwise the research group could not remain viable. Without some form of equilibrium valuation model this, however, is difficult to quantify. Many research groups now offer other consultancy services or provide promotional material based on surveys. The collapse of the property market in the early 1990s saw a reduction in the size of some research groups and the establishment of independent organisations.

One implication of understanding market efficiency and property valuation is that firms offering property investment advice are really in the information business.

Different forms of market efficiency

So far we have discussed market efficiency in general terms. There are, however, different versions of the efficient market hypothesis that depend on the amount of information contained in market values and prices. Because property is infrequently traded valuations assume greater importance in the marketplace and this has a direct bearing on the efficient allocation of funds. We showed earlier that when the market is in equilibrium, valuations are a good proxy for prices. Tests of market efficiency are also tests of how good valuers are at impounding new information into valuations.

A market is said to be efficient if prices fully and instantaneously reflect all available, relevant information. The price at which an asset will trade will, therefore, be an accurate signal for capital allocation. Although the emphasis in the property market must switch from prices to valuations it is nevertheless essential to know whether valuations are efficient. If there are significant differences between prices and valuations this could signal the conditions under which an investor could earn excess returns.

The conditions necessary for an efficient market can be contrasted with those of a perfect market, in which case the following conditions must hold:

● Markets must be frictionless, i.e. there should be no transaction costs or taxes, and all assets must be perfectly divisible and marketable.
● Information should be costless and received simultaneously by all individuals.
● All investors should be rational and depending on their risk preferences prefer more return to less.

If a perfect market exists, then it will be both allocationally and operationally efficient. In other words, funds will be distributed in an optimal manner without cost.

The idea of a perfect market is, of course, very restrictive and generally not essential to ensure that the market is efficient. For example, a market can still be efficient even if it involves transaction costs and assets cannot be split into small parts. In addition, a market may exhibit imperfect competition yet still be efficient. Similarly the existence of costless information is not necessarily a precondition for market efficiency.

These points are, of course, important as far as property is concerned because its lumpiness prevents investors from acquiring a small proportion of the equity of a property other than through some other product such as a property bond or a unit trust. In addition, transaction and marketing costs for property tend to be relatively high, and this prevents frequent trading. These factors will mean that the property market is imperfect but this does not imply that it is inefficient.

Fama (1970) formalised the process of testing for market efficiency in relation to the level of available information, based on the following three forms suggested by Roberts (1967):

- **Weak form efficiency**: no investor can earn excess returns from trading rules based on a past series of prices
- **Semi-strong form efficiency**: no investor can earn excess returns from trading rules based on publicly available information
- **Strong form efficiency**: no investor can earn excess returns from any information whether publicly available or not.

Note that each of these has been written in terms of a trading rule. The idea is that abnormal returns are only possible by exploiting different levels of information. The efficient markets hypothesis suggests that this is likely to be difficult. We will look at some of the evidence in the appendices, but for the moment we will focus on what these different forms of efficiency mean for property investors.

Weak form efficiency

A market is said to be weak form efficient if its prices reflect all historic market information. In property terms this means that all historic information about the location of a building, its quality, type of tenant, lease structure, and so on are already incorporated into the current value. Historic information has no further value, as it cannot be exploited to earn abnormal returns. So if you are given a time-series of values for a property you cannot use this to forecast what the future value is likely to

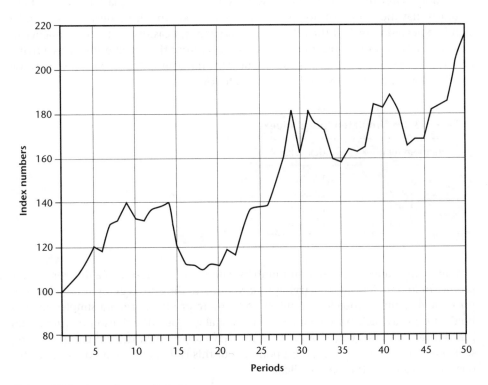

Figure 13.3 A random walk index

be. We have already suggested that the reason for this is that values will only change in response to new information. Even if you see patterns emerging in the sequence of valuations this is just the cumulative effect of incorporating new information. Take a look at Figure 13.3.

This could represent the pattern of a regularly valued property. It appears to have picked up some cycles in the market and by the time you have got to period 50 it looks as though its value will carry on rising. Although this illustration appears to have picked up market cycles around a rising trend it has nothing to do with any investment asset whatsoever. We constructed this index by plotting the cumulative effect of a series of random numbers. The way we have done this is as follows. Prices should only change if new information becomes available. The current price, P_t, of an asset will, therefore, be equal to its previous price, P_{t-1}, plus a random amount, e_t, representing the impact of new information. You can write this as follows:

$$P_t = P_{t-1} + e_t \tag{13.2}$$

If the prices are in log form then the difference between them would be equal to the rate of return:

$$P_t - P_{t-1} = e_t = r_t \tag{13.3}$$

One important implication of equation 13.3 is that the rate of return is equal to the random term. It follows that in an efficient market the sequence of returns must also be random. We will return to this issue in Appendix 13A. In equation 13.2 we have assumed that the error term follows a normal distribution with a mean of zero and a standard deviation of 5. If the first price is 100 you can easily construct a sequence of new prices. For example, our first random drawing from the distribution gives a figure of 4.452 so the next price is 104.452. If you continue this process you can summarise the first few numbers of our 'price' index as follows:

Table 13.4 ● Simulated 'price' index

Random number	Index value
	100.000
4.452	104.452
2.562	107.128
5.270	112.773

A different sequence of random numbers will, of course, result in a different index profile. In an efficient market trying to develop a trading strategy by using charts of price movements is, therefore, unlikely to be more profitable than a simple buy and hold strategy, as each price change is unpredictable. You should also note the cycles that appear in our sequence of prices. These have arisen even though the underlying sequence is random. The important point about this is that although cycles occur this does not mean that they are predictable.

If cycles were predictable then it would be possible to earn superior returns by trading on the basis of those cycles. However, if they were really predictable they would almost certainly self-destruct as investors recognised that there was an upswing in the market and would begin to bid up prices. The excess demand would soon eliminate the opportunity to earn abnormal returns as prices once again move towards their equilibrium value.

If there is a lot of competition in the market then property prices will reflect their true value. By this we mean that prices will incorporate all relevant information available to investors at the time they are agreed. There is nothing in this that suggests valuers should be trying to forecast future market prices. In an efficient market this would not be possible. Having said this the RICS introduced a valuation concept known as the *Estimated Realisation Price* that is intended to do just this. Given that it takes some months to sell a property, valuers are required to estimate what they believe a property would sell for several months in the future. If the market only exhibits a small degree of efficiency, then it is unlikely that this form of valuation will survive, as valuers are unlikely to take on the role of fortune-tellers.

Current evidence suggests that the property market is weak form efficient. This means that it is impossible to earn abnormal returns by developing a trading strategy based on trying to follow market trends. This approach is known as *technical analysis* and relies on following charts that plot market movements. In a weak form efficient market this approach is worthless as a tool for improving investment strategy.

Semi-strong form efficiency

A market is said to be semi-strong form efficient if prices fully reflect all public information. This would include all published reports including financial statements, newspaper reports, government statements and any other market data. A good example of this in the property market would be a planning authority decision to change the use of some land. Once the public is aware of this information it should be immediately reflected in land values.

The underlying principle behind semi-strong form market efficiency is that the market may have got it wrong so prices do not fully reflect all public information. If this is true, then in-depth research of a market, known as *fundamental analysis*, should identify mispriced properties. However, the cost of undertaking the research may be so high that the possibility of earning abnormal returns may quickly disappear. If the market is semi-strong form efficient, then all this information is already incorporated into prices.

An example of public information made available through the property press is that relating to reversionary sales. This is a property that is for sale under a current lease agreement that has an imminent reversion to its full market rental. This type of property is very popular and some commentators have suggested that the reason for this is because they are always undervalued. It is not clear, however, whether the term *undervalued* implies any trade-off between risk and return although the implication is that purchase of these properties would lead to abnormal returns. If, however, the market is semi-strong form efficient, then information concerning the reversions should have been incorporated into prices. There may have been some cases of mispricing taking place, but it is hard to believe that in a reasonably competitive market reversionary properties remain consistently undervalued for long periods.

Research in the USA (Linneman 1986) using the physical characteristics of residential properties as proxies for current public information found that the market was semi-strong form efficient after transactions costs were taken into consideration.

Strong form efficiency

A market is strong form efficient if prices reflect all information, both public and private. Private information refers to information that is known to only a few people. The most obvious example would be individuals with inside information who are able to exploit this to their own advantage. If the market is strong form efficient, then prices should already reflect this information. The evidence from the securities market suggests that it is probably inefficient at this level, but bear in mind that acting on insider information is illegal so the costs associated with this activity are quite substantial.

Acting on privileged information in the property market is not, in most cases, illegal. An individual who buys a site knowing that the local authority are planning to change its use to a higher value can legitimately capitalise on that information. However, once this information is publicly known the change in value will be quickly incorporated into the value of all subsequent sales.

Oliver Marriott (1969) in *The Property Boom* records an interesting example of how a 1960s developer exploited a situation similar to this. The Euston Centre in London involved redeveloping a site for office use. However, because the local authority wanted to build an underpass on part of the land on which they had previously granted outline planning consent for office use, it became possible for the developer to increase the density of development beyond what would normally have been agreed. However, the problem that the developer faced was that he didn't own all the land. With the prospect of a successful planning consent being widely known it would be easy for small landowners to hold the developer to ransom. Stock Conversion was the developer and Joe Levy, a director and estate agent acting for the company, got round this problem by forming a consortium of estate agents.

> He knew that if his firm alone were to attempt to buy from all the many different owners, freeholders, leaseholders and sub-leaseholders, his intention might become apparent and there would be two great dangers. Owners might dream up an exaggerated idea of the value, to him, of their properties or some small-time property dealers might compete against him in order to hold him to ransom. In either case his ultimate profit on the redevelopment could be either sharply slimmed down or wiped out entirely. Levy brought in three other agents to help his strategy.
> (*The Property Boom*, 1969)

It took four years to acquire the site and at no time did a notice board get erected indicating that only one developer was involved. Because of the unique situation surrounding this development Stock Conversion was able to capitalise on information that was available to only a few people. However, prices did vary wildly. In one case Levy bought two adjoining semi-derelict cottages that were worth about £1,000 each. One was bought for £1,800 and the other for £45,000!

The low prices could only be secured when information about development was not publicly known. Although this is equivalent to insider information there is no guarantee that the developer could always earn an abnormal return so that the market could still be efficient, even at the strong form level. In the case of the Euston Centre much of the profit that was earned was due to a substantial increase in rental values that took place before the development was completed. Had this not happened the profit might have been less substantial.

There are a number of examples in property where a change in use can trigger a substantial increase in land value so that a developer can earn abnormal returns by keeping information secret for as long as possible. At a less serious level a good example of this can be found in the film *Superman*. The story revolves round Lex Luthor acquiring cheap land on the eastern side of the San Andreas fault in California. In order to increase its value Lex Luthor planted a series of atomic bombs along the fault line with the intention of eliminating the existing coastline. Had he been successful the land he had bought would have become the new West Coast of America and land values would have soared. He was able to buy the land cheaply because only he knew about the potential change in land value. Fortunately, Superman also spotted his plan and was able to save the day. You may have thought that *Superman* was just an entertaining film. However, it was really a case study in strong form market efficiency in the property market and how difficult it is to make abnormal returns.

Gaylon Greer undertook the only formal test of strong form efficiency in 1974 using a sample of real estate agents with inside information. The research was based on data from 135 transactions between 1968 and 1973 and investigated whether a group of traders with advance information about forthcoming property sales were able to earn abnormal returns. Using the efficient markets model this study rejected the hypothesis that the real estate market was inefficient.

General conclusions about market efficiency

Because of its importance to investors it is not surprising that, in the securities literature, more papers have been written on market efficiency than any other area of financial economics. Evidence in real estate markets is less prolific but is growing. An excellent review of current research and issues can be found in Gatzlaff and Tirtiroglu (1995).

The evidence from both the USA and UK suggests that property markets have some inefficiencies, but the costs of locating mispriced assets are likely to wipe out any potential gains. The greatest benefits for investors are likely to come at the strong form level although the costs of securing the benefits are likely to account for a significant proportion of any profits. On average investors are probably compensated for the risks they are taking on.

> Trying to consistently locate underpriced properties is a bit like taking part in a lottery – it is a game worth winning but not necessarily a game worth playing.

Despite the evidence in support of market efficiency it is still common to see anecdotal reports, usually from valuers, suggesting that the property market is grossly inefficient. Many of these are based on single transactions with no reference to risk. However, the real test of whether this view is *correct* is to analyse the performance of publicly traded portfolios such as property bonds and property companies. If those valuers are correct, then the performance of property portfolios should record consistent abnormal performance. We look at this issue in Chapter 16 when we cover performance measurement. However, it will probably come as no surprise to know that our results show no evidence of significant abnormal returns.

There is an interesting paradox in the view taken by valuers. If they really believe the market is grossly inefficient this also implies that they are unable to process relevant information when estimating values. The more they argue that the market is inefficient the less credibility they are giving to the valuation profession.

Asset pricing and market efficiency

We mentioned earlier that there is a relationship between the capital asset pricing model, CAPM, and the efficient markets hypothesis, EMH. If relevant information is efficiently impounded into asset prices, then the CAPM can be used to determine the correct expected rate of return. If, however, the CAPM identifies that an asset is under- or overpriced, this raises questions as to why this should be the case. It may be due to information not being fully incorporated into prices. Alternatively, there may be a number of important behavioural factors that have an influence on price. Our discussion on sticky prices in Appendix 12A showed that the combination of a number of different valuation practices could easily induce high serial correlation into a time-series of returns. This is clearly a behavioural issue and a simple test of market efficiency would reject the belief that the market was efficient at the weak form level.

A number of researchers are beginning to look into these issues and it should be possible to develop a link between behavioural psychology and finance that could offer significant insights into the way valuations and prices are formed in property markets. (See, for example, Arrow 1982; DeBondt and Thaler 1985, 1987; Levy 1998; Shiller 1984, 1986, 1990; Shefrin and Statman 1985.)

Summary

Market efficiency is one of the most important ideas in finance. It is concerned with how information is incorporated into values and prices. In an efficient market, prices will reflect all knowable information so that it is difficult to earn abnormal returns. Although there is a widespread belief that property markets are inefficient the real test of this view is whether property investors can earn abnormal returns consistently over many periods. The evidence suggests that this is not the case.

The efficient market hypothesis comes in three forms: weak form, semi-strong form and strong form. In each case the set of information becomes more stringent. There is probably a case to be made for believing that the property market is inefficient at the strong form level, but at present there is insufficient evidence to support or reject this belief.

This chapter has two appendices that deal with more advanced topics.

Appendix 13A: Fair game, martingale and random walk models

In this appendix we introduce you to the basic forms of model that describe the way asset returns evolve. These models are frequently drawn upon when tests of market efficiency are being undertaken.

Appendix 13B: Tests of weak form market efficiency

In this appendix we undertake a test of weak form market efficiency of the UK property market. This is probably the easiest test to carry out and has direct relevance to those financial institutions that hold property as a long-term investment.

Chapter 13: Summary table

1. Market efficiency is one of the most important ideas in finance and is concerned with the way information is impounded into prices. In property you have to focus on valuations but the same principles apply.

2. Although property is lumpy, difficult to sell and incurs high transaction costs, this does not imply that valuations are informationally inefficient. This just highlights the difference between operational efficiency and allocational or informational efficiency.

3. It is common for valuers to argue that the property market is inefficient. There is, however, no compelling evidence to believe that this is true. The real test of inefficiency is whether investors can consistently earn abnormal returns.

4. The efficient markets hypothesis has three forms:
   ● weak form efficiency
   ● semi-strong form efficiency
   ● strong form efficiency
   At each level of efficiency the information set used to form valuations and prices becomes more stringent.

5. The property market is more likely to be inefficient at the strong form level as property investors may be able to capitalise on private information. There is, however, limited information available to analyse this issue.

6. In an efficient market valuation models are not required. Prices will reach their equilibrium level through the process of buying and selling. The role of valuation models is to identify equilibrium market values. If the model is successful the equilibrium values can be used to establish whether a property is under- or over-priced.

7. An important implication of market efficiency is to recognise that professional property firms are really in the information business. The better their information systems the better their advice.

Problems

1. What do you understand by the term 'efficient markets'?

2. What are the characteristics of the property market that make it operationally inefficient?

3. What is the relevance of valuation models in an efficient market?

4. Name the three types of market efficiency and explain their relevance to the property market.

5. Does the evidence suggest that property markets are grossly inefficient?

6. If the property market is inefficient what would this imply for investors in property?

7. Are there situations in which it would be possible for investors in property to earn abnormal returns?

Selected references

Arrow, K.J. (1982) Risk perceptions in psychology and economics. *Economic Enquiry* **4**, 1–19.

Brown, G.R. (1985) The information content of property valuations. *Journal of Valuation* **3** (4), 350–62.

DeBondt, F.M. and Thaler, R. (1985) Does the stock market overreact? *Journal of Finance* **40**, 793–805.

Fama, E.F. (1970) Efficient capital markets: A review of theory and empirical work. *Journal of Finance* **XXV** (2), 383–417.

Fama, E.F., Fisher, L., Jensen, M.C. and Roll, R. (1969) The adjustment of stock prices to new information. *International Economic Review* **X** (1), 1–21.

Gatzlaff, D.H. and Tirtiroglu, D. (1995) Real estate market efficiency: Issues and evidence. *Journal of Real Estate Literature* **3** (2).

Gau, G. (1984) Weak form tests of the efficiency of real estate investment markets. *The Financial Review* **19** (4), 301–20.

Greer, G. (1974) Risk, return and efficiency in the market for real property. University of Colorado, PhD.

Hendershott, P. (1998) Equilibrium models in real estate research: A survey. *Journal of Real Estate Literature* **6**, 13–25.

Jensen, M.C. and Bennington, G.A. (1970) Random walks and technical theories: Some additional evidence. *Journal of Finance* **XXV** (2), 469–82.

Levy, D.S. (1998) Client influence on reported values. University of Auckland, Paper presented at the RICS Cutting Edge, Property Research Conference, De Montfort University, UK.

Marriot, O. (1969) *The Property Boom*, Pan Books, London.

Pines, H.A. (1983) The psychology of investor decision making. *AAII Journal* **5** (September), 10–17.

Quigley, J. and Van Order, R. (1990) Efficiency in the mortgage market: The borrower's perspective. *AREUEA Journal* **18**, 237–52.

Roberts, H. (1959) Stock market patterns and financial analysis: Methodological suggestions. *Journal of Finance* **XIV** (1), 1–10.

Roberts, H. (1967) Statistical versus clinical prediction of the stock market. Unpublished paper presented at the Seminar on the Analysis of Security Prices. University of Chicago.

Scholes, M. (1972) The market for securities: Substitution versus price pressure and the effects of information on share prices. *Journal of Business* **XLV** (2).

Shefrin, H.M. and Statman, M. (1985) The disposition to sell winners too early and ride losers too long: Theory and evidence. *Journal of Finance* **40**, 777–90.

Shiller, R. (1981) The use of volatility measures in assessing market efficiency. *Journal of Finance* **36**, 291–304.

Shiller, R. (1990) Market volatility and investor behaviour. *American Economic Review* **80** (58), 62, Papers and proceedings.

Shiller, R. (1992) Volatility in the US and Japanese stock markets. *Journal of Applied Corporate Finance* **5** (Spring), 4–35.

Skantz, T.R. and Strickland, T.H. (1987) Efficient markets in real estate. *Journal of Real Estate Research* **2**, 75–83.

Appendix 13A
Fair game, martingale and random walk models

The idea that an efficient market reflects all information is so general that it is not testable. In order to formalise the information content of prices Fama (1970) classified efficient markets into fair game, martingale and random walk models, the last being special cases of fair game models.

The fair game model

The basic idea behind a fair game model is that the return on an asset is a function of its risk. This can be expressed as:

$$e_{j,t+1} = r_{j,t+1} - E(r_{j,t+1}|\phi_t)$$
(13A.1)

where

$e_{j,t+1}$ = difference between actual and expected return
$r_{j,t+1}$ = return on asset j from period t to $t+1$
ϕ_t = information set available at time t.

The expected value of the difference is zero:

$$e_{j,t+1} = E[r_{j,t+1} - E(r_{j,t+1}|\phi_t)] = 0$$
(13A.2)

For a fair game to exist on average across a large sample, the expected return on an asset must equal its actual return. This does not imply that returns are positive, but it does imply that expectations are not biased.

The martingale and submartingale

A popular model used for testing the efficient markets hypothesis is the martingale. If returns follow a stochastic process it will be a martingale if:

$$E(r_{j,t+1}|\phi_t) = r_{j,t}$$
(13A.3)

This implies that the best forecast of $r_{j,t+1}$ is $r_{j,t}$, given the relevant information set available at time t. If, however,

$$E(r_{j,t+1}|\phi_t) > r_{j,t}$$
(13A.4)

then the returns process becomes a submartingale.
Substituting equation 13A.3 into 13A.2 gives:

$$e_{j,t+1} = E(r_{j,t+1} - r_{j,t}) = 0$$
(13A.5)

A sequence of returns is considered to be a martingale only if $e_{j,t+1} = 0$ is a fair game. The returns on assets will be a fair game if the present value of a series of prices and dividends is a martingale.

The random walk model

By contrast, the random walk model implies that there is no difference between a distribution of returns conditional on a subset of information and an unconditional distribution. In returns form this can be written as:

$$f(r_{j,t+1}|\phi_t) = f(r_{j,t+1}) \tag{13A.6}$$

A random walk requires much more stringent conditions than fair game or martingale models because the returns are expected to be the same with or without the information set. If returns follow a random walk, then the mean of the underlying distribution does not change over time and a fair game results.

The empirical implication of a random walk is that all returns are independent drawings taken from the same distribution. Thus a random walk requires the serial correlation between returns to be zero for all lags. However, evidence of significant serial correlation is not inconsistent with a fair game.

Arising from these concepts are two important ideas:

1. Prices follow a martingale if markets are efficient.
2. If asset returns follow a fair game then prices are the present value of expected future cash flows.

This second point is shown in the following sections that have been adapted from Gatzlaff and Tirtiroglu (1995).

Prices follow a martingale

You can write the total return on an asset between periods $t–1$ and t in terms of its price, P, and income received, a, as follows:

$$r_t = \frac{P_t + P_{t-1} + a_t}{P_{t-1}} \tag{13A.7}$$

If the market is a fair game then the expected return will equal the actual return:

$$E(r_{t+1}) = r \tag{13A.8}$$

where r is a constant return.

Substituting equation 13A.7 in 13A.8 gives:

$$E\left(\frac{P_{t+1} - P_t + a_{t+1}}{P_t}\right) = r \tag{13A.9}$$

By rearranging you can express the current price as:

$$P_t = \frac{E(P_{t+1} + a_{t+1})}{1 + r} \tag{13A.10}$$

If the market is efficient then prices will follow equation 13A.10. Note, however, that tests of market efficiency that do not include income will not imply a martingale unless the income is constant.

Prices are present values

Samuelson (1965, 1973) showed that if returns follow a fair game, then asset prices equal the present value of expected future cash flows.

From equation 13A.10 you can write the price in period $t+1$ as:

$$P_{t+1} = \frac{E(P_{t+2} + a_{t+2})}{1 + r}$$

(13A.11)

Substituting this back into equation 13A.10 gives:

$$P_t = \frac{E\left[\dfrac{E(P_{t+2} + a_{t+2})}{1 + r} + a_{t+1}\right]}{1 + r}$$

(13A.12)

By continuously repeating this process it can be shown that after n iterations the present value becomes:

$$P_t = \sum_{i=0}^{i=n} \frac{E(a_{t+i})}{(1 + r)^i} + \frac{E(P_{t+n})}{(1 + r)^n}$$

(13A.13)

At the limit the expression on the extreme right-hand side of equation 13A.13 converges to zero so you will end up with the standard present value model:

$$P_t = \sum_{i=0}^{i=n} \frac{E(a_{t+i})}{(1 + r)^i}$$

(13A.14)

This shows that in an efficient market current prices are the present value of expected future cash flows. It should be evident from this that abnormal returns can only be earned if there are inefficiencies in the market that can be exploited net of transaction costs.

Selected references

Fama, E.F. (1970) Efficient capital markets: A review of theory and empirical work. *Journal of Finance* **XXV** (2), 383–417.

Gatzlaff, D.H. and Tirtiroglu, D. (1995) Real estate market efficiency: Issues and evidence. *Journal of Real Estate Literature* **3** (2).

Samuelson, P. (1965) Proof that properly anticipated prices fluctuate randomly. *Industrial Management Review* **6**, 41–9.

Samuelson, P. (1973) Proof that properly discounted present values of assets vibrate randomly. *Bell Journal of Economics* **4**, 369–74.

Appendix 13B
Tests of weak form market efficiency

In this appendix we present the results of some tests of weak form market efficiency based on UK returns data. This is particularly important for institutional investors holding large portfolios of property. If the market were inefficient at this level it would imply that investors could create profitable trading strategies by plotting the performance of individual properties and using this information to signal a potential sale. Our interest is, therefore, in the efficiency of *individual* property returns. We will also look at the efficiency of index returns but the effects of aggregation and cross-correlation will distort our results.

Most of the empirical tests of weak form efficiency focus on the random walk. This states that changes in prices (or returns) are independent and identically distributed. This implies that there should be no relationship between current returns and previous returns. In Chapter 13 we plotted current returns for the FTA Property Share Index against returns in the previous month (see Figure 13.1) and showed that the relationship was not very strong. If you plot current returns against returns lagged by two periods, you get a similar relationship. If the market strictly followed a random walk, then you would expect the correlation between current and lagged returns to be indistinguishable from zero for all lags.

However, we also pointed out that our forecast of expected returns was based on an information set. We wrote the expected return for asset j in period $t+1$ as $E(r_{j,t+1}|\phi_t)$. In a market that is weak form efficient the information set ϕ_t is just the past sequence of returns namely, $r_{j,t}, r_{j,t-1}, r_{j,t-2}, \ldots r_{j,t-n}$. As the expected return in period $t+1$ can depend on the observed return in period t the serial correlation need not be zero. Thus serial correlation within single period returns is not inconsistent with a fair game but is inconsistent with a random walk.

Testing the random walk hypothesis for property

The random walk hypothesis described above has been tested (Brown 1985) by examining the serial correlation coefficients for a large sample of commercial properties. The serial correlation coefficient is just a more formal way of estimating the relationship between current and lagged returns. We show how you can estimate the serial correlation coefficient for different lags in Table 13B.1.

This shows a sequence of fourteen returns in the first column. In each of the other columns the series is lagged by different periods. For example, if you wanted to estimate how correlated current returns were with the returns in the previous period you would lag the returns by one period. This is shown in the column headed 1. You would then estimate the coefficient of correlation between the overlapping returns. The figure in this case is –0.06, implying a low correlation between current and lagged returns. This figure is known as the first-order serial correlation because it only involves a lag of one period. Note that you lose two observations as a result of lagging the returns. If you wanted to estimate the correlation between current returns and those lagged by three periods you would use the overlapping returns shown in the table. The coefficient in this case is –0.21 and is known as the third-order serial correlation. If you look at the overlapping parts you will see that you lose six observations, so, depending on how many observations you start with, there is clearly a limit to how far you can take this.

We use this process to estimate the serial correlation coefficients for UK commercial property over different periods.

Table 13B.1 ● Estimating serial correlation coefficients

	Original series	Order of lag 1	Order of lag 2	Order of lag 3
1	2.15			
2	0.02	2.15		
3	1.96	0.02	2.15	
4	−4.67	1.96	0.02	2.15
5	−2.53	−4.67	1.96	0.02
6	9.90	−2.53	−4.67	1.96
7	0.56	9.90	−2.53	−4.67
8	6.22	0.56	9.90	−2.53
9	0.57	6.22	0.56	9.90
10	−4.25	0.57	6.22	0.56
11	−1.99	−4.25	0.57	6.22
12	8.62	−1.99	−4.25	0.57
13	3.52	8.62	−1.99	−4.25
14	1.99	3.52	8.62	−1.99
		1.99	3.52	8.62
			1.99	3.52
				1.99
Correlation:		**−0.06**	**−0.27**	**−0.21**

January 1979 to December 1982:
Monthly, quarterly and half-yearly returns

The first UK analysis of weak form efficiency was undertaken using a sample of 135 monthly valued properties over the period January 1979 to December 1982. The sample consisted of 46 retail, 39 office and 50 industrial properties. Continuously compounded returns were computed, thus enabling returns to be obtained for periods longer than one month merely by adding returns. A summary of the average serial correlation coefficients is given in Table 13B.2.

In all cases the absolute value of the correlation coefficients is low. This would seem to imply that the property market is efficient at the weak form level. It is not a random walk but complies with the requirements of a fair game. As discounted present values follow a martingale this also provides evidence that valuations are present values.

At the portfolio level the coefficients are also small. These are summarised in Table 13B.3 for both equal-weighted and value-weighted portfolios. In this example the portfolios were constructed by combining the cash flows. The first-order figures are larger than the averages in Table 13B.2 but this can be accounted for by the effect of averaging. If the underlying series is random, the effect of averaging would result in a maximum first-order serial correlation coefficient of 0.25. None of the first-order coefficients is significantly different from 0.25.

Table 13B.2 ● Average serial correlation coefficients for each sector, January 1979 to December 1982

	Monthly						Quarterly			Half-yearly
	1	2	3	4	5	6	1	2	3	1
Retail (46)	0.027	−0.037	0.024	0.002	−0.021	0.003	−0.012	0.015	−0.021	−0.020
Office (39)	−0.027	−0.107	0.087	−0.023	0.048	−0.011	−0.077	−0.053	0.003	−0.233
Industrial (50)	−0.039	−0.003	0.041	0.004	0.009	0.016	0.017	0.005	−0.072	−0.104

Table 13B.3 ● Serial correlation coefficients for equal- and value-weighted portfolios

Equal-weighted portfolio	Monthly						Quarterly			Half-yearly
	1	2	3	4	5	6	1	2	3	1
Retail (46)	0.038	0.192	0.094	−0.153	0.069	−0.010	0.115	0.212	0.215	0.367
Office (39)	0.234	−0.162	0.188	0.032	−0.271	−0.062	−0.010	0.047	0.196	−0.161
Industrial (50)	0.375	0.364	0.244	0.057	0.098	0.148	0.266	0.090	−0.088	−0.123
PF(EW) (135)	0.346	0.096	0.220	−0.056	−0.080	0.021	0.131	0.068	0.175	−0.026

Value-weighted portfolio	Monthly						Quarterly			Half-yearly
	1	2	3	4	5	6	1	2	3	1
Retail (46)	0.274	0.223	0.175	−0.010	0.174	0.016	0.303	0.279	0.296	0.405
Office (39)	0.221	−0.094	0.009	−0.018	−0.154	0.043	−0.119	0.041	0.228	−0.051
Industrial (50)	0.184	0.213	0.187	−0.025	0.025	0.146	0.085	0.117	−0.067	−0.242
PF(VW) (135)	0.375	0.108	0.165	−0.017	0.033	0.094	0.104	0.119	0.248	0.053

From these results it would appear that there is little dependence between successive changes in property valuation. What evidence there is, is insufficient to enable an investor to construct a profitable trading strategy based on a time-series examination of property valuations, assuming that valuations are a good proxy for traded prices.

December 1987 to November 1992:
Monthly and quarterly results

The results above represent the first test of market efficiency based on a reliable sample of property data. Since that time more extensive databases have become available and it is now possible to provide more up-to-date results. In this section we cover the period December 1987 to November 1992 and in the following section, December 1992 to November 1997.

Table 13B.4 ● Average correlation coefficients, December 1987 to November 1992

	Monthly						Quarterly			
	1	2	3	4	5	6	1	2	3	4
Retail (40)	0.143	0.154	0.141	0.080	0.050	0.070	0.287	0.085	0.046	−0.051
St. Dev.	0.156	0.141	0.130	0.111	0.133	0.128	0.206	0.213	0.175	0.173
Office (30)	0.220	0.219	0.221	0.196	0.182	0.164	0.414	0.336	0.276	0.180
St. Dev.	0.152	0.127	0.147	0.143	0.142	0.149	0.228	0.219	0.238	0.243
Industrial (40)	0.191	0.171	0.204	0.163	0.136	0.127	0.394	0.283	0.212	0.064
St. Dev.	0.137	0.146	0.135	0.145	0.144	0.117	0.215	0.213	0.185	0.208
All property (100)	0.180	0.179	0.184	0.140	0.115	0.115	0.357	0.220	0.165	0.053
St. Dev.	0.153	0.141	0.141	0.141	0.150	0.137	0.223	0.242	0.222	0.227

Table 13B.5 ● Correlation coefficients for sector index returns, December 1987 to November 1992

	Monthly						Quarterly			
	1	2	3	4	5	6	1	2	3	4
Retail (40)	0.769	0.639	0.633	0.528	0.463	0.394	0.723	0.488	0.404	0.165
Office (30)	0.795	0.742	0.734	0.712	0.740	0.724	0.820	0.831	0.633	0.432
Industrial (40)	0.764	0.791	0.663	0.690	0.572	0.525	0.844	0.668	0.468	0.248
All property (100)	0.848	0.835	0.781	0.742	0.690	0.644	0.853	0.745	0.562	0.320
St. Dev.	0.122	0.120	0.118	0.116	0.114	0.112	0.197	0.186	0.175	0.164

In Table 13B.4 we summarise the average correlation coefficients for each sector of the market based on monthly and quarterly returns. We also show the standard deviation of the sample in each period to give an indication of the distribution of the coefficients. You will see that none of the coefficients is significantly different from zero. This applies to both monthly and quarterly returns.

In addition to the above we also averaged the returns in each sector to give an index of returns and re-estimated the serial correlation coefficients. These are summarised in Table 13B.5.

Averaging the returns has introduced serial correlation not present in the individual property returns. All the correlation coefficients are significantly different from zero and the first-order serial correlation coefficients are also significantly different from 0.25.

Clearly, these results differ from those for individual properties and it follows that it would be wrong to draw conclusions about the efficiency of the property market based on evidence drawn solely from index returns.

We have extended these correlation coefficients and plotted a comparison in Figure 13B.1.

Given that our main interest is in the return characteristics of individual properties this evidence also confirms that the property market is weak form efficient.

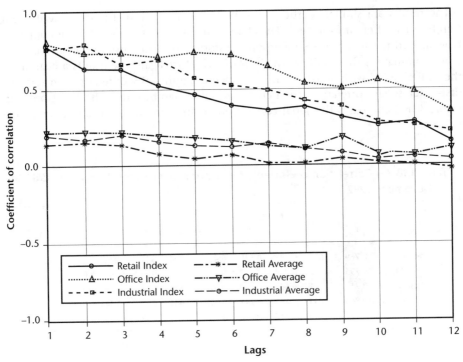

Figure 13B.1 Sample average and index serial correlation coefficients. Monthly returns from 1986 to 1992

December 1992 to November 1997: Monthly and quarterly results

The previous period covered a time when the UK property market went through a major boom in values. It is useful, therefore, to examine the following period when the UK economy was in recession, the property market collapsed and after a number of years gradually began to show signs of recovery. The average serial correlation figures are summarised in Table 13B.6.

Table 13B.6 ● Average correlation coefficients, December 1992 to November 1997

| | Monthly | | | | | | Quarterly | | | |
	1	2	3	4	5	6	1	2	3	4
Retail (40)	0.134	0.079	0.115	0.100	0.066	0.053	0.272	0.113	−0.019	−0.089
St. Dev.	*0.125*	*0.132*	*0.140*	*0.161*	*0.134*	*0.124*	*0.213*	*0.236*	*0.189*	*0.186*
Office (30)	0.227	0.169	0.150	0.072	0.095	0.038	0.277	0.048	−0.081	−0.098
St. Dev.	*0.228*	*0.160*	*0.165*	*0.147*	*0.128*	*0.115*	*0.223*	*0.204*	*0.180*	*0.272*
Industrial (40)	0.162	0.100	0.198	0.133	0.044	0.090	0.321	0.107	−0.056	−0.135
St. Dev.	*0.186*	*0.186*	*0.182*	*0.177*	*0.142*	*0.141*	*0.245*	*0.244*	*0.258*	*0.239*
All property (100)	0.170	0.113	0.150	0.101	0.068	0.060	0.288	0.092	−0.049	−0.106
St .Dev.	*0.184*	*0.163*	*0.165*	*0.163*	*0.136*	*0.129*	*0.227*	*0.231*	*0.212*	*0.231*

The results are similar to the earlier period with none of the coefficients being significantly different from zero. The change in market conditions does not appear to have altered the way valuers incorporate information into current valuations. Table 13B.7 summarises the results at the index level. Once again the results are similar to the earlier period with all the coefficients being significantly different from zero. The first-order serial correlation coefficients are also significantly different from 0.25. Figure 13B.2 compares the serial correlation coefficients for both sample and index returns.

Table 13B.7 ● Correlation coefficients for sector index returns, December 1986 to November 1992

	Monthly						Quarterly			
---	1	2	3	4	5	6	1	2	3	4
Retail (40)	0.769	0.639	0.633	0.528	0.463	0.394	0.723	0.488	0.404	0.165
Office (30)	0.795	0.742	0.734	0.712	0.740	0.724	0.820	0.831	0.633	0.432
Industrial (40)	0.764	0.791	0.663	0.690	0.572	0.525	0.844	0.668	0.468	0.248
All property (100)	0.848	0.835	0.781	0.742	0.690	0.644	0.853	0.745	0.562	0.320
St. Dev.	0.122	0.120	0.118	0.116	0.114	0.112	0.197	0.186	0.175	0.164

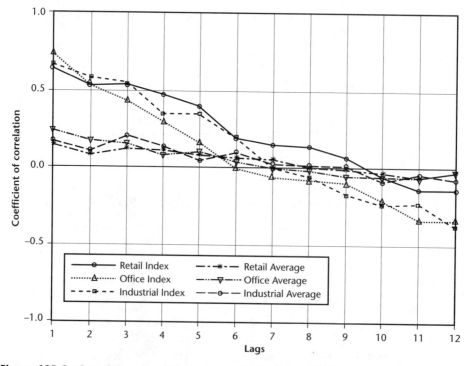

Figure 13B.2 Sample average and index serial correlation coefficients. Monthly returns from 1992 to 1997

1987 to 1996:
Annual returns

Our results so far have been based on monthly valuations and they show a consistent pattern in terms of serial correlation. However, the majority of properties are valued annually so it is essential to see whether the results we obtained with high-frequency data also apply at the annual level.

Our analysis is based on the annual returns of 250 properties from each sector of the market from 1987 to 1996. Table 13B.8 summarises the results.

Table 13B.8 ● Annual serial correlation coefficients, 1987–96

| | Annual | | | |
	1	2	3	4
Retail (250)	0.092	−0.225	−0.302	−0.149
St. Dev.	0.292	0.298	0.351	0.416
Office (250)	0.163	−0.143	−0.307	−0.160
St. Dev.	0.298	0.302	0.371	0.452
Industrial (250)	0.124	−0.144	−0.157	−0.024
St. Dev.	0.254	0.308	0.320	0.404
All property (750)	0.126	−0.171	−0.256	−0.111
St. Dev.	0.283	0.305	0.355	0.429

Once again the sample serial correlation figures for individual properties for each lag are insignificantly different from zero. When averaged into portfolios we get the results shown in Table 13B.9.

Table 13B.9 ● Annual serial correlation coefficients, 1987–96

| | Annual | | | |
	1	2	3	4
Retail (250)	0.329	−0.400	−0.611	−0.315
Office (250)	0.465	−0.225	−0.675	−0.315
Industrial (250)	0.334	−0.103	−0.203	0.041
All property (750)	0.379	−0.243	−0.537	−0.191
St. Dev.	0.237	0.211	0.184	0.158

In this case none of the first-order serial correlation coefficients is significantly different from either zero or 0.25. However, there is a significantly negative relationship between current returns and those lagged by three years. This probably reflects the severe downturn in the market that took place round about 1992–93. However, as far as developing a trading strategy is concerned the insignificant first-order serial correlation coefficient would seem to rule out the possibility that using past information is likely to result in a profitable strategy.

Conclusion

Our results have covered different time intervals and embrace seventeen years of returns. Even though we have reported monthly, quarterly and annual figures the results present a consistent picture. Changes in individual valuations appear to comply with the requirements of a fair game and are on the whole not predictable. This is good news for valuers as it implies that they are doing a good job of impounding information into valuations.

At the index level the results are mixed. Monthly and quarterly returns show strong serial dependence, but this disappears at the annual level. This finding is in line with the results that we reported earlier on sticky valuations.

Selected references

Brown, G.R. (1985) The importance of information in assessing value. *Journal of Valuation* **3** (4), 343–9.

Brown, G.R. (1991) *Property Investment and the Capital Markets*, London: Chapman & Hall.

Hedging against inflation

Introduction

Historically, property has been regarded as a good hedge against inflation and has probably formed a major part of institutional investment portfolios purely on this basis.

This chapter considers this important aspect of property and investigates the tests that need to be carried out in order to establish whether property adequately hedges against inflation and performs better or worse than other assets. There have been a number of studies in the USA that have dealt with this issue and there is a growing body of literature in the UK.

The development of inflation

The evidence suggests that there is no single cause for inflation. There are, however, some initiating influences on the demand and supply side that can be seen to contribute to the development of an inflationary economy. If, for example, the demand for goods and services exceeds supply then prices will be bid up. In this case the direction of cause is from demand to inflation. In other words there is too much money chasing too few goods. A good example of this occurred in 1922 when the German Central Bank printed billions of paper marks, which then went into circulation chasing too few goods. Prices rose causing *demand-pull* inflation with a vengeance.

This is essentially the monetarist view of inflation, which anticipates a continuous inflationary spiral if the quantity of money is increased as prices rise. Not surprisingly, the monetarist cure is to restrict the money supply as prices rise-maintaining its increase at a rate appropriate for the real rate of growth of the economy.

Inflation can, however, also be started on the supply side, causing what is known as *cost-push* inflation. An example of this was the five-fold increase in oil prices in 1973–74 which triggered world-wide inflation. Cost-push inflation usually follows from demand-pull. Once prices start to rise trade unions seek compensating wage rises related not only to current increases but also to the expectation of future price rises. Prices are, therefore, bid up.

In simple terms this is what causes inflation although it is difficult to distinguish between the two effects.

As far as capital assets are concerned – and this includes property – inflation will have the effect of increasing the monetary value of future earnings or rents, which will in turn be reflected in capital values. Clearly some assets will respond better to inflation than others. From the investors' point of view there is a need to protect the purchasing power of savings so they will try to seek out those assets which will provide a hedge against inflation. Institutional investors are also aware of this problem as they have a long-term liability to maintain the real value of personal pensions.

To determine which assets are hedges against inflation it is necessary to understand what an inflation hedge means.

Hedging against inflation

One of the common areas of confusion that students experience when discussing inflation hedges is the difference between high real rates of return and hedging against inflation. We can illustrate the difference with a simple example. Assume, for example, that you invest in two assets, A and B, over the ten-year period 1989–98. The returns on each asset, together with the rate of inflation, are given in Table 14.1.

The asset returns are in nominal terms as they incorporate the effects of inflation. If you look at the time-series of returns you will see that Asset B has outperformed Asset A and is much less volatile. You are also interested to know how these assets have performed in real terms, as one of the reasons for investing in these assets was to protect the purchasing power of your fund.

We showed in Part 1 that the relationship between nominal returns and real returns can be expressed as:

$$1 + r_n = (1 + r_r)(1 + \Delta) \tag{14.1}$$

where r_n is the nominal return, r_r is the real rate of return and Δ represents the rate of inflation.

Table 14.1 ● Asset returns and inflation

Year	Asset A	Asset B	Inflation
1989	6.00	15.00	6.75
1990	7.00	14.00	7.68
1991	11.00	13.00	9.31
1992	2.00	15.50	4.45
1993	2.00	16.00	2.57
1994	−1.00	11.00	1.93
1995	5.00	15.00	6.18
1996	3.00	13.00	2.45
1997	4.00	12.00	3.62
1998	3.00	14.20	2.87
Average	4.20	13.87	4.78
St. Dev.	3.29	1.60	2.55

Table 14.2 ● Real returns for Assets A and B

Year	Asset A	Asset B
1989	−0.70	7.73
1990	−0.63	5.87
1991	1.55	3.38
1992	−2.35	10.58
1993	−0.56	13.09
1994	−2.87	8.90
1995	−1.11	8.31
1996	0.54	10.30
1997	0.37	8.09
1998	0.13	11.01
Average	−0.56	8.72
St. Dev.	1.33	2.76

By rearranging equation 14.1 you can find the real rate of return in each period. For example, the real return on Asset A in period 1 can be estimated as follows:

$$r_r = \frac{1 + r_n}{1 + \Delta} - 1 = \frac{1.0600}{1.0675} - 1 = -0.0070 = -0.70\%$$

We have summarised the real returns for Assets A and B in Table 14.2.

Although Asset B still outperforms Asset A, its standard deviation of returns now exceeds A's. The lower variation in the real returns of Asset A means that you can be more certain about the actual outcome. There is, however, a lot of uncertainty in the real returns of Asset B. You can see why this is the case in Figures 14.1a and 14.1b.

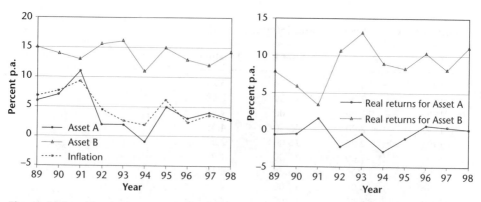

Figure 14.1a Nominal returns and inflation   **Figure 14.1b** Real returns

Figure 14.1a shows that over the period 1989–98 the nominal returns for Asset A move in line with the rate of inflation, whereas Asset B shows much less variability. The close relationship between the returns on Asset A and inflation implies that it is hedging against changes in the rate of inflation. The difference between the rate of inflation and the returns on Asset A has much less variability. You can see this in Figure 14.1b, which plots the real returns for Assets A and B over time. Asset A shows a real return that fluctuates within a narrow range round a constant value, whereas Asset B shows a lot of variation, which implies that the real return is not constant and does not, therefore, hedge against inflation.

This simple example highlights the fact that it is possible to have high average real rates of return that do not hedge against inflation. If it is important for investors to protect their purchasing power, then including assets in a portfolio that hedge against inflation will go some way towards achieving that goal.

This example also offers a simple way of visualising whether an asset hedges against inflation. Plotting the asset returns against inflation provides a good indication of how they move relative to each over time. You will see from Figures 14.2a and 14.2b that the returns on Asset A are positively correlated with inflation, whereas Asset B shows a negative relationship.

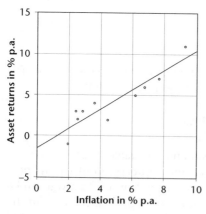

Figure 14.2a Asset A versus inflation

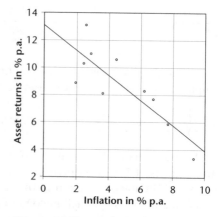

Figure 14.2b Asset B versus inflation

We will draw on this idea as we develop a test for inflation hedging.

Inflation and asset performance – the record

A broad understanding of inflation hedging can be seen by plotting an index of the retail price against similar indexes for the main asset classes. This is shown in Figure 14.3.

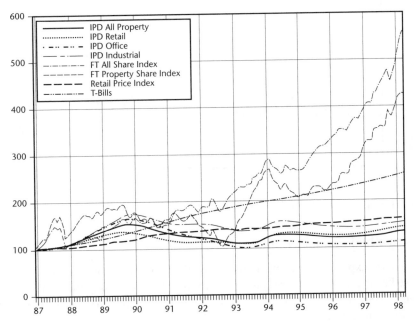

Figure 14.3 Inflation and index comparison

We have used monthly data for this graph and have included the IPD capital growth index for each sector. You should note that because the IPD monthly index is highly smoothed the profile of capital growth will not fully reflect the true volatility of monthly changes, although the general trend is valid. What is clear from this graph is that over short periods property can both outperform and underperform inflation. In the long run, however, capital values generally move in line with inflation.

When you look at the equity indexes it will be seen that in the long run both the FT All Share Index and the FT Property Share Index have outperformed inflation. It looks from these data that the equity markets are able to offer high real returns but are not a good hedge against inflation. This can be seen more clearly in Figure 14.4. Over the eleven-year period 1987–98 property has slightly underperformed inflation, whereas the other asset classes have outperformed.

Although this type of analysis is useful in terms of visualising the performance of different asset classes, it is not a reliable test of inflation hedging. The reason for this is that the results will vary depending on which data the index numbers are based. Clearly, a more rigorous approach is needed.

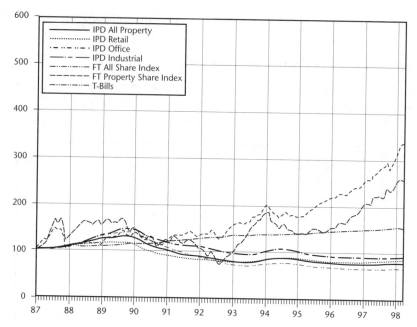

Figure 14.4 Inflation-adjusted index comparison

Defining a hedge against inflation

If returns are expressed in continuous terms, the nominal return on an asset can be expressed as the sum of the real rate of return and the rate of inflation.[1] When prices are being fixed the market will use all available information to assess each of these components in expectations form.

> Investors will fix the price of an asset at the beginning of the period so that the expected nominal return will be the sum of the appropriate expected real rate of return and the best possible assessment of expected inflation.

This relationship was first put forward by Irving Fisher in 1930. He argued that the expected real return on an asset is determined by factors such as the productivity of capital, the investor's time preference and his taste for risk. He also argued that expected real returns and expected inflation are unrelated.

This general approach to the definition of nominal returns is valid, irrespective of the period over which returns are measured. Thus, as a first attempt at getting closer to deciding whether property is a hedge against inflation, you could compare the internal rate of return of a number of portfolios back to their date of purchase with the estimated rate over the same period. The internal rates of return calculated for each portfolio take account of the initial value and current value, together with the size and timing of each of the acquisitions and cash flows for each property. The rate of return

---

[1] In discrete terms $(1 + r_n) = (1 + r_r)(1 + \Delta)$. Taking logs gives $\ln(1 + r_n) = \ln(1 + r_r) + \ln(1 + \Delta)$.

calculated in this way is money-weighted because it takes account of cash flows into and out of the portfolio. It therefore represents the return on a managed portfolio. The comparable rate of inflation is estimated from the retail price index and is found by taking index values at the same dates as the initial and current portfolio values and measuring the annual increase over the period. This is actually the time-weighted rate of return, but because there are no intermediate cash flows it will be exactly the same as the money-weighted rate of return. The two returns are, therefore, comparable.

Using this approach we estimated the internal rate of return for 27 portfolios and compared these with similar returns estimated from the retail price index over progressively longer holding periods. The data were recorded in 1983 and the oldest portfolio was 35 years. Figure 14.5 plots the results.

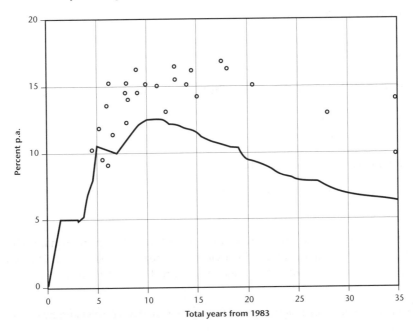

Figure 14.5 Property portfolio returns and inflation

As the nominal returns for each portfolio incorporate the effects of inflation the internal rates of return calculated for a group of portfolios should show a positive relationship with similar returns estimated for the retail price index if property is hedging against inflation. As expected, this is what happens. Almost without exception all the returns are above the retail price index line, indicating that over long periods property shows positive real rates of return. We have used the total age of the portfolios in this example. Had we used the portfolio duration, the relationship would probably be stronger.

Another way of looking at this issue is to strip out the effects of inflation from the cash flows of each of the properties in order to arrive at a cash flow in real terms. The relationship between the real and nominal cash flow can be accounted for by the rate of inflation. You can adjust the cash flows to account for inflation by writing the real rate of return as follows:

$$1 + r_{rt} = \frac{(1 + r_{nt})}{(1 + \Delta_t)} \tag{14.2}$$

However, we can also write the nominal return and the rate of inflation in terms of changes in their absolute values.

Using capital values

$$1 + r_{nt} = \frac{V_t}{V_{t-1}} \tag{14.3}$$

Using the retail price index

$$1 + \Delta_t = \frac{RPI_t}{RPI_{t-1}} \tag{14.4}$$

Substituting these into equation 14.2 gives the following real rate of return:

$$1 + r_{rt} = \frac{V_t}{V_{t-1}} \div \frac{RPI_t}{RPI_{t-1}} \tag{14.5}$$

By rearranging you get the following:

$$1 + r_{rt} = \frac{V_t}{RPI_t} \div \frac{V_{t-1}}{RPI_{t-1}} \tag{14.6}$$

This shows that the real rate of return can be estimated from nominal cash flows that are converted to real cash flows by dividing by the retail price index. This is a very useful technique as it simplifies the calculation of real rates of return.

> Nominal cash flows can easily be converted to real cash flows by dividing by the retail price index.

To show how this works in practice Table 14.3 summarises both the nominal returns for Asset A and the inflation rate taken from Table 14.1 in index form. You will see that the average real return and standard deviation are exactly the same as the figures we calculated for Table 14.2.

By using this method all the cash flows for the 27 portfolios were converted using the retail price index so that the rate of return could be estimated in real terms. The results of plotting the real returns against the total age of each portfolio are shown in Figure 14.6.

If you were to regress real returns against total age it would be possible to see whether age has any impact on explaining real returns. The regression line is also shown in Figure 14.6.

Table 14.3 ● Asset returns and inflation

Year	Asset A	RPI	(Asset A ÷ RPI) × 100	r_{rt}
1988	100.00	100.00	100.00	
1989	106.00	106.75	99.29	−0.70
1990	113.42	114.95	98.67	−0.63
1991	125.89	125.65	100.19	1.55
1992	128.41	131.24	97.85	−2.35
1993	130.98	134.61	97.30	−0.56
1994	129.67	137.21	94.50	−2.87
1995	136.16	145.69	93.45	−1.11
1996	140.24	149.26	93.96	0.54
1997	145.85	154.67	94.30	0.37
1998	150.23	159.10	94.42	0.13
			Average	−0.56
			St. Dev.	1.33

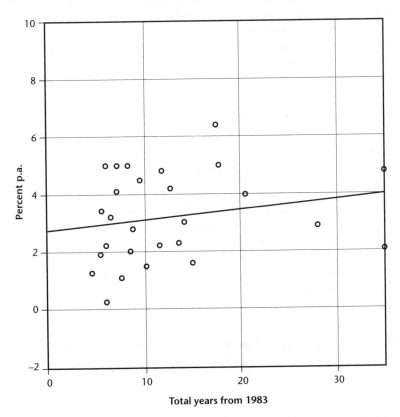

Figure 14.6 Real rates of return and portfolio age

You will see that the regression line is close to horizontal, indicating that there is no significant relationship. The age of a portfolio appears to have no impact on determining real returns. From this analysis it is also possible to show that on average, over a period of 35 years, investors have received a real rate of return in the region of 2.77% p.a. You can also say that there is a 95% probability that the real return has been in the region of 1.77%–3.77% p.a. If the past is any guide to the future you can say that investors in property can, on average, expect to earn real returns in this order.

Although this analysis gives some indication of the quality of property as a hedge against inflation it is still not a conclusive test. In fact, we have yet to provide a suitable definition and test for a hedge against inflation.

To tackle this problem you have to look in more depth at the way assets are priced and how expected nominal returns are expressed. In continuous terms we have shown that expected nominal returns could be expressed as the sum of the *expected* real rate of return and the *expected* rate of inflation. The important point to note is that everything is drafted in terms of expectations, even inflation. Observed changes in the retail price index, however, not only include expected inflation but also an additional shock, which can be either negative or positive, which alters the final outcome. Thus, if investors have to forecast what inflation is going to be next year the consensus view would represent the expected value based on the best estimate of economic conditions. In twelve months' time economic conditions may turn out to be completely different, causing the retail price index to differ from expectations. Inflation can, therefore, be split into two components representing the expected and unexpected changes that occur.

> Observed inflation = expected inflation + unexpected inflation

This separation of inflation into two components gives a better way of defining an asset as a hedge against inflation. For example:

- If there is a one-to-one relationship between observed returns and expected inflation, then the asset is a hedge against expected inflation.
- If there is a one-to one relationship between the observed returns and unexpected inflation, then the asset is a hedge against unexpected inflation.
- If there is a one-to-one relationship between the observed returns and both expected and unexpected inflation, then the asset can be regarded as a complete hedge against inflation.

This approach is economically sound and can be tested over a number of periods.

> An asset is a complete hedge against inflation if there is a one-to-one relationship between observed returns and both expected and unexpected inflation.

A test of inflation hedging

The classic work in this area is a paper by Fama and Schwert (1977) in which they established a methodology and examined the hedging characteristics of a wide range of assets, including residential real estate, in the USA over the period 1953–71. Assuming continuous returns Fama and Schwert formalised the definition of nominal returns proposed by Irving Fisher in the following manner:

$$E(r_{jt}|\phi_{t-1}) = E(r_{rjt}|\phi_{t-1}) + E(\Delta_t|\phi_{t-1})$$
(14.7)

Although this looks a bit complicated it is essentially the same as equation 14.1 written in continuous returns. The left-hand side, $E(r_{jt}|\phi_{t-1})$, is just the expected nominal return on asset j in period t, subject to all the information available at the beginning of the period, i.e., $t–1$. This is captured by the symbol ϕ_{t-1}. On the right-hand side we have the expected real rate of return, $E(r_{rjt}|\phi_{t-1})$, and the expected rate of inflation $E(\Delta_t|\phi_{t-1})$.

The expectations operator, E, is important in this equation but to make the notation simpler to follow we will drop the symbol for the information set. We will assume, therefore, that whenever returns are expressed in terms of expectations they are always subject to the information available at the beginning of the period. You can, therefore, write equation 14.7 as:

$$E(r_{jt}) = E(r_{rjt}) + E(\Delta_t)$$
(14.8)

In setting the nominal return $E(r_{jt})$ for the period from $t–1$ to t, the market uses the information available at the beginning of the period to determine the expected rate of inflation and expected real rate of return, including an adjustment for risk. This assumes that the market is an efficient processor of information.

Fisher had previously argued that the real and monetary sectors of the economy were independent of each other. The expected real rate of return given in equation 14.8 is, therefore, determined by factors such as the productivity of capital, time preference and attitude to risk, and will be independent of the expected rate of inflation. Assuming that it is possible to measure the expected rate of inflation running a regression of nominal returns against expected inflation it should be possible to test the joint hypothesis that:

● the market is efficient
● the expected real return and the rate of inflation are independent

Writing equation 14.8 in the form of the following regression equation can test these propositions:

$$r_{jt} = \alpha_j + \beta_j E(\Delta_t) + e_{jt}$$
(14.9)

You can interpret the coefficients from this model as follows:

● α_j should be equal to the real rate of return
● β_j should be statistically indistinguishable from 1.0 if the asset is a hedge against expected inflation. This is also consistent with the view that real returns and inflation are unrelated. In other words, expected inflation and nominal returns will move together, but this will have no effect on the expected real rate of return.
● e_{jt} is the error term, or residual, from the regression and should be serially uncorrelated. In other words, there should be no pattern in the residuals indicating that the market is efficient.

This simple model relates nominal returns to expected inflation. However, you are also interested in knowing whether nominal returns are related to unexpected inflation. This is just the difference between observed and expected inflation. You can write this as follows:

Unexpected inflation $= \Delta_t - E(\Delta_t)$ (14.10)

With this extra piece of information we can write the full regression model as:

$$r_{jt} = \alpha_j + \beta_j E(\Delta_t) + \gamma_j [\Delta_t - E(\Delta_t)] + u_{jt}$$ (14.11)

If the asset is a hedge against unexpected inflation then $\gamma_j = 1.0$.

This model now covers both components of inflation. For an asset to be a complete hedge against inflation you should expect to see $\beta_j = \gamma_j = 1.0$.

The Fisher model implies that all assets should have a coefficient for β_j equal to 1.0. However, we have no prior belief about the relationship between nominal returns and unexpected inflation except that it is likely to differ with different assets. Property is an asset class that is widely believed to be a hedge against inflation. If it responds well to unexpected changes in the rate of inflation, then the coefficient relative to unexpected inflation should be positive.

Before you can use this model there are some other issues that need to be resolved.

Assessing expected inflation

The method of analysis we have described represents the standard approach for testing whether an asset is a hedge against inflation. It relies, however, on being able to estimate expected inflation reliably, as it is not directly observable. The way Fama overcame this was to use the returns on Treasury Bills as a proxy for expected inflation. He argued that because Treasury Bills are short-term investments they will have incorporated the effect of expected inflation but will not have had time to adjust to any unexpected changes. However, before using Treasury Bills in his analysis Fama (1975) tested to see whether they were a good proxy for expected inflation. He did this as follows:

The return on a Treasury Bill that matures at time t will be known in advance. If the bill market is efficient and real returns are constant, the nominal return on Treasury Bills should be equal to the expected real rate of return plus the expected rate of inflation. If r_{bt} represents the return on 90-day Treasury Bills in period t you can write this in terms of its expected real rate of return $E(r_{rt})$ and the expected rate of inflation $E(\Delta_t)$ as follows:

$$r_{bt} = E(r_{rt}) + E(\Delta_t)$$ (14.12)

Rearranging gives the expected rate of inflation as follows:

$$E(\Delta_t) = -E(r_{rt}) + r_{bt}$$ (14.13)

Fama tested whether Treasury Bills were a good proxy for expected inflation by running the following regression:

$$\Delta_t = \alpha + \beta r_{bt} + e_t$$ (14.14)

If this relationship holds, then β should be statistically indistinguishable from 1.0 and Treasury Bill rates can be used as a proxy for expected inflation. The intercept term, α, should also represent the real rate of return. The results that Fama obtained are shown in Table 14.4.

Table 14.4 ● **Treasury Bill rates as proxies for expected inflation, 1953–71**

| | Sample size | α | β | $\bar{R}^2$ | Serial correlation in residuals for following lags | | |
					1	2	3
Monthly	223	−0.0007	0.98	0.29	0.10	0.12	−0.02
		(0.0003)	(0.10)				
Quarterly	74	−0.0023	0.93	0.48	0.00	0.04	0.10
		(0.0011)	(0.11)				
Half-yearly	24	−0.0097	1.06	0.83	0.00	−0.04	0.16
		(0.0024)	(0.10)				

Returns on six-month Treasury Bills were only available from 1959.
Standard errors are shown in brackets.

Each of the regression analyses has slope coefficients that are statistically indistinguishable from 1.0. The serial correlation coefficients are all close to zero. These findings imply that Treasury Bill rates are good proxies for expected inflation. On this basis the unexpected component of inflation can be calculated by subtracting Treasury Bill rates from the observed rates of inflation. Equation 14.11 can therefore be tested using the following:

$$r_{jt} = \alpha_j + \beta_j r_{bt} + \gamma_j [\Delta_t - r_{bt}] + u_{jt} \tag{14.15}$$

Before presenting the results of Fama and Schwert's analysis it is as well to point out that this method of estimating expected inflation has been criticised on the grounds that it assumes real rates of return are constant. Although this was true over the period used by Fama and Schwert, it transpired that for other periods real rates of return were not constant. Fama and Gibbons (1982) subsequently addressed this issue by estimating expected inflation using a moving average process. Hartzell, Hekman and Miles (1986) also used this approach when analysing the inflation-hedging characteristics of US commercial property. They looked at whether Treasury Bills acted as a proxy for expected inflation and produced the results shown in Table 14.5.

From this it will be seen that over the period 1973–83 Treasury Bills acted as a poor proxy for expected inflation. The same was also true for the sub-periods examined. The Durbin-Watson statistic tests for the presence of serial correlation in the residual errors from the regression. The low figures imply that there is some evidence of positive serial correlation, implying that the real rates of return were not constant or that the equation is mis-specified in some way.

It should be clear from this discussion that the debate concerning the appropriate method for estimating expected inflation is still open.

Table 14.5 ● Treasury Bill rates as proxies for expected inflation, 1973–83

	α	β	$\bar{R}^2$	DW
1973–83	0.013	0.338	0.08	0.89
	(0.004)	(0.183)		
1976–83	0.010	0.393	0.11	0.98
	(0.005)	(0.203)		
1978–83	0.007	0.500	0.09	0.78
	(0.011)	(0.382)		

DW is the Durbin-Watson statistic for serial correlation.
Standard errors are shown in brackets.

The Fama and Schwert results

Using data collected over the period 1953–71 Fama and Schwert (1977) analysed the inflation-hedging properties of common stocks, US Treasury Bills, longer-term US Government Bonds, Human Capital and Residential Real Estate using the model described above. They used the returns of three-month Treasury Bills as a proxy for expected inflation.

The data used for real estate were the home purchase price component of the Consumer Price Index. The purchase price index was based on the purchase price of homes with mortgages newly issued by the Federal Housing Association. The index was expressed as a price per square foot and was adjusted to take account of differences in quality between individual properties. It was, however, a three-month moving average because the price of a property was reported only at the time it was insured and so there was a lag of 1–3 months between the price being determined and the time it was reflected in the index. In addition, the sample was not representative of all residential property.

A general picture of the inflation-hedging properties of each asset class, obtained by comparing inflation rates with average annualised returns for each asset, is shown in Table 14.6.

As the rate of inflation increases over each sub-period it will be seen that the returns on real estate and Treasury Bills correspond exactly to the ordering of average nominal returns. The same is true to a lesser extent with long-term Government Bonds and human capital. Common stocks appear, however, to be negatively related to changes in inflation and as such did not provide a good hedge. Despite this negative relationship the average returns on stocks were high and so observed real returns were positive, although they did not move in line with inflation.

Using the model shown in equation 14.15 for relating nominal returns to both expected and unexpected inflation Fama and Schwert analysed the inflation-hedging characteristics of each asset class. A summary of their results for US residential real estate is given in Table 14.7 for monthly, quarterly and half-yearly returns.

Table 14.6 ● Comparison of inflation and US assets using average annualised nominal returns

Asset	1953–57	1958–62	1963–67	1968–71	1971–75
Inflation	1.3	1.3	2.3	5.1	7.1
Treasury Bills					
1 month	1.9	2.2	3.7	5.5	5.7
2 month	2.1	2.7	4.0	5.9	6.0
3 month	2.3	3.0	4.1	6.1	6.4
Government Bonds					
1 year	2.3	3.5	3.6	6.1	N/A
2 year	2.7	3.6	3.2	5.7	N/A
3 year	2.6	3.7	2.9	5.1	N/A
4 year	2.4	3.3	2.6	4.5	N/A
Real estate	1.0	0.6	1.7	5.9	6.2
Human capital	2.2	3.4	5.2	4.7	6.1
Common stocks					
Value-weighted	12.3	12.8	12.5	3.0	1.6
Equal-weighted	10.5	14.4	18.5	3.3	−0.6

N/A: not available.
All figures in % p.a.

Table 14.7 ● US residential real estate as a hedge against inflation (after Fama and Schwert)

	α Real return	β Expected inflation	γ Unexpected inflation	$\bar{R}^2$
Monthly	−0.0012 (0.0005)	1.19 (0.16)	0.31 (0.11)	0.21
Quarterly	−0.0032 (0.0019)	1.15 (0.19)	0.56 (0.20)	0.35
Half-yearly	−0.0054 (0.0073)	1.27 (0.24)	1.14 (0.49)	0.60

Standard errors are shown in brackets.

These results show that irrespective of period, residential property acts as a hedge against expected inflation. With regard to unexpected inflation it is only half-yearly returns that show a coefficient that is statistically indistinguishable from 1.0. However, the coefficients for monthly and quarterly returns are significantly different from zero, which would imply that they are a better hedge against longer-term, unexpected inflation. Fama and Schwert suggested that this result may be due to measurement errors in the property data because the returns were derived from a three-month moving average. The property transaction usually took place between one and three months before the date they were included in the index. Because of this the correlation between nominal returns and unexpected inflation could be spread over a six-month period. On the basis of this evidence they suggest that property is a complete hedge against both expected and unexpected inflation even on a monthly basis. They verify this by using a technique developed by Scholes and Williams (1977), which involves regressing nominal rates of return on expected inflation as well as current and lagged values of unexpected inflation over a six-month period. The model they used was:

$$r_{jt} = \alpha_j + \beta_j r_{bt} + \sum_{i=0}^{i=6} \gamma_i [\Delta_{t-i} - r_{b,t-i}] + \eta_{jt} \tag{14.16}$$

The summation captures the lagged values of unexpected inflation over a six-month period. The sum of the regression coefficients provides a consistent estimate of the relationship between the true return from property and the unexpected monthly inflation rate. Using this technique they found that the γ coefficient was 0.88 with a standard error of 0.29. The coefficient for unexpected inflation was, therefore, statistically indistinguishable from 1.0.

This result confirms that property appears to act as a complete hedge against inflation so that the real rate of return is unrelated to the inflation rate. This does not imply, however, that the real rate of return is certain. The $\bar{R}^2$ value for half-yearly returns given in Table 14.7 shows that 60% of the variation in returns could be explained by inflation. The remaining 40% is still unexplained.

Of the other assets tested by Fama and Schwert all, with the exception of stocks, were a complete hedge against expected inflation. There was, however, less consistency with unexpected inflation. Over the period covered, stocks were negatively related to both expected and unexpected inflation. Contrary to popular belief stocks did not appear to act as a hedge against inflation, although they did provide high real rates of return.

More recent studies in the UK suggest that commercial property is a hedge against unexpected inflation, but is less successful in hedging against expected inflation. We cover some of these results in the appendix to this chapter.

Summary

Understanding whether property is a hedge against inflation is important if investors aim to protect the real purchasing power of their investments. In this chapter we showed that although it was possible for an asset to have high real rates of return it could fail to act as a hedge against inflation.

In order to test whether an asset is a hedge against inflation we showed that observed inflation could be split into two components. One part reflects expected inflation and the other, unexpected inflation. An asset would be regarded as being a complete hedge against inflation if a one-to-one relationship existed between each component. The asset would be regarded as being a partial hedge against inflation if there was a one-to-one relationship with only one component. However, in order to run this model we pointed out that you need to have an estimate of expected inflation. Fama and Schwert used Treasury Bills as a proxy for expected inflation and undertook the original tests of inflation hedging. A critical assumption underlying this choice was that the real return on Treasury Bills was constant. Although this was satisfactory over the period they analysed it turned out that in later periods the real rate of return was not constant so that Treasury Bills were not a good proxy for expected inflation. As expected inflation is unobservable, identifying a suitable proxy still remains an issue worthy of research.

Fama and Schwert's original study showed that of all the asset classes they examined only US residential real estate proved to be a complete hedge against inflation. They also showed that it was a better hedge against unexpected inflation in the long term than the short term. Their analysis did not, however, cover commercial real estate.

This chapter has one appendix.

Appendix 14A: Empirical studies on inflation hedging

This appendix briefly reviews some of the international tests of inflation hedging that have been carried out. These have largely focused on the commercial property market.

Chapter 14: Summary table

1. The causes of inflation are not clearly defined but arise from a combination of *demand-pull* and *cost-push* inflation. It is not easy to separate the two effects.	
2. If investors are keen to protect the purchasing power of their assets then they will want to ensure that they hold investments that hedge against inflation.	
3. Inflation can be split into two components: expected inflation and unexpected inflation.	Observed inflation = expected inflation + unexpected inflation
4. An asset is said to be a complete hedge against inflation if there is a one-to-one relationship between observed returns and each component of inflation.	

5. Fama formalised a test of inflation hedging to reflect both expected inflation and unexpected inflation.

$$r_{jt} = \alpha_j + \beta_j E(\Delta_t) + \gamma_j[\Delta_t - E(\Delta_t)] + u_{jt}$$

6. The results of this test should be interpreted as follows:
   ● If β_j = 1.0 the asset is a hedge against expected inflation
   ● If γ_j = 1.0 the asset is a hedge against unexpected inflation
   ● If $\beta_j = \gamma_j$ = 1.0 the asset is a complete hedge against inflation

7. As expected inflation is unobservable a proxy needs to be used.

   Treasury Bills are frequently used as a proxy for expected inflation

8. Treasury Bills only work if their real return is constant. This is not always the case.

9. Fama and Schwert's analysis showed that US residential real estate was the only asset class that provided a complete hedge against inflation.

10. Real estate also appeared to be a better hedge against unexpected inflation in the long term rather than the short term.

Problems

1. How would you define a hedge against inflation?

2. Why is it important for investors to include assets in their portfolios that do hedge against inflation?

3. How would you convert a series of nominal returns to real returns?

4. What are the two components of observed inflation and why do they arise?

5. Discuss the formal model of inflation hedging.

6. How would you interpret the regression coefficients in an inflation-hedging test?

7. How would you estimate expected inflation?

8. Discuss some of the problems associated with estimating expected inflation.

9. Is property likely to be a better hedge against short-term or long-term inflation?

10. If an asset has a high real rate of return does this mean that it has hedged against inflation?

Selected references

Fama, E.F. (1975) Short-term interest rates as predictors of inflation. *American Economic Review* 65 (June), 269–82.

Fama, E.F. and Schivert, G.W. (1977) Asset returns and inflation. *Journal of Financial Economics* 5 115–46.

Hartzell, D., Hekman, J.S. and Miles, M. (1987) Real estate returns and inflation. *AREUEA Journal* 15 (1), 617–37.

Scholes, M. and Williams, J. (1977) Estimating betas with non-synchronous data. University of Chicago, Working paper.

Appendix 14A
Empirical studies on inflation hedging

In this appendix we briefly summarise some of the tests that have been undertaken internationally to examine whether property is a hedge against inflation. This is not a comprehensive study and interested readers should refer to the special issue of the *Journal of Property Finance*[1] for a more detailed examination of some of the issues concerning inflation hedging.

Chapter 14 outlined the approach developed by Fama and Schwert (1977) for testing whether an asset is a hedge against inflation. They examined a wide range of assets over an 18-year period (1953–71) and came to the conclusion that residential real estate was the only asset class that fully hedged against both components of inflation.

There are a number of problems with their approach, which are particularly important when it is applied to commercial property.

- All tests need a reliable time-series of property returns. Until quite recently this has been very difficult. In the UK the introduction of the IPD database has eased this problem, although problems of confidentiality still restrict the availability of information.
- The Fama and Schwert test assumed that the real returns on Treasury Bills are constant. This enabled them to use these bills as a proxy for expected inflation.
- Expected inflation is unobservable so that the success of any test will rely on the validity of the proxy being used.
- Tests have to be carried out using valuations. It should be stressed that tests based on valuations may not be the same as similar tests using prices.
- The results of tests based on 'backed out' market prices which rely on some form of statistical deserialising model will depend on the return-generating process implied by the model used.

Given these additional problems associated with property you can never be sure that the results provide definitive answers to the question of inflation hedging. You should, however, be able to identify some general trends.

Do property values reflect lagged inflation?

The simplest test for a relationship between inflation and property is to look at the cross-correlation between the rate of inflation and the returns from each sector of the property market. Using a reliable sample of property data over a four-year period from January 1979 to December 1982 we estimated continuous rates of returns for both equal-weighted and value-weighted portfolios. The correlation between inflation and each sector is shown in Table 14A.1. A comparison is also shown with the returns on the FT All Share Index.

---

[1]The special issue dealing with inflation was *Journal of Property Finance* (1996), Vol. 7, No. 1.

Table 14A.1 • Inflation and correlation with property and equities, January 1979 to December 1982

Monthly returns	Industrial	Office	Retail	Portfolio	FT
Portfolio EW	0.53	0.34	0.25	0.41	
Portfolio VW	0.40	0.40	0.25	0.44	0.06

EW = equal-weighted portfolio.
VW = value-weighted portfolio.

Table 14A.2 • Property returns and lagged inflation, January 1979 to December 1982

Sector		Lag in months					
		0	1	3	6	9	12
Industrial	EW	0.53	0.25	0.31	−0.06	0.19	0.09
	VW	0.40	0.29	0.24	−0.04	0.11	0.05
Office	EW	0.34	0.03	0.41	0.06	0.24	0.48
	VW	0.40	−0.05	0.41	0.08	0.34	0.46
Retail	EW	0.25	0.18	0.41	0.08	−0.05	0.33
	VW	0.25	0.34	0.51	0.17	−0.03	0.26
Portfolio	EW	0.41	0.15	0.45	0.05	0.16	0.41
	VW	0.44	0.17	0.48	0.09	0.23	0.39

These results show a high level of correlation between inflation and each sector of the property market. By contrast the FT All Share Index shows little correlation with inflation. Although this provides some evidence of the hedging capability of property a further question that needs to be asked is whether the returns from property respond to current changes in the rate of inflation or whether they react more slowly. This can be examined by lagging the returns for inflation and measuring the effect on the coefficient of correlation. The results are shown in Table 14A.2.

Although there is some evidence of strong positive association between property returns and lagged inflation, particularly after three months and twelve months, the relationship in the current month still remains very strong. This is also true when returns and inflation are calculated over longer holding periods, as shown in Table 14A.3 for half-yearly returns. Again, it will be seen that inflation twelve months ago has an impact on current returns but the effect of current inflation appears to be more significant.

This, of course, is not a direct test of inflation hedging as described in Chapter 14, but it does at least show that property is responsive to current changes in inflation. The belief that it takes some time for inflation to work its way into changes in valuation appears to have weak support.

The model developed by Fama and Schwert can be tested using this sample and by estimating expected inflation using a simple AR1 autoregressive model. The results are given in Table 14A.4.

Table 14A.3 ● Property returns and lagged inflation, January 1979 to December 1982

Sector		Lag in half-yearly returns		
		0	1	2
Industrial	EW	0.86	−0.21	0.35
	VW	0.87	−0.26	0.64
Office	EW	0.76	−0.09	0.73
	VW	0.86	0.11	0.63
Retail	EW	0.88	0.26	0.75
	VW	0.93	0.41	0.61
Portfolio	EW	0.87	−0.03	0.67
	VW	0.94	0.11	0.67

Table 14A.4 ● Inflation hedging, January 1979 to December 1982 (monthly returns)

	α real return	β expected inflation	γ unexpected inflation	$\bar{R}^2$
Portfolio returns	0.0046	0.941	0.723	0.16
	(0.005)	(0.563)	(0.236)	

The intercept term shows that the average annual real rate of return over the period was 5.66% p.a. The standard error shows, however, that it is statistically indistinguishable from zero. The coefficient for expected inflation is statistically indistinguishable from 1.0 but is only 1.67 standard errors from zero. Although you can't reject that this is zero at the 95% level you can at the 90% level. You should also bear in mind that as there is probably some error in the measurement of the variables, the coefficients will be biased downwards. The coefficient for unexpected inflation is indistinguishable from 1.0 and is also significantly different from zero. These results support those of Fama and Schwert. Note also that the $\bar{R}^2$ value is only 0.16, which again is in line with their findings for residential property. This result implies that only 16% of the variation in returns of commercial property could be explained by inflation. There are clearly other factors at work which explain changes in property values.

More extensive tests have been carried out by a number of researchers.

International tests of inflation hedging

The most difficult part of testing whether an asset is a hedge against inflation is estimating the expected rate of inflation. We showed in Chapter 14 that Fama and Schwert used Treasury Bills as a proxy for expected inflation. Later, Fama and Gibbons (1982) used an autoregressive model. Given that expected inflation is unobservable, a number of estimation methods have been proposed. In fact, a lot of the research into inflation hedging centres on deciding what should be regarded as a suitable proxy. We have briefly summarised some of the methods used and the main findings of tests of inflation hedging that have been carried out round the world. This is not intended to be comprehensive but should give an idea of the approaches that have been adopted.

UK studies

Limmack and Ward 1988

This test used a ten-year sample of quarterly returns over the period January 1976 to March 1986 taken from the Jones Lang Wootton database. They estimated expected inflation using two approaches:

- The first followed Fama's earlier methodology using the yield on three-month Treasury Bills calculated on the last day of the previous quarter to estimate expected inflation for the following quarter. Subtracting this from the observed inflation rate, estimated using the Retail Price Index, gave a measure of unexpected inflation.
- The alternative approach used an autoregressive integrated moving average model to estimate expected inflation on a rolling predictor basis using past data on a quarterly inflation rate.

Using the first approach they showed that property was a hedge against expected inflation but was a poor hedge against unexpected inflation. The only exception to this was the industrial sector. In all cases the explanatory power of the models was low, indicating that inflation explained only part of the total returns.

The alternative approach, using a rolling autoregressive model, used estimates of the expected rate of inflation by allowing the real rate of return to vary. The results in this case were broadly in line with the first approach concerning expected inflation. Only the office sector was significantly different from 1.00. There was, however, a significant improvement with regard to unexpected inflation. Each sector had a coefficient that was indistinguishable from 1.00. The explanatory power of each of the models still remained low.

Tarbert 1996

Tarbert used three approaches to estimate the expected rate of inflation:

- The first used Treasury Bills as a proxy for expected inflation.
- The second approach adopted an ARIMA model to generate estimates of the real rate of return. The expected rate of inflation was then calculated by taking the difference between the nominal rate of return and the forecast value of the real rate of return.
- The third approach used the difference between the yields on index-linked gilts and conventional gilts.

In all cases once the expected rate of inflation has been estimated the unexpected component of inflation could be found by subtracting from the observed rate of inflation.

Tarbert's results show that the choice of estimation procedure can have a dramatic difference on the results. Using Treasury Bills commercial property did not hedge against expected inflation but fully hedged against unexpected inflation. These results were reversed when the ARIMA model was used.

Using the difference between index-linked gilts and conventional gilts showed that property did not hedge against either expected inflation or unexpected inflation.

Barber White 1995

The Barber White report is probably the most extensive that has been produced in the UK and, using quarterly returns, covers the period 1967–94. Although the techniques used in the analysis are sophisticated, the report unfortunately gives very little information about the statistics surrounding their results. The early part of the data series they used was interpolated to estimate quarterly values from annual data. This process could, therefore, induce bias into the series. They used an ARIMA model to estimate expected inflation and their results showed that commercial property only hedged against unexpected inflation.

US studies

Hartzell, Hekman and Miles 1986

This study was based on an analysis of 300 commercial properties taken from a Commingled Real Estate fund with quarterly returns over the ten-year period 1973 to 1983. They used two methods to estimate expected inflation: Treasury Bills and an ARIMA model. They constructed two samples from their data covering a 40-quarter and 20-quarter period. Many of the acquisitions of new properties were made within the first 20 quarters and the growth and cash flows reflected this. The second period was not influenced to the same degree and was felt to be more representative of the long-run income-producing ability of the portfolios. Their results showed that commercial real estate provided a hedge against both expected and unexpected inflation.

Australian studies

Newell 1996

The study by Newell is interesting as it uses the results of surveys undertaken by the Westpac Bank to monitor investors' beliefs concerning expected inflation. This is the only study that uses an index of market sentiment to estimate inflationary expectations. Regressing observed inflation against the Westpac proxy tested the validity of this approach. The results showed that there was a one-to-one relationship and the relationship had an explanatory power of 76%. Adopting this proxy Newell shows that commercial property hedges against expected inflation but the results are mixed as far as unexpected inflation is concerned.

Swiss studies

Hamelink and Hoesli 1996

The study undertaken by Hamelink and Hoesli focused on apartment property in Geneva using annual returns over the ten-year period 1982 to 1992. They used four approaches to estimate expected inflation:

- Contemporaneous inflation on the assumption that expectations are perfect and there is no unexpected inflation.
- An AR(1) model in which current inflation is specified as a linear function of lagged inflation.
- The third approach uses the errors from the AR(1) model as part of an ARCH process. This stands for Autoregressive Conditional Heteroskedasticity and implies that the variance of a series is conditional on past innovations. Hamelink and Hoesli also allowed the mean and variance in their model to adjust to different regimes. This is known as the qualitative threshold ARCH, or QTARCH model.
- The fourth approach uses the more common ARCH in mean model, i.e. ARCH-M.

The analysis showed that only those estimates of expected inflation based on the AR(1) and QTARCH model, enabled property to hedge against expected inflation. Apartment buildings appeared to offer no hedge against unexpected inflation.

Hong Kong studies

Ganesan and Chiang 1998

Hong Kong offers an interesting case study because of the linked exchange rate system between the Hong Kong and US dollar. This was fixed in 1983 at HK$ 7.8 = US$ 1.0. Ganesan and Chiang argue that because local rates follow US interest rates Hong Kong does not have the monetary tools to fight inflation. Estimates of expected inflation using ARIMA models are therefore inappropriate. Since 1987 real interest rates have fluctuated within a narrow range of –2%. Using this figure for the real rate of return they estimate the annual expected rate of inflation to be the annual deposit rate plus 2%.

Their results showed that each of the property sectors hedged against unexpected inflation. However, only the commercial, i.e. the retail sector, and residential property also provided a hedge against expected inflation. The office and industrial sectors showed a negative relationship with expected inflation. The explanatory power of each of the models was very low.

The results of these studies are summarised in Table 14A.5.

Table 14A.5 ● Summary of inflation-hedging studies

Author	Period	Frequency	Exp Inf	Sector	Inflation Expected	Inflation Unexpected	$\bar{R}^2$
USA							
Fama and Schwert	1953–71	Monthly	T-Bills	Residential	✓	✗	0.21
		Quarterly			✓	✗	0.35
		Half-yearly			✓	✓	0.60
Hartzell et al.	1973–83	Quarterly	T-Bills	Commercial	✓	✓	0.40
			ARIMA		✓	✓	0.36
	1978–83		T-Bills		✓	✓	0.56
			ARIMA		✓	✓	0.53
UK							
Brown	1979–82	Monthly		Commercial	✓	✓	0.16
Limmack and Ward	1976–86	Quarterly	T-Bills	Retail	✓	✗	0.18
				Office	✓	✗	0.05
				Industrial	✓	✗	0.27
				All Property	✓	✗	0.19
			ARIMA	Retail	✗	✓	0.12
				Office	✗	✓	0.03
				Industrial	✓	✓	0.25
				All Property	✓	✓	0.14
Tarbert	1978–95	Quarterly	T-Bills	Retail	✗	✓	0.12
				Office	✗	✓	0.16
				Industrial	✗	✓	0.15
				All Property	✗	✓	0.18
			ARIMA	Retail	✓	✗	0.04
				Office	✓	✗	0.03
				Industrial	✓	✗	0.06
				All Property	✓	✗	0.02
			Gilt-Indx	Retail	✗	✗	0.31
				Office	✗	✗	0.46
				Industrial	✗	✗	0.19
				All Property	✗	✗	0.42
Barber White	1967–94	Quarterly	ARIMA	Retail	✗	✓	NA
				Office	✗	✓	NA
				Industrial	✗	✓	NA
				All Property	✗	✓	NA
AUSTRALIA							
Newell	1984–95	Half-yearly	Survey	Retail	✓	✗	0.35
				Office	✓	✓	0.60
				Industrial	✓	✗	0.27
				All Property	✓	✓	0.57
SWITZERLAND							
Hamelink and Hoesli	1982–92	Annual	Current	Apartments	✗	–	0.01
			AR(1)		✓	✗	0.03
			QTARCH		✓	✗	0.11
			ARCH-M		✗	✗	0.05
HONG KONG							
Ganesan and Chiang	1984–94	Quarterly	Riskless + 2.0%	Office	✗	✓	0.12
				Retail	✓	✓	−0.01
				Industrial	✗	✓	0.02
				Residential	✓	✓	0.01

Other studies

There are two other studies that are worth mentioning. These are by Matysiak et al. (1996) and Barkham et al. (1996). They differ from the conventional approaches in that they focus on whether property acts as a hedge against inflation in the long term. Matysiak et al. use a multivariate cointegration approach over the period 1963–93 and show that property returns reflect both expected and unexpected components of inflation in the long term. However, there is no support for a similar finding in the short term. The study by Barkham et al. arrives at a similar conclusion although it also shows that in the short term there is some link to value. It is interesting to note that these more sophisticated approaches confirm the earlier findings of Fama and Schwert, which showed that property was probably a better hedge against longer-term inflation.

Selected references

Barber White (1995) *Property and Inflation: The Hedging Characteristics of Commercial Property*, London: Barber White Property Economics.

Barkham, R. and Ward, C.W.R. (1996) The inflation-hedging characteristics of UK property. *Journal of Property Finance* **7** (1), 62–76.

Brown, G.R. (1991) *Property Investment and the Capital Markets*, London: Chapman & Hall.

Fama, E.F. and Gibbons, M. (1982) Inflation, real returns and capital investment. *Journal of Monetary Economics* **9** (3).

Fama, E.F. and Schwert, G.W. (1977) Asset returns and inflation. *Journal of Financial Economics* **5**, 115–46.

Fisher, I. (1930) *The Theory of Interest*, London: Macmillan.

Ganesan, S. and Chiang, Y.H. (1998) The inflation hedging characteristics of real and financial assets in Hong Kong. *Journal of Real Estate Portfolio Management* **4** (1), 55–68.

Hamelink, F. and Hoesli, M. (1996) Swiss real estate as a hedge against inflation: New evidence using hedonic and autoregressive models. *Journal of Property Finance* **7** (1), 33–49.

Hartzell, D., Hekman, J.S. and Miles, M. (1987) Real estate returns and inflation. *AREUEA Journal* **15** (1), 617–37.

Limmack, R.J. and Ward, C.W.R. (1988) Property returns and inflation. *Land Development Studies* **5**, 47–55.

Matysiak, G.A., Hoesli, M., MacGregor, B.D. and Nanthakumaran, N. (1996) The long term inflation hedging characteristics of UK commercial property. *Journal of Property Finance* **7** (1), 50–61.

Newell, G. (1996) The inflation hedging characteristic of Australian commercial property: 1984–1995. *Journal of Property Finance* **7** (1), 6–20.

Scholes, M. and Williams, J.T. (1977) Estimating betas with nonsynchronous data. University of Chicago, Working paper.

Tarbert, H. (1996) Is commercial property a hedge against inflation? A cointegration approach. *Journal of Property Finance* **7** (1), 77–98.

Developing
a portfolio strategy

Introduction

So far we have discussed a number of important investment issues and applied them to property. Although the current state of property research is not as advanced as the equities market, you should by now have a reasonable idea of areas such as diversification, risk analysis, inflation hedging and market efficiency. However, because you have to deal with valuations that are largely matters of opinion you can never be certain that our findings would be the same had we used prices. This position is unlikely to change in the near future. You will have to accept that as databases improve and information becomes more accessible the difference between valuations and prices will reduce. With this background we will examine some of the issues that are important in developing a portfolio strategy. We will bring together a number of the areas we have covered and develop a general approach that we believe is economically valid.

Some common misconceptions

Whatever approach you decide to take in developing an investment strategy you need to ask two important questions:

1. Can professional advisers utilise costly information in such a way that underpriced properties can be selected?
2. Is professional advice sufficiently good that positive abnormal returns can be earned consistently from period to period?

The first of these is an *ex-ante* exercise and deals with strategy. The second is *ex-post* and deals with performance measurement.

> Investment strategy is concerned with *ex-ante* decisions.
> Performance measurement is concerned with *ex-post* evaluation.

We will look at performance measurement in Chapter 16. In this chapter we will try to answer the first question by raising a number of related issues that are poorly understood in the marketplace. Our discussion will be based on the research we have described throughout this book. Given this background we can discuss strategies that have a sound economic basis. We cannot, however, offer any sure-fire solutions to success. You should by now have realised that property is a risky business.

The framework for establishing a property strategy and evaluating performance is the security market line we introduced in Chapter 10. The basic premise is that a trade-off exists between risk and expected return, and underpriced assets will lie above the line. Part of a good strategy is to locate underpriced assets. This view of investment is closely tied in with the idea of efficient markets that we discussed in detail in Chapter 13. With this in mind we can now address a number of common misconceptions that appear to influence the behaviour of property investors.

The property market is grossly inefficient

This is a view often argued by professional valuers. However, if it were true, then it would always be possible to identify mispriced properties and the consequences would be quite profound. Positive abnormal performance would be guaranteed and investors would buy property in preference to other asset classes. Unfortunately, the evidence of abnormal performance does not support this. Property, on average, appears to be correctly valued. The view taken by valuers is understandable when based on limited evidence gleaned from a few abnormal transactions that receive headline status in the property press. The market, however, is not made up of abnormal transactions. The majority of properties almost certainly reflect a trade-off between expected return and the risk taken on by investors.

This does not mean that underpriced properties do not exist. From time to time abnormal returns will be earned in the property market, but there are probably substantial costs associated with trying to locate underpriced properties. As databases of information become more widely used inefficiencies in the market are likely to reduce.

Property offers stable returns

This is another common view held by professional advisers. In fact, this has been suggested as one of the main reasons for investing in property. Unfortunately, this view is largely illusory and is probably based on the idea that rent received under a lease is fixed for long periods and is generally guaranteed. However, income returns are only one component of total return. What investors are interested in are total returns because this is what influences their long-term wealth position. Total returns are therefore made up of two components: the return on income ($\hat{y}$) and the growth in capital value (g). We can write this for property P as:

$$r_p = \hat{y}_p + g_p \tag{15.1}$$

You will see that if professional advisers focus solely on the income yield ($\hat{y}$) they are ignoring a large portion of the total return. It is also the most volatile portion.

If wealth-maximisation is an important aspect of investment strategy, then investors should be concerned with total returns. Relying on income yields as the basis for making investment decisions is unlikely to produce a strategy that will be consistent with the long-term goals of the investor.

Property is a long-term investment

This is an interesting view and probably has its roots in history. It is really based on the idea that if you measure returns over long periods all intermediate changes in value will be irrelevant and you will be left with an average return that is more in line with expectations.

Although this sounds reasonable it is important to draw a distinction between average annualised returns and your terminal wealth position. After all, investors are more concerned with the final value of their investment calculated by compounding the annual rates of return rather than shocks to the average annualised rate of return.

For example, if you owned a property that had a standard deviation of returns of 15% p.a. and you had an investment horizon, T, of five years the average annualised standard deviation of your investment measured over the five years would be estimated as follows:

$$\sigma_T = \frac{\sigma}{\sqrt{T}} = \frac{15}{\sqrt{5}} = 6.71\% \text{ p.a.}$$

However, common sense suggests that with the passage of time there will be more uncertainty in the terminal value of your investment, not less. In this case you would estimate the standard deviation of your terminal wealth position as follows:

$$\sigma_T = \sigma\sqrt{T} = 15 \times \sqrt{5} = 33.54\% \text{ p.a.}$$

The uncertainty in your terminal value has more than doubled!

This is the result for one property. You can see the effect that this would have on a portfolio by combining a number of properties that have similar standard deviations. Using our sample of monthly valued properties over the period 1992–97 we selected 14 properties. Assuming that they each have the same initial capital value we have plotted the change in values over the five-year time horizon. These are shown in Figure 15.1.

Even over a short time horizon of five years the terminal values range from 100 to 230. If you refer to Appendix 12C you will see why there is so much volatility in the terminal wealth.

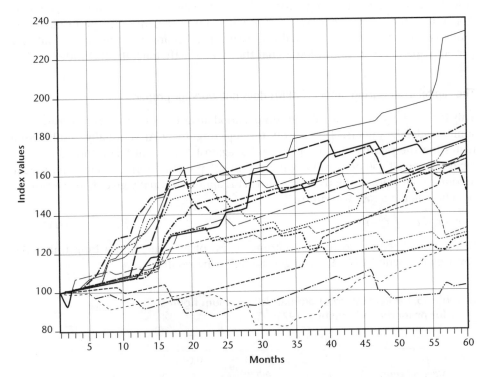

Figure 15.1 Terminal wealth position of properties with same variance, 1992–97

Property portfolios are well diversified

Once again this is a commonly held view that is based on a naïve understanding of diversification. The argument usually revolves around the belief that a portfolio is well diversified if it has property holdings in sectors of the market that are geographically widespread over each sector. As a result it is not uncommon to see professional reports that discuss the performance of small portfolios containing a statement implying that the portfolio is well diversified across all sectors of the market.

This is certainly one view of diversification but it is not one that has a lot of economic validity. We showed in Chapter 11 that diversification is a single period concept that is concerned with the reduction in risk by combining assets. We also showed that it is very difficult to construct highly diversified portfolios. Even some of the largest commercial portfolios are poorly diversified.

The objective of a strategy is to track an index

With the publication of the IPD Annual Index it has become popular to use this as a benchmark that should at least be met. Tracking the IPD Index is therefore one objective that many investors are keen to achieve. We have shown, however, that this is almost impossible to achieve. The composition of the IPD Index and most portfolios is so different that the tracking error is likely to be large. We discuss tracking errors in Appendix 16D when we cover performance measurement. The performance of property funds may move up and down with general changes in the market, but on a period-by-period basis it is unlikely that they will exactly track the IPD Index.

The capital asset pricing model (CAPM) does not work for property

This is probably one of the most misunderstood areas by both property investors and some academic valuers. The reason for rejecting the CAPM usually results from regressing the returns on a property index against the FT All Share Index. Let's see what happens if you do this. We will work in risk premium form so that you can take account of changes in the riskless return. This approach usually gives better estimates of beta. The model we will run is:

$$r_p - r_f = \alpha + \beta(r_e - r_f) \tag{15.2}$$

Using annual returns so that smoothing is less of an issue, and a long time-series covering the period 1971–97, you get the following results:

Table 15.1 ● Regression of annual risk premium figures for property and equities, 1971–97

	α	β	$\bar{R}^2$
$r_p - r_f$	1.698	0.073	0.043
Standard errors	2.431	0.070	

Both the intercept term and the slope coefficient are statistically indistinguishable from zero. At first sight this would seem to reject the CAPM. However, this regression really has nothing to do with the CAPM. All it is telling us is that the equity market explains very little about the variation in property returns. To appreciate this point you have to understand that you are really concerned with two betas.

● The first beta was developed to simplify the calculations needed for a full portfolio analysis. It was proposed as a means of estimating the covariance between assets. The idea was suggested by Markowitz (1958) and later developed by Sharpe (1963) into the single index model. The principle was that the co-movement between assets could be related to some common factor, such as the returns on an index.

Estimating the beta for each asset dramatically reduces the number of covariance terms needed for the calculations.

● The second beta came along in 1964 and focused on what the market for all capital assets would look like if every investor made decisions according to the ideas suggested by Markowitz. The mathematics for the second beta looked exactly the same as the first, except that the calculations are now related to a value-weighted index consisting of *every* asset in the marketplace. This became known as the Market Portfolio and its relationship with expected returns became known as the Capital Asset Pricing Model. It is a highly specific model that is concerned with estimating the expected returns on assets.

You will see from this that the FT All Share Index is likely to be a poor proxy for the market portfolio. Not only does it exclude a high proportion of commercial and residential property, it also excludes art objects, human capital and other forms of non-tradable asset. For the CAPM to work properly the definition of the market portfolio is very important. Unfortunately, the market portfolio is not observable and although the economic basis of the model is sound, it still remains difficult to prove. If tests are like the one we carried out above, the results will almost certainly cause the CAPM to be rejected.

There is another misconception concerning the CAPM that is widespread in the property market. This says that the CAPM applies to the equity market only. However, there is nothing in the theory that says that this should be the case. The conditions that were proposed in order to develop the model are fairly stringent and in many cases it is true that they are violated by property. However, the CAPM is a general equilibrium asset-pricing model and is quite capable of accommodating property.

There is one final point that needs to be borne in mind with the CAPM and that is that it is an *ex-ante* model. It is based on expectations. Although betas are often estimated from historic data, portfolio theory requires forecasts. As a result *ex-ante* estimates of beta are just as valid as historic regression betas that are adjusted to reflect investor expectations.

Strategy and the investment process

Strategy and performance measurement is an interrelated process. Strategy identifies the investment objectives for a fund, which are evaluated some time later by performance measurement. A process of review should then follow, during which individual properties are evaluated and changes to the portfolio are then suggested to keep the fund in line with the agreed strategy. We summarise this process in Figure 15.2.

The development of a viable strategy revolves around an understanding of portfolio theory and the characteristics of property. It also involves identifying, in consultation with your client, what the overall objective for the fund should be. This may be influenced by the tax status of the fund, but is also likely to revolve around some general notion that relates to growth prospects. This is just another way of highlighting the fact that the fund has different views concerning risk. So it is also important to try to evaluate the risk profile of the fund. What you are interested in is finding out how risk-averse the fund is likely to be. This will give you a better indication of the type of properties you should be examining.

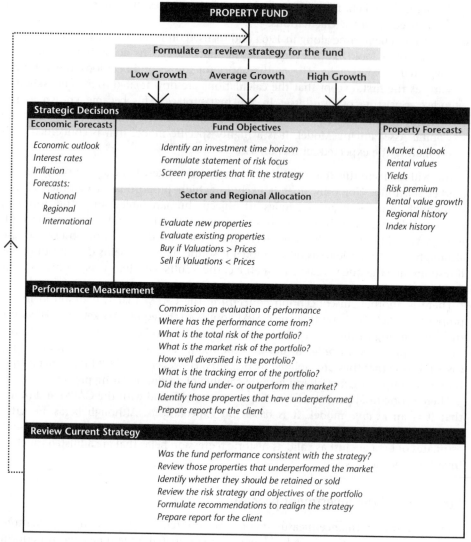

Figure 15.2 The investment process

From this discussion together with what you have learnt in other parts of this book you can summarise the characteristics of property as an investment class as follows:

- valuations are probably a fair reflection of market prices
- property is better at hedging inflation in the long term
- the returns from individual properties are not highly correlated
- individual properties carry high levels of specific risk
- most portfolios hold fewer than 50 properties and are poorly diversified
- property portfolios have high tracking errors so that it is not possible to track an index.

With these points in mind it is possible to consider what these imply in terms of developing a portfolio strategy.

Active–passive strategies

We showed in Chapter 11 that property portfolios tend to be poorly diversified. One of the criticisms frequently levelled at the efficient markets hypothesis is that investors do not believe that assets are fairly priced so that there are always mispriced assets waiting to be bought. However, the more people who believe that the market is not efficient the more competitive it is likely to become. This in turn makes it more efficient. As the main objective of developing an investment strategy is to locate underpriced properties the fact that investors are operating in a reasonably competitive market suggests that this can only be achieved through three sources:

● luck
● inside information
● superior forecasting ability

This is an interesting idea that has a direct bearing on the type of strategies that can be developed.

Portfolio strategy and forecasting ability

In essence portfolio strategy depends on your forecasting ability. These can be considered in relation to two extremes: *perfect forecasting ability* and *no forecasting ability*.

If you possess perfect forecasting ability you will be able to predict with complete certainty those properties that will show superior performance. The strategy that should be adopted in this case is to invest as much as possible in those properties that you know are underpriced because you are guaranteed to earn abnormal returns.

At the other end of the spectrum let us assume that you have no forecasting ability whatsoever. Here again your strategy is also straightforward. All you have to do is follow the herd and construct a portfolio that tracks an index. In this case there will be no abnormal performance, but you will at least have the comfort of knowing that the fund performance has been no better nor worse than average.

> *Perfect forecasting ability* suggests that investors should buy those properties they know are underpriced. This will guarantee abnormal returns.
> *No forecasting ability* suggests that investors should track an index so that performance is in line with the average. There will be no abnormal returns.

The active–passive strategy

The problem really comes if you have *some* forecasting ability. Recognising the differences in forecasting ability has led to a widely recognised approach to investment known as the active–passive strategy. This suggests that the investment process can be split into two parts.

● The first part is to create a portfolio that tracks an index. All the specific risk is eliminated through diversification so that the returns move in line with an index. The penalty for doing this, as mentioned above, is that it is not possible to outperform the index.

● The second part reserves a proportion of funds that can be used to back your beliefs concerning forecasts of performance for individual assets. If you are able to capitalise on this part successfully, then over time the performance of your portfolio should be better than a managed portfolio carrying the same level of market risk. If, of course, your forecasts were not so good then your performance will be below that of the managed portfolio.

The active–passive strategy tries to identify those assets that have an intrinsic value that is different from their current value. This requires some knowledge of the risk class of the asset in order to determine whether it is under- or overpriced. In terms of the security market we discussed earlier this would be represented by asset U in Figure 15.3.

Applying this idea to the property market leaves you with an interesting situation. Property investors and their advisers frequently believe they have perfect forecasting ability, but behave as if they have none. In other words, every property recommended for purchase is believed to be underpriced, but the strategy many investors try to pursue is to track an index.

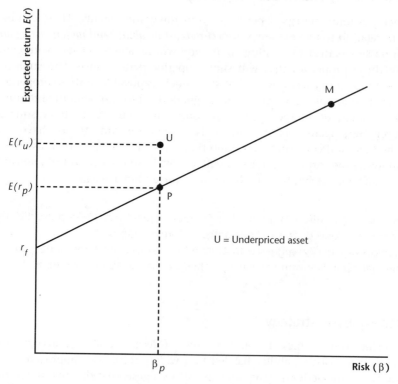

Figure 15.3 Selection of underpriced assets

> Property investors believe they have perfect forecasting ability but often behave as if they have none!

This raises two questions:

1. Is it possible to track an index with a property portfolio?
2. Is this a viable strategy to pursue?

Tracking an index with a property portfolio

We have already shown in Chapter 11 that because it is so difficult to achieve highly diversified portfolios of property, it will be very difficult to track an index with a property portfolio. In order to track an index the portfolio should

- have a high $\bar{R}^2$ value, and
- have a beta equal to 1.0.

In other words, the property market should explain a high proportion of the variance in returns of the property portfolio and they should both be similar in composition.

You should recall from Chapter 11 that it is very difficult to achieve a property portfolio with a high $\bar{R}^2$ value. We also showed that for an equally weighted portfolio approximately 200 properties would be needed to achieve an $\bar{R}^2$ of 95%. If the effect of value weighting is taken into consideration, the figure is likely to be much higher unless there are some properties that are highly correlated with the market.

It is useful to make a similar comparison with the equity market. Table 15.2 shows that it is much easier to achieve highly diversified portfolios with equities than with property. Although our figures are based on data for the period 1979–82 you will find that you will get similar results for other periods. Since most portfolios hold fewer than 50 properties and very few portfolios hold over 170 properties it is almost impossible to achieve a portfolio that will track an index.

Although there may be a desire for property investors to track an index, the practicalities of investment in property make this almost impossible. IPD have examined this issue and have shown that the tracking errors of commercial property funds can vary from 2% to 18% p.a. and there is no relationship with the total risk of a fund. Figure 15.4, prepared by IPD, shows this relationship and also confirms how difficult it would be to track an index.

After undertaking an extensive analysis IPD came to the following conclusions about those funds that had high tracking errors.

Table 15.2 • Diversification of property and equity markets compared, 1979–82

% diversification	Number of properties	Number of equities
95%	171	44
99%	895	228

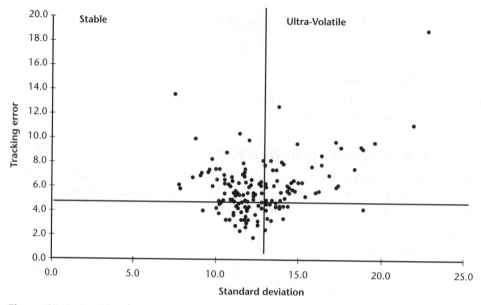

Figure 15.4 Tracking error and standard deviation (courtesy of IPD)

- The funds were generally small
- They actively managed their portfolios
- They had high levels of specific risk
- They had sold underperforming assets
- They had made lower transactions profits
- They had suffered development losses

The conclusions reached by IPD confirm our analysis of risk reduction and diversification given in Chapter 11.

Although it is clear that tracking an index on a period-by-period basis is almost impossible, this does not mean, however, that the rationale for following this type of strategy is unrealistic. The reason for this is that many investors tend to hold special properties for long periods. It is not unusual, for example, for investors to hold trophy properties as a core component in their portfolios. Each of these will, of course, have their own level of systematic risk. As they get older expectations of future growth will reduce and the systematic risk will decline. A fund may, for example, have decided that it wishes to establish a high-growth portfolio. This implies that on average the portfolio beta should be greater than 1.0. As the properties age, and assuming that they are not actively managed in any way, their betas will decline. The portfolio will, therefore, fall into a lower market risk class and have a lower expected return. As the observed returns will fluctuate round the expected value-changes in market risk can have an important impact on performance. This effect is illustrated in Figure 15.5.

The target return for this fund is currently 15% and its target beta, β_T, is slightly greater than 1.0. This could be regarded as a growth fund. However, because a number of the properties have aged the actual beta, β_A, is only 0.65 and its expected return is 13.5%. The shaded areas show the upside for this fund relative to the target position.

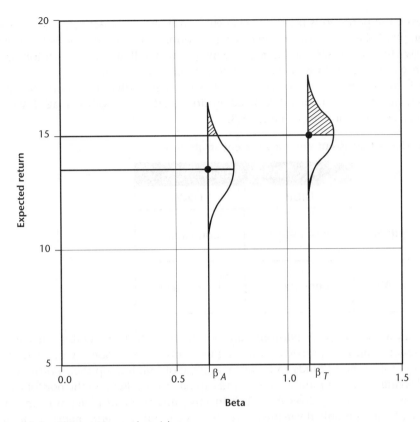

Figure 15.5 Changes in market risk

We have illustrated this point in relation to a change in the growth potential of standing investments. We have pointed out that this implies that the properties are not actively managed. This is particularly important for index construction, as it is possible that some commercial indexes may be tracking changes in the age of a portfolio as well as overall market movements.

The same effect could, of course, be observed as more properties are added into the portfolio. It is, therefore, useful to track the expectations of a fund in relation to changes in systematic risk. At present we know little about fund objectives in relation to differences in systematic risk. We will look at changes in systematic risk, as more properties are included in a portfolio, when we examine performance measurement in Chapter 16.

Consistent and inconsistent strategies

Our discussion so far leads us on to what can be considered consistent and inconsistent strategies (Brealey 1983).

If a portfolio is highly diversified with a high $\bar{R}^2$ value, then it should reduce the turnover of its assets in order to minimise management charges. The aim of the portfolio in this case should be to track an index. This is a consistent strategy. If, however, the portfolio is poorly diversified then it should be actively managed with the emphasis being placed on forecasting abnormal returns. This too is a consistent strategy. In both cases the strategy being pursued follows from partitioning the variance of returns into systematic and non-systematic components.

An inconsistent strategy would be to have a highly diversified portfolio that is actively managed or a poorly diversified portfolio that is inactively managed. We have summarised these options in Table 15.3.

Table 15.3 ● Consistent and inconsistent strategies

		Trading Activity	
		HIGH	**LOW**
Diversification	**HIGH**	Inconsistent	**Consistent**
	LOW	**Consistent**	Inconsistent

We know that property portfolios are poorly diversified. In addition, it has been common to consider property as a long-term investment. Some years ago it was common for property funds to follow a strategy of building up their portfolios and then leaving them to produce income and capital growth. Because the portfolios were small they were poorly diversified. The inactive management policy was, therefore, consistent with a highly diversified portfolio. As a result the performance of the portfolios was almost certainly due to non-market factors and probably owed more to chance than good management. We will look at this in more detail in Chapter 16.

We should point out that it cannot be assumed that this inconsistent strategy will always produce poor results, as in some periods the returns may be spectacularly good. Providing a convincing explanation for the results against a predetermined policy may, however, be more difficult to justify. This would be more marked during a downturn in the property market.

Property selection

Identifying individual properties that are underpriced in an economic sense is difficult to achieve. The market abounds with comments on the relative merits of individual properties but there is, at present, no consensus view within the property industry as to how properties should be defined in terms of being under- or overpriced. This, of course, contrasts with the economic view that assets should be priced in relation to their expected return. Differences between observed and expected returns will indicate whether an asset is under- or overpriced. The property market is, however, yield-driven, the main purpose of which is to estimate capital values. As yields represent a combination of both total return and rental value growth their use as a means of identifying underpriced properties, in an economic sense, is not clear and random selection may prove to be just as successful.

Selecting properties by using yields does not guarantee that underpriced properties can be identified.
Random selection of properties may be just as successful.

These are, of course, contentious statements. However, it is not enough for a valuer to suggest that a property is undervalued merely on the basis of yields and intuition. There needs to be some economic reference point based on expected returns and risk. However, valuers rarely make use of these concepts when evaluating property.

There is, of course, plenty of research and advice concerning the prospects for individual properties, but whether this can be converted into information that is profitable is open to debate. If information is widely available, then there is every likelihood that it will already be impounded into values. Unless the professional adviser or investor has access to information that is not widely known, or is contemplating the purchase of a property where the information set differs significantly from that used for open market valuations, it is unlikely that he or she will be able consistently to acquire underpriced properties. In addition, the high cost of research could well erode any potential gains that have been identified.

This view has significant implications for property research organisations. Without a formal theory of market equilibrium it is doubtful whether the research function can identify underpriced properties other than by chance.

Without a formal theory of market equilibrium it is doubtful whether research organisations can identify underpriced properties, other than by chance.

This is a very strong statement. However, when we discuss performance measurement we will show that there is no evidence to support the view that professional advisers can consistently outperform the market. You shouldn't be too surprised by this. In an efficient market this is what you would expect. There will be some evidence of abnormal returns, but you would not expect it to be statistically significant. Similar results also exist in the stockmarket.

The only thing that should surprise you is that despite the widespread belief amongst professional advisers that the property market is inefficient, they do not seem able to consistently exploit that information.

The starting point for identifying underpriced properties is to recognise that property is part of a much larger investment market and that the theory of risk, expected return and equilibrium that we have discussed throughout this book applies as much to property as to any other investment sector. Although much has been written about property there is nothing in the literature that substantiates the view that property is so different from all other markets that it requires a whole new theory of investment. Pursuing this logic the next step is to accept that the market only rewards investors for taking on that part of risk that they cannot diversify away, i.e. systematic or market risk.

The concept of market risk and the diversification of specific risk are likely to be around for some time. These are robust ideas that apply to all risky assets. Although the accurate pricing of assets using the CAPM may not be feasible you should also realise that this may not be the goal that investors want to achieve. For example, there is probably more merit in trying to establish the ranking of property assets relative to a broad-based index of property. If the IPD Index is regarded as the market for property, then selecting properties that appear mispriced relative to that index provides a viable way to proceed.

> If the IPD Index represents the 'market' for property, then a viable strategy is to identify properties that appear mispriced relative to that index.

Although the mathematics of selection will not change, this approach bypasses the need to use the CAPM. The process of selection then focuses on the following activities:

● Forecast the expected return on the market
● Forecast the risk of individual properties
● Estimate the expected return for individual properties
● Identify those properties that appear under- or overpriced.

You should notice that everything in this list is drafted in terms of forecasts or expectations. Depending on your forecasting skill your job is to try to forecast the shape of the *ex-post* security market line. Assuming that you have decided on a suitable investment horizon let's look at some possible outcomes.

● If you have no forecasting skill your security market line will be upward-sloping and will offer you an expected return for taking on extra risk that is in line with the long-term average. You will assess each property relative to the slope of the line and hope that over your investment horizon your expectations are realised and you have made good decisions.
● If you have some forecasting skill, or have bought in the results of a forecasting service, you may believe that the *ex-post* security market line over your investment horizon has a different slope to the long-term average. This could be upward or downward. Once again you make your choice of properties relative to this line and evaluate your performance at the end of the period. If your forecasts were right, then you will have secured some positive abnormal returns.

You will see that your choice of properties, or any investment asset, depends on your forecast of what you believe is going to happen in the market. You then try to identify those properties that are likely to offer abnormal returns on an *ex-ante* basis. This is the role of property analysis, the results of which can then be fed into a system of recommendations for buying, selling or holding property. This ties in with the general framework of risk and return that we have also discussed. It should be clear, therefore, that it is difficult to make valid buy–sell recommendations without having some knowledge of the following:

● The risk class of each property
● A forecast of market expectations
● An estimate of the expected return

This is not just a scientific exercise. There is a lot of skill required in estimating each of these elements, but the important point to appreciate is that it ties in the selection of property with capital market theory. This is also consistent with maximising net present value. The general framework is therefore as follows:

Table 15.4 ● Property recommendations and net present value

Recommendation	Net present value
Buy	Positive
Sell	Negative
Hold	Zero

If this type of analysis is carried out against a specific time horizon, the results represent an economically defensible approach to the problem of property selection. Whether your selection proves to be worthwhile will depend on the quality of the forecasts used to implement the model.

In identifying whether a property is under- or overpriced all available information concerning that property has to be processed in a better than average way. If, as is often suggested, the property market were really inefficient, then there should be ample opportunity to earn abnormal returns. Due to the lack of a central marketplace where properties can be bought and sold, the flow of information is not as readily accessible. To overcome this the market uses agents, with a wide network of contacts, to fill the information void. The greater the number of agents operating in a particular sector or region the greater the flow of information which then leads to an increase in efficiency. This would also occur if the proposals for a securitised market were accepted and interests in commercial properties became more frequently traded.

> Because there is no central marketplace for buying and selling property, agents fill the information void by building up a network of contacts. The more extensive the network the greater is the pricing efficiency of the market.

Processing information

The ability to identify underpriced properties depends on how well information can be processed. If all research departments are reviewing the same markets in the same way, then they should arrive at a consensus view concerning future prospects. Given this framework it is the unconventional view that will achieve the greatest rewards.

At present, recommendations for property purchases make no reference to forecasts of abnormal returns. There are two approaches currently used in the market to identify whether a property is under- or overpriced. These are making a comparison of equivalent yields or internal rates of return.

Equivalent yields

This is one of the main pieces of information used for deciding whether to purchase a property. The decision to buy is frequently made by comparing the yield on a property with the prime yield. If there is a difference it is sometimes suggested that this will signal that the property is under- or overpriced. In simple terms equivalent yields can be regarded as the difference between expected returns and growth rates. There is an infinite combination of these two factors that will give the same yield. If investors are interested in maximising their long-term wealth position, then the rate of return is the appropriate measure to use. A comparison of yields will only result in the selection of underpriced assets merely by chance.

Internal rate of return

As an alternative, the cash flows for a property are sometimes projected over a number of years and the internal rate of return is then estimated. This is more defensible and is widely used. However, the decision to accept or reject a property depends on making a comparison between the internal rate of return and a target return. This figure is often fixed as a company target and is applied as a constant cut-off rate to all properties. To be accepted, each property has to achieve returns in excess of the cut-off rate irrespective of the risk class in which they lie. This process causes potentially profitable low-risk properties to be rejected and pushes the fund towards accepting higher-risk property, some of which may be overpriced. Over time the fund will become more risky.

If both these approaches were, however, consistently successful the results of selecting properties would show up as positive abnormal returns in a performance analysis. Chapter 16 shows that this is not the case. The internal rate of return approach is partly valid, but could be improved by making an allowance for the risk of each property.

Identifying abnormal returns

Property selection is really concerned with identifying positive abnormal returns as this will lead to an increase in net present value. If, for property J you know the expected risk adjusted return, $E(r_j)$, and compare this with its internal rate of return, r_j, then the difference would be a measure of the abnormal return α_j:

$$\alpha_j = r_j - E(r_j) \tag{15.3}$$

If this is positive then the property is worth buying. You can formalise this process in three steps and make use of traditional valuation and modern investment techniques, incorporating the detailed knowledge and forecasting skill of the valuer.

Step 1. Estimate the current property value

This can be determined by using the standard equivalent yield model:

$$V_j = \frac{a_j}{y_j} + \frac{R_j - a_j}{y_j (1 + y_j)^n} \tag{15.4}$$

The current value of property J is related to its current rental value, R, and passing income, a, both of which are capitalised at the equivalent yield, y. In this case the lease is assumed to have n years to run before the rent is next reviewed. The model incorporates the experience of the valuer in assessing both the equivalent yield and the rental value.

On its own this estimate cannot tell you whether the property is under- or over-valued.

Step 2. Estimate the market risk and expected return for the property

An important step in evaluating the property is to know something about its risk class. This is an *ex-ante* exercise. Using the equivalent yield model together with similar information for the market it is possible to estimate the market risk as described in Appendix 10F. This process again takes into consideration the experience of the valuer and estimates the market risk on the assumption that the property would be held in perpetuity. This would be the approach to adopt if you wanted to value the property.

However, if you have a short-term investment horizon you might want to estimate the market risk using a scenario approach. You should recall from Part 1 this also draws on the experience of the valuer, together with other market forecasts. In both cases you are trying to estimate the risk of the property relative to the property market. This is not a direct application of the CAPM although the maths looks exactly the same.

Assuming you have estimated the market risk for property J as β_j and you also have an estimate for the market risk premium you can estimate the expected return from:

$$E(r_j) = r_f + \beta_j[E(r_m) - r_f] \tag{15.5}$$

This provides you with a benchmark return against which you can evaluate an individual property.

Step 3. Estimate the internal rate of return based on forecasts of rental value growth

Based on a detailed examination of the location of the property you need to estimate a separate forecast of rental value growth. Substituting this into a cash flow model for the property it is possible to estimate the internal rate of return that will give the same present value as estimated using the equivalent yield. If you were proposing to hold the property in perpetuity then the model you can use in this case would be:

$$V_j = \frac{a_j[1 - (1 + r_j)^{-n}]}{r_j} + \frac{R_j[1 + E(g_j)]^n}{r_j(1 + r_j)^n} \left\{ \frac{(1 + r_j)^p - 1}{(1 + r_j)^p - [1 + E(g_j)]^p} \right\} \tag{15.6}$$

This is just the value of property J valued part-way through a rent review where

a_j = passing rent
R_j = the rental value
$E(g_j)$ = rental value growth
n = number of years to the next rent review
p = the rent review period

The values given in equations 15.4 and 15.6 are economically equivalent so they can be set equal to each other.

If you compare the internal rate of return from step 3 with the expected return in step 2 you can then estimate the abnormal return and decide whether the property is under- or overpriced.

Example

Analysing single properties

Let's assume that you have an investment horizon of five years and that you have only one property to examine: we will call the property X. You are given the following information.

Table 15.5 ● Property details

Property X	
Current income p.a.	£68,000
Current rental value	£77,000
Equivalent yield	6.5%
Years to next review	2.5

Step 1

Following step 1 you can estimate the expected value as follows:

$$V_X = \frac{£68,000}{0.065} + \frac{£77,000 - £68,000}{0.065\,(1 + 0.065)^{2.5}} = £1,164,446$$

If you were examining a property that was available for purchase you should also know its price, P_X. You could then make a direct comparison between these two figures and decide whether or not to buy. You would do this if your value exceeded the purchase price:

$$\text{Buy if } V_X > P_X \tag{15.7}$$

This would imply that you believe the property is worth more than its price and as a result is mispriced. However, you should investigate this further as small changes in yield have a significant impact on value.

If, however, you already held the property you really want to know whether it is under- or overvalued relative to your investment horizon and the property market as a whole. To decide whether this represents a fair value you need to estimate the market risk, β_X, of the property.

Steps 2 and 3

If you have a relatively short investment horizon you can use the scenario approach we described in Part 1 and combine steps 2 and 3. Remember that your estimate of market risk is intended to represent what you *expect* the risk to be. It is a forecast of how volatile you believe the returns on property X are likely to be relative to the market as a whole.

You have already estimated the current value using the equivalent yield model and arrived at a figure of £1,164,446. Given your investment horizon of five years you estimate what you believe the property will be worth at the end of that time assuming a range of different market conditions. We have summarised one possible scenario in Table 15.6.

Table 15.6 ● Forecast values for property X after five years

Current value	Income	Market conditions	Growth forecast in % p.a.	Value after five years	IRR
£1,164,446	£68,000	Above average	22.00%	£3,166,079	26.27%
£1,164,446	£68,000	Average	11.00%	£1,944,071	15.64%
£1,164,446	£68,000	Below average	1.00%	£1,231,423	6.84%

The estimated values could be based on experience or by using a commercial market forecast applicable to the property location. The internal rates of return are estimated by projecting the cash flows over five years and assuming that the property is then sold. To simplify matters we have assumed that the income remains constant.

To estimate the market risk you also need similar estimates of the returns you would expect for each set of market conditions together with their probability. All the calculations are shown in Table 15.7.

You will see from this that over the investment horizon of five years the expected market return is 13.00% and the expected property return is 17.95%. We have also estimated the market variance and covariance between the property returns and the market. With this additional information you can estimate the market risk of the property as follows:

$$\beta_x = \frac{Cov(r_x, r_m)}{Var(r_m)} = \frac{30.24}{25.20} = 1.20$$

This indicates that the property is 20% more volatile than the market.

In order to decide whether this property is under- or overvalued in relation to your investment horizon you need to know the certain return that you could earn over the same period. This represents the benchmark against which you would evaluate any property. You can find this in the financial press by referring to the return on government securities with a five-year maturity. Let's assume that this is 7.00% p.a. As you have estimated the property market return to be 13.00% this implies that over the next five years you will be expecting a risk premium of 6.00% p.a. This is clearly

Table 15.7 ● Estimating the market risk

Market conditions	Prob.	Market return (r_m)	Deviation from mean	Property return (r_x)	Deviation from mean	Market variance[1]	Covariance[2]
Above average	0.30	20.00%	7.00%	26.27%	8.32%	14.70%	17.47%
Average	0.60	11.00%	-2.00%	15.64%	-2.31%	2.40%	2.77%
Below average	0.10	4.00%	-9.00%	6.84%	-11.11%	8.10%	9.99%
Expected values		13.00%		17.95%		25.20%	30.24%

higher than the 2.00% long-term average used in the market and implies that you believe that the property market is moving into a more risky phase.

With this additional information you can estimate the expected return for the property as follows:

$$E(r_x) = r_f + \beta_x[E(r_m) - r_f] \tag{15.8}$$

$$E(r_x) = 0.065 + 1.20\,[0.06] = 0.142$$

The expected return for this property is, therefore, 14.2%. Comparing this with the expected return of 17.95% estimated from Table 15.7 you will see that the abnormal return is 3.75%:

$$\alpha_x = r_x - E(r_x)$$

$$\alpha_x = 17.95\% - 14.20\% = 3.75\%$$

As this is positive you can say that the property is worth more than its current value. Another way of looking at this is to say that the inclusion of this property in your portfolio is helping to increase the net present value.

You would need to evaluate the project in the same way each year and decide whether it should be retained or sold.

Analysing large groups of properties

The approach we have just described can be applied to a small number of properties and relies upon making an estimate of the market risk premium based on your estimate of market conditions over a short time horizon. We know, however, that the premium is likely to change over time and will depend on the aggregate risk-aversion. If you have a large sample of properties you can investigate this issue over a much longer time horizon as well as identify those properties that are under- or overpriced.

If, for example, you were responsible for managing a large portfolio of properties that are held as standing investments you should be able to obtain a forecast of the long-term expected rental value growth for each property. Each forecast would be

---

[1] The market variance is estimated by multiplying the squared deviation by the probability. For example, $0.3 \times 7.00\%^2 = 14.70\%$.

[2] The covariance is the product of the deviations multiplied by the probability. For example, $0.3 \times 7.00\% \times 8.32\% = 17.47\%$.

made from an economic assessment of the prospects for each location but would also be required as part of the regular valuation exercise. Armed with this information, the latest valuation and the details of the lease structures, you can estimate the IRR for each property using equation 15.6.

$$V_j = \frac{a_j[1 - (1 + r_j)^{-n}]}{r_j} + \frac{R_j \, [1 + E(g_j)]^n}{r_j \, (1 + r_j)^n} \left\{ \frac{(1 + r_j)^p - 1}{(1 + r_j)^p - [1 + E(g_j)]^p} \right\}$$

Using this equation you can estimate the internal rate of return r_j, as long as you know the open market value V_j, the passing rent a_j, the rental value R_j, the number of years to the next review n, the rent review period p, and you have an estimate of the expected growth $E(g_j)$.

To analyse the aggregate risk-aversion in the market you do, however, need to estimate the market risk of each property. In this case you are assuming an infinite time horizon, so you could use the model shown in Appendix 10F or you could extend the scenario approach to embrace an infinitely long time horizon. The next step is to plot the internal rate of return for each property against the market risk and estimate the regression line between the two sets of data. We have done this with a large sample of properties and obtained the results shown in Figure 15.6.

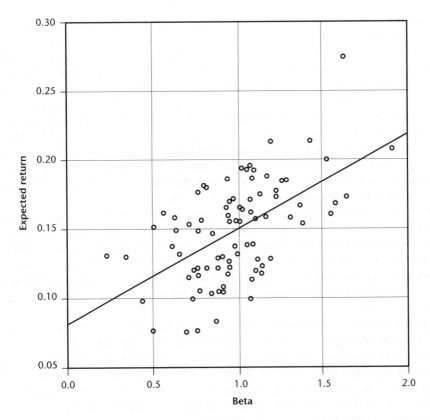

Figure 15.6 Abnormal returns and aggregate risk-aversion

As the values are based on current information the slope of the line will change over time and will tell you something about the aggregate aversion to risk. This is potentially useful as it may contain information about future changes in the market. For example, the illustration shows a strong positive relationship between risk and return with a market risk premium in the order of 7%. This implies that, based on this hypothetical sample of data, you would expect prices to fall in the future in order to justify the high returns.

The illustration also shows those properties that are both under- and overpriced. If this type of analysis is undertaken on a continuous basis, it could provide useful signals for portfolio revision and restructuring of standing investments.

Sector and regional allocation

The selection of individual properties is part of a much larger area of strategy concerning the allocation of funds to both sectors and regions.

We have shown earlier that the most important aspect influencing diversification is the correlation structure. We have also shown that most property portfolios tend to be small so that it is difficult to track an index. In fact, most of the performance comes from the residual risk component. When we looked at the correlation structure between individual properties across sectors it appeared that there was no strong relationship. This seems to imply that there is no significant advantage in terms of risk reduction to be gained by diversifying across sectors. If diversification is a goal that investors want to pursue, then diversifying within any sector is likely to prove just as effective.

However, few investors pursue this type of strategy. They prefer to spread their funds across sectors in order to take advantage of any superior returns that may be earned when one sector does better than another. It would, therefore, be useful to know when sectors are mispriced at the aggregate level, as this would provide a useful guide when searching for prospective properties. There is another reason for doing this. Most of the sector analyses that are undertaken to investigate asset allocation make use of aggregate data. We have shown you that the tracking error for most commercial property portfolios is so large that it is unlikely that they are able to take advantage of the allocation recommendations made in these studies.

The same principle will apply at the regional level. Small portfolios containing about 50 properties will find it hard to capitalise on specific allocation recommendations concerning regional investment. Most of their performance will come from the specific risk they hold so that they need to focus on individual property selection as opposed to regional allocation. As the portfolios get bigger, sector and regional allocations may become more important, but specific risk will still play an important role in decision-making.

If all properties have the same correlation structure those sectors or regions that appear to be underpriced will heavily influence the investment decision. In this respect Lee (1998) has shown that fund managers should pay more attention to sector allocation than to regional spread. Recommendations on sector or regional spread should, therefore, focus on any mispricing that may occur due to high or low demand. At the regional level there may be geographic areas that are doing well but the performance effects have not been incorporated into prices.

You can examine this idea to see whether any sectors appear to be mispriced by examining the abnormal returns within each sector. The reason mispricing may occur is because the index of returns for each sector will contain specific risk. Remember that an index only tracks the performance of a sample of properties. Even though the sample may be large it will still have some specific risk. To give you an idea of what is involved you can make an estimate of the specific risk that you are likely to experience in the IPD Annual Index.

By using the ideas we developed in Chapter 11 you can assume that the risk of the average property is 25% p.a. If all the specific risk in an index could be diversified away you can also assume that the risk in the index will reduce to 10% p.a. With this information you can estimate the residual risk for any size portfolio. We showed in Chapter 11 that the variance of a portfolio of size n could be related to the number of properties as follows:

$$\sigma_p^2 = A + \frac{B}{n} \tag{15.9}$$

where A and B are constants. This is just the sum of the systematic and residual risks of the portfolio, where both are expressed in variance terms. Another way of writing the total variance of the portfolio is:

$$\sigma_p^2 = \beta_p^2 \sigma_m^2 + \sigma_e^2 \tag{15.10}$$

From which you will see:

$$\sigma_e^2 = \frac{B}{n} \tag{15.11}$$

To estimate the residual risk you need to estimate the value of B. To find this you can write two expressions. The first gives the variance of the average property and the second the variance of a fully diversified portfolio with no residual risk as follows:

$$A + B = \beta_p^2 \sigma_m^2 + \sigma_e^2 \tag{15.12}$$

$$A = \beta_p^2 \sigma_m^2 \tag{15.13}$$

Subtracting gives:

$$(A + B) - A = \sigma_e^2 = B \tag{15.14}$$

If you resist the temptation of eliminating A from this expression you should recognise that $(A + B)$ represents the average property risk and A the market risk, both of which you know. They do, however, have to be squared so that they are expressed in variance terms. You now have everything to estimate the residual risk:

$$\sigma_e^2 = 25^2 - 10^2 = 525$$

The average number of properties for each sector of the IPD Annual Index is about 4,500. Substituting these figures into equation 15.11 gives:

$$\sigma_{4,500}^2 = \frac{525}{4,500} = 0.1167$$

In standard deviation terms the residual risk is 0.34% p.a. This is, of course, an approximate figure and will vary with each sector. It is also based on the naïve investor concept, which assumes equal investment in each property and that the variance and covariance for all properties is the same. The IPD All Property Index holds about 14,000 properties. Even at this level the residual risk is still about 0.20% p.a. Given these figures you shouldn't be too surprised to find some evidence of mispricing between the observed return for each sector and the expected return based on the market risk for each sector.

We have analysed each sector of the market to identify periods of mispricing and have summarised the results in Figures 15.7–15.9.

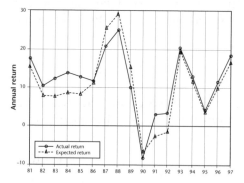

Figure 15.7 Actual and expected returns: retail sector, 1981–97

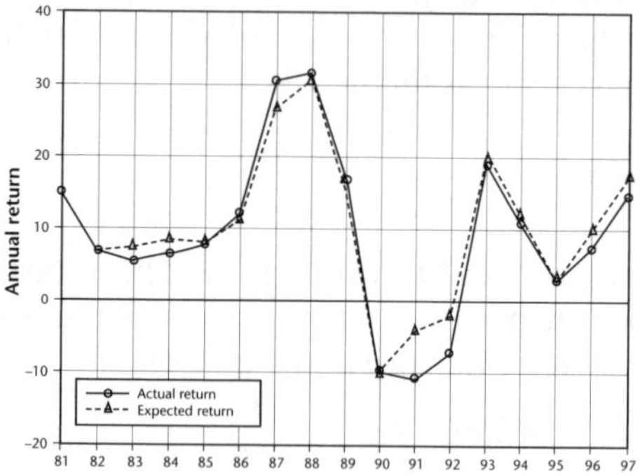

Figure 15.8 Actual and expected returns: office sector, 1981–97

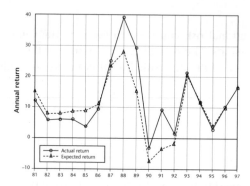

Figure 15.9 Actual and expected returns: industrial sector, 1981–97

Our aim in undertaking this analysis is to identify periods of abnormal return that would signal a buy–sell strategy. In principle these would be identified when a difference occurs between observed and expected returns. Figure 15.10 summarises the periods of mispricing.

We have also shown a 2% margin on either side of zero. This is intended to represent costs that would be incurred on buying or selling. It would be difficult to earn any profits within this margin.

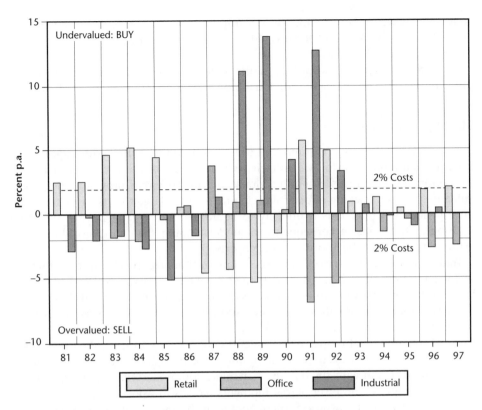

Figure 15.10 Abnormal performance for UK property, 1981–97

Given our discussion on the residual risk in each sector our estimates of abnormal returns will be subject to some variation. In addition, we will later show that the methods used to calculate index returns can introduce absolute errors in the region of 0.5% in the return calculations. If you want to be 95% certain that there is some mispricing in the marketplace, then you need to take the different sources of error into consideration to estimate the outer boundaries between which it is likely that there is no mispricing. You can estimate this as follows:

Margin = Transaction costs + (1.96 × Specific risk) + Index return error

Margin = 2% + (1.96 × 0.67%) + 0.5% = 3.17%

This is, of course, an average figure and assumes the worst case. It should be adjusted for each sector. What it does show, however, is that there may be a margin in excess of 3% on either side of zero that needs to be taken into consideration before making any comments about significant abnormal performance. With this additional information you will see that the majority of the abnormal returns are within this range, implying that periods of abnormal return are difficult to locate. The industrial sector did, however, show evidence of significant abnormal returns during the late 1980s. Since 1993 there has been no evidence of abnormal returns that could easily be exploited at the index level.

These results give an indication, at the aggregate level, of when to move into different sectors. The choice of individual properties is of course a separate issue.

Strategy guidelines

In developing a strategy it is important to bear in mind that the performance of the average institutional portfolio is unlikely to benefit from recommendations based on the performance of large sector and regional indices. They may provide some general guidance, but the tracking error of most portfolios is so large that their performance on a period-by-period basis is unlikely to be influenced by general asset allocation decisions. This is just a consequence of understanding that it is very difficult to achieve highly diversified portfolios of property.

Traditional portfolio strategy suggests a top-down approach. This implies that the sector allocation should be chosen first. The next level is the regional allocation followed by the allocation to individual assets. In property it is more likely to be the other way round. Although a broad indication of the allocation to sectors is likely to be useful in terms of identifying a general risk class most decisions will be made at the individual property level. Identifying whether an individual property is under- or overpriced is likely to be more important than ensuring that the commitment of funds fits in with the output of an allocation model. Having said this, when we looked at the use of lower partial moments models in Appendix 10C we showed that, irrespective of risk-aversion, there appears to be some evidence to suggest that investors should hold approximately 20% of their funds in the office sector. Changes in risk-aversion will then be related to the proportion of funds held in retail and industrial property.

> Identifying whether an individual property is under- or overpriced is likely to be more important than ensuring that the commitment of funds fits in with the output of an allocation model.

Given this background we can, nevertheless, offer some general comments that may be helpful in developing a strategy:

● Decide on an investment objective for the property fund. The aim should be to choose a category such as a growth fund, an income fund or a balanced fund. The choice may be influenced by the tax position of the fund or by other issues such as the need to meet certain objectives, or specific legal requirements. Each of these groups tells you something about the market risk of the fund that will influence the average long-term performance.

● Keep the market risk of the fund in line with the investment objectives. This requires that the market risk of the fund be monitored on a regular basis.

- Forecast the expected risk premium for the property market over different time horizons. This can be used to estimate expected returns.
- Analyse the properties within the portfolio in addition to those that have been earmarked for purchase to identify whether they are under- or overvalued.
- Actively manage the portfolio to ensure that its market risk stays in line with the stated objectives of the fund and that disposals and purchases that are made will contribute to positive net present values.

What is important to recognise is that there are only two things that can increase investment success:

1. Improve forecasting skill.
2. Use correct decision models.

Using good forecasts with poor decision models will not improve performance. We can't offer any magic recipes that will guarantee outstanding performance. What we can be sure of, however, is that get-rich-quick schemes are unlikely to turn every property investor into a millionaire. The competitive nature of the property market will ensure that, on average, most properties will be fairly priced. In a competitive market a strategy that is based on sound economic principles, but which is allowed to indulge any special knowledge available to an investor, may in the long run prove to be successful.

There is one final point that we need to make before we leave this section. We showed in Chapter 9 that individual property returns tend to be positively skewed. Investors like positive skewness because it offers the potential for high returns. Skewness, however, can be quickly diversified away so there is probably some incentive for investors to hold small portfolios as this would increase their chances of capitalising on any abnormal increases in return.

Risk management

Another important aspect of strategy is risk management. The risk of each sector of the market can change over time and will be reflected in changes in market risk. We have estimated these changes on an annual basis and summarised them in Figure 15.11.

Individual portfolios will, of course, behave differently but the clear message is that the volatility of portfolios, relative to the overall property market, will not remain constant. If you add to this changes in both the riskless rate of return and the market premium you will see that there is likely to be a lot of change in the expected performance of portfolios.

Changes in expected performance constitute an unavoidable risk for investors, especially if they are unable to buy or sell properties quickly enough to take advantage of shifts in the market. One way of reducing this risk is to make use of derivatives. This is a relatively new area for property but it is likely to grow in importance. At present the use of derivatives is not widely understood but it can provide the opportunity for property investors to hedge against expected changes in the market. As this is such an important area we have covered it in more detail in Appendix 15B.

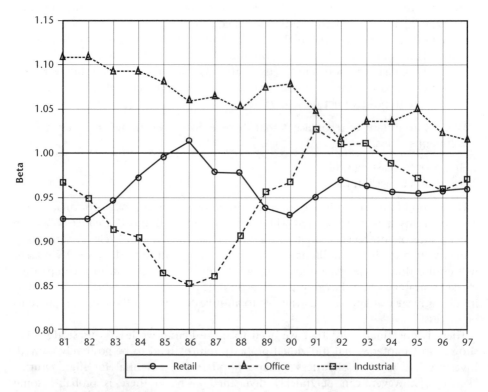

Figure 15.11   Profile of market risk, 1981–97

Summary

There is currently no established theory of property strategy that ties property investment into the capital markets. The market tends to be deal-driven with the emphasis being on selecting individual properties. However, because the specific risk element of property is so high and property portfolios tend to be small it turns out that this is not such a bad strategy to follow, at least in principle. The difficulty in operationalising it, however, comes in identifying whether individual properties are under- or overpriced. Traditional property valuation texts pay little attention to concepts such as market equilibrium so that investment decisions are made without reference to any formal benchmark.

In this chapter we have addressed these issues and have shown how to tie together the forecasting skill of the investor with some knowledge of the capital market so that viable investment decisions could be made. We also have shown that an understanding of the way markets work leads to the development of the active–passive strategy. In property, however, the active part is the most important element affecting performance.

This chapter has three appendices that address some issues that are important in understanding portfolio strategy.

Appendix 15A: Estimating the risk premium

Understanding the risk premium is an important part of investing in property. The conventional view is that it is in the region of 2%. This appendix examines this issue.

Appendix 15B: Using derivatives to control portfolio risk

As property becomes a more important part of the capital markets it is becoming essential to gain a better understanding of how risk can be controlled. This appendix looks at the role of derivatives as a means of controlling risk.

Appendix 15C: Property performance indices

This appendix provides a brief overview of some of the more important property indices available in the UK.

Chapter 15: Summary table

1. There is no established theory of property strategy that ties property into the capital markets.	
2. Property investors need answers to the following questions: ● Can professional advisers utilise costly information in a way that underpriced properties can be selected? ● Is professional advice sufficiently good that positive abnormal returns can be earned consistently from period to period?	The first question deals with strategy and the second with performance measurement.
3. A good strategy should build on our understanding of portfolio theory and the way that assets are priced.	
4. There are only three ways that an investor can earn abnormal returns: ● Good luck ● Inside information ● Superior forecasting ability	These imply that investors may have perfect forecasting skill or no forecasting skill.

5. With perfect forecasting skill you should buy those properties that you *know* are undervalued.	This strategy will guarantee abnormal returns.
6. With no forecasting skill you should aim to track an index so that your performance is in line with the average.	This strategy will guarantee no abnormal returns.
7. If you have some forecasting skill you should follow the active–passive strategy. The passive part tracks an index and the active part exploits any mispricing.	
8. Property investors believe they have perfect forecasting skill but behave as if they have none.	
9. As most property portfolios are poorly diversified it is difficult to track an index. This implies that investors are, by default, following an active strategy.	
10. Portfolio theory also suggests that there are consistent and inconsistent strategies.	If your portfolio is poorly diversified it should be actively managed. This is a consistent strategy.
11. Property selection should be undertaken within a capital market framework. Investors should try to estimate the expected return and use this as the benchmark against which to make an investment decision.	Without a good economic benchmark it is difficult to know whether underpriced properties can be selected other than by chance.
12. There does not appear to be any compelling reason to believe that investors would improve their diversification position by diversifying across sectors or regions.	Research suggests, however, that the choice of sector is more important than region.
13. Irrespective of risk-aversion it would appear that a core holding of 20% is a good starting point. Changes in risk-aversion can be adjusted by altering the percentage of funds in retail and industrial.	
14. It is important to track the market risk of your fund to ensure that it does not drift from expectations.	
15. Selecting properties that are undervalued and generate positive NPVs will in the long run produce better performance.	

Problems

1. What are the main issues in developing a portfolio strategy?

2. Discuss some of the popular misconceptions concerning property.

3. What are the main investment characteristics of property portfolios that will affect the development of a strategy?

4. If you have perfect forecasting ability, how would you exploit this in developing a strategy?

5. If you have no forecasting ability, how would you exploit this in developing a strategy?

6. Discuss the active–passive strategy and how it could be exploited in a property portfolio.

7. One strategy often followed by property investors is to track the IPD Index. Is this possible?

8. Discuss the steps you would need to take to estimate whether a property was under- or overvalued.

9. Which is more important, sector or regional diversification?

10. Discuss why it is important to track the market risk of a portfolio.

11. What role do forecasting services play in developing a portfolio strategy?

Selected references

Bernstein, P.L. and Damodaran, A. (1998) *Investment Management*, Wiley Frontiers in Finance, New York: John Wiley & Sons.

Brealey, R.A. (1983) *An Introduction to Risk and Return*, 2nd edn. Oxford: Basil Blackwell.

Brealey, R.A. (1986) Active–passive management. *Risk Management Service* 3 (1), 3–5.

Brown, G.R. (1993) Investment skill and portfolio management. *Journal of Property Valuation and Investment* 11 (3), 241–7.

Brown, G.R. (1996) Buy–sell strategies in the Hong Kong commercial property market. University of Salford.

Brown, G.R. and Chau, K.W. (1997) Excess returns in the Hong Kong commercial property market. *Journal of Real Estate Research* 14 (1/2), 91–106.

Brown, G.R. and Newell, G. (1996) Buy–sell opportunities in the Sydney CBD office market: 1984–95. University of Salford.

Brown, G.R. and Schuck, E.J. (1996) Optimal portfolio allocations to real estate. *Journal of Real Estate Portfolio Management* 2 (1), 63–74.

Diaz, J. (1990) The process of selecting comparable sales. *The Appraisal Journal* (October), 539–40.

Fama, E.F. and Schwert, G.W. (1977) Asset returns and inflation. *Journal of Financial Economics* 5, 115–46.

Firstenberg, P.B., Ross, S.A. and Zisler, R. (1987) Managing real estate portfolios. In *Real Estate Research*. Goldman Sachs.

Firstenberg, P.B., Ross, S.A. and Zisler, R. (1988) Real estate: the whole story. *Journal of Portfolio Management* (Spring), 23–32.

Fogler, H.R. (1984) 20% in real estate: Can theory justify it? *Journal of Portfolio Management* **10** (2), 6–13.

Haugen, R.A. (1993) *Modern Investment Theory*, 3rd edn. Englewood Cliffs, NJ: Prentice-Hall International.

Lee, S. (1997) Performing with style. University of Reading.

Lee, S. (1998) Sector and regional factors in real estate returns. University of Reading.

Lizieri, C. and Satchell, S. (1996) Property company performance and real interest rates: a regime-switching approach. University of Reading.

MacGregor, B.D. and Nanthakumaran, N. (1992) The allocation to property in the multi-asset portfolio: the evidence and theory reconsidered. *Journal of Property Research* **9**, 5–32.

Markowitz, H.M. (1959) *Portfolio Selection: Efficient Diversification of Investments*, A Cowles Foundation Monograph, New Haven: Yale University Press.

Markowitz, H.M. (1984) The 'two beta' trap. *Journal of Portfolio Management* **11** (1), 12–20.

Sharpe, W.F. (1963) A simplified model for portfolio analysis. *Management Science* **IX** (2), 277–93.

Sharpe, W.F. (1964) Capital asset prices: A theory of market equilibrium under conditions of risk. *Journal of Finance* (September), 425–42.

Appendix 15A
Estimating the risk premium

It is a widely held belief that the premium earned from investing in property is in the order of 2% p.a. over the riskless return on long-term government securities. This figure is adopted without question as the basis for establishing target rates of return, and is often applied to each sector of the market as well as to individual properties, irrespective of differences in risk class.

In this appendix we examine a number of approaches to estimating the risk premium. In doing this we draw a distinction between the expected premium used for valuation purposes, and the historic premium earned by investing in property. In the long run these figures should be close to each other, but over short periods there are bound to be differences.

Defining the risk premium

Many finance textbooks devote a chapter to the cost of equity. The reason for this is that the development of financial theory has revolved round estimating the expected return offered by different classes of asset. From our discussion in earlier chapters you should be aware that investors require a higher return to compensate for taking on extra risk. In order to choose an appropriate cost of equity you need to consider the relationship between risk and return. We have also shown that one of the important insights arising out of portfolio theory is that investors are not compensated for all the risk they take on, only that which they cannot eliminate through diversification. One way to capture this is to use the capital asset pricing model (CAPM) we discussed in Chapter 10. You will recall that this model decomposes the total return into two components.

- The return on a *risk-free* asset such as government stock, and
- An additional return needed to compensate for the uncertainty associated with undertaking a risky investment.

It is the second component that defines the risk premium. In a CAPM framework the expected return for asset *j* can be written as follows:

$$E(r_j) = r_f + \beta_j[E(r_m) - r_f]$$ (15A.1)

where $\beta_j[E(r_m) - r_f]$ is the risk premium for the asset. The expression in the square brackets is the *market risk premium*. The risk of the asset relative to the market is captured by β_j. An important component in this model is the risk-free rate of return as this provides the baseline against which the expected return on risky assets is estimated. The combination of the risk-free rate of return and the risk premium gives the expected return, and it is this that determines the price of the asset.

> The market prices risky assets in relation to their expected returns taking account of a premium, over the riskless return, needed to compensate for the additional risk of the asset.

The risk-free rate of return

You can define the risk-free rate of return as the certain return that can be earned over a specified period. The yield on a fixed-income government security that guarantees a fixed payment at a known point in the future is often used as the risk-free return. Typical examples include a short-term three-month Treasury Bill or, for longer periods, a bond maturing in 10 or 15 years' time. You will see from equation 15A.1 that the risk-less return is an important part of the CAPM. It is important because it is the rate of return that causes investors to make a choice between risk-free saving and investment.

The CAPM is a single-period model. However, it doesn't define how long that single period should be. What is clear is that when estimating the risk premium it is important to use a riskless return that matches the time horizon over which the returns on your risky asset are measured. The riskless return must, therefore, have two important properties that follow from the CAPM:

- it should have no variance so that the return is guaranteed
- it should have no covariance with the market returns

Meeting these requirements can, however, cause problems in choosing the correct return.

Treasury Bills are probably one of the safest investments, as there is little risk of default and given their short term there is little variation in price. Long-term bonds, by contrast, fluctuate in price in line with changes in interest rates, although if held to maturity they can still be regarded as being riskless. The price at which the bonds are bought will influence the return that is earned on maturity. Even though the return on government securities can be regarded as being riskless up to the date of maturity, it should be noted that their real rate of return remains uncertain, as there will be uncertainty about the rate of inflation.

In Chapter 6 we looked at the term structure of riskless interest rates. We showed that the annualised rates of interest are not necessarily the same for loans of differing maturity. The annual rates are influenced by changes in expectations concerning future interest rates. For example, the annualised interest rates on a two-year loan might be higher than a one-year rate if short-term interest rates are expected to rise in the future. At other times short-term interest rates might be lower than long-term rates. In Chapter 6 we offered a number of reasons for these differences. The yield curves that we illustrated were for zero-coupon bonds. These bonds have no inter-mediate cash flow but pay out a guaranteed amount on maturity. Unfortunately, zero-coupon bonds are unlikely to exist for all desired maturities. In a CAPM framework the yield to use is one with an effective maturity, called the duration, that is equal to the desired maturity of the investment. In practice a single rate is generally employed.

Historic and expected risk premia

In a valuation framework the risk premium should be forward-looking, reflecting the uncertainty of *future* cash flows. This is consistent with using the risk premium to estimate the expected value of an asset. In practice, however, historic estimates are usually taken as the starting point in estimating the expected risk premium. The realised market risk premium is simply the difference between the return on the risky portfolio and the risk-free return measured over the same period. In a CAPM frame-work the risk premium should, however, be estimated on a forward-looking basis, using the expected long-term return on the market less the long-term, risk-free rate.

Using historic returns to forecast the expected risk premium, even using data over periods as long as 50 years, can be suspect for a number of reasons. First, the data may suffer from extreme variance. Second, there may have been structural changes in the commercial property markets so that the use of historic data is unlikely to reflect the riskiness of future performance. For example, the lease structures in the 1950s and 1960s were very different from those that exist today. Even the recent experience of the 1990s has seen changes in the traditional lease. This was highlighted in the recent RICS research report entitled *Right Space: Right Price? Changing Lease Structures in Commercial Markets* (1998). The upshot is that taking past performance figures as a guide to estimating the expected risk premium is likely to be fraught with problems. A few unusually high or low returns can distort the underlying average.

> Expected values are assessed using expected risk premium figures. Historic pre-mium figures may not be a good guide to estimating expected risk premia.

In the following analysis we draw a distinction between estimating the *ex-post* and the *ex-ante* risk premium. In the first case we use historic data and subtract a periodic risk-free return that coincides with the period over which the returns are measured. The riskless return in this case is usually based on Treasury Bills. In the second case we develop a simple expectations model and try to extract the expected risk premium from information about current property market yields. The appropriate risk-free return in this case is the return on long-dated gilts. Our real interest in this case is to see how valid is the traditional 2% risk premium.

The *ex-post* risk premium

Method A. Cash flow analysis

In this approach we estimate the long-term risk premium that has been earned by holding a portfolio consisting of a large number of properties. This is often what is of real interest to investors, as over time they will have made decisions concerning which properties to buy. However, simply calculating the internal rate of return on a port-folio and subtracting from it the redemption yield on long-term government stock with the same maturity is inappropriate. The acquisition costs and cash flow of the properties that are added into the portfolio will influence the return on the portfolio. The way round this is to focus solely on the additional return that has been earned as a result of adding properties into the portfolio. By stripping out the influence of investing in a riskless asset that coincides with the risky cash flows it is possible to express the portfolio cash flows in risk premium form. The internal rate of return represents the risk premium. In order to do this you need some way of removing the effect of the riskless return from the risky cash flows. The methodology can be developed as follows.

In a single-period context the risk premium is merely the difference between the actual returns and the riskless rate of return. If you work in continuous returns you can write this as follows:

$$p = r_p - r_f \tag{15A.2}$$

where p is the premium, r_p is the nominal property return, r_f is the risk-free rate of return.

Taking antilogs gives:

$$1 + p = \frac{(1 + r_p)}{(1 + r_f)} \tag{15A.3}$$

If you let V_t and I_t represent an index of nominal and riskless returns in period t you can write changes in their values as follows:

$$(1 + r_p) = \frac{V_t}{V_{t-1}} \tag{15A.4}$$

and

$$(1 + r_f) = \frac{I_t}{I_{t-1}} \tag{15A.5}$$

Substituting these back into equation 15A.2 and rearranging gives:

$$p = \left(\frac{V_t}{I_t}\right) \div \left(\frac{V_{t-1}}{I_{t-1}}\right) - 1 \tag{15A.6}$$

This shows that in a single-period context you can estimate the risk premium by dividing the values at the beginning and end of the period by the riskless index so that the change in value is expressed in risk premium form. You can extend this idea over a number of periods. Dividing the cash flow in each period by a riskless index enables the internal rate of return to be estimated in risk premium form. This was the principle followed by Emary (1985), who analysed a portfolio made up from a sample of 350 properties. The cash flows extended over the 29-year period 1956–85. The riskless index was estimated from the monthly returns on three-month Treasury Bills. This ensured that there was a riskless index number whenever a cash flow occurred. The resulting money-weighted premia for each sector, over different sub-periods, are summarised in Table 15A.1.

Table 15A.1 ● Money-weighted risk premium figures

	Risk premium % p.a. for different sub-periods			
	1956–85	1980–85	1984–85	Sample size
Portfolio	1.80%	-2.20%	-4.80%	350
Retail	3.70%	0.10%	3.60%	144
Office	0.70%	-1.80%	-6.70%	94
Industrial	0.80%	-4.90%	-9.40%	112

There are two points to notice from this analysis. First, the average risk premium measured over the whole period for the total portfolio is close to 2.0%. Second, the spread of premium figures in each sub-period increases as the period over which the premium is measured decreases. The negative risk premium over the shorter periods indicates that it is not always possible to achieve positive returns, so the common view concerning the 2% risk premium only has validity in terms of long-term expectations. In other words, the longer a property is held the more likely the expected return will be realised.

Method B. Direct observation

This is the most direct method for obtaining estimates of the risk premium for property and involves subtracting the risk-free rate of return from the observed returns in each period. However, to be consistent, the choice of risk-free rate needs to match the holding period of the investment returns. For example, if you are measuring returns annually, then the appropriate risk-free rate of return needs to coincide with a one-year holding period. The risk premium then tells you what extra return you earned by taking on the risk of investing in property.

Using this principle we estimated the risk premium using the returns from published property indexes for monthly, quarterly and annual holding periods. We also examined the risk premium at the individual property level by using the following datasets:

● The IPD monthly data series for the period 1987–98. This is used to estimate both the monthly and quarterly returns.
● A long-run annual aggregate property index covering the period 1921–97. The data were made available by IPD.
● Subsets of these data covering each sector of the market over the period 1971–96.
● A sample of monthly valued properties covering the periods 1988–92 and 1993–97.

The risk-free rate employed in the analysis is the return on Treasury Bills over one month, three months and one year.

Monthly and quarterly data

Figure 15A.1 shows the monthly risk premium for the IPD All Property return series. There are discernible trends in this series together with a lot of variability.

A similar profile of risk premium figures can be observed for each sector. We have summarised the annualised premium figures in Table 15A.2. In annualising the standard deviations we have ignored the added complication of serial correlation so these figures will be understated.

In terms of the 2% target premium you are more concerned with the position at the all property level. We have, therefore, estimated the standard error of the mean premium figures. At the all property level the 95% confidence range for the average premium is 0.79% to 2.00%. This is quite wide and the 2% premium lies at the extreme of the range.

The corresponding risk premium profile for quarterly returns is shown in Figure 15A.2.

Table 15A.2 ● Annualised *ex-post* risk premia for IPD monthly returns, 1987–98

Sector	All property	Retail	Office	Industrial
Risk premium	1.40%	1.14%	0.32%	4.39%
St. Dev.	3.55%	3.30%	4.26%	3.79%
St. error of mean	0.31%	0.29%	0.38%	0.34%

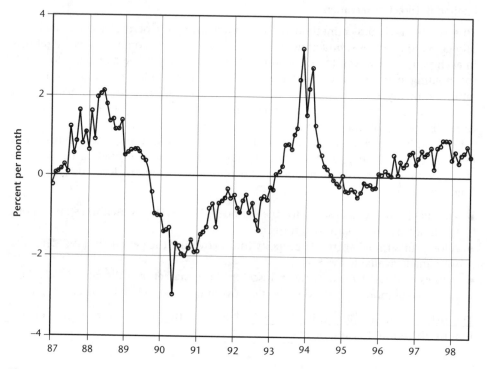

Figure 15A.1 Monthly risk premium: IPD All Property Index, 1987–98

Like the monthly returns this also shows a high degree of trending and variability. Summary statistics for the annualised quarterly premium figures are shown in Table 15A.3.

The 95% confidence range for the average all property risk premium in this case is from –0.29% to 3.35%. Note that not only does the 2% premium lie within this range, but so does zero. These figures are, of course, influenced by events that took place in the property market during the period 1987–98. You will see that the risk premium for offices is the lowest of the three sectors, followed by the retail sector. The figure for the industrial sector is by far the largest. All sectors do, however, exhibit considerable variation in the risk premium.

Table 15A.3 ● Annualised *ex-post* risk premia, IPD quarterly returns (%)

Sector	All property	Retail	Office	Industrial
Risk premium	1.53%	1.26%	0.46%	4.61%
St. Dev.	6.09%	5.61%	7.20%	6.50%
St. error of mean	0.93%	0.86%	1.10%	0.99%

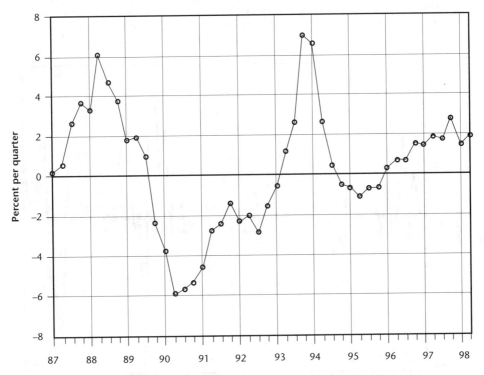

Figure 15A.2 Quarterly risk premium: IPD All Property Index, 1987–98

Annual data

From the above it could be argued that even with a time span of almost twelve years the monthly and quarterly figures may not provide a reliable guide to the average risk premium. One reason for this is that the data cover only one property cycle. A longer run of data spanning a number of cycles may therefore provide a more accurate reflection of the underlying risk premium.

IPD have quite recently constructed a long-term annual return series covering the period 1921–97. This is the longest series of property returns currently available and is con-structed from an IPD data series from 1971 to 1997 together with a series for 1921–70 from data collected by Peter Scott and published in his book *The Property Masters*. A full account of the data and the reliability of the earlier figures are provided in the IPD research report *Property Cycles 1921–1997*.

Table 15A.4 ● Annual average risk premia and variability (in % p.a.)

Period	1921–38 17 years	1921–97 76 years	1947–70 23 years	1947–97 50 years	1971–97 26 years
Risk premium	3.84%	3.36%	3.69%	3.19%	2.74%
St. Dev.	10.23%	10.19%	6.21%	10.23%	12.92%
St. error of mean	2.48%	1.17%	1.29%	1.45%	2.53%
Premium –95%	–1.02%	1.07%	1.16%	0.35%	–2.22%
Premium +95%	8.70%	5.65%	6.22%	6.03%	7.70%

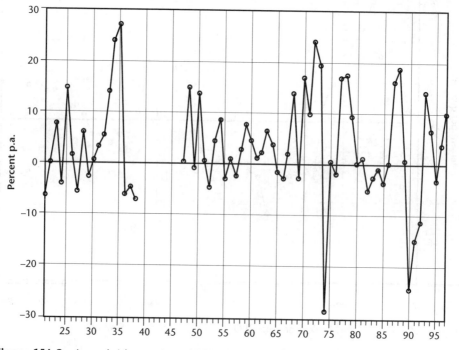

Figure 15A.3   Annual risk premium: 1921–97

Figure 15A.3 shows the profile of the annual risk premia for the period 1921–97. There is a break in the data during 1939–46 when insufficient data were available.

This series covers a number of property cycles and shows that the risk premium exhibits considerable variation over the period. There are also a number of periods when the premium is negative. The average figure for the whole period is 3.36%, which is higher than the 2% typically assumed. There is some evidence of kurtosis, indicating more extreme values than would be the case for a normal distribution, but this is not statistically significant. Table 15A.4 shows how the risk premium varied over five intervals.

Table 15A.5 ● Annual sector risk premia, 1971–97 (%)

Sector	All property	Retail	Office	Industrial
Risk premium	2.74%	3.73%	1.73%	4.38%
St. Dev.	12.92%	11.57%	14.54%	11.96%
St. error of mean	2.53%	2.27%	2.85%	2.35%

Over the long term there appears to be a strong consistency in the average values. The period 1971–97 covers the IPD long-term data series, and the risk premium is seen to be lower than values before this period. This may reflect the quality of the data prior to the rigorous data validation undertaken by IPD. However, the differences in average values for each period are all within a relatively small range.

The standard error of the mean risk premium figures is quite large and the traditional 2% premium still lies within the 95% confidence bands. Taking the whole 76 years you can be reasonably certain that the average risk premium is positive so that investors did receive compensation for investing in property.

By way of comparison the average equity risk premium for the period 1921–97 was 10.18%. This also included the period 1939–46, but the figure is considerably higher than the average of 3.36% for property.[1] Investors have, therefore, received a higher premium for investing in equities, which reflects the more risky nature of this type of investment. However, measurement of the equity risk premium is not without problems. The fact that it is so large has puzzled financial economists since 1985, and economists Mehra and Prescott have argued that it is too high to be consistent with current theory.

Using the IPD long-term series from 1970 you can investigate the annual property risk premium at the sector level. These are summarised in Table 15A.5.

Although there is some variation in the figures you cannot reject the proposition that the average risk premium for each sector over the period 1971–9, has been significantly different from 2%. However, the standard errors are so large that you also can't reject the proposition that the risk premium figures have been significantly different from zero. Historically, this shows that there is a lot of variation in the average risk premium. You should draw some comfort from the fact that the average figure is positive.

Over periods of up to 76 years the historic average risk premium has been higher than the target value of 2%, and has been much closer to 3%.
Statistically, however, you cannot reject the 2% risk premium.

[1] If you assume that the risk premium figures represent equilibrium positions then property and equities should both lie on the security market line. This implies that the beta of property relative to the equity market is about 0.33. You can find this by dividing the risk premium figures, i.e. 3.36/10.18 = 0.33.

This simple analysis shows that there is a lot of variation in the risk premium across sectors. It also implies that there is a lot of variation between properties so that it is important to consider the appropriate risk premium to use on a property-by-property basis. It is to this issue that we now turn.

Property risk premium at the individual property level

An analysis at the individual property level is of interest to anyone who wishes to understand the range of excess returns that have been earned. The results reported in this section are based on 40 retail, 30 office and 30 industrial properties over the periods 1987–92 and 1993–97. Tables 15A.6 and 15A.7 summarise the distribution of average annualised premium values for both monthly and quarterly returns estimated across the sample.

You will see from Table 15A.6 that there have been considerable differences in the risk premium both between sectors and within each five-year period. An additional feature is that during 1988–92 the retail and office sectors returned a negative average risk premium while the industrial sector offered a positive premium. The corresponding figures for the quarterly returns are given in Table 15A.7.

If you look at the quarterly risk premium you reach the same conclusion that was reached with the monthly data. Individual risk premia exhibit considerable differences between each period. Both the retail and office sectors have a negative premium in the first period whereas the industrial sector has a positive premium. The average for all

Table 15A.6 ● Distribution of average annualised *ex-post* risk premia, monthly returns (%)

	All property 100 properties		Retail 40 properties		Office 30 properties		Industrial 30 properties	
	88–92	93–97	88–92	93–97	88–92	93–97	88–92	93–97
Risk premium	−0.92%	4.66%	−5.83%	5.04%	−1.40%	4.46%	6.11%	4.35%
St. Dev.	2.40%	1.11%	1.45%	1.09%	2.81%	1.19%	1.36%	1.09%
St. error of mean	0.24%	0.11%	0.23%	0.17%	0.51%	0.22%	0.25%	0.20%

Table 15A.7 ● Average annualised *ex-post* risk premia, quarterly returns (%)

	All property 100 properties		Retail 40 properties		Office 30 properties		Industrial 30 properties	
	88–92	93–97	88–92	93–97	88–92	93–97	88–92	93–97
Risk premium	−0.51%	4.89%	−5.63%	5.25%	−0.89%	4.74%	6.69%	4.57%
St. Dev.	4.23%	1.96%	2.48%	1.93%	4.93%	2.10%	2.46%	1.89%
St. error of mean	0.43%	0.20%	0.39%	0.31%	0.90%	0.38%	0.45%	0.35%

sectors over the five years from 1993 has been high relative to the expected figure of 2%. Compared with the long-run sector averages given in Table 15A.5 the last five years are higher, particularly in the case of retail.

The *ex-ante* risk premium

Our analysis so far has been based on historical data. Although this gives a good idea of what investors have earned over long periods the results could well be influenced by events that were unforeseen. Interesting though this is, valuers and investors are more concerned with what the risk premium is *expected* to be. The reason for this is that valuations are based on expected cash flows. What is also important is that for freehold valuations the sequence of cash flows is effectively perpetual. Given this widely accepted valuation framework it will be clear that what has happened in the past has no bearing on expected performance. It is, therefore, sensible to turn our attention to estimating what you expect the risk premium to be, based on current information concerning property in a wider economic framework.

There are a number of ways of approaching this problem but in this appendix we will use a simple model that makes use of information that is familiar to most valuers.

You know that it is possible to value a property in two ways. The first is to use the equivalent yield model and assume that the yield captures all the current market information concerning expected growth and return. The second approach is to use a model that is more explicit in defining the expected rate of return and growth in rental value. Despite the differences in approach these models should both arrive at the same value. The important point to note in using the yield model is that it should capture current market opinion concerning the expected premium. What you are trying to do is extract the risk premium from the equivalent yield. If you review some of the material in Chapter 3 you will see that you can write this equality as follows:

$$\frac{a}{y} + \frac{R - a}{y(1 + y)^n} = a \left[\frac{1 - (1 + r)^{-n}}{r} \right] + \frac{R(1 + g)^n}{r(1 + r)^n} \left[\frac{(1 + r)^p - 1}{(1 + r)^p - (1 + g)^p} \right] \quad (15A.7)$$

where

a and R = the current income and rental value
n = the number of years to the next review
p = the rent review period
y = the equivalent yield
r = the required return
g = the expected growth in rental values

Another way of expressing the expected return is as the sum of the risk-free rate of return, r_f, measured on long-dated gilts and the risk premium, p. We can write this as:

$$r = r_f + p \quad (15A.8)$$

If you combine this with equation 15A.7 you will see that each parameter is observable, with the exception of the risk premium and the expected growth rate. As you are trying to estimate the risk premium this means that you should focus your attention on estimating the expected growth in rental value.

Two possible proxies come to mind. One is to use a forecast of expected inflation on the assumption that property is likely to hedge against inflation over long periods. You should recall from Chapter 14 that the evidence suggests that property is a better hedge against inflation in the long term, rather than the short term. An alternative view would be to use a forecast of Gross Domestic Product. The argument here is that growth in rental values would be linked to the performance of the economy as whole. Whatever approach is adopted it is clear that the growth forecast is an important factor influencing the expected risk premium.

To give you an idea of how this model could work in practice we will estimate the expected risk premium assuming two cases. The first is that all properties are fully rented so that the equivalent yield is equal to the initial yield. The second case assumes that rental values are in excess of the passing income and there are two and a half years, on average, to the next review.

We have taken average values from the IPD monthly index over the period 1986–97 and obtained comparable average figures for the return on Treasury Bills and the retail price index. You will see that in this case we are assuming that rental values in the long term will move in line with the rate of inflation. By substituting these figures into equation 15A.7 you can easily solve for the risk premium. You will, however, have to solve this by iteration.

Table 15A.8 summarises our results and provides two values for the risk premium.

Based on these figures the expected risk premium appears to be in the range 1.86%–3.12% p.a. As these are close to the 2% figures used in the market it implies that this widely used premium is not unreasonable. However, as far as this analysis is concerned there are a number of important points that need to be made:

● The premium figures only apply at the all property level. Each sector of the market and individual properties will have different expected premium figures and will need to be estimated separately.

● Our model has assumed a constant growth rate in perpetuity. This is clearly unrealistic and it may be that a model incorporating multiple growth rates offers additional insights.

● The model is very sensitive to the inputs. A small change in some of the values can cause a large change in the risk premium figures.

Table 15A.8 ● Estimating the *ex-ante* risk premium

	Income yield	Equivalent yield
Average yield	7.10%	8.40%
Expected return on T-Bills	9.10%	9.10%
Expected rate of inflation	4.40%	4.40%
Years to next rent review	0 years	2.5 years
Rent review period	5 years	5 years
Ratio of rental value to income	1.00	1.16
Expected risk premium	1.86%	3.12%
Expected return	10.96%	12.22%

Despite these difficulties it is reassuring to see that the estimated figures embrace some of the empirical estimates we have reported.

Selected references

Clinebell, J.M., Kahl, D.R. and Stevens, J.L. (1994) Time series properties of the equity risk premium. *Journal of Financial Research* **XVII** (1), 105–16.

Emary, R. (1985) Property risk premia. University of Reading, Unpublished MPhil dissertation.

FitzGerald, A., Semple, R. and Reynolds, J. (1992a) The equity risk premium puzzle. Equity Briefing Paper 24. County NatWest.

FitzGerald, A., Semple, R. and Reynolds, J. (1992b) Solving the risk premium puzzle. Equity Briefing Paper 26. County NatWest.

Lizieri, C., Crosby, N., Gibson, V., Murdoch, S. and Ward, C.W.R. (1997) *Right Space, Right Place? A Study of the Impact of Changing Business Patterns on the Property Market.* London: RICS.

Scott, M. (1992) The cost of equity capital and the risk premium on equities. *Applied Financial Economics* **2**, 21–32.

Scott, P. (1996) *The Property Masters*, London: E. & F.N. Spon.

Siegel, J.L. (1992) The equity premium: Stock and bond returns since 1802. *Financial Analysts Journal* (Jan/Feb), 28–46.

Yamaguchi, K. (1994) Estimating the equity risk premium from downside probability. *Journal of Portfolio Management* (Summer), 17–27.

Appendix 15B
Using derivatives to control portfolio risk

In this appendix we will show you how a derivatives contract can be used to hedge portfolio risk. At present there are few derivative contracts based on commercial property so the opportunities for controlling risk are limited. Nevertheless this is an area of growing importance and there are several players who are exploring initiatives that could extend the range and use of derivatives.

In comparison with other assets such as bonds and equities, property has a number of characteristics that expose investors to unavoidable risk during periods of high volatility. These include illiquidity, indivisibility and high transaction costs. In combination these factors can seriously frustrate strategic and tactical asset allocation decisions. However, by taking advantage of a property derivatives market investors can significantly reduce these risks by hedging against adverse movements in the commercial property market. We will consider the use of forward contracts.

Forward contracts

A forward contract is an agreement to buy or sell an asset at a future date for a certain price that is determined today. Forward contracts are private agreements between two parties and are not traded on any exchange. They are, therefore, described as over-the-counter (OTC) or off-exchange forward contracts (OFC).

One party to the forward contract assumes a *long position* by agreeing to buy the asset for a certain price at a specified date in the future, known as the maturity date.

The other party assumes a *short position*, agreeing to sell the asset at the same date for the agreed price. To date, only a limited number of forward contracts have been issued for commercial property.

Property Index Forwards (PIFs)

Property Index Forwards, also known as PIFs, are off-exchange forward contracts that offer a derivative exposure to the UK commercial property market. The first two PIFs were launched by BZW (now Barclays Capital) in November 1996, with one maturing in December 1997 and the other in December 1998. It is anticipated that further contracts will also be issued.

Trading in PIFs is undertaken by Barclays' market makers, who quote indicative bid/offer prices that are displayed by Reuters. PIFs contracts, therefore, provide investors with exposure to changes in UK commercial property values, as measured by the Investment Property Databank (IPD) Capital Growth Index. The contracts pay an amount equal to the difference between the purchase price and the value of the IPD Annual Capital Growth Index. The PIF contract that matured in 1997 provided purchasers with a capital gain of 9.6% from the date of issue.

How can PIFs be used?

As with any derivative instrument there will always be an element of speculation. This is a normal part of the arbitrage process that helps ensure that the derivatives are fairly priced. Speculators play an important role in ensuring that there is sufficient volume of trade to justify the existence of derivatives.

The most important category of PIF user is drawn from professional investors actively involved in managing property portfolios. However, as the role of these instruments becomes better understood and they become more widely used, other investors are likely to be attracted into the marketplace. These may include:

● Equity and bond portfolio managers wishing to diversify across assets into areas that have low correlation with the main investment instruments under their management.
● Corporate treasurers wishing to hedge against falling or rising property values prior to a valuation or balance sheet reporting exercise.
● Financial institutions whose mortgage books may require hedging when rising interest rates lead to mortgage defaults, which in turn leads to selling property in a falling market.
● Real estate managers intending to enter the property market at some later date but wishing to take advantage of prevailing buoyant market conditions.

Discussions with property advisers suggest that there is a widespread requirement for forward contracts such as PIFs, and for other derivative-based property instruments. A common view is that access to a range of derivative instruments, such as financial options and real options, could have considerable impact on property investment strategy.

Hedging property risk

Hedging is a way of arranging two opposite positions, such that the losses from one position are offset by profits from the other position. In other words, a hedger wishes to eliminate exposure to changes in value by taking on one risk to offset another.

We can illustrate the way in which PIFs can help to protect a property portfolio against unexpected changes in the market with a simple graph. Figure 15B.1 illustrates the idea.

The portfolio pay-off line shows the profit and loss that accrue to an investor who takes a long position in a property portfolio. The value is determined by the current market price of properties held. If the portfolio moves in line with the IPD Index, then any departure from the current value of 100 represents a profit or loss.

Suppose now that you forecast a fall in property prices by the end of the year. One way of minimising your potential loss is to sell your property holdings and move into other assets. Unfortunately, in a downturn your portfolio is likely to be illiquid so that you won't be able to sell your properties quickly enough. Even if you could organise some quick sales you will more than likely have to accept lower prices than expected in order to stimulate some sales. Your selling strategy, therefore, results in much greater losses than anticipated.

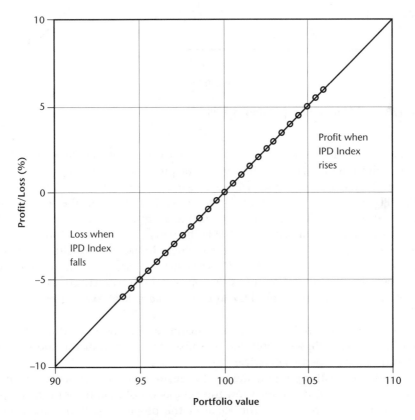

Figure 15B.1 Taking a long position in a property portfolio

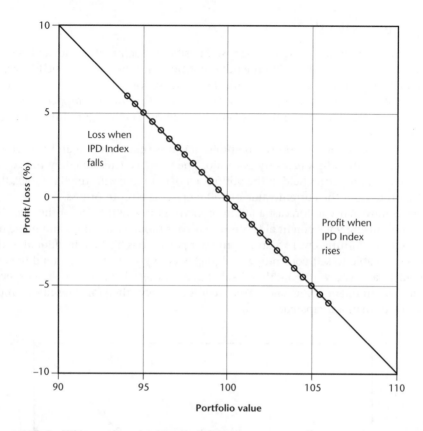

Figure 15B.2 Taking a short position in a PIF

An alternative way to minimise your loss is to make use of PIF contracts. The principle is illustrated in Figure 15B.2, where the property fund manager takes a short position in the forward market and agrees to sell a PIF for 100.

If the IPD Index falls in value to 94 by the end of the year, the fund manager could buy at 94 and sell at 100 thereby making a profit that would offset the loss. A strategy that allows short sales will enable the party running the position to realise a profit even when the property market is falling. The position would be reversed if the index increased in value. If the PIFs were held in isolation without having an underlying property portfolio, the situation would be described as uncovered. However, our interest is in using PIFs to control the risk of existing property portfolios.

From a hedging perspective, an ideal outcome would be one where the losses realised in the 'real' property portfolio are offset by gains from the short position undertaken in the property derivative.

Figure 15B.3 shows this position and can be regarded as a perfect hedge. The points that run along the horizontal line show the net pay-off of holding both the property portfolio and a PIFs contract. If the value of the property portfolio falls over the

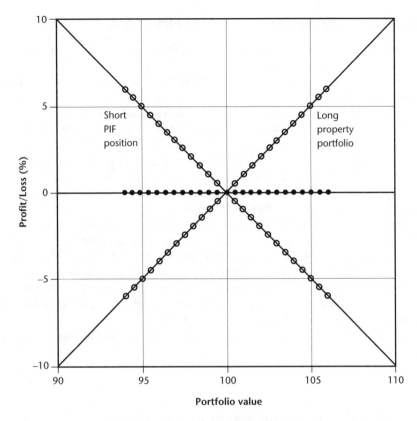

Figure 15B.3   A hedged portfolio

period, the losses are offset by gains from the PIFs contract. For example, a 6% fall in value in the property portfolio is offset by a 6% gain in the short PIFs position. This combination of a pre-existing long position in the property portfolio and the short forward position in the PIFs contract effectively creates a negatively correlated two-asset portfolio. The offsetting positions in each portfolio result in zero movement away from the current 100% valuation.

   Such an outcome ignores, of course, the impact of transaction costs that will reduce the value of the property portfolio. The fact remains, however, that the PIF derivative contract acts in such a way that it allows the user to lock into the current market price. In the absence of default risk, this results in a known pay-off at some specified date in the future.

> The value of a PIF contract is that it allows the user to lock into the current market price. In the absence of default risk this results in a known pay-off at some specified date in the future.
> This, together with the fact that forward contracts are a liquid form of investment, makes PIFs useful for hedging property risk.

Measuring portfolio sensitivity to market movements

There are, however, a number of aspects relating to the hedging approach we described that need to be considered. Figures 15B.1–15B.3, for example, assumed that there was a perfect relationship between property and the PIF. This implies that a 1% change in the value of the property portfolio would be exactly matched by a 1% change in the value of the PIF. In practice, this is unlikely to be the case. The reason for this is that the investment performance of most property portfolios is likely to reflect the characteristics of the individual properties held, rather than broad market movement as measured by the IPD Index. We discussed this in Chapter 11 and showed that property portfolios tend to be poorly diversified and poorly correlated with market movements. However, it is still possible to hedge that component of investment performance that is accounted for by general market movements.

In order to achieve this, the relationship that exists between the property portfolio and the PIF instrument needs to be established for hedging purposes. With sufficient data, regression analysis provides one way of estimating this relationship. In this case the regression analysis seeks to determine the relationship between a dependent variable, and one or more explanatory variables. This approach will, of course, require past performance data on the property portfolio's returns and the IPD Index returns, on which the PIF contracts are written.

Assuming these data are available the regression model would take the following form:

$$r_{P_t} = \alpha + \beta r_{IPD_t} + \varepsilon_t \tag{15B.1}$$

where

r_{P_t} represents the return on the property portfolio at time t
r_{IPD_t} represents the return on the IPD Index at time t
α and β are the parameters for the portfolio, whose values are to be estimated
ε_t is an error term.
(The error term represents the returns of the property portfolio that are not explained by the IPD Index.)

The beta (β) coefficient plays an important role in that it measures the relationship that exists between the returns on the property portfolio and the returns on the IPD Index. In other words, it measures the sensitivity of the portfolio returns relative to movements in the IPD Index. If the property portfolio moves in line with the IPD Index then alpha (α) will be zero and beta 1. Depending on the composition of the portfolio it is more likely, however, that beta will take on values that are either less than or greater than 1. The estimated beta can be used to calculate the total value of PIFs required to hedge the portfolio.

Once the extent of the market exposure, as measured by beta, has been identified, the problem facing the PIFs user is to determine the appropriate size of hedge that needs to be put in place. A simple way of doing this is to take the current value of the property portfolio, V_p, and divide it by the current value of the PIFs index, V_{PIF}, that is being quoted. The value of β_p from the regression model can then be used to scale the size of the notional principal, N_p, required for the hedge. The relationship between these values is shown in equation 15B.2.

$$N_P = \frac{V_P}{V_{PIF}} \, \beta_P \qquad\qquad (15B.2)$$

To see how you would use this in practice let us look at a simple example.

Example

Assume that you are a fund manager responsible for a property portfolio valued at £10,000,000. You are concerned that over the coming year the value of your fund is likely to decline. Rising interest rates, increasing void rates and a depressed outlook for commercial property have contributed to this view. To protect the value of your portfolio against falling market prices you decide to hedge your position by using PIFs. You estimate the β value of your portfolio relative to the IPD Index at 0.8. The current forward quotation for the PIFs is 100.

Using these figures you can determine the appropriate value of the short position that you would have to take. This represents the value of PIFs contracts that, in theory, you would have to buy to protect the value of your portfolio. From equation 15B.2 you can estimate the notional principal, N_P, as follows:

$$N_P = \frac{£10,000,000}{100} \cdot 0.8 = £8,000,000 \qquad\qquad (15B.3)$$

By taking a short position in PIF contracts with a notional principal of £8,000,000, which you agree to sell at 100, you will adequately hedge against the fall in your £10,000,000 portfolio.

To illustrate that this strategy works, assume that by the time the PIF contract matures the IPD Index has fallen to 98. Because of the fall in value you are able to buy PIF contracts equal to your notional principal for only £7,840,000. You calculate this as follows:

$$N_P \frac{IPD_t}{IPD_{t-1}} = £8,000,000 \times \frac{98}{100} = £7,840,000$$

By taking a short position you have agreed to sell these at the index value of 100, so you make a profit of £160,000.

Because of the fall in the market the value of your property portfolio has fallen from £10,000,000 to £9,840,000. You calculate this using equation 15B.4:

$$V_{P,t} = V_{P,t-1} + V_{P,t-1} \left(\frac{I_t - I_{t-1}}{I_{t-1}} \right) \beta_P \qquad\qquad (15B.4)$$

where

$V_{P,t}$ is the value of portfolio P at time t
$V_{P,t-1}$ is its value in the previous period
I_t is the value of the IPD Index at time t
I_{t-1} is its value in the previous period

Substituting the portfolio and index values gives:

$$V_{P,t} = £10,000,000 + £10,000,000 \left(\frac{98 - 100}{100} \right) 0.80 = £9,840,000$$

To see how the use of PIFs hedges against the fall in the market you can draw up the balance sheet shown in Table 15B.1.

Table 15B.1 ● Hedging risk in a property portfolio

	Property portfolio	Forward market (PIF)
Current position	£10,000,000	£8,000,000 (Sell short)
At maturity of PIF contract	£9,840,000	£7,840,000 (Buy)
Profit/Loss	–£160,000	£160,000

The £160,000 loss made by the property portfolio has been exactly offset by the £160,000 profit made by taking a short position in the forward market.

Clearly a number of simplifying assumptions have been made in arriving at this result and, in reality, it is most unlikely that a perfect hedge would be established. Nevertheless the example serves to illustrate how the use of cash settled forward contracts can help to cushion falls in property market prices without liquidating, or partially liquidating, the underlying portfolio. You should also note that as far as the forward contract is concerned, no money changes hands until the contract matures.

Other uses of PIFs

In principle, the liquid nature of PIFs provides the opportunity for effectively managing property portfolio risk that should appeal to short-term investors. We have shown how PIFs can be used to hedge a portfolio against expected falls in the market.

It is also possible to use PIFs to alter the exposure of the portfolio to potential market movement. For example, if the property fund manager took the view that the market would continue to rise it would be possible, by increasing the portfolio β, to gear up the exposure of the fund to market movements. As a result, PIFs may be used as either a hedging instrument or a pre-positioning instrument, depending on the prospective outlook for the market.

There is, however, an important caveat. Most commercial property portfolios are poorly diversified, with the result that a high proportion of the portfolio return is not accounted for by general market movements. There are also many portfolios that have a concentration of investments in particular sectors such as retail, office or industrial. In addition, a portfolio may be dominated by one or more high-value properties whose performance will greatly influence overall portfolio performance. In the former case, forward contracts taken out on specific sectors, if such instruments were available, would provide a better hedge in accounting for systematic risk exposure.

Because most property portfolios are poorly diversified this implies that hedging risk by using PIFs is unlikely to provide complete protection against the volatility in a property portfolio. In order to accomplish this it would be necessary to incorporate other property-related instruments into the analysis, enabling more comprehensive portfolio protection. However, consideration of this and the implementation of dynamic hedging strategies would take us beyond our immediate task. Ideally, more focused futures and forwards instruments need to be developed, but PIFs have provided a good start.

Securitisation

Our discussion on PIFs has assumed that investors hold portfolios of real property. The benefit is that the portfolios produce a rental income stream and there is usually some capital growth. The returns tend to have low correlation with other assets so that including property in a mixed-asset portfolio generally shows an improvement in the trade-off between risk and return. An additional advantage is that the underlying assets can be used as security for loan purposes.

However, there are a number of disadvantages to owning property. For example:

- property is illiquid and is not easily sold
- transaction costs are high
- management costs are high
- maintenance costs can be high
- shifting property sectors in response to market movements is not easy

As a result of these conflicting positions there has been a move towards developing products that offer the investment benefits of real property without the ownership problems. This is known collectively as securitisation or unitisation. All this means is that trading can take place in paper securities that are backed by direct investment in property. Each security would represent a small proportion of the underlying property. The advantage to investors is that they could take a position in the property market without any of the difficulties of property ownership.

Discussions and proposals on securitisation have been going on for a number of years and as an idea it clearly offers a number of advantages to investors. For example:

- it offers improved liquidity
- greater asset allocation opportunities
- opportunities for small investors to own part of a large building
- opportunities for large investors to diversify across a range of buildings
- it offers a way of raising equity capital for development projects
- the value of the traded securities would give an instant valuation of the property
- shares in the underlying properties could be traded on the stock exchange
- trading could take place quickly
- the returns on property securities could be more easily geared

These are clearly attractive and as a result there have been a number of attempts in the UK to securitise individual properties. The following give an indication of products that have been developed.

Property Income Certificates (PINCs)

These were designed to offer investors a share of the rental income stream of property.

Single Property Ownership Trusts (SPOTs)

This, as its name implies, was to be set up like a unit trust, based only on a single property.

Single Asset Property Companies (SAPCOs)

This was also based on a single property but was to be operated more like company shares.

Unfortunately none of these proposals has been successful largely due to difficulties with taxation. The difficulty of introducing these products was exacerbated by the state of the property market at the time they were proposed. There was also concern that there might not be sufficient interest in the secondary market to generate speculation. This is an important factor in developing this type of market.

More conventional products already exist that provide investors with the opportunity to take a position in a commercial property portfolio without the problems of ownership. Property Unit Trusts and Property Bonds have, for example, existed since the 1960s. The prices of the units are related to the underlying property valuations which are usually undertaken monthly.

However, none of these offers the investor the opportunity to take a position in each sector of the market. As an alternative to this, AMP in London have proposed the introduction of an over-the-counter (OTC) property forward market based on the IPD Monthly Indices. This is called the Real Estate Index Market (REIM). By offering forward contracts on a monthly basis AMP would be able to overcome many of the problems associated with high-frequency indices. As yet REIMs have not been formally introduced.

Despite the problems associated with securitisation the opportunity still exists to develop a product based on short-term movements in the market. To be successful the index would need to be updated on a real-time basis and be sufficiently volatile to pick up rapid changes in the market. Volatility is important in order to create speculation. Without this it would be difficult to create an active market.

At present no such index exists, as the highest-frequency index is monthly and there is a delay of a few weeks between collection and reporting. In addition, because the returns on monthly indices are highly smoothed and predictable, trading in derivative products based on the indices is unlikely to generate speculation. However, some positive work is being undertaken in this area. If you assume, for example, that the annual volatility in a large commercial property index is about 10% p.a., this implies that the volatility per day is about 0.5%.[1] This is probably much larger than most investors realise, but it does suggest that there is sufficient volatility in the property market to encourage speculation in derivative products.

---

[1] You can estimate this as follows. Assuming that the returns are independent the daily volatility would be calculated as $10\% \div \sqrt{365} = 0.52\%$.

If property investors could have access to such products then they would be able to quickly vary their exposure to each sector of the market in response to changing conditions. This would offer opportunities for risk management that at present do not exist.

Selected references

Adams, A. and Baum, A. Property securitisation: premium or discount? City University.

Adams, A. and Venmore-Rowland, P. (1991) Proposed property investment vehicles: will they work? *Journal of Property Valuation and Investment* 9, 287–93.

AMP (1995) *The Real Estate Market Index (REIM): A Concept Document*. London.

Brown, G.R. and Matysiak, G.A. (1995) Developing a real time property valuation index. University of Salford, Working paper.

Brown, G.R. and Matysiak, G.A. (1996) A real-time property index. *Estates Gazette*, No. 9628, 128–30.

Gelbtuch, H.C. and Lipkin, P. (1992) Real estate securitisation. *The Appraisal Journal* (July), 323–30.

Jaffee, D.M. and Renaud, B. (1995) Securitisation in European mortgage markets. University of California. Paper presented at the International Real Estate Conference, Stockholm.

RICS (1985) *The Unitisation of Real Property*. GCPPA/Report (85) 34 London.

Appendix 15C
Property performance indices

The measurement of commercial property performance is now a well-established feature of the property market. In the UK the main provider of these services is the Investment Property Databank (IPD). They offer an annual performance measurement and ranking service of commercial property portfolios. In order to do this the evaluation of investment performance requires a suitable standard against which to compare investment returns. Fund mangers should be able to compare their performance relative to the whole market, a sub-market, their peer group or some user-defined benchmark. From the investor's point of view the requirement for an overall measure of property market performance arises for the following reasons:

● the need to evaluate property market performance relative to other asset classes
● the identification of property selection skills
● the isolation of active performance from general market movements
● the identification of management skills

We will look at these in more detail in Chapter 16. In this appendix we provide an overview of the main commercial property measures that are available.

Investment markets and indicators of performance

A characteristic of well-established investment markets is the existence of indices recording their performance. For example, in the UK there are several UK gilts price indices categorised by both bond maturity and coupon yield. There are also a number of share indices. These include the FT 30 Index as well as the FTSE Actuaries share indices which include the FTSE 100, FTSE Small Cap and the FTSE All-Share index. Industry sector indices covering, for example, consumer goods and financials are also available. More globally, the FT/S&P Actuaries World Indices report daily index (price) figures in a number of currencies for national and regional markets. In the equities markets a number of different performance measures will be found. For example, there are price indices, price/earnings ratios and dividend yield indices. Most of these are routinely reported in the financial press.

Performance measurement statistics for investment categories such as unit trusts or investment funds are also regularly reported in the financial press. At the fund level performance measures from the Combined Actuarial Performance Statistics (CAPS) or from World Markets (WM) are regularly reported for pension funds.

Clearly, investment performance indices are important, so it should come as no surprise to find that there are a number of indices that track the performance of the property market.

Types of property indices

Property indices may be constructed in one of two ways:

● as portfolio-based indices, or
● as barometer or market-type indices based on a hypothetical portfolio of rent points.

Both types of index are useful but are designed for different purposes.

Portfolio-based indices measure rental values, capital values and total rates of return of actual rented properties. Different indices of this type are likely to provide different results because the underlying portfolio of properties will vary in size, location and the weighting scheme employed between each sector of the property market. The rates of return will be *money-weighted*, meaning that the timing and magnitude of the cash flows into the portfolio making up the index will influence the results. As the valuations will rely heavily on comparable evidence of sales of similar properties in the same area, there are likely to be delays in reflecting underlying market movements. See Chapter 12 on smoothing for a fuller discussion of the issues. The main use of this type of index is for portfolio performance measurement.

The *market barometer* index aims to track movements in the property market by estimating open market rentals on a number of hypothetical rack-rented properties. Being based on valuers' estimates of rental value and yield, these measures should provide an earlier indicator of market changes than portfolio-based indices. The purpose of this type of index is to provide market-responsive measures that reflect a wide and, therefore, comprehensive view of market sentiment. The main use of this type of index is to highlight short-term changes in the level of the market at the regional and local level. An index of this type is unsuitable for portfolio performance measurement since investors could not closely match its movement with an actual portfolio of property holdings.

Given that there is no central marketplace and that indices are based on valuations, a commercial property index cannot, therefore, be viewed in the same way as a transactions-based index, such as the FT All-Share Index or the FTSE 100.

Property indices

When considering how to construct a property index a number of issues need to be taken into account.

1. The first concerns the population being measured. This will, by construction, define the property 'market'. The types of question that arise here are, is the index to include secondary properties, prime properties or all properties? Should the index include retail, office, industrial, out-of-town shopping centres or some other category?

2. It will not be possible to collect information on all properties in the market, and consequently, a sample will need to be selected. The important questions which then arise are: which properties and in what locations? Given the heterogeneous nature of the market, it is important to select a *representative* sample that will reflect the underlying trend of the market. The composition of each index by category of property is likely to vary. Indeed, the relative weighting of the sectors may turn out to be arbitrary so it is important to decide how much weighting should be attributed to the various sectors. In practice, the weightings of the component categories within the IPD Annual Index are often used. For example Jones Lang Wootton and Richard Ellis create notional market portfolios by including selected properties which they actively manage, and weighting the retail, office and industrial sectors in line with the IPD sectors.

3. It is important to ensure that the index reflects the broad, underlying trend being measured and not the idiosyncratic nature of the properties held. This requires that the index be well diversified, reflecting the underlying systematic risk impact on performance. Our discussion in Chapter 11 on constructing property portfolios showed how difficult this could be in practice.

4. In the securities markets indices are generally constructed from transaction prices, which, for actively traded stocks, are likely to exhibit continuous fluctuations. It is much more difficult to produce similar indices for commercial property. As sales for individual properties occur infrequently, published indices are by necessity compiled from valuations. The basis of the valuation is subjective and therefore suffers from some uncertainty. In thin markets current valuations may give the erroneous impression of a slow adjustment in prices. Construction of property indices is further confounded because the valuation of each property is seldom carried out at a single point in time. Chapter 12 provides a discussion on these effects at the index level.

From these points you will see that the property market faces a number of difficulties in producing an acceptable property index. In the securities market there is a centralised marketplace where data are readily available for the construction of up-to-date indices that reflect the particular market as a whole. The absence of a central marketplace for property means that only sample data are available so that indices may not be representative of the population at large. As a result different indices can report different results, even though they are tracking the same market. Furthermore, given the heterogeneity of property it is difficult to define categories clearly. It is important to recognise that there are likely to be differences between valuation returns and actual market returns. Also, it should be pointed out that even if a transactions-based index were to be constructed, sampling error would still be present (Miles et al. 1991).

UK commercial property indices

The Society of Property Researchers carried out a user survey of commercial property performance measures in 1994 in order to elicit views on various indices. They were interested to see how the indices were used and what improvements users would like to see. One of the reported findings was that the main purpose was as a reference of the state of the market. Clearly, it is important that the reported measures should reflect the underlying market trends and not the idiosyncratic features of the constituent properties.

The longest continually reported series are those provided by Hillier Parker (now CB Hillier Parker) and Jones Lang Wootton (now Jones Lang Lasalle).

The *CB Hillier Parker* indices were designed to track current market movements. This market method uses open market rental values and yields estimated from a representative sample at different 'rent points', rather than specific properties. The measure reflects the best rent obtainable assuming it is available on the open market. Essentially, what is effectively being measured is a property with vacant possession. It is likely that the measures reported by this type of index will provide a leading indicator of actual portfolio performance trends.

The *Jones Lang Wootton Index* employs a portfolio method where the performance of a *representative* portfolio of actual properties is measured. The portfolio index reflects factors such as voids, rent-free periods and other tenant inducements.

Although most properties are valued annually there are, nevertheless, a substantial number of investment-grade properties that are valued quarterly or monthly. These are usually tied to other investment products such as property unit trusts or property bonds where the unit prices are fixed in relation to the value of the underlying properties. Using these properties, indices have also been produced that track the movement of the property market on a more frequent basis. The largest monthly index is produced by IPD. It uses a much smaller sample than the IPD Annual Index and at September 1998 comprised 56 funds containing 2,780 properties valued at £7.75 billion. The composition of the index is different from the annual index although the overall trends are the same. In addition to IPD, Richard Ellis also produces a monthly index, although this is based on a smaller sample of properties. Jones Lang Wootton produces the only index based on formal quarterly valuations. Table 15C.1 provides broad details of the most frequently reported monthly and quarterly indices.

Table 15C.2 provides further details of the main types of commercial property indices. This offers a broad overview of reported information. You should consult the appropriate publication produced by each organisation in order to obtain a full description of each index and method of construction.

In addition to the above, the Valuation Office produces reports for a variety of locations showing rental values for the retail, office and industrial sectors. The indices provide measures of rental growth, capital growth and total rates of return. Yields are also available.

Table 15C.1 ● Comparison of high-frequency indices

Measurer	Number of properties	Capital value £billion (date)
IPD Monthly	2,812	£7.86 (Oct '98)
Richard Ellis Monthly	412	£2.40 (Oct '98)
JLW Quarterly	177	£0.42 (Sept '98)

Table 15C.2 ● Comparison of UK commercial property indices

Source	Nature of business	Types of indices/ measures	Sector & spatial coverage	Frequency and start date
Investment Property Databank	Performance measurement organisation	RV/C/T/Y	R/O/I/A: L/RG/N	Monthly: Dec 1986 Annual: 1971
CB Hillier Parker	Surveyor/Fund Manager	RV/C/T/Y	R/O/I/RW/SM/A: L/RG/N	Quarterly: Aug 1990 Bi-Annual: May 1977 Annual: May 1972
Jones Lang Wootton	Surveyor/Fund Manager	RV/C/T/Y	R/O/I/A: L/RG/N	Quarterly: June 1977 Bi-Annual: Mar 83/92/93 Annual: June 1967
Richard Ellis	Surveyor/Fund Manager	RV/C/T/Y	R/O/I/A: RG/N	Monthly: Mar 1987 Annual: Mar 1978
Healey & Baker	Surveyor/Fund Manager	RV/Y	R/O/I/A: L/RG/N	Quarterly: Jan 1984 Bi-Annual: June 1977
Chesterton	Surveyor/Fund Manager	RV/C/Y	R/O/I/A: L/RG/N	Monthly: June 1990
Weatherall Green & Smith	Surveyor/Fund Manager	RV/C/Y	R/O/I/A: N	Quarterly: Dec 1979

Key: **Types of index:**
RV: rental value growth; C: capital growth; T: total return; Y: yield.

Sector and spatial coverage:
R: Retail; O: Office; I: Industrial; A: All Property; RW: Retail Warehouse; SM: Supermarket;
L: Local centre level; RG: Regional level; N: National level.

The Investment Property Databank (IPD) Annual Index is the most widely used measure of UK property performance. Founded in 1985, IPD is an independent organisation that collects property data and provides a performance measurement service. The property database held by IPD is the largest source of investment property in the UK. Annual performance figures span the period from 1 January to 31 December and are reported, on average, at the end of the first quarter in the following year. As at the end of 1997, there were almost 14,000 properties in the database valued in excess of £65 billion. This represents over 90 per cent, by value, of the commercial property investment market. The index now reflects information on 247 property portfolios containing 13,721 properties. The majority of the information relates to properties owned by pension funds and insurance companies. However, other groups, including property companies, have also begun to deposit information with IPD. Given such a large independent database the IPD performance figures provide benchmark measures of the universe of UK investment properties.

IPD produce an Annual Digest which analyses in detail the performance of the database properties. You should consult this document in order to obtain insights into the various dimensions of performance that are unavailable elsewhere. The most comprehensive recorded performance data commence in 1981, although performance figures are available back to 1971 in the IPD Long Run Index.

Much of the published data are available at the regional or national level with statistics on local data being more limited. Many of the indices classify property by broad use type such as retail, office and industrial, and by regional administrative boundaries defined by the Office of National Statistics, ONS (formerly the Central Statistical Office, CSO).

By using the three broad classifications in any analysis the implicit assumption is that there is a high degree of similarity *within* each sector and a low degree of similarity *between* them (Hoesli et al. 1997). The value of grouping the data by broad use type and administrative region has, therefore, begun to be the subject of more detailed research. Changes in planning controls and user requirements have blurred the distinction between the various categories. For example, the distinction between some office and industrial uses is now less clear. In addition, the growth in warehousing, the emergence of a leisure sector and the different types of retail property, such as out-of-town shopping, retail warehouse parks and factory outlets, have meant that the traditional use classifications of retail, office and industrial are too broadly based. The identification of homogeneous property groupings in terms of risk and return could offer more meaningful classifications which may enable more effective and efficient portfolio risk control. An appropriate classification will also permit economically meaningful models of property market behaviour to be developed for forecasting purposes. Much work still remains to be done in this area before a consensus picture emerges.

Other issues surrounding the construction of property indices include:

● the calculation of returns
● how outgoing expenditures such as refurbishment costs are treated
● the impact of management and transaction costs
● the treatment of transactions
● the effect of developments

A discussion of how these are treated in different indices can be found in Morrell (1991).

A criticism often levelled against commercial property indices is that the time taken between collecting the data and reporting the index numbers tends to be long. However, currently available best practice reflects a trade-off between an acceptable sample and the administration involved in order to calculate the index numbers within an acceptable timescale. Another issue that affects all property indices to some degree is that the changes in value are highly smoothed. As a result property indices tend to track general trends in the market rather than discrete changes reflecting the arrival of new information. This effect is more pronounced at the monthly level.

Index performance

The three most quoted commercial property indices in the UK are those published by the Investment Property Databank (IPD), Jones Lang Wootton (JLW) and Richard Ellis (RE). It is useful, therefore, to compare the performance of these indices. We will focus on the IPD Annual Index and a comparison of quarterly figures. We looked at the monthly statistics in Chapter 9.

IPD Annual Index from 1970

A comparison of the capital growth of each sector of the UK commercial property market is given in Figure 15C.1.

You will see from this that over the 27-year period the retail sector has offered the best performance. This is consistent with the generally lower yields found in this sector. Also, for the majority of the period the industrial sector has offered the lowest growth. Again, this is consistent with the higher yields found in this sector.

Figure 15C.2 summarises the annual growth per period. You will see that there is a close association between the growth in each sector and that the range is large.

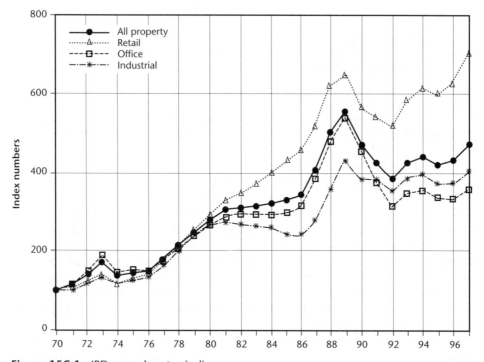

Figure 15C.1 IPD annual sector indices

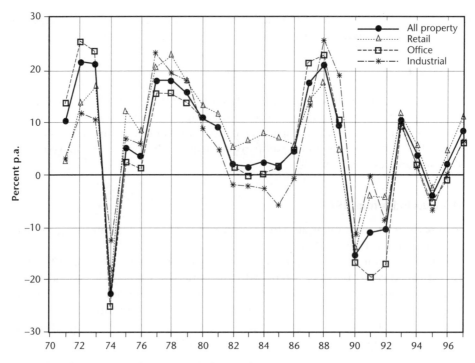

Figure 15C.2   IPD annual sector capital growth

A summary of the main statistics is given in Table 15C.3.

The capital growth is more or less normally distributed with some evidence of slight negative skewness. At the all-property level the standard deviation of the capital growth is about half that of the equities market. The other main feature that you should be interested in is the serial correlation in the growth figures. This indicates whether there is a strong association between changes in value over time. You will see from this table that the highest positive serial correlation occurs in the first period (lag). The figures then drop rapidly.

The association between each sector can be seen in the cross-correlation coefficients. These are summarised in Table 15C.4. The figures are all positive and high, which indicates that the sectors generally move in the same direction.

Although the Annual Index is often used as the benchmark for performance measurement purposes there are other indices available that track changes in the market at monthly and quarterly intervals. An important issue in viewing these indices is in knowing whether they are all tracking the same general changes in the market. We have examined this by estimating annual equivalent changes from the monthly and quarterly indices produced by IPD, JLW and RE. The annual changes are shown in Figure 15C.3 over a shorter period from 1986. We have also included the IPD annual returns for comparison.

Although the size and the composition of each index are different, it is reassuring to see that there is close correspondence between the annual figures. This implies that, at the annual level, each index is generally tracking the same market.

Table 15C.3 ● IPD annual capital growth statistics from 1970

		Mean	St. Dev.	Skew	Kurt	J–B	Serial correlation			
							1	2	3	4
IPD	All Property	5.70%	11.36%	−0.66	3.06	1.95	0.29	−0.09	−0.33	−0.16
	Retail	7.18%	9.99%	−1.01	4.03	5.78	0.21	0.02	−0.08	−0.09
	Office	4.65%	13.24%	−0.54	2.80	1.34	0.37	−0.08	−0.36	−0.19
	Industrial	5.09%	10.41%	0.21	2.28	0.79	0.35	0.00	−0.33	−0.23

J–B: Jarque–Bera statistic.

Table 15C.4 ● Cross-correlation between sectors

	All property	Retail	Office	Industrial
All property	1.00			
Retail	0.93	1.00		
Office	0.99	0.87	1.00	
Industrial	0.87	0.83	0.82	1.00

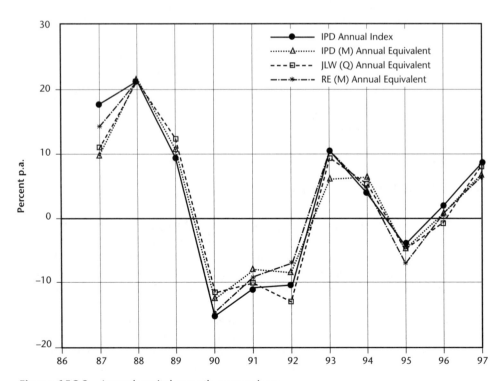

Figure 15C.3 Annual capital growth comparison

Quarterly indices

With higher-frequency indices differences in sample size are likely to have more effect on periodic performance. You can see this in Figures 15C.4a–15C.4d, where we have compared the index numbers prepared by the IPD, JLW and RE on a sector basis. To make the figures comparable we have estimated quarterly changes in value for the IPD and RE monthly series. The JLW series is, however, based on quarterly valuations.

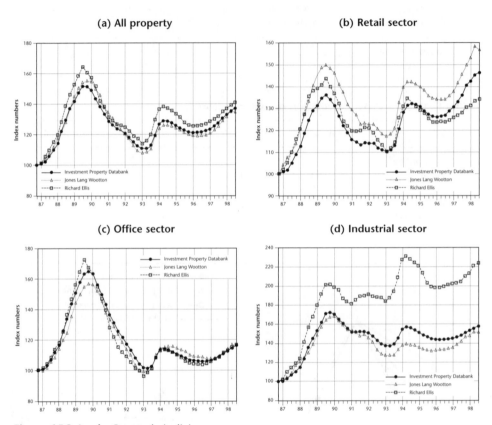

Figure 15C.4a–d Quarterly indicies

With the exception of industrial property the sectors generally track each other quite well. You should not expect an exact correspondence, as there will be differences in both systematic and specific risk. In addition, the value weighting of properties in each index will also influence performance on a period-by-period basis. This probably accounts for the differences in performance of the Richard Ellis industrial property index.

It is also useful to make a comparison between the periodic growth in each index. We have done this on a company basis and summarised the results in Figures 15C.5a–15C.5c. Each graph is drawn to the same scale. You can see that growth in each period exhibits the same general trends although there are differences in the sector variation between different firms.

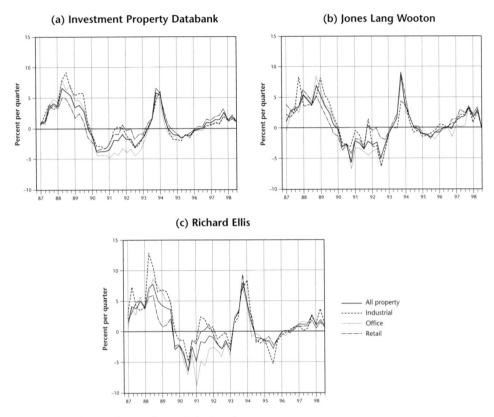

Figure 15C.5a–c Quarterly capital growth

The trending in each of the growth series is shown in the serial correlation figures which we have summarised in Table 15C.5. We have also summarised the main distributional statistics from which you will see that the quarterly index growth figures are approximately normal. There is also a high level of serial correlation in the quarterly figures, which gradually dies away.

Table 15C.5 ● Comparison of quarterly indexes (1986:Q4 to 1998:Q3)

| | | Mean | St. Dev. | Skew | Kurt | J–B | Serial correlation | | | |
							1	2	3	4
IPD	All Property	0.66	2.76	0.38	2.38	1.92	0.87	0.67	0.44	0.23
	Retail	0.81	2.35	0.35	2.85	0.98	0.82	0.59	0.32	0.09
	Office	0.31	3.39	0.32	2.31	1.73	0.89	0.75	0.55	0.37
	Industrial	0.96	3.07	0.83	3.02	5.44	0.85	0.61	0.40	0.21
JLW	All Property	0.63	3.04	0.25	2.72	0.66	0.79	0.66	0.47	0.27
	Retail	0.96	2.84	0.49	3.01	1.91	0.75	0.56	0.35	0.17
	Office	0.32	3.44	0.29	3.02	0.68	0.77	0.65	0.50	0.29
	Industrial	0.87	2.99	0.36	3.16	1.06	0.71	0.58	0.39	0.26

Table 15C.5 continued

		Mean	St. Dev.	Skew	Kurt	J–B	Serial correlation 1	2	3	4
RE	All Property	0.72	3.30	0.28	2.65	0.87	0.79	0.63	0.38	0.19
	Retail	0.62	2.87	0.48	3.96	3.66	0.69	0.49	0.18	0.02
	Office	0.32	3.99	0.03	2.47	0.56	0.80	0.71	0.49	0.29
	Industrial	1.70	3.83	0.81	3.55	5.80	0.74	0.50	0.32	0.19

J–B: Jarque–Bera statistic.

Monthly figures

IPD and Richard Ellis produce the two monthly property indices available in the UK. They both track the institutional property market but differ in size. We showed in Table 15C.1 that at the end of October 1998 the IPD Index consisted of 2,812 properties with a capital value of about £7.86 billion. The Richard Ellis is smaller, consisting of 412 properties with a capital value close to £2.4 billion.

Figures 15C.6A–15C.6D show the relative tracking of these indices at the all property and sector level.

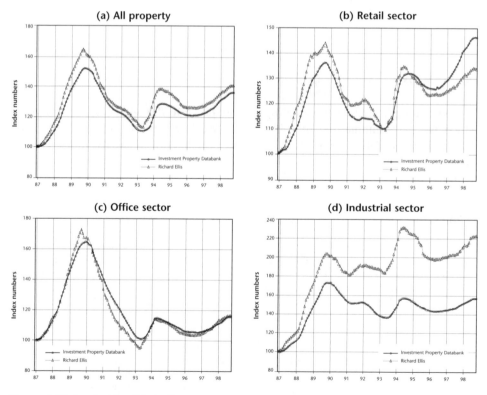

Figure 15C.6a–d Monthly Indices

You will see that the indices broadly track each other, with the exception of the industrial sector. This was also the case using quarterly figures. The corresponding monthly capital growth rates for each sector are shown in Figures 15C.7a and 15C.7b.

The overall measures of association between the capital growth figures between the two indices at the all-property level and at the sector level are summarised in the correlation matrix in Table 15C.6.

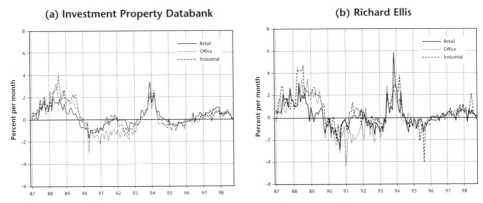

Figure 15C.7a–b Monthly capital growth

Table 15C.6 ● Monthly correlation measures between IPD and RE capital growth rates

	IPD All Property	IPD Retail	IPD Office	IPD Industrial
RE All Property	0.89			
RE Retail		0.78		
RE Office			0.83	
RE Industrial				0.84

The higher correlation coefficient between the all-property indices reflects the higher diversification at this level. Although the correlation figures are generally high it is still possible to see differences in the performance of each index.

The summary statistics for each index are reported in Table 15C.7.

From these figures it appears that the capital growth for the office sector for both the IPD and Richard Ellis is normally distributed, whereas normality does not hold for the other sectors. The large value for the Jarque–Bera statistic for the Richard Ellis retail sector can be partly explained by a number of large monthly growth rates in the months around the beginning of 1994. At the all-property level, capital growth rates are normally distributed for both the IPD and Richard Ellis indices. You will also notice that the serial correlation between monthly growth rates is high and dies away very slowly. This is further evidence of the smoothing phenomenon in high-frequency indices that we discussed in Chapter 12.

Table 15C.7 ● Comparison of monthly indices, December 1986–October 1998

| | | Mean | St. Dev. | Skew | Kurt | J–B | Serial correlation | | | |
							1	2	3	4
IPD	All Property	0.21	0.94	0.41	2.90	3.96	0.90	0.86	0.83	0.76
	Retail	0.27	0.82	0.56	3.95	12.76	0.86	0.80	0.76	0.69
	Office	0.10	1.71	0.29	2.85	2.11	0.87	0.84	0.83	0.78
	Industrial	0.32	1.05	0.86	3.47	18.82	0.89	0.84	0.80	0.72
RE	All Property	0.24	1.16	0.35	3.26	3.31	0.83	0.79	0.69	0.69
	Retail	0.20	1.09	1.24	7.93	180.27	0.65	0.63	0.50	0.48
	Office	0.11	1.43	-0.07	3.05	0.12	0.78	0.74	0.68	0.70
	Industrial	0.56	1.39	0.56	4.29	17.31	0.76	0.69	0.65	0.55

J–B: Jarque–Bera statistic.

Other issues

The number of commercial property transactions relative to the amount of investment property held is very small. Consequently, it is not possible to have a transactions-based index such as those that are found in other major investment markets. What this means is that in order to construct a capital value or total returns index, the calculations have to rely on valuations. We discussed the issues of valuations versus prices at the individual property level in Chapter 7. In a well-diversified property index the impact of random valuation errors is expected to vanish. However, in different market conditions it is still possible to find some bias between valuations and prices.

If you are interested in knowing something about the current state of the market rather than some time after the event, it is necessary to collect and process information on a continuous basis. In an ideal world, a real-time, transactions-based commercial property index would exist. However, given that there is no central marketplace, coupled with the paucity of property transactions, this index does not exist. However, an attainable objective is a computer-based data capture and processing system which provides rapid reporting of a valuation-based index. This would be equivalent to a real-time, valuation-based index. The success of such an index will, however, depend on the following conditions being satisfied:

● the index should capture underlying market movements and be acceptable to users
● the data requirements should be minimal
● the index numbers should be updated soon after data collection
● the index numbers should be produced independently
● the index should not require the use of any confidential data
● the index numbers should be instantly accessible

Given the widespread use of on-line computing facilities we believe that, in time, commercial property investors will routinely have access to real-time, valuation-based indices.

Selected references

Dunse, N., Jones, C., Orr, A. and Tarbert, H. (1998) The extent and limitations of local commercial property market data. *Journal of Property Valuation and Investment* **16** (5), 455–73.

Gordon, J. (1990) *Property Performance Indices in the United Kingdom and the US*. New York: Baring Institutional Realty Advisors Inc.

Hoesli, M., Lizieri, C., and MacGregor, B.D. (1997) The spatial dimensions of the investment performance of UK commercial property. *Urban Studies* **34** (9), 1475–94.

Miles, M., Guilkey, D. and Shears, D. (1991) A transaction based real estate index: is it possible? *Journal of Property Research* **8**, 203–17.

Morrell, G.D. (1991) Property performance analysis and performance indices: A review. *Journal of Property Research* **8**, 29–50.

Performance measurement

Introduction

If investors are prepared to pay a premium for bearing risk, then risk must play an important part in explaining performance. Much of this book has been concerned with investigating risk and its importance in property investment. We have shown how it can be reduced and have explained that it is an important factor in determining the prices at which property will trade.

Even without any formal understanding of risk or how it can be measured professional property investors recognise its importance and try to reduce it by creating portfolios. However, when it comes to measuring performance, risk receives relatively little attention.

In this chapter we introduce you to the reasons for measuring performance and discuss the measures of returns that are commonly used. We will also explain performance attribution and show how this fits into the models of diversification that we covered earlier. We do this in a context that both excludes and includes risk. We also show that the standard measures of performance that have been developed in the finance literature can be applied to commercial property.

This is an important chapter because it provides the basis for evaluating the decisions that you made as part of developing your investment strategy. Without some way of monitoring your performance you can't tell whether your decisions were good or bad. The results of a performance analysis are therefore an important part of reviewing your strategy.

Some of the more advanced topics of performance measurement are covered in the appendices.

Communication, accountability and research

There are three main reasons for undertaking performance measurement: communication, accountability and research.

Communication

Communication is important because portfolio results must be conveyed to the trustees or shareholders of a fund to show that targets are being met, to review existing and future strategies and to advise on any changes that need to be made. Without this reporting function it is impossible to make any valid decisions concerning the portfolio.

Accountability

Because investment decisions are made on behalf of other people, accountability is likely to become more important as professional advisers are called upon to justify their advice. If there is a trend towards terms of appointment that focus on achieving target rates of return, then there needs to be greater awareness of the risks involved. A valid justification of investment decisions can only be made within a framework that embraces both risk and return.

The investor has two main objectives when making an investment decision. These are maximising wealth and efficiently allocating resources. Performance measurement looks at these aspects in a way that should make professional advisers accountable for their actions.

Research

The third reason for undertaking performance measurement is to provide information that can be used for research purposes. This is important for professional advisers in a world where accountability becomes a driving force. Performance measurement of individual properties, therefore, provides the basis for developing databases that can be used to carry out empirical analysis. It is only through research that you can develop a better understanding of the property sector as an asset class.

As a specialist field, performance measurement is relatively new. In the equities market it began in the early 1970s but did not have an impact on property until the late 1970s. Performance measurement systems for equities are also available that take risk into consideration. This is still not commonplace in commercial property, although standard measures of total risk are now more frequently published. Awareness and understanding of risk in performance measurement is still relatively limited. Part of the reason for this has been the focus on teaching traditional methods of valuation which fail to place property in a capital market context. This is, however, gradually changing. Another reason has been the lack of quality data which has given rise to poor measures of risk. This too is also changing. Despite these difficulties it is important to recognise that risk is an important aspect of performance and should be incorporated into the performance process.

We will look at performance measurement as it is currently undertaken, but will also discuss ways in which risk can be incorporated into the analysis.

Objectives of a performance measurement system

There are two main objectives that performance measurement tries to fulfil.

External

This covers the measurement of performance against pre-set targets. These may be established in the marketplace or by the trustees of a fund. In addition, the measurement system should be able to compare the performance of the portfolio against other funds as well as with other investments. It is at this level that the need to make an assessment of the riskiness of property relative to other funds or investments becomes important. The direct comparison of returns of assets in different risk classes could give a misleading ranking of results.

Internal

This is concerned with the comparison of returns of individual properties and tries to explain why one property has performed better than another. It also leads directly to the rebalancing of the portfolio in response to those sectors that are performing badly. Adjusting the portfolio weights is one way of trying to maximise the performance of the portfolio in the long term and is part of the continuing evolution of the investment strategy. It will be seen, therefore, that portfolio strategy and performance measurement go hand in hand. This, of course, reinforces the need for a valid system of measuring performance.

Bearing in mind that professional advice is not free it makes sense to monitor whether it is good or bad. It is very difficult, however, to determine whether investment performance is due to skill or just good luck.

If professional advice is costly then it makes sense to monitor whether it is good or bad. It is also important to recognise that each investment decision carries with it some level of risk. A proper evaluation of professional advice should take this into consideration.

It is not sufficient just to measure performance. It is essential to give some weight to the measures achieved and to establish where the performance is coming from. A good performance measurement system will, therefore, try to answer a number of important questions, such as:

- What returns have been achieved?
- How do these returns compare with other portfolios and assets?
- Has the timing of purchases been good?
- Has selection ability been good?
- Can good performance be achieved consistently from period to period?
- What is the risk profile of the portfolio?
- How well diversified is the portfolio?
- Where are the returns coming from, i.e. is it skill or is it chance?

Two of these topics – timing and selection – require special attention.

Timing

This is concerned with whether properties have been acquired in full knowledge that the market is going to rise or fall in the future.

Selection

Selection is concerned with whether properties have been acquired that are under-priced in an economic sense.

These two aspects are at the root of many of the strategies pursued in the market-place. Professional investors always believe they are buying underpriced properties at the right time. A good system should distinguish between these different sources of performance and try to identify whether, after the event, the decisions were correct.

Performance measurement is really an extension of the security market line we discussed in Chapter 10. You will recall that we showed that under- and overvalued assets would lie above or below the security market line and correctly valued assets would lie on the line. Deviations would represent abnormal performance and it is this aspect that we are interested in. Figure 15.3 (see page 498) summarised this position.

Note that the focus is on value not price. It is not possible to liquidate a property portfolio when you want to measure its performance, so you have to rely on valuations. We investigated the relationship between valuations and prices in Chapter 7 from which you will recall that we showed that valuations were a good proxy for prices in an equilibrium market, but tended to lag price changes in both rising and falling markets. This phenomenon is known as smoothing.

The other aspect of the security market line that is important is the market portfolio. Strictly speaking in a CAPM world the market portfolio, M, is made up of every risky asset. If you define the market portfolio in this way then you have a specific form of the model that deals with the way assets are priced. This, however, is not so important for performance measurement as you are really interested in knowing how well your portfolio has performed relative to some benchmark. Although the mathematics is the same the two approaches have different economic meanings.

Given this background there are three aspects to performance measurement that need to be addressed: measuring rates of return, choosing a benchmark against which to make a comparison and analysing the results.

Measuring returns

Although measuring the rate of return on a property or portfolio may seem relatively straightforward it is, nevertheless, fraught with difficulties. For example, should the returns be *money-weighted* or *time-weighted*? Each has a specific role to play in understanding performance, but it is important to appreciate that you are really concerned with measuring the relative skill of managers and how they have utilised resources.

As relative skill is being measured it is not necessary to allow for the effect of general economic conditions. For example, it is easier to earn high returns in a rising market, but should you be congratulated for doing this? Similarly, should you be blamed if the returns on your portfolio go down when the market is falling? These are general market influences that affect all players. However, if you are successful in selecting underpriced properties or managing your portfolio, then it should still be possible to identify relative skill. It is, therefore, important to use the correct calculation for the rate of return.

We discussed some of the issues surrounding different methods of calculating returns in Appendix 9C and pointed out that the difference in methodology is important in measuring performance. The conventional approach to performance measurement is to compare portfolio returns over a series of intervals with the corresponding returns from a benchmark. The returns for both the portfolio and the benchmark would be estimated as follows:

$$r_p = \frac{V_{t+1} + a_t}{V_t} - 1 \tag{16.1}$$

This would be compared with the expected return obtained from the single-period capital asset pricing model:

$$E(r_p) = r_f + \beta_p[E(r_m) - r_f] \tag{16.2}$$

The difference between what you expected and what you achieved identifies the abnormal return:

$$\text{Abnormal return} = r_p - E(r_p) \tag{16.3}$$

If this is positive you have done better than expected and if it is negative you have done worse. This is what the security market line implies, so this approach to performance measurement fits in with financial theory.

If, however, you wanted to measure the return over two periods but you had acquired some additional assets at the end of the first period your return calculation would reflect the impact of the cash flowing into the fund and would not be measuring true fund performance. The way round this is to use a measure of return that neutralises this effect. This simple example illustrates the difference between money-weighted and time-weighted rates of return. As you will see, each of these returns has a role to play in performance measurement.

Time-weighted and money-weighted rates of return

We can illustrate the difference between money-weighted and time-weighted rates of return with a simple example.

Assume that you invest £100 in a project that has a life of five years. It produces no income but generates the following changes in value:

Table 16.1 ● Changes in investment value

Periods	Market growth	Value of investment
End year 0		£100.00
End year 1	5%	£105.00
End year 2	10%	£115.50
End year 3	20%	£138.60
End year 4	2%	£141.37
End year 5	4%	£147.03

At the end of five years your investment of £100 has grown to £147.03. The question you need to ask is, what rate of return have you earned on your investment? To find this out we will estimate both the time-weighted and money-weighted rates of return.

The time-weighted rate of return

The time-weighted rate of return is just the geometric mean rate of return and is calculated by taking the nth root of the product of all the intermediate returns. You can write this as follows:

$$TWRR = \sqrt[5]{(1.05 \times 1.10 \times 1.20 \times 1.02 \times 1.04)} - 1$$

$$TWRR = 0.08012 = 8.014\% \text{ p.a.}$$

In Appendix 9C we also showed that the geometric mean return could be calculated using logs as follows:

Table 16.2 ● Estimating the geometric mean return

Period	1+return	ln(1+r)
End year 1	1.05	0.0488
End year 2	1.10	0.0953
End year 3	1.20	0.1823
End year 4	1.02	0.0198
End year 5	1.04	0.0392
	Average	0.0771

The time-weighted, or geometric, mean return can be estimated from:

$$TWRR = e^{0.07709} - 1$$

$$TWRR = 0.08014 = 8.014\% \text{ p.a.}$$

The time-weighted rate of return (TWRR) is the geometric mean return of all the sub-period returns. It neutralises the effect of cash flowing into and out of the fund.

The money-weighted rate of return

The money-weighted rate of return takes account of cash flowing into and out of the fund and is just the internal rate of return. It is calculated by finding the return that makes the terminal value of the portfolio, together with any intermediate cash flow, equal to the initial value.

The money-weighted rate of return (MWRR) is just the internal rate of return. It is a measure of the absolute return earned by taking account of cash flowing into and out of the fund.

In our example you have no intermediate cash flows so the money-weighted rate of return can be found as follows:

$$£100.00 = \frac{£147.03}{(1 + MWRR)^5}$$

$$MWRR = 0.08014 = 8.014\% \text{ p.a.}$$

Because you have no intermediate cash flows the TWRR and the MWRR are identical. This will be the case irrespective of the period over which the returns are measured. However, differences between the two measures will occur when inter-mediate cash flows are involved. We can illustrate the principles involved by using a two-period example that covers both rising and falling markets.

Case 1. Rising market

Assume that you have £200 to invest. The market is rising so you decide to invest £100 in some stocks. By the end of the first year the market has increased by 15% and the forecast is that it will continue to rise. You are encouraged by this news and decide to invest the remaining £100. During the second year the market increases by 35%. What rate of return have you earned?

If you consider this as two separate investments they can be summarised as follows:

Table 16.3 ● Cash flows in a rising market

End year	% growth	First investment	Second investment	End year values
0		£100.00		£100.00
1	15%	£115.00	£100.00	£215.00
2	35%	£155.25	£135.00	£290.25

You can calculate the time-weighted rate of return as before:

$$TWRR = \sqrt{(1.15 \times 1.35)} - 1$$

$$TWRR = 0.2459 = 24.59\% \text{ p.a.}$$

Calculating the money-weighted rate of return is more complicated because there are intermediate cash flows. The final value of your investment is £290.25 but this has been created by two separate investments. The relevant figures are shown in bold type in Table 16.3. If you let your cash investments take on a negative sign and the final portfolio value a positive sign you can estimate the money-weighted rate of return as follows:

$$0 = -£100 + \frac{-£100}{(1 + MWRR)} + \frac{£290.25}{(1 + MWRR)^2}$$

$$MWRR = 0.2755 = 27.55\% \text{ p.a.}$$

Case 2. Falling market

Assume now that the market conditions are reversed. In this case your initial investment of £100 has grown by 35% at the end of the first year and this encourages you to make a similar investment at the beginning of the second year in the hope that the high return will continue. Unfortunately, the market takes a turn for the worse and the return in the second year is only 15%. What rate of return have you now earned?
   The cash flows can be summarised as follows:

Table 16.4 ● Cash flows in a falling market

End year	% growth	First investment	Second investment	End year values
0		£100.00		£100.00
1	35%	£135.00	£100.00	£235.00
2	15%	£155.25	£115.00	£270.25

The calculation of the time-weighted return is exactly the same as before. The fact that the returns have been reversed makes no difference to the calculation.

$$TWRR = \sqrt{(1.35 \times 1.15)} - 1$$

$$TWRR = 0.2459 = 24.59\% \text{ p.a.}$$

The calculation of your money-weighted rate of return is the same as before although the change in market conditions has altered the final value:

$$0 = -£100 + \frac{-£100}{(1 + MWRR)} + \frac{£270.25}{(1 + MWRR)^2}$$

$$MWRR = 0.2183 = 21.83\% \text{ p.a.}$$

You will see from these figures that when the market was rising you made a good timing decision by committing extra funds to the project in the second year. When, however, the market was falling your decision to invest additional funds in the second year was not so good. We can summarise these positions as follows:

Table 16.5 ● Comparison of timing skill

Market conditions	MWRR	TWRR	Difference
Rising	27.55%	24.59%	2.96%
Falling	21.83%	24.59%	-2.76%

Looking at the TWRRs in isolation cannot tell you whether you have demonstrated any skill in selecting underpriced assets. These returns need to be compared with what you would expect to have earned given the riskiness of the assets. This is what you learnt from the security market line. If there is a difference between these two figures then you could identify whether you earned any abnormal returns. What the TWRR does is to neutralise the timing effect of cash flows into and out of your fund and so measures your relative skill.

The MWRR by contrast takes account of cash flows into and out of the fund so that the difference between the MWRR and TWRR provides you with information about the timing skill of the investor. In the first case you earned an additional return of 2.96% by investing at the right time. In the second case the additional investment was made at the wrong time so that the difference between MWRR and TWRR is –2.76%. This example highlights some simple rules:

If MWRR > TWRR then the timing of investment into and out of the fund has been good.
If MWRR < TWRR then the timing of investment into and out of the fund has been poor.
The difference between MWRR and TWRR provides a measure of timing skill.
As performance measurement is concerned with measuring relative skill you should compare TWRRs.

However, in terms of performance you are really concerned with measuring the selection skill of one fund relative to another. If a fund doubles in size over the measurement period, then this effect needs to be neutralised if you are to say anything about selection skill. It is for this reason that the time-weighted rate of return is the preferred return to use in performance measurement.

Calculating time-weighted rates of return

We have already shown you how to estimate the TWRR in our simple example. When you have more complex cash flows you need a more general approach that is able to cope with the additional complexities. This is particularly important in terms of measuring the TWRR for an index of properties where the rental cash flows can be spread over a year. There are two common methods used for calculating TWRR: the exact method and the linked internal rate of return.

The exact method

This approach highlights the main problem associated with calculating the TWRR. A valuation is required every time there is a cash flow into and out of the fund. Each of these has to be precisely dated in order to produce an accurate measure of return. The MWRR also requires the precise dating of cash flows, but it has the advantage that it requires only two valuations: one at the beginning of the period and one at the end.

The formula proposed by the Bank Administration Institute (1968) for calculating the exact TWRR is as follows:

$$TWRR_C = \frac{1}{t_f - t_0} \left[\ln \left(\frac{V_f}{V_0} \right) - \sum_{j=1}^{n} \ln \left(\frac{V_j + C_j}{V_j} \right) \right] \qquad (16.4)$$

where

C_j = net amount of the jth cash flow where flows into the fund are positive
V_0 = initial value of the fund
V_f = final value of the fund
V_j = fund value immediately before the jth cash flow
$t_f - t_0$ = time in years from beginning to the end of the period under consideration
$TWRR_C$ = time-weighted rate of return, compounded continuously.

This procedure is equivalent to calculating continuous internal rates of return (i.e. MWRRs) for each sub-period, when a cash flow occurs, and then taking the average by weighting each return by the length of its corresponding sub-period. You can see how this works by using the cash flows given in Table 16.4 for the falling market situation over the two-year time horizon. Substituting the appropriate figures gives:

$$TWRR_C = \frac{1}{2} \left\{ \ln \left(\frac{270.25}{100.00} \right) - \left[\ln \left(\frac{135.00 + 100.00}{135.00} \right) + \ln \left(\frac{270.25}{270.25} \right) \right] \right\}$$

$$TWRR_C = \frac{1}{2} [0.9941 - (0.5543 + 0)]$$

$$TWRR_C = 0.2199 = 21.99\% \text{ p.a.}$$

This final figure is the continuously compounded rate of return. From Appendix 9C we showed that discrete and continuous rates of return are related as follows:

$$1 + TWRR_D = e^{TWRR_C} \tag{16.5}$$

where $TWRR_D$ equals the discrete rate of return and $TWRR_C$ is the continuous rate of return.

By rearranging you can estimate $TWRR_D$ as follows:

$$TWRR_D = e^{TWRR_C} - 1$$

$$TWRR_D = e^{0.2199}$$

$$TWRR_D = 0.2459 = 24.59\% \text{ p.a.}$$

This is the figure we estimated in our example. Remember, however, that the value in using continuous rates of return is that they tend to be normally distributed and are, therefore, more appropriate in a portfolio context.

This example does, of course, highlight the difficulties that can arise if the dating of cash flows is not exact. We chose a simple example with annual cash flows to illustrate the method of calculation. The rent received under the terms of a property lease may, however, be quarterly in advance. There may also be a delay between the lease date and the actual date the rent is received. You will see from equation 16.4 that a valuation is needed at the date of each cash flow. Sometimes this is not possible so that approximations have to be made that can lead to errors in the calculation of the TWRR.

In general, if rental income is received quarterly then it is important to have quarterly valuations. Similarly if cash flows are received monthly, valuations must also be undertaken monthly. This clearly introduces an additional cost associated with frequent valuations that will reduce the return. Using less frequent valuations, however, also introduces errors into the return calculation. The technique that has been proposed to reduce this problem is to use the linked internal rate of return.

The linked internal rate of return

This method divides the time span over which the time-weighted rate of return is estimated into sub-periods. Knowing the value of the fund at the beginning and end of each sub-period, together with the timing of cash flows into and out of the fund, it is possible to compute the internal rate of return for each sub-period. The time-weighted rate of return is then calculated by taking an average of the internal rates of return assuming they are continuously compounded on an annual basis. The weight used for each sub-period is related to its length. We can also illustrate this method with a simple example.

Assume you want to estimate the annual time-weighted rate of return for a property that has irregular valuations and cash flows over a number of periods. We will assume that the main unit of time is quarterly. The cash flows and calculations are shown in Table 16.6.

Table 16.6 • Calculation of linked internal rate of return

	Qtr	Value	Income	Return per quarter	Annualised return	Continuous annual return	Number of periods	Weight	Weighted return
Dec.	0	£10,000							
Mar.	1		£100						
Jun.	2		£100						
Sep.	3								
Dec.	4	£12,000	£100	0.0537	0.2328	0.2093	4	0.267	0.0558
Mar.	5								
Jun.	6	£12,500		0.0249	0.1034	0.0984	2	0.133	0.0131
Sep.	7		£100						
Dec.	8								
Mar.	9		£120						
Jun.	10	£15,000		0.0508	0.2194	0.1983	4	0.267	0.0529
Sep.	11								
Dec.	12		£120						
Jan.	13		£120						
Mar.	14								
Sep.	15	£18,000		0.0402	0.1706	0.1575	5	0.333	0.0525
							15	1.000	**0.1743**

The calculations can be undertaken on a step-by-step basis.

Step 1. Estimate the quarterly internal rate of return for each sub-period

This is estimated whenever there is a valuation at the beginning and end of a sub-period. The first sub-period runs from quarters 0 to 4. The internal rate of return is estimated from the following:

$$-£10,000 = \frac{£100}{(1 + r_q)} + \frac{£100}{(1 + r_q)^2} + \frac{£12,000 + £100}{(1 + r_q)^4}$$

Note that there is no cash flow in the third quarter. Solving this equation gives a quarterly return of 0.0537 or 5.37%.

Step 2. Estimate the annual continuous rate of return

As the return is estimated on a quarterly basis it is first converted to its annual equivalent as follows:

$$(1 + r_{quarterly})^4 = (1 + r_{annual})$$

$$(1.0537)^4 = 1.2328$$

This is equivalent to 23.28% p.a. By taking the natural log you convert this to a continuous rate of return as follows:

$$\ln(1.2328) = 0.2093$$

The first sub-period therefore has a continuous rate of return of 20.93% p.a.

Step 3. Estimate the weighted return for each sub-period

As the cash flow covers a fifteen-month period you need to estimate what contribution the return for each sub-period makes to the overall return. As your first sub-period covers four months you can express this as a percentage of the total 15-month period as 0.267 (i.e. 4/15, or 26.7%). You can now apply this weight to the sub-period annual return:

$$\text{Weighted return} = 0.2093 \times 0.267 = 0.0558$$

The first sub-period, therefore, contributes 5.58% to the weighted annual return. You estimate the effect of each sub-period by repeating steps 1–3. You will see that the second sub-period only covers two quarters and contributes 1.31% to the weighted annual return. Adding all the weighted returns together gives an annual continuous rate of return of 17.43%. You can convert this to a discrete rate of return by taking antilogs:

$$r_D = e^{0.1743} - 1 = 1.1904 - 1 = 0.1904, \text{ or } 19.04\%$$

This figure is an approximation of the time-weighted rate of return because valuations were not available at the time of every cash flow.

You can also estimate the money-weighted rate of return because you know the value at the beginning and end of the fifteen-quarter period as well as the intermediate cash flows. This is just a simple internal rate of return calculation:

$$-£10,000 = \frac{£100}{(1+r)} + \frac{£100}{(1+r)^2} + \frac{£100}{(1+r)^4} + \frac{£100}{(1+r)^7} + \frac{£120}{(1+r)^9} + \frac{£120}{(1+r)^{12}} + \frac{£120}{(1+r)^{13}} + \frac{£18,000}{(1+r)^{15}}$$

Solving this gives a quarterly internal rate of return of 0.0440 which is equivalent to a discrete annual return of 18.81%.

You will see from this calculation that the difference between the money-weighted and time-weighted rate of return is –0.23%. As this figure is very small it is difficult to make any comment about timing skill.

However, before leaving this example we should emphasise that by using the linked internal rate of return the estimates are an approximation of the true return and are subject to error. The absolute error in annual returns will depend on the precision in dating the cash flows as well as the frequency of the valuations. For example, the Bank Administration Institute report on *Measuring Investment Performance* (1968) summarised the results of research into the typical mean absolute errors in annual returns in using the linked internal rate of return method. Table 16.7 is adapted from this report

Table 16.7 ● Mean absolute errors (% p.a.) using the linked internal rate of return

Dating precision of cash flows	Frequency of valuations			
	Monthly	Quarterly	Semi-annually	Annually
Daily	0.04	0.45	0.56	0.60
Monthly	0.12	0.48	0.59	0.62
Quarterly		0.51	0.61	0.64
Semi-annually			0.67	0.62
Annually				0.69

These figures are based on moderate growth. In our example the valuations are approximately annual and the cash flows occur either quarterly or semi-annually. On this basis the absolute error in the linked internal rate of return is likely to be between 0.62% and 0.64% p.a. If you take an average of 0.63% this implies that the true time-weighted rate of return lies in the range 17.43% ± 0.63%. The top and bottom end of this range give continuous returns of 18.06% and 16.80%. The discrete equivalents are 19.79% and 18.29%. The money-weighted rate of return of 18.81% is only 0.52% greater than 18.29%. Even allowing for the errors in calculation there is still little evidence to suggest that, in this example, the timing skill was good.

The holding period return and the mean fund concept

The linked internal rate of return is a general approach used to approximate the time-weighted rate of return. We have shown you how it can be used to estimate the annual time-weighted rate of return from data that are spread over a number of periods. Performance measurement, however, is generally undertaken on a yearly basis so it is important to estimate the time-weighted rate of return for a portfolio over regular holding periods. In order to do this you need a method of calculation that is easy to estimate yet produces accurate results.

Let us start with a property that has a valuation at the beginning and end of a holding period of V_{t-1} and V_t. The holding period can be one month, one quarter or a year. Let us also assume that the rent is received in a single payment at the same time as the end-of-period valuation. Given this cash-flow profile you can write the following present value:

$$V_{t-1} = \frac{V_t + a}{(1 + r)}$$ (16.6)

To make what follows a little easier to follow you can rearrange this as follows:

$$V_t - V_{t-1} (1 + r) + a = 0$$ (16.7)

Solving for r gives the internal rate of return. This, however, only really works with simple cash flows that occur at one point in time. When you start to look at property portfolios it will be clear that the timing of cash flows over the holding period will be complex so that using equation 16.7 will result in returns that differ considerably from the exact rate of return. The way round this is to use what is known as the *mean fund concept*. To make the calculations more realistic you need to include both net income and capital expenditure incurred on improvements throughout the period.

If you let NI equal the net income and CI the capital improvements the difference between these two amounts will give the net cash flow at one point in time. If you have n of these cash flows in each sub-period you can rewrite equation 16.7 as:

$$V_t - V_{t-1}(1 + r_s)^n + \sum_{j=1}^{n} (NI_j - CI_j)(1 + r_s)^{n-j} = 0$$ (16.8)

This is just a slightly expanded version of equation 16.7 related to the return over each sub-period, r_s, and compounded to the end of the holding period. This is in effect what you did with the linked internal rate of return. However, in this case you are more interested in the return over the whole period rather than each sub-period. This is easily changed by recognising that the holding period return, r, over n sub-periods can be written as:

$$(1 + r_s)^n = (1 + r)$$ (16.9)

and the return for each sub-period cash flow can be expressed as a proportion of the total period:

$$(1 + r_s)^{n-j} = (1 + r)^{1-p}$$ (16.10)

This is exactly how we dealt with the linked internal rate of return.

Substituting these changes in equation 16.8 gives:

$$V_t - V_{t-1}(1 + r) + \sum_{j=1}^{n} (NI_j - CI_j)(1 + r)^{1-Pj} = 0 \qquad (16.11)$$

Solving for r will give the holding period return.

Although this is based on the linked internal rate of return it is not, however, in the form generally used for estimating portfolio returns. To develop a more useful formula you have to recognise that the value at the end of the holding period, V_t, is really just a function of $(1 + r)$. You can see this if you rearrange equation 16.11. You can then use a Taylor expansion to work out all the terms in this function. As this is a little complicated we will spare you the details. However, the net result of doing this is to end up with the following revised expression for the holding period return.

$$r = \frac{V_t - V_{t-1} + \sum_{j=1}^{n} (NI_j - CI_j)}{V_{t-1} - \sum_{j=1}^{n} (NI_j - CI_j)(1 - p_j)} \qquad (16.12)$$

To simplify this further you have to make some assumptions about the dating of cash flows so that the number of sub-periods in the calculation can be reduced. We will consider two cases.

Case 1

Assume that the net income arises at the end of the holding period and all the capital improvements arise in the middle of the holding period. This gives you two sub-periods that are equal in length. By letting the sum of the net income and capital improvements equal NI_t and CI_t you can write the following expressions for total return, capital growth and income return.

Holding period total return

$$r = \frac{V_t - V_{t-1} - CI_t + NI_t}{V_{t-1} + 0.5CI_t} \qquad (16.13)$$

Holding period capital growth

$$g = \frac{V_t - V_{t-1} - CI_t}{V_{t-1} + 0.5CI_t} \qquad (16.14)$$

Holding period income return

$$\hat{y} = \frac{NI_t}{V_{t-1} + 0.5CI_t} \qquad (16.15)$$

Case 2

As an alternative to the above you can assume that both the net income and the capital improvements occur at the middle of the holding period. This assumption gives:

Holding period total return

$$r = \frac{V_t - V_{t-1} - CI_t + NI_t}{V_{t-1} + 0.5CI_t - 0.5NI_t}$$

(16.16)

Holding period capital growth

$$g = \frac{V_t - V_{t-1} - CI_t}{V_{t-1} + 0.5CI_t - 0.5NI_t}$$

(16.17)

Holding period income return

$$\hat{y} = \frac{NI_t}{V_{t-1} + 0.5CI_t - 0.5NI_t}$$

(16.18)

The second case is also the approach adopted by the Investment Property Databank (IPD) for calculating the performance measures of standing investments. If you assume that a portfolio holds n properties then you can estimate aggregate measures for a portfolio as follows:

Total return (standing investments)

$$r = \frac{\sum_{i=1}^{i=n}(V_{i,t} - V_{i,t-1} - CI_{i,t} + NI_{i,t})}{\sum_{i=1}^{i=n}(V_{i,t-1} + 0.5CI_{i,t} - 0.5NI_{i,t})}$$

(16.19)

Capital growth (standing investments)

$$g = \frac{\sum_{i=1}^{i=n}(V_{i,t} - V_{i,t-1} - CI_{i,t})}{\sum_{i=1}^{i=n}(V_{i,t-1} + 0.5CI_{i,t} - 0.5NI_{i,t})}$$

(16.20)

Income return (standing investments)

$$\hat{y} = \frac{\sum_{i=1}^{i=n} NI_{i,t}}{\sum_{i=1}^{i=n}(V_{i,t-1} + 0.5CI_{i,t} - 0.5NI_{i,t})}$$

(16.21)

Taking the natural log of these returns will give their continuous equivalents.

The measures given in equations 16.19–21 are for standing investments only. IPD also have a version of these calculations that include both transactions and development costs. However, as these involve more complex expressions we will spare you the details.

Although these measures of return are widely used in practice you will see from the way they have been developed that they are approximations of the true time-weighted rate of return. There are no empirical tests in the UK to compare the accuracy of conventional property return calculations with exact methods. It is likely, however, that the reported returns could have mean absolute errors of up to 0.5% p.a. This clearly points to the need to develop better estimation techniques for calculating returns. The main problem is to estimate a value for each property at the time of each cash flow. Without this information the return calculations are always going to be an approximation. One approach that may produce better results would be to use regression analysis. This method would identify those factors that were important in explaining values whenever a cash flow took place. The regression model would then be used to identify the value of all non-valued properties at the same point in time. When used in the analysis of equity portfolios regression models have been shown to reduce the error in estimating returns by a factor of about three. Given the magnitude of errors that could occur this approach is certainly worth developing.

Choosing a benchmark

Having discussed how to estimate the returns on a portfolio it is important to compare those returns against some peer-group benchmark. The difference between the achieved returns and the benchmark should offer some evidence of abnormal performance. It is at this point, however, that you are likely to run into problems of theory versus practice.

At the theoretical level you are trying to identify abnormal performance relative to the security market line. This means using an index of property returns that is *ex-ante* efficient. However, you can only construct such an index if you know the expected return and variance of every property in the marketplace. If you were able to do this you would be able to construct an efficient portfolio so that every property would lie on the security market line and there would be no abnormal performance. This is just a logical outcome of the theory surrounding the capital asset pricing model. In an *ex-ante* efficient world you can't distinguish between under- or overpriced properties and performance measurement is not required!

This, however, is the theory. In practice, you don't know the true expected return and variance of any property. You can only estimate what these are likely to be, and because you are dealing with estimates the performance of a property index will not be mean-variance efficient, implying that you should be able to identify winners and losers. As long as fund managers have different views concerning the expected return and variance of individual properties it should be possible to rank the performance of properties and portfolios relative to a mean-variance inefficient index.

The sting in the tail, however, is that if you use another index you will get a different ranking of properties. Although this may seem to be a severe criticism of performance measurement it can be largely avoided if you decide in advance which benchmark index you want to use. Your investment strategy then revolves around trying to identify those properties that you believed are mispriced, or valued, relative to that benchmark.

> Different indices will give a different ranking of properties so it is important to decide what target you are aiming to beat at the time the strategy is being set.

In the UK the IPD index is generally regarded as the target to beat.

Introducing risk

It is at this point that it is important to address the issue of risk. At present commercial property performance measurement systems assume that all properties lie within the same risk class. This implies that every property is as risky as the benchmark, so that a direct comparison of the portfolio and index returns is adequate for ranking performance. This is illustrated in Figure 16.1 on the basis of the security market line discussed earlier. It will also be seen that the ranking of returns is independent of market conditions.

However, you know from Chapter 9 that individual properties carry different levels of risk so that in this illustration the performance analysis is only strictly valid when the return on the market is the same as the risk-free rate of return. In this case the security market line would be horizontal. However, the more usual situation is for the security market line to be either upward- or downward-sloping. If risk were taken into consideration it would not be unusual to find properties with the same total return differing in terms of abnormal performance because of differences in their risk. Remember that you are interested in trying to maximise abnormal performance because it is related to net present value. If you ignore risk you can't be sure that the reported 'abnormal' performance will contribute to increasing your net present value. Figure 16.2 shows the abnormal returns if risk is taken into consideration.

This approach is correct in principle, but once again you are up against theory versus practice. In theory you should make an allowance for risk, as it is an important factor in determining the value of properties. In practice, you can't be sure about how to measure risk. For most properties you won't have the luxury of an accurate time-series of returns that can be used to estimate the market risk of each property. Even if this did exist you would still be faced with new properties that would have no time-series at all.

This may seem to be an insurmountable problem. However, it is important to realise that what you are really interested in is an *ex-ante* measure of risk. You need to estimate the risk of an investment based on what you *expect* to happen not what has

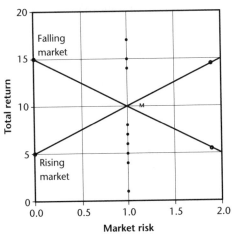

Figure 16.1 Abnormal performance ignoring risk-adjusted returns

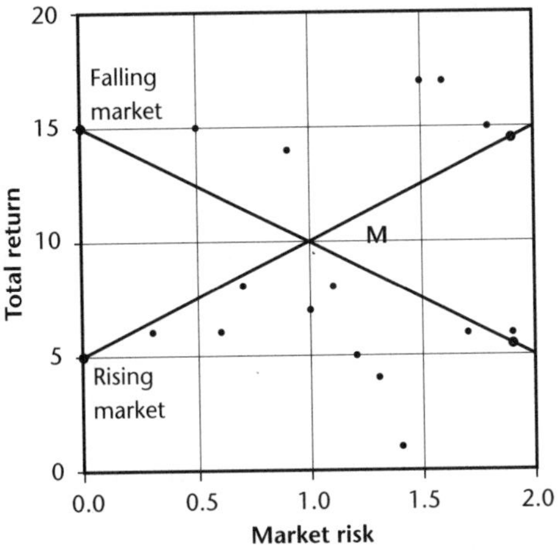

Figure 16.2 Abnormal performance assuming risk-adjusted returns

happened in the past. Regression methods use historic data to estimate risk usually as a matter of convenience. Using this approach the risk estimates will be influenced by events that took place in the past. In the stock market the use of five years of monthly data is usually regarded as a reasonable compromise between the influence of past events and obtaining a measure of market risk that is unbiased. However, even with this volume of data the risk estimates are still adjusted towards the grand mean in order to arrive at an expected measure of risk. So you don't need to rely on regression methods to estimate the risk of property.

> We don't need to rely on regression models to estimate the risk of property. Other approaches may be just as valid and more appropriate in a property context.

As performance measurement is concerned with the difference between what you expected and what you achieved then using an *ex-ante* model of risk may be helpful in establishing the risk of a property at the beginning of the measurement period.

This, of course, is not the only way of dealing with risk. Another way would be to compare the performance of a portfolio directly with a peer group. For example, if you were the manager of a property fund that specialised in industrial investment it would not make sense to compare your performance with portfolios that also held retail and offices. Choosing a peer group is one way of identifying a broad risk classification.

> Performance measurement is a bit like a race. You need to know who you are competing with before you start otherwise you won't know whether your efforts are likely to be worthwhile.

You will see from this discussion that there are a number of ways that you can deal with risk:

- You can ignore risk completely and assume that all properties are as risky as the market.
- You can assume that your portfolio should be compared with peer-group portfolios that are believed to be in the same risk class.
- You can explicitly allow for risk by making use of an *ex-ante* risk model.

The decision is not clear-cut because they all have advantages and disadvantages. The market tends to favour the first two, but this does not mean that the results can be regarded as definitive. We tend to favour the last method because we have shown that there is a lot of risk associated with property investment and we believe that this should be factored into performance measurement. There are, of course, a lot of problems with risk-adjusted performance measurement. However, as risk is an important issue influencing return it seems logical to acknowledge that it should also influence your interpretation of performance.

Attribution analysis

Earlier in this chapter we pointed out that performance measurement is concerned with identifying the relative skill of fund managers. We also showed that you needed to estimate time-weighted rates of return in order to identify relative skill. However, just knowing that your returns have been better than a competitor's doesn't tell you where the extra performance has come from. There is, therefore, a lot of interest in attribution analysis. This is intended to identify the sources of return so that this information can be used to improve investment strategy. As the process is fairly complex we have covered the main techniques that are used in Appendix 16C. You will also see that we cover attribution analysis with and without risk being taken into consideration.

The IPD standard comparative analysis

As part of the process of identifying performance and attribution, modern performance systems also provide a lot of information about the structure of a portfolio relative to the market average. For example, the IPD comparative performance system covers three main topics: *measurement, evaluation* and *income analysis*. As this system is widely used in the marketplace you should be aware of its main components.

We have summarised the structure of a typical analysis prepared by IPD in Appendix 16A. You will see that a number of the topics covered have already been discussed in this chapter. Specific details concerning attribution analysis and other aspects of risk measurement are discussed in some of the other appendices.[1]

---

[1] More detailed information on the IPD comparative analysis is available from the Investment Property Databank, 7/8 Greenland Place, London NW1 0AP, UK.

This report provides a comprehensive analysis of fund performance in comparison with the IPD Index. It also includes a lot of information that would enable the analysis to be extended to embrace more information on the risk characteristics of the fund. By incorporating risk in a more formal way it would be possible to provide information on the following:

- the risk class of the fund
- the total risk and residual risk of the fund
- the risk-adjusted abnormal return earned by the fund
- the net present value impact of management decisions
- the level of diversification in the fund
- the expected return for the fund and each property
- the expected growth of the fund and
- the current percentage reduction in risk

Including risk in the analysis provides a finer level of information concerning performance. This should not, however, be regarded as competing with the standard methods of analysis used in the market. However, we have shown that property portfolios are risky and poorly diversified. It makes sense, therefore, to acknowledge this fact and to understand the risk characteristics of each fund.

We develop this idea further in Appendix 16D, where we draw together a number of ideas developed throughout this book. The estimation of risk is a complex issue and is clearly subject to error. However, the errors are no greater than those that exist in the assumptions underlying other methods of performance measurement.

We anticipate that the techniques developed to estimate risk will improve significantly over the next few years so that risk measures will become an important part of performance measurement. It is, however, important to understand the issues involved, as they will have a direct bearing on the future development of property investment strategy.

Summary

Performance measurement is a way of evaluating whether your investment strategy has been worthwhile. The results of undertaking a performance analysis can be used to re-evaluate your strategy and take remedial actions. We showed that there are three main reasons why performance measurement is undertaken. These are: communication, accountability and research.

The results of performance measurement provide a way of evaluating the performance of a fund relative to other investments and portfolios. This represents an external objective of performance measurement. An internal objective is to analyse the returns of individual properties relative to each other and decide whether they are under- or overvalued. We showed that performance measurement is really just an extension of the security market line. If you have good forecasting ability and your selection strategy is good, then you should be able to select underpriced properties that lie above the line. Performance measurement will tell you whether you have picked winners or losers.

A major issue in evaluating performance is to estimate the rate of return. We discussed the differences between money-weighted and time-weighted rates of return and showed that if you are trying to measure the relative skill of fund managers, then the time-weighted rate of return is the appropriate measure to use.

The choice of a suitable benchmark is an important issue in understanding performance measurement. In the UK the IPD Index, because of its size and independence, can be regarded as the benchmark. However, comparing returns relative to the index implies that each property or portfolio carries the same risk as the market. You need to have some way of categorising the risk class of your investments. Making a comparison against a peer group of similar investments usually does this. However, a better way is to estimate the risk of each property. This enables you to determine whether your investment decisions are adding value to your portfolio.

Performance measurement is a complex issue. This chapter has a number of appendices devoted to advanced topics.

Appendix 16A: The IPD standard comparative analysis

This appendix provides an overview of the main components contained in the industry standard system of performance measurement.

Appendix 16B: Risk-adjusted measures of performance

This appendix discusses some of the risk-adjusted measures that are used to rank performance.

Appendix 16C: Attribution analysis

Attribution analysis is used to identify what part of performance is contributing to returns. This appendix covers this topic with and without taking risk into consideration.

Appendix 16D: Example portfolio analysis

This appendix provides a simplified portfolio analysis by focusing on attribution. The standard approach is compared with a risk-adjusted approach to highlight the value in recognising the importance of risk.

Appendix 16E: Tracking errors

This appendix shows you how to estimate the tracking error in your portfolio relative to a benchmark portfolio.

Appendix 16F: Some common questions concerning performance

In this appendix we cover a number of common questions concerning the perform-ance of a portfolio and provide answers that show you how performance is related to portfolio theory and diversification.

Appendix 16G: The performance of property bonds

The analysis is based on managed portfolios of property. If professional advisers show evidence of selection skill, it should show up in this analysis.

Appendix 16H: A time-varying analysis of property company performance

This appendix examines the performance of property shares. We use an established approach to performance analysis, as in Appendix G, but introduce a time-varying ele-ment. If professional advisers show evidence of selection skill, then it should show up in this analysis.

Chapter 16: Summary table

1. Performance measurement is required to evaluate, after the event, whether investment decisions were good or bad.

2. There are three main reasons for undertaking performance measurement. These are: ● Communication ● Accountability ● Research	Accountability is important because performance measurement checks to see whether investor wealth is being maximised and resources are being allocated efficiently.

3. A performance measurements system has two main objectives.
   ● *External*: Are pre-set targets being met and what is the performance like relative to other assets?
   ● *Internal*: How has one property performed relative to another?

4. If professional advice is costly, it makes sense to monitor whether it is good or bad. It is also important to recognise that each investment decision carries with it some level of risk. A proper evaluation of professional advice should take this into consideration.

Risk is important in making property investment decisions but receives little attention in performance measurement.

5. Performance measurement is really an extension of the security market line. If selection skill has been good then it should show up as positive abnormal performance.

6. Total returns can be either time-weighted or money-weighted.
   ● *Time-weighted return (TWRR)*: This is the geometric mean of the periodic returns. It neutralises the timing of cash flows into and out of the fund.
   ● *Money-weighted return (MWRR)*: This is the internal rate of return taking account of the cash flows.

You should measure performance using time-weighted rates of return, as you are concerned with measuring the relative skill of fund managers.

7. If **MWRR > TWRR** then the timing of investment into and out of the fund has been good. If **MWRR < TWRR** then the timing of investment into and out of the fund has been poor.

The difference between MWRR and TWRR provides a measure of timing skill.

8. The calculation of TWRR requires a valuation every time there is a cash flow. In practice this is not possible so that approximations have to be used.

Depending on the dating of cash flows there could be an absolute error in annual returns of approximately 0.5%.

9. The method most frequently used to overcome inaccurate approximations is the *linked internal rate of return*.

An extension of this method is used to estimate the returns for most commercial property portfolios.

10. The choice of a suitable benchmark for comparison purposes should be representative of the market as a whole or a peer-group of comparable investments.

In the UK the IPD Index is generally regarded as the appropriate benchmark.

11. Risk is an important part of measuring performance. You should either address it explicitly or approximate it using peer group comparisons.

12. Attribution analysis is undertaken in comparison with a benchmark and is concerned with where the sources of performance come from.

Problems

1. What are the main reasons for undertaking performance measurement?

2. Why is it important to consider risk when undertaking an analysis of performance?

3. Discuss the differences between timing skill and selection skill.

4. How does performance measurement relate to the security market line?

5. What is the difference between the time-weighted and money-weighted rate of return?

6. Which method of return is most appropriate for performance measurement?

7. Discuss the methods used in practice to estimate time-weighted rates of return and explain why the results are only approximations of the true returns.

8. Discuss how you would choose an appropriate benchmark to use when measuring portfolio performance.

9. If risk is not taken into consideration is it possible to identify abnormal performance?

10. What is attribution analysis?

Selected references

Andrews, C., Ford, D. and Mallinson, K. (1986) The design of index funds and alternative methods of replication. *The Investment Analyst* **82**, 16–23.

Ang, J.S. and Chua, J.H. (1979) Composite measures for the evaluation of investment performance. *Journal of Financial and Quantitative Analysis* **14** (2), 361–84.

Bank Administration Institute (1968) *Measuring the Investment Performance of Pension Funds*.

Brown, G.R. (1985a) Explaining portfolio performance. *Estates Gazette* 1335–38. No. 276.

Brown, G.R. (1985b) Property investment and performance measurement: a reply. *Journal of Valuation* **4** (1), 33–44.

Brown, G.R. and Matysiak, G.A. (1995) Using commercial property indices for measuring portfolio performance. *Journal of Property Finance* **6** (3), 27–38. Paper presented at the RICS Cutting Edge Conference, Aberdeen, 1995.

Burns, W. and Epley, D. (1982) The performance of portfolios of REIT's and stocks. *Journal of Portfolio Management* (Spring), 37–42.

IPD (1998) IPD Standard Comparative Report. London: Investment Property Databank.

Appendix 16A
The IPD standard comparative analysis

The IPD standard comparative analysis provides a detailed analysis of the performance of a fund relative to the IPD Index and the universe of funds being analysed. In the following sections we have summarised the level of detail provided by IPD in the analysis of a portfolio.

The report is divided into three parts covering measurement, evaluation and income analysis.

Measurement

This part of the analysis provides a factual description of the returns and structure of the portfolio. For each measure the emphasis is on providing a comparative analysis with the IPD Index as well as with a peer group and other asset classes. Also covered is an analysis of the risk of each asset class together with the correlation between assets.

1 Portfolio returns

1.1 Portfolio returns and ranking

Returns per year and annualised over longer holding periods. The performance of the fund is compared with IPD Index and ranked against the universe of funds.

1.2 Long-term portfolio returns

Comparison of time-weighted and money-weighted annualised rates of return over longer holding periods. A comparison of performance is also made in real terms.

1.3 Three- and five-year rolling returns

Comparison of performance relative to the IPD Index over three- and five-year periods and ranking relative to the universe of funds being measured.

1.4 Portfolio returns: Types of investor

This section provides a comparative ranking against different types of fund such as life funds, property unit trusts, unit-linked funds, etc.

1.5 Portfolio returns: Property and other assets

Analysis of annual returns in comparison with other asset classes such as FT property shares, WM equities, gilts, cash, etc. Annualised comparisons are made over longer holding periods. In addition, a comparison is made with property yields and equity dividend yields as well as with the gross redemption yield on gilts.

1.6 Risk and diversification

This section of the report provides an analysis of risk and return for the fund, the IPD Index and the quartile values for the universe of funds being analysed. The analysis provides a comparison of average returns, standard deviations, tracking errors, risk-adjusted returns (i.e. the reward-to-risk ratio) and the Sharpe ratio. Where appropriate this information is also provided for a number of other asset classes. In addition the correlation coefficient between assets is also provided.

1.7 Impact of transactions and developments

The impact of transactions and developments on the total return is analysed on a yearly basis. This is also calculated on an annualised basis over longer holding periods.

1.8 Capital growth and income return

This section provides an analysis of capital growth and income return for all properties and standing investments on an annual basis. Annualised figures are also provided over longer holding periods.

2 Activity and structure

2.1 Fund size and investment flows: Year of analysis

A comparison of the fund is made with the IPD Index of gross purchase expenditure, other capital expenditure, development expenditure and net sales.

2.2 Investment history

This provides an annual breakdown of the investment history of the fund. This includes purchases, sales and turnover and includes the number of properties in the fund.

2.3 Net investment by market segment

This section provides a comparative analysis on an annual basis of investment in different sectors of the property market. The figures are also annualised over longer holding periods.

2.4 Portfolio structure by market segment: History

This section shows how the asset allocation for the fund has changed over time.

2.5 Portfolio structure by market segment: Year of analysis

This provides a more detailed comparative analysis of asset allocation on a sector and regional basis in the year of analysis

2.6 Portfolio structure by property type: Year of analysis

This is similar to 2.5 but provides a detailed comparative analysis of different types of property within each sector grouping.

2.7 Portfolio characteristics: Year of analysis

This section provides a comparative overview of the fund in terms of capital value, tenure, age and yield band.

Evaluation

The evaluation part of the analysis is concerned with the returns earned by the fund in comparison with the IPD Index. This embraces attribution analysis and covers both timing and stock selection.

3 Attribution

3.1 Total return by market segment: Year of analysis

This provides a comparative attribution by total return on a sector and regional basis.

3.2 Capital employed by market segment: Year of analysis

This is similar to the above, but provides a comparative analysis in terms of the percentage of capital employed.

3.3 Attribution of fund return by market segment: Year of analysis

This provides an analysis of the components of relative return on a sector and regional basis for standing investments.

3.4 Individual property contributions to relative return in year of analysis

This section provides an analysis of contribution to return made by the top and bottom ten standing investments.

4 Long-term attribution

4.1 Attribution of relative portfolio return: History

This provides a breakdown of the main components that have contributed to the relative return.

4.2 Returns by market segment: History

This provides a sector and regional breakdown of the returns on funds standing investments. These are provided on an annual basis and annualised over longer holding periods.

4.3 Attribution of relative returns: History

Similar to 4.2 except that relative returns are used.

5 Capital and income returns

5.1 Capital and income returns: Year of analysis

This provides a comparative analysis of total return split into capital growth and income returns.

5.2 Rental value growth and yields: Year of analysis

This provides a comparative analysis of the effect that the shift in yields has on capital values.

5.3 Constituents of total return: History

This section provides a detailed breakdown on a year-by-year basis of the components of total return. Annualised values over longer periods are also provided.

5.4 Rental value growth by market segment

Annual growth in rental values on a sector and regional basis. Annualised values over longer periods are also provided.

5.5 Yields and yield impact by market segment

Analysis by sector and region of equivalent yields and the impact that the change in yields has on capital growth.

Income analysis

An important part of the assessment of a fund is to understand the covenant strength and structure of the income received. The future growth in rental value is also a vital component of the performance of the fund.

6 Income composition

6.1 Concentration of income: Year of analysis

Comparison with IPD of the lease composition and concentration of income in the fund.

6.2 Analysis of vacancies

Comparative analysis of the vacancies in the fund, by type and timing. This also includes the length of the vacancies and the impact on income.

7 Income prospects

7.1 Income security and growth potential

Comparative analysis of income security and growth potential.

7.2 Future cashflow at current rental value

Comparative analysis of the distribution of rent reviews and lease expiries.

7.3 Equivalent yield: Initial yield ratio

This provides a comparative analysis of the reversionary potential of the fund.

The full IPD report provides the results in both numerical and graphical form. The method of presentation and level of detail are revised from time to time and discussed with a consultative group. Further details may be obtained from:

Investment Property Databank
7/8 Greenland Place
London NW1 0AP

Tel: +44 (0)171 482 5149
Fax: +44 (0)171 267 0208
e-mail: manager@ipdindex.co.uk

Appendix 16B
Risk-adjusted measures of performance

Given that a positive relationship exists between market risk and expected return it is useful to capture both dimensions in some measure of performance. The three most widely used measures are those proposed by Sharpe, Treynor and Jensen. Each of these provides a single number that can be used for ranking purposes.

The Sharpe ratio

This is estimated by calculating the ratio of the average risk premium for a portfolio divided by its total risk. The ratio can be represented as follows:

$$S = \frac{\bar{r} - r_f}{\sigma} \tag{16B.1}$$

where S is the Sharpe ratio.

The resulting number is a risk premium per unit of risk. It is a measure of desirability so that the portfolio with the highest ratio will indicate the highest trade-off between risk and return. Because it takes both risk and return into consideration it avoids the temptation to rank portfolios solely in terms of total return. We can show how the Sharpe ratio is measured by using annual returns for the IPD Index over the period 1985–97. The figures we shall use are as follows:

Table 16B.1 ● IPD annual returns, 1985–97

	All properties	Retail	Office	Industrial	T-Bills
1986	0.11	0.12	0.12	0.09	0.10
1987	0.26	0.21	0.31	0.25	0.09
1988	0.30	0.25	0.32	0.39	0.10
1989	0.15	0.10	0.17	0.29	0.13
1990	−0.08	−0.08	−0.10	−0.04	0.14
1991	−0.03	0.03	−0.11	0.09	0.11
1992	−0.02	0.03	−0.07	0.02	0.09
1993	0.20	0.20	0.19	0.21	0.05
1994	0.12	0.13	0.11	0.12	0.05
1995	0.04	0.04	0.03	0.03	0.06
1996	0.10	0.12	0.07	0.10	0.06
1997	0.17	0.19	0.14	0.16	0.07
G. Mean	0.10	0.11	0.09	0.14	0.09
St. Dev.	0.11	0.09	0.14	0.12	

For each sector we have estimated the geometric mean return and standard deviation. The Sharpe ratio for all property can be estimated as follows:

$$S_{ALL} = \frac{0.10 - 0.09}{0.11} = 0.09$$

The other sectors can be compared with all property by estimating their Sharpe ratios. The results are summarised in Table 16B.2.

The higher the value of the Sharpe ratio the more desirable is the portfolio. You will see that over the twelve-year period 1986–97 the industrial sector had the highest ranking, followed by the retail and office sectors. Each of the ratios represents the slope of a line from the risk-free rate of return to the average return on the portfolio plotted in risk-return space. Figure 16B.1 shows that the Sharpe ratio can be considered to be a series of rays from the risk-free rate of return with the ranking related to their slope.

In performing the above analysis we have used the IPD annual returns. We did this for a reason. The IPD sector returns represent highly diversified portfolios of property. The Sharpe ratio really only works for diversified portfolios that do not contain any unsystematic risk. It is not, therefore, appropriate for ranking the performance of individual properties.

The Sharpe ratio can only be used to rank the performance of diversified portfolios. It should not be used to rank individual assets.

Table 16B.2 ● Ranking by Sharpe ratios, 1985–97

Sector	Sharpe ratio	Sector ranking
All property	0.09	
Retail	0.22	2
Office	0.00	3
Industrial	0.42	1

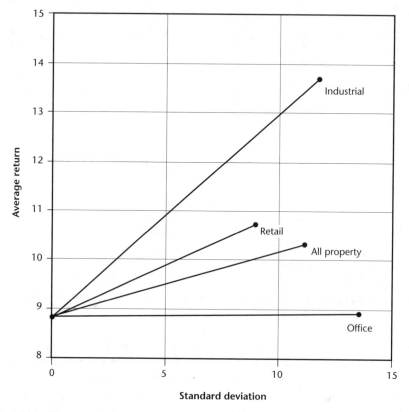

Figure 16B.1 Sharpe ratio, 1985–97

You will recall from Chapter 11 that it is very difficult to construct highly diversified portfolios of property. Even the IPD Index contains specific risk. This means that there will be errors in the measurement of the Sharpe ratio, although the ranking of sectors may remain unchanged.

The majority of property portfolios are relatively small and contain a lot of unsystematic risk so that the Sharpe ratio will not provide a reliable method of ranking portfolio performance.

The Treynor Index

The Treynor Index also measures desirability but uses systematic risk instead of total risk, and is calculated from the following:

$$T = \frac{\bar{r} - r_f}{\beta} \tag{16B.2}$$

Because Treynor's measure uses systematic risk it can be used to evaluate the performance of both portfolios and single assets and is therefore more appropriate for property.

> The Treynor Index can be used to rank the performance of both diversified portfolios and single assets.

Using the data from Table 16B.1 we have estimated the systematic risk for each sector as follows:

Table 16B.3 ● Systematic risk, 1985–97

Sector	Systematic risk
All property	1.00
Retail	1.19
Office	0.81
Industrial	0.85

The Treynor Index for the retail sector can be estimated from the following:

$$T_{RET} = \frac{0.11 - 0.09}{1.19} = 0.02$$

The ranking for each sector is shown in Table 16B.4.

The ranking can again be related to the slope of the line from the risk-free rate of return to the average return on the portfolio or asset, plotted in β-return space. This gives the same ranking as before. Figure 16B.2 summarises the results.

Table 16B.4 ● Ranking by Treynor Index, 1985–97

Sector	Treynor Index	Sector ranking
All property	0.01	
Retail	0.02	2
Office	0.00	3
Industrial	0.06	1

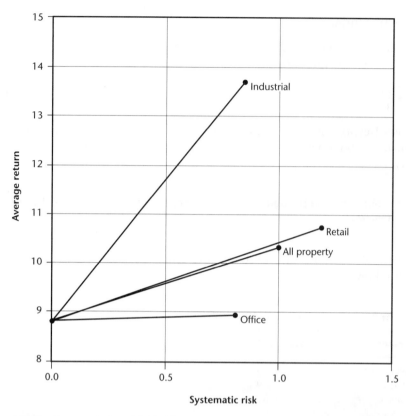

Figure 16B.2 Treynor Index, 1985–97

The Jensen measure

Jensen takes a different approach from Sharpe's and Treynor's and uses the security market line to focus on abnormal performance.

You will recall that the equation for the expected return of an asset *j* lying on the security market line is as follows:

$$E(r_j) = r_f + \beta_j\,[E(r_m) - r_f] \tag{16B.3}$$

In Chapter 10 we showed that assets that lie above the security market line are under-priced and those that lie below the line are overpriced. This is illustrated in Figure 16B.3.

Using this principle Jensen measures the desirability of a portfolio as the vertical distance that each portfolio lies above or below the line. This can be incorporated into equation 16B.3 as follows:

$$E(r_j) = r_f + \alpha_j + \beta_j[E(r_m) - r_f] \tag{16B.4}$$

The Jensen measure is really an indication of abnormal performance and can be estimated from the following regression model:

$$E(r_{jt}) - r_{ft} = \alpha_j + \beta_j[E(r_{mt}) - r_{ft}] + e_{jt} \tag{16B.5}$$

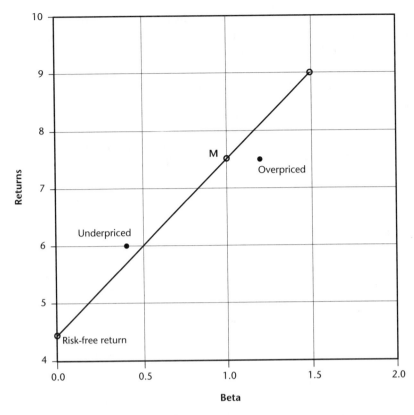

Figure 16B.3 Under- and overpriced assets

Because the value of α is equivalent to the intercept term in a regression model it is often referred to as Jensen's alpha. Jensen suggests fitting this equation by using a different value for the risk-free rate in each period. This is why we have shown a time subscript for the risk-free rate of return. By doing this we are able to keep the variation in the level of interest rates constant while abnormal performance is being estimated. The results for each sector are shown in Table 16B.5.

The measures of abnormal performance for each sector are close to zero. None is statistically significant at the 95% level. For large portfolios this is what we should

Table 16B.5 ● Jensen's abnormal performance, 1985–97

Sector	Jensen's alpha	t-value for alpha	Beta coefficient	t-value for beta
Retail	−0.007	−0.62	1.139	11.59
Office	0.012	1.93	0.849	19.36
Industrial	−0.030	−1.69	0.932	6.99

expect. Abnormal performance should be diversified away unless there is some evidence of mispricing. Because the Jensen approach relies on systematic risk it can also be applied to both portfolios and single assets.

> Jensen's alpha can be used to rank the performance of both diversified portfolios and single assets.

You will see from Table 16B.5 that the β coefficients differ slightly from those shown in Table 16B.3. The reason for this can be seen from equation 16B.5, which is estimated in risk premium form. Allowing the risk-free rate to change over time gives rise to slight differences in the calculation of beta.

Using risk-adjusted performance measures

Although the measures we have discussed appear to be different they are just linear transformations of each other. As far as property is concerned fund managers should be interested in knowing the performance ranking of both individual properties and portfolios. From the above discussion the only methods that satisfy this requirement are those that make use of systematic risk. In this respect the Jensen method offers the greatest scope for performance evaluation as it enables individual assets as well as portfolios to be ranked by abnormal performance. As net present value is related to abnormal performance it is possible to evaluate the effect of portfolio decisions in both relative and absolute terms. Each of the measures that use systematic risk does not rely upon beta being estimated using regression analysis. Estimates of risk can be made at the beginning of the period and the measure of performance made at the end of the period. *Ex-ante* models have a valuable role to play in this respect.

> Performance measures that use systematic risk do not rely upon regression analysis. *Ex-ante* models can be used at the beginning of an evaluation period so that performance can be measured at the end of the period.

All the measures of performance we have discussed are, however, biased against high-risk portfolios and assets. This arises because of differences in borrowing and lending rates, which causes the security market line to be non-linear. Higher-risk portfolios and assets tend, therefore, to have lower expected returns than predicted if these two rates were the same.

It has been suggested that the use of semi-variance will result in unbiased estimates of performance. As semi-variance is a measure of downside risk it follows more closely the preferences of investors. However, as semi-variance is just a special case of the lower partial moments we discussed in Appendix 10C it is more appropriate to rank assets using a given order for the lower partial moment. If, for an order n, we call the reward to lower partial moment $RLPM_n$, the performance measure can be written as:

$$RLPM_n = \frac{\bar{r} - r_f}{LPM_n} \qquad (16B.6)$$

Table 16B.6 ● Reward to lower partial moment, 1986–97

Sector	LPM 0.5	LPM 2.0	LPM 3.0
Retail	1.417	0.265	0.199
Office	−0.031	−0.006	−0.005
Industrial	1.994	0.653	0.528

Note: LPM 2.0 is equal to the semi-variance.

We showed how to estimate lower partial moments in Appendix 10C and summarise the results for the returns estimated over the period 1986–97 in Table 16B.6. Increases in the LPM value indicate increasing risk-aversion.

Our previous analysis covered the period 1981–97 and showed that the ranking of sectors changed as investors became more averse to risk. Over this shorter period the ranking of sectors has remained the same and confirms the rankings we found using both the Sharpe and Treynor measures.

Using lower partial moments does, however, make more sense as different groups of investors have different attitudes to risk. At present, however, we don't know much about the risk attitudes of different groups of property investor.

Selected references

Ang, J.S. and Chua, J.H. (1979) Composite measures for the evaluation of investment performance. *Journal of Financial and Quantitative Analysis* **14** (2), 361–84.

Jensen, M.C. (1968) The performance of mutual funds in the period 1945–1964. *Journal of Finance* **23** (2), 389–416.

Jensen, M.C. (1969) Risk, the pricing of capital assets and the evaluation of investment portfolios. *Journal of Business* **42** (2), 167–85.

Sharpe, W.F. (1966) Mutual fund performance. *Journal of Business* **39** (1), 119–38.

Sharpe, W.F. and Cooper, G.M. (1972) Risk-return classes of New York Stock Exchange common stocks, 1931–67. *Financial Analysts Journal* **28** (2), 413–46.

Treynor, J.L. (1965) How to rate management of investment funds. *Harvard Business Review* **43** (1), 63–75.

Treynor, J.L. and Mazuy, K.K. (1966) Can mutual funds outguess the market? *Harvard Business Review* **44** (4), 131–6.

Appendix 16C
Attribution analysis

In Chapter 16 we discussed how to calculate the return on a portfolio. On its own this measure of performance will tell you very little about the investment process. A fund manager might have achieved good returns in one year as a result of a lucky investment. Alternatively, the performance might have been the result of investment skill. Being able to identify the sources of performance will help you decide whether a fund manager is pursuing an agreed investment strategy. It is for this reason that fund managers are interested in attribution analysis.

In this appendix we will look at two approaches to attribution analysis:

● The first approach compares the performance of different parts of a fund with similar groupings in a benchmark index. This approach addresses risk in a general way by assuming that each grouping represents a specific risk class.
● The second approach explicitly allows for risk in order to evaluate selection and diversification skills.

We will, therefore, discuss various ways in which the performance of a portfolio can be analysed. Not every performance measurement system uses the methods we describe.

Benchmark attribution analysis

Return difference

The starting point is to compare the fund returns with the returns on a benchmark index in order to evaluate the difference between the joint effect of return and weighting. We can represent this as follows:

$$\Delta_p = (r_p w_p - r_I w_I) \tag{16C.1}$$

where

Δ_p = difference in returns between the contribution of the fund and the index
$r_p w_p$ = weighted return for sector of fund
$r_I w_I$ = weighted return for sector index

Each sector is split into different regions. You estimate the return on the properties within each region together with the weight that they represent of the whole portfolio. Similar figures for the universe of properties within each region are available from IPD. Given this information you can use equation 16C.1 to estimate the relative contribution made by your portfolio. We illustrate this in Table 16C.1 for one sample region.

Although your fund has slightly higher weighting (20.80%) than the IPD Index (18.20%) for this region the lower return has resulted in a lower contribution to the overall portfolio return. The fund and IPD contributions are calculated as follows:

Fund contribution = 11.30 × 0.2080 = 2.35%

IPD contribution = 14.60 × 0.1820 = 2.66%

The difference between these two figures shows how your fund has performed relative to the market. Equation 16C.1 captures these calculations in one step and indicates that the performance of Retail South in the fund has contributed a negative return of –0.31% relative to the IPD Retail Index.

Given this figure it is also useful to know whether the difference in contribution arises from timing or selection skill.

Table 16C.1 ● Relative performance

	Fund		IPD		Contribution		Equation 16C.1
	Return	Weight	Return	Weight	Fund	IPD	Fund – IPD
Retail South	11.30%	20.80%	14.60%	18.20%	2.35%	2.66%	–0.31%

Industry or timing skill (structure)

This is a measure of your success in investing in a sector or region that you believe is likely to perform well. If your timing is right, then by over-weighting in specific sectors and regions your fund should perform better than average. This component of attribution implies that timing skill is influenced by the difference between the proportion of funds committed to the portfolio and the index. You can write this as:

$$\text{Timing} = r_I[w_P - w_I] \tag{16C.2}$$

Using the figures from Table 16C.1 the attribution associated with timing can be estimated from:

$$\text{Timing} = 14.60 \times (0.2080 - 0.1820) = 0.38\%$$

In this case the timing showed that there was some evidence of timing skill, albeit small.

Sector score

This is a measure of the relative contribution to performance made by investing in sectors that you believe will perform better than the IPD Index. You can write this as follows:

$$\text{Sector score} = (w_P - w_I)(r_I - r_{IPD}) \tag{16C.3}$$

where r_{IPD} = the return on the IPD Index.
  If you expand equation 16C.3 you get:

$$\text{Sector score} = r_I(w_P - w_I) - r_{IPD}(w_P - w_I) \tag{16C.4}$$

You will see that the first part is the same as the measure of industry or timing skill we showed in equation 16C.2. The second part represents the timing skill you would have earned by investing in the IPD Index. If the return on the IPD Index is 18.41% the sector score can be estimated as:

$$\text{Sector score} = 0.38 - [18.41 \times (0.2080 - 0.1820)] = -0.10\%$$

This shows that the contribution made by investing in this sector was slightly less than the contribution made by the market.

Property selection score

IPD also report a property selection score. This is a measure of stock selection and is concerned with the choice of individual properties. Given that you have many properties available for purchase you will choose to select those properties that fit in with a predetermined profile. For example, your fund may prefer individual retail properties as opposed to large shopping centres. Your job is to identify those properties that you believe are underpriced. Choices such as this are concerned with selection. If your research is correct then evidence of skill will show up in a difference in portfolio returns relative to the index. We can capture this effect as follows:

$$\text{Property score} = w_P(r_P - r_I) \tag{16C.5}$$

Once again we can use the figures from Table 16C.1. The attribution associated with selection skill can be estimated as:

$$\text{Property score} = 0.2080 \times (11.30 - 14.60) = -0.69\%$$

In this case stock selection has not been so good and has wiped out the benefits achieved by good timing within the sector.

Aggregating the attribution scores

If you take equations 16C.2 and 16C.5 and add them together you get the following:

$$\text{Timing} + \text{Property score} = r_I(w_P - w_I) + w_P(r_P - r_I) = (r_P w_P - r_I w_I) \tag{16C.6}$$

This is the same as equation 16C.1, which gave the difference between the weighted returns. This shows that you have decomposed the return difference for each sector or region into its timing and property selection components. Adding the timing score of 0.38 to the property score of –0.69 gives –0.31, which is the figure shown in Table 16C.1.

However, the sum of the sector score and the property score for each sector or region will not add up to the return difference. In this case the figures are (–0.10) + (–0.69) which give –0.79. You can see why these figures don't give the same answer by adding equations 16C.3 and 16C.5 as follows:

$$\text{Sector score} + \text{Property score} = (w_P - w_I)(r_I - r_{IPD}) + w_P (r_P - r_I) \tag{16C.7}$$

You can simplify this to give:

$$\text{Sector score} + \text{Property score} = (r_P w_P - r_I w_I) + r_{IPD} (w_I - w_P) \tag{16C.8}$$

You will see that the first part is the same as equation 16C.6 and represents the return difference. The extra component relates to the market effect and shows that the sum of the two scores cannot add up to the return difference at the sector level. However, if you total the scores over the whole portfolio you will see that the sum of the weights for both the portfolio, w_P, and the index, w_I, will equal 100%. The difference between w_P and w_I is, therefore, equal to zero so that at the portfolio level the sum of the sector and property scores will be equal to the return difference.

So far we have illustrated these calculations using only one sector and region. A full attribution analysis usually covers all sectors and regions. We summarise a full analysis in Table 16C.2.

Table 16C.2 • Portfolio attribution analysis

	FUND Return	FUND Weight	IPD Return	IPD Weight	Contribution Fund	Contribution IPD	Fund–IPD	Attribution Scores Sector	Attribution Scores Timing	Attribution Scores Property
Retail South	11.30	20.80	14.60	18.20	2.35	2.66	-0.31	-0.10	0.38	-0.69
Retail North	15.50	7.70	18.00	11.90	1.19	2.14	-0.95	0.02	-0.76	-0.19
Shopping Centres		0.00	11.60	1.00	0.00	0.12	-0.12	0.07	-0.12	0.00
Retail Warehouses	37.70	1.50	29.20	1.70	0.57	0.50	0.07	-0.02	-0.06	0.13
Totals		30.00		32.80			-1.31	-0.03	-0.55	-0.75
City Offices	17.70	0.60	24.40	5.80	0.11	1.42	-1.31	-0.31	-1.27	-0.04
West End Offices	27.70	7.80	33.00	7.80	2.16	2.57	-0.41	0.00	0.00	-0.41
South East Offices	22.10	14.80	17.40	17.90	3.27	3.11	0.16	0.03	-0.54	0.70
Provincial Offices	12.70	20.60	13.00	16.70	2.62	2.17	0.45	-0.21	0.51	-0.06
Totals		43.80		48.20			-1.20	-0.49	-1.30	0.18
South East Industrial	16.90	15.40	18.30	11.00	2.60	2.01	0.59	0.00	0.81	-0.22
Provincial Industrial	17.60	10.90	19.50	7.00	1.90	1.37	0.54	0.04	0.74	-0.21
Totals		26.30		18.00			1.15	0.04	1.57	-0.42
Other	0.00	0.00	34.00	1.00	0.00	0.34	-0.34	-0.16	-0.34	0.00
Totals		0.00		1.00			-0.34	-0.16	-0.34	0.00
		100.00		100.00						
Totals					16.78	18.41	-1.64	-0.65	-0.65	-0.99

This analysis covers a one-year period and shows that the fund did not perform as well as the IPD Index over the same period. The difference between the two returns at the portfolio level was –1.64%. This was made up of –0.99 for property selection and –0.65 for timing. The only sector that provided a positive contribution was industrial where the difference between the fund and IPD was 1.15%. If you look at the attribution columns you will see that this figure can be split into 1.57% for the timing of investment and –0.42% for the property component. The sector component is also positive implying that investment in this sector outperformed a similar investment made in the market. From this you can say that the fund manager was not very good at selecting industrial properties but benefited from the positive performance of the industrial sector as a whole.

Based on this analysis we have summarised the fund manager's overall skill in Table 16C.3.

Table 16C.3 ● Assessing the skill of the fund manager

Sector	Sector choice	Timing skill	Selection skill
Retail	NO EFFECT	POOR	POOR
Office	POOR	POOR	GOOD
Industrial	GOOD	GOOD	POOR
Other	POOR	POOR	NO EFFECT
Portfolio	POOR	POOR	POOR

During the year of analysis the overall performance wasn't very good. It would, however, be unfair to make a judgement about the skill of a manager based on the results of one year. In fact, part of the role of performance measurement is to use the results as a means of reviewing investment strategy and to make changes as required. Over time the results of performance measurement should confirm whether the strategy being pursued is working.

Risk-adjusted attribution analysis

The attribution analysis outlined above makes use of sector and regional groupings that attempt to define broad risk classes. There is no guarantee, however, that those geographical groupings do identify differences in risk. We showed in Chapter 9 that there is a lot of risk associated with property so it may well be possible that a different set of groupings would show different performance. On the positive side regional groupings do provide investors with familiar areas that might influence investment decisions.

However, we have also shown that most portfolios tend to be relatively small so there will be a lot of specific risk associated with fund performance. Diversifying across a number of regions in an attempt to replicate the regional weighting of the IPD Index may be misguided for the majority of funds. As most properties are bought in the belief that they are underpriced, this implies that selection skill should play an important role in performance measurement. In addition to this, risk-averse investors generally dominate the market so you should expect to see some evidence of premiums for bearing risk.

Although this approach clearly leads us into the area of risk-adjusted performance measurement it does not imply that a long time-series of data is needed in order to estimate the risk parameters. We previously pointed out that portfolio theory is drafted in terms of expectations so there is clearly some merit in developing *ex-ante* measures of risk. As far as performance measurement is concerned what is needed is an estimate of the expected risk at the beginning of the assessment period. At the end of the period the risk has been resolved and you can measure the difference between what was expected and what was achieved. This, of course, is the principle embodied in the security market line.

The choice of an appropriate risk measure is debatable. Investors do not generally hold highly diversified portfolios nor do they confine themselves to a single asset. The appropriate risk measure is neither beta nor total risk but somewhere between the two. A composite risk measure is difficult to achieve so the argument for using beta is that it acts as a proxy for the true risk when measured against an index that is representative of market trends. The same argument holds true for the valuation of property. Although individual investors hold poorly diversified portfolios, the open market valuation of a property is estimated as if it were part of a highly diversified portfolio. This ensures consistency in the valuation process and also helps to explain why the expected risk premium is generally in the region of 2% p.a. The actual price achieved for a property depends on an individual investor's perception of the added value that a particular property can offer.

Performance measurement is therefore concerned with identifying relative skill and whether managers are able to add value to the portfolio. If they have some skill in identifying underpriced properties, or managing portfolios, managers should be able to do this on an *ex-ante* basis. Performance measurement should be able to identify abnormal returns after taking into consideration differences in the risk class of each sector or property.

Estimating a risk-adjusted return for each property is effectively estimating its benchmark return. This implies that a fund manager could have achieved the benchmark return by investing a proportion of funds in an index and the remainder in a riskless asset. The exact proportion of funds to use is related to the market risk. For example, if a property or portfolio had a beta of 0.6 this would imply that investing 60% of funds in the index and the remaining 40% in the risk-free return would have produced a return equal to the benchmark return. This is a passive strategy. The fund manager, by contrast, takes a more active approach by investing in a risky property and tries to perform better than the benchmark.

Abnormal returns

The difference between the active and passive returns is the abnormal return. This can be either positive or negative depending on whether the performance is superior or inferior. The abnormal return can also be expressed in terms of a net present value so that the value of management skill can be considered in absolute terms. If you assume a one-year time horizon and you know the value of a property at the end of the period, you can write the present value and expected value as follows:

$$V_0 = \frac{V_1 + a}{1 + r} \qquad (16C.9)$$

where r = internal rate of return, and

$$E(V_0) = \frac{V_1 + a}{1 + E(r)} \qquad (16C.10)$$

The difference between these two expressions gives the net present value:

$$NPV_0 = E(V_0) - V_0 \qquad (16C.11)$$

$$NPV_0 = (V_1 + a) \left\{ \frac{r - E(r)}{(1 + r)[1 + E(r)]} \right\} \qquad (16C.12)$$

For example, assume you are evaluating a property that has a capital value of £1,250,000 at the end of 1998 and the rent received is £100,000. The capital value of the property at the end of 1997 was £1,200,000. From this information you estimate that the internal rate of return is 12.50% and the growth in capital value is 4.17%. Assuming that you have also estimated the expected return to be 10% you can calculate the net present value at the end of 1997 using equation 16C.12 as follows:

$$NPV_{1997} = (£1,250,000 + £100,000) \left[\frac{0.125 - 0.100}{(1.125)(1.100)} \right] = £27,273$$

This transaction, therefore, showed a positive increase in value of £27,273. The abnormal return in this case was 2.5% (i.e. 12.50% – 10.00%). Had the net present value been zero this would have implied that the property was correctly valued. However, in this case management skill was able to show an increase in value – or was it just good luck? The abnormal return of 2.5% has a lot of uncertainty attached to it, so although this figure appears to imply management skill it could really be a chance event.

The information ratio

One way to resolve this is to calculate what is known as the *information ratio*. This is the abnormal return divided by the residual standard deviation. This is exactly the same as the *t*-value and would imply that that a low abnormal return with a high information ratio is better than a high abnormal return with a low information ratio. If in our example you assume that the residual standard deviation was 6% p.a. the information ratio would be 0.42 (i.e. 2.5%/6.0%). This low ratio implies that the abnormal return is not significantly different from zero so it doesn't really provide any conclusive evidence of management skill.

Attribution analysis and risk

Given that we have estimated an abnormal return it is useful to see how it is made up. This is exactly the same approach we took with the benchmark attribution analysis. Assuming that we have estimated the portfolio beta, β_p, the expected return over the period of analysis will be given by:

$$E(r_p) = r_f + \beta_p(r_m - r_f) \tag{16C.13}$$

The observed return, r_p, is likely to differ from this figure. Subtracting the expected return from the observed return gives the abnormal return:

$$r_p - E(r_p) = r_p - [r_f + \beta_p(r_m - r_f)] \tag{16C.14}$$

This is also equal to Jensen's alpha which we covered in Appendix 16A. The abnormal return only arises because the portfolio has not diversified down to the systematic risk level. The investor is, therefore, exposed to the total risk of the portfolio and not just to systematic risk. You will recall that you can write the total risk of the portfolio as:

$$\sigma_p^2 = \beta_p^2 \sigma_m^2 + \sigma_e^2 \tag{16C.15}$$

As the residual risk, σ_e^2, has not been diversified away, you need to ask whether the difference between the observed and expected returns has provided compensation for the extra risk taken on as a result of the reduction in diversification. This can be determined by estimating a hypothetical beta, β_h, that would result if the portfolio was highly diversified and contained no residual risk. By letting σ_e^2 equal zero equation 16C.15 can be rewritten as:

$$\sigma_p^2 = \beta_h^2 \sigma_m^2 \tag{16C.16}$$

Rearranging gives:

$$\beta_h = \frac{\sigma_p}{\sigma_m} \tag{16C.17}$$

At this level of risk the portfolio has the following expected return:

$$E(r_h) = r_f + \beta_h(r_m - r_f) \tag{16C.18}$$

The abnormal return can be represented as the sum of these two components:

$$r_p - E(r) = [E(r_h) - E(r)] + [r_p - E(r_h)] \tag{16C.19}$$

- The difference between $E(r_h)$ and $E(r)$ is the return if only systematic risk is taken into consideration. This proportion of abnormal return is therefore due to *diversification*.
- The difference between r_p and $E(r_h)$ is the abnormal return adjusted for the fact that the portfolio is not efficiently diversified. This *net selectivity* represents the performance of the fund adjusted for poor diversification.

This decomposition is shown in Figure 16C.1.

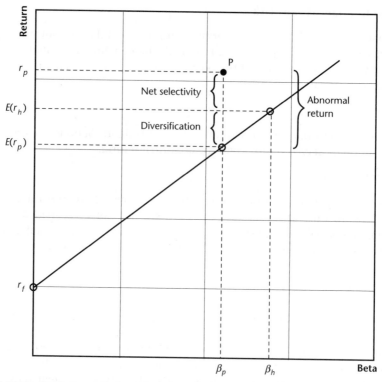

Figure 16C.1 Portfolio analysis and performance attribution

We can illustrate the ideas behind this type of attribution analysis with a simple example. Assume that you are measuring the performance of a portfolio over a one-year period and you have the following information.

Table 16C.4 ● Portfolio and market data

Portfolio	
Reported return	25.50%
Standard deviation	15.50%
Systematic risk	1.15%
Market	
Market return	12.50%
Standard deviation	10.50%
Risk-free return	6.50%

From these data you could derive the following.

Step 1. Estimate the abnormal return

To estimate the abnormal return, calculate the expected return using equation 16C.13.

$$E(r_p) = 6.5\% + 1.15(12.5\% - 6.5\%) = 13.40\%$$

The abnormal return is just the difference between the observed and expected return:

$$r_p - E(r_p) = 25.50\% - 13.40\% = 12.10\%$$

Step 2. Estimate the hypothetical beta

Estimation of the market risk of the portfolio with the same total risk comes from equation 16C.17:

$$\beta_h = \frac{15.50}{10.50} = 1.48$$

Step 3. Estimate the expected return using the hypothetical beta

This comes from equation 16C.18:

$$E(r_h) = 6.50\% + 1.48(12.5\% - 6.5\%) = 15.38\%$$

This is the expected portfolio return assuming that all the risk has been diversified away.

Step 4. Decompose the abnormal return

Equation 16C.19 decomposes the abnormal return into components of diversification and net selectivity.

Diversification

$$E(r_h) - E(r) = (15.38\% - 13.40\%) = 1.98\%$$

Net selectivity

$$r_p - E(r_h) = (25.50\% - 15.38\%) = 10.12\%$$

The sum of these components equals the abnormal return of 12.10%.

You will see from this that the net selection component is positive. This implies that the portfolio has adequately compensated the investor for the additional risk taken on due to the fact that the portfolio is poorly diversified. You will also notice that most of the abnormal return can be attributed to net selectivity. This is what you would expect from most property portfolios as they tend to be poorly diversified.

Market timing

So far we have based our calculations on the beta of the property at the beginning of the estimation period. However, a fund is likely to have a long-term risk position that it wishes to maintain. This would be decided by the trustees of the fund and be built into the buying and selling strategy that is pursued. The observed portfolio beta is, therefore, likely to differ from the long-term beta because of market timing decisions affecting the buying and selling strategy. If you let β_L represent the long-term target beta and β_p the current beta the difference in the returns calculated for each beta will capture the return from market timing. This is given as follows:

$$E(r_p) - E(r_L) = (\beta_p - \beta_L)(r_m - r_f)$$ 16C.20

If you assume that the fund managers are aiming to keep a long-term beta of, say, 1.0, you can estimate the effect of timing on the performance of the portfolio using the information from Table 16C.4:

$$E(r_p) - E(r_L) = (1.15 - 1.00)(12.5\% - 6.5\%) = 0.9\%$$

The effect of market timing has in this case only contributed 0.9% to the overall abnormal performance.

You will see that taking risk into consideration offers the opportunity to investigate performance in more detail. If it is ignored, then differences in performance between individual properties or funds could be due to differences in risk as opposed to difference in skill. This is clearly an important area of performance measurement. However, the estimation of risk still needs further investigation.

Selected references

Brinson, G.P., Hood, R. and Beebower, G.L. (1995) Determinants of portfolio performance. *Financial Analysts Journal* **51** (1), 133–48.

Dietz, P.O. (1966) *Pension Funds: Measuring Investment Performance*, New York: The Free Press.

Fama, E.F. (1972) Components of investment performance. *Journal of Finance* **27** (3), 551–67.

Posey, A. (1996) How to evaluate manager style and skill. *Pension Management* (February).

Sharpe, W.F. (1992) Asset allocation: Management style and performance attribution. *Journal of Portfolio Management* (Winter), 7–19.

Singer, B.D. (1996) Evaluation of portfolio performance: Attribution analysis. *Journal of Performance Measurement* (Winter), 45–55.

Sortino, F.A. and Forssey, H.J. (1996) Style risk: Resolving the time sensitivity problem. *Journal of Performance Measurement* (Fall).

Spaulding, D. (1997) *Measuring Investment Performance*, New York: McGraw-Hill.

Surz, R.J. (1994) Portfolio opportunity distributions: An innovation in performance evaluation. *Journal of Investing* (Summer).

Appendix 16D
Example portfolio analysis

This appendix brings together a number of ideas developed throughout this book. Our intention is to shed some light on the measurement of portfolio performance and to offer evidence, if it exists, of superior management skill. We will undertake the analysis in two ways. The first will use benchmark measures of performance and attribution analysis. The second approach will extend this analysis by incorporating risk and will use the attribution analysis described in Appendix 16C. We will focus more on risk-adjusted methods as these have the potential for offering greater insights into the way the portfolio is really performing. We will draw on some of the measures

Table 16D.1 • Portfolio and IPD summary data

Sample property portfolio	1996 £	1997 £	ERV 1996 £	Rent 1996 £	Net Inc 1997 £	Weight 96	Beta	Return
Ret	46,760,000	50,922,000	4,803,200	4,934,400	3,341,700	29.22%	1.091	16.05%
Off	54,845,000	51,690,000	4,212,500	5,454,000	4,457,600	34.27%	0.979	2.38%
Ind	58,410,000	59,845,000	8,251,700	5,737,400	5,531,100	36.50%	0.811	11.93%
	160,015,006	162,457,000	17,267,400	16,125,800	13,330,400	100.00%	0.952	9.92%
							IPD Annual Index	
					Retail	49.20%	1.094	18.50%
					Office	37.20%	0.930	14.50%
					Industrial	13.60%	0.833	16.50%
					Portfolio	100.00%	1.000	16.80%

of performance used by IPD, but will also introduce others that rely upon some estimate of risk.

Before we start, we should point out that the portfolio we use in the analysis is drawn from a random sample of properties. No attempt has been made to select the properties. Although it could be argued that this is bound to show no evidence of superior skill we will, in later appendices, analyse the performance of property companies and property bonds. These represent managed funds so if there is evidence of superior management skill it should show up in the performance of these funds.

The analysis covers a one-year period, December 1996 to December 1997. The market during this period was quite buoyant with the IPD Annual Index reporting a return of 16.8%. All sectors showed an increase in return over the previous year so if managers had any timing ability it should show up in the analysis.

Benchmark portfolio analysis

In this part of the analysis we will examine performance at the sector level. This is because we are making a comparison with the universe of properties represented by the IPD annual index. It would, of course, be possible to take the analysis down to the regional level as long as the portfolio is split up into the same regions as identified by IPD. In our example we do not have enough information to identify the regions involved so we will confine the analysis to a comparison of sectors. The principle remains the same, however, irrespective of the level of disaggregation. We have summarised the main details of the portfolio and the IPD Annual Index in Table 16D.1.

The analysis proceeds in four steps.

Step 1. Estimate the return difference

This measures how well the fund has performed relative to the benchmark. It is another way of looking at abnormal return assuming that the portfolio risk is the same as the market. The calculation uses the following equation:

$$\Delta_p = r_p w_p - r_I w_I \tag{16D.1}$$

For example, using the retail sector you would calculate the return difference as follows:

$$\Delta_p = (16.05\% \times 0.2922) - (18.50\% \times 0.4918) = -4.41\%$$

Table 16D.2 summarises the results for each sector.

Table 16D.2 ● Sector abnormal returns

Sector	Sample portfolio Return	Weight	IPD Annual Index Return	Weight	Return difference
Retail	16.05%	0.292	18.50%	0.492	–4.41%
Office	2.38%	0.343	14.50%	0.372	–4.57%
Industrial	11.93%	0.365	16.50%	0.136	2.10%
Portfolio	9.92%	1.000	16.80%	1.000	–6.88%

You will see that, with the exception of the office sector, the weightings differ considerably from the IPD sectors. Had this been a managed portfolio the difference in weightings might have reflected some timing ability. The only sector that performed well relative to the market sectors was industrial. Overall the return difference was –6.88%. This can be split into two components. One part will reflect timing and the other, selection.

Step 2. Estimate the industry or timing score (structure)

If the fund manager had believed that one sector would have performed better than another then over-weighting in that sector would, hopefully, have led to improved returns. The timing component can, therefore, be estimated from the following:

$$\text{Timing score} = r_I(w_p - w_I) \tag{16D.2}$$

Using the retail sector as an example:

$$\text{Timing} = 18.50\%(0.2922 - 0.4918) = -3.6926\%$$

The low allocation to the retail sector was clearly a wrong move!

Step 3. Estimate the sector score

We showed in Appendix 16C how to estimate what is known as the sector score. This can be calculated from:

$$\text{Sector score} = (w_p - w_I)(r_I - r_{IPD}) \tag{16D.3}$$

Using the retail sector gives:

$$\text{Sector score} = (0.2922 - 0.4918)(18.50\% - 16.80\%) = -0.34$$

This shows that relative to the IPD Index the weighting in the retail sector reduced the overall portfolio return by 0.34%.

Step 4. Estimate the property selection score

If the fund manager was successful in choosing underpriced properties then this should show up in a positive property score. This can be analysed as follows:

$$\text{Property score} = w_p(r_p - r_I) \tag{16D.4}$$

Once again we will use the retail sector as an example.

$$\text{Property score} = 0.2922(16.05\% - 18.50\%) = -0.72\%$$

Selection skill in this sector was also poor. We have summarised the results for each sector in Table 16D.3.

Table 16D.3 • Analysis of timing and selection skill

Sector	Return difference	Sector score	Timing score	Property score
Retail	−4.41%	−0.34%	−3.70%	−0.72%
Office	−4.57%	0.07%	−0.42%	−4.16%
Industrial	2.10%	−0.07%	3.77%	−1.67%
Portfolio	−6.88%	−0.34%	−0.34%	−6.54%

On the basis of this analysis we can draw some general conclusions about the performance of the fund. At the portfolio level the difference in returns between the fund and the IPD Index is dominated by selection skill. Although the overall result for the fund is disappointing the fact that selection skill dominates performance is in line with our findings in Chapter 11. We showed that it was very difficult to create highly diversified portfolios of property so that the level of residual risk is likely to be high. For a fund manager to perform well with high residual risk most of the emphasis will be placed on selection skill. We can, therefore, summarise the performance as follows.

Table 16D.4 • Portfolio performance

Sector	Sector	Timing	Selection
Retail	POOR	POOR	POOR
Office	NO EFFECT	NO EFFECT	POOR
Industrial	NO EFFECT	GOOD	POOR
Portfolio	POOR	POOR	POOR

This fund didn't do too well during 1996–97. The selection skills of the manager could be improved with better forecasting. At least the performance measurement process has helped to identify those areas that would benefit from better research.

This analysis just represents one year in the life of the portfolio. A full analysis would extend this over a number of years so that the skill of the fund manager can be analysed in more depth. The IPD system follows a similar approach but attributes performance to structure and selection only. It is possible to have a different number of attribution components and place different interpretations on them. There is no universally agreed method.

This type of analysis can only go so far. It would, for example, be useful to know more about the level of diversification in the portfolio and to have some evidence of the residual risk. It would also be useful to know how portfolio decisions affect the absolute value of the portfolio in terms of changes in net present value. In order to do this we need to extend the analysis to take account of risk.

Risk-adjusted portfolio analysis

The benchmark method of analysis treats risk in a broad sense by making a comparison between the performance of different parts of the portfolio and similar groupings in the universe of all property. IPD do this by making a comparison at the regional and sector level. They also undertake an analysis at the individual property level by making comparisons with the peer group within which each property lies.

By taking risk into consideration it is possible to address differences in each property by specifically identifying the risk class within which they lie. The performance comparison is then with a naïvely diversified portfolio with the same risk. This is just a straightforward application of the security market line. Taking risk into consideration does, however, offer a number of additional insights concerning diversification and risk-reduction that the benchmark approach is unable to address.

The following analysis will, therefore, draw on a number of topics covered throughout this book. Using our sample of 36 randomly selected properties we will estimate the following:

● market risk
● total risk
● expected return
● abnormal return
● net present value
● expected growth

With this information it is possible to analyse the portfolio in terms of diversification and percentage reduction in risk.

The principle involved in this analysis is to estimate the risk that investors expected at the beginning of the evaluation period and then assess the performance at the end of the period. This way you will be comparing the difference between what you expected with what you earned. There are four steps involved in this level of analysis.

Step 1. Estimate the market risk for each property

The first step involves estimating the market risk of each property. We have used the duration approach we outlined in Appendix 10F, but have made some simplifications because we have limited information concerning each property. The market risk is estimated relative to the IPD All Property Index. This, however, is not the only way to estimate risk. We have previously discussed a scenario approach and this is equally valid.

Step 2. Estimate the expected and abnormal return for each property

Given estimates of market risk for each property it is possible to estimate the expected return and abnormal return for each property. The riskless return and IPD All Property return over the period were 6.64% and 16.80%. The expected return is estimated using the security market line.

$$E(r_j) = r_f + \beta_j(r_m - r_f) \tag{16D.5}$$

Taking the retail sector of our portfolio as an example, the expected return can be estimated as:

$$E(r_j) = 6.64\% + 1.011(16.80\% - 6.64\%) = 16.91\%$$

As the actual return earned over the period was 16.05% you can estimate the abnormal return as follows:

Abnormal return = 16.05% − 16.91% = −0.87%

Table 16D.5 summarises the results for each sector of the market.

Table 16D.5 ● Expected returns and abnormal performance

Sector	Weight	Beta	Return	Exp Ret	Ab Ret	Wtd Ab Ret
Retail	0.2922	1.011	16.05%	16.91%	−0.87%	−0.25%
Office	0.3427	0.986	2.38%	16.66%	−14.29%	−4.90%
Industrial	0.3650	0.871	11.93%	15.49%	−3.56%	−1.30%
Portfolio		0.952	9.86%			−6.45%

There are clearly differences between this approach and the benchmark method discussed above, but in essence they are the same. Although there may be differences in abnormal performance at the sector level you would expect greater similarity at the portfolio level. Our analysis shows an abnormal return of −6.45% whereas the benchmark approach recorded a figure of −6.88%.

Step 3. Estimate the net present value of each property

The abnormal returns we estimated in step 2 are given in relative terms. It would, however, be useful to know what the abnormal returns mean in terms of changes in net present value. We showed in Appendix 16C how to calculate this using the following equation:

$$NPV_0 = (V_1 + a) \left\{ \frac{r - E(r)}{(1 + r)[1 + E(r)]} \right\} \tag{16D.6}$$

$r - E(r)$ is just the abnormal return. Using the figures for the retail sector the abnormal return can be converted to a net present value as follows:

$$NPV_0 = (£50,922,000 + £3,341,700) \left[\frac{0.1605 - 0.1691}{(1.605)(1.1691)} \right] = -£347,962$$

This sector has a negative NPV at the beginning of 1996. In other words, the performance of retail properties over the year has caused an immediate decrease of £347,962 in the value of the sector. Another way of interpreting the negative NPV is to say that in 1996 the retail sector was overvalued by this amount.

This type of analysis can also be carried out at the individual property level and will help to identify those properties that are under- or overvalued.

Step 4. Estimate the expected growth in rental value

The final part of the analysis is to estimate the expected growth, g, based on an estimate of the expected return, $E(r)$. By assuming that each property is valued part-way through a rent review period you can write the value as:

$$V = \frac{a\{1 - [1 + E(r)]^{-n}\}}{E(r)} + \frac{R(1 + g)^n}{E(r)[1 + E(r)]^n} \left\{ \frac{[1 + E(r)]^p - 1}{[1 + E(r)]^p - [1 + g]^p} \right\} \qquad (16D.7)$$

In this expression n represents the number of years to the next rent review and p represents the rent review period. This is quite a complex expression and the expected growth rate, g, can only be solved by iteration. To show how this works we have summarised the components for the retail sector as follows:

Table 16D.6 ● Estimating the capital growth for the retail sector

Retail sector	
Capital value	£46,760,000
Rental value	£4,803,200
Income	£3,341,700
Expected return	0.1691
Number of years to rent review	2.5 years
Rent review period	5 years

Substituting these figures into equation 16D.7 the expected growth in perpetuity is estimated to be 8.38% p.a. There are, however, a number of important points to consider when interpreting this figure:

● We have used the expected return to estimate the growth rate. It would be incorrect to use the riskless return on long-dated gilts or the expected return on the market as these impose specific assumptions about risk.
● The calculation estimates the expected growth in rental value that merely justifies the capital value.
● The calculation estimates the expected growth in perpetuity.
● The calculation also assumes that the conditions recorded over the period of analysis remain unchanged.

However, as you move through time, market conditions will change and you can build up a distribution of expected growth. Alternatively, you could estimate the long-term expected growth from a long-term estimate of the expected return. This also requires an estimate of the long-term market risk premium. Appendix 15A discussed the risk premium in more detail. If you estimate the expected growth in this way you can compare the figures with a long-term forecast of growth. If, for example, you believe that property offers a hedge against inflation in the long term then an inflation forecast might be a good target to use. If your calculated growth is greater than this figure then you could argue that the property is undervalued. Similarly, if the growth is less than this figure, the property may be overvalued. This is clearly a dynamic process so that it is as well to check the expected growth with forecasts of growth on a regular basis.

This analysis does not, however, tell you anything about the actual growth that will be achieved.

Example portfolio analysis

We have summarised the results of steps 1–4 for each property shown in Table 16D.7. We estimated the expected growth by assuming that each property has a five-year rent review period and the next rent review occurs in 2.5 years' time. A more formal analysis would allow for differences in rent review structure.

Table 16D.7 ● Portfolio performance analysis

Analysis period: 1996–97
Portfolio name: Sample Portfolio
Capital value: £160,015,000 (1996)

PROPERTY ANALYSIS

	Property weight	Beta 96	Wtd beta	Exp return	Wtd exp return	Property return	Wtd prop return	Abn return	Wtd ab ret	Exp growth	Wtd exp growth	Net present value
Retail												
R1	3.12%	1.101	0.034	17.82%	0.56%	27.89%	0.87%	10.07%	0.31%	11.68%	0.36%	427,420
R2	0.56%	1.370	0.008	20.56%	0.12%	24.44%	0.14%	3.88%	0.02%	16.07%	0.09%	28,982
R3	2.97%	1.133	0.034	18.15%	0.54%	3.12%	0.09%	-15.03%	-0.45%	12.64%	0.38%	-604,180
R4	0.30%	0.862	0.003	15.39%	0.05%	8.97%	0.03%	-6.42%	-0.02%	7.11%	0.02%	-27,096
R5	0.98%	0.727	0.007	14.02%	0.14%	6.11%	0.06%	-7.91%	-0.08%	3.63%	0.04%	-109,313
R6	0.72%	1.200	0.009	18.83%	0.14%	16.15%	0.12%	-2.68%	-0.02%	13.48%	0.10%	-25,946
R7	2.46%	1.315	0.032	20.00%	0.49%	9.61%	0.24%	-10.39%	-0.26%	15.35%	0.38%	-340,950
R8	7.50%	0.434	0.033	11.05%	0.83%	13.20%	0.99%	2.15%	0.16%	0.00%	0.00%	232,422
R9	7.50%	1.077	0.081	17.58%	1.32%	28.90%	2.17%	11.32%	0.85%	11.73%	0.88%	1,154,899
R10	2.75%	1.917	0.053	26.11%	0.72%	-3.41%	-0.09%	-29.52%	-0.81%	23.64%	0.65%	-1,030,049
R11	0.35%	0.862	0.003	15.40%	0.05%	24.09%	0.08%	8.69%	0.03%	7.32%	0.03%	42,178
Sector Averages:		1.091		17.72%		14.46%		-3.26%		11.15%		
St. Dev.		0.368		3.74%		10.26%		11.77%		6.16%		
	29.22%		0.296		4.94%		4.69%		-0.25%		2.92%	-£251,633
Office												
O1	0.54%	1.581	0.009	22.70%	0.12%	7.25%	0.04%	-15.45%	-0.08%	19.10%	0.10%	-108,945
O2	3.12%	0.836	0.026	15.13%	0.47%	18.89%	0.59%	3.76%	0.12%	6.98%	0.22%	163,275
O3	4.06%	0.943	0.038	16.22%	0.66%	12.08%	0.49%	-4.14%	-0.17%	8.92%	0.36%	-231,338
O4	1.24%	0.506	0.006	11.78%	0.15%	-26.09%	-0.32%	-37.88%	-0.47%	0.00%	0.00%	-670,872
O5	5.81%	0.758	0.044	14.35%	0.83%	5.79%	0.34%	-8.56%	-0.50%	5.28%	0.31%	-695,858
O6	2.53%	1.167	0.030	18.50%	0.47%	6.14%	0.16%	-12.36%	-0.31%	13.50%	0.34%	-422,319
O7	1.34%	0.934	0.013	16.13%	0.22%	22.42%	0.30%	6.29%	0.08%	9.51%	0.13%	116,481
O8	8.12%	1.289	0.105	19.73%	1.60%	-15.72%	-1.28%	-35.45%	-2.88%	15.30%	1.24%	-3,848,898
O9	1.75%	0.934	0.016	16.13%	0.28%	15.09%	0.26%	-1.05%	-0.02%	9.16%	0.16%	-25,277
O10	3.87%	0.878	0.034	15.56%	0.60%	4.68%	0.18%	-10.89%	-0.42%	7.75%	0.30%	-584,010
O11	1.87%	0.940	0.018	16.19%	0.30%	2.93%	0.05%	-13.26%	-0.25%	9.23%	0.17%	-342,352
Sector Averages:		0.979		16.58%		4.86%		-11.72%		9.52%		
St. Dev.		0.270		2.75%		13.67%		13.52%		4.86%		
	34.27%		0.338		5.71%		0.81%		-4.90%		3.34%	-£6,650,112

Table 16D.7 continued

Analysis period: 1996–97
Portfolio name: Sample Portfolio
Capital value: £160,015,000 (1996)

PROPERTY ANALYSIS

	Property weight	Beta 96	Wtd beta	Exp return	Wtd exp return	Property return	Wtd prop return	Abn return	Wtd ab ret	Exp growth	Wtd exp growth	Net present value
Industry												
I1	3.78%	0.752	0.028	14.28%	0.54%	19.94%	0.75%	5.66%	0.21%	4.82%	0.18%	299,459
I2	3.26%	0.797	0.026	14.74%	0.48%	15.69%	0.51%	0.95%	0.03%	5.27%	0.17%	43,131
I3	0.62%	0.903	0.006	15.82%	0.10%	14.11%	0.09%	-1.71%	-0.01%	8.23%	0.05%	-14,758
I4	5.00%	1.071	0.054	17.52%	0.88%	10.09%	0.50%	-7.43%	-0.37%	11.49%	0.57%	-505,682
I5	5.60%	1.138	0.064	18.20%	1.02%	2.67%	0.15%	-15.54%	-0.87%	12.66%	0.71%	-1,178,243
I6	0.03%	0.690	0.000	13.66%	0.00%	30.20%	0.01%	16.54%	0.01%	2.25%	0.00%	7,278
I7	0.84%	0.648	0.005	13.23%	0.11%	11.51%	0.10%	-1.71%	-0.01%	1.38%	0.01%	-20,440
I8	1.44%	1.097	0.016	17.79%	0.26%	15.14%	0.22%	-2.65%	-0.04%	12.19%	0.18%	-51,726
I9	1.91%	0.710	0.014	13.85%	0.26%	10.75%	0.20%	-3.10%	-0.06%	2.65%	0.05%	-83,145
I10	6.03%	0.787	0.047	14.64%	0.88%	11.90%	0.72%	-2.74%	-0.17%	5.57%	0.34%	-230,553
I11	2.37%	0.707	0.017	13.82%	0.33%	11.41%	0.27%	-2.41%	-0.06%	3.55%	0.08%	-80,430
I12	0.89%	0.340	0.003	10.09%	0.09%	10.32%	0.09%	0.22%	0.00%	0.00%	0.00%	2,859
I13	3.50%	0.764	0.027	14.40%	0.50%	15.11%	0.53%	0.70%	0.02%	4.33%	0.15%	34,385
I14	1.22%	0.946	0.012	16.25%	0.20%	17.05%	0.21%	0.80%	0.01%	9.29%	0.11%	13,407
Sector Averages:		0.811		14.88%		13.99%		-0.89%		5.98%		
St. Dev.		0.202		2.06%		5.96%		6.70%		3.98%		
	36.50%		0.318		5.65%		4.35%		-1.30%		2.61%	-£1,764,457
	100.00%		0.952		16.31%		9.86%		-6.45%		8.87%	-£8,666,202

You will see that the overall performance was not good. Although the portfolio earned a positive return of 9.86% its expected return was 16.31% for a market risk of 0.952. The net effect was a negative abnormal return of –6.45%, which translated into a negative net present value of –£8,666,202 or 5.4% of the initial portfolio value. Relative to the market in 1996 the portfolio was overvalued.

We have also summarised the performance of each sector in Figures 16D.1–16D.3 by plotting the actual return for each property against its market risk. The security market line for the property sector is also shown. Those properties lying above the line are undervalued and those below the line overvalued.

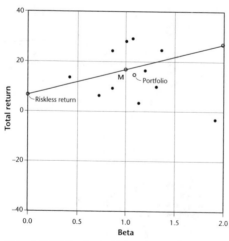

Figure 16D.1 Sample portfolio: retail sector, 1996–97

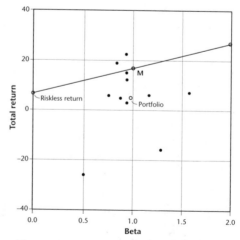

Figure 16D.2 Sample portfolio: office sector, 1996–97

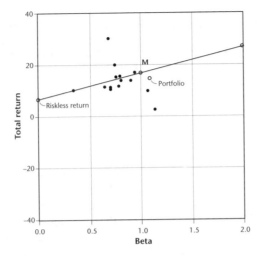

Figure 16D.3 Sample portfolio: industrial sector, 1996–97

Tracking the portfolio market risk

An important part of portfolio strategy and performance measurement is knowing the target risk class of the portfolio. The fund manager in consultation with the trustees of a fund will determine the appropriate target. It may be that the trustees wish to pursue a growth policy, or they may be more interested in income returns. Each of these targets implies something about the risk class of the portfolio. For example, a high beta portfolio would imply high expected growth. Alternatively a low beta portfolio would imply low expected growth. We have already seen that the retail sector tends to have high betas and the industrial sector low betas. Our sample portfolio shows a wide range of betas within each sector (Table 16D.8).

The target beta is important because if affects the expected return on the portfolio, which in turn influences the abnormal return. In addition, as properties begin to age, their growth expectations will decline. Without active management it is possible that the market risk of the portfolio will decline over time. Knowing the market risk and expected return of a portfolio is important because the actual returns in each period will fluctuate round the expected return. In some periods you may observe positive abnormal returns and in other periods negative abnormal returns. Unless there is some evidence of superior skill your best estimate of the average abnormal return is that it will be zero.

The reason this is important is that a fund may be pursuing a high-growth policy and so should, therefore, have a high target beta. However, its selection policy may put it into a low beta category. If the security market line is upward-sloping the average performance of the fund relative to expectations would imply that the portfolio is overvalued. Although fund managers may not currently estimate the risk class of a portfolio they will be able to measure the return and will see that, over a number of years, it is underperforming the market.

Table 16D.8 ● Range of property market risk for sample portfolio

Sector	Average beta	Standard deviation
Retail	1.091	0.368
Office	0.979	0.270
Industrial	0.811	0.202

The greatest influence on the market risk of the portfolio is the capital value weighting of each property that is purchased. Unlike equities, property portfolios tend to be built up by acquiring one property after another. Pursuing a target policy in this case means buying properties that fit some agreed criteria, such as age, location, quality of building and tenant, and growth potential. However, if the capital values of the properties vary widely, then the market risk of the portfolio will be influenced by the largest-value properties and will change as each new property is acquired.

We have given an example of how this process will work in practice. Our sample of 36 properties is randomly selected across sectors in order to replicate a hypothetical buying policy. As each new property is acquired the market risk of the portfolio is re-estimated. Remember that the portfolio market risk is just the weighted average of the component properties. The results of this exercise are shown in Figure 16D.4.

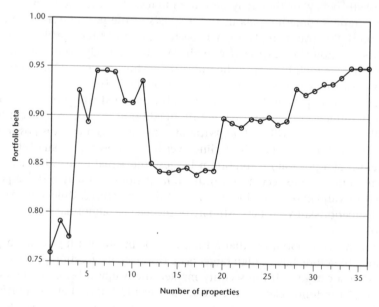

Figure 16D.4 Changes in portfolio market risk

This just shows one buying sequence to illustrate how the market risk changes as extra properties are added into the portfolio. Some other grouping of the same properties would result in a different profile. However, they would all end up with the same market risk level.

You will notice that there is a lot of fluctuation in the market risk. As more properties are added the risk gradually increases and eventually settles at a figure of 0.952. If the fund wanted to pursue a growth policy it would need a beta in excess of 1.00. It will be seen from this illustration that the sequence of purchases has resulted in a risk position for the portfolio that is consistently less than 1.00. This has happened even though a lot of the properties have individual betas greater than 1.0.

To analyse the portfolio in more depth you have to assess the total risk of each property.

Risk assessment of individual properties

One of the major difficulties with the risk assessment of property is that there is usually an insufficient time-series of returns available to measure the standard deviation of returns. In many cases a fund may acquire a new property and have no history of its returns. Despite these difficulties it is still possible to estimate the *expected* risk. In fact, this is more in the spirit of portfolio theory and we described a model in Appendix 10F that could be used to do this. Other models based on identifying the outcome under different scenarios are also possible, but for the remainder of this chapter we will use the duration approach described in Appendix 10F. We will also make the simplifying assumption that the income is fixed over the evaluation period so that the variance of returns will be equal to the variance of the capital growth rates. In Appendix 10F we showed that the variance of the capital growth rate of property j is equal to:

$$Var(g_j) = D_j^2 Var(dy_j) \qquad (16D.8)$$

The square root of this gives the property risk and shows that it is the product of the duration and the standard deviation of the change in yield. We estimate this by calculating the duration for each property and using the standard deviation for the change in yield on a sector basis. A more formal analysis would estimate this on a property-by-property basis. We estimated the average standard deviation of the change in yield for each sector from the time-series of yields taken from our sample (not reported). We also estimated a similar figure for the whole market taken from IPD data as we will need this figure later, when we decompose the risk estimates. These figures are summarised in Table 16D.9.

For example, if you take a single property from the industrial sector and estimate its duration to be 9.47 years you can approximate its total risk as follows:

Table 16D.9 ● Standard deviation of yield changes

Retail	0.0120
Office	0.0137
Industrial	0.0123
IPD All Property	0.0036

Property risk = $9.47 \times 0.0123 = 0.1165 = 11.65\%$

This can be split into its market risk and residual risk components as follows:

Total risk = Market risk + Residual risk

$$\sigma_j^2 = \beta_j^2 \sigma_m^2 + \sigma_e^2 \qquad\qquad (16D.9)$$

We have already estimated the beta of each property but we don't as yet have an estimate for the total risk of the market. By using IPD market data we estimated the duration for the all property index to be 14.204 years. The risk of the property market at the end of 1996 is, therefore:

$$\sigma_m = D_m \sigma_{\Delta y_m} = 14.204 \times 0.00357 = 0.0507 = 5.07\% \text{ p.a.}$$

With this figure you can now decompose the total risk of the property, assuming that it has a beta relative to the IPD Index of 0.69. We discussed the principles behind this decomposition in Chapter 10. The calculations are shown in Table 16D.10.

In comparison to the total risk the residual risk component is quite high. This is the portion of risk that can be diversified away by including the property in a portfolio. If the diversification is successful most of this risk will disappear. If not, then a lot of it will remain and influence the performance of the portfolio on a period-by-period basis.

Using the method of calculation outlined above we have summarised the risk of each property in Table 16D.11.

Table 16D.10 ● Decomposition of total risk

		Variance	Standard deviation
Total risk	σ_j^2	$0.1165^2 = 0.01357$	11.65%
Market risk	$\beta_j^2 \sigma_m^2$	$0.69^2 \times 0.0507^2 = 0.0012$	3.50%
Residual risk	$\sigma_j^2 - \beta_j^2 \sigma_m^2$	$0.01357 - 0.0012$	11.12%

Table 16D.11 ● Risk analysis

Analysis period: 1996–97
Portfolio name: Sample Portfolio
Market Standard Deviation (IPD All Property): 5.07% p.a.

RISK ANALYSIS

		Beta	Total risk	Variance	Market standard deviation	Residual variance	Residual standard deviation
Retail	R1	1.101	18.12%	328.43%	5.58%	328.42%	18.12%
	R2	1.370	22.56%	509.10%	6.95%	509.09%	22.56%
	R3	1.133	18.65%	347.99%	5.74%	347.99%	18.65%
	R4	0.862	14.19%	201.26%	4.37%	201.26%	14.19%
	R5	0.727	11.96%	143.12%	3.68%	143.12%	11.96%
	R6	1.200	19.75%	390.23%	6.08%	390.22%	19.75%
	R7	1.315	21.65%	468.51%	6.66%	468.50%	21.64%
	R8	0.434	7.15%	51.10%	2.20%	51.10%	7.15%
	R9	1.077	17.73%	314.43%	5.46%	314.43%	17.73%
	R10	1.917	31.56%	996.16%	9.72%	996.15%	31.56%
	R11	0.862	14.19%	201.46%	4.37%	201.45%	14.19%
Sector Averages:		**1.091**	**17.96%**		**5.53%**		**17.96%**
St. Dev.:		0.368	6.07%		1.87%		6.07%
Office	O1	1.581	29.72%	883.31%	8.02%	819.06%	28.62%
	O2	0.836	15.71%	246.90%	4.24%	228.94%	15.13%
	O3	0.943	17.72%	314.16%	4.78%	291.31%	17.07%
	O4	0.506	9.52%	90.60%	2.57%	84.01%	9.17%
	O5	0.758	14.26%	203.30%	3.85%	188.51%	13.73%
	O6	1.167	21.94%	481.54%	5.92%	446.52%	21.13%
	O7	0.934	17.56%	308.42%	4.74%	285.99%	16.91%
	O8	1.289	24.23%	586.89%	6.53%	544.20%	23.33%
	O9	0.934	17.57%	308.59%	4.74%	286.14%	16.92%
	O10	0.878	16.51%	272.57%	4.45%	252.75%	15.90%
	O11	0.940	17.66%	311.94%	4.76%	289.25%	17.01%
Sector Averages:		**0.979**	**18.40%**		**4.96%**		**17.72%**
St. Dev.:		0.270	5.08%		1.37%		4.89%
Industry	I1	0.752	12.69%	161.03%	3.81%	146.50%	12.10%
	I2	0.797	13.46%	181.13%	4.04%	164.78%	12.84%
	I3	0.903	15.25%	232.52%	4.58%	211.54%	14.54%
	I4	1.071	18.07%	326.56%	5.43%	297.10%	17.24%
	I5	1.138	19.21%	368.98%	5.77%	335.68%	18.32%
	I6	0.690	11.65%	135.81%	3.50%	123.55%	11.12%
	I7	0.648	10.94%	119.68%	3.29%	108.88%	10.43%
	I8	1.097	18.52%	342.96%	5.56%	312.01%	17.66%
	I9	0.710	11.98%	143.50%	3.60%	130.55%	11.43%
	I10	0.787	13.28%	176.40%	3.99%	160.48%	12.67%
	I11	0.707	11.93%	142.35%	3.58%	129.51%	11.38%
	I12	0.340	5.74%	32.94%	1.72%	29.97%	5.47%
	I13	0.764	12.90%	166.30%	3.87%	151.29%	12.30%
	I14	0.946	15.96%	254.69%	4.79%	231.71%	15.22%
Sector Averages:		**0.811**	**13.68%**		**4.11%**		**13.05%**
St. Dev.:		0.202	3.42%		1.03%		3.26%
Portfolio Averages:			**16.43%**		**4.80%**		**5.59%**
St. Dev.:			5.34%		1.55%		8.86%

Portfolio risk

Now that we have estimated the beta and total risk for each property it is possible to use these to calculate the risk of the portfolio. This is not an optimisation problem as we will use the weights determined by the capital value of each property.

We discussed portfolio risk in Chapter 10 and showed that it could be estimated from the following:

$$\sigma_p^2 = \sum_{i=1}^{n} x_i \sigma_i^2 + \sum_{i=1}^{n} \sum_{\substack{j=1; \\ j \neq i}}^{n} x_i x_j \sigma_{ij} \qquad (16D.10)$$

This is just the sum of all the variances and covariances weighted by the capital value of each property.

You can easily calculate the first part of this expression from our risk estimates and the capital value of each property. The covariance is a little more complicated but is easily solved by making use of the single index model. We also discussed this in Chapter 10 and showed that the covariance could be related to the market variance and the beta of each asset in the following way:

$$\sigma_{ij} = \beta_i \beta_j \sigma_m^2 \qquad (16D.11)$$

For example, using the information given in Table 16D.11, assume that you want to estimate the covariance between property O4 and I8. The beta of O4 is 0.506 and for I8 it is 1.097. Using our estimate of 5.07% for the market risk you can estimate the covariance as:

$$\sigma_{O4,I8} = 0.506 \times 1.097 \times (5.07)^2 = 14.268\%$$

Although you only need to estimate the covariance to calculate the portfolio risk you can take this calculation a little further. As the covariance term is not too easy to interpret it is frequently converted into the coefficient of correlation by dividing the covariance by the product of the standard deviations of each asset. In this example the standard deviations of O4 and I8 are 9.52% and 18.52%. The coefficient of correlation between O4 and I8 is therefore:

$$\rho_{O4,I8} = \frac{0.506 \times 1.097 \times (5.07)^2}{9.52 \times 18.52} = 0.081 \qquad (16D.12)$$

This shows that the correlation between these two properties is low. This is in line with our discussion in Chapter 9 concerning the distributional characteristics of property. The low correlation is probably a result of location and other factors that are specific to these properties. Bear in mind that this is the expected correlation. After the event there may be a number of factors that would cause the observed correlation to differ from this figure.

By using the properties of the single index model to estimate the covariance term you can write the portfolio risk as follows:

$$\sigma_p^2 = \sum_{i=1}^{n} x_i \sigma_i^2 + \sigma_m^2 \sum_{i=1}^{n} \sum_{\substack{j=1; \\ j \neq i}}^{n} x_i x_j \beta_i \beta_j \qquad (16D.13)$$

Substituting the appropriate figures the portfolio risk is 5.977% p.a. This figure can be decomposed into its market and residual risk elements so that you can get a better understanding of the diversification and risk-reduction potential of the portfolio (Table 16D.12).

Table 16D.12 ● Decomposition of portfolio total risk

	Calculation	Variance	Standard deviation
Average property risk	$\bar{\sigma}_j^2$		16.43%
Total portfolio risk	σ_j^2	0.00356	5.97%
Portfolio market risk	$\beta_j^2 \sigma_m^2$	$0.952^2 \times 0.0507^2 = 0.00233$	4.82%
Residual risk	$\sigma_j^2 - \beta_j^2 \sigma_m^2$	0.00356 – 0.00233	3.53%

Although the portfolio holds 36 properties the residual risk is 3.53% p.a. This is quite high and shows that there will be a lot of deviation from the expected return in each year. The high residual risk is a function of the portfolio diversification. This is analysed in Table 16D.13.

Table 16D.13 ● Diversification and risk reduction

	Calculation		
Average property risk	$\bar{\sigma}_j$		16.43%
Diversification: R^2	$\dfrac{\beta_j^2 \sigma_m^2}{\sigma_j^2}$	$\dfrac{0.952^2 \times 5.07^2}{5.97^2}$	65.45%
Risk-reduction	$\dfrac{\bar{\sigma}_j - \sigma_j}{\bar{\sigma}_j}$	$\dfrac{16.43 - 5.97}{16.43}$	63.66%
Maximum risk-reduction	$\dfrac{\bar{\sigma}_j - \beta_j \sigma_m}{\bar{\sigma}_j}$	$\dfrac{16.43 - 4.82}{16.43}$	70.66%

This portfolio is 65.45% diversified. A highly diversified portfolio would have a figure close to 95%. Given the high residual risk in the portfolio you are left with the conclusion that this portfolio is poorly diversified. This explains the high residual risk.

On the positive side the portfolio has achieved a level of risk-reduction of 63.66%. However, had it been possible to diversify away all the residual risk the reduction in risk would have increased to 70.66%. This portfolio still has a lot of risk-reduction potential although in practice it may be difficult to achieve.

Risk-reduction and portfolio size

In Figure 16D.4 we illustrated how the market risk changed as the portfolio increased in size. We can undertake a similar exercise with the total risk. We discussed the effect of risk-reduction and portfolio size in some detail in Chapter 11. You would normally expect the total risk of the portfolio to reduce as more properties are added. Whether this happens in practice depends on the risk of each property, the covariance structure and the value of each property. Given this information we have plotted the reduction in risk as more properties are included in the portfolio. This can also be compared with a naïve policy of equal investment by making the following assumptions:

● the total risk of each property is equal to the average risk of all the properties in the portfolio
● the correlation structure between each property is equal to the average correlation
● the minimum risk for the portfolio is equal to the average covariance

With these assumptions it is possible to estimate the parameters of an equally weighted risk-reduction profile. You will recall that the reduction in risk for an equally weighted portfolio is given by:

$$\sigma_p^2 = A + B \left(\frac{1}{n} \right)$$
(16D.14)

where A is equal to the systematic risk and $(A + B)$ is equal to the average property risk.
These figures can be estimated from our estimates of the total risk and betas for each property together with the total risk of the IPD All Property Index.

$$A = \bar{\beta}^2 \sigma_m^2 = 0.9476^2 \times 5.07^2 = 23.0816\%$$

$$A + B = 16.430^2 = 269.90\%$$

The difference between these figures gives $B = 246.86\%$.
Our risk-reduction equation for this portfolio is, therefore:

$$\sigma_p^2 = 23.0816 + 246.86 \left(\frac{1}{n} \right)$$

We have plotted this equation in Figure 16D.5 together with the profile of our randomly selected portfolio. You will see that the reduction in risk is fairly steady, although for most portfolio sizes the risk is greater than the naïve portfolio.
Every portfolio will have its own naïve risk-reduction profile which can be estimated from the average property risk and market risk for the portfolio. Knowing the composition of different portfolios is important in understanding risk-reduction and portfolio size. For example, it would be misleading to examine a large number of portfolios by plotting standard deviation against the number of properties. The reason for this is that each portfolio is likely to lie in a different risk class and a plot of standard deviation against portfolio size would not necessarily confirm any reduction in risk.
In Appendix 11E we examined the effect that differences in value weighting would have on risk-reduction for the naïve investor. We estimated an equal-weighted equivalent portfolio size from the reciprocal of the sum of the squared property weights. Given our sample portfolio you can test to see whether this provides a useful estimate of performance.
Our sample portfolio holds 36 properties. Taking value weighting into consideration we estimated the equal-weighted equivalent to be 22 properties. This implies that

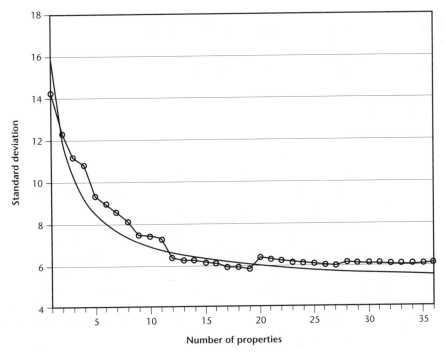

Figure 16D.5 Sample portfolio compared with equal weighting

although the portfolio is holding 36 properties it is behaving more like an equal-weighted naïve portfolio consisting of 22 properties. We can use this to estimate the risk of the portfolio by substituting into equation 16D.14:

$$\sigma_{22} = \left[23.081 + 246.86 \left(\frac{1}{22} \right) \right] = 5.86\%$$

The true portfolio risk is 5.98%. The difference between these two figures is 0.12% and is due to the covariance structure in the value-weighted portfolio. The model developed in Appendix 11E assumes that the correlation between each property is the same.

Using the equal-weighted equivalent provides a simple guide to ranking portfolios in terms of diversification. However, it is not possible to quantify the diversification without a full risk analysis.

Analysis of abnormal return

We showed earlier that the abnormal return earned by this portfolio is –6.45%. This was also similar to the figure we got using the standard benchmark method of analysis. On its own this figure does not mean a great deal because it has to be related to the residual risk of the portfolio. The abnormal return results from the fact that the portfolio is poorly diversified, so the fund manager is in effect placing bets on individual properties that may produce better than expected returns. If you look at the number of positive and negative abnormal returns you will see that some of the bets paid off and some didn't. These are shown in Table 16D.14.

Table 16D.14 • Comparison of abnormal performance

Abnormal performance by number of properties	Value-weighted returns
13 properties > 0%	1.87%
23 properties < 0%	-8.32%
Aggregate abnormal performance	-6.45%

Over half the properties in this portfolio performed badly during the year.

We know, however, that the portfolio is only 65% diversified and the residual risk is 3.53% p.a. If the fund manager really has selection skill he or she should be able to exploit this position by managing the portfolio or by selecting properties that would contribute to positive abnormal returns. The figure of –6.45% is merely one observation in a time-series of abnormal returns that will fluctuate around some average figure. The fact that it is negative in one year cannot be taken as confirmation of consistent poor management. If, however, you are trying to evaluate the skill of the portfolio manager you need to know the target value for the abnormal return. This is the return needed to justify taking on the additional risk arising from the portfolio not being efficiently diversified.

Fortunately, you can find what this figure should be by using the principles of portfolio theory and assuming that the investor maintains the same level of risk indifference to both the systematic and residual risk components of the portfolio (Rudd and Clasing 1982). The target abnormal return can be found by equating the mean-variance ratio for the active part of the portfolio to the same ratio for the passive or target position.

$$\frac{\alpha_p}{\sigma_e^2} = \frac{\beta_p[E(r_m) - r_f]}{\beta_p^2 \sigma_m^2} \tag{16D.15}$$

$$\alpha_p = \frac{[E(r_m) - r_f]\sigma_e^2}{\beta_p \sigma_m^2} \tag{16D.16}$$

To use this formula you need to have long-term positions. Let us assume therefore that the fund manager's target position is to have a beta of 1.0 so that the portfolio is generally tracking the market. Assume also that the market risk premium is believed to be 2% and the risk of the property market is on average believed to be 5% p.a. As we have estimated the residual risk for the portfolio you can find the target abnormal return as follows:

$$\alpha_p = \frac{2\% \times (3.533\%)^2}{(5\%)^2} = 1.00\%$$

The information ratio is just the abnormal return divided by the residual risk.

$$\text{Information ratio} = \frac{1.00\%}{3.533\%} = 0.28$$

The abnormal return represents the compensation required to justify taking on the extra risk in the portfolio by not being efficiently diversified. As shown by the information ratio it is not significantly different from zero. It is, however, the figure around which the observed abnormal returns will fluctuate from year to year. In some years the return may be significant but in others it may not. The observed abnormal return for the sample portfolio is −6.45%.

You can find whether this differs significantly from the target abnormal return by estimating the following t value:

$$\frac{\alpha_p - ABR}{\sigma_e} = \frac{1.00 - 6.45}{3.533} = -1.54$$

The figure is over 80% significant, but it is unfortunate that it is negative. However, the result of one year's performance doesn't really confirm whether the strategy being pursued is working or not. What you would like to know is how long it would take before you could confirm that the investment strategy was providing statistically significant returns.

Assume that the portfolio maintains its residual risk at a constant level of 3.533% p.a. As you measure the compound abnormal performance over longer periods the residual risk will reduce at a rate that is inversely proportional to the square root of time. As a fund manager you are really more concerned with delivering positive abnormal returns so the appropriate test to use is a one-tailed t-test with a significance value of 1.64. As the observed abnormal return will fluctuate round the target value you can write the significance of the target as follows:

$$\frac{\alpha_p}{\sigma_e/\sqrt{T}} = 1.64 \qquad\qquad (16D.17)$$

where T represents the number of periods involved.

By substituting our figures we can solve for T as follows:

$$\frac{1.00\%}{3.533\%/\sqrt{T}} = 1.64$$

$T = 33.57$ years

On this evidence it would take over 33 years before you can be certain that the strategy being pursued by the fund manager is profitable.

It is difficult to read a lot into this figure other than that it may be difficult to be absolutely certain that professional investment advice is really delivering statistically significant abnormal performance. The figure is also very sensitive to the inputs. For example, if the property market risk increased from 5% to 8% the period would increase to over 220 years! Alternatively, by keeping the property market risk at 5% but reducing the residual risk of the portfolio to 2% the time would drop to just over 13 years. The message from this is that portfolio management is important in trying to ensure better than average returns. This means improving forecasting skills through better research.

Diversification, selection and timing skill

The final part of our analysis is to ask whether the abnormal return earned compensated investors for the additional risk associated with the imperfect diversification. In order to understand this we will summarise the results of our portfolio analysis (Table 16D.15).

Table 16D.15 ● Summary of results

		Sample portfolio (p)	IPD Annual Index (m)
Riskless return	r_f	6.64%	6.64%
Observed return	r	9.86%	16.80%
Beta	β	0.952	1.000
Portfolio risk	σ	5.979%	5.07%
Portfolio market risk	$\beta\sigma_m$	4.824%	
Residual risk	σ_e	3.533%	0.00%
Expected return	$E(r_p) = r_f + \beta(r_m - r_f)$	16.31%	16.80%
Abnormal return	$\alpha_p = r_p - E(r_p)$	-6.45%	

There are four steps involved in decomposing the abnormal return into its diversification, net selection and timing components.

Step 1. Estimate the hypothetical beta and expected return

This is just the beta of the portfolio assuming all the residual risk has been diversified away:

$$\beta_h = \frac{\sigma_p}{\sigma_m} = \frac{5.979}{5.07} = 1.18$$

The expected return based on this beta is:

$$E(r_h) = r_r + \beta_h(r_m - r_f) = 6.64\% + 1.18(16.80\% - 6.64\%) = 18.62\%$$

Step 2. Estimate the return due to diversification

Had all the risk in the portfolio been diversifiable the expected return on the portfolio would have been 18.62%. We know, however, that the market risk of the portfolio is 0.952 and expected return is 16.31%. The difference between these two figures gives the compensation earned as a result of poor diversification.

$$\text{Diversification} = E(r_h) - E(r_p) = 18.62\% - 16.31\% = 2.31\%$$

The figure is positive. This means that the portfolio provided adequate return to compensate for the poor diversification.

Step 3. Estimate the return due to selection

This is just the difference between the actual return and the expected return based on the hypothetical market risk:

Net selectivity = $r_p - E(r_h)$ = 9.86% – 18.62% = –8.76%

The negative figure shows that the selection component during the year has not been good and failed to provide compensation for the poor diversification. You will see that the sum of the diversification and selection components adds up to –6.45%, which is the abnormal return. This decomposition is shown in Figure 16D.6.

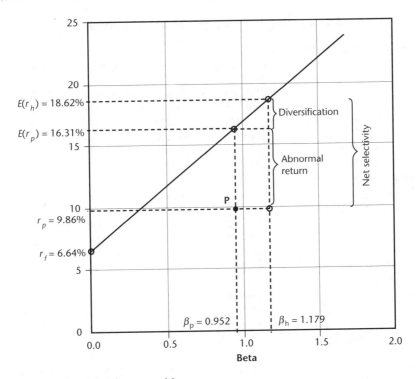

Figure 16D.6 Portfolio decomposition

Step 4. Estimate the effect due to market timing

In order to estimate the effect of timing you will need to know the target risk class for the portfolio. This is the long-term beta related to the policy established by the trustees of the portfolio. Let us assume that the intention is to maintain a risk position that is equal to the market. This means trying to maintain a beta equal to 1.0. Timing is concerned with the shift in the position of the portfolio relative to the target position. If it has been possible to forecast correctly the movement of the market, shifting the risk class may have contributed to an increase in return. The return from timing is just the difference between the expected return on the portfolio based on the observed market risk and the target market risk. You can calculate this as follows:

Timing $= E(r_p) - E(r_L) = (\beta_p - \beta_L)(r_m - r_f) = (0.952 - 1.00)(16.80 - 6.64) = -0.49\%$

The negative return due to timing implies that the weighting towards low beta properties was not a good move. This shows that it is important to monitor the risk class of the portfolio to ensure that it stays within the target limits.

This type of analysis can, of course, be undertaken for each sector. Table 16D.16 summarises these results on the assumption that the target beta for each sector is the same as the sector betas estimated from the IPD Annual Index. The results broadly confirm the benchmark approach but provide additional insights into performance that can be used to develop portfolio strategy.

Table 16D.16 ● Sector performance analysis of sample portfolio

Sample portfolio sector analysis, 1996–97	All property	Retail	Office	Industrial
IPD annual return	16.80%	18.50%	14.50%	16.50%
IPD sector risk	5.070%	4.817%	4.759%	6.033%
IPD sector betas	1.000	1.094	0.930	0.833
IPD expected return	10.10%	10.39%	9.71%	9.30%
IPD sector weights		47.78%	36.13%	13.25%
Riskless return	6.640%			
Sample portfolio				
Sector weights		29.22%	34.27%	36.51%
Beta (value-weighted)	0.952	1.011	0.986	0.871
Beta (equal-weighted)	0.948	1.090	0.979	0.811
Total return	9.857%	16.047%	2.373%	11.928%
Expected return	16.308%	16.916%	16.661%	15.488%
Expected growth	6.678%	7.718%	9.761%	3.017%
Risk analysis				
Total risk	5.978%	8.142%	8.662%	6.589%
Market risk	4.824%	5.128%	5.001%	4.416%
Residual risk	3.531%	6.325%	7.073%	4.891%
Sector diversification				
Number of properties	36	11	11	14
% diversification	65.12%	39.66%	33.33%	44.90%
Risk-reduction	63.49%	54.65%	52.92%	51.86%
Max. possible risk-reduction	70.54%	71.44%	72.82%	67.73%
Abnormal return analysis				
Abnormal return	−6.45%	−0.87%	−14.29%	−3.56%
Return due to diversification	2.31%	6.04%	7.34%	4.36%
Return due to selection	−8.76%	−6.91%	−21.63%	−7.92%
Timing analysis				
Target beta	1.00	1.09	0.93	0.83
Return due to timing	−0.49%	−0.84%	0.57%	0.39%
Performance measures				
Jensen	−6.45	−0.87	−14.29	−3.56
Treynor	3.38	9.30	−4.32	6.07
Sharpe	0.54	1.56	−0.49	0.80

Table 16D.17 ● Summary of risk-adjusted performance measures for sample portfolio

Sector	Beta	Return	Total risk	Jensen Index	Treynor Index	Sharpe Index
Retail	1.011	16.05%	6.59%	−0.87	9.31	1.16
Office	0.986	2.38%	8.66%	−14.29	−4.32	−0.49
Industrial	0.871	11.93%	8.14%	−3.56	6.07	0.80
All property	0.952	9.86%	5.97%	−6.45	3.38	0.54
IPD All Property	1.000	16.80%	5.07%	0.00	10.16	2.00

Note: The risk-free rate is 6.64% p.a.

The abnormal return we used in these calculations is just Jensen's alpha we described in Appendix 16A. The other performance measure we recommended was Treynor's index. We have estimated these figures for each sector and summarised them in Table 16D.17. For completeness we have also included the Sharpe Index. However, as each sector is poorly diversified the Sharpe ratio will give biased results.

The ranking of sectors is the same for each performance measure and no sector has outperformed the IPD Index.

Selected references

Bank Administration Institute (1968) *Measuring the Investment Performance of Pension Funds*, Park Ridge, Illinois.

Fama, E.F. (1972) Components of investment performance. *Journal of Finance* **27** (3), 551–67.

Francis, J.C. (1986) *Investments*, 4th edn. New York: McGraw-Hill.

Francis, J.C. and Archer, S.H. (1979) *Portfolio Analysis*, Prentice-Hall Foundations of Finance Series, 2nd edn. Englewood Cliffs, NJ: Prentice-Hall Inc.

IPD (1998) IPD Standard Comparative Report. London: Investment Property Databank.

Jensen, M.C. (1969) The performance of mutual funds in the period 1945–1964. *Journal of Finance* **23** (2), 389–416.

Jensen, M.C. (1998) Risk, the pricing of capital assets and the evaluation of investment portfolios. *Journal of Business* **42** (2), 167–85.

Levy, H. and Sarnat, M. (1984) *Portfolio and Investment Selection: Theory and Practice*, Englewood Cliffs, NJ: Prentice-Hall International.

Rudd, A. and Clasing, H.K. (1982) *Modern Portfolio Theory: The Principles of Investment Management*, Homewood, Illinois: Dow Jones-Irwin.

Schuck, E.J. and Brown, G.R. (1997) Value weighting and real estate portfolio risk. *Journal of Property Research* **14** (3), 169–87.

Singer, B.D. (1996) Evaluation of portfolio performance: Attribution analysis. *Journal of Performance Measurement* (Winter), 45–55.

Spaulding, D. (1997) *Measuring Investment Performance*, New York: McGraw-Hill.

Treynor, J.L. (1965) How to rate management of investment funds. *Harvard Business Review* **43** (1), 63–75.

Appendix 16E
Tracking errors

Performance measurement is usually a single-period exercise. However, investors are also interested to know how well their portfolio returns track the benchmark over a number of periods. This can be found by estimating the tracking error.

Assume that the return on a portfolio in period t is r_{pt} and the equivalent benchmark return is r_{bt}. The benchmark could be the IPD Index or some subset of the IPD Index that represents a suitable comparison for the portfolio. The benchmark will, of course, be better diversified than the portfolio and it is the difference in diversification that causes their returns to differ on a period-by-period basis. What investors are interested in knowing is the variation in this difference. This is the tracking error.

Dropping the time subscripts for simplicity, you can write the difference in the portfolio return and the benchmark return as α so that:

$$\alpha = r_p - r_b \tag{16E.1}$$

This is the same as the abnormal return we discussed earlier. The variation in this figure can be written as follows:

$$Var(r_p - r_b) = Var(r_p) + Var(r_b) - 2Cov(r_p, r_b) \tag{16E.2}$$

Assuming that you can estimate the variance of both the portfolio and benchmark returns the only difficult part is estimating the covariance. However, if you assume that the single index model is a valid description of the returns-generating process the covariance between the portfolio returns and the benchmark, $Cov(r_p, r_b)$, can also be written as:

$$Cov(r_p, r_b) = \beta_p \beta_b Var(r_m) \tag{16E.3}$$

where

r_m = the expected market return
r_p = the portfolio return
r_b = the benchmark return
β_p = portfolio beta
β_b = benchmark beta

Substituting equation 16E.3 back into equation 16E.2 gives:

$$Var(r_p - r_b) = Var(r_p) + Var(r_b) - 2\beta_p \beta_b Var(r_m) \tag{16E.4}$$

Example

To see how this works in practice assume that you want to estimate the tracking error of the retail sector portfolio we analysed in Appendix 16D relative to the IPD retail sector. Table 16E.1 summarises the information you need to estimate this figure.

Table 16E.1 ● Parameters for estimating tracking error

Retail portfolio	σ_p	8.142%
IPD retail sector	σ_b	4.817%
IPD All Property	σ_m	5.07%
Retail portfolio beta	β_p	1.011
IPD retail beta	β_b	1.094

Substituting into equation 16E.4 gives the following:

$$Var(r_p - r_b) = 8.142^2 + 4.817^2 - 2 \times 1.011 \times 1.094 \times 5.07^2 = 32.63$$

Taking the square root gives a tracking error of 5.71% per annum expressed in terms of standard deviations. Assuming the parameters we used remain constant this figure implies that in each year there will be 68% probability that the portfolio will miss the IPD retail returns by ±5.71%. This figure is quite high but bear in mind that the retail portfolio only contains 11 properties so is very poorly diversified. In Appendix 16D we showed that the portfolio was about 40% diversified so the low tracking error is not unexpected.

Another way of looking at this is to specify a target tracking error and then work back to find what this implies in terms of the portfolio. Assume for example that you would like to track the IPD retail sector within a standard deviation of 0.5%. By substituting this into equation 16E.4 you can estimate the variance of the retail portfolio that would justify this tracking error.

$$Var(r_p) + 4.817^2 - 2 \times 1.01 \times 1.09 \times 5.07^2 = 0.50^2$$

$$Var(r_p) = 33.64\%$$

$$\sigma_p = 5.80\%$$

At present the retail portfolio has a standard deviation of 8.142% but would need to reduce this to 5.800% if the intention is to achieve a tracking error of 0.50%. If you have no forecasting skill and view every property as having the same average risk and covariance you can estimate the number of properties that would be needed to get close to this tracking error.

To estimate this figure you need to know the average property risk and the average covariance for the portfolio. We estimated the total risk for each property in Table 16D.11. The average property risk for the retail sector is 17.96% p.a. If you assume that the market risk of the sector portfolio remains unchanged at 1.094 you can estimate the average covariance for the portfolio from:

$$\text{Average portfolio covariance} = \beta_p^2 \sigma_m^2 = 1.094^2 \times 5.07^2 = 30.54 \qquad (16\text{E}.5)$$

In Chapter 11 we showed that the portfolio risk can be written as:

$$\sigma_p^2 = A + B \left(\frac{1}{n} \right) \qquad (16\text{E}.6)$$

where A equals the average covariance and $(A + B)$ equals the average property risk.

As both these figures have been estimated you can write the equation as:

$$\sigma_p^2 = 30.54 + 292.02 \left(\frac{1}{n}\right)$$

By setting this equation equal to the target variance of $(5.80\%)^2$ you can estimate the number of properties needed to meet the target tracking error:

$$5.800^2 = 30.54 + 292.02 \left(\frac{1}{n}\right)$$

$n = 94$ properties.

This is considerably larger than the current retail portfolio and shows how difficult it is to achieve high tracking errors.

Selected reference

Brown, G.R. and Matysiak, G.A. (1995) Using commercial property indices for measuring portfolio performance. *Journal of Property Finance* **6** (3), 27–38. Paper presented at the RICS Cutting Edge Conference, Aberdeen, 1995.

Appendix 16F
Some common questions concerning performance

Understanding the results of portfolio performance analysis requires some knowledge of concepts such as market risk and how effective diversification is likely to be in constructing property portfolios. This appendix is in the form of an imaginary conversation between a fund manager and professional adviser. The intention is to reinforce some of the important ideas raised in this chapter.

Q1: The IPD Annual Index has reported a total return over the year of 16.80%. Why has my performance differed from this figure even though I hold properties in the same sectors?
Your portfolio is much smaller than the IPD Index so the performance of individual properties will have a greater influence on your annual return. You are in effect placing bets on the performance of specific properties and locations. Depending on your selection and management skill, some may have outperformed the index whereas others may not. As you add more properties to your portfolio a lot of the variation in annual returns will be washed away so that your portfolio will tend to move more in line with the market. It will, however, be difficult for you to diversify away completely the effect of specific properties. As a result, although the performance of your portfolio will tend to move in line with the market your return in any year will still be affected by the performance of individual properties.

Q2: I have looked at the return from other indexes and find that I have performed better than some but worse than others. How can I judge my own performance?
In looking at the results from other indexes it is important to examine how they have been constructed. For example, an index based on a very small sample may show more

variation from year to year than one using a large sample. In addition you should also check to see how representative is the sample. Does it, for example, track the movement of prime property or cover a cross-section of the market? Differences in construction will affect the results from year to year so it would not be unusual to find that your own portfolio underperforms some indexes but outperforms others. In trying to judge your own performance against an index you should choose the one that most closely resembles your own portfolio. Not every index provider supplies detailed information on the composition of the index although this is important for performance measurement purposes. The IPD Index does supply detailed information on its composition and covers a high proportion of institutional investment. It is widely recognised and provides a good indicator for comparison purposes. What is important is that you should choose your benchmark index in advance of your portfolio management decisions. After all, you can always find some index that you have outperformed after you have measured your results!

Q3: Is it possible for my portfolio consistently to outperform the index?
This depends on your forecasting ability. If you are good at picking properties that are undervalued then you will outperform the index. However, to do this consistently from period to period would require exceptional skill. Look at Appendices 16G and 16H. There appears to be little evidence that it is possible for managed portfolios to consistently outperform the market.

Q4: Can I construct a portfolio that will always give the same return as the IPD Index?
In order to perform exactly in line with the index it would be necessary to hold every property in the index. This is clearly impossible so you should aim to try to work within an acceptable tracking error. The smaller your target tracking error the more properties you will need to hold. We gave an example in Appendix 16E and showed that to maintain a tracking error of 0.5% you would need to hold at least 95 equal-valued properties. If value weighting is taken into consideration the figure is much greater. If you bear in mind that most portfolios tend to hold about 40 properties you will see that trying to track an index will not be easy. Tracking an index may seem like a good idea, but it should also be clear that it would not be possible to outperform the index by holding the index. If you believe that you have some skill in choosing properties you stand a better chance of achieving better than average performance.

Q5: My portfolio contains a large number of properties. Am I better diversified than a portfolio holding half as many properties?
As your portfolio increases in size you can diversify away a lot of the variation in annual returns. However, most of your reduction in risk will occur by holding a relatively small number of properties. If you look at our results in Chapter 11 you will see that most of the reduction in risk occurs within the first 10–15 properties. At this level you will begin to establish the risk class of your portfolio. This identifies your volatility relative to the market. Your portfolio will, however, still carry a lot of risk that is attributable to the performance of individual properties. Diversifying away this residual risk will be difficult and is only likely to be achieved by holding many thousands of properties. Assuming that your risk class does not change, the residual

risk in your portfolio will determine how much variation you would expect to observe in each period relative to your expected return. The capital value of each property will play an important role here.

The important message is that you can reduce the risk in your portfolio down to its market risk level by holding relatively few properties, but it is very difficult for a portfolio to be highly diversified so that it will track the performance of the IPD Index. A portfolio holding 100 properties may, for example, have the same market risk as one holding 50 properties. They will both have the same expected return but you would *expect* the smaller portfolio to show greater deviation from its expected return than the larger portfolio. We say *expect* because the capital value of the properties plays an important role in performance. The 100-property portfolio may therefore be more volatile than the 50-property portfolio because of differences in value weighting. You can only be certain about the diversification in your portfolio by undertaking the type of analysis described in Appendix 16D.

Q6: Can I rank the performance of my portfolio with other portfolios by using one-year and five-year return figures?
Both figures can be used to rank your performance but the results will be misleading because you are assuming that each portfolio carries the same level of risk. In practice, each portfolio will probably lie in different risk classes and have different levels of diversification that will be influenced by the type of properties held, the sectors in which they lie and their capital values. These differences will alter the ranking unless their effects are taken into consideration. As you measure the returns over longer holding periods the variation in average annualised returns will begin to diversify away so the portfolios will probably begin to rank in relation to their market risk levels. This may be misleading because the variation in cumulative returns will almost certainly increase.

Q7: I like to invest in fringe properties because prime is too expensive. What effect will this have on my portfolio returns?
If there is a lot of competition for prime property it could well mean that some properties may be overpriced. In this instance, looking at fringe properties could reveal some underpriced opportunities. Securing underpriced properties will improve the performance of your portfolio. What must be borne in mind, however, is the effect these properties will have on the overall riskiness of your portfolio. It may well be that fringe properties are more risky than prime. The problem is how to identify whether a property is underpriced. This requires some knowledge of its risk and expected return.

Q8: If I have the highest return in one year am I likely to have the highest return next year?
The performance of your portfolio will depend on the number and value of the properties you hold, together with your level of diversification. In addition it will depend on the timing of your purchases and your forecasting ability concerning the future prospects of individual properties. In any particular year your total return will depend not only on how your portfolio has reacted to market movements but also on the performance of individual properties. If your portfolio is reasonably well diversified, then any excess return earned will be the result of specific properties that have provided extra return not influenced by general market movements. Excess returns of

this nature may well be the result of skill in choosing properties. Alternatively, they may just be the result of good luck. The problem from the investor's point of view is that it is difficult to tell the difference. As a result the abnormal return relative to the market may in one year be positive and in another, negative.

Because positive and negative abnormal returns are just as likely to occur it follows that having the highest return in one year does not necessarily mean this will happen in the following year.

Appendix 16G
The performance of property bonds

In Appendix 16D we examined the performance of a portfolio that was constructed by randomly selecting a group of 36 properties. We showed that during the period of analysis the portfolio was poorly diversified and that most of the performance came from selection skill. We also showed that there was no significant evidence of superior management skill. Our results could, of course, be influenced by the fact that we had randomly selected the properties.

In this appendix we investigate this further by analysing the performance of a group of managed property bonds. Although the data we have used are a little historic, the period of analysis has similarities with the more recent period in that it covers a property boom followed by a collapse. What follows is the result of a study of the performance of a group of property bonds over the nine-year period 1973–82. Property bonds are important because they represent a wide range of professionally managed property portfolios so their results can be considered typical of investment management practice. If there is evidence of management skill and selection ability then it should show up in these data.

Making property investment decisions

If property portfolios are poorly diversified they should offer the opportunity for abnormal returns. The methodology for testing this proposition is that suggested by Jensen (1968) in the analysis of mutual funds in the United States. The approach he adopted was to assume that the capital market is in equilibrium so that the expected return on any asset, P, over t periods can be expressed as:

$$E(r_{pt}) = r_{ft} + \beta_p[E(r_{mt}) - r_{ft}]$$ (16G.1)

In risk premium form this can be written as:

$$E(r_{pt}) - r_{ft} = \beta_p[E(r_{mt}) - r_{ft}]$$ (16G.2)

In terms of expectations this equation will yield no abnormal performance. *Ex-post*, however, the record may show that realised returns have differed from expectations, in which case the empirical counterpart of equation 16G.2 can be written as the following regression model:

$$r_{pt} - r_{ft} = \alpha + \beta_p[r_{mt} - r_{ft}] + e_t$$ (16G.3)

Table 16G.1 ● Property bond performance using quarterly returns, 1973–82

Property bond	α	Standard error	β	Standard error	$\bar{R}^2$	Durbin–Watson
Abbey	−0.49%	0.80	1.47*	0.228	0.52	2.24
M&G	0.03%	0.40	1.02	0.141	0.58	2.31
Guardian	0.08%	0.30	0.96	0.095	0.73	1.65
Cannon	0.13%	0.30	0.71*	0.086	0.65	1.97
Hambro	0.22%	0.20	0.72*	0.049	0.85	2.04
Hill Samuel	−0.01%	0.30	1.21*	0.082	0.85	2.36
Merchant Investors	−0.13%	0.10	1.28*	0.122	0.75	2.13
Tyndall	−1.15%	0.90	1.51*	0.153	0.72	2.56
S&P	0.27%	0.40	0.95	0.114	0.65	2.26
Averages	**−0.12%**		**1.09**		**0.70**	

* Coefficients are significantly different from 1.0 at the 95% level.

Expressing the model in risk premium form, and allowing the risk-free rate to vary over time, overcomes the problem of non-stationarity of the riskless rate. Table 16G.1 shows the results of this analysis using continuously compounded quarterly returns from a sample of nine property bonds from the second quarter of 1973 to the fourth quarter of 1982. The return on the Money Management equally weighted bond index was used as a proxy for the market portfolio and cash on deposit was used as the risk-free rate of return.

Differences in systematic risk, β, will also reflect differences in liquidity. However, any values for α that are statistically significant would imply superior selection or management skill.

There are two important facts to note from Table 16G.1.

1. All the $\bar{R}^2$ values are low in comparison with a portfolio that would be considered well diversified. The average value is 0.7 and confirms the results given in Chapter 11. This value is also in line with the diversification figures shown in the sample portfolio analysis given in Appendix 16D and confirms that property portfolios tend to be poorly diversified.
2. None of the α values is statistically different from zero. It would appear that although positive and negative abnormal returns can be earned, it is not possible to sustain the abnormal performance over long periods. As a result their risk class will heavily influence the long-term performance of the property bonds.

Of the nine bonds analysed, only Abbey, Hill Samuel, Merchant Investors and Tyndall had levels of market risk that were statistically greater than 1.00. These bonds appear to be pursuing a strategy of growth. The market risk of Cannon and Hambro were significantly less than one and M&G and Guardian were indistinguishable from 1.0.

The Durbin–Watson statistic shows that in seven out of the nine portfolios examined there is some evidence of negative serial correlation in the residuals implying that over the period analysed values were following a cyclical pattern.

Table 16G.2 ● Decomposition of quarterly abnormal returns, 1973–82

Property bond	Abnormal return	Diversification	Net selectivity
Abbey	−0.490	−0.034	−0.524
M&G	0.030	−0.019	0.011
Guardian	0.080	−0.022	0.058
Cannon	0.130	−0.011	0.119
Hambro	0.220	−0.004	0.216
Hill Samuel	−0.010	−0.007	−0.017
Merchant Investors	−0.130	−0.013	−0.143
Tyndall	−1.150	−0.015	−1.165
S&P	0.270	−0.014	0.256
Averages	**−0.117**	**−0.015**	**−0.132**

Table 16G.3 ● Systematic risk over non-overlapping periods

Property bond	1973–77	1978–82
Abbey	1.52	1.11
M&G	1.13	0.67
Guardian	0.94	0.97
Cannon	0.74	0.47
Hambro	0.69	0.92
Hill Samuel	1.21	1.09
Merchant Investors	1.31	1.09
Tyndall	1.49	0.89
S&P	1.02	0.59
Averages	**1.12**	**0.87**

Another way of examining the performance is to decompose the abnormal returns in the manner suggested by Fama (1972). We used this approach in Appendix 16D. The abnormal return can be decomposed into a portion due to diversification and the remainder due to the ability to pick underpriced properties. You may need to refer to Appendix 16D to find out more about this approach. The results are shown in Table 16G.2.

The diversification components are small and consistently negative implying that none of the bonds was able to compensate investors for the poor diversification. By contrast, the net selectivity components are much larger. The majority are positive implying that there is some selection skill that compensated for the imperfect diversification. However, as we have seen this is not statistically significant.

The information on systematic risk can also be used to determine whether investors have some preference for a specified risk class. If there is a preference, then a portfolio in a high-risk class in one period should also exhibit a similar risk preference in the following period. Table 16G.3 shows the systematic risk of each bond calculated over two non-overlapping four-year periods.

You will see that there is a considerable change in a number of the beta estimates for each sub-period. The second, more recent period shows a lower average systematic risk. This could be due to an increase in the average level of liquidity or a change in the management policy or the type of properties held. As the cost of managing property tends to be high, the risk class of the underlying property should remain fairly constant from period to period. This will be more significant for portfolios holding large numbers of properties. Changes in the systematic risk of property bonds will, therefore, be influenced more by changes in liquidity. As the period 1978–82 covered a downturn in the UK property market it was not unusual to see property companies reducing their levels of borrowing. The reduction in debt would cause the betas to drop. The rank-order correlation coefficient between the two sets of figures is 0.546 (t =1.72). Although this is not high, the relationship is positive. Thus the underlying property is likely to stay within the same risk class although the fund manager can change this relationship by altering the liquidity.

To summarise, the performance of property bonds gives rise to the following conclusions:

1. Most property portfolios tend to be poorly diversified.
2. On average, no property bond showed better performance than a market-based portfolio with the same risk.
3. Although there is some evidence to suggest that portfolio managers can pick under-priced properties, they are not able to do this consistently from period to period.
4. There is a positive relationship between the risk class in non-overlapping periods although this is not strong and is influenced by changes in liquidity.
5. The average return measured in the long run is more likely to be influenced by the market risk of the portfolio.

Selected references

Brown, G.R. (1987) The performance of property bonds. *Estates Gazette*, 1273–4, No. 281.
Brown, G.R. (1991) *Property Investment and the Capital Markets*, London: Chapman & Hall.

Appendix 16H
A time-varying analysis of property company performance

In Appendix 16G we used Jensen's measure of excess return to estimate the abnormal performance of property bonds. Our results showed that although there was some evidence of selection skill it could not be sustained over the nine-year period of analysis. Abnormal performance was not, therefore, significantly different from zero. In this appendix we take this idea further by investigating the performance of publicly quoted property companies. However, instead of assuming that excess returns and systematic risk remain constant we allow them to vary over time.

Background

Property companies are specialised portfolios of direct property holdings and are often poorly diversified. The results of analysing their performance could, therefore, offer insights into whether investing in property companies would provide abnormal performance relative to broadly based, highly diversified portfolios of securities such as unit trusts or investment trusts.

Property companies differ in many respects. The size of each company and the types of the property held suggest that selection ability could play an important role in determining the characteristics of each firm. Differences in trading activity and gearing, together with their impact on specific and systematic risk, will all have an effect on the ability of property companies to deliver performance.

We showed in Chapter 11 that it is very difficult to create highly diversified portfolios of property. If the performance of the underlying properties is translated into share prices, then by looking at the secondary market it may be possible indirectly to obtain an assessment of the underlying performance of property company assets and, by implication, an assessment of the selection skills of property company investment managers.

Detecting investment forecasting ability

Fama (1972) has identified forecasting ability at two levels, namely:

- micro-forecasting (investment selectivity), and
- macro-forecasting (market timing)

Micro-forecasting

This refers to selection skill in identifying under- or overvalued investments, and involves analysis at the individual asset level. The process involves identifying those investments whose expected returns exceed a broad market measure after controlling for risk. The key component concerns the ability to forecast specific risk. In the context of property company performance this involves the experience of the property investment surveyor who employs the 'traditional approach' and assembles portfolios on a property-by-property basis, without regard to any concepts that relate to modern portfolio theory.

Macro-forecasting

This is concerned with anticipating broad market movements. Traditionally this has not been the approach used to build up property investment portfolios. However, this top-down approach is increasingly receiving attention, particularly amongst the larger institutional investors, as a result of the development of commercial property market forecasting services, leading to structured property portfolio investment strategies.

In this appendix we investigate property company share performance. The results of the analysis may be interpreted as providing indirect evidence of the performance of the underlying property assets. If the UK commercial property market is co-integrated with the property share market, in the sense of Engle and Granger (1987), the respective risk-adjusted returns should track each other. Consequently, we are looking for selection ability in the choice of properties by measuring abnormal returns in the secondary market for shares. That is to say, we look for evidence of property company management displaying superior selection ability, which is reflected in positive abnormal equity returns.

In line with previous studies investigating abnormal performance the single index market model is employed, which proposes an *ex-post* relationship between the portfolio and market excess returns given by equation 16H.1:

$$r_{jt} = \beta_{jt} r_{mt} + \varepsilon_{jt} \tag{16H.1}$$

where

r_{jt} = the risk premium earned by property company j
r_{mt} = the risk premium of the market portfolio
β_j = the sensitivity of the property company return relative to the market portfolio
ε_{jt} = a random error term with $E(\varepsilon_{jt}) = 0$ and $E(\varepsilon_{jt}, r_{mt}) = 0$

If the managers of the jth property company have superior property selection ability, due to specialised knowledge of niche property sub-markets, they will select properties such that $\varepsilon_{jt} > 0$. The portfolio will, therefore, earn a rate of return in excess of the expected return as determined by β_j and r_{jt}. The potential abnormal return can be accommodated by allowing a non-zero constant term in equation 16H.1. This is Jensen's measure of excess performance (Jensen 1968).

$$r_{jt} = \alpha_j + \beta_{jt} r_{mt} + \mu_{jt} \tag{16H.2}$$

The error term μ_{jt} now has the property $E(\mu_{jt}) = 0$.

A positive value of the term α_j can be interpreted as the ability of the property portfolio managers to forecast property prices. Conversely, a negative value will signify poor selection ability. A value of $\alpha_j = 0$ suggests that performance is in line with a random selection buy and hold strategy, implying that there is no evidence of selection ability.

Market timing turns on adjusting the portfolio's sensitivity to anticipated market movements. For example, if the market is expected to rise or fall then the risk level of the portfolio β_j is increased or lowered. Exposure to the market can be achieved in a number of ways such as changing the property mix or the leverage. It has been shown (Jensen 1968) that selection and timing ability need to be modelled simultaneously, otherwise any empirically derived estimates of α_j and β_j will be biased and, therefore, provide invalid inferences of investment ability. There are a number of issues surrounding risk-adjusted performance measures, including the selection of an appropriate benchmark (see, for example, Grindblatt and Titman 1989).

The case for time-varying parameters

Estimating equation 16H.2 by ordinary least squares (OLS) implicitly assumes that β_j is constant. This is based on an assumed constant correlation structure between the portfolio and market excess returns. However, beta is a measure of the correlation between two expectations, which can vary over time and is, therefore, unlikely to be static. An example of changing expectations may arise when the market corrects for

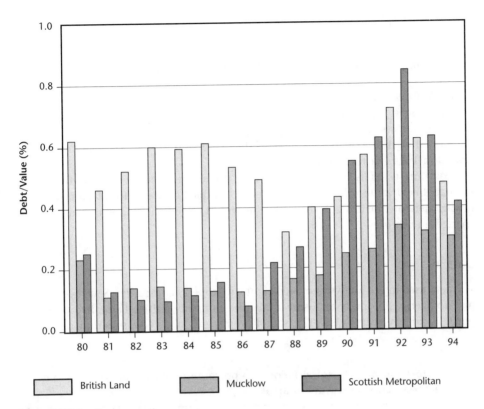

Figure 16H.1 Gearing ratios

the underpricing of 'loser' shares and the overpricing of 'winner' shares. Property analysts are also concerned with net asset values (NAVs) and the discount to NAVs. As there can be considerable variation in these figures changes in their value will also have an effect on share price movements. Finally, property companies tend to be highly geared and the combination of these effects implies that β_j will vary over time. As an example of the level of gearing Figure 16H.1 shows the percentage debt to value for three property companies.

In a study of UK unit trusts Black et al. (1992) use an econometric approach known as the Kalman filter to allow β_j to vary. However, they keep their estimates of abnormal performance, α_j, constant. We also employ the same approach, but we believe that keeping α_j constant may be unduly restrictive, particularly when looking at property company performance. We therefore adopt a more general approach that allows both α_j and β_j to vary over time.

This discussion implies that a formulation of the time-varying parameter profiles is required. In order to develop this we assume that *changes* in the parameter values are random. The reasoning underlying this assumption is that changes in α_j and β_j reflect the random arrival of new information. The profiles of α_j and β_j, therefore, evolve over time according to the following laws of motion:

$$\alpha_{jt} = \alpha_{jt-1} + \eta_{jt} \qquad\qquad (16\text{H}.3)$$

$$\beta_{jt} = \beta_{jt-1} + v_{jt} \qquad\qquad (16\text{H}.4)$$

where η_{jt} and v_{jt} are white noise with $E(\eta_{jt}) = E(v_{jt}) = E(\eta_{jt}, v_{jt}) = 0$.

By reformulating the system in 'state space' form, equation 16H.2 can be written as a measurement equation with the parameter profiles given by equations 16H.3 and 16H.4 as transition equations. Employing maximum likelihood estimation and the Kalman filter it is possible to recover the parameter values (see Harvey 1993, or Hamilton 1994, for further details).

As our interest is in stock selection we do not address issues of market timing. The estimated beta value will reflect the combined impact of the various factors discussed. It will, therefore, be difficult to isolate the impact of general market movements from changes in gearing.

Data

The data used in the analysis covered eighteen property companies. Seventeen of these had no overseas property exposure. Only one company, British Land, had 6–7% of its portfolio in overseas assets. The sample represents a diverse selection of property

Table 16H.1 ● Market capitalisation as a percentage of FT property company sector and main investment areas

Property company	% of sector	Principal investment areas		
		Retail	Office	Industrial
Land Securities	21.80	■	■	
British Land	8.20	■	■	
Great Portland Estates	4.00	■	■	
Frogmore Estates	1.60	■	■	
Bilton	1.50	■	■	■
Town Centre Securities	0.90	■		
Greycoat	0.90	■	■	
Wates	1.00	■		
Mucklow	1.00			■
Scottish Metropolitan Properties	0.70	■	■	■
Southend Properties	0.30	■	■	
London Merchant Securities	1.70	■	■	
Burford Holdings	2.10	■	■	
Evans of Leeds	1.00	■	■	
Chesterfield Property	0.70	■	■	
Tops Estate	0.60	■	■	
St Mowden Properties	0.40	■	■	
Trafford Park	0.40		■	■
Total	**48.80**			

companies with different representations of property holdings across geographic locations, portfolio size and 'use' type including offices, industrials and retail sector holdings. The total market capitalisation of the traded property company sector, as of January 1995, was some £14 billion, representing 1.8% of the FT All Share Index. The sample used in the analysis represents almost half, by market capitalisation, of the total UK traded property companies. Table 16H.1 provides details of the proportion that each company represents of the total FT property sector. Also included is an indication of the main property sectors in which each company specialises.

The largest valued company is Land Securities, having a market capitalisation of some £3 billion and representing almost 22% of the property sector. The Land Securities portfolio is dominated by retail and office holdings, with some 40% of the portfolio held in central London offices. British Land is the next largest portfolio in the sample, having a market capitalisation of £1.1 billion. The portfolio consists, predominantly, of retail and office holdings. British Land is a good example of a company whose beta is likely to have changed over the last five years or so. The composition of the properties held has altered from some 70% central London office representation to less than 25%.

Empirical results

The analysis has been undertaken using monthly and quarterly total rates of return over the period January 1980 to February 1995. The three-month Treasury Bill rate is used as the risk-free rate in the calculation of excess returns. The period of analysis encompasses both boom and slump environments in the direct property market. Monthly and quarterly total rates of return (capital and income) were obtained from mid-market closing prices provided by Datastream.

Due to changes in liquidity and long refurbishment and development time horizons, the underlying performance of property may take time to translate into share prices. Property portfolio managers base their investment decisions on expected returns over longer time horizons than would be the case with other asset categories. Commercial property investment horizons will often be based on long-term return expectations. It should be recognised that, if performance evaluation is undertaken over an inappropriate period, the results may be biased. However, irrespective of any linkages that may exist between the commercial property market and the property share market, an analysis of monthly and quarterly share data should enable a comparison with investment in other equity sectors to be made.

Discussions with market-makers revealed that the bid–offer spreads for property company shares can vary and will depend on a number of factors, including market conditions and the level of trading volume. Large capitalised stocks such as Land Securities would typically have a spread of 1%. In this study we have applied a constant 1% spread across all property companies, recognising that the results may overstate the actual performance figures for some of the companies analysed.

OLS estimates of equation 16H.1, for monthly and quarterly returns, were obtained in order to facilitate a comparison with the time-varying parameter estimates. The monthly and quarterly results are summarised in Table 16H.2.

Table 16H.2 ● Monthly and quarterly OLS parameter values

	Monthly			Quarterly		
	α	β	$\bar{R}^2$	α	β	$\bar{R}^2$
Land Securities	−1.733*	0.818	0.44	−1.568	0.886	0.41
	(0.283)	(0.068)		(1.121)	(0.139)	
British Land	−1.143*	1.070	0.39	−1.442	1.199	0.40
	(0.414)	(0.100)		(1.559)	(0.194)	
Great Portland Estates	−1.488*	0.919	0.35	−2.480	0.939	0.38
	(0.383)	(0.092)		(1.278)	(0.159)	
Frogmore Estates	−0.802*	0.970	0.41	−0.342	0.979	0.35
	(0.359)	(0.087)		(1.417)	(0.176)	
Bilton	−1.294*	0.809	0.31	−1.745	0.956	0.26
	(0.376)	(0.091)		(1.701)	(0.211)	
Town Centre Securities	−1.235*	1.077	0.43	−1.681	1.076	0.44
	(0.381)	(0.092)		(1.275)	(0.158)	
Greycoat	−2.612*	1.204	0.21	−4.855	1.149	0.16
	(0.718)	(0.174)		(2.794)	(0.347)	
Wates	−2.128*	1.300	0.40	−4.210	1.473	0.47
	(0.634)	(0.145)		(2.283)	(0.252)	
Mucklow	−1.044*	0.751	0.31	−1.097	0.889	0.34
	(0.349)	(0.084)		(1.298)	(0.161)	
Scottish Metropolitan Properties	−1.762*	0.985	0.26	−3.378	1.175	0.29
	(0.520)	(0.126)		(1.957)	(0.243)	
Southend Properties	−0.301	1.170	0.17	3.873	1.266	0.11
	(0.806)	(0.195)		(3.762)	(0.467)	
London Merchant Securities	−1.741*	1.034	0.38	−2.819	0.9025	0.28
	(0.409)	(0.099)		(1.530)	(0.190)	
Burford Holdings	0.584	0.635	0.06	3.233	0.356	0.01
	(1.319)	(0.295)		(4.329)	(0.581)	
Evans of Leeds	−0.794*	1.050	0.40	−0.254	0.988	0.36
	(0.398)	(0.096)		(1.384)	(0.172)	
Chesterfield Property	−1.530*	1.0331	0.26	−2.495	1.074	0.24
	(0.541)	(0.130)		(2.036)	(0.253)	
Tops Estate	1.604	1.403	0.07	8.742	2.006	0.08
	(1.763)	(0.416)		(8.972)	(1.029)	
St Mowden Properties	−0.175	1.721	0.38	1.044	2.180	0.61
	(0.971)	(0.216)		(2.884)	(0.307)	
Trafford Park	−0.853	0.858	0.23	−0.485	0.850	0.25
	(0.484)	(0.117)		(1.570)	(0.195)	

Note: The figures in brackets are standard errors.
* Significant negative return at the 5% level.

For returns measured over monthly time horizons, thirteen companies produced significantly negative abnormal returns, the remaining five having statistically insignificant abnormal performance figures at the 5% level. The range of low R^2 values is indicative of the fact that property portfolios are not well diversified, containing low levels of systematic risk. These results again support our findings in Chapter 11.

The figures from Black et al. (1992), covering a similar period of analysis, showed that the majority of unit trusts had R^2 values in excess of 0.80. This is not unexpected, as unit trust portfolios will be more highly diversified than their property portfolio counterparts. Also, one third of the unit trusts outperformed the market compared with a two-thirds underperformance by the property companies. The low levels of property portfolio diversification were not, therefore, compensated for by an abnormal (selectivity) return component, in the majority of cases performing worse than a buy-and-hold strategy.

A more realistic performance measurement horizon for commercial property is likely to be of a longer duration than a monthly profile, as it takes some time to achieve the target structure of a property portfolio. As a comparison, Table 16H.2 also shows the OLS results using quarterly returns. Over the longer horizon *no* property company shows an abnormal return that is significantly different from zero at the 5% level.

Irrespective of the differences between the monthly and quarterly figures the OLS estimates will be biased as the parameters are expected to vary over time. In order to show the variation, we report the results of the time-varying parameter estimates in Tables 16H.3 and 4 based on the quarterly data. Given the liquidity issues discussed earlier this may be a more appropriate measurement period.

Table 16H.3 • Quarterly time-varying Jensen α_{jt} values, January 1980 to February 1995

Property company	Average value	Minimum	Maximum	Standard deviation	ADF
Land Securities	−1.68	−2.03	−1.24	0.24	−3.55*
British Land	−1.65	−2.50	−1.00	0.37	−2.62
Great Portland Estates	−2.63	−3.34	−1.76	0.40	−2.30
Frogmore Estates	−0.47	−1.17	+0.36	0.33	−2.48
Bilton	−2.08	−2.71	−1.31	0.42	−1.48
Town Centre Securities	−1.80	−2.26	−1.24	0.28	−2.55
Greycoat	−4.81	−8.13	−3.34	1.05	−2.42
Wates	−4.08	−5.76	−3.44	0.56	−2.06
Mucklow	−1.45	−2.27	−0.74	0.54	−1.28
Scottish Metropolitan Properties	−3.42	−4.75	−2.49	0.53	−2.40
Southend Properties	+4.02	+1.28	+7.95	1.88	−1.58
London Merchant Securities	−3.33	−4.17	−2.72	0.36	−1.46
Burford Holdings	+3.49	+1.83	+6.99	1.25	−2.80
Evans of Leeds	−0.43	−1.14	+0.31	0.40	−1.18
Chesterfield Property	−2.69	−4.54	−1.76	0.53	−3.08*
Tops Estate	+3.34	+1.38	+5.64	1.24	−0.65
St Mowden Properties	+0.45	−0.82	+1.54	0.62	−1.61
Trafford Park	−0.68	−1.44	+0.62	0.51	−2.03

Note: ADF is the Augmented Dickey-Fuller test for non-stationarity of the Jensen measure.
* Stationarity at the 5% level of significance.

Table 16H.4 ● Quarterly time-varying β_{jt} values, January 1980 to February 1995

Property company	Average value	Minimum	Maximum	Standard deviation	ADF
Land Securities	0.88	0.81	0.92	0.03	−1.91
British Land	1.18	1.08	1.24	0.05	−1.15
Great Portland Estates	0.93	0.81	1.01	0.07	−1.35
Frogmore Estates	0.96	0.84	1.04	0.06	−1.48
Bilton	0.93	0.82	1.03	0.06	−1.23
Town Centre Securities	1.07	0.95	1.11	0.04	−1.81
Greycoat	1.11	1.02	1.26	0.05	−2.01
Wates	1.46	1.38	1.53	0.04	−1.32
Mucklow	0.88	0.82	0.93	0.02	−2.48
Scottish Metropolitan Properties	1.14	0.92	1.32	0.13	−1.31
Southend Properties	1.17	0.68	1.38	0.21	−1.62
London Merchant Securities	0.87	0.74	0.92	0.04	−3.52*
Burford Holdings	0.31	0.02	0.46	0.13	−2.55
Evans of Leeds	0.98	0.83	1.03	0.04	−1.78
Chesterfield Property	1.03	0.85	1.18	0.11	−0.79
Tops Estate	1.46	1.34	1.61	0.07	−0.71
St Mowden Properties	2.18	2.11	2.29	0.04	−2.96
Trafford Park	0.83	0.73	0.90	0.05	−1.92

Note: ADF is the Augmented Dickey-Fuller test for non-stationarity of the beta coefficient.
* Stationarity at the 5% level of significance.

These figures show that most of the property companies displayed negative abnormal returns, albeit with a time-varying pattern. The OLS quarterly regression results reported in Table 16H.2 indicated that in all cases the negative abnormal returns were not significantly different from zero at the 5% level. Over time, however, there can be considerable variation in the quarterly figures, the extent of which is shown in Table 16H.3. The time-varying Jensen measures show that in eleven cases abnormal performance was negative in each quarter, showing no tendency towards positive abnormal performance. Analysis of the time-varying confidence intervals confirms that these abnormal returns remained statistically indistinguishable from zero. Three companies, Southend Properties, Burford Holdings and Tops Estate, exhibited positive abnormal returns in each quarter, although the figures were not significantly different from zero. Interestingly, these three companies also had the smallest $\bar{R}^2$ values, indicating that market movements accounted for only a small proportion of the return. Of the remaining companies, three registered positive returns in 1988–89, but recorded negative figures in other periods.

Merely looking at the statistically insignificant abnormal performance figures reported in Table 16H.2, it is not possible to obtain a picture of the variation in the underlying performance. By employing a time-varying parameter approach it is seen that greater insight into the quarterly profile of abnormal returns is revealed.

These findings qualify the apparently neutral abnormal quarterly performance figures reported in Table 16H.2, providing evidence of an enduring underperformance profile for many property companies, with no support for the argument that positive abnormal returns will eventually flow through. There appears, therefore, to be no evidence of property managers displaying consistently superior selection skills. The results contrast sharply with those reported by Black et al. (1992), where the majority of the unit trusts in their sample provided higher risk-adjusted returns than could be obtained from merely holding a well-diversified portfolio of shares; in these cases fund managers were able to add value. This does not appear to have been the case for the majority of property companies investigated in this study.

In the majority of cases the average values of the time-varying betas are in the neighbourhood of their OLS estimate. However, for all of the property companies the beta values show variation over time. The general level of these values is high, reflecting the high levels of gearing.

Figure 16H.2 provides a sample of time-varying α_{jt} and β_{jt} profiles together with their 95% confidence bands.

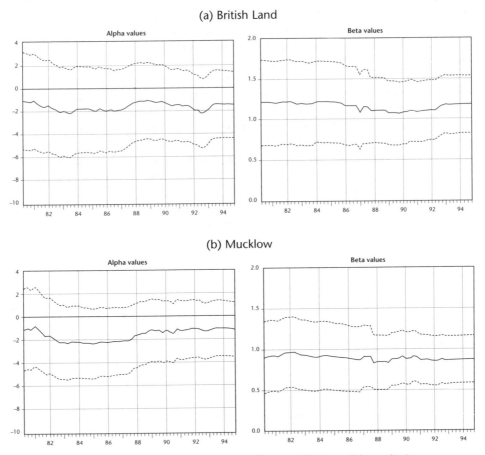

Figure 16H.2 a–c Time-varying parameter profiles and 95% confidence limits

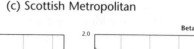

(c) Scottish Metropolitan

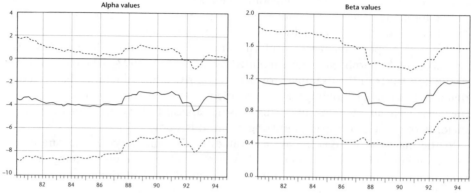

Figure 16H.2 continued

For all of the property companies investigated the predominant pattern was one of α_{jt} values being statistically indistinguishable from zero. As regards the time-varying β_{jt} values the profiles show that these also exhibit a lot of variation.

Tables 16H.3 and 16H.4 also report summary measures of the Augmented Dickey-Fuller (ADF) test for the stationarity of the estimated abnormal returns and beta measures. For the Jensen measure, the ADF test shows that in sixteen cases the series contain a unit root, implying that abnormal returns do not revert to an underlying mean. As regards the estimated betas, the ADF test indicates that in all but one case the coefficient is non-stationary, again implying that there is no tendency for the coefficients to revert to a mean value. These results are in line with the findings of Black et al. (1992), where stationarity of the beta coefficients was found only in the case of three out of thirty unit trusts. An implication of the existence of time-varying betas is that in order to obtain measures of the underlying time-varying asset risk premium the impact of factors such as the gearing level may need to be explicitly taken into account in arriving at the conditional value of beta.

Selected references

Adams, A. and Venmore-Rowland, P. (1990) Property share valuation. *Journal of Valuation* **8**, 127–42.

Ball, R. and Kothari, S.P. (1989) Nonstationary expected returns: Implications for tests of market efficiency and serial correlation in returns. *Journal of Financial Economics* **25**, 51–74.

Black, A., Fraser, P. and Power, D. (1992) UK unit trust performance 1980–1989: a passive time-varying approach. *Journal of Banking and Finance* **16** (1015), 1033.

Coggin, T.D., Fabozzi, F.J. and Rahman, S. (1993) The investment performance of US equity pension fund managers: An empirical investigation. *Journal of Finance* **48**, 1040–55.

Engle, R.E. and Granger, C.W.J. (1987) Cointegration and error-correction: representation, estimation and testing. *Econometrica* **55**, 251–76.

Fama, E.F. (1972) Components of investment performance. *Journal of Finance* **27** (3), 551–67.

Grindblatt, M. and Titman, S. (1989) Portfolio performance evaluation: old issues and new insights. *Review of Financial Studies* **2**, 393–421.

Hamilton, J.D. (1994) *Time Series Analysis*, Princeton, NJ: Princeton University Press.

Harvey, A.C. (1990) *The Econometric Analysis of Time Series*, London: Philip Allan.

Harvey, A.C. (1993) *Time Series Models*, New York: Harvester-Wheatsheaf.

Jensen, M.C. (1968) The performance of mutual funds in the period 1945–1964. *Journal of Finance* **23** (2), 389–416.

Quantitative techniques

Introduction

Throughout this book we have used a number of techniques that rely on an understanding of statistics and econometrics. This reflects the way financial research has developed over the last forty years. As property research embraces these ideas it is not surprising to see these techniques gradually being applied in a wider context. In this chapter we review some of the essential mathematical material that you will encounter in the text. We have presented this in an introductory fashion and have illustrated key points with worked examples.

One of the main reasons for making use of quantitative techniques to analyse property is to gain insights into the way that the market operates. This offers two main advantages. First, it may be possible to identify those factors that explain the behaviour of property sub-markets. Second, it may be possible to develop models that can forecast market movements. These are, of course, important fields of study and econometrics helps to answer some important questions. As you become more familiar with some of the research that has been undertaken you will begin to appreciate that many of the techniques we describe are successfully being used to forecast market movements and explain property cycles.

Our intention in this chapter is to cover a few important ideas in outline. References to more advanced material can be found at the end of the chapter.

Some basic definitions and notation

Variables

A variable represents some characteristic being measured. Examples of these would include rental value, capital value, yield, total return and vacancy rate. Examples of common abbreviations for property variables are: capital value by the letter V; total return by the letter r; yield by y; and years purchase by YP. When an algebraic expression is used to show the relationship between several variables, the variables are clearly defined so that there is no ambiguity about their meaning.

Coefficients

In an expression such as $7x^2$, the number 7 is referred to as the coefficient with the variable x taking on different values.

Suffixes

A suffix is used to distinguish between the individual values of a variable. For example, a portfolio may hold five individual properties each with a capital value $V_1, V_2, V_3 ... V_5$. Where there is a large number of observations, the most general abbreviation in this example would be $V_1, V_2, V_3 ... V_n$, where n is the number of properties and any individual observation would be referenced as V_i.

Integers

An integer is a positive or negative whole number.

Using shorthand symbols

Greek symbols are often employed as a shorthand way of expressing a mathematical operation. In this section we provide examples of some of the more commonly encountered expressions.

Summation

The symbol for addition, also known as summation, is sigma, i.e. Σ. For example, suppose the five properties above had capital values of £20m, £30m, £40m, £50m and

£60m and you want to write a simple expression representing the sum of each value. Using a summation sign this can be written as:

$$\sum_{i=1}^{i=5} V_i = \sum (20 + 30 + 40 + 50 + 60) = £200m \tag{17.1}$$

The range of the summation is defined over properties 1 to 5.

Products

A shorthand way of writing the product of a series of numbers is to use the Greek symbol pi, Π. Using the above example, if we wanted to know the product of all the values we could write it as follows:

$$\prod_{i=1}^{i=5} V_i = \prod (20 \times 30 \times 40 \times 50 \times 60) = £72,000,000m \tag{17.2}$$

Inequalities

The following symbols, known as inequalities, are frequently encountered.

Table 17.1 ● Inequalities

Inequality	Meaning
$x > y$	x is greater than y
$x \geq y$	x is greater than or equal to y
$x < y$	x is less than y
$x \leq y$	x is less than or equal to y

Other symbols frequently encountered are:

Table 17.2 ● More inequalities

Symbol	Meaning
$x \neq y$	x not equal to y
$x \cong 5$	x approximately equal to 5
$x \equiv y$	x is equivalent/identical to y
$x \pm 5$	x plus or minus 5

Exponents

If n is a positive integer, the expression x^n means that x is multiplied by itself n times i.e. $x^n = x.x.x. \dots x$, where there are n terms of x. This is also known as raising x to the power of n. The value of x is known as the base, and n is termed an *index*, *power* or *exponent*.

If n is equal to 1 the expression is simply written as x. If, however, n is equal to 0 then any non-zero value of x will be equal to 1. For example, $x^0 = 1$. If $x = 3$, then $3^0 = 1$.

In the following examples we summarise the *rules of exponents*. If m and n are integers then:

Table 17.3 ● Rules of exponents

Rule	Let $x = 3$, $y = 5$, $m = 4$ and $n = 6$
$\dfrac{1}{x^m} = x^{-m}$	$\dfrac{1}{3^4} = 3^{-4} = 0.012346$
$x^m(x^n) = x^{m+n}$	$3^4(3^6) = 3^{4+6} = 3^{10} = 59{,}049$
$\dfrac{x^m}{x^n} = x^{m-n}$	$\dfrac{x^4}{x^6} = 3^{4-6} = 3^{-2} = \dfrac{1}{3^2} = \dfrac{1}{9} = 0.111111$
$(x^m)^n = x^{mn}$	$(3^4)^6 = 3^{4\times6} = 3^{24} = 282{,}429{,}536{,}000$
$(x^my^m) = (xy)^m$	$(3^4 \times 5^4) = (3 \times 5)^4 = 50{,}625$
$\dfrac{x^m}{y^m} = \left(\dfrac{x}{y}\right)^m$	$\dfrac{3^4}{5^4} = \left(\dfrac{3}{5}\right)^4 = 0.1296$
$\sqrt{x} = x^{\frac{1}{2}}$	$\sqrt{3} = 3^{\frac{1}{2}} = 1.732051$
$\sqrt[m]{x} = x^{\frac{1}{m}}$	$\sqrt[4]{3} = 3^{\frac{1}{4}} = 1.316074$
$\sqrt[m]{x^n} = (x^{\frac{1}{m}})^n = x^{\frac{n}{m}}$	$\sqrt[4]{3^6} = (3^{\frac{1}{4}})^6 = 3^{\frac{6}{4}} = 5.196152$
$(x^{\frac{1}{m}})(y^{\frac{1}{m}}) = \sqrt[m]{xy} = (xy)^{\frac{1}{m}}$	$(3^{\frac{1}{4}})(5^{\frac{1}{4}}) = \sqrt[4]{} \times 5 = (3 \times 5)^{\frac{1}{4}} = 1.967990$

Exponential functions

The previous section described the power function of the form $y = x^n$, where the base x can take any value and n is a *constant*. In this section we describe the situation where x is a constant and the exponent n is allowed to vary. This situation is frequently encountered when dealing with growth rates and compound interest situations.

The equation $y = ab^x$, where $a > 0$ and $a \neq 1$ is called an *exponential function*. Here, a is constant, b is the constant base value and x is a variable figure. A commonly used expression is the *natural exponential function*, written as $y = e^x$ or $y = \exp(x)$. In this case value of the base is given the special symbol e, which is approximately equal to 2.71828. The reason for using e is that it is mathematically convenient in a number of situations. These would include compounding on a continuous basis and in the calculation of rates of change and other growth situations. We have made use of this idea throughout this book.

The relationship between exponential functions and growth rates can be seen in the following graph, which plots the general function of $y = ab^x$ for different values of b, over a range of x values.

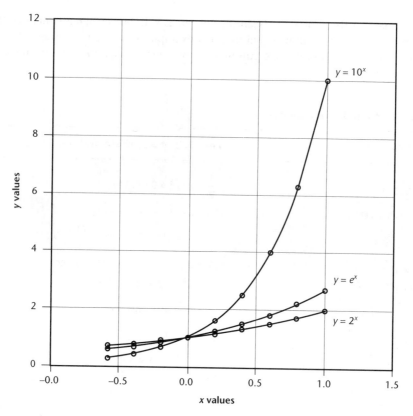

Figure 17.1 Exponential functions

Logarithms

A logarithm is the power to which a base must be raised in order to equal a given number. For example, you know that 6 and 36 are related to each other by $6^2 = 36$. You can, therefore, state the exponent 2 to be the log of 36 to the base 6.

In the expression $y = b^x$, the value of x is the logarithm of y to the base b. This is written as $x = \log_b y$. You could, therefore, write our example as $\log_6 36 = 2$. If the base b is equal to 10, $\log_{10} y$ is called a *common logarithm*. If the base is equal to the exponential value e, $\log_e y$ is called the *natural logarithm* which is abbreviated to ln y. Natural logarithms are convenient to work with and are frequently encountered in applied studies.

Just as in the case of exponents, there are a number of rules governing the manipulation of logarithms. If b, x and y are positive numbers, and $b \neq 1$ the following rules, shown in Table 17.4, apply.

The use of logarithms arises in many situations, including the calculation of growth rates, continuous rates of return, as well as the solution to simple exponential equations and the transformation of non-linear functions in regression analysis.

Table 17.4 ● Log rules

Rule	Let $b = e = 2.718282$, $x = 3$, $y = 4$ and $n = 9$
$\log_b (1) = 0$	$\ln 1 = 0$
$\log_b(xy) = \log_b x + \log_b y$	$\ln (3 \times 5) = \ln 3 + \ln 4 = 1.098612 + 1.386294 = 2.484906$
$\log_b\left(\dfrac{x}{y}\right) = \log_b x - \log_b y$	$\ln(\frac{3}{4}) = \ln 3 - \ln 4 = 1.098612 - 1.386294 = -0.287682$
$\log_b (y^n) = n\log_b y$	$\ln(4^9) = 9\ln 4 = 9 \times 1.386294 = 12.476646$
$\log_b (\sqrt[n]{y}) = \dfrac{1}{n} \log_b y$	$\ln(\sqrt[9]{4}) = \frac{1}{9} \ln 4 = \frac{1}{9} \times 1.386294 = 0.154033$

In addition logarithms can also be used to find unknown values in an equation. For example, what is the value of x that satisfies the equation $4 \times 9^x = 12$? Using logs to the base e you could write this as follows:

$$x\ln(9) = \frac{12}{4}$$

$$x = \frac{3}{2.1972}$$

$$x = 1.3654$$

Logarithms, therefore, provide a convenient way of manipulating data involving the multiplication and division of numbers and for solving equations.

From the examples we have given it will be seen that there is an inverse relationship between an exponential function and its logarithm. Recall that $\ln x$ signifies the power to which e must be raised in order to get x. It follows therefore that $e^{\ln x} = x$.

If, for example, you have $\ln x = 2.5$ and you want to know the value of x that satisfies this equation, you can set both sides of the equation as exponents of e in order to eliminate the *ln* expression:

$$e^{\ln x} = e^{2.5}$$

$$x = e^{2.5}$$

$$x = 12.182494$$

Obtaining an unknown value from a logarithm is frequently undertaken. An example of this procedure is given in the section on *Indices and geometric averages*.

Exponential and logarithmic calculations can readily be undertaken on a calculator by making use of the y^x or e^x keys, the $\ln x$ key, or the exp( ) function on a spreadsheet.

Example 1

Assume you invest £100 with a view to accumulating £1,000 at some point in the future. The investment earns a fixed annual rate of interest of 6%, payable annually. How long do you have to hold the investment so that it yields £1,000?

This is an exponential equation problem and the use of logarithms helps in obtaining the answer. Let A = the accumulated value, P = the amount invested, i = annual rate of interest and n = number of years invested. The relationship between the current and future value after n years can be written as:

$$A = P(1 + i)^n \tag{17.3}$$

Taking logs gives:

$$\ln A = \ln P + n\ln(1 + i) \tag{17.4}$$

You can solve for n by substituting the appropriate figures:

$$n = \frac{\ln A - \ln P}{\ln(1 + i)} = \frac{\ln 1000 - \ln 100}{\ln(1 + 0.06)} = \frac{6.908 - 4.605}{.0583} = 39.516 \text{ years}$$

Thus, at a rate of 6% p.a. it will take just over 39.5 years for the initial investment to grow to £1,000. In this example we used natural logs. You would have arrived at the same answer had you used logs to any base value.

It is sometimes convenient to express the proportionate growth in a variable by considering it as the difference between two natural logarithms. For example, the change in the value of x between periods t and $t-1$ can be expressed as:

$$\ln x_t - \ln x_{t-1} = \ln\left(\frac{x_t}{x_{t-1}}\right) = \ln\left(\frac{x_t - x_{t-1}}{x_{t-1}}\right) = \ln(1 + g_t) \tag{17.5}$$

If the proportionate growth $\left(\dfrac{x_t - x_{t-1}}{x_{t-1}}\right) = g_t$ is relatively small, a useful approximation for the growth rate is given by $\ln(1 + g) = g$.

Example 2

Consider the following values taken from the IPD annual total return index.

Table 17.5 ● IPD total return index values

Year	Index value
1994	384
1995	396
1996	435

The annual total returns, converted to percentages, obtained from the above approximation are compared with the accurate calculation in Table 17.6.

Table 17.6 ● Comparison of growth rates

	Approximate growth p.a.	Accurate growth p.a.
Period	$\ln\left(\dfrac{Index\ value_t}{Index\ value_{t-1}}\right)$	$\left(\dfrac{Index\ value_t - Index\ value_{t-1}}{Index\ value_{t-1}}\right)$
1994–95	3.08%	3.12%
1995–96	9.39%	9.85%

Although the figures are similar it should be noted that the larger the rate of return the larger will be the difference between the two sets of figures. A cautionary note should be added to the use of reported index numbers as shown in the above calculation. The actual rates of return reported by IPD were 3.3% in 1994–95 and 9.6% in 1995–96. These differ from our calculations because IPD have reported rounded index figures. The use of rounded figures can result in significant differences between calculated figures and reported figures. This applies to all index figures reported by surveying practices and to other official financial and economic data.

Linear and quadratic equations

An equation is a mathematical relationship between a number of variables. A linear equation has the form $y = a + bx$, which is the equation of a line with intercept a and slope b. A quadratic equation has the form $y = ax^2 + bx + c$, where a, b and c are constants.

Example

Assume you have two equations, $y = 10 + 0.5x$ and $y = 10 + 0.75x$. Both have identical intercepts but the slope of the second equation is 50 per cent greater than that of the first equation.

An equation may also be expressed as a function so that $y = f(x)$. For example, the linear equation may be written as $y = a + bx = f(x)$ and the quadratic equation as $y = ax^2 + bx + c = f(x)$. The expression $y = f(x)$ is read 'y is a function of the variable x'. For different values of the variable x, values of y can be obtained from the equations and can be represented in tabular or graphical form.

The functional form is a useful shorthand notation for making statements about relationships. For example, if commercial property yields, y_p, depend in some way on a target rate of return, r_p, the expected rental growth, g_p, and depreciation, d_p, this may be expressed as:

$$y_p = f(r_p, g_p, d_p) \tag{17.6}$$

Although the precise relationship between the variables needs to be spelled out, the expression does capture those elements that are considered to be the most important systematic influences determining yields. The relationship says that any change in the variables on the right-hand side will *cause* a change in yields. In mathematical terms the variable y_p is described as the *dependent* variable and r_p, g_p and d_p are the *independent* variables. Forecasting models attempt to explain and measure the change in a dependent variable in terms of a number of independent variables. This is often accomplished by using regression analysis.

Graphical representation of functions

When graphing a function such as $y = f(x)$, the variable x is shown on the horizontal axis and the variable y on the vertical axis. As noted above, the equation of a line is given by $y = ax + b$ where a is the *intercept* on the y axis, and b is the *slope* of the line. The intercept crosses the y axis at the point where $x = 0$. The slope indicates the steepness and direction of the line and is measured by the change in y divided by the change in x. The greater the absolute value of b, the steeper the line.

Example

Table 17.7 shows the values corresponding to the equation of three different lines. The first two have a positive slope, one being 0.25 and the other 0.75. The third line has a negative slope of 0.80. All the lines have an identical y intercept equal to 1.

Table 17.7 ● Straight line equations

x values	y = 1 + 0.25x	y = 1 + 0.75x	y = 1 − 0.80x
−3	0.25	−1.25	3.40
−2	0.50	−0.50	2.60
−1	0.75	0.25	1.80
0	1.00	1.00	1.00
1	1.25	1.75	0.20
2	1.50	2.50	−0.60
3	1.75	3.25	−1.40

A graph of each of these lines is shown in Figure 17.2.

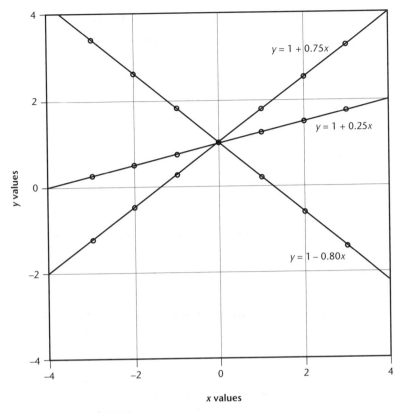

Figure 17.2 Linear functions

Arithmetic and geometric progressions

In this section we will discuss some of the series often used in investment mathematics. A series consists of a number of quantities, each of which is formed from one or more of the preceding quantities according to some fixed rule. The successive quantities are called *terms* of the series. Many of the standard formulas used in valuation models are based on geometric series. As this is such an important area, it is useful to know how the sum of these series can be summarised in closed form solutions.

Arithmetic progressions

A series of numbers is said to follow an arithmetic progression when the numbers increase or decrease by a common amount. The first n terms of an arithmetic series can be expressed as:

$$S_n = A + (A + d) + (A + 2d) + ...(A + (n - 1)d) \qquad (17.7)$$

where A = the first term of the series, d = the common difference and n = number of terms in the series.

If you write the final term as l, another way of writing this is:

$$S_n = A + (A + d) + (A + 2d) + ... + (l - 2d) + (l - d) + l \qquad (17.8)$$

where

$$l = A + (n - 1)d \qquad (17.9)$$

You can also express the series in reverse order:

$$S_n = l + (l - d) + (l - 2d) + ... + (A + 2d) + (A + d) + A \qquad (17.10)$$

If you add equations 17.7 and 17.10 together you get:

$$2S_n = (A + l) + (A + l) + (A + l) + ...$$

$$2S_n = n(A + l) \qquad (17.11)$$

Substituting our expression for l from equation 17.9 and rearranging gives the sum of the first n terms as follows:

$$S_n = \frac{1}{2} n[2A + (n - 1)d] \qquad (17.12)$$

Note that as the number of terms gets larger the sum of the series approaches infinity.

Example

Find the sum of the first ten terms of the series $3 + 6 + 9 + ...$
Here $A = 3$, $d = 3$ and $n = 10$. The sum of the series is, therefore:

$$S_{10} = \frac{10}{2} (2 \times 3 + 9 \times 3) = 165$$

Geometric progressions

Quantities are said to follow a geometric progression when the ratio of any one term to the preceding term is constant. You will find this relationship frequently occurring in compounding and discounting situations. The relationship between each value is called the common ratio. You can write the sum, S_n, of the first n terms of a geometric progression as:

$$S_n = A + AR_c + AR_c^2 + AR_c^3 + ... + AR_c^{n-2} + AR_c^{n-1} \qquad (17.13)$$

where, A = the first term of the series, R_c = the common ratio and n = number of terms in the series.

By multiplying both sides by the common ratio you get:

$$R_c S_n = AR_c + AR_c^2 + AR_c^3 + ... + AR_c^{n-1} + AR_c^2 \qquad (17.14)$$

Subtracting equation 17.14 from 17.13 gives:

$$S_n - R_c S_n = A - AR_c^n \qquad (17.15)$$

$$S_n = \frac{A(1 - R_c^n)}{1 - R_c} \quad \text{subject to } R_c \neq 1 \qquad (17.16)$$

We use this formula in Chapter 3 to derive the present value of a perpetually growing income stream.

Example

Find the sum of the first eight terms of the series $2 + 6 + 18 + 54 \ldots$

Here $A = 2$, $R_c = 3$ and $n = 8$. The sum of the series is:

$$S_8 = \frac{2(1 - 3^8)}{1 - 3} = 6{,}560$$

If the ratio R_c lies in the range $-1 < r < 1$ and the number of terms n increases indefinitely (i.e. tends towards infinity), the series is said to be convergent and its sum S_n converges to the value given by the following formula:

$$S_\infty = \frac{A}{1 - R_c} \qquad (17.17)$$

Example

Find the sum of the series $1 + \frac{1}{2} + \frac{1}{4} + \frac{1}{8} + \ldots$ as n tends to infinity.

Here $A = 1$ and $R_c = \frac{1}{2}$. The first 3, 4 and 5 terms have sums of 1.75, 1.875 and 1.9375. The sum is gradually increasing and is approaching a limiting value given by:

$$S_\infty = \frac{1}{1 - \frac{1}{2}} = 2$$

Indices and geometric averages

Many commercial property measures are provided in terms of an index number. Common examples would be capital growth, rental value and total return indices. Indices are a useful way of tracking market changes and trends in a particular sector of the economy. Many published financial and economic data are also presented in index form. Here we provide a brief overview on the use of such indices. See Appendix 15C for a discussion on property performance indices.

An index number is a summary measure, provided by a single number, which gives the average value of a set of related items. The number is usually expressed as a percentage of their average value at some base period. For example, Table 17.8 shows the total capital value of properties held in the IPD database in 1981, 1988 and 1996. If 1981 is taken as the base period against which all future periods will be compared, the capital value in 1981 is arbitrarily assigned a value of 100. The reason 100 is chosen is that future values will show the percentage change that has occurred since the 1981 base date.

In order to arrive at any index number, the capital value in the year in question is divided by the value in the base year and multiplied by 100. The index numbers are shown to one decimal place, rounded up.

Table 17.8 ● Capital values and index numbers

Year	Capital value (£m)	Index number
1981	17,842.37	100.0
1988	45,970.88	257.7
1996	52,651.99	295.1

The growth, g, in an index between periods t–1 and t is given by:

$$g = \frac{I_t - I_{t-1}}{I_{t-1}} = \frac{I_t}{I_{t-1}} - 1 \qquad\qquad (17.18)$$

Dividing the index values in one period by the previous period, $\dfrac{I_t}{I_{t-1}}$, is therefore equal to 1 plus the growth rate over the period, $1 + g$.

Over the period 1981–96 the total capital value of the funds reporting to IPD increased by 295.1%. The average annual growth, g, over the 15 years can be expressed as:

$$295.1 = 100(1 + g)^{15}$$

Taking logarithms gives:

$$\ln 295.1 = \ln 100 - 15\ln(1 + g)$$

$$\ln(1 + g) = \frac{\ln 295.1 - \ln 100}{15} = \frac{5.687 - 4.605}{15} = 0.072$$

$$1 + g = 1.0748$$

$$g = 0.0748 \cong 7.48\%$$

Hence, the value of funds contributing to the IPD Index has grown by almost 7.48% each year. This figure is a combination of growth in existing capital values together with the value of new funds joining the IPD Index. In any one year actual growth will differ from the calculated average. The average figure that we have calculated is known as the *geometric* average growth, reflecting the compounding nature of the calculation. You will see that in order to calculate the average only the beginning and end values are required.

In Chapter 14 we looked at the inflation hedging characteristics of property. We used these ideas to estimate the nominal returns and also showed how to take account of inflation. You might want to review that chapter to see how these ideas can be put into practice.

Index numbers were originally developed to measure the changes in price levels and now measure a diversity of things such as retail sales, manufacturing output, FT All Share Index and property performance. There are a number of ways in which economic and financial indices may be constructed and weighted, the discussion of which is beyond this introduction. The bibliography provides references for the interested reader.

Statistical issues

In this section we will outline some of the main statistical concepts employed throughout the book. As it is not possible to provide a comprehensive treatment of the various topics, we have provided only a brief outline. Readers should consult the selected references given in the bibliography for more information.

Descriptive statistics

We provided a brief description of some of the main descriptive statistics in Appendices 9B and 9C when we discussed the distributional characteristics of property. You may find it useful to review that material.

In Appendix 9C we discussed a number of measures of dispersion. One additional measure of dispersion that is often used in performance measurement is based on the use of quartiles. There are three measures involved:

The lower quartile range

The lower quartile range is the value in a series such that one quarter of the observations lie below it.

The upper quartile range

The upper quartile range is the value in a series such that one quarter of the observations lie above it.

The inter-quartile range

The inter-quartile range (IQR) is the difference between these two values:

IQR = upper quartile – lower quartile

One feature of the IQR is that it is not affected by extreme values.

Frequency distributions and histograms

It is also useful to depict data graphically using a histogram or a relative frequency distribution. A histogram is a bar chart with each bar showing the number of values of a variable that fall into a predefined interval. If the value of each bar is divided by the total number of observations, the resulting figure is known as a relative frequency distribution. This has the same shape as the histogram, but the bar heights will now show the percentage of values falling into each value category. A cumulative frequency distribution shows, for each asset class, the total number of observations in all classes up to and including that class. A cumulative frequency curve is also known as an ogive.

Probability concepts

Continuous random variables

A continuous random variable is one that assumes outcomes over a continuous range of real numbers. The probabilities of the outcomes are characterised by what is known as a probability density function, or *pdf* for short. The density function has the property that the total area under the function is equal to 1.

A random variable is a variable whose value is subject to uncertainty. The value of a random variable is associated with some probability of being observed. A discrete random variable can only assume distinct values. For example, tossing a coin can only result in one of two values: heads or tails. The roll of a die can result in one of six possible outcomes, the numbers 1 through 6. This contrasts with a continuous random variable, which can assume an infinite number of values. For example, suppose that the hands of a clock stop. The random variable here is the time at which the clock stopped. There are an infinite number of positions between 0 and 12 at which the clock could have stopped, so that the probability that the time is any particular value is zero. However, the probability that the time lies within a particular *interval* is non-zero and can be found. Continuous distributions often arise in situations where measurements are taken on finer and finer intervals, rather than counting outcomes. A continuous variable is one that can assume any value in a given range.

For a discrete random variable the probability of the outcome of any value x_i is characterised by a probability function, $p(x_i)$. The probability function has the property that the probability of each outcome must lie between 0 and 1, and the sum of the probabilities must add up to 1. That is:

$$0 \le p(x_i) \le 1$$

$$\sum_i p(x_i) = 1 \tag{17.19}$$

The set of all possible values or outcomes that a random variable can take on, together with their associated probabilities, is called a probability distribution. For example, suppose that you represent the outlook for the commercial property market in a year's time as shown in Table 17.9.

Table 17.9 ● Probability distribution

Market conditions	Total return	Probability p_i
Slump	−5.0%	0.40
No change	8.0%	0.50
Boom	20.0%	0.10

This shows the probability of all *anticipated* market outcomes and their associated anticipated total rates of return.

In some situations you may be interested in finding the probability that a variable would take on a value that is less than or equal to a given number. The cumulative distribution function, often denoted by $P(x)$ or $F(x)$, specifies the probability that the random variable will assume a value less than or equal to a specified value. If, for example, $x_1, x_2, \ldots x_m$ are the values of a random variable given in increasing order of size, so that $x_1 < x_2 < x_3 \ldots <x_m$ then the cumulative probability, $F(x_k)$, of a value x_k is given by:

$$F(x_k) = f(x_1) + f(x_2) + \ldots + f(x_k) = \sum_{i=1}^{k} f(x_i) \qquad (17.20)$$

The expectation operator

The expected value, or mean, of a probability distribution, denoted by $E(x)$ or μ, is given by:

$$E(x) = \sum_{i=1}^{i=n} x_i p(x_i) \qquad (17.21)$$

This is a measure of the central tendency of a distribution. For example, given the market conditions identified in Table 17.9 and using the properties of a summation you would calculate the expected return as:

$$E(r) = (-5.0\% \times 0.4) + (8.0\% \times 0.5) + (20.0\% \times 0.1) = -4.0\%$$

The expected value function has a number of general properties which can be used in a number of cases. For example, there may be a need to calculate the expected value of a sum or combination of random variables. For example, suppose that you had expected returns for the retail, office and industrial sectors and you wanted to know what the expected return on a portfolio of these sectors would be. The application of a few simple rules enables you to work this out. You can also use some simple rules to estimate other statistical moments such as the variance, skewness and kurtosis.

The following provides a series of alternative expressions for common statements relating to two random variables x and y, which have a joint probability distribution $p(x,j)$, together with constants k, a, b, c and d. You will see that by combining some elementary algebra with the expectation operator you can express a number of statistical functions in terms of some common expressions.

The expected value

$$E(kx) = kE(x) \qquad (17.22)$$
$$E(bx + c) = bE(x) + c \qquad (17.23)$$
$$E(x + y) = E(x) + E(y) \qquad (17.24)$$
$$E(ax + by) = aE(x) + bE(y) \qquad (17.25)$$

If x and y are independent then the expected value of their product can be written as:

$$E(xy) = E(x)E(y) \qquad (17.26)$$

When the variables are correlated you need to take into consideration how they co-vary. However, before doing this we will look at some cases of using the expectation operator to estimate the variance.

The variance

$$Var(x) = E[x - E(x)]^2 \tag{17.27}$$
$$= E\{x^2 - 2xE(x) + [E(x)]^2\} \tag{17.28}$$
$$= E(x^2) - 2E(x)E(x) + [E(x)]^2 \tag{17.29}$$
$$= E(x^2) - [E(x)]^2 \tag{17.30}$$

If a probability is assigned to each outcome then equation 17.30 can be written as:

$$Var(x) = E(x^2) - [E(x)]^2 = \sum_{i=1}^{i=n} x_i^2 P_{x_i} - \mu^2 \tag{17.31}$$

Using the figures given in Table 17.9 the variance can be estimated as:

$$Var(x) = [(-5^2 \times 0.4) + (8^2 \times 0.5) + (20^2 \times 0.1)] - 4^2$$

$$Var(x) = 82 - 16 = 66$$

Taking the square root gives a standard deviation of 8.12%.

Another common expression for the variance involves variables and constants.

$$Var(ax + b) = E[(ax + b) - E(ax + b)]^2 \tag{17.32}$$
$$= E[(ax + b) - aE(x) - b]^2 \tag{17.33}$$
$$= Ea^2[x - E(x)]^2 \tag{17.34}$$
$$= a^2 Var(x) \tag{17.35}$$

Similarly:

$$Var(ax) = a^2 Var(x) \tag{17.36}$$

If x and y are independent of each other then:

$$Var(ax + by) = a^2 Var(x) + b^2 Var(y) \tag{17.37}$$

If x and y are not independent then equation 17.37 becomes:

$$Var(ax + by) = a^2 Var(x) + b^2 Var(y) + 2abCov(x,y) \tag{17.38}$$

You should recognise this as the variance of a two-asset portfolio we discussed in Chapter 10.

The covariance

$$Cov(x,y) = E\{[x - E(x)][y - E(y)]\} \tag{17.39}$$
$$= E[xy - xE(y) - yE(x) + E(x)E(y)] \tag{17.40}$$
$$= E(xy) - E(x)E(y) - E(y)E(x) + E(x)E(y) \tag{17.41}$$
$$= E(xy) - E(x)E(y) \tag{17.42}$$

From this you will see that the expected value of the product of two random variables can be written as:

$$E(xy) = E(x)E(y) + Cov(x,y) \qquad (17.43)$$

This is a more general expression for the product of two random variables. You will see that equation 17.7 will only be equal to equation 17.10 if $Cov(x,y) = 0$.

In Chapter 10 we pointed out that the covariance of returns is the most important factor influencing diversification. If the covariance between x and y is zero, the variables are said to be uncorrelated. In an intuitive sense, independence rules out any kind of relationship between two variables and implies a zero covariance. However, the converse is not necessarily true. It is possible to have zero covariance between two variables yet they may not be independent. The reason for this is that covariance only measures the *linear* relationship between variables. However, it is possible that two variables may be related in a *non-linear* way. This is something that you should be aware of when looking at covariance or correlation measures, as dismissing *any* association on the basis of these measures may be wrong.

The covariance is often difficult to interpret because it is affected by the scale of the variables. This can be overcome by dividing the covariance by the product of the standard deviations of each variable. This measures the degree of linear association between the variables and is known as the coefficient of correlation. For two random variables x and y it can be written as:

$$\rho_{x,y} = \frac{Cov(x,y)}{\sigma_x \sigma_y} \qquad (17.44)$$

The coefficient lies in the range -1 to $+1$ and measures the degree of the relationship between two random variables. A positive value indicates the existence of a positive relationship and a negative value the presence of a negative relationship. Values close to -1 or to $+1$ indicate a high degree of association between the variables. A coefficient with a value close to zero indicates a weak or no relationship.

Some other expressions involving the covariance are as follows:

$$Cov(x,k) = E(xk) - E(x)E(k) \qquad (17.45)$$
$$= kE(x) - kE(x) = 0 \qquad (17.46)$$
$$Cov[(ax + b),(cy + d)] = E\{[(ax + b) - E(ax + b)][(cy + d) - E(cy + d)]\} \qquad (17.47)$$
$$= E\{[ax + b - aE(x) - b][cy + d - cE(y) - d]\} \qquad (17.48)$$
$$= E\{a[x - E(x)]c[y - E(y)]\} \qquad (17.49)$$
$$= acE\{[x - E(x)][y - E(y)]\} \qquad (17.50)$$
$$= acCov(x,y) \qquad (17.51)$$

By similar reasoning:

$$Cov[(ax + bz),y] = aCov(x,y) + bCov(z,y) \qquad (17.52)$$

The skewness and kurtosis

Higher-order moments can also be derived in a similar manner. You will recall that the skewness and kurtosis are the third and fourth moments of a distribution and can be written as:

$$M_3 = E[x - E(x)]^3 = E(x^3) - 3E(x^2)E(x) + 2[E(x)]^3 \tag{17.53}$$

$$M_4 = E[x - E(x)]^4 = 2E(x^4) - 8E(x)E(x^3) + 6[E(x^2)]^2 \tag{17.54}$$

Probability distributions

There are many probability distributions that characterise the properties of random variables. Some are appropriate for discrete random variables and include binomial and Poisson distributions. For continuous variables a normal, lognormal or t-distribution are more appropriate. Many continuous distributions can assume different shapes and sizes, depending on the value of attendant parameters. It is common to find skewed distributions and symmetric distributions. We gave examples of these in Appendix 9B.

The normal distribution

The normal distribution is frequently encountered in economics and statistics. It is a continuous bell-shaped curve that is symmetrical about its mean value, μ. It is the most commonly used of all probability distributions in statistical analysis. The distributions of many phenomena in the real world conform to a normal distribution. An important statistical concept underlying this common occurrence is known as the central limit theorem. This implies that the sum of a sequence of random numbers will tend towards a normal distribution as the sample increases indefinitely.

A normal distribution with a mean μ and variance σ^2 is often expressed as $N(\mu,\sigma^2)$. For example, $N(10,144)$ would represent a normal distribution with a mean value of 10 and variance of 144, or equivalently, a standard deviation of 12. One of the important properties of the normal distribution is that irrespective of the value of the variance, it is possible to make probability statements about the proportion of the distribution that lies within certain boundaries. For example, approximately 68% of the area under the curve lies within one standard deviation, 95% of the area is within 1.96 standard deviations and approximately 99.7% of the area is within three standard deviations. These numbers enable a rough assessment of how likely a value is to have arisen from a given distribution. For example, if an observed value is more than three standard deviations from the mean value, the likelihood of its having originated from the given distribution is small. The normal distribution is used in hypothesis testing and in working out the probability that values will lie within a particular range, or fall below or exceed a specified value. We used this important idea in Appendix 7D when we examined the margin of error in valuations.

The standard normal distribution

There are an infinite number of normal distributions, each depending on the value of the mean and variance. To calculate probabilities in each situation would be a complex and time-consuming task. However, it is possible to convert any normal distribution into what is known as the standard normal distribution. Subtracting the mean value and dividing by the standard deviation makes the conversion. The advantage of doing this is that the area under the curve is standardised so that you can use tabulated values found in most statistical textbooks. As a result of the conversion the standard normal distribution has a mean of zero and a variance equal to one, denoted by $N(0,1)$.

An introduction to confidence intervals and hypothesis testing

Confidence intervals

In this section we look at statistical inference. This describes the procedures employed in using observed data to draw conclusions about the population or the process that generated the data. The process is called hypothesis testing.

A hypothesis test is a procedure that addresses the question of whether the *difference* between an estimated value, based on a sample of data, and the hypothesised population value is significant or merely due to chance. The way to do this is to construct a test statistic that is usually based on the assumption that there is no difference between the population and the sample. The significance test partitions the set of possible values into an acceptance or rejection region.

Assume that over a number of years you have collected a series of annual rates of return for a portfolio of commercial properties. You have also collected the annual risk-free rate of return. By subtracting these figures from the property returns in each period you then estimate the average risk premium, $\bar{x}_1$. The question you now ask is: how good is this estimate in representing the average risk premium for the whole property market? Using *sample* data to estimate the values of *population* parameters and the estimation of confidence intervals and hypothesis testing is known as statistical inference.

So far you have estimated the average risk premium from one sample. If you took another sample and again calculated the average risk premium you should not be surprised if the value differed from the first sample. Given reasonably large sample values, say greater than 30 observations, the distribution of many averages will be approximately normally distributed with mean value μ and standard deviation equal to $\frac{\sigma}{\sqrt{n}}$, where n is the sample size. This result follows from the central limit theorem.

The standard deviation of the distribution of the averages is called the *standard error of the mean*. As the distribution of the sample means is normal, given the rule-of-thumb figures provided in the discussion of the normal distribution, 95% of them will lie within 1.96 standard errors of the population mean. This enables a *confidence interval* to be constructed that is likely to contain the unknown population mean with a probability of 0.95. This interval is expressed as:

$$p\left[\left(\bar{x} - 1.96\frac{\sigma}{\sqrt{n}}\right) \leq \mu \leq \left(\bar{x} + 1.96\frac{\sigma}{\sqrt{n}}\right)\right] = 0.95 \qquad (17.55)$$

This implies that there is a 95% probability that the population mean, μ, will lie within the interval $\left(\bar{x} \pm 1.96 \dfrac{\sigma}{\sqrt{n}} \right)$. If it were possible to estimate the mean and confidence interval from many samples, 95% of the confidence intervals would contain the unknown population mean. The remaining 5% would lie outside this range. In most situations, however, only a single sample will be available so it is not possible to know whether the resulting confidence interval actually contains the population mean. All that can be said is that as long as the sample is a representative drawing from the population the confidence interval is more likely to contain the unknown population mean.

You should note that there is nothing special about a 95% level of confidence. This is a commonly used value that is suitable in most cases. However, depending on the application and the quality of the data you may wish to calculate 90% or 99% confidence intervals. Statistical tables can be used to provide the appropriate values for any given probability. If the sample size is less than 30 observations, the values from a t-distribution table should be used. A t-distribution is a symmetric probability distribution like the normal distribution. It is, however, flatter and has longer tails. The use of confidence levels does, however, raise issues about errors of interpretation. There are two types that may be encountered.

Type I error

This occurs when the test is rejected when it is in fact true.

Type II error

This occurs when the test is accepted when it is in fact false.

For further details you should refer to one of the references at the end of this chapter.

Hypothesis tests

An important application of probability distributions in financial analysis is *hypothesis testing*. For example, the expected risk premium for the property market is frequently cited as being 2%. With a sufficiently large sample of property returns you can test the hypothesis that the historic premium confirms the expected value. We discussed this in detail in Appendix 15A.

The null hypothesis

In order to undertake a statistical test it is necessary to pose the question in such a way that the test can be rejected. The convention is to use what is known as the *null hypothesis*. This is usually abbreviated to H_0. The hypothesis is simply a statement about a population value. For example, in the risk premium example the null hypothesis is that the risk premium of the property sample is not significantly different from the expected value of 2%. The established methodology is therefore to have a null hypothesis that is considered valid, unless it is disproved by the evidence.

The second part of the test consists of posing an *alternative hypothesis* to the null, which is usually abbreviated to H_A. This will depend on prior knowledge concerning the situation in hand. You may, for example, suspect that the average risk premium is less than or greater than 2%. Alternatively you may have no prior belief concerning the premium. In this case the alternative hypothesis would be that it is not equal to 2%. This situation can be summarised as:

H_0: average risk premium = 2%

H_A: average risk premium ≠ 2%

You will recall that the calculated value for the average risk premium estimated from a sample has a standard error. The probability that the expected population value of 2% will lie within a range of values will depend on the size of this standard error. Given this uncertainty you are testing to see if the average value of the risk premium is *statistically different* from a figure of 2%. The question that arises is what does statistically different mean?

The next step in hypothesis testing is to devise some criterion, or rule, that will enable you to decide whether the null hypothesis should or should not be rejected in favour of the alternative hypothesis. The criterion defines a test statistic that is calculated from the data. If its value falls within what is known as the *region of rejection* or the *critical region*, the null hypothesis is rejected. If the statistic does not fall within this region the hypothesis is not rejected. The region of non-rejection is called the *acceptance region*. The boundary between the rejection and the acceptance regions is called the *critical value*. Statistical tests can be two-sided (two-tailed) or one-sided (one-tailed). This will depend on your prior beliefs about the value of the parameter under the alternative hypothesis. The conclusion of a test is simply to say that the result is *significant* or *not significant*. The probability of rejecting the null hypothesis, H_0, when it is true is called the significance level. The value typically chosen for the significance level is 5%, or sometimes 1%. A statistically significant result means that the sampling variation is unlikely to explain the discrepancy between the null hypothesis and the sample value. A statistically insignificant result means that sampling variation is a likely explanation of the discrepancy between the null hypothesis and the sample value.

An introduction to regression analysis

Often, you will be concerned with the relationship among a number of variables. For example, you may want to know how retail rental growth depends on retail sales or on the growth in the economy at large. Alternatively, you may want to know whether property yields are related to the yields on other assets. Regression analysis helps to address these questions and to quantify the extent of the underlying relationships. Results based on regression analysis have been reported in various chapters throughout the book and it is, therefore, important to understand the basic principles. In this section we can only provide a brief overview. In order to obtain a working knowledge the reader should consult the applied papers referred to in the appropriate chapters and the statistical sources in the selected references.

Table 17.10 ● Individual property returns and associated market returns

	Returns											
Property r_p	−4.0	−2.5	−1.0	0.5	2.0	2.0	3.0	6.0	5.0	8.0	10.0	12.0
Market r_m	−3.0	−1.0	−1.5	−1.0	2.0	3.0	3.5	5.0	8.0	10.0	12.0	15.0

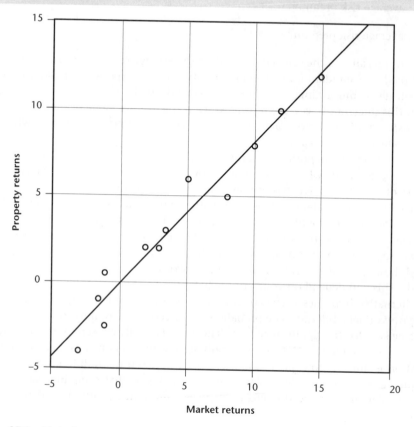

Figure 17.3 Plot of property returns and the market

To provide you with an introduction to regression analysis we will only consider a two-variable equation. You may, therefore, wish to predict the value of one variable given the value of another variable. The variable that is being *explained* or *predicted, Y,* is known as the *dependent* variable and the variable that is used to make the prediction, *X*, is known as the *independent* or *explanatory* variable.

A regression analysis seeks to determine the relationship between the dependent variable and one or more explanatory variables. For example, Table 17.10 shows twelve rates of return for both an individual property and the market. What you are trying to do is capture the relationship between the two sets of data. Figure 17.3 plots a graph of the data in the form of a scatter plot, from which you will see that the relationship is approximately linear.

The idea behind regression analysis is to find the *line of best fit*. For example in general terms, Y may be related to X in a linear manner so that the regression equation will take the following linear form:

$$Y_i = \beta_0 + \beta_1 X_i + \varepsilon_i \qquad (17.56)$$

This equation tells you that the value of Y will depend on the value of X and on some random factor ε_i known as the *disturbance term*. The values β_0 and β_1 are the *regression parameters* that need to be estimated. Depending on the problem being examined, observations on the X and Y variables can be taken from a variety of sources with the subscript denoting the ith observation. In such instances the data would be described as *cross-sectional*. If the observations are collected over a number of periods the data would be described as being *time-series*. It is also possible to combine cross-sectional and time-series data to give what is known as *pooled time-series and cross-sectional data*. This would apply, for example, if you had collected data on retail rental levels in different locations over time.

The random error term is very important in regression analysis as it introduces uncertainty into the value of Y_i. For example, you may find that retail sales may help to explain retail rents, but the relationship is not perfect. There will always be specific considerations for any one property that will influence the rent. If it is believed that retail sales are the only systematic impact on rents, the distribution of other property-specific factors is assumed to be a random variable. This means that the value of rental level, Y_i, will also be a random variable with the result that it cannot be forecast exactly. You will see that Y_i will have a probability distribution so that statements about its expected value, therefore, need to be made in statistical terms.

Provided that certain assumptions about the disturbance term are met, estimates of the parameters β_0 and β_1 can be obtained by a process known as *ordinary least squares*, or *OLS* for short. All this does is to find an equation for the regression line that minimises the sum of the squared errors of each observation from the line. A statistical package or a spreadsheet can be employed to estimate the equation. Additional statistics will also be reported, together with the coefficient estimates. These will include the standard error of the coefficient estimates, the equation standard error and the coefficient of multiple determination. This is called R-squared or simply R^2. We discuss this further in Appendix 17A. Other statistics will also be reported, enabling further statistical tests of the robustness of the estimated relationship and the properties of the error term.

An analysis of the data in Table 17.10 would involve regressing the property returns against the market returns. You will find that in this case the influence of the market factor is statistically significant at the 5% level. Also, the R^2 value is 95%, implying that the market explains about 95% of the variation in the property returns. Using a spreadsheet you should estimate the regression equation in order to verify these findings.

We next look at testing the regression coefficients in a little more detail.

Example

The regression results reported in Table 17.11 relate the excess returns on a property, r_{pt}, to the excess returns on a market index r_{mt}, both in period t. The results are based on 20 monthly observations. The task is to test whether the property has delivered significant abnormal returns and whether the beta of the property is equal to 1. This is an application of the Jensen measure of performance we discussed in Appendix 16B.

Table 17.11 ● Estimates of regression parameters

Regression equation: $r_{pt} = \hat{\beta}_0 + \hat{\beta}_1 r_{mt} + \varepsilon_t$

	Parameter estimates		Sample size
$\hat{\beta}_0$	$\hat{\beta}_1$	R^2	
0.44 (3.36)	0.85 (0.05)	0.863	20

Note: Standard errors are shown in brackets.

Given these results we want to test whether $\hat{\beta}_0 = 0$ and $\hat{\beta}_1 = 1$. Our prior hypothesis is that excess returns are zero, i.e.

$$H_0 : \beta_0 = 0$$

The alternative hypothesis is that excess returns are positive, i.e.

$$H_A : \beta_0 > 0$$

You should note that this is a one-tail test because you are only interested in testing for the significance of a positive value of excess returns.

As noted above, a test statistic needs to be calculated. Since two degrees of freedom are used up for calculating β_0 and β_1, the number of degrees of freedom is $n - 2$. The test statistic is found from:

$$t_{n-2} = \frac{\hat{\beta}_0 - \beta_0}{\sigma_{\hat{\beta}_0}} \qquad (17.57)$$

where $\hat{\beta}_0$ is the estimated value, β_0 the hypothesised value and $\sigma_{\hat{\beta}_0}$ is the standard error of the estimate $\hat{\beta}_0$.

As there are twenty observations we use the t-distribution, the number of degrees of freedom being 18. Substituting the figures from Table 17.11 gives:

$$t_{18} = \frac{0.44 - 0}{3.36} = 0.13$$

For a one-tail test at the 5% level, the value of t_{18} from a table of the t-distribution is equal to 1.734. Since our calculated value of 0.13 is less than this, we cannot reject the null hypothesis. This would be interpreted as providing no statistical support for abnormal returns.

In order to test whether the slope coefficient is significantly different from 1, the null hypothesis is that the slope coefficient is equal to 1:

$$H_0 : \beta_1 = 1$$

The alternative hypothesis is that it is not equal to 1:

$$H_A : \beta_1 \neq 1$$

As we have no prior views about the value of the slope coefficient it could be less than 1 or greater than 1. In this case you have a two-tailed test.

The test statistic is found from:

$$t_{n-2} = \frac{\hat{\beta}_1 - \beta_1}{\sigma_{\hat{\beta}_1}} \tag{17.58}$$

where $\hat{\beta}_1$ is the estimated value, β_1 is the hypothesised value and $\sigma_{\hat{\beta}_1}$ is the standard error of the estimate $\hat{\beta}_1$.

Substituting the regression results gives:

$$t_{18} = \frac{0.85 - 1}{0.05} = -3.00$$

The tabled value for a two-tailed t-distribution at the 5% level, with 18 degrees of freedom, is 2.101. Since the calculated absolute value of 3 exceeds this figure we reject the null in favour of the alternative. That is, the slope coefficient cannot be regarded as being statistically close to the value of 1.

It is possible to undertake other diagnostic tests regarding the validity of the estimated regression coefficients; however, this would take us beyond the introduction provided here. Further information can be found in the references.

Multiple regression

Multiple regression is just an extension of the simple regression model. In this case, however, the variable Y is explained by several other variables. The equation now takes the form:

$$Y_i = \beta_0 + \beta_1 X_1 + \beta_2 X_2 + \dots + \beta_k X_k + \varepsilon_i \tag{17.59}$$

where the Xs represent the independent variables. There are, however, a number of additional complications that arise when there is more than one independent variable. Again, you should refer to the references for further details.

Summary

This chapter has provided an outline of some of the important statistical concepts that are frequently used in applied property research. We described some basic techniques used in algebraic manipulation and showed the importance of graphing functions.

Many of the valuation models we derived make use of geometric progressions. Knowing how to sum geometric progressions over a fixed number of terms as well as in perpetuity provides the basic building blocks for developing complex valuation models.

The second part of the chapter discussed some important statistical and probability concepts. We introduced and discussed the use of the expectation operator and derived a number of key statistical expressions. We also discussed one of the most important distributions. This is the normal distribution. It has well-known properties and can be easily manipulated. We made use of the normal distribution to develop the idea of confidence intervals and hypothesis testing.

The final part of the chapter introduced regression analysis. We used the principles we developed for describing confidence intervals and hypothesis testing to set up a null hypothesis and to interpret the output from a regression analysis.

This chapter has two appendices.

Appendix 17A: The explanatory power of the estimated regression equation

As regression analysis is widely used in practice we provide a more detailed treatment of the explanatory power of the model.

Appendix 17B: Property datasets

In this appendix we provide datasets of property returns compiled by the Investment Property Databank. These can be used to explore some of the econometric techniques we have described.

Problems

1. Using the annual total returns for property, equities and gilts given in Appendix 17B re-estimate the total return indices so that they have a base value of 100 in 1980.

2. Estimate the following summary statistics for the sector and regional data:
   (a) arithmetic and geometric mean returns
   (b) standard deviation
   (c) skewness and kurtosis
   Which sector is the most volatile?

3. Rank the returns for property, equities and gilts using the Sharpe ratio.

4. Assuming that the returns are normally distributed, what is the probability of getting an annual return in excess of zero in each of the three asset classes?

5. Using the three property sectors including equities and gilts, calculate the coefficient of correlation between the asset classes. Using a spreadsheet optimiser estimate the efficient frontier that excludes and includes the property sectors. Compare the results.

6. Use a spreadsheet to regress the returns on property against gilts and property against equities:

    (a)   How would you interpret the regression coefficients?

    (b)   What are the standard errors of the coefficients?

    (c)   What are the 95% confidence intervals for the slope coefficient?

    (d)   What is the R^2 value in each case?

7. Take the square root of the R^2 value in each case and compare your results with the corresponding coefficient of correlation. What do you observe?

Selected references

Fogler, H.R. and Ganapathy, S. (1980) *Financial Econometrics for Researchers in Finance and Accounting*, Englewood Cliffs, NJ: Prentice Hall.

Griffiths, W., Hill, C. and Judge, G. (1993) *Learning and Practicing Econometrics*, New York: McGraw-Hill.

Gujarati, D.N. (1995) *Basic Econometrics*, 3rd edn. New York: McGraw-Hill.

Hill, C., Griffiths, W. and Judge, G. (1997) *Undergraduate Econometrics*, New York: John Wiley & Sons.

Johnston, J. and DiNardo, J. (1997) *Econometric Methods*, 4th edn. New York: McGraw-Hill.

Kmenta, J. (1986) *Elements of Econometrics*, 2nd edn. New York: Macmillan.

Mood, A.M. and Graybill, F.A. (1963) *Introduction to the Theory of Statistics*, New York: McGraw-Hill.

Salvatore, D. (1982) *Statistics and Econometrics*, Schaum's Outline Series, New York: McGraw-Hill.

Appendix 17A
The explanatory power of the estimated regression equation

In this appendix we discuss the explanatory power of a regression model. This is a useful area to understand because it also provides an explanation for the split that we gave in Chapter 10 between market risk and residual risk. You will also see that the explanatory power of a regression model is another way of looking at diversification.

In Chapter 17 we showed how you could use regression analysis to estimate a linear relationship between a dependent and independent variable. It is useful, however, to know what proportion of the variation in the dependent variable can be explained by the independent variable. This is known as the goodness of fit and is usually measured by the *coefficient of determination* or R^2 value.

If you had a series of observations for variable Y_i, your best guess of any individual value for Y_i would be given by the mean of all the observations, $\bar{Y}$. In practice it is unlikely that this average would represent a good estimate for each value of Y_i so that relying on this single figure would result in a lot of error. If, however, you had some other variable, X_i, and it was possible to estimate a linear relationship between Y_i and X_i, this would enable you to make a much better prediction about any individual value for Y_i. Regression analysis identifies this relationship and helps you to make statements about Y_i *conditional* on values of X_i.

Analysing variation

Having estimated a regression equation it is necessary to examine how well it explains variations in the dependent variable Y_i.

Assuming that each value of Y is only related to a single variable X, each observed value of Y_i can be written in terms of the regression equation as follows:

$$Y_i = \beta_0 + \beta_1 X_i + \varepsilon_i \qquad (17A.1)$$

The fitted values of Y_i and the estimated regression beta coefficients, all identified by a hat value, ^, are given by the estimated regression line:

$$\hat{Y}_i = \hat{\beta}_0 + \hat{\beta}_1 X_i \qquad (17A.2)$$

A single observation Y_i can be expressed in terms of its deviation from the mean values as follows:

$$(Y_i - \bar{Y}) = \text{Total the deviation of } Y_i \text{ from the mean, } \bar{Y} \qquad (17A.3)$$

This can be split into two components. The first is the deviation of Y_i from the mean $\bar{Y}$ that can be explained by the regression:

$$(\hat{Y}_i - \bar{Y}) = \text{Explained deviation of } Y_i \text{ from } \bar{Y} \qquad (17A.4)$$

The second part is the deviation of Y_i from the mean, $\bar{Y}$, that is not explained by the regression:

$$(Y_i - \hat{Y}_i) = \text{Unexplained deviation of } Y_i \text{ from } \bar{Y} \qquad (17A.5)$$

This decomposition is shown in Figure 17A.1.

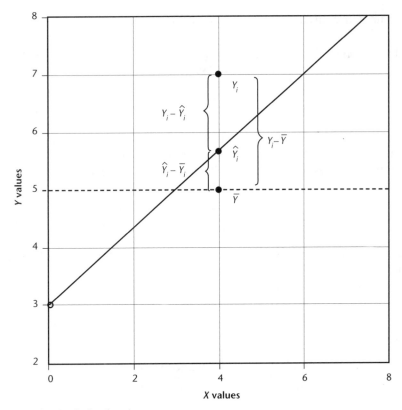

Figure 17A.1 Analysis of variance

The next step is to square all the deviations and add them together. This defines each component of total variation in the dependent variable Y_i as follows.

Total sum of squared deviations (TSS)

$$\sum (Y_i - \bar{Y})^2 = \sum y_i^2 \qquad (17A.6)$$

Regression (explained) sum of squared deviations (RSS)

$$\sum (\hat{Y}_i - \bar{Y})^2 = \sum \hat{y}_i^2 \qquad (17A.7)$$

Error (unexplained) sum of squared deviations (ESS)

$$\sum (Y_i - \hat{Y}_i)^2 = \sum e_i^2 \qquad (17A.8)$$

The total sum of squares, TSS, can be written as the sum of RSS and ESS:

$$\sum (Y_i - \bar{Y})^2 = \sum (\hat{Y}_i - \bar{Y})^2 + \sum (Y_i - \hat{Y}_i)^2 \qquad (17A.9)$$

Writing this in deviation form gives:

$$\sum y_i^2 = \sum \hat{y}_i^2 + \sum e_i^2 \qquad (17A.10)$$

You can summarise this decomposition as follows:

Total variation in Y TSS $\sum y_i^2$		Explained variation in Y RSS $\sum \hat{y}_i^2$		Residual variation in Y ESS $\sum e_i^2$
	=		+	

The explanatory power of the model is represented by the coefficient of determination, which is also called R^2. This is the proportion of total variation in Y that can be explained by the regression of Y on the regressor, or independent, variables.

From the above the R^2 value can be estimated from the following:

$$R^2 = \frac{\text{Explained variation in } Y}{\text{Total variation in } Y} = \frac{RSS}{TSS} \tag{17A.11}$$

Using the deviation expression in equation 17A.10 the R^2 value can be found by dividing through by $\sum y_i^2$:

$$\frac{\sum y_i^2}{\sum y_i^2} = \frac{\sum \hat{y}_i^2}{\sum y_i^2} + \frac{\sum e_i^2}{\sum y_i^2} \tag{17A.12}$$

This can also be expressed as:

$$1 = \frac{\text{Explained variation in } Y}{\text{Total variation in } Y} + \frac{\text{Unexplained variation in } Y}{\text{Total variation in } Y} \tag{17A.13}$$

The R^2 value is then given by:

$$R^2 = \frac{RSS}{TSS} = \frac{\sum \hat{y}_i^2}{\sum y_i^2} \tag{17A.14}$$

You will see that the larger RSS is relative to TSS the higher the R^2 value. Another way of looking at this is to recognise that as the residual variation $\sum e_i^2$ gets smaller, there will be less error in the regression so that the R^2 value will increase. At the limit $\sum e_i^2 = 0$ and the R^2 value will equal 1.0.

The range of values that R^2 can take on will lie in the interval $0 \le R^2 \le 1$ as $0 \le ESS \le TSS$.

In multiple regression, the inclusion of additional independent variables will always tend, to a greater or lesser extent, to increase the R^2 value even if the additional variables have no relationship, or effect, on the dependent variable, Y. You should, therefore, be careful in attaching too much importance to the significance of R^2 when a number of independent variables are used in the regression. One way to account for the inflated value of R^2 is to adjust its value to take account of the number of independent variables. This revised measure is known as R-bar squared, or $\bar{R}^2$.

$$\bar{R}^2 = 1 - (1 - R^2)\left(\frac{n-1}{n-k}\right) \tag{17A.15}$$

where n is the number of observations and k is the number of variables in the model, including the intercept term.

Cautionary warning

Both the R^2 and $\bar{R}^2$ values should be regarded as summary statistics, providing an indication of the overall goodness of fit. A more formal approach would be to test the overall significance of these values, and therefore the regression equation, using the F-test (see Gujarati 1995 for further details).

In order to determine the validity of any estimated regression equation a number of tests should be undertaken. Discussion of these topics is beyond this introductory appendix and will depend on the application being investigated. However, you should be interested in asking the following questions:

- Are the variables *individually* significant?
- What is the equation's standard error?
- Does the estimated equation make sense?
- Do the estimated coefficients have the expected sign?
- Are the estimated coefficients stable over time?
- Does the estimated equation forecast well out of sample?
- Do the residuals display a normal distribution pattern and satisfy the underlying assumptions for using the ordinary least squares (OLS) estimation procedure?

The choice of a valid relationship should not be determined on the basis of the highest R^2 value. The estimated relationship should make both theoretical and logical sense and display a random pattern in the residuals! Many econometric software packages now provide readily available, and easy to use, procedures for undertaking statistical tests enabling robust analysis of regression results. Interested readers should consult the references in Chapter 17 in order to gain further insights into an understanding of regression analysis.

Appendix 17B
Property datasets

The following datasets have been based on information supplied by the Investment Property Databank. They provide an overview of the performance of the UK commercial property sector and offer the opportunity to explore some of the ideas we have discussed in this book.

Market standing investment performance (% p.a.)

	Total return				Income return				Capital growth				ERV growth				Equivalent yield			
	All	Ret	Off	Ind	All	Ret	Off	Ind	All	Ret	Off	Ind	All	Ret	Off	Ind	All	Ret	Off	Ind
1971	16.1	8.0	19.2	11.8	5.0	5.4	4.7	8.5	11.1	2.6	14.6	3.3	–	–	–	–	–	–	–	–
1972	29.5	20.5	33.4	22.0	5.2	5.8	4.5	9.2	24.2	14.7	28.9	12.8	–	–	–	–	–	–	–	–
1973	28.5	24.0	30.8	20.0	4.7	5.7	4.0	8.4	23.8	18.3	26.8	11.7	–	–	–	–	–	–	–	–
1974	-16.2	-14.3	-18.7	-4.5	4.3	4.3	3.7	7.8	-20.4	-18.7	-22.4	-12.2	–	–	–	–	–	–	–	–
1975	11.5	18.5	8.1	16.5	6.1	5.5	5.6	9.5	5.4	12.9	2.5	7.0	–	–	–	–	–	–	–	–
1976	9.4	13.7	7.1	14.5	6.1	5.5	5.9	8.6	3.3	8.2	1.2	5.9	1.6	7.2	-0.4	6.6	9.1	8.2	9.0	11.7
1977	26.5	29.7	23.4	34.8	6.9	7.1	6.5	8.6	19.6	22.6	16.9	26.1	4.7	5.4	3.6	7.4	7.9	7.7	7.6	9.1
1978	25.7	31.5	22.8	28.7	6.2	6.0	5.9	7.4	19.5	25.5	16.9	21.3	9.8	12.4	8.8	9.3	7.3	7.4	6.9	8.5
1979	23.0	25.2	20.4	27.5	6.0	5.5	5.7	7.6	17.0	19.7	14.7	19.9	14.6	16.4	13.2	16.6	7.2	7.1	6.9	8.4
1980	17.5	19.4	16.9	17.1	6.0	5.4	5.7	7.6	11.5	14.0	11.2	9.5	12.5	14.1	11.5	13.5	7.4	7.2	6.9	8.8
1981	15.0	17.4	15.1	12.1	5.7	5.1	5.6	7.4	9.4	12.3	9.5	4.7	7.8	9.1	8.1	5.0	7.6	7.4	7.2	9.0
1982	7.5	10.4	6.7	5.7	5.6	5.1	5.5	7.4	1.9	5.3	1.3	-1.7	3.8	5.7	3.3	2.1	7.6	7.4	7.2	9.2
1983	7.6	12.3	5.5	6.1	5.9	5.5	5.8	8.0	1.6	6.8	-0.3	-1.9	2.8	4.9	2.4	1.2	7.6	7.2	7.3	9.6
1984	8.6	13.8	6.4	6.0	6.2	5.6	6.1	8.6	2.4	8.3	0.3	-2.5	4.2	7.2	2.9	2.9	7.7	7.1	7.4	9.8
1985	8.3	12.7	7.6	3.6	6.4	5.6	6.4	9.2	1.8	7.1	1.2	-5.6	6.4	9.4	6.0	2.6	7.8	7.0	7.6	10.4
1986	11.1	11.7	11.8	9.3	6.6	5.6	6.6	10.1	4.5	6.1	5.2	-0.8	9.8	9.7	11.7	4.4	8.0	7.0	8.0	10.8
1987	25.8	20.8	30.6	24.8	6.7	5.7	6.7	10.4	19.1	15.1	23.9	14.4	19.1	14.6	24.8	11.7	7.7	7.0	7.7	10.3
1988	29.7	24.9	31.6	39.0	6.2	5.4	6.0	9.6	23.5	19.4	25.6	29.4	22.8	19.5	25.3	22.3	7.4	6.7	7.5	9.4
1989	15.4	9.9	16.6	29.1	5.6	5.1	5.5	8.2	9.8	4.8	11.1	20.9	15.0	14.1	14.3	21.0	7.7	7.3	7.6	9.3
1990	-8.4	-8.3	-9.9	-3.5	5.8	5.5	5.5	7.5	-14.2	-13.8	-15.4	-11.1	2.8	4.5	0.5	6.8	9.2	8.8	9.0	11.0
1991	-3.2	3.2	-10.8	9.1	7.3	7.1	7.0	9.3	-10.5	-3.9	-17.8	-0.1	-8.5	-2.2	-15.0	-1.9	9.7	8.8	9.8	10.9
1992	-1.7	3.5	-7.3	1.5	8.3	7.7	8.5	9.7	-10.0	-4.2	-15.7	-8.2	-11.9	-3.4	-20.4	-8.8	9.9	9.1	10.3	11.4
1993	20.0	20.4	19.2	20.9	9.1	8.1	9.7	10.6	10.8	12.3	9.5	10.3	-7.9	-1.9	-13.8	-8.9	8.6	8.0	8.7	9.8
1994	12.0	13.0	10.9	11.8	8.1	7.2	8.5	9.5	4.0	5.8	2.4	2.3	-0.8	0.2	-1.2	-3.0	8.0	7.5	8.1	9.3
1995	3.5	4.1	2.9	2.7	7.6	6.8	8.0	9.2	-4.1	-2.8	-5.1	-6.5	0.3	1.8	-0.8	-1.5	8.2	7.7	8.2	9.7
1996	10.0	11.7	7.5	10.3	8.0	7.1	8.4	9.9	2.0	4.6	-0.9	0.3	3.3	4.7	2.3	1.3	8.0	7.5	8.2	9.6
1997	16.8	18.5	14.5	16.5	7.8	7.0	8.3	9.8	9.0	11.5	6.1	6.6	8.0	7.8	9.8	5.3	7.6	7.1	7.9	9.0
Annualised																				
1970-97	12.3	13.4	11.1	14.1	6.4	6.0	6.3	8.8	5.9	7.4	4.8	5.2	n/a	n/a	n/a	n/a				
1970-80	16.3	16.8	15.4	18.4	5.7	5.6	5.2	8.3	10.7	11.2	10.1	10.0	n/a	n/a	n/a	n/a				
1980-90	11.6	12.2	11.6	12.6	6.1	5.4	6.0	8.6	5.5	6.8	5.6	3.9	9.3	9.8	9.6	7.8				
1987-97	8.8	9.7	6.7	13.1	7.4	6.7	7.5	9.3	1.4	3.0	-0.9	3.7	1.8	4.3	-0.8	2.8				
1992-97	12.3	13.4	10.8	12.3	8.1	7.3	8.6	9.8	4.2	6.1	2.3	2.5	0.5	2.5	-1.0	-1.5				

Source: The Investment Property Databank.

IPD market performance: Market segments – total return (% p.a.)

	1981	1982	1983	1984	1985	1986	1987	1988	1989	1990	1991	1992	1993	1994	1995	1996	1997
Standard Shops	**18.8**	**10.3**	**12.6**	**14.4**	**13.5**	**12.5**	**22.1**	**26.2**	**9.1**	**-8.9**	**1.2**	**0.5**	**19.1**	**11.1**	**1.4**	**9.2**	**16.3**
Central London	10.1	1.3	9.8	14.4	16.0	16.1	33.6	34.9	10.9	-9.7	-7.4	-5.3	18.7	15.2	5.3	15.7	25.9
Rest of London	19.5	10.9	13.6	13.5	13.0	15.0	23.5	27.7	7.4	-10.5	2.3	-0.8	15.9	9.5	0.7	8.9	15.8
Southern England	22.7	13.8	14.1	15.1	13.9	11.6	19.9	24.4	8.2	-9.3	1.8	0.0	17.9	8.5	-1.3	6.8	12.0
Rest of UK	19.9	11.3	11.8	14.0	12.4	10.9	18.2	22.9	9.8	-7.4	4.8	3.9	21.3	12.3	2.4	8.5	16.0
Shopping Centres	**15.5**	**10.5**	**12.1**	**13.8**	**12.2**	**10.4**	**19.8**	**23.0**	**11.8**	**-6.6**	**2.4**	**3.8**	**16.9**	**13.6**	**5.0**	**12.7**	**17.4**
London	–	10.5	10.4	9.6	11.2	14.4	22.3	12.7	3.2	-3.0	-4.2	1.1	15.8	12.4	4.7	10.1	18.8
Southern England	17.3	12.4	14.6	15.9	13.3	10.7	18.3	25.4	11.5	-9.8	2.1	2.2	13.4	10.6	5.8	13.2	17.7
Rest of UK	16.2	9.3	11.0	13.9	11.7	8.8	20.1	24.1	13.9	-4.9	4.9	5.9	20.0	16.0	4.4	13.2	16.9
Retail Warehouses	**14.3**	**11.9**	**8.4**	**12.8**	**12.4**	**15.3**	**18.2**	**25.8**	**10.1**	**-12.7**	**14.1**	**14.4**	**35.4**	**18.6**	**8.7**	**15.9**	**26.2**
London	–	12.0	9.9	11.9	10.6	12.0	21.3	23.3	6.3	-12.2	13.1	14.0	33.6	17.9	6.8	13.7	27.2
Southern England	11.0	6.9	10.8	15.0	17.2	17.1	16.0	25.2	8.7	-14.7	16.3	12.7	34.9	17.2	7.1	15.5	25.7
Rest of UK	16.0	16.0	5.8	11.8	9.6	16.0	19.8	29.4	15.9	-10.1	11.7	16.9	36.7	20.3	10.9	16.8	26.5
Dept/Variety Stores	**15.5**	**10.0**	**12.3**	**11.0**	**9.1**	**11.0**	**17.2**	**23.0**	**7.1**	**-6.6**	**7.8**	**6.9**	**22.3**	**13.3**	**5.6**	**10.8**	**15.9**
Supermarkets	**16.2**	**11.0**	**10.6**	**12.0**	**9.4**	**11.6**	**14.8**	**17.4**	**11.0**	**-5.5**	**10.6**	**9.0**	**27.8**	**11.5**	**5.6**	**10.1**	**15.1**
Other Retail	**19.9**	**11.4**	**12.5**	**13.2**	**14.9**	**10.9**	**20.7**	**24.8**	**11.8**	**-4.7**	**5.0**	**2.9**	**19.3**	**11.5**	**2.8**	**9.4**	**15.8**
Standard Offices	**15.1**	**6.7**	**5.5**	**6.4**	**7.6**	**11.8**	**30.6**	**31.6**	**16.6**	**-9.9**	**-11.3**	**-7.2**	**19.4**	**10.8**	**2.8**	**7.2**	**14.2**
Central London	16.3	6.6	5.1	7.3	10.9	18.5	39.8	31.7	13.4	-12.1	-17.7	-10.1	20.3	12.2	4.8	7.6	15.7
Rest of London	12.9	4.6	4.8	2.1	0.8	3.0	21.4	37.2	18.9	-7.2	-6.5	-8.5	16.1	6.3	-1.3	8.5	16.7
Southern England	15.2	8.5	6.4	7.6	5.2	1.7	13.8	28.1	20.3	-9.4	-3.0	-4.8	18.5	8.6	1.2	7.7	13.6
Rest of UK	12.3	7.8	7.0	6.3	5.0	3.9	15.3	29.4	33.8	0.8	5.3	2.0	19.6	12.0	1.2	4.1	8.0
Office Parks	–	–	–	–	7.0	10.5	22.0	24.6	19.4	-9.3	1.6	-7.6	16.6	12.3	3.7	10.7	17.4
Standard Industrials	**11.9**	**5.7**	**6.0**	**5.5**	**3.4**	**9.4**	**25.7**	**40.2**	**29.1**	**-3.2**	**9.4**	**1.7**	**19.8**	**11.5**	**2.7**	**10.6**	**17.3**
London	12.0	6.1	6.7	6.1	4.3	10.5	25.8	41.4	28.0	-4.0	7.5	0.4	19.9	9.5	4.2	12.2	21.0
Southern England	13.8	6.1	7.1	6.6	3.0	9.4	27.4	39.8	28.3	-5.1	8.5	-0.5	18.5	11.1	1.1	10.1	17.5
Rest of UK	8.7	4.7	3.3	3.0	3.0	8.1	21.8	39.5	33.3	3.9	14.5	8.5	22.5	14.2	4.2	10.4	14.7
Industrial Parks	13.2	6.2	7.7	10.7	6.7	7.3	19.3	33.8	28.8	-7.1	6.1	-1.4	19.7	12.5	3.2	10.7	16.2
Distribution WHs	15.2	4.6	6.1	8.0	0.8	11.3	23.9	35.2	30.2	2.0	13.8	5.9	30.9	12.5	2.6	8.3	13.8
Other Property	9.0	4.3	6.0	5.4	-7.2	-3.5	8.2	22.6	13.3	3.5	-0.3	2.4	17.9	15.6	18.4	15.5	16.2
All Property	**15.0**	**7.5**	**7.6**	**8.6**	**8.3**	**11.1**	**25.8**	**29.7**	**15.4**	**-8.4**	**-3.2**	**-1.7**	**20.0**	**12.0**	**3.5**	**10.0**	**16.8**

Source: The Investment Property Databank.

Total returns

	Property	Gilts	Equities	T-Bills	RPI
1971	16.13	27.30	45.20	6.20	9.00
1972	29.46	−3.80	21.70	5.40	7.60
1973	28.50	−8.90	−32.10	9.00	10.60
1974	−16.15	−15.20	−49.40	12.60	19.10
1975	11.46	36.80	149.60	10.80	24.90
1976	9.43	13.70	−1.10	11.30	15.10
1977	26.52	44.80	57.20	9.40	12.10
1978	25.73	−1.80	12.10	8.10	8.40
1979	22.99	4.10	9.70	13.50	17.30
1980	17.48	20.90	34.10	17.20	15.10
1981	15.05	1.80	12.20	13.80	12.00
1982	7.51	51.30	28.80	12.40	5.40
1983	7.59	15.90	28.40	10.10	5.30
1984	8.63	6.80	29.80	9.50	4.60
1985	8.25	11.00	21.60	11.90	5.60
1986	11.08	11.00	26.40	10.90	3.72
1987	25.75	16.30	8.40	9.60	3.70
1988	29.69	9.40	12.80	11.00	6.75
1989	15.40	5.90	33.50	14.60	7.68
1990	−8.42	5.60	−6.70	15.90	9.31
1991	−3.18	18.90	16.90	11.60	4.45
1992	−1.69	18.40	19.90	9.50	2.57
1993	19.96	28.80	27.40	5.90	1.93
1994	12.01	−11.30	−4.10	5.40	2.88
1995	3.55	19.00	23.10	6.70	3.21
1996	9.95	7.70	15.10	6.20	2.45
1997	16.81	19.40	24.50	6.90	3.63

Index numbers

	Property	Gilts	Equities	T-Bills	RPI
	100.00	100.00	100.00	100.00	100.00
	116.13	127.30	145.20	106.20	109.00
	150.34	122.46	176.71	111.93	117.28
	193.18	111.56	119.99	122.01	129.72
	161.98	94.61	60.71	137.38	154.49
	180.54	129.42	151.54	152.22	192.96
	197.55	147.15	149.87	169.42	222.10
	249.95	213.08	235.60	185.35	248.97
	314.27	209.24	264.10	200.36	269.88
	386.52	217.82	289.72	227.41	316.57
	454.07	263.34	388.52	266.52	364.38
	522.40	268.08	435.92	303.30	408.10
	561.66	405.61	561.46	340.91	430.14
	604.26	470.10	720.92	375.34	452.94
	656.38	502.07	935.75	411.00	473.77
	710.54	557.30	1137.87	459.91	500.30
	789.29	618.60	1438.27	510.04	518.92
	992.56	719.43	1559.09	559.00	538.12
	1287.20	787.06	1758.65	620.49	574.44
	1485.46	833.49	2347.80	711.08	618.54
	1360.44	880.17	2190.50	824.15	676.14
	1317.16	1046.52	2560.69	919.75	706.24
	1294.88	1239.08	3070.27	1007.12	724.40
	1553.30	1595.93	3911.52	1066.54	738.41
	1739.84	1415.59	3751.15	1124.14	759.69
	1801.59	1684.56	4617.66	1199.46	784.07
	1980.93	1814.27	5314.93	1273.82	803.27
	2313.87	2166.24	6617.09	1361.71	832.43

Source: The Investment Property Databank.

CHAPTER 18

Some unanswered questions

Learning objectives

After reading this chapter you will understand the following:

● Areas of property research that are not well understood

● Emerging areas that need further investigation

Introduction

Over the last twenty years technology has played an important role in the way businesses operate. Traditional views are changing as we approach the twenty-first century. Information is now seen as a commodity that can be traded. Property markets have shifted from local deal-oriented businesses to international markets that are research-driven.

In this book we have introduced some of the techniques that are important in viewing property as an information business. Many of the new ideas that will be developed in property investment will try to identify exploitable inefficiencies in the way information is impounded into prices.

In this chapter we identify a number of areas that we believe are, as yet, unresolved. This does not mean, however, that research is not being carried out in these areas. Our view is that some of the results are not yet conclusive and offer the potential for further work. Our list of topics is not conclusive, but they appeared to us to have a direct bearing on the way information influences the property market.

1. What objectives do funds follow?

We have talked a lot about the objectives of a fund in relation to the type of portfolios that should be held. However, we still don't know a great deal about the objectives that property funds are trying to pursue. Allied to this is our belief that funds may believe that they are pursuing one strategy but are in reality following another. Broad groupings such as retail, office and industrial may not be fine enough if there is an overlap in the risk–return groupings. The real issue concerns risk-aversion. Different groups of property investor may, for example, have different views concerning risk-aversion. Other than broad generalisations such as a fund is trying to pursue a growth or income policy, this area is as yet unexplored.

One way, for example, of trying to reconcile the differences between theory and practice is to use style analysis. This technique was developed by Sharpe in 1988 and provides a means of tracking, over time, the asset allocation that funds have made relative to a number of broadly based market indices. This technique has produced a number of valuable insights into the performance of equity portfolios and could have potential for identifying performance decisions of different groups of property investor. There are also issues relating to the size and diversification of property portfolios in the use of style analysis, but as yet these are unresolved.

2. How do you measure risk?

Much of this book has been concerned with risk and return and what this means in terms of diversification. In fact, the whole of financial theory is dominated by risk. Clearly, this is something that is not going to go away so it is important for property investors and their advisers to know something about risk.

There are two aspects to this topic. One concerns the estimation of *ex-post* risk and the other *ex-ante* risk. Of these, *ex-ante* risk is the most important as it influences the prices at which assets trade. It is also the most difficult to estimate. We have offered some guidance on ways in which risk can be estimated in an *ex-ante* framework, but have also assumed that the standard deviation of returns is the appropriate measure to use. However, we have also shown that there are other measures of risk that can be used in a portfolio context which may prove more appropriate in relation to the risk-aversion of different classes of investor. Given this framework the way forward may be to use simulation models. This would be particularly relevant for properties that have no history of returns. As an important first step it is necessary to identify the types of risk to which an investor or fund is exposed. Decisions can then be made about how risks should be controlled. In principle, the risks to which a fund is exposed should depend on its objectives. Consequently, it is necessary to establish what these objectives are. This is clearly a very big area of research, but at present there is very little that is being done.

3. Do property indices have to be smooth?

We devoted a whole chapter to smoothing. It is probably fair to say that we probably know quite a bit about the effects of smoothing and how this is likely to affect the performance of property indices. However, despite the advances that have been made in this area, there seems to be some reluctance on the part of index providers routinely to adjust the performance of high-frequency property indices to reflect this effect.

Smoothing at the individual property level does not seem to be too much of a problem. In fact, smoothing at the individual property level can be regarded as reflecting the efficient use of available information. However, at the index level there does appear to be a strong correlation across the sample of properties in both current and previous periods that introduces high levels of smoothing.

At the practical level, high-frequency indices tend to track general trends rather than market changes. This severely limits the use of these indices for risk management purposes. In time we envisage that this will have to change although there will also need to be some agreement of the method that is used to remove the effect of index smoothing. It may also be that limited transactions-based indices emerge, restricted to transactions in local areas or reflecting auctions-based data. Alternatively, indices based on methodologies such as repeat sales may emerge. There are a number of possibilities but, as yet, this remains unresolved.

4. Can risk be controlled with derivative products?

One of the main findings that we have tried to reinforce in this book is that investment in property is a risky business. Institutions investing in property will tend to hold poorly diversified portfolios of property that carry high levels of residual risk. This suggests that there may well be opportunities for risk control and management that could help investors to create more highly diversified portfolios. The principle here is to capture the benefits of taking a position in property as an asset class without the management responsibilities of ownership. This is clearly an attractive idea that opens up the opportunity for more effective risk management. However, for it to work effectively there would need to be a number of investment products based on property that investors could buy and sell quickly and easily.

Although some attempts have been made to securitise individual properties none has been very successful. A more useful way forward may be to develop a number of derivative products based on high-frequency property indices. These could be available at both the sector and regional levels. The resulting indices would, however, need to be free of smoothing effects, otherwise the movements in the index numbers would be predictable and would be unlikely to stimulate sufficient trades.

This whole area is as yet unresolved but is clearly an important part of the development of a more liquid property market.

5. Do investors make efficient use of information?

Information is the lifeblood of the property market. Without a free flow of information it would not be possible for investors to know the price of property in relation to other asset classes.

At its simplest level there is a direct relationship between information and price. This is what the efficient market hypothesis tells us. However, the real issue in property is that there may be opportunities that could be exploited to offer abnormal returns.

...se would arise because the flow of information is restricted in some way. The question that arises is, how do investors identify and make use of such information?

There are probably a number of different levels to this problem. The most obvious starting point is to identify whether different sectors of the market are under- or over-priced. Given that property indices only record the performance of a sample of properties it is possible that mispricing at the sector level could be identified. This would then provide a clue as to which regions or individual locations within a sector should be investigated in more depth. This is, of course, a strategic issue that revolves around trying to identify the alpha values that we discussed in our chapter on strategy.

This approach points to the need for highly organised research units that are able to develop products that can identify mispriced assets. However, it is not clear whether commercial research organisations approach the role of property selection in this manner.

6. Do behavioural issues influence value?

In a market in which information is freely available and trading takes place on a continuous basis you would expect investors to act in a rational manner and arrive at values that represent a fair reflection of market prices. However, what if the behaviour of investors is not rational? This would create anomalies in the market that cannot be explained in terms of traditional financial models.

A good example of this would be where a valuer uses a sample of properties to value a whole portfolio. In this case the value of a large proportion of the portfolio is influenced by the value of a small number of properties. The portfolio valuation in this case has little to do with market forces and more to do with the behaviour of the valuer. This is an easy example to appreciate, but the same effect can be experienced at the individual property level where valuers are influenced by the anchoring effect of other information. These behavioural issues can be quite important and could lead to valuations that are not fair reflections of market price.

Similar effects can be observed in the stock market and some research is being undertaken to investigate these issues in more detail. However, it is one thing to say that the phenomenon exists and another thing to prove it. What is needed is a formal theory of asset pricing that allows the effect of behavioural issues to be isolated and tested. This is a potentially valuable avenue for research, but at present there are a number of issues in the development of testable models that remain unresolved.

7. Is depreciation important to investors?

The effect of depreciation on property values was first raised by Norman Bowie in 1983. Since then a number of studies have investigated the sources of depreciation and attempted to quantify it. However, very little has been done to determine whether valuations adequately reflect the fact that properties do age. In a reasonably efficient market it seems strange to believe that valuations would not adjust to reflect the fact that property is ageing. It is, of course, useful to know what parts of a building suffer most from depreciation, but it is not as easy to isolate the effect of depreciation on changes in yields.

We do not believe that depreciation is as much of a problem as it was made out to be. Valuers know that buildings age. They also know that land changes in value. This information is readily observable and in combination should be accounted for in the choice of property yield. The extent to which yields *fully* reflect depreciation at any particular point in time may be unresolved, but we don't believe that markets continually, and systematically, underestimate the impact of depreciation.

8. Are property yields influenced by the term structure of interest rates?

A more important issue is the relationship between changes in the term structure of interest rates and changes in property yields. At present we know very little about this. Yields are a combination of growth in rental value and the expected rate of return. The difference between these two figures produces the yield. However, if interest rates shift by 1% it is not entirely clear what effect this will have on changes in property yields in each sector. It may, for example, have no impact because of a compensating effect in the expected rate of rental value growth. At present this is unresolved, but it would be useful to know how the yields in different sectors respond to changes in interest rates.

9. What do we really know about international property investment?

In recent years there has been a lot of interest in international property investment. A number of studies have been undertaken to investigate the effect of constructing international property portfolios. The rationale for doing this is not only to gain some international property exposure but also to achieve more effective reduction in risk. Research in this area has followed on from similar research in the equities market. We have chosen not to cover this area in depth because we believe that there are a number of unresolved issues concerning the quality of the data and methodologies being used.

In principle, international diversification offers a lot of potential. However, most of the studies that have examined this issue have made use of a Markowitz model to estimate the optimal proportion of funds to invest in each country. Although this seems reasonable, the procedure may well be suspect when using property data. We have already alluded to some of the problems. For example:

- Basing an optimal allocation on index returns may not be very helpful if investors cannot replicate the same risk-return characteristics of the indices in each country.
- There may be differences in the way the local indices are constructed. For example, a number of property indices in Singapore are based on prices not valuations. It would be invalid to use an asset allocation model that mixes valuations and prices unless it can be shown that they are a perfect substitute for each other.
- Where valuations are used as a proxy for prices it is important to know how robust is the relationship in different market environments.
- We don't know much about the attitude of investors to the risk of international investment and why they want to take on an additional level of currency risk.

We feel that it is probably too early to make definitive statements about international asset allocation decisions until some of these issues have been resolved.

10. Why do investors like property?

We have adapted this question from Jaffe and Sirmans. Their view was that as property becomes more integrated into the world capital markets it is not clear why investors should continue to like property. They argue that traditional economic views of property are not overwhelming reasons for holding property.

Property often offers tax advantages, but that too is probably not sufficient to encourage investors to hold property. One plausible reason could lie in our results on diversification and the distributional characteristics of property. From our research it would appear that most investors hold poorly diversified portfolios of property. Most individuals are likely to hold a portfolio of one property. We also showed that individual property returns tend to be positively skewed. Investors like positively skewed returns and at times when demand is high there are opportunities for earning high returns. There is also no capital gains tax for individuals selling their principal private residence. Although it cannot be guaranteed as a strategy, poorly diversified investment in property does offer the opportunity for exploiting positively skewed returns. This may be one reason. There may be other behavioural reasons why investors are attracted to property. However, the issue still remains unresolved.

11. What is the relationship of property to the wider economy?

Although there has been some research on capturing the lagged effects between property and the wider economy as well as between different property sectors, there has been little theoretical formulation of these interrelationships. Currently, there are no theoretical models integrating the spatial aspects of property with its role as a financial asset within the wider macro-economy. Furthermore, the nature of spatial interactions between regions and between locations within regions is poorly understood. An understanding of spatial dependence is important in delineating homogeneous markets and in constructing efficient investment portfolios. We believe these to be fruitful areas for further research.

Selected references

Bowie, N. (1983) The depreciation of buildings. *Journal of Valuation* 2 (1), 5–13.

Jaffe, A.C. and Sirmans, C.F. (1995) *Fundamentals of Real Estate Investment*, 3rd edn. Englewood Cliffs, NJ: Prentice Hall.

Sharpe, W.F. (1988) Determining a fund's effective asset mix. *Investment Management Review* (Nov/Dec), 59–69.

Bibliography

Adams, A. and Venmore-Rowland, P. (1990) Property share valuation. *Journal of Valuation* **8**, 127–42.

Adams, A. and Venmore-Rowland, P. (1991) Proposed property investment vehicles: will they work? *Journal of Property Valuation and Investment* **9**, 287–93.

Adams, A., Booth, P. and Venmore-Rowland, P. (1993) An actuarial approach to property valuation. *University of Edinburgh Department of Business Studies* **93.2**, 1–40.

Alvayay, J.R. and Ordway, N. (1994) *Determinants of shopping centre vacancy rate.* California State University.

AMP (1995) *The Real Estate Market Index (REIM): A concept document.* London.

Andrews, C., Ford, D. and Mallinson, K. (1986) The design of index funds and alternative methods of replication. *The Investment Analyst* **82**, 16–23.

Ang, J.S. and Chua, J.H. (1979) Composite measures for the evaluation of investment performance. *Journal of Financial and Quantitative Analysis* **14** (2), 361–84.

Arrow, K.J. (1982) Risk perceptions in psychology and economics. *Economic Enquiry* **4**, 1–19.

Bagnani, E.S., Milonas, N.T., Saunders, A. and Avlos, N.G. (1997) Managers, owners, and the pricing of risky debt: An empirical analysis. *Journal of Finance* **XLIX** (2), 453–77.

Ball, M., Lizieri, C. and MacGregor, B.D. (1998) *The economics of commercial property markets,* London: Routledge.

Ball, R. and Kothari, S.P. (1989) Nonstationary expected returns: Implications for tests of market efficiency and serial correlation in returns. *Journal of Financial Economics* **25**, 51–74.

Bank Administration Institute (1968) *Measuring the investment performance of pension funds.*

Barber White (1995) *Property and inflation: The hedging characteristics of commercial property.* London: Barber White Property Economics.

Barkham, R. and Geltner, D. (1994) Unsmoothing British valuation-based returns without assuming an efficient market. *Journal of Property Research* **11**, 81–95.

Barkham, R. and Ward, C.W.R. (1996) The inflation-hedging characteristics of UK property. *Journal of Property Finance* **7** (1), 62–76.

Batchelor, R. (1980) Rational expectations, efficient markets and economic policy. *City University Annual Monetary Review* **2**, 15–25.

Baum, A. and Crosby, N. (1995) *Property Investment Appraisal,* 2nd edn. London: Routledge.

Baum, A. and MacGregor, B.D. (1992) The initial yield revealed: explicit valuations and the future of property investment. *Journal of Property Valuation and Investment* **10**, 709–26.

Beja, A. (1971) The structure of the cost of capital under uncertainty. *Review of Economic Studies* **38**, 359–68.

Benjamin, J.D. and Chinloy, P.T. (1994) *Measuring returns to innovation in real estate services.* American University.

Benjamin, J.D., Jud, D.G. and Winkler, D.T. (1994) *An analysis of shopping center investment.* University of North Carolina.

Bera, A.K. and Jarque, C.M. (1981) *An efficient large-sample test for normality of observations and regression residuals.* Australian National University (WP 040).

Bernstein, P.L. and Damodaran, A. (1998) *Investment Management*, Wiley Frontiers in Finance, New York: John Wiley.

Black, A., Fraser, P. and Power, D. (1992) UK unit trust performance 1980–1989: a passive time-varying approach. *Journal of Banking and Finance* **16** (1015), 1033.

Black, F. and Scholes, M. (1972) The pricing of options and corporate liabilities. *Journal of Political Economy* **81** (637), 659.

Blundell, G. and Ward, C.W.R. (1987) Property portfolio allocation: a multi factor model. *Land Development Studies* **4**, 145–56.

Bollerslev, T. and Wooldridge, J.M. (1992) Quasi-maximum likelihood estimation and inference in dynamic models with time-varying covariances. *Econometric Reviews* **1** (2), 143–72.

Bollerslev, T., Chou, R.Y. and Kroner, K.F. (1992) ARCH modeling in finance. *Journal of Econometrics* **52**, 5–59.

Boquist, J.A., Racette, G.A. and Schlarbaum, G.G. (1975) Duration and risk assessment for bonds and common stocks. *Journal of Finance* **XXX** (5), 1360–5.

Bowie, N. (1983) The depreciation of buildings. *Journal of Valuation*, **2** (1), 5–13.

Boyd, J.W. and Ziobrowski, A.J. (1993) *Leverage and real estate investment in mixed asset portfolios.*

Brealey, R.A. (1983) *An introduction to risk and return*, 2nd edn. Oxford: Basil Blackwell.

Brealey, R.A. (1986) Active-passive management. *Risk Management Service* **3** (1), 3–5.

Brealey, R.A. (1997) *The distribution and independence of successive rates of return from the British equity market.* London Business School.

Brealey, R.A. and Myers, S.C. (1996) *Principles of Corporate Finance*, 5th edn. New York: McGraw-Hill.

Brinson, G.P., Hood, R. and Beebower, G.L. (1995) Determinants of portfolio performance. *Financial Analysts Journal* **51** (1), 133–48.

Brown, G.R. (1983) Making property investment decisions via capital market theory. *Journal of Valuation* **2** (2), 142–60.

Brown, G.R. (1985a) The information content of property valuations. *Journal of Valuation* **3** (4), 350–62.

Brown, G.R. (1985b) The importance of information in assessing value. *Journal of Valuation* **3** (4), 343–9.

Brown, G.R. (1986) A note on the analysis of depreciation and obsolesence. *Journal of Valuation* **4** (3), 230–8.

Brown, G.R. (1987) The performance of property bonds. *Estates Gazette* 1273–4.

Brown, G.R. (1988a) Reducing the dispersion of returns in UK real estate. *Journal of Valuation* **6** (2), 127–47.

Brown, G.R. (1988b) Portfolio theory and property investment analysis. In: MacLeary, A. and Nanthakumaran, N. (eds) *Property Investment Theory*, pp. 110–33. London: E. & F.N. Spon.

Brown, G.R. (1991a) *Property Investment and the Capital Markets*, London: Chapman & Hall.

Brown, G.R. (1991b) Property Indexes. In: Venmore-Rowland, P. and Brandon, P. (eds) *Investment, procurement and performance in construction*, London: E. & F.N. Spon.

Brown, G.R. (1992) Valuation accuracy: developing the economic issues. *Journal of Property Research* **9**, 199–207.

Brown, G.R. (1993) Investment skill and portfolio management. *Journal of Property Valuation and Investment* **11** (3), 241–47.

Brown, G.R. (1995) Estimating effective rents. *Journal of Property Finance* **6** (2), 33–42.

Brown, G.R. (1997) Reducing the dispersion of returns in UK real estate portfolios. *Journal of Real Estate Portfolio Management* **3** (2), 1–12.

Brown, G.R. and Chau, K.W. (1997) Excess returns in the Hong Kong commercial property market. *Journal of Real Estate Research* **14** (2).

Brown, G.R. and Matysiak, G.A. (1995) Using commercial property indices for measuring portfolio performance. *Journal of Property Finance* **6** (3), 27–38.

Brown, G.R. and Matysiak, G.A. (1997a) A note on the periodic conversion of measures of risk. *Journal of Property Research* **13**, 13–16.

Brown, G.R. and Matysiak, G.A. (1997b) Sticky valuations, aggregation effects and property indices. *Journal of Real Estate Finance and Economics* **20** (1).

Brown, G.R. and Matysiak, G.A. (1998) Valuation smoothing without temporal aggregation. *Journal of Property Research* **15** (2), 1–15.

Brown, G.R. and Schuck, E.J. (1996) Optimal portfolio allocations to real estate. *Journal of Real Estate Portfolio Management* **2** (1), 63–74.

Brown, G.R., Matysiak, G.A. and Shepherd, M.C. (1998) Valuation uncertainty and the Mallinson report. *Journal of Property Research* **14**.

Burns, W. and Epley, D. (1982) The performance of portfolios of REIT's and stocks. *Journal of Portfolio Management* (Spring), 37–42.

Byrne, P. (1996) *Risk, uncertainty and decision-making in property development*, London: E. & F.N. Spon.

Byrne, P. and Lee, S. (1994) Computing Markowitz efficient frontiers using a spreadsheet optimiser. *Journal of Property Finance* **5** (1), 58–66.

Byrne, P. and Lee, S. (1995) Is there a place for property in the multi-asset portfolio? *Journal of Property Finance* **6** (3), 60–83.

Byrne, P. and Lee, S. (1997) Real estate portfolio analysis under conditions of non-normality: the case of NCREIF. *Journal of Real Estate Portfolio Management* **3** (1), 37–46.

Calatchi, R.F. and Rosenberg, S.B. (1992) *Property finance: an international perspective*, London: Euromoney Books.

Casabona, P.A., Fabozzi, F.J. and Francis, J.C. (1994) How to apply duration to equity analysis. *Journal of Portfolio Management* (Winter), 52–8.

Chan, K., Hendershott, P. and Sanders, A. (1990) Risk and return on real estate: evidence from equity REIT's. *AREUEA Journal* **18** (4), 431–52.

Chinloy, P.T., Cho, M. and Megbolugbe, I. (1997) Appraisals, transaction incentives and smoothing. *Journal of Real Estate Finance and Economics* **14**, 89–111.

Clinebell, J.M., Kahl, D.R. and Stevens, J.L. (1994) Time series properties of the equity risk premium. *Journal of Financial Research* **XVII** (1), 105–16.

Coggin, T.D., Fabozzi, F.J. and Rahman, S. (1993) The investment performance of US equity pension fund managers: An empirical investigation. *Journal of Finance* **48**, 1040–55.

Cohen, K.J. and Pogue, J. (1967) An empirical evaluation of alternative portfolio selection models. *Journal of Business* **46** (April), 166–93.

Cohen, K.J., Maier, S.F., Schwartz, R.A. and Whitcomb, D.K. (1986) *The microstructure of securities markets*, Englewood Cliffs, NJ: Prentice-Hall.

Cox, S., Ross, S.A. and Rubinstein, M. (1979) Option pricing: a simplified approach. *Journal of Financial Economics* **9** (September), 229–63.

Darlow, C. (1984) *Valuation and development appraisal*, London: Estates Gazette.

DeBondt, F.M. and Thaler, R. (1985) Does stock market overreact? *Journal of Finance* **40**, 793–805.

deRoos, J.A. (1994) *Smoothing in the appraisal of real estate.* Cornell University.

Diaz, J. (1990) The process of selecting comparable sales. *The Appraisal Journal* (October).

Diaz, J. (1997) An investigation into the impact of previous expert estimates on appraisal judgement. *Journal of Real Estate Research* **13** (1).

Diaz, J. and Wolverton, M.L. (1998) A longitudinal examination of the appraisal smoothing hypothesis. *Real Estate Economics* **26** (2).

Dietz, P.O. (1966) *Pension funds: Measuring investment performance*, New York: The Free Press.

Drivers Jonas (1988) Technical appendix to the variance in valuations. London: Investment Property Databank.

Dunse, N., Jones, C., Orr, A. and Tarbert, H. (1998) The extent and limitations of local commercial property market data. *Journal of Property Valuation and Investment* **16** (5), 455–73.

Efron, B. and Tibshirani, R. (1993) *An introduction to the bootstrap*, London: Chapman and Hall.

Elton, E.J. and Gruber, M.J. (1977) Risk reduction and portfolio size: An analytical solution. *Journal of Business* **50** (4), 415–37.

Elton, E.J. and Gruber, M.J. (1981) *Modern portfolio theory and investment analysis*, 5th edn. New York: John Wiley.

Emary, R. (1985) *Property risk premia*. University of Reading.

Engle, R.E. and Granger, C.W.J. (1987) Cointegration and error-correction: representation, estimation and testing. *Econometrica* **55**, 251–76.

Evans, J.L. and Archer, S.H. (1968) Diversification and the reduction of dispersion. *Journal of Finance* **23** (4), 761–7.

Fabozzi, F.J. (1996) *Bond markets, analysis and strategies*, 3rd edn. Englewood Cliffs, NJ: Prentice-Hall.

Fama, E.F. (1965) The behavior of stock market prices. *Journal of Business* **38** (1), 34–105.

Fama, E.F. (1970) Efficient capital markets: A review of theory and empirical work. *Journal of Finance* **XXV** (2), 383–417.

Fama, E.F. (1971) Risk, return and equilibrium. *Journal of Political Economy* **79** (1), 30–55.

Fama, E.F. (1972) Components of investment performance. *Journal of Finance* **27** (3), 551–67.

Fama, E.F. (1975) Short term interest rates as predictors of inflation. *American Economic Review* **65** (June), 269–82.

Fama, E.F. (1976) *Foundations of finance*, Oxford: Blackwell.

Fama, E.F. and Gibbons, M. (1982) Inflation, real returns and capital investment. *Journal of Monetary Economics* **9** (3).

Fama, E.F. and Schwert, G.W. (1977) Asset returns and inflation. *Journal of Financial Economics* **5**, 115–46.

Finnerty, J.D. (1996) *Project financing: asset based financial engineering*, Wiley Frontiers in Finance, New York: John Wiley.

Firstenberg, P.B., Ross, S.A. and Zisler, R. (1987) Managing real estate portfolios. In: *Real Estate Research*. Goldman Sachs.

Firstenberg, P.B., Ross, S.A. and Zisler, R. (1988) Real estate: the whole story. *Journal of Portfolio Management* (Spring), 23–32.

Fisher, I. (1930) *The theory of interest*, London: Macmillan.

Fisher, J.D., Geltner, D. and Webb, B. (1992) *Historical value indices of commercial real estate*. Indiana University.

Fisher, J.D., Geltner, D. and Webb, B. (1994) Value indices of commercial real estate: a comparison of index construction methods. *Journal of Real Estate Finance and Economics* **9**, 137–64.

FitzGerald, A., Semple, R. and Reynolds, J. (1992a) *The equity risk premium puzzle*. Equity Briefing Paper 24. County NatWest.

FitzGerald, A., Semple, R. and Reynolds, J. (1992b) *Solving the risk premium puzzle*. Equity Briefing Paper 26. County NatWest.

Fogler, H.R. (1984) 20% in real estate: Can theory justify it? *Journal of Portfolio Management* **10** (2), 6–13.

Fogler, H.R. and Ganapathy, S. (1980) *Financial econometrics for researchers in finance and accounting*, Englewood Cliffs, NJ: Prentice-Hall.

Francis, J.C. (1986) *Investments*, 4th edn. New York: McGraw-Hill.

Francis, J.C. and Archer, S.H. (1979) *Portfolio analysis*, Prentice-Hall Foundations of Finance Series, 2nd edn. Englewood Cliffs, NJ: Prentice-Hall.

Francis, J.C. and Taylor, R.W. (1992) *Investments*, Schaum's Outline Series, New York: McGraw-Hill.

Franks, J., Broyles, J.E. and Carleton, W.T. (1985) *Corporate finance: concepts and applications*, California: Kent Publishing Company.

French, K.R., Schwert, G.W. and Stambarugh, R.F. (1987) Expected stock returns and volatility. *Journal of Financial Economics* **19**, 3–29.

Friedman, H.C. (1970) Real estate investment and portfolio theory. *Journal of Financial and Quantitative Analysis* (April), 861–74.

Ganesan, S. and Chiang, Y.H. (1998) The inflation hedging characteristics of real and financial assets in Hong Kong. *Journal of Real Estate Portfolio Management* **4** (1), 55–68.

Gatzlaff, D.H. and Tirtiroglu, D. (1995) Real estate market efficiency: Issues and evidence. *Journal of Real Estate Literature* **3** (2).

Gau, G. (1984) Weak form tests of the efficiency of real estate investment markets. *The Financial Review* **19** (4), 301–20.

Gelbtuch, H.C. and Lipkin, P. (1992) Real estate securitisation. *The Appraisal Journal* (July), 323–30.

Geltner, D. (1989a) Bias in appraisal based returns. *AREUEA Journal* **17** (3), 338–52.

Geltner, D. (1989b) Estimating real estate's systematic risk from aggregate level appraisal-based returns. *AREUEA Journal* **17** (4), 463–81.

Geltner, D. (1991) Smoothing in appraisal based returns. *Journal of Real Estate Finance and Economics* **4**, 327–45.

Geltner, D. (1993a) Temporal aggregation in real estate return indices. *AREUEA Journal* **21** (2), 141–66.

Geltner, D. (1993b) Estimating market values from appraisal values without assuming an efficient market. *Journal of Real Estate Research* **8** (3), 325–45.

Giacotto, C. and Clapp, J. (1992) Appraisal based real estate returns under alternative market regimes. *AREUEA Journal* **20** (1), 1–24.

Giliberto, M. (1990) Equity REIT's and portfolio diversification. *Journal of Real Estate Research* **5**, 259–64.

Giliberto, M. (1993) Measuring real estate returns: the hedged REIT index. *Journal of Portfolio Management* (Spring), 94–9.

Goodman, L.A. (1960) On the exact variance of products. *American Statistical Association Journal* **55**, 708–13.

Gordon, J. (1990) *Property performance indices in the United Kingdom and the US.* New York: Baring Institutional Realty Advisors Inc.

Gould, J.B. and Sorensen, E.H. (1996) Duration: A factor in equity pricing. *Journal of Portfolio Management* (Fall), 38–43.

Graff, R.A. (1998) The impact of seasonality on investment statistics derived from quarterrly returns. *Journal of Real Estate Portfolio Management* **4** (1), 1–16.

Greer, G. (1974) *Risk, return and efficiency in the market for real property.* University of Colorado. PhD.

Grenadier, S.R. (1995) The valuation of leasing contracts: a real options approach. *Journal of Financial Economics* **38**, 297–331.

Griffiths, W., Hill, C. and Judge, G. (1993) *Learning and practicing econometrics,* New York: McGraw-Hill.

Grindblatt, M. and Titman, S. (1989) Portfolio performance evaluation: old issues and new insights. *Review of Financial Studies* **2**, 393–421.

Gujarati, D.N. (1995) *Basic econometrics,* 3rd edn. New York: McGraw-Hill.

Hager, D. and Lord, D. (1985) *The property market, property valuations and property performance measurement.* Institute of Actuaries.

Hamelink, F. and Hoesli, M. (1996) Swiss real estate as a hedge against inflation: New evidence using hedonic and autoregressive models. *Journal of Property Finance* **7** (1), 33–49.

Hamelink, F., MacGregor, B.D., Nanthakumaran, N. and Orr, A. (1998) *The duration of UK commercial property.* University of Aberdeen.

Hamilton, J.D. (1994) *Time series analysis,* Princeton, NJ: Princeton University Press.

Harrington, D.R. (1987) *Modern portfolio theory, the capital asset pricing model and arbitrage pricing theory: a user's guide,* 2nd edn. Englewood Cliffs, NJ: Prentice-Hall.

Hartzell, D., Hekman, J.S. and Miles, M. (1987) Real estate returns and inflation. *AREUEA Journal* **15** (1), 617–37.

Harvey, A.C. (1990) *The econometric analysis of time series,* London: Philip Allan.

Harvey, A.C. (1993) *Time series models,* New York: Harvester Wheatsheaf.

Haugen, R.A. (1993) *Modern investment theory,* 3rd edn. Englewood Cliffs, NJ: Prentice-Hall.

Hendershott, P. (1998) Equilibrium models in real estate research: A survey. *Journal of Real Estate Literature* **6**, 13–25.

Hertz, D.B. (1964) Risk analysis in capital investment. *Harvard Business Review* **42** (1), 95–106.

Hertz, D.B. and Thomas, H. (1983) *Risk analysis and its applications*, Chichester: John Wiley.

Hertz, D.B. and Thomas, H. (1984) *Practical risk analysis: An approach through case histories*, Chichester: John Wiley.

Hicks, J.R. (1946) *Value and Capital*, 2nd edn. London: Oxford University Press.

Hill, C., Griffiths, W. and Judge, G. (1997) *Undergraduate econometrics*, New York: John Wiley.

Hillier, F.S. (1963) The derivation of probabilistic information for the evaluation of risky investments. *Management Science* **9** (3), 443–57.

Hillier, F.S. (1965) Supplement to the derivation of probabilistic information for the evaluation of risky investments. *Management Science* **11** (3), 485–7.

Hoag, J. (1980) Towards indices of real estate value and return. *Journal of Finance* **35**, 569–80.

Hoesli, M., Lizieri, C. and MacGregor, B.D. (1997) The spatial dimensions of the investment performance of UK commercial property. *Urban Studies* **34** (9), 1475–94.

Hopewell, M.H. and Kaufman, G.G. (1973) Bond price volatility and term to maturity: A generalized respecification. *American Economic Review* **63** (4), 749–53.

Hull, J.C. (1980) *The evaluation of risk in business investment*, Oxford: Pergamon Press.

Hutchison, N., MacGregor, B.D., Nanthakumaran, N., Adair, A. and McGreal, S. (1996) *Variations in the capital valuations of UK commercial property*, London: RICS.

Ibbotson, R.G., Siegal, L.B. and Love, K.S. (1985) World wealth: Market values and returns. *Journal of Portfolio Management* (Fall), 4–23.

Ingersoll, J.E. and Ross, S.A. (1992) Waiting to invest: Investment and uncertainty. *Journal of Business* **65** (1), 1–29.

IPD (1998) *IPD Standard Comparative Report*. London: Investment Property Databank.

IPD/Drivers Jonas (1988) *The variance in valuations*. London: Investment Property Databank.

Isaac, D. (1996) *Property development appraisal and finance*, London: Macmillan.

Jacob, N.L. (1974) A limited diversification portfolio selection model for the small investor. *Journal of Finance* (June), 847–56.

Jaffe, A.C. and Sirmans, C.F. (1995) *Fundamentals of Real Estate Investment*, 3rd edn. Englewood Cliffs, NJ: Prentice-Hall.

Jaffee, D.M. and Renaud, B. (1995) *Securitisation in European mortgage markets*. University of California.

Jarque, C.M. and Bera, A.K. (1987) A test for normality of observations and regression residuals. *International Statistical Review* **55**, 163–72.

Jarrow, R. (1978) The relationship between yield, risk and return of corporate bonds. *Journal of Finance* **XXXIII** (4), 1235–40.

Jefferies, R. (1994) Lease incentives and effective rents: a decapitalisation model. *Journal of Property Valuation and Investment* **12**, 21–42.

Jensen, M.C. (1968) The performance of mutual funds in the period 1945–1964. *Journal of Finance* **23** (2), 389–416.

Jensen, M.C. (1969) Risk, the pricing of capital assets and the evaluation of investment portfolios. *Journal of Business* **42** (2), 167–85.

Jensen, M.C. and Bennington, G.A. (1970) Random walks and technical theories: Some additional evidence. *Journal of Finance* **XXV** (2), 469–82.

Johnston, J. and DiNardo, J. (1997) *Econometric methods*, 4th edn. New York: McGraw-Hill.

Kerson, J.S. (1994) Trading in fundamental real estate risk with market-hedged equity indexes. *Bankers Trust Research*, 1–15.

Kiley, M.T. (1996) *The lead of output over inflation in sticky prices*. Federal Reserve Board, Washington.

Kmenta, J. (1986) *Elements of econometrics*, 2nd edn. New York: Macmillan.

Konno, H. and Yamazaki, H. (1991) Mean absolute deviation portfolio optimisation model and its application to the Tokyo Stock Market. *Management Science* **37** (5), 519–31.

Kuhle, J. (1987) Portfolio diversification and return benefits – common stock versus REIT's. *Journal of Real Estate Research* **2**, 1–9.

Lai, T.-Y. and Wang, K. (1998) Appraisal smoothing: the other side of the story. *Real Estate Economics* **26** (3), 511–35.

Lanstein, R. and Sharpe, W.F. (1978) Duration and security risk. *Journal of Financial and Quantitative Analysis* (Proceedings Issue – November), 653–68.

Lee, S. (1989) Property returns in a portfolio context. *Journal of Valuation* **7**, 248–58.

Levy, H. and Sarnat, M. (1984) *Portfolio and investment selection: Theory and practice*, Englewood Cliffs, NJ: Prentice-Hall.

Limmack, R.J. and Ward, C.W.R. (1988) Property returns and inflation. *Land Development Studies* **5**, 47–55.

Lintner, J. (1965) Security prices, risk and maximal gains from diversification. *Journal of Finance*, 587–615.

Liu, C., Hartzell, D., Grisson, T. and Greig, W. (1990) The composition of the market portfolio and real estate investment performance. *AREUEA Journal* **18**, 49–75.

Livingston, M. (1978) Duration and risk assessment for bonds and common stocks: A note. *Journal of Finance* **XXXIII** (1), 293–5.

Lizieri, C. and Venmore-Rowland, P. (1991) Valuation accuracy: a contribution to the debate. *Journal of Property Research* **8** (2), 115–22.

Lizieri, C. and Venmore-Rowland, P. (1993) Valuations, prices and the market: a rejoinder. *Journal of Property Research* **10** (2), 77–84.

Lizieri, C., Crosby, N., Gibson, V., Murdoch, S. and Ward, C.W.R. (1997) *Right space, right place? A study of the impact of changing business patterns on the property market.* London: RICS.

Locke, S.M. (1990) Property investment analysis using adjusted present values. *Appraisal Journal* (July), 373–78.

Lusht, K.M. (1997) *Real Estate Valuation*, Chicago: Irwin.

MacGregor, B.D. and Nanthakumaran, N. (1992) The allocation to property in the multi-asset portfolio: the evidence and theory reconsidered. *Journal of Property Research* **9**, 5–32.

Maitland-Smith, J. (1996) *Value indices of commercial real estate: a Markov switching process?* University of Reading.

Mallinson, M. (1994) *Report of the President's Working Party on commercial property valuations*, London: RICS.

Margrabe, W. (1978) The value of an option to exchange one asset for another. *Journal of Finance* **33** (March), 177–86.

Markowitz, H.M. (1952) Portfolio selection. *Journal of Finance* **12** (March), 77–91.

Markowitz, H.M. (1959) *Portfolio selection: Efficient diversification of investments*, A. Cowles Foundation Monograph, New Haven, CT: Yale University Press.

Markowitz, H.M. (1984) The 'two beta' trap. *Journal of Portfolio Management* **11** (1), 12–20.

Marriott, O. (1969) *The Property Boom*, London: Pan Books Ltd.

Matysiak, G.A. (1993) Optimizing property portfolio holdings: a scenario based approach. *Journal of Property Finance* **4** (3/4), 68–75.

Matysiak, G.A. and Brown, G.R. (1997) A time-varying analysis of abnormal performance of UK property companies. *Applied Financial Economics* **7**, 367–77.

Matysiak, G.A. and Wang, P. (1995) Commercial property market prices and valuations: analysing the correspondence. *Journal of Property Research* **12** (3), 181–202.

Matysiak, G.A., Hoesli, M., MacGregor, B.D. and Nanthakumaran, N. (1996) The long term inflation hedging characteristics of UK commercial property. *Journal of Property Finance* **7** (1), 50–61.

Mayers, D. (1972) Nonmarketable assets and capital market equilibrium under uncertainty. In: Jensen, M.C. (ed.) *Studies in the Theory of Capital Markets*, New York: Praeger.

Mayers, D. (1973) Nonmarketable assets and the determination of capital asset prices in the absence of a riskless asset. *Journal of Business* **46** (2), 258–67.

Mayers, D. (1976) Nonmarketable assets, market segmentation and the level of asset prices. *Journal of Financial and Quantitative Analysis* **11** (1), 1–12.

Meiselman, D. (1962) *The term structure of interest rates*, Englewood Cliffs, NJ: Prentice-Hall.

Michaelsen, J.B. (1973) *The term structure of interest rates*, Monetary Economics, New York: Intext Educational Publishers.

Michaud, R.O. (1989) The Markowitz optimisation enigma: is 'optimised' optimal? *Financial Analysts Journal* (Jan/Feb), 31–42.

Miles, M., Guilkey, D. and Shears, D. (1991) A transaction based real estate index: is it possible? *Journal of Property Research* **8**, 203–17.

Miles, M., Guilkey, D., Webb, B. and Hunter, K. (1992) *An empirical evaluation of the reliability of commercial appraisals 1978–1990.* Prudential Real Estate Investors

Miles, M., Hartzell, D. and Guilkey, D. (1990) A different look at commercial real estate returns. *AREUEA Journal* **18**, 403–30.

Modigliani, F. and Miller, M.H. (1958) The cost of capital, corporation finance and the theory of investment. *American Economic Review* **48**, 261–97.

Mood, A.M. and Graybill, F.A. (1963) *Introduction to the theory of statistics*, New York: McGraw-Hill.

Morrell, G.D. (1991) Property performance analysis and performance indices: A review. *Journal of Property Research* **8**, 29–50.

Morrell, G.D. (1993) Value weighting and the variability of real estate returns: implications for portfolio construction and performance evaluation. *Journal of Property Research* **10**, 167–83.

Mussa, M. (1981) Sticky prices and disequilibrium in a rational model of the inflationary process. *American Economic Review* **71**, 1020–7.

Nawrocki, D.N. (1983) A comparison of risk measures when used in a simple portfolio selection heuristic. *Journal of Business Finance and Accounting* **10** (2), 183–94.

Nawrocki, D.N. (1991) Optimal algorithms and lower partial moments: Ex post results. *Applied Economics* **23** (March), 465–70.

Nawrocki, D.N. and Staples, K. (1989) A customised LPM risk measure for portfolio analysis. *Applied Economics* **21** (February), 205–18.

Nelson, C.R. (1972) *The term structure of interest rates*, New York: Basic Books.

Newell, G. (1996) The inflation hedging characteristic of Australian commercial property: 1984–1995. *Journal of Property Finance* **7** (1), 6–20.

Newell, G. and Kishore, R. (1998) Are valuations an effective proxy for property sales? *The Valuer and Land Economist* **35** (2), 150–3.

Newell, G. and MacFarlane, J. (1995) Improved risk estimation using appraisal-smoothed real estate returns. *Journal of Real Estate Portfolio Management* **1** (1), 51–7.

Newell, G. and MacFarlane, J. (1996) Risk estimation and appraisal smoothing in UK property returns. *Journal of Property Research* **13** (1), 1–12.

Newell, G. and MacFarlane, J. (1998) The effect of seasonality of valuations on property risk. *Journal of Property Research* **15** (3), 167–82.

Officer, R.R. (1972) The distribution of stock returns. *Journal of the American Statistical Association* **67**, 807–12.

Phyrr, S.A. (1973) A computer simulation model to measure the risk in real estate investment. *AREUEA Journal* **1** (1), 48–78.

Pines, H.A. (1983) The psychology of investor decision making. *AAII Journal* **5** (September), 10–17.

Posey, A. (1996) How to evaluate manager style and skill. *Pension Management* (February).

Quan, D. and Quigley, J. (1989) Inferring an investment return series for real estate from observations on sales. *AREUEA Journal* **17** (2), 218–30.

Quan, D. and Quigley, J. (1991) Price formation and the appraisal function in real estate markets. *Journal of Real Estate Finance and Economics* **4** (2), 127–46.

Quigg, L. (1993) Empirical testing of real option-pricing models. *Journal of Finance* **XLVIII** (2), 621–40.

Rao, R.K.S. (1987) *Financial management*, New York: Macmillan.

Reilly, F.K. and Sidhu, R.S. (1980) The many uses of bond duration. *Financial Analysts Journal* (July–August), 58–72.

Rendleman, R. and Bartter, B. (1979) Two state option pricing. *Journal of Finance* **34** (December), 1093–10.

RICS (1985) *The unitisation of real property.* London: RICS.

Roberts, H. (1959) Stock market patterns and financial analysis: Methodological suggestions. *Journal of Finance* **XIV** (1), 1–10.

Rorke, H.C. (1974) On the portfolio effects of nonmarketable assets: Government transfers and human capital payments. *Journal of Financial and Quantitative Analysis* **9** (2), 167–77.

Ross, S.A. and Zisler, R. (1987a) Managing real estate portfolios, Part 2: Risk and return in real estate. In: *Real Estate Research*. Goldman Sachs.

Ross, S.A. and Zisler, R. (1987b) Managing real estate portfolios, Part 3: A close look at equity real estate risk. In: *Real Estate Research*. Goldman Sachs.

Ross, S.A. and Zisler, R. (1991) Risk and return in real estate. *Journal of Real Estate Finance and Economics* **4** (2), 175–90.

Rudd, A. and Clasing, H.K. (1982) *Modern portfolio theory: The principles of investment management*, Homewood, IL: Dow Jones-Irwin.

Rydin, Y.J., Rodney, W. and Orr, C. (1990) Why do institutions invest in property? *Journal of Property Finance* **1** (2), 250–8.

Salvatore, D. (1982) *Statistics and econometrics*, Schaum's Outline Series, New York: McGraw-Hill.

Samuelson, P. (1965) Proof that properly anticipated prices fluctuate randomly. *Industrial Management Review* **6**, 41–9.

Samuelson, P. (1973) Proof that properly discounted present values of assets vibrate randomly. *Bell Journal of Economics* **4**, 369–74.

Saunders, A., Ward, C.W.R. and Woodward, R. (1980) Stochastic dominance and the performance of UK unit trusts. *Journal of Financial and Quantitative Analysis* **15** (2), 323–30.

Schaefer, S.M. and Schwartz, E.S. (1987) Time dependent variance and the pricing of bond options. *Journal of Finance* **XLII** (5), 1113–28.

Scholes, M. (1972) The market for securities: Substitution versus price pressure and the effects of information on share prices. *Journal of Business* **XLV** (2).

Scholes, M. and Williams, J.T. (1977) *Estimating betas with nonsynchronous data*. University of Chicago.

Schuck, E.J. and Brown, G.R. (1997) Value weighting and real estate portfolio risk. *Journal of Property Research* **14** (3), 169–87.

Scott, M. (1992) The cost of equity capital and the risk premium on equities. *Applied Financial Economics* **2**, 21–32.

Scott, P. (1996) The property masters, London: E. & F.N. Spon.

Shapiro, A.C. (1991) *Modern corporate finance*, New York: Macmillan.

Sharpe, W.F. (1963) A simplified model for portfolio analysis. *Management Science* **IX** (2), 277–93.

Sharpe, W.F. (1964) Capital asset prices: A theory of market equilibrium under conditions of risk. *Journal of Finance* (Sept), 425–42.

Sharpe, W.F. (1966) Mutual fund performance. *Journal of Business* **39** (1), 119–38.

Sharpe, W.F. (1970) *Portfolio theory and capital markets*, McGraw-Hill Series in Finance, New York: McGraw-Hill.

Sharpe, W.F. (1971) Mean-absolute-deviation characteristic lines for securities and portfolios. *Management Science* **18** (2), B1–B13

Sharpe, W.F. (1985) *Investments*, 3rd edn. Englewood Cliffs, NJ: Prentice-Hall.

Sharpe, W.F. (1988) Determining a fund's effective asset mix. *Investment Management Review* (Nov/Dec), 59–69.

Sharpe, W.F. (1992) Asset allocation: Management style and performance attribution. *Journal of Portfolio Management* (Winter), 7–19.

Sharpe, W.F. and Cooper, G.M. (1972) Risk-return classes of New York Stock Exchange common stocks, 1931–67. *Financial Analysts Journal* **28** (2), 413–46.

Shefrin, H.M. and Statman, M. (1985) The disposition to sell winners too early and ride losers too long: Theory and evidence. *Journal of Finance* **40**, 777–90.

Shiller, R. (1981) The use of volatility measures in assessing market efficiency. *Journal of Finance* **36**, 291–304.

Shiller, R. (1990) Market volatility and investor behaviour. *American Economic Review* **80** (58), 62.

Shiller, R. (1992) Volatility in the US and Japanese stock markets. *Journal of Applied Corporate Finance* **5** (Spring), 4–35.

Siegel, J.L. (1992) The equity premium: Stock and bond returns since 1802. *Financial Analysts Journal* (Jan/Feb), 28–46.

Singer, B.D. (1996) Evaluation of portfolio performance: Attribution analysis. *Journal of Performance Measurement* (Winter), 45–55.

Skantz, T.R. and Strickland, T.H. (1987) Efficient markets in real estate. *Journal of Real Estate Research* **2**, 75–83.

Sortino, F.A. and Forssey, H.J. (1996) Style risk: Resolving the time sensitivity problem. *Journal of Performance Measurement* (Fall).

Spaulding, D. (1997) *Measuring investment performance*, New York: McGraw-Hill.

Surz, R.J. (1994) Portfolio opportunity distributions: An innovation in performance evaluation. *Journal of Investing* (Summer).

Surz, R.J. (1996) Portfolio opportunity distributions: A solution to the problems with benchmarks and peer groups. *Journal of Performance Measurement* (Winter).

Tarbert, H. (1996) Is commercial property a hedge against inflation? A cointegration approach. *Journal of Property Finance* **7** (1), 77–98.

Tirtiroglu, D. (1997) Valuation of real estate assets using the adjusted present value method. *Journal of Property Finance* **8** (1), 7–23.

Treynor, J.L. (1965) How to rate management of investment funds. *Harvard Business Review* **43** (1), 63–75.

Treynor, J.L. and Mazuy, K.K. (1966) Can mutual funds outguess the market? *Harvard Business Review* **44** (4), 131–6.

Van Horne, J. (1995) *Financial management and policy*, 10th edn. Englewood Cliffs, NJ: Prentice-Hall.

Wagle, B. (1967) A statistical analysis of risk in capital investment projects. *Operational Research Quarterly* **18** (1), 13–33.

Ward, C.W.R. (1988) Asset pricing models and property as a long term investment: The contribution of duration. In: MacLeary, A.R. and Nanthakumaran, N. (eds) *Property Investment Theory*, pp. 134–45. London: E. & F.N. Spon.

Webb, B., Miles, M. and Guilkey, D. (1992) Transaction driven commercial real estate returns: the panacea to asset allocation models? *AREUEA Journal* **20**, 325–57.

Webb, J. and Rubens, J. (1988) How much in real estate?: a surprising answer. *Journal of Portfolio Management* (Spring), 10–13.

Webb, R.B. (1994) On the reliability of commercial appraisals: an analysis of the properties sold from the Russell-NCREIF Index (1978–1992). *Real Estate Finance* **11** (1), 62–5.

Wheaton, W. and Torto, R. (1989) Income and appraised values: a re-examination of the FRC returns data. *AREUEA Journal* **17**, 439–49.

Whipple, R.T.M. (1995) *Property valuation and analysis*, Sydney: Law Book Co.

Willemain, T.R. (1994) Bootstrapping on a shoestring: resampling using spreadsheets. *The American Statistician* **48** (1), 40–2.

Williams, J.T. (1978) Risk, human capital and the investor's portfolio. *Journal of Business* **1**, 65–89.

Working, H. (1960) Note on the correlation of the first differences of averages in a random chain. *Econometrica* **28**, 916–18.

Yamaguchi, K. (1994) Estimating the equity risk premium from downside probability. *Journal of Portfolio Management* (Summer), 17–27.

Young, M.S. and Graff, R.A. (1995) Real estate is not normal: a fresh look at real estate returns distributions. *Journal of Real Estate Finance and Economics* **10**, 225–59.

Index